Programming the Web using XHTML and JavaScript

Larry Randles Lagerstrom
The University of California-Davis

 **Learning Solutions**

Boston   Burr Ridge, IL Dubuque, IA New York San Francisco St. Louis
Bangkok Bogotá Caracas Lisbon London Madrid
Mexico City Milan New Delhi Seoul Singapore Sydney Taipei Toronto

The **McGraw·Hill** Companies

Programming the Web Using XHTML and JavaScript

5 6 7 8 9 0 KNG KNG 14 13 12 11

ISBN-13: 978-0-07-739625-1
ISBN-10: 0-07-739625-1

Learning Solutions Representative: Shirley Grall
Production Editor: Kelly Heinrichs
Printer/Binder: King Printing

JavaScript Quick Reference

JavaScript Objects, Methods, and Properties
See Appendix F.

JavaScript Errors and Error Messages
See Appendix G.

Script Element with Alert Box and Comments
```
<script type="text/javascript">
    alert("Hello, world!")      //This is a single-line comment
    /*This is a multiple-line
        comment*/
</script>
```

Loading a New Document
```
location.href = "http://www.yahoo.com"
```

Accessing Document Properties
```
alert("The title is " + document.title +
    "and the background color is " + document.bgColor)
```

Declaring and Initializing Variables
```
var firstNum, secondNum
var thirdNum = 56
secondNum = 37        //This is an assignment statement
var answer1 = 4.962                     //number value
var answer2 = "Hello! How are you?"     //string value
var answer3 = true                      //boolean value
answer1 = 19.3          //Changing the value to 19.3
```

Using the Prompt and Confirm Boxes
```
var theName 5 prompt("Please enter your name:", " ")
var userAnswer 5 confirm("Are you sure?")
```

Declaring a Function with No Parameters
```
function someName() {
    //JavaScript instructions go here
}
```

Calling a Function with No Parameters
```
someName()
```

Declaring a Function with Parameters
```
function sampleFunction(a, b, c) {
    alert(a)
    alert(c)
    alert(b)
}
```

Calling a Function with Parameters
```
sampleFunction("Bill", "Sarah", "Theresa")
```

Declaring a Function with a Local Variable
```
function someName() {
    var theResult
    //Rest of function's code goes here
}
```

Declaring a Function that Returns a Value
```
function calculateAve(num1,num2,num3) {
    var average = (num1+num2+num3)/3
    return average
}
```

Calling a Function that Returns a Value
```
var theResult
theResult = calculateAve(8, 3, 12)
```

```
var n1 = 8, n2 = 3, n3 = 12
theResult = calculateAve(n1, n2, n3)
```

Declaring a Function that Receives a Form with Textboxes nameBox and messageBox
```
function displayMessage(f) {
    f.messageBox.value = "Hi" + f.nameBox.value
}
```

Calling the displayMessage() Function Above and Passing a Form Named userInfoForm
```
displayMessage(userInfoForm)
```

Calling Function via onclick Event Handler
```
<input type="button" name="b1"
    value="Click here!" onclick="sampleFunction()" />
```

Calling Function via onchange Event Handler
```
<input type="text" name="nameBox" size="30"
    onchange="sampleFunction()" />
```

Mathematical Operators
```
var result, firstNum, secondNum, thirdNum
firstNum = firstNum + 1    //Incrementing firstNum
result = firstNum + secondNum – thirdNum
result = firstNum*secondNum        //Multiply
result = firstNum/secondNum        //Divide
firstNum++          //Same as firstNum = firstNum + 1
firstNum--          //Same as firstNum = firstNum – 1
firstNum+=7         //Same as firstNum = firstNum + 7
firstNum–=7         //Same as firstNum = firstNum – 7
firstNum*=7         //Same as firstNum = firstNum*7
firstNum/=7         //Same as firstNum = firstNum/7
```

Order of Operations when No Parentheses
1. Increment and decrement (++ and --), left to right
1. Multiply and divide, from left to right
2. Add and subtract, from left to right

Using the Math Object
```
var result, theNum = 36
result = Math.sqrt(theNum)          //Square root
result = Math.pow(theNum, 2)        //Squaring
result = Math.round(theNum)         //Rounding to nearest int
result = Math.floor(theNum)         //Truncating decimal part
theNum = Math.random()      //Random no. between 0 and 1
```

Converting a String to a Number
```
var theStr = "72.95", theNum
theNum = parseFloat(theStr)
```

Basic Conditional Statement (pseudocode)
```
if (some condition is true) {
    //JavaScript instructions to execute
}
```

Compound Conditional Statement
```
if (some condition is true) {      //This is pseudocode
    //JavaScript instructions to execute
}
else if (another condition is true) {
    //Second block of instructions
}
else if (yet another condition is true) {
```

```
    //Third block of instructions
}
else {
    //Fourth block of instructions
}
```

Relational and Logical Operators
```
==, <, >, <=, >=, != (latter is the not-equal operator)
&& (and), || (or), ! (not)
```

Using Relational and Logical Operators
```
if ((firstNum > 12) && (firstNum < 25)) {
    alert("The number is between 12 and 25")
}
else {
    alert("The number is out of bounds")
}
if ((firstNum > 5) || (secondNum > 9)) {
    alert("firstNum is > 5 or secondNum is > 9, or both")
}
```

Transfering the Value of Textbox box1 to box2 (both in the form named test)
```
document.test.box2.value = document.test.box1.value
```

Testing the Value of a Checkbox
```
if (document.options.sunroofCB.checked==true) {
    //JavaScript code goes here
}
```

Testing Value of Third Radio Button in a Set
```
if (document.survey.sodaRB[2].checked==true) {
    document.survey.messageBox.value="Good!"
}
```

Concatenating (Joining) Strings
```
var greeting, userName = "Jenny"
greeting = "How are you, " + userName + "?"
```

Converting String to Uppercase or Lowercase
```
var stringA, stringB, myString = "Hello, Fred!"
stringA = myString.toLowerCase()      //"hello, fred!"
stringB = myString.toUpperCase()      //"HELLO, FRED!"
```

Getting Number of Characters in a String
```
var nmbrChars = greeting.length
```

Extracting a Character or Substring
```
var letters, theWord= "gigabyte", someLetter
letters = theWord.substring(2,5)      //Value is "gab"
someLetter = theWord.charAt(3)        //Value is "a"
```

Splitting a String
```
var name1, name2, name3
var customerNames = "John, Jill, Jim"
name1 = customerName.split(", ")[0]    //Value is "John"
name2 = customerName.split(", ")[1]    //Value is "Jill"
name3 = customerName.split(", ")[2]    //Value is "Jim"
```

Three Types of Loops: for, while, do-while
```
var ctr
for (ctr = 1; ctr <= 3; ctr=ctr+1) {
    alert("The value of ctr is: " + ctr)
}
ctr = 1
```

```
while (ctr <= 3) {
    alert("The value of ctr is: " + ctr)
    ctr = ctr + 1
}
ctr = 1
do {
    alert("The value of ctr is: " + ctr)
    ctr = ctr + 1
} while (ctr <= 3)
```

Creating and Filling Arrays
```
var sampleArray = new Array(3)
sampleArray[0] = "Hi there!"
sampleArray[2] = false
sampleArray[1] = 12.6
var daysOfWeek = new Array("Sun", "Mon", "Tue", "Wed", "Thu",
    "Fri", "Sat")
var daysOfWeek2 = ["Sun", "Mon", "Tue", "Wed", "Thu", "Fri", "Sat"]
```

Creating a Cookie Named userName with the Value "Heidi" and a 6-month Exp. Date
```
var theName = "Heidi"
var expDate = new Date()     //Get today's date and set it
expDate.setMonth(expDate.getMonth()+6) //6 mos. ahead
document.cookie = "userName=" + theName + ";expires=" +
    expDate.toGMTString()
```

Reading the Cookie's Name and Value
```
var theCookieName = document.cookie.split("=")[0]
var theCookieValue = document.cookie.split("=")[1]
```

Constructor Function for an Object with 3 Properties Named name, address, and phone
```
function adrEntry(n, a, p) {
    this.name = n
    this.address = a
    this.phone = p
}
```

Creating an Object Using the Constructor Above and Accessing the Object Properties
```
var firstAdr = new adrEntry("Bill", "123 Main", "321-4567")
alert("The phone number for Bill is: " + firstAdr.phone)
```

Calling a Function from a Frame Document when the Function is in the Frameset Doc
```
parent.someFunction()
```

Writing HTML Text and Tags to a Frame Named rightFrame
```
var firstName = "Jamie"   //This code is in frameset doc
rightFrame.document.write("<strong>The surfer's first name
    is:</strong> " + firstName)
rightFrame.document.close()
```

Opening a Document in a New Window
```
var sampleWindow = window.open("DocToDisplay.htm",
    "smpWin", "toolbar,scrollbars,resizable,width=250,
    height=200,left=80,top=50,screenX=80,screenY=50")
```

Bringing Window to Front; Closing Window
```
windowA.focus()   //Bring window A to front
if (windowB.closed == false) {   //If window B not closed,
    windowB.close()   // close it
}
```

Programming the Web Using
XHTML and JavaScript

Larry Randles Lagerstrom

University of California-Davis

McGraw-Hill
Irwin

Boston   Burr Ridge, IL   Dubuque, IA   Madison, WI   New York   San Francisco   St. Louis
Bangkok   Bogotá   Caracas   Kuala Lumpur   Lisbon   London   Madrid   Mexico City
Milan   Montreal   New Delhi   Santiago   Seoul   Singapore   Sydney   Taipei   Toronto

InformationTechnology

Information Technology at McGraw-Hill/Irwin

At McGraw-Hill Higher education, we publish instructional materials for the higher education market. In order to expand the tools of higher learning, we publish everything you may need: texts, lab manuals, study guides, testing materials, software, and multimedia products—the Total Solution.

We realize that technology has created and will continue to create new mediums for professors and students to use in managing resources and communicating information to one another. McGraw-Hill/Irwin continues to provide the most flexible and complete teaching and learning tools available as well as offer solutions to the changing world of teaching and learning. McGraw-Hill/Irwin is dedicated to providing the tools for today's instructors and students which will enable them to successfully navigate the world of Information Technology.

- Seminar Series and Focus Groups—McGraw-Hill/Irwin's seminar series and focus groups are offered across the country every year. At the seminar series we provide you with the latest technology products and encourage collaboration among teaching professionals. We conduct many focus groups year round where we can hear from you what we need to publish.

- ITAP—Information Technology Advisory Panel. This is a "super focus group," where we gather many of the country's top IT educators for three days to tell us how to publish the best IT texts possible. ITAP's are very instrumental in driving our publishing plans.

- McGraw-Hill/Osborne—This leading trade division company of family of McGraw-Hill Companies is known for its best-selling Internet titles, Harley Hahn's Internet & Web yellow pages, and the Internet Complete Reference. If we don't have it in our CIT/MIS, you can find it at Osborne. For more information, visit Osborne at **www.osborne.com**.

- Digital Solutions—Whether you want to teach a class online or just post your "bricks-n-mortar" class syllabus, McGraw-Hill/Irwin is committed to publishing digital solutions. Taking your course online doesn't have to be a solitary adventure, nor does it have to be a difficult one. We offer several solutions that will allow you to enjoy all the benefits of having your course material online.

- Packaging Options—For more information about our discount options, contact your McGraw-Hill/Irwin Sales representative at 1-800-338-3987 or visit our website at **www.mhhe.com/it**.

McGraw-Hill Higher Education

A Division of The McGraw-Hill Companies

PROGRAMMING THE WEB USING XHTML AND JAVASCRIPT
Published by McGraw-Hill/Irwin, a business unit of The McGraw-Hill Companies, Inc., 1221 Avenue of the Americas, New York, NY, 10020. Copyright © 2003 by The McGraw-Hill Companies, Inc. All rights reserved. No part of this publication may be reproduced or distributed in any form or by any means, or stored in a database or retrival system, without the prior written consent of The McGraw-Hill Companies, Inc., including, but not limited to, in any network or other electronic storage or transmission, or broadcast for distance learning. Some ancillaries, including electronic and print components, may not be available to customers outside the United States.

This book is printed on acid-free paper.

domestic   1 2 3 4 5 6 7 8 9 0 DOC/DOC 0 9 8 7 6 5 4 3 2
international 1 2 3 4 5 6 7 8 9 0 DOC/DOC 0 9 8 7 6 5 4 3 2

ISBN 0-07-256031-2

Publisher: *George Werthman*
Sponsoring editor: *Steve Schuetz*
Developmental editor: *Diana Del Castillo*
Manager, Marketing and Sales: *Paul Murphy*
Media producer: *Greg Bates*
Project manager: *Destiny Rynne*
Lead production supervisor: *Heather D. Burbridge*
Senior designer: *Pam Verros*
Senior supplement producer: *Rose M. Range*
Senior digital content specialist: *Brian Nacik*
Cover design: *Adam C. Rooke*
Interior design: *Maureen McCutcheon*
Typeface: *10/12 New Baskerville*
Compositor: *Black Dot Group*
Printer: *R. R. Donnelley*

Library of Congress Cataloging-in-Publication Data

Lagerstrom, Larry Randles.
    Programming the Web using XHTML and JavaScript / Larry Randles Lagerstrom.
      p. cm.
    ISBN 0-07-256031-2 (alk. paper) – ISBN 0-07-119997-7 (international : alk. paper)
    1. Internet programming. 2. XHTML (Document markup language) 3. JavaScript
    (Computer program language) I. Title.
    QA76.625 .L34 2003
    005.2'76—dc21

                                                     2002071929

INTERNATIONAL EDITION ISBN 0-07-119997-7
Copyright © 2003. Exclusive rights by The McGraw-Hill Companies, Inc. for manufacture and export. This book cannot be re-exported from the country to which it is sold by McGraw-Hill. The International Edition is not available in North America.

www.mhhe.com

Preface

To the Instructor

Programming the Web Using XHTML and JavaScript has been designed to meet the needs of three types of increasingly popular courses.

Web Authoring Courses

The first type consists of introductory Web Authoring courses. Many community colleges, university extension programs, and technical schools have added such courses to their programs in the last few years to meet the demand for training and retraining in Internet technologies. *Programming the Web* provides a solid and up-to-date introduction to HTML, including XHTML, style sheets, and forms.

Web Scripting Courses

Such Internet education programs typically also offer a more advanced course on Web Scripting using JavaScript, the primary client-side scripting language of the Internet. Many students in these web scripting courses are coming to the course as web page designers who want to become familiar with the capabilities of JavaScript. They often have little or no experience in computer programming, and they are easily overwhelmed by the subject as normally presented in trade books on JavaScript. In contrast, *Programming the Web* provides a more suitable introduction to JavaScript, paying careful attention to the concepts where novice programmers and nontechnical students encounter the most difficulty.

CS 0 Courses

The third type of course includes the so-called "CS 0" courses: computer science service courses that introduce non-CS majors to computers and/or the Internet. A recent report from the National Academy of Sciences on "Being Fluent with Information Technology" (1999) recommends that an introduction to programming be included in these courses. The question arises, however, as to what programming language would be most suitable for nontechnical students. Given the importance of the Internet and its allure for students, a well-designed curriculum based on HTML and JavaScript is arguably the best way to fulfill this recommendation, and many CS 0 courses are going in that direction. *Programming the Web* fits well within such a curriculum, as it provides a gently sloping introduction to programming in general and HTML and JavaScript in particular. It also allows the instructor to choose how far and how deep to go into programming matters. (Suggested coverage for various types of courses is given in the Instructor's Manual.)

Other features of the text include:

- Up to date coverage of the nature of XHTML and its relationship to HTML. (This is a continuing source of confusion, even among many web designers.)
- Adherence to the World Wide Web Consortium's emphasis on the distinction between structure and presentation in web page coding.
- An early (but optional) introduction to the use of cascading style sheets in HTML to specify web page presentation.
- A smooth yet substantial introduction to JavaScript programming, using numerous examples and everyday metaphors (e.g., visualizing an array as a set of cubbyholes or post office boxes).
- A concern for not trying to introduce too many things at once and a practice of using the familiar to learn about the unfamiliar (e.g., easy-to-understand alert boxes are used to introduce and highlight important aspects of variables, functions, and parameters).

To the Student:

The World Wide Web needs little introduction. In less than a decade during the 1990s it went from a useful scheme for information sharing at a European physics laboratory to a worldwide phenomenon that is having profound effects on society, culture, business, education, and technology. Arthur C. Clarke, the noted author of *2001: A Space Odyssey* among many other works, once remarked that "Any sufficiently advanced technology is indistinguishable from magic." To many people, the World Wide Web is just that: magic. How web pages get created and then pulled out of cyberspace and displayed on a computer screen is a wondrous mystery to them. If you are reading this book, however, you presumably have an interest in demystifying some of that magic and even acquiring some of the knowledge and skills of the web magicians themselves. This book will help you do that. It will take you back behind the scenes of the Web and introduce you to Hypertext Markup Language (HTML), the language used to create web pages.

But we won't stop with HTML. By next learning a programming language called JavaScript, you will be able to create web pages that actually respond to and interact with the web surfer. You will learn how to make online calculators, quizzes, image rollovers, slide shows, and much more. Although learning a programming language is not always easy, we will try to give the educational road a gentle upward slope, and in the end you will find the journey well worth the effort. Even if you do not pursue a career as a web designer or programmer, the technical knowledge and skills you acquire will serve you well and open doors throughout your career, whatever field you might be in.

Key Features

Programming the Web includes a number of key features that are designed to increase its pedagogical effectiveness:

- **Side-by-side comparisons of source code and the corresponding browser display**, using screen shots from Notepad and Internet Explorer.
- **Error Alert icons** placed in the margin to warn students of common errors.
- **Important icons** placed in the margin to highlight useful programming tips and advice.
- **QuickCheck questions** at the end of every section to help students check their understanding of the material.
- **Comprehensive end-of-chapter material**, including:

    Key terms listed at the end of chapter. These key terms are highlighted in bold color in the text when first introduced.

    Code examples that review the syntax and use of all the HTML and/or JavaScript elements covered in the chapter.

    Summary list of all the "error alerts" and important items in the chapter.

    Review questions (in multiple-choice, fill-in-the-blank, and short-answer formats).

    Exercises that cover the main topics of the chapter which may be assigned as homework problems.

- **Debugging exercises** for practice with identifying programming errors.
- **Detailed laboratory exercises for each chapter**, most of which are designed to be completed in a two-hour lab session.
- **Sitebuilding exercises** (Appendix A)

    This series of five exercises leads students through a step-by-step process of creating a sophisticated, JavaScript-powered website. The exercises, which are listed in Appendix A, are designed to be done at strategic points throughout the text. Students may either do the exercises as they come up in the text, thus gradually assembling the website over the course of the term, or they may wait until all the pertinent material has been covered and then focus solely on the sitebuilding exercises as an end-of-term programing project.

    To provide a focus, three types of projects are suggested:

    1. A Company/Organization Information Site
    2. A Distance Learning Site
    3. An Electronic Commerce Site

Each sitebuilding exercise outlines certain features to add to the site, based on the material just covered and the project chosen. For example, Sitebuilding Exercise 3 ("Adding Interactive Features") suggests implementing a customer survey for the Company Information site, or an online exam for the Distance Learning site, or an order form calculator for the Electronic Commerce site (among other ideas).

- **Reference appendices**
  Although *Programming the Web* is not intended to be a comprehensive reference for all aspects of HTML and JavaScript, it includes sufficient reference material so that students can use the book as a resource guide for building JavaScript-powered websites. This material is divided into nine appendixes:

  A. Sitebuilding Exercises
  B. HTML and XHTML Elements
  C. Converting HTML to XHTML
  D. Basic Style Properties and Values
  E. Color and Character Codes
  F. JavaScript Versions, Objects, and Reserved Words
  G. Common HTML and JavaScript Errors
  H. Publishing a Web Page on the Internet
  I. Tools and Resources

Instructor's Resource Kit

The Instructor's Resource Kit is a CD-ROM containing the Instructor's Manual in both MS Word and .pdf formats, Brownstone test-generating software, and accompanying test item files in both MS Word and .pdf formats for each chapter.

Instructor's Manual

- Chapter learning objectives per chapter
- Chapter outline with teaching tips
- Several suggested course outlines, depicting a time table and schedule for covering chapter content
- Answers to end-of-chapter Review Questions

Test Bank

The Test Bank, using Diploma Network Testing Software by Brownstone, contains 850 questions with the page reference to the text.

There are 50 questions per chapter. The Test Bank consists of 20 multiple choice, 15 true/false, 10 fill-in and 5 short answer questions per chapter.

Custom Website: (http://www.mhhe.com/lagerstrom)

The Custom Website includes code examples from the text, additional problems, and the Instructor's Resource Kit.

Digital Solutions for Instructors and Students:

PageOut is our Course Website Development Center that offers a syllabus page, URL, Custom Website content, online quizzes, gradebook, discussion board, and an area for student web pages. For more information, visit the PageOut website at www.pageout.net.

Acknowledgements

The material in *Programming the Web* has been field-tested in several types of courses and academic settings. It had its start in 1996 as a lab manual for Interdepartmental Studies 110—"Introduction to Computers"—at the University of California at Berkeley. The 4,000 students who passed through the course in the years 1996–2000 made many useful suggestions as to how the material could be improved, as did the dozens of teaching assistants who were involved. Three head teaching assistants deserve special recognition for their help and coolness under fire: Chris Ritter, Susan Shepler, and Mohamed Abdel-Kader. More recently, students in Engineering 7—"The Technology and Culture of the Internet"—at the University of California at Davis and in the U. C. Davis Extension course "Web Page JavaScripting" have tested revised versions of the original material. Several anonymous reviewers also provided very helpful feedback and made the final result much better than it would have been. Any errors that remain are my own.

Finally, important contributions were made in their own way by Ron and Velma Lagerstrom, Tirso and Lois Serrano, Roy and Delfa Randles, and most of all by Lori, Ryan, and Linnea Randles Lagerstrom.

Brief Contents

Contents

CHAPTER 7

Introduction to Programming and JavaScript   177

CHAPTER 8

Objects and Variables   211

Introduction to the Internet

LEARNING OBJECTIVES

1. Learn about the Internet's origins in the 1960s, motivated by the twin ideas of connecting dissimilar networks and creating a more robust distributed network model.

2. Understand how information travels over the Internet via packets and routers.

3. Learn how Internet addresses work.

4. Learn about the early services available on the Internet, how software is layered on the Internet, and the origins of the World Wide Web.

5. Understand what goes on behind the scenes when a browser loads a web page.

The Origins of the Internet

In simplest terms, the Internet is a network of computer networks, or an **internetwork** (thus the name). Although it burst into prominence in the 1990s, its origins go back to the 1960s, when officials at the U.S. Defense Department's Advanced Research Projects Agency (ARPA) became frustrated that they were always having to switch back and forth between different computer networks in order to communicate with their research projects at universities around the country. Bob Taylor, the official in charge of overseeing the agency's computing projects, actually had to have three different computers in his office, each with different log-in and operating procedures. In 1966 he therefore came up with a vision of somehow connecting these dissimilar computer networks together in such a way that the user would only have to deal with a generic set of log-in and operating procedures. The result, after three years of work, was **ARPANET.** At first it only connected computers at four sites: the University of California at Los Angeles, the University of California at Santa Barbara, the University of Utah, and the Stanford Research Institute.

Over time, however, more and more computers and networks were connected, primarily at universities and a few government agencies, and ARPANET became an essential tool for researchers around the country to communicate with each other and share documents and software.

There was another defense-related factor that motivated the early development of the ARPANET. The Cold War between the United States and the former Soviet Union was at its height in the 1960s, and many people were concerned about the possibility of nuclear war. Among other things, the Defense Department worried about how it would keep its communication and computer networks operational in such an event. A common design for a computer network was to have one or a few central computers that acted as hubs to control the rest of the network. Any and all information sent from one computer on the network to another was routed through one of the hubs. That meant, however, that if a hub computer was disabled, much of the network would go down with it.

A researcher named Paul Baran therefore came up with the idea of a **distributed network** that had no central hub (Figure 1.1). If one computer was disabled, the network was designed to route the flow of information around it. The ARPANET design was not based on the hub model, and although surviving a nuclear war was not the original inspiration for the ARPANET, Baran's idea of a distributed network provided additional motivation to develop it.

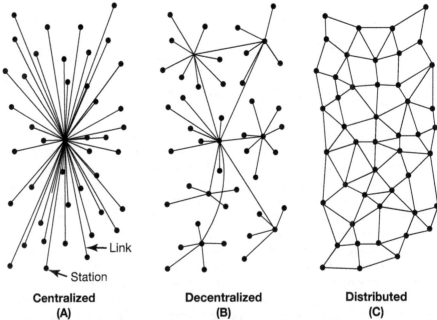

Centralized
(A)

Decentralized
(B)

Distributed
(C)

FIGURE 1.1.   Paul Baran's original diagram comparing a distributed network design with network designs using a single hub (centralized) or multiple hubs (decentralized)

The ARPANET grew quickly and by the mid-1980s had over 1,000 computers or **hosts**, mainly at government and university sites. In 1986 the National Science Foundation was given responsibility to expand the network and open it up to organizations without a military connection. (Most universities received some sort of defense funding, such as research grants, and so were eligible for the ARPANET.) By this time, many people had started to call it the Internet.

Packets and Routers

Without a central hub to direct traffic flow, how would a distributed network work? In the modern design of the Internet, the central hub is replaced by numerous connectors called **routers**. A router is most simply a special-purpose computer running special-purpose software that enables it to connect the network of networks that make up the Internet. Routers may be thought of as the traffic cops of the Internet, in charge of directing and routing the network's traffic.

The traffic itself consists of **packets**. When sending a file or message over the network from one computer to another, the file is broken up into packets (Figure 1.2). Typical packet sizes used on the Internet range from under 100 bytes up to 1,500 bytes. Each packet includes "header" information that lists the filename, the origin and destination computers, and the order number of the packet; for example (in English terms), "packet #5 of 22 total for the file named such and so."

These packets are then sent out over the network. The nearest router receives them, checks their destination, and then sends them on to another router that is closer to the final destination. An individual packet typically goes through a number of routers before it arrives at its destination. Once all the packets arrive, the file is reconstituted by reassembling the packets in the proper order.

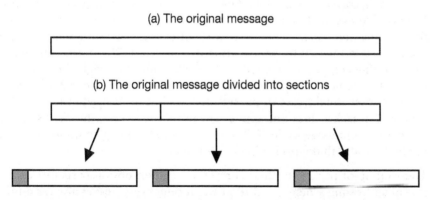

(a) The original message

(b) The original message divided into sections

(c) The sections put into packets, with header information added (shaded)

FIGURE 1.2. Breaking a message into packets

This method of traffic control and flow is called **packet-switching**, where "switching" means "routing," not "interchanging." (Think of a railroad yard where the railcars are switched onto different tracks depending on their destination.) The Internet and similarly designed networks are known as packet-switched networks. The whole process is like mailing a five-page letter to a friend through the regular postal service, but instead of sending it all in one envelope, putting each page in its own envelope and mailing them all separately.

The routers on the network are constantly communicating with each other in order to have up-to-the-second "traffic reports." If, for example, one router is experiencing very heavy traffic loads or goes offline for some reason, the other routers will send packets around it (i.e., to other routers) until the traffic subsides or the router is back online. A packet may therefore take a very circuitous route to its destination. And, in fact, the individual packets that make up a file may not even take the same route through the network. Some packets of a file sent from a computer in San Francisco to a computer in Boston, for example, may end up traveling through routers in Albuquerque, Dallas, and Atlanta while others may take a northerly route through routers in Seattle, Chicago, and New York.

TCP/IP and Domain Names

During the Internet's early growth, it went through several redesigns to improve and standardize its operating procedures. The most significant standardization occurred in 1983, when the network was converted to what was called **TCP/IP**.

IP, standing for Internet Protocol, is the software that runs the routers, performing the basic task of moving packets as quickly as possible from router to router. One thing it doesn't do, however, is check to see whether the packets reach their correct destination. That's where TCP, or Transmission Control Protocol, comes in. TCP is the software that breaks messages into packets at the sending end. After the packets are sent over the network and routed to the correct destination by routers using IP software, TCP software running on the receiving computer recombines the packets into the original message. As part of this recombining process, TCP also provides an error-checking mechanism in order to take care of packets that are lost or delayed in transit. Very simply, if a packet does not appear at the receiving end, the TCP software there sends a message to the TCP software on the sending computer requesting that it transmit the packet in question again.

The routing of packets to their correct destination obviously requires some sort of addressing scheme, and IP provides one. Every host computer on the Internet is given a unique **IP address**, made up of four numbers, such as 192.56.215.131, where each of the numbers may be between 0 and 255.

Using all possible combinations of the four numbers in an IP address yields approximately 4 billion addresses. Originally this number seemed to provide ample room for expansion. But the explosive growth of the Internet in the 1990s quickly ate into the reserve. In addition, it was clear that the trend was toward even greater growth, especially as more and more handheld computers and other small devices were connected to the Internet (often via wireless connections). In the mid-1990s, therefore, the **Internet Engineering Task Force (IETF)**, a large open community of network researchers, operators, and suppliers, proposed an updated version of IP, known as **IPv6**, for "Internet Protocol version 6." (The current version is IP version 4. IP version 5 was a limited experimental version that did not see wide use.)

IPv6 allows for 64 billion billion billion addresses, enough so that we could assign an IP address to every grain of sand on the Earth if we so desired. Another important feature of IPv6 is that it is able to coexist with IPv4. This means that it can be gradually implemented into the existing Internet without having to take on the impossible task of upgrading everything at once.

The IP addressing schemes based on numbers suit computers just fine, but they are a little too sparse for humans. Imagine the confusion and consternation that would result if there were no street names but just address numbers. Instead of "we live at 216 Main Street," it might be "we live at 192.56.215.131." An Internet **domain name system (DNS)** is therefore laid on top of the IP addressing system for the sake of us humans.

At the broadest level, the Internet is divided into different country domains, consisting of all the hosts on the network in that country. Then, within each country or **top-level domain**, the hosts are grouped according to the organization to which they belong. (Sometimes the country domain is first broken into smaller subdomains, like states or provinces, and then further divided into cities before being divided into organizations.) Finally, the host itself is given a name. Instead of referring to a host by its IP address, 192.56.215.131 or whatever, we can refer to it using the general syntax below:

> *hostname.organizationname.countryname*

With this syntax, it's not necessary that every host on the network have a different name. Two different organizations in the same country may use identical host names, but the full name will be different because the organization names are different.

Special codes are used for the country name. For example, the United States is .us, the United Kingdom is .uk, Germany is .de (for Deutschland), and so on. There's even one for Antarctica, .aq. The period is pronounced as "dot," hence "dot UK," and so on. A few examples:

> *www.ox.ac.uk (Oxford University)*
> *www.louvre.fr (official site of the Louvre Museum in Paris)*
> *www.mos.ru (City of Moscow site)*

> *www.ci.sf.ca.us (City of San Francisco site)*
> *www.tpn.aq (the Tasmanian Polar Network)*

An alternative scheme, however, is used for many hosts in the United States. Instead of the top-level domain being the country code, it consists of a code corresponding to the type of organization to which the host belongs. The codes for the major types are .edu, .com, .gov, .mil, and .org for educational, commercial, government, military, and nonprofit organizations, respectively. There's also net, used especially for networking companies and organizations. A special organization with a charter from the U.S. government, the **Internet Corporation for Assigned Names and Numbers (ICANN)**, oversees the management and assignment of names, as well as IP addresses. A few examples:

> *socrates.berkeley.edu*
> *www.redcross.org*
> *www.att.net*
> *developer.intel.com*
> *www.whitehouse.gov*
> *www.edwards.af.mil (Edwards Air Force Base)*

Note that the .com, .org, and .net top-level domains are not strictly regulated. It's possible, for example, for any organization to use the org designation, whether or not it's a nonprofit. In practice, however, .org often does signify a nonprofit organization. In addition, several new top-level domains were approved by ICANN in 2001, including .museum, .aero, and .biz (the latter because of the run on .com names in the late 1990s).

Anyone may register a domain name with a .com, .org, or .net extension. Although ICANN is in overall charge of registration, in practice it certifies certain **domain name registrars** to manage the process, such as Network Solutions (www.netsol.com) and Register.com (www.register.com). These companies register names for an annual fee usually ranging from about $20 to $100, depending on the registrar and the type of name. The real challenge is finding a domain name that has not already been registered, especially in the .com domain. Some countries with desirable top-level domain names have seized the opportunity and gotten into the domain name business for themselves. Tuvalu, for example, has the country abbreviation .tv. It is more than happy to register domain names with that extension for anyone who pays the requested fee, whether they live in Tuvalu or not. (Television stations are especially encouraged to apply.)

Some people register domain names simply for speculative purposes, hoping to sell the rights later at a profit. Occasionally someone strikes it rich this way, especially if he or she had the foresight early on in the game to register a name like internet.com. But trademark issues come into play. If a domain name like microsoft.com were available, you might be able to register it, although you couldn't use it as the courts have ruled that such names can only be used by the trademark owner.

By itself, the domain name is simply that: a name. It only becomes meaningful when it is associated with an IP address, because the numbered IP addresses of computers on the network are what is used in the transmission of information across the network. In order to associate a domain name with a specific IP address, the domain name must be listed in a special database similar to a phone book. For a given domain name, the database lists the corresponding IP address. This database is stored on a **DNS server** (or simply a **name server**) on the network. We will discuss servers in more detail later in this chapter. For now, you may consider a server to be a computer on a network that is set up to serve information to other computers on the network whenever they request it. So when a computer on the network wants to send information to another computer and has the domain name but not the IP address of that computer, it first sends the domain name to a DNS server. The DNS server looks up the corresponding IP address and sends it back to the computer. The computer then knows where to send its message.

Basic Services from FTP to the WWW

In addition to the basic transmission and addressing protocols of TCP/IP, the Internet uses other software protocols to provide various services to its users. Among the earliest services made available were FTP, telnet, and electronic mail.

FTP stands for file transfer protocol and, as the name implies, allows Internet users to transfer or download files from another computer on the network to their own. The **telnet** protocol allows the user to connect and log in (usually via a password) to a remote computer on the network in order to access its resources. For example, a user might telnet to a certain computer to access a library database. Sometimes called remote log-in, telnet is also used as a verb, as in "If you telnet to such-and-such computer, you'll be able to access that library database." FTP may be used similarly: "If you FTP to that computer on the network, you'll find a nice site with a lot of software you can download."

Internet services like FTP and telnet are **layered** on top of TCP/IP. This means that any messages that are sent across the network from one computer to another computer via these services go through several layers of processing. Consider the case of making a telnet connection from computer A to computer B (Figure 1.3). To do so, computer A must be running telnet software that can call computer B and request a connection, and computer B must be running a slightly different version of telnet software that is capable of receiving the request and establishing the connection via the appropriate login procedures. This requires that the telnet programs on computers A and B send several messages back and forth to each other to get everything sorted out. When the telnet software on computer A sends a message to computer B, it does not send it directly, but hands it off to the TCP software on computer A. The TCP software breaks the message into packets and adds the necessary error-checking material. It then hands off the packets to the IP software running on computer A, which does its job by sending the packets to the nearest router on the network. The packets are passed from router to router on the network, each of which is running IP software, until the packets reach computer B.

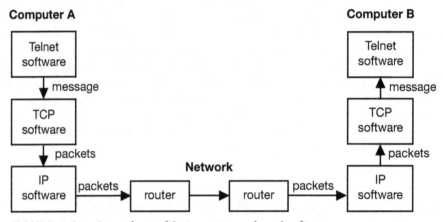

FIGURE 1.3.   Layering of Internet services/software

At computer B, the process is reversed. The IP software running on computer B receives the packets and hands them off to the TCP software running on computer B. The TCP software performs its job by recombining the packets into the original message (checking for errors in the process) and passing them to the telnet software running on computer B. The telnet software then reads the message and takes appropriate action. If that action involves sending a message back to the telnet software on computer A, the whole process starts again, but this time going from computer B to computer A.

While network services like FTP and telnet found immediate use on the early Internet, electronic mail was the software application that more than anything else jumpstarted it. Invented in 1971–1972 by Ray Tomlinson, electronic mail began as a jury-rigged "hack" of early file transfer software so that users could send messages to each other. E-mail quickly became a preferred means of communicating among university researchers and students, and to this day remains one of the main reasons why people decide to get an Internet connection and go online.

The other main reason for the explosion of interest in the Internet during the 1990s was of course the World Wide Web. The basic protocol for the Web was created from 1989 to 1991 by Tim Berners-Lee at the European high energy physics lab called CERN. Berners-Lee was looking for a way to access and share documents across all the different research groups at CERN. Although everybody was connected to the CERN computer network (and the network, in turn, was connected to the Internet), it was difficult to locate and share information. Files could be transferred back and forth, but file formats varied from group to group. Moreover, even if a person could locate the desired file on the network and download it, the person might not have the correct software to view it. And when everything did work, the process was cumbersome. Berners-Lee dreamed of being able to directly access and display any information on his computer.

To make his vision a reality, he built on an idea that had been around for a long time: **hypertext**. To understand the concept of hypertext, imagine that you are reading a magazine article (the paper-based kind) and you come across a footnote or reference to another article that looks like something you would like to read. To do so, you would probably have to go to a library, find the magazine in question, and look up the article. But what if you could do all that electronically? What if the original magazine was an electronic magazine that you could access over a computer network and display its contents on the screen? And what if, when you saw the footnote, you could simply click on it with the mouse and thereby direct the computer to retrieve and display the footnoted article? Then, perhaps in the second article, you might see another interesting footnote. Click on that footnote and you would quickly have that article on the screen ready to peruse. Decide to go back to the previous article? Just click a "Back" button. And so on and so forth.

Hypertext is very much like browsing through an encyclopedia or a library, following your interests wherever they may lead. It makes possible a more random, nonsequential type of reading experience than the linear flow of a regular book. And it doesn't have to be just footnotes and other academic trappings. Hyperlinks can be built right into the text of a document. Key words, for example, in a magazine article may be made into hyperlinks—when the user clicks on one of the key words, a definition or further explanation of it might appear. Or the names of key people mentioned might be hyperlinks that, when clicked, would pop up a screen of biographical information.

To allow the creation of hypertext documents, Berners-Lee invented a special kind of document formatting or "markup" language, called **hypertext markup language (HTML)**, as well as a transmission protocol called **hypertext transfer protocol (HTTP)** to make it possible to send and receive HTML documents over a network. He also created **browser** software that could read the HTML formatting instructions in an HTML document that the computer had received and display the document on a computer monitor. Put it all together, and you had what Berners-Lee called the **World Wide Web (WWW)**.

Berners-Lee and CERN offered HTML and HTTP for free to the Internet community in 1991, which generated immediate interest. From 1991 to 1994 WWW-related network traffic at CERN grew 1,000 percent each year. It was an event half a world away, however, that triggered the Internet revolution of the 1990s.

The first PC versions of HTML and HTTP worked with software that used a text-based user interface, with no icons, images, mouse pointer, and so on. A group of graduate students at the University of Illinois, led by Marc Andreesen, decided to bring the browser into the GUI (graphical user interface) world. In 1993 they created browser software they called Mosaic that allowed the user to easily browse the hyperlinked paths and documents (pages) of the Web and, even better, to download and display images on web pages. The key members of the Mosaic team soon left the University to found a company first called Mosaic and then, after the University protested, renamed Netscape. It was the Netscape Navigator browser of 1994 that propelled the World Wide Web to a world-wide phenomenon. The next year Microsoft followed with its own browser software, Internet Explorer. Other browsers also exist, such as the Opera browser developed by a group in Norway, although Explorer and Navigator dominate the market.

URLs and Client-Server Computing

What exactly goes on when you use browser software to visit a web page or two or three?

Unless you click on a hyperlink that automatically displays a web page for you, to visit a web page you first need to know its **uniform resource locator**, or **URL**. (URL is pronounced "U-R-L" by some, "earl" by others. In addition, some people prefer the term "uniform resource identifier," or URI.) A URL tells where to find a document and how to retrieve it. Earlier we covered the IP addressing and domain name systems, which supply unique addresses for each computer connected to the Internet. Any given computer, however, obviously contains thousands of files, so we need to be more specific if we are to retrieve a certain document. In short, we need to specify two things:

1.   The exact location of the document, i.e., the computer on which it may be found and where it is stored on that computer.

2.   The method or protocol by which to retrieve and display the document.

These two things are given by the URL. Consider the following example:

http://universityextension.ucdavis.edu/distancelearning/index.htm

The first part—the http://—specifies the protocol, or set of rules, for transmitting the document across the network. Other possibilities would include the Internet services FTP and telnet, or ftp:// and telnet://.

The second part—universityextension.ucdavis.edu—is the combination hostname/domain name: ucdavis.edu refers to the local ucdavis domain within the top-level educational domain edu, and universityextension is the name of a host computer within the ucdavis domain.

The third part gives the pathname of a document on the universityextension host, in this case /distancelearning/index.htm. That is, the index.htm document is stored in the distancelearning folder (or directory). (While URLs with more complex syntax than these examples may also occur, this is the basic form.) In a real sense, a URL is very much like the pathname of a file on a hard disk, but here the hard disk is the whole Internet.

Now that we know how to specify a Web page to visit via its URL, the next question is what happens when we instruct our Web browser to go there. To answer this question, we need to know about the **client-server model**. In this case, our PC is the **client** and the computer on which the Web page document resides is the **server**. The name server comes from the fact that its job is to serve documents to other computers on the network whenever it receives a request to do so.

Sometimes the terms client and server refer more specifically to the software running on the computers involved, not the computers themselves. A web browser is sometimes called a web client or web client software. E-mail applications like Microsoft's Outlook and Qualcomm's Eudora programs are called e-mail clients. On the server end of the connection, a computer may be running several types of server software at the same time, such as web server software and FTP server software. A computer may also act as a client and a server simultaneously. It's possible to set up a PC to run web server software that processes web page requests while at the same time the PC is running web client software (e.g., Navigator or Explorer) to browse the Web.

When browser software is given the URL for a web page stored on a computer somewhere, it sends a request to the web server software on that computer, asking that the web page document in question be sent. This document, known as the **source document**, contains the HTML instructions that tell the browser how to display the web page. Assuming that the source document exists and it is in its proper place, the server responds to the request by sending it (Figure 1.4). (At this point it goes through the usual layered processing of the Internet involving TCP and IP.) When the document arrives at the client (our PC in this example), the browser software takes the document, interprets the HTML instructions (or code) in it, and displays the document on the screen.

Note two things about this process: First, when you visit a web page, you don't actually go there—the document containing the HTML code for the web page is sent to you and then displayed on your computer. Second, after the HTML document arrives the connection is broken. This is very different from the other network we all use: the phone network. In the case of a phone call, the connection between you and the person at the other end persists until the end of the call. The Internet, however, is more like a document delivery

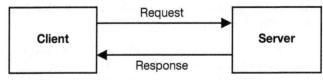

FIGURE 1.4. The client-server model

service. The client sends a request to a server for a specific file, and then the server responds to that request by sending it back.

The final, and biggest, mystery in this process concerns the HTML source document. What kind of instructions does it contain? And how can we create our own web pages using these source documents? The rest of this book provides some answers.

Lab Exercises 1.1, 1.2, 1.3, and 1.4 may be done at this point.

Key Terms

ARPANET
browser
client
client-server model
distributed network
DNS server
domain name registrars
domain name system (DNS)
FTP
host
hypertext

hypertext markup language (HTML)
hypertext transfer protocol (HTTP)
Internet Corporation for Assigned Names and Numbers (ICANN)
Internet Engineering Task Force (IETF)
internetwork
IP address
IPv6
layering

name server
packet
packet-switching
router
server
source document
TCP/IP
telnet
top-level domain
uniform resource locator (URL)
World Wide Web (WWW)

Review Questions

1. Where does the name Internet come from?
2. List the two factors that motivated the early development of ARPANET.
3. Routers may be thought of as the _____ of the Internet.
4. The Internet uses a method of traffic control and flow known as _____ .
5. Which of the following provides an error-checking mechanism that takes care of packets that are lost or delayed in transit?
   a. Transmission Control Protocol (TCP)
   b. Internet Protocol (IP)
   c. Hypertext Transfer Protocol (HTTP)
   d. Internet Error Checking Protocol (IECP)
6. Which of the following is an example of an IP address?
   a. www.whitehouse.gov
   b. http://www.whitehouse.gov/history/index.htm

    c. .gov

    d. 216.43.187.162

7. What is the purpose of the domain name system?

8. Explain the meaning of each part of the following domain name: socrates.berkeley.edu.

9. True or false: Tim Berners-Lee invented the idea of hypertext.

10. Explain the meaning of each part of the following URL: http://socrates.berkeley.edu/courses/history/hist181.html.

11. When you are browsing the Web and viewing web pages, your computer is acting as a:

    a. telnet

    b. client

    c. server

    d. packet

Exercises

1. Briefly define and/or explain the following terms: distributed network, router, packet-switching.

2. Explain how the domain name system works and why it's useful.

3. What is the purpose of HTTP?

4. Using a search engine or Internet directory like www.google.com or www.yahoo.com, search for information on Bob Taylor, Paul Baran, and Tim Berners-Lee. List at least one interesting tidbit of information you find for each one. (Tip: Don't just enter the name, or you may get too many search hits to be useful. Try entering the name plus "origins of Internet", "history of Internet", "ARPANET", or "history of World Wide Web".)

5. Using an Internet directory like www.yahoo.com or www.lycos.com, browse around and try to find at least one URL example for each of the top-level domains .com, .edu, .org, .net, .gov, and .mil. Also find URLs with top-level domains from at least five other countries besides the United States.

6. Using the online dictionary found at www.webopedia.com, read its definitions for TCP/IP, IP address, and HTTP and summarize their key points.

7. Go to www.cybergeography.com and click on the link for "Atlas of Cyberspaces." Explore the various examples of how people have attempted to map the Internet and its various parts. Pick three categories of maps and give a brief description of the purpose of that type of map (i.e., what does it map?). As part of your description, draw a sample sketch of what such a map looks like.

8. Explain how a video rental store provides a rough analogy to the World Wide Web.

Exercise 1.1: Thinking about Web Page Design

Lab Exercises

In this chapter we considered how a web page works in the sense of how HTML works. But there's also another sense of "how a web page works" that's equally as important: the layout and design of the web page. There are many web pages that have innovative and slick HTML code but are poorly designed in terms of the user experience. To explore this aspect of how web pages work, visit at least three of the web sites below and analyze their layout and design. Write a brief summary of what you found, comparing and contrasting the web pages. What was good, and what was bad? Some questions to consider:

1. How long do you have to wait for the page to load and be displayed?

2. Is the design clean and easy to follow or cluttered?

3. Is color used appropriately or is it jarring to the eye?

4. Are graphic images used appropriately? Do they enhance or detract from the site?

5. How easy is it to navigate around the site and find information?

6. If you were looking for an address and a phone number for the organization, could you easily find it?

Suggested websites:

www.ucdavis.edu	www.sun.com	www.lycos.com
www.berkeley.edu	www.dell.com	www.excite.com
www.stanford.edu	www.zdnet.com	www.google.com
www.intel.com	www.cnet.com	www.cocacola.com
www.microsoft.com	www.internet.com	www.pepsi.com
www.apple.com	www.yahoo.com	www.7up.com

Exercise 1.2: Behind the Scenes of a Web Page

You can actually see the HTML source code for any document that is currently displayed in your browser window. To see how this works, first go to a web page of your choosing (the simpler the web page, the better for this exercise). Once you see the web page displayed in your browser window, go to the View menu and select Source (in Explorer) or Page Source (in Navigator). A window will come up that displays the HTML source code for the web page. Take a look at it and see if you can match up some of the HTML code with the corresponding items that are displayed on the web page. Write down a few things you notice about the HTML code (anything at all will do). (Note: Some web pages use a technique known as frames, in which the browser window is divided into multiple independent panes. If you try the View Source method and don't get much information and if you're using a two-button mouse, try right-clicking in one of the frames and choosing View Source from the menu that pops up.)

Exercise 1.3: Comparing Browsers

One nice feature of HTML and web browsers is that they are very similar across computer platforms, such as Intel/Windows ("Wintel") machines vs. Macintosh machines vs. Unix machines. This means that it does not matter what type of computer you have at home, in the office, or at school, or which web browser software you are using. Any or all of them may be used to create and view web pages.

On the other hand, however, some differences do exist between the two major browsers, Netscape Navigator and Internet Explorer, in how they interpret and display HTML source documents. Older versions of each browser, which many web surfers may still be using, also do not implement the newer features of HTML. Finally, the same web page may display slightly differently on a Wintel machine than on a Macintosh machine because of differences in monitor hardware and software. Good web designers will always check for such differences in how their web pages display.

If you have access to both Explorer and Navigator, check the home page of your school or organization in both browsers and write down any differences that you see. (Compare, for example, colors, type styles and size, layout positions, and so on.) If you have time, go back to some of the previous web pages you visited in Exercise 1.1 and compare them in the two browsers.

Exercise 1.4: Tracing Packets

It's possible to get an idea of how packets travel over the Internet by using two simple utility programs that come with many operating systems. On most Windows and Unix systems you may use a program called ping to measure the round trip time of a packet sent to a given Internet host, specified either by its domain name or by its IP address.

To do so on a Windows system (Windows 98 or later), open an MS-DOS window by going to the Start menu and choosing Programs and then MS-DOS Prompt. When the MS-DOS window opens with its command-line prompt, type ping followed by a domain name (e.g., yahoo.com) or an IP address and then press Enter, as shown below with the prompt C:\WINDOWS>:

```
C:\WINDOWS>ping yahoo.com
```

The ping program will send three or four packets to the specified domain and then display the round trip times in milliseconds (thousandths of a second) of each packet. If network traffic is heavy and/or key routers are out of commission, the trip times will be lengthened.

For a Unix system, the procedure is the same: enter ping followed by a domain name or IP address at the Unix prompt.

For a Macintosh system, you will probably need to download a utility program like MacPing, available at websites like download.com or tucows.com.

Note: Because pinging a web server is a method used in Denial of Service hacking attacks, some web servers refuse ping requests.

A second utility program allows you to trace the route a packet travels to the destination domain, as it hops from router to router. On a Windows system, you enter tracert and the domain name at the prompt. On a Unix system it's usually traceroute and the domain name. And for Macintosh systems, download and use a program like WhatRoute or VisualRoute. All these programs will display the names and IP addresses of the routers that a packet passes through on the way to the specified destination. (The VisualRoute program even displays the route on a world map.)

Using the ping and trace route programs, explore the round trip times and routes of packets to at least five different web servers. Choose websites at different places around the world.

Creating a Basic Web Page

2

LEARNING OBJECTIVES

1. Learn how HTML uses tags and elements in a source document to define the structure of a web page.

2. Learn how to create a simple web page using a text editor.

3. Understand the reasons behind the development of the latest version of HTML (XHTML) and the new requirements for source documents and HTML elements.

4. Understand that the browser will ignore extra spaces and line breaks in the HTML source document so that line breaks and paragraph divisions must be specified in the HTML code itself.

5. Learn how to use a variety of basic HTML elements for headers, font size, block quotations, strong text, emphasized text, and comments.

The HTML Source Document

In Chapter 1 we learned about the client-server model and how a web page works. To review: When you connect to a web page by entering its URL into the browser (or by clicking on a hyperlink), the browser instructs your computer to send a message out over the Internet to the computer specified by that URL and requests that it send back a certain document (also specified in the URL). This document is the **HTML source document** for that web page. The source document contains HTML **source code** (instructions) that describes the content and layout of the page. It's called source code because this code is the source of the web page. In other words, the HTML code tells the browser what to display and how to lay it out. When your computer receives the source document in reply, your browser software interprets the HTML code in the source document and displays the resulting web page—its text, graphics, links, etc.—according to the HTML instructions.

Clearly much of the magic of the World Wide Web must reside in this HTML source document. The first point to be made about the source document is that it's a **text-only document**. No matter how fancy the web page, no matter how many images, animations, or whatever it has, the foundation of it all is a simple text document. (This of course raises the question of how we get things like images on a web page if the only thing in the source document is text. The answer will have to wait until Chapter 5.)

The second point is that the text in the source document consists of two things: (1) the actual text to be displayed on the web page, and (2) special markers called **elements** and **tags**, which specify the structure of the web page such as headings, paragraphs, and so on. These elements are what HTML is all about. The purpose of HTML is to use these elements to define the headings, paragraphs, and other elements that make up the structure of a web page. Another way to say this is that HTML elements *classify the contents* of the web page. They tell the browser whether a given section of text is a header or a regular paragraph or something else.

Consider, for example, how we would use HTML to classify the contents of this chapter and turn it into a web page. The most obvious elements of the web page would be the chapter's five major section headings:

The HTML Source Document
Creating a Source Document
HTML, XML, and XHTML
Paragraphs and Line Breaks
Adding More Tags

Some of these sections are further divided into subsections, each with its own heading. The *HTML, XML, and XHTML* section, for example, has the following subsection headings:

Writing and Indenting HTML Code
From HTML to XHTML
Creating an XHTML Source Document

Each of these subsections, in turn, is made up of paragraphs.

To represent this structure using HTML code in the source document, we use pairs of tags for each element, with different types of tags indicating the different types of elements. The major headings, for example, are marked using the beginning header 1 tag <h1> and the ending header 1 tag </h1>. As a pair, they make up the header 1 element. We see that tags are set off from the regular text by < > symbols. The closing tag contains a / before the h1 to indicate the termination of the header 1 element. Between each pair of header 1 tags we put the text for the header:

```
<h1>The HTML Source Document</h1>
...
<h1>Creating a Source Document</h1>
...
<h1>HTML, XML, and XHTML</h1>
...
<h1>Paragraphs and Line Breaks</h1>
...
<h1>Adding More Tags</h1>
```

When the browser sees these tags in a source document, it displays the text in between the <h1> and </h1> tags in a style appropriate for a major heading (usually in large bold type, although the style can be customized, as we'll see in Chapter 3).

Similarly, we use header 2 tags for the subsection headings. For example:

```
<h1>HTML, XML, and XHTML</h1>
   <h2>Writing and Indenting HTML Code</h2>
   <h2>From HTML to XHMTL</h2>
   <h2>Creating an XHTML Source Document</h2>
```

And to mark the paragraphs we use the <p> and </p> tags. The first paragraph in the section "The HTML Source Document" starts with the sentence: "In Chapter 1 we learned about the client-server model and how a web page works . . ." The second paragraph starts with: "Clearly much of the magic of the World Wide Web must reside in this HTML source document . . ." Therefore, the code for the first section of the source document would be:

```
<h1>The HTML Source Document</h1>
<p> In Chapter 1 we learned about the client-server model
and how a web page works . . . </p>
<p> Clearly much of the magic of the World Wide Web must
reside in this HTML source document . . . </p>
```

Putting all this together, we have what is called the **body** element of the source document. The body contains the HTML elements and text that end up being displayed by the browser as the Web page. It is marked off by the <body> and </body> tags.

```
<body>
<h1>The HTML Source Document</h1>
<p> In Chapter 1 we learned about the "client-server
model" and how a web page works . . . </p>
</body>
```

This code does not quite make a complete source document, however. Before the body element we also need a **head** element, marked by the <head> and </head> tags. The head contains special information such as the tags that define the document's title:

```
<head>
  <title>Creating a Basic Web Page</title>
</head>
```

The text within the title element (Creating a Basic Web Page, in this case) appears in the title bar of the browser window when it loads the source document and displays the results. This title is also used when a web surfer adds the page to his or her bookmark or Favorites list.

Together, the <body> and <head> elements make up the two major sections of the source document. Finally, we enclose the complete source code inside <html> and </html> tags, which signify that it is HTML code that defines a web page.

We now have a complete, albeit relatively simple, source document that defines the structure of the web page. Figure 2.1 shows the source code for our sample document (with a lot of content still to be filled in) and Figure 2.2 shows how the browser displays the first part of it. Don't worry at this point about understanding the details of the tags used in the source code. We will cover them later in this chapter. For now you should focus on the larger picture, which is that the code in the source document defines the structure and classifies the content of the web page. Note also that we have used an actual screen shot of the browser window in Figure 2.2 so that you can see the title in the title bar at the top of the window (Creating a Basic Web Page). Depending on the browser used, the window and buttons may look different than shown. (We used Explorer here. Note that for this example we set up the browser's View options to include the buttons and address bar at the top of the window, the scrollbar on the right side, and the status bar at the bottom. Usually we will leave those out and just show the title bar and menu bar of the browser window. We also set the browser's Text Size setting to smallest instead of medium. If you were to view this document in your browser, the text might appear larger.)

At this point you may have a number of unanswered questions such as "Do you have to type the tags in lowercase as shown?" or "Does it matter if a pair of tags (and any text and/or other tags inside them) is on the same line or not?" or "Do you have to indent certain lines as shown?" and "How exactly do you create the source document?" The next section will describe how to make a source document and then we will deal with some of these **syntax** issues. (Syntax simply refers to the rules for how something needs to be written and punctuated.)

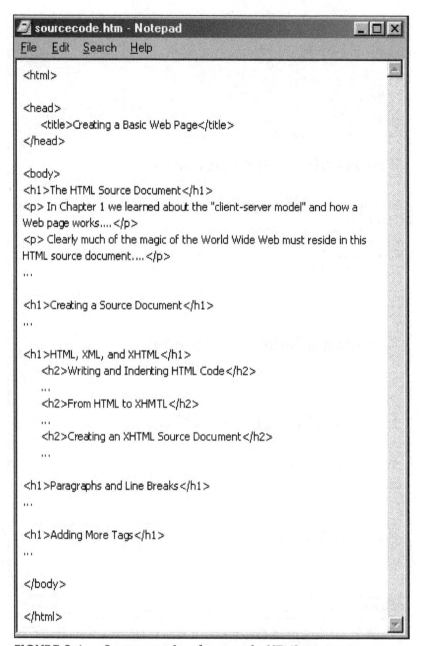

```
sourcecode.htm - Notepad
File   Edit   Search   Help

<html>

<head>
    <title>Creating a Basic Web Page</title>
</head>

<body>
<h1>The HTML Source Document</h1>
<p> In Chapter 1 we learned about the "client-server model" and how a
Web page works....</p>
<p> Clearly much of the magic of the World Wide Web must reside in this
HTML source document....</p>
...

<h1>Creating a Source Document</h1>
...

<h1>HTML, XML, and XHTML</h1>
    <h2>Writing and Indenting HTML Code</h2>
    ...
    <h2>From HTML to XHMTL</h2>
    ...
    <h2>Creating an XHTML Source Document</h2>
    ...

<h1>Paragraphs and Line Breaks</h1>
...

<h1>Adding More Tags</h1>
...

</body>

</html>
```

**FIGURE 2.1.   Source code of a sample HTML source
document showing the basic structure of the document**

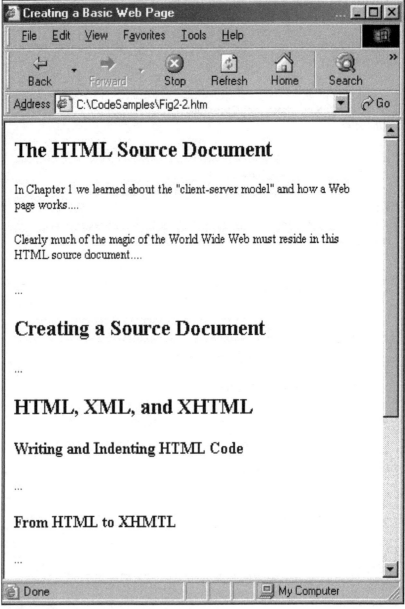

FIGURE 2.2.   Browser display of the first part of the Figure 2.1 source document

QuickCheck Questions

1. What is the purpose of HTML code?
2. What are the two major elements of a source document?
3. What's the difference between a tag and an element?
4. How do you create a title for a web page, and where is it displayed by the browser?

Creating a Source Document

Now that we know the basic idea of how HTML works—using tags in the source document to specify the structure of a web page—the next step is to create an actual source document.

To do this we use a simple text processor, such as Notepad, SimpleText, or pico. Notepad comes free with the Windows operating system, SimpleText comes free with the Macintosh operating system, and pico is one of several text editors that is usually available on Unix systems. All three allow the user to create text-only documents, which are documents that do not contain any hidden formatting characters (e.g., to indicate margins, font size, font type, bold text, and so on). The only things saved in the document are the actual characters that the user has typed. (Another popular choice on Windows systems is a text processor named TextPad. It has a number of features that Notepad lacks, such as automatic display of HTML tags in color to distinguish them from regular text. A trial copy may be downloaded from www.textpad.com.)

The HTML source document needs to be a text-only document because HTML has its own special characters—the tags—which it uses to tell the browser how to display the document. If there were other non-HTML special characters in the document, the browser would display them as regular text, with confusing results.

Even though you may create text-only documents using Microsoft Word's Save As . . . option, it is not recommended to do so because the latest versions of Word have HTML capabilities built in. What this means in practice is that when you open an HTML source document in Word in order to make changes to the HTML code, Word reads the document as HTML instead of text-only and therefore displays it as a browser would.

IMPORTANT

It's also possible to create HTML source documents by using HTML editor software like Microsoft FrontPage, Macromedia Dreamweaver, or Adobe GoLive. Microsoft Word also has limited HTML editing capabilities. An HTML editor allows the user to create web pages (i.e., the HTML source documents) without having to know any HTML. Even professional web designers who are experts in HTML often use HTML editors to speed up the process of creating complex web pages. The convenience of an HTML editor does come with some limitations, however. Coding directly in HTML offers more power and flexibility to the serious or even semi-serious web designer. Anyone who wants to do more than just dabble in web page creation needs to have a good understanding of HTML itself.

Now, open up a text processor like Notepad or SimpleText (in your mind if not in actual practice), and we'll create our first HTML source document.

Figure 2.3 shows the bare-bones structure of a source document: the <head> and <body> elements contained within the <html> element and the <title> element within the <head> element. We also have included a sample line of text in the <body> element.

FIGURE 2.3.   The structure of an HTML source document

Before we can see how the browser will display this simple source code, we need to save it and create a source document. We will assume that we have been typing the above code using the Notepad program that comes with the Windows operating system. (Notepad may be opened by going to the Start menu and selecting Programs and then Accessories, where you should see it in the list of files.) When we save our work for the first time, we of course need to choose a filename for our document. We may name the document whatever we want (as long as it's a legal filename), with one exception and one caveat.

The exception is that the file must have a **.htm extension** (pronounced "dot-HTM") at the end of the name, because it signifies that the document is an HTML source document. (You may also save it with the four-letter extension, **.html**.) The caveat is that even though it's legal to put spaces and a few other special characters in file names, it's best to avoid them when naming HTML files.

Restrict yourself to letters and numbers. If you want to create a multiple-word filename, you may separate the words with the underscore (_) character or capitalize the separate words. Or you may simply write it as all lowercase letters.

For example, we might name our source document WebPage1.htm, or simple_web_page.htm, or SimpleWebPage.htm, or even simplewebpage.htm. It's good to use descriptive filenames, as we have done in the latter three cases. On the other hand, don't make your filenames too long and involved, because long names are more easily mistyped. In addition, some people prefer using all lowercase letters because the Unix operating system, which is the operating system used by the majority of web servers on the Internet, distinguishes between uppercase and lowercase letters (i.e., it's case-sensitive). If you always write your filenames in all lowercase letters, you never have to worry about typing a lowercase letter when it should be an uppercase letter. In what follows we will assume that we named the source document simplewebpage.htm.

Note a quirk of Notepad and some other text editors: When you save a file for the first time, a .txt extension is appended to the filename. This extension signifies that the file is a text-only file. For example, if we specify the name *simplewebpage*, then the full filename becomes *simplewebpage.txt*. Or, if we specify the name *simplewebpage.htm*, the file is saved with the name *simplewebpage.htm.txt*. Even though the HTML source document is a text-only file, it must have a .html or .htm extension at the end, not .txt. The solution is simple. When you save the file for the first time using Notepad's Save dialog box, put quotation marks at the beginning and end of the filename: "simplewebpage.htm". Doing so indicates to Notepad that you want the filename to be exactly as you specify it, and it won't add the .txt extension, unless of course you add it yourself.

If you are using your own Windows computer, you may create a more permanent solution to this .txt problem by making sure that Windows knows about .htm files. To do so, open a Windows Explorer window and select Folder Options under the View menu. Click the File Types tab in the window that appears, and then the New Type button. An Add New File Type box will appear with text boxes labeled Description of type and Associated extension (plus a few other boxes). In the Description box enter HTML source file and in the Associated extension box enter .htm. Click OK twice and you're done.

Once the source document has been saved properly, the next step is to open the browser (Netscape Navigator, Internet Explorer, or whatever) while keeping Notepad (with your HTML document) open at the same time. We want to be able to see both the source document and the browser display side by side.

The method of opening the simplewebpage.htm document from within the browser varies slightly depending on which browser is used. If it's Navigator version 6 or later, we select Open File . . . from the File menu. In earlier versions of Navigator, we select Open Page . . . from the File menu, and then click on the Choose File button on the right side of the dialog box that appears. Using Explorer, we select Open from the File menu and then click on the Browse button. These actions call up the normal Open File dialog box, at which point we may find the simplewebpage.htm file in the listings and open it. You may also more quickly open the document in the browser by dragging the document's icon into the open browser window.

Figure 2.4 shows the resulting display in the browser. Note that the Address line shows that Explorer is displaying a local HTML file from a folder on one of the computer's disks (a folder named CodeSamples on the C: drive in this case), instead of a source document that it has downloaded from another computer on the Internet (signified by a full URL such as http://www.someplace.com/simplewebpage.htm).

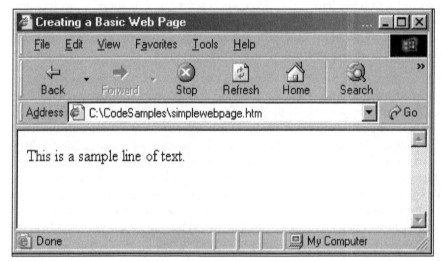

FIGURE 2.4.   Browser display of the Figure 2.3 source document

IMPORTANT

Also note that this means that your computer does not have to be connected to the Internet for you to create and view a web page. You can run your browser in offline mode and simply use it to display the HTML source documents that you have made and saved on your hard drive.

Once you have created an HTML source document using a text editor and opened it in the browser, you change and fine-tune the web page by going back and forth between the text editor and the browser. You add some HTML code to the source document or modify the existing code, save the changes, and then open the document again in the browser to see the results. When opening the document, you don't have to use the Open File command again. Instead, simply click the Reload button (in Navigator) or the Refresh button (in Explorer), and the browser will retrieve the source document again (now changed) and display it.

A common mistake in this editing process is to forget to save the changes you made to the source document. If you don't save the new version of the document, the browser will reload the previously existing version and nothing will change in the browser's display. Another common mistake is to open multiple copies of the source document in multiple windows of Notepad. Doing so makes it difficult to remember which copy is the currently saved version.

QuickCheck Questions

1. Why does the HTML source document need to be a text-only document?
2. What are the rules for giving a name to an HTML source document?

Lab Exercise 2.1, "A Simple Web Page," may be done at this point.

HTML, XML, and XHTML

At the end of the first section, we noted some common questions about the syntax of HTML code such as "Do you have to type the tags in lowercase?" or "Does it matter if a pair of tags (and any text and/or other tags inside them) is on the same line or not?" and "Do you have to indent certain lines?" The latter two questions are easily answered: They're both "No." The first question, however, will lead us into a discussion of the nature of HTML itself.

Writing and Indenting HTML Code

Taking the easy questions first, we have wide leeway in how we write HTML code. For example, we may write:

```
<head>
<title>Creating a Basic Web Page</title>
</head>
```

Or we may write:

```
<head>
<title>
Creating a Basic Web Page
</title>
</head>
```

Or:

```
<head><title>Creating a Basic Web Page</title></head>
```

Or even something like:

```
<head><title>
Creating a Basic Web
Page</title>
</head>
```

There are two key rules limiting these variations. First, the text in question (Creating a Basic Web Page in this case) must be enclosed within the tags that apply to it (<title> and </title> in this case). Second, different elements must be **nested** properly within each other and not overlapped. In this case, the <title> element should be nested inside the <head> element. The following two examples are incorrect because the </title> tag comes after the </head> tag:

```
<head><title>Creating a Basic Web Page</head></title>
```

Or:

```
<head>
<title>
Creating a Basic Web Page
</head>
</title>
```

IMPORTANT

As to the question of indenting, it's recommended but not required. It's always a good idea to make your HTML code readable to humans (including yourself), even though it doesn't matter to the browser. When the browser loads a source document and begins to display it, it starts at the top and works its way down to the bottom. In doing so, it ignores all extra **whitespace** (tabs and extra spaces) and the line breaks as well. Some web designers prefer to use multiple levels of indentation, while others prefer just one or two levels. Although we have not yet seen examples of more complex code where indentation really comes into play, you can see the possibilities from the examples below.

Multiple levels of indentation:

```
<html>
     <head>
       <title>Creating a Basic Web page</title>
     </head>
       . . .
</html>
```

Fewer levels of indentation:

```
<html>
<head>
    <title>Creating a Basic Web page</title>
</head>
  . . .
</html>
```

The key point is not to use a certain number of levels of indentation, but to use enough indentation so that your code is easy to read and understand.

From HTML to XHTML

The first question we raised above, regarding the use of lowercase characters in HTML tags, would seem to be just as straightforward as the questions regarding tags on the same line and indenting, but in fact it is not. Lowercase characters actually played a key role in the evolution of HTML itself.

In its early years especially, HTML evolved in a haphazard fashion. After Tim Berners-Lee introduced the language in the early 1990s, the designers of the Mosaic and Netscape Navigator browsers extended it in many ways. Even though a **World Wide Web Consortium** (the **W3C**, at www.w3.org) was created in 1994 to specify an official version of HTML, it had difficulty holding back first Netscape and then Microsoft when it introduced Explorer. Both companies were locked in a race to add ever more features to their browsers. Many web page designers, for their part, aggravated the situation by racing to use as many cutting-edge features and techniques as they could on their web pages. The result was an increasingly complex language and increasingly complex browsers that required megabytes of hard drive space and memory.

By the late 1990s the W3C had been able to exert a little more control over the process and standardize what was called version 4 of HTML. But Explorer and Navigator often played fast and loose with the official version, each in their own way. And the problem of complexity remained. For browsers designed to run on personal computers, this looseness and complexity does not pose a major problem. PCs have plenty of memory and storage space. Everyone could see, however, that a new generation of web-enabled devices like hand-held computers and cell phones was on the way. The W3C, in fact, estimated that by 2002 up to 75 percent of computers connected to the Internet would be small web-enabled devices. (Like many predictions, their timing was overly optimistic, although clearly the trend is in that direction.) Such devices do not have the memory and storage space to handle a full-featured browser displaying full-featured web pages. Nor would most web pages, which are designed to be viewed on PC monitors, display well on the screens of small devices.

There was clearly a need for a simpler, more standardized version of HTML that would work well, whatever the viewing device. To answer this need, the W3C decided that instead of making an HTML version 5, it would turn to a different language that it had been developing: **Extensible Markup Language**, or **XML**. The primary motivation for the creation of XML was the need to send data over the Internet in a universal, structured format, especially as electronic commerce and data exchange over the Internet began to take off in the 1990s.

At its heart, XML is a set of rules that lets web designers classify their data in a way customized to their needs by creating new types of tags. Thus the name extensible: XML allows designers to extend the language to fit their needs. For example, an online car dealership might organize and store information about their automobiles using tags like `<make>`, `<model>`, `<year>`,

<numberofdoors>, <color>, and so on. Or a hospital might use customized tags for its online system of patient records like <patient>, <billingad-dress>, <healthplan>, and <physician>. (HMTL does not have these capabilities. All its tags, with only a couple of exceptions, are predefined.)

The W3C decided that the best approach to solve HTML's problems would be to reorganize and reformulate it from the ground up using XML rules and philosophy. Because this new version of HTML would not be based on earlier versions of HTML but on XML, it was named **Extensible Hypertext Markup Language** or **XHTML**. The first version of XHTML was officially released in January 2000. Navigator 6 and Explorer 6 both support XML for the most part, and therefore also support XHTML. (A listing of XML-compatible browsers may be found at www.xmlsoftware.com/browsers/. Note also that XHTML is not XML. If you want the full customization capabilities of XML, you have to use it, not XHTML.)

In order to ensure that XML is universal—that it works no matter the device being used—it has some very strict syntax rules. As an XML-based language, XHTML inherits these rules (and their benefits). And thus we come back to where we started this discussion: the question of lowercase characters in tag names. HTML version 4 is *not* a **case-sensitive** language. This means, for example, that it makes no distinction between <body>, <BODY>, and <bOdY>. All three variations are legal HTML code and signify the same thing (although the last one would certainly not be recommended). But XML is a case-sensitive language: The way you type the name of an element matters. The W3C chose to use lowercase letters for XHTML tags, and therefore in XHTML only <body> is allowed.

We also briefly mentioned above that tags must be nested properly. Even though this rule applies in HTML, many browsers were designed to ignore the rule and accept overlapping tags as legal. An XHTML-compatible browser must not.

As yet another example, sometimes it's possible to leave off an ending tag, like </body>, with no ill effects: Many browsers will still display the web page. A browser that follows the XHTML rules, however, will not do so.

You may think that some of these rules, such as the lowercase restriction, are needlessly restrictive. What does it matter if all tag names are lowercase, especially if browsers can be designed to handle it? But the more exceptions the language has, the more complex the browser needs to be to handle all of them. And the more complex the browser, the more memory and storage space it requires. And the greater the memory and storage requirements, the less likely it will work well on devices like handheld computers and cell phones.

Creating an XHTML Source Document

In Figure 2.3 we reviewed the required elements that make up an HTML source document: the <head> and <body> elements enclosed in the <html> element plus the <title> element in the <head>. It doesn't take much to make this into an XHTML source document. We first add the following cryptic lines at the very beginning before the <html> tag:

```
<?xml version="1.0"?>
<!DOCTYPE html PUBLIC
    "-//W3C//DTD XHTML 1.0 Transitional//EN"
    "http://www/w3/org/TR/xhtml/11/DTD/xhtml11-
        transitional.dtd">
```

The first line is an **XML declaration** that indicates, or declares, to the browser the version of XML used for the document's code. In other words, our newly modified document is actually now an XML document. But of course it is not just any XML document: It is an XML document that uses custom tags as defined by the W3C's XHTML specification. If a browser is going to be able to recognize and correctly display the tags contained in the document, it needs to know about the XHTML specification. The last four lines in the code above give this information to the browser. These lines (which may be written all on one line) make up what is called a **Document Type Definition (DTD)**. As the name implies, the DTD specifies what type of document this is—in this case, an XHTML document. We will have more to say about the details of the DTD in the next chapter.

The final change we need to make involves the <html> tag. It becomes:

```
<html xmlns="http://www.w3.org/1999/xhtml">
```

The xmlns that we added stands for **XML namespace**. A namespace helps the browser keep track of what all the custom XML tag names mean, especially if the same name is used for different tags. It's possible to envision a scenario, for example, where you want to use some of your own custom XML tags in a web page you are creating using XHTML. If the topic of your web page is books and literature, you might create an XML tag named <title> to indicate the title of a book. But this <title> tag has the same name as the XHTML <title> tag that is used to delineate the title of the web page. You can imagine the confusion that would result if the browser did not have any way to know which tag is which. A namespace lessens the confusion by providing the browser with information on the meaning of the tags in the document. By adding the above xmlns information to the <html> tag, we are telling the browser that all tags contained within the <html> element belong to the XHTML namespace as defined by the W3C and located at the given URL.

We will not encounter situations such as this dual <title> tag in this book, because the subject here is learning to use XHTML, not how to use XML to create custom tags. Including the xmlns information in the <html> tag is nevertheless required for a valid XHTML document. Putting all this together, Figure 2.5 shows a simple but complete XHTML document. (We have saved it under the name sourcecode.htm, a name we will often use for our code samples.)

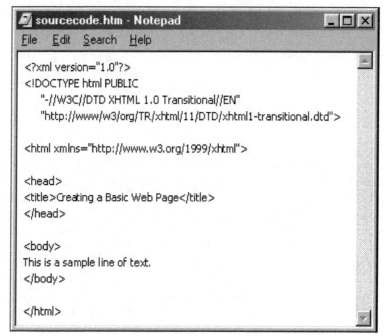

FIGURE 2.5.   A basic XHTML source document

At this point you might ask the question: "What about the millions of existing web pages that follow the old rules (or lack of them)? Will they suddenly cease to work?" Because there is such a large installed base of web pages created under the old rules of HTML version 4 and before, it is likely that the major PC browsers will continue to recognize old HTML code and display it properly. But as browsers are designed for new devices like handheld computers and cell phones, it's likely that only XHTML-based web pages will work on them. Serious web designers are already using XHTML rules for their new web pages and rewriting their previous web pages to be compatible with XHTML. Semi-serious web designers should do likewise. Fortunately, the gap between XHTML and HTML is not that great. As we progress in our journey through XHTML, we will point out the key differences between it and the older versions of HTML.

IMPORTANT

Note: The term "HTML" is still used in a general sense to refer to the language itself, whether it be XHMTL or HTML version 4 or HTML version whatever. We will use it in that sense throughout the book. When it's important to make the distinction between XHTML and HTML version 4 (or older versions), we will use those more precise terms. We also will not always include the necessary DTD and namespace information in our HTML and JavaScript examples, in order to save space and focus on the essential points.

The <meta> Element

The XML and DTD specifications in the source document provide information to the browser about what kind of code the document contains. It's often also useful to indicate something about the content of the document. We do this by adding one or more <meta> elements inside the <head> element. The <meta> element is used to specify keywords that describe a document's contents as well as a short description. (The word "meta" comes from the Greek word for "about," thus the name: A <meta> element has information about the document.) Including <meta> elements in the source document makes it easier for search engines and Internet directories to categorize it. For example, if we were creating a web page for an online store named "Aromatic Coffee and Tea" that sells specialized coffees and teas from around the world, we might include the following <meta> elements in the <head> element:

```
<head>
  <title>Aromatic Coffee and Tea</title>
  <meta name="keywords" content="coffee, tea, exotic,
    imported" />
  <meta name="description"
    content="Wholesaler and retailer of coffees and teas
      from around the world" />
</head>
```

Note the syntax of the <meta> tag. After the word "meta" we have two parts, one labeled "name" and one labeled "content." These are known as tag **attributes** and are used to specify various options that the tag may use. In this case, the name attribute specifies whether the <meta> tag is being used to define the document's keywords or the document's description. The content attribute then specifies the actual keywords or description, respectively. Attributes like these are used in many HTML elements, and we will cover them in more detail in Chapter 4.

You might also notice that there is no ending </meta> tag. It's just the single tag <meta> (with a slash at the end) instead of <meta> . . . </meta>. This type of HTML element is known as an empty element. We will learn more about empty elements and their syntax in the section "The
 Element" below.

QuickCheck Questions

1. How do you correctly nest elements?
2. Why is XHTML a case-sensitive language? What does it mean?
3. What are the three things that need to be added to an HTML version 4 source document to make it an XHTML source document?

Paragraphs and Line Breaks

When discussing the whys and wherefores of indenting HTML source code in the previous section, we explained that when the browser loads a source document, it ignores all extra whitespace (tabs and extra spaces) as well as the line breaks in the HTML code. But if the browser ignores line breaks in the source code, how does it know when to display a new line on the web page?

To begin to understand how line breaks work in HTML, consider the three examples in Figure 2.6. We see that despite the differences in line breaks and spacing in their source code, they all display identically in the browser. (We just show the <body> element, not the whole source document.)

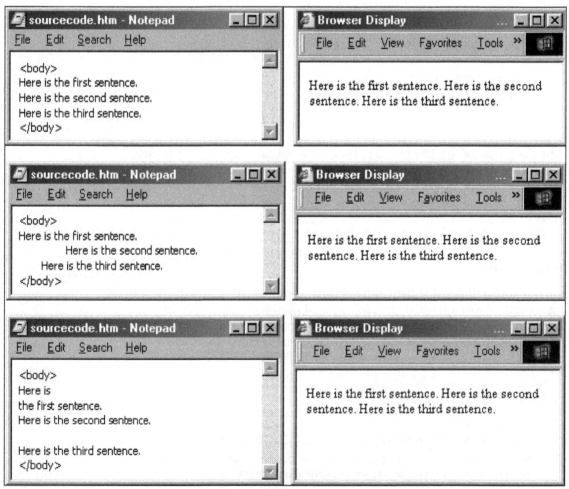

FIGURE 2.6.   Line breaks in the source code but not in the browser display

The reason for the identical displays is that HTML uses elements, and only elements, to define the structure of the document. The browser ignores all line breaks, extra spaces, and tabs in the source code and displays everything on the same line until it comes to the right edge of its window, at which point it wraps the text around to the next line.

The <p> Element

If we can't designate a line break by typing the Enter key in the source document but must use elements instead, what do we use? The most common element to use is the paragraph element, <p> and </p>, which we first saw in the section "The HTML Source Document" above. The <p> element classifies a block of text as a paragraph. Explorer and Navigator will normally display this text as single spaced, wrapping the text around at the right edge of the browser window. They also insert a blank line at the beginning and end. (We say "normally" because, as we will see in Chapter 3, it's possible to customize how the browser displays the paragraph.)

Figure 2.7 shows several examples of the <p> element. Note how the first example puts the third sentence on a line by itself with blank lines above and below it. The second example (sentences six, seven, and eight) and the third example (sentences nine and ten) show how we would normally write the <p> element in the source code. By putting the <p> and </p> tags on lines by themselves, it makes the code easier to read and more clearly shows where the paragraphs are. (But it makes no difference to the browser, of course.)

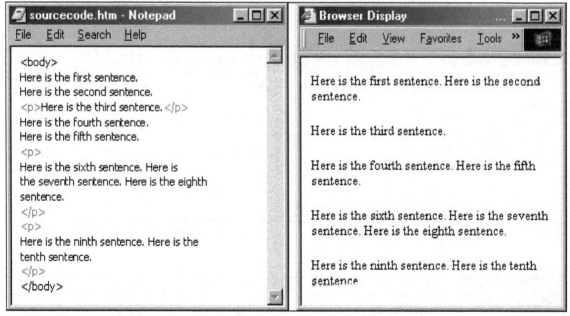

FIGURE 2.7.   Using the <p> element

If you used the View Source option discussed in the Chapter 1 Exercises to view the HTML code underlying various web pages, you may have seen many <p> tags that lacked their ending </p> tags. The reason for this is that early versions of HTML (before version 3.0) only defined a <p> tag, not a full <p> . . . </p> element. Many web pages were therefore designed using just <p> tags, because it's an easy way to generate a blank line in the browser display. And many amateur web designers continue to use the <p> tag by itself. You should not, however. XHMTL requires that every <p> tag have a corresponding </p> tag.

If you have a pre-XHTML source document that uses <p> tags without ending </p> tags, such as that shown in Figure 2.8, you may make it XHTML-compliant simply by adding a </p> tag immediately after each <p> tag (Figure 2.9).

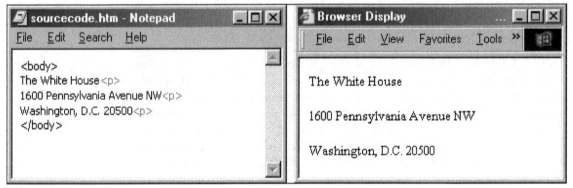

FIGURE 2.8.   The blank line effect of a single <p> tag (not XHTML-compliant)

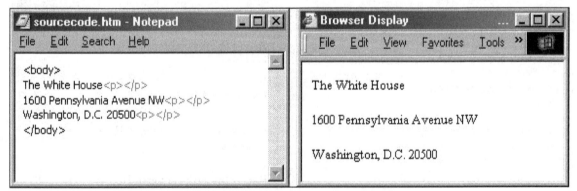

FIGURE 2.9.   Making the code from Figure 2.8 XHTML-compliant

IMPORTANT

In general, however, it is better to put the text in question inside the <p> element, as shown in Figure 2.10. The main reason for doing so will come up in Chapter 3. There we will learn that we can only apply various type styles (bold, italic, font, font size, etc.) to the text of a paragraph if it is enclosed between <p> and </p> tags.

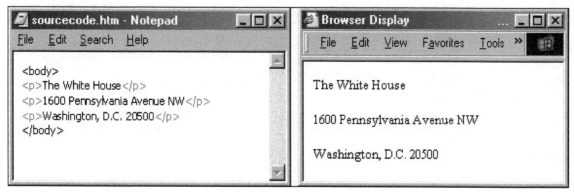

FIGURE 2.10.   The proper way to use the `<p>` element

You might be wondering how older browsers handle newer tags they don't know anything about, like the `</p>` tag. The solution is simple: Web browsers are designed to ignore any tag they do not understand. On the one hand, this means you don't have to worry about using newer HTML tags that an up-to-date browser implements but that an older browser does not. If a web surfer views your page using an older browser, the browser will simply skip over any tags unknown to it.

On the other hand, you do need to know whether a tag is so new that most browsers haven't implemented it. If you use the new tag, your page may not display correctly for most people. Good web page designers want their pages to display correctly as much as possible, no matter which browser a surfer may be using.

IMPORTANT

The `<br />` Element

Occasionally we need to specify a line break at a certain point in a web page. We have seen that the `<p>` element generates a line break but also adds a blank line as well. If we just want the line break, we use the break tag, `<br>`. This tag is an exception to the rule that elements always have separate beginning and ending tags. There is no `</br>` tag. As previously mentioned when we discussed the `<meta>` element, we call such tags **empty elements**. Prior to XHTML, the `<br>` tag and other empty elements were used just as they were. But XHTML requires some indication that an element is empty, so we must add an ending slash (/) to the tag: instead of `<br>` we write `<br />`.

If you look carefully at `<br />` you will notice that there is a space between the r and the /. This space is not required by XHTML but is included for reasons of backward compatibility. Some older browsers do not display line breaks correctly if the space is absent.

Figure 2.11 shows the effects of the `<br />` element. (As the fourth sentence is too long for the window, the browser breaks it and wraps the text.)

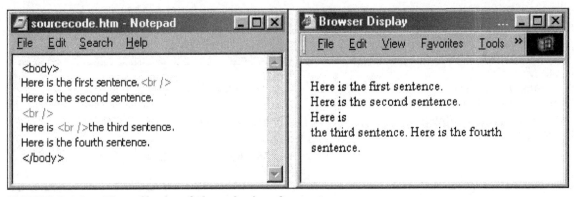

FIGURE 2.11.   The effects of the <br /> element

The <br /> tag is most useful when you need to have the browser display lines of poetry or someone's address (Figure 2.12).

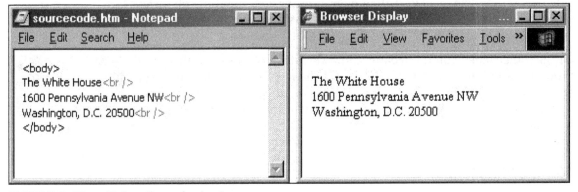

FIGURE 2.12.   Using the <br /> tag

QuickCheck Questions

1. How does the browser display blank lines, tabs, and extra spaces that are in the source document?
2. Why is it a good idea to use the <p> element instead of just a <p> tag?
3. If the browser encounters a tag it doesn't understand, what does it do?
4. What is an empty element? What are the rules for writing an empty element in XHTML?

Lab Exercise 2.2, "Lines and Paragraphs," may be done at this point.

Adding More Tags

You can create a web page just with the elements we have introduced so far, but HTML obviously offers much more. We survey a number of basic elements below, including the six levels of headers, strong and emphasized text, block quotations, and font size.

Headers

In the section "The HTML Source Document," we introduced the header elements <h1> and <h2> as two of the major HTML elements used to define the structure of a web page. HTML actually has six levels of headers, using the tags <h1> . . . </h1>, <h2> . . . </h2>, and so on up to <h6> . . . </h6>. On personal computer browsers like Explorer and Navigator, the default setting for the display of text inside a header element is boldface type and a different size, depending on the header level. Header 1 represents the most important headings and header 6 the least important. The default settings on the Windows versions of Explorer and Navigator display header text ranging in size from 24-point text for header 1 to 8-point text for header 6. The browser also puts a blank line both before and after the header text. (Other browsers, such as those designed for handheld computers, may have a different default display for headers. As we've mentioned before, we'll learn how to customize the display in Chapter 3.)

Figure 2.13 shows a code sample for each header level and Figure 2.14 shows the results in Explorer. (Note that in Figure 2.13 we left off the necessary XHTML introductory material as well as the <head> element, as we previously mentioned we would do in order to focus on the key parts of the example code and reduce clutter. In Figure 2.14 we use an actual screen shot with the text size set to the browser's default value of medium so that you can see

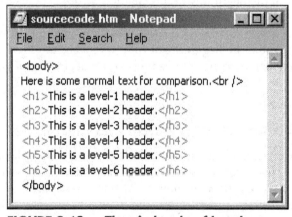

FIGURE 2.13.   The six levels of headers

the relative size of the type compared to the browser window. For more on how the user may set the browser's text size, see the section "A Few Words about Fonts" later in this chapter.)

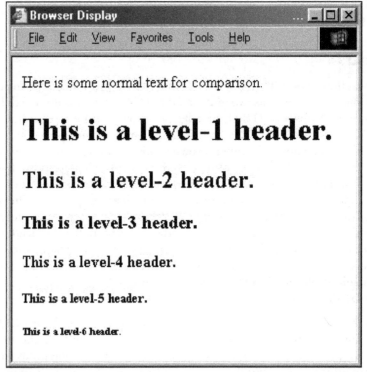

FIGURE 2.14.   Browser display of headers

As mentioned at the beginning of this chapter, we use headers to specify headings for the various sections and subsections of a web page. You might, for instance, use a level-1 header for a large "Welcome" message or other heading that would appear at the beginning of your web page, and then use one of the lower-level headers to create subheadings at the beginning of each section in your page.

The <em> and <strong> Elements

So far we have learned how to use HTML elements that classify the major parts of a web page, such as headers and paragraphs. Often we need to classify smaller parts within those elements. Within a paragraph, for example, we might want a word or a phrase to receive special emphasis. We can use the <em> and <strong> elements to do so.

The <em> element marks the section of text within it as emphasized, and the <strong> element marks the text within it as strong or strongly emphasized. Browsers designed for personal computers, like Navigator and Explorer, will usually display text in the <em> element in italic and text in the <strong> element in bold. Figures 2.15 and 2.16 show some sample code for each and the displayed results.

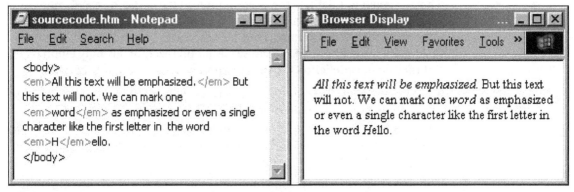

FIGURE 2.15.   Creating sections of emphasized text using the <em> element

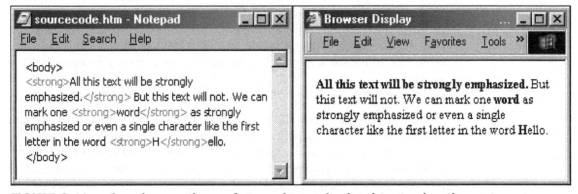

FIGURE 2.16.   Creating sections of strongly emphasized text using the <strong> element

We can get similar results in Navigator and Explorer by using the italic element and the bold element. The <i> and </i> tags mark text that the browser displays in italic and, as you might expect, the <b> and </b> tags mark text to be displayed in bold. (The early versions of HTML also defined a <u> element for underlining text, but it is rarely used as browsers traditionally use underlining to indicate hyperlinks.)

The <i> and <b> elements are among the first tags most people learn, and it would seem that they would be preferred over the <em> and <strong>

elements, if for no other reason than that they're shorter to type. But note an important difference between them. The `<b>` element defines the display, or **presentation**, of text as bold. The `<strong>` element, in contrast, does not determine the presentation. Depending on the device and the browser, the text may be displayed as bold or it may be presented in an entirely different manner.

The same distinction may be made between the `<i>` and `<em>` elements. The `<i>` element defines the presentation as italic; the `<em>` element does not define the presentation. The `<em>` and `<strong>` elements are structural or **content-based elements**: They classify certain content within the source document (usually a word or phrase) as emphasized or strongly emphasized. But they do not predefine the presentation of the content within them.

The presentation does not necessarily even have to be visual. Browsers designed for visually impaired people use speech synthesis to "speak" a source document out loud. Such browsers might use one type of inflection for text that is classified as emphasized and another for text that is classified as strongly emphasized.

This point about the distinction between **structure** and presentation is extremely important. At the beginning of this chapter we stated that the primary purpose of HTML is to define the structure of a web page by classifying its various text elements. In the haphazard early years of HTML, however, the browser companies and many web designers began to use tags to define not only the structure but also the presentation of the web page. The problem with this approach is that it results in web pages that display well only in a browser running on a personal computer (or on a similar computer, like a workstation). If we want the web page to display well on other devices, we would have to create separate versions of the page for each type of device.

By defining the presentation separately from the structure, we get rid of much of this problem. The structure of the page is defined in the HTML source document and the rules for the presentation of the various structural elements used (headers, paragraphs, and so on) are defined elsewhere, either in the browser itself (as in, for example, a special speech synthesis browser) or in a separate style sheet definition (the subject of the next chapter). (Note that what we are calling presentation is also called layout, style, and/or display.)

The W3C—via XML, XHTML, and style sheets—has sought to recapture the original emphasis on separating structure from presentation so that source documents can be displayed appropriately no matter the device, without having to create separate source documents for every type of device. The separation also makes for more modular and better HTML code.

At this point, you probably won't be able to fully understand the significance of this separation, because we haven't done much with HTML yet. When we cover style sheets in the next chapter, you will see the power of creating web pages in this way.

For now the advice is to use the <em> and <strong> elements instead of the <i> and <b> elements, because they do not predetermine the presentation of the page and are therefore more flexible. (Although it is not incorrect to use the <i> and <b> elements—they are still part of XHTML.)

IMPORTANT

Block-Level vs. Inline Elements

If we want to classify some text to be both a header and emphasized, we simply include an <em> element inside the header element:

```
<h2><em>This header will be both bold and
italicized</em></h2>
```

In Navigator and Explorer the normal presentation of this text will be large and bold (because it's a header 2) and italicized (because it's emphasized). You might wonder, however, whether we could also write this with the <h2> element inside the <em> element, like this:

```
<em><h2>Will this header be both bold and
italicized?</h2></em>
```

The answer (in XHTML) is that we cannot, because <em> and <h2> are different kinds of tags. Header elements are designed to be **block-level elements**, meaning that they define a complete section or block of text. The browser indicates the extent of the block by putting a blank line both before and after it. When you use header elements, you don't have to combine them with a <p> element to get a line break. It's already built into it. Paragraph elements themselves are a basic form of block-level elements and the <body> element is another example.

Elements like <em> and <strong>, on the other hand, are **inline elements** because they're used to define the structure of a sequence of characters within a line of text, or even a single character. Inline elements may not contain a block-level element but may be used within a block. (In older versions of HTML this distinction between block-level and inline elements is also true, although the browsers often ignore it and display the incorrect code anyway.)

Anything may be put inside a block-level element, including another block-level element. The <body> element, for example, obviously contains all manner of other block-level tags.

The <blockquote> Element

A block-level element that is occasionally useful is the <blockquote> element. You use it when you want to classify a block of text as a long quotation. In Explorer and Navigator, the default presentation for the <blockquote> element is to indent the whole block of text (Figure 2.17).

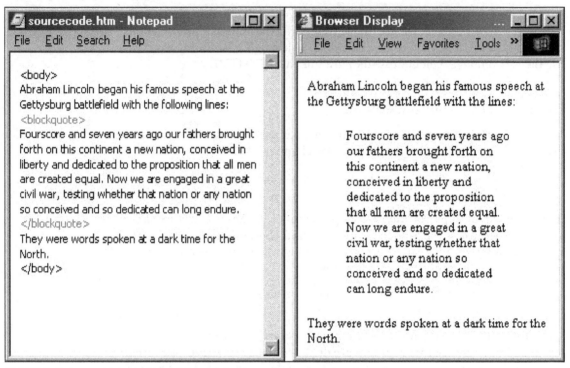

FIGURE 2.17.   Using the <blockquote> element

Font Size

You should not use a header element just to make some text bold, unless it's actually a header. To do otherwise would be to misclassify the text. Use the <strong> element instead. Nor should you use a header element just to change the font size of some text. Instead we use the <big> and </big> tags to mark text that is to be big and the <small> and </small> tags to mark text that is to be "small." The examples shown in Figure 2.18 give you an idea of the presentation of these elements in Explorer when the default text size is set to medium. (Navigator is similar.)

The actual presentation of big and small text will vary from user to user, depending on which font and font size the user has chosen for the default browser font (discussed in more detail below). But you can see that big text will be slightly larger than the normal display font (which is usually 12-point size) and small text will be slightly smaller. (Even more size flexibility is provided via style sheets.)

A Few Words about Fonts

After learning about the <big> and <small> elements, an obvious question is can we specify the font itself? In Chapter 3 we will learn that the text font may be set using style sheets or using the <font> element. But we will also learn that the <font> element is a classic example of an element that defines

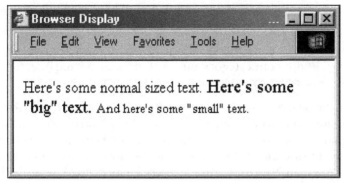

FIGURE 2.18.   Effects of the <big> and <small> elements on text size

presentation, not structure. The preferred way to specify the font is through the use of style sheets.

The question also applies to another issue of web page design. Who should have control over how the web page looks on the screen, the web page designer or the surfer? Early browsers were designed to give control over the font selection to the surfer, not to the designer, on the principle of surfer freedom. Given this freedom and the means to implement it, the surfer could customize the browser display to his or her own liking. The means to implement this freedom came from the browser software, which allowed the surfer to choose the default font in which text would be displayed. Both major browsers still allow this choice.

In Netscape Navigator, the surfer may set a **variable width** default font and a **fixed width** default font. Internet Explorer version 5 or before calls it proportional instead of variable width. Explorer version 6 labels the two types the Web page font and the plain text font, respectively. Variable width means that the letters in the font take up varying amounts of horizontal space on the line. The font of this sentence is an example. The letter i, for instance, takes up less space than the letter m. The letters in a fixed width or monospaced font take up the same amount of space on the line, no matter how narrow or wide they may be. `This sentence is an example of a fixed font, named Courier.` Most fonts are variable width.

To set the default fonts and font sizes for Navigator, select Preferences under the Edit menu and then, when the Preferences dialog box appears, check the listings on the left side under the heading Categories. If you see Fonts listed, click on it. If you don't see Fonts listed, first click on the main category named Appearances. Fonts should then appear as a subcategory under Appearances.

In Explorer, select Internet Options under the Tools menu. Then click the General tab and click the Fonts button. To change the default font size, click the Accessibility button. (The idea is that visually impaired surfers would want to choose a larger size for the default font.) You may also temporarily change the text size by selecting Text Size under the View menu and choose either

Largest, Larger, Medium, Smaller, or Smallest (where Medium represents the default text size that has been set).

Note that the surfer can actually choose any font, even a proportional font, for the Fixed Width Font category and any font, even a fixed one, for the Variable Width Font category.

In general, the browser uses the variable width font for the web page text and the fixed width font in pop-up dialog boxes. However, as noted above, the web page designer may override the browser settings and specify the font style and display using various means. The surfer may prevent this override from occurring via the Fonts dialog box in Navigator and the Accessibility dialog box in Explorer (as alluded to above). The disadvantage is that many web pages will not display well as they have been custom designed to use a certain font style and font size.

Comments about Comments

Sometimes you will want to write notes or make **comments** about the HTML code you have written. These comments are for your benefit (e.g., to remind you how a certain piece of HTML code works), or for the benefit of future editors of your HTML document (special instructions, for example). You do not want these comments to be displayed by the browser. To keep them from being seen by the surfer, you put them inside the comment tag:

```
<!-- comments go here -->
```

Anything inside the comment tag will be ignored by the browser (Figure 2.19).

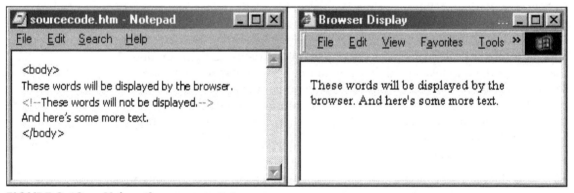

FIGURE 2.19.   Using the comment tag

Note that even though the comment tag looks like an empty element (no ending tag), it does not take a slash at the end (/>).

Comments may be spread over several lines in the source document:

```
<body>
<!-These words won't be seen by
```

```
anyone even though they're broken between lines->
</body>
```

Comments are also useful when you're experimenting with HTML code or modifying code you have previously written. Sometimes you want to take out a block of HTML tags and text and see how the document displays without it. You could simply cut it out and paste it back in later if you decide to keep it. But it's easier and faster to surround the code with the comment tag, i.e., put a <!-- at the beginning of the section and a --> at the end of the section. The browser ignores everything inside, including any HTML tags. In the code in Figure 2.20, for example, the browser will ignore the <blockquote> element and not display it.

IMPORTANT

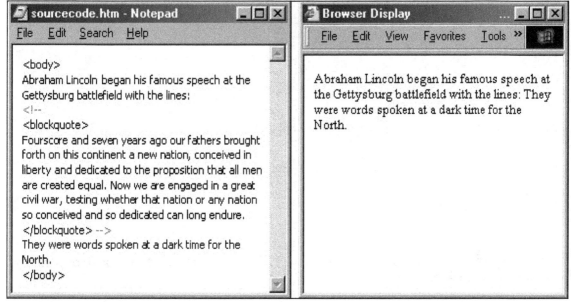

FIGURE 2.20.   Commenting out HTML code

Lab Exercise 2.3, "Adding More Tags," may be done at this point.

QuickCheck Questions

1. Which header element is the most prominent level, <h1> or <h6>?
2. What's the difference between using the <em> element and the <i> element?
3. What is the difference between a block-level element and an inline element? Give an example of each.
4. What is the difference between a variable width font and a fixed width font?
5. Write the line of HTML code that would instruct the browser to display the sentence "Welcome to my Web page" as (a) emphasized text, (b) strongly emphasized text, and (c) both emphasized and strongly emphasized text.

Key Terms

.htm extension
.html extension
attribute
block-level element
body
case sensitive
comments
content-based elements
Document Type Definition (DTD)
element
empty element

Extensible Hypertext Markup
 Language (XHTML)
Extensible Markup Language
 (XML)
fixed width font
head
HTML source document
inline element
nested elements
presentation
source code

structure
syntax
tag
text-only document
variable width font
whitespace
World Wide Web Consortium
 (W3C)
XML declaration
XML namespace

Code Summary

1. Creating a Source Document

The basic structure of a source document (HTML version 4):

```
<html>
<head>
   <title>Creating a Basic Web Page</title>
</head>
<body>
This is a sample line of text.
</body>
</html>
```

Defining the title for a web page (code is put in the <head> element and title will be displayed in the browser window's title bar):

```
<title>Larry's Web Page</title>
```

2. HTML, XML, and XHTML

Adding the XML declaration and the Document Type Definition for XHTML to the beginning of a source document:

```
<?xml version="1.0"?>
<!DOCTYPE html PUBLIC
   "-//W3C//DTD XHTML 1.0 Transitional//EN"
   "http://www.w3.org/TR/xhtml/11/DTD/xhtml1-transitional.dtd">
```

Adding the XML namespace information to the <html> tag:

```
<html xmlns="http://www.w3.org/1999/xhtml">
```

Using the <meta> element (within the <head> element) to describe the content of a web page via a list of keywords and/or a short description:

```
<meta name="keywords" content="coffee, tea, exotic, imported" />
<meta name="description"
   content="Wholesaler and retailer of coffees and teas from around the world" />
```

3. Paragraphs and Line Breaks

Defining a paragraph, with blank lines before and after it:

```
<p>Here is the first sentence of the paragraph. Here is the second sentence. Here is the
third sentence.</p><p>This sentence will be the first in a new paragraph . . . </p>
```

Inserting a blank line between blocks of text using just the <p> tag (not recommended):

```
Here is the first sentence.<p>Here is the second sentence, which will be the start of a
new paragraph. Here is the third sentence.
```

Making the previous example XHTML-compliant:

```
Here is the first sentence.<p></p>Here is the second sentence, which will be the start
of a new paragraph. Here is the third sentence.
```

Inserting a line break:

```
This line will be<br /> broken after the fourth word.
```

4. Adding More Tags

Specifying headers (most important to least important, level 1 to level 6):

```
<h1>This is a level-1 header.</h1>
...
<h6>This is a level-6 header.</h6>
```

Specifying text as emphasized (usually displayed as italic):

```
<em>This sentence will probably be displayed in italic.</em>
```

Specifying text as strong (usually displayed as bold):

```
<strong>This sentence will probably be displayed in bold.</strong>
```

Specifying text to be displayed in italic (not recommended):

```
<i>This sentence will be displayed in italics.</i>
```

Specifying text to be displayed in bold (not recommended):

```
<b>This sentence will be displayed in bold.</b>
```

Specifying a block quotation:

```
<blockquote>Fourscore and seven years ago our fathers brought forth on this continent a
new nation, conceived in liberty and dedicated to the proposition that all men are created
equal.</blockquote>
```

Specifying text to be slightly larger or slightly smaller than normal size:

```
<big>This sentence will be displayed slightly larger than normal.</big>
<small>This sentence will be displayed slightly smaller than normal.</small>
```

Inserting a comment into the HTML code:

```
<!-- comments go here -->
```

It's best not to use Microsoft Word to create an HTML source document, because when you open it again Word will display it as a browser would and you won't be able to edit the source code. Use a text processor like Notepad (Windows) or SimpleText (Macintosh) instead.

The source document must be saved with a .htm or .html extension.

In naming a source document, use only letters, numbers, and the underscore (_) character. In particular, don't use spaces.

When saving a file using Notepad (and some other text processors), watch that it doesn't add an extra .txt extension to the filename.

You don't have to be connected to the Internet to create a source document and view it in the browser.

When you are editing a source document, don't forget to save the changes you made before you view it in the browser. If you don't save the new version of the document, when you reload the document in the browser it will display the previously existing version and nothing will change in the display.

HTML elements must be nested properly within each other, not overlapped.

Indent your HTML code for readability.

Design your web pages to be XHTML-compatible.

Avoid using paragraph elements without text inside.

Design your web pages to display correctly no matter which browser a surfer may be using. Be cautious about using HTML tags that are supported only by the newest browser versions or that are supported only by Explorer and not by Navigator, or vice versa.

For backward compatibility, put a space before the "/" in empty elements like the `<br />` element.

Avoid using HTML elements that predefine the presentation, such as `<b>` and `<i>`.

Inline elements may not contain a block-level element.

Avoid using elements for things they are not intended for, such as using header elements simply to make (non-header) text big and bold.

Comment your HTML code.

Use comments to comment out code during debugging.

1. True or false: HTML version 4 tags are case sensitive.
2. True or false: XHTML tags are case sensitive.
3. Which of the following would display the first word (and only the first word) in the line of text "Welcome to my Web page" in emphasized text?
   a. `Welcome<em> to my Web page`
   b. `<em>Welcome to my Web page`
   c. `<em>Welcome</em> to my Web page`
   d. `<em Welcome /em> to my Web page`
4. Why isn't it a good idea to use Microsoft Word to create and edit an HTML source document?
5. What are the two major sections within an HTML source document?
6. True or false: When saving an HTML source document, the three-letter extension .htm must be used.
7. Which of the following are legal names for a source document?
   a. WebPage2.htm
   b. simple_web_page.htm
   c. simplewebpage.htm
   d. SimpleWebPage
8. True or false: In order to check how an HTML source document you have created will be displayed in a web browser, you must be connected to the Internet.

9. Which of the following is used to create an empty paragraph in XHTML?

  a. `<p>`
  b. `<p />`
  c. `<p></p>`
  d. `<p /p>`

10. Web browsers are designed to _____ any tag that they do not understand.

11. Which of the following are block-level elements?

  a. `<big> . . . </big>`
  b. `<h2> . . . </h2>`
  c. `<strong> . . . </strong>`
  d. `<p> . . . </p>`

12. A font in which each character occupies the same amount of space on the line is called a _____ font or a _____ font. A font in which each character occupies differing amounts of space on the line is called a _____ font or a _____ font.

13. True or false: The `<strong>` and `<b>` elements are equivalent.

1. Briefly define the following terms: tag, element, block-level element, inline element.

2. Is there a major difference between using a .htm extension as opposed to a .html extension for a source document?

3. Write the HTML code for a complete XHTML source document with the text "Welcome to my Web page!" as a header 1. Give the document the title "Basic Web Page."

4. What is the purpose of adding the "xmlns" information to the `<html>` tag?

5. Write the code for a `<body>` element of a source document that contains a header 2 element with the text "Section 1. All About Computers" followed by two header 3 elements with the text "Part A. The CPU" and "Part B. The Operating System" respectively.

6. Write the code for a `<body>` element of a source document that contains a paragraph with the following text: Thomas Jefferson was only 33 years old when he was chosen in June 1776 to write the first draft of the Declaration of Independence. Mark the 33 as emphasized text and the Declaration of Independence as strongly emphasized.

7. Write the code for a `<body>` element of a source document that contains two paragraphs. The first paragraph should have the following two sentences: Alexander Graham Bell introduced his telephone invention to the public at the Philadelphia Centennial Exposition of 1876. Bell was a teacher of deaf students who was interested in developing devices that could help their learning. The second paragraph should be: The distinguished visitor Emporer Don Pedro of Brazil was rendered almost speechless by the marvel. The word speechless should be marked as larger than normal type.

8. Why not use a `<h1>` or `<h2>` element when you want to have some regular text displayed as big and bold?

9. Write the HTML code that would display the last lines from Robert Frost's famous poem using the `<blockquote>` element.

  I shall be telling this with a sigh
  Somewhere ages and ages hence:
  Two roads diverged in a wood, and I—
  I took the one less traveled by,
  And that has made all the difference.

Hint: You will need to use more tags than just the blockquote element.

1. Assuming that the following code is intended to be XHTML-compliant, identify the errors in it and then sketch on paper how the browser would display it once the errors were corrected.

```
<html>
<head>
   <title>Sample Web Page<title>
</head>
<body>
<em><h2>Welcome to my Web page!</h2></em>
<strong>Here are some samples of my HTML expertise:</strong><br>
<BIG>Here's some big text.</BIG><br>
<smaller>Here's some smaller text.</smaller><br>
<p>And here's a new paragraph to round things out.

</html>
```

Note: Many of the Problems above may also be done as lab exercises.

Exercise 2.1: A Simple Web Page

The best way to learn HTML is to stop reading and start experimenting. That is, don't just read this textbook straight through, but stop occasionally and try things out. You will find one or more hands-on exercises in each chapter that provide suggestions (or assignments, if you are using this textbook in a course). When a paragraph in an exercise begins with a check box ❑, it means that the paragraph contains some specific instructions for you to do.

❑ Open Notepad (or the equivalent—in the directions below we will refer to Notepad) so that you have a new Untitled document. You should be able to find Notepad by going to the Windows Start menu and selecting Programs and then Accessories. (If Notepad is already open, select New from the File menu.)

❑ Type in the HTML code shown in Figure 2.3, but use a title with your name in it and add a "Welcome to my Web page" message in the body. Don't forget the slashes in the ending tags!

❑ After you have typed the HTML code, save the document. We suggest "simplewebpage.htm" as a name (without the quotation marks).

Whatever name you choose, don't make it too long and be sure to include the .htm extension at the end of the name, because it signifies that the document is an HTML source document. (You may also save it with a .html extension.)

If you are in a computer lab setting, make sure that you save it on your floppy disk (or removable hard disk). If the name of your floppy disk does not appear at the top of the Save As dialog box where it says Save in:, click on the Save in: textbox to get the drop-down menu and then double-click on 3½ Floppy (A:) before saving it.

❑ Now that you have saved your source document, go to Netscape Navigator or Internet Explorer (if it isn't open, use the Start menu to open it). Keep Notepad and your HTML document open at the same time (i.e., don't quit Notepad or close your HTML document).

❑ If you're using Navigator, select Open Page . . . from the File menu, and then click on the Choose File button on the right side of the dialog box that appears. If you're using Explorer, select Open from the File menu and then click on the Browse button. Find your new source document, simplewebpage.htm (or whatever you named it), and open it. You should see something like Figure 2.4.

❑ Now return to Notepad and the simplewebpage.htm document (select the Notepad button from the Taskbar at the bottom of the screen or, if you can see part of the document's window, just click in it). Add some text of your choosing to the `<body>` element of the HTML document after the "Welcome" message. Then add examples of the `<em>` and `<strong>` elements. Don't spend too much time composing the text. Just type it in and put the various tags wherever.

❑ Once you have written some HTML code, save the changes. Then switch back to your web browser and simply click on the Refresh button (for Explorer) or Reload button (for Navigator) on the toolbar near the top of the window.

The browser will retrieve, reload, and display the current HTML document—whatever it may be, whether a local HTML document or some distant HTML document on a computer halfway around the world. The additions you made to your simplewebpage.htm document should be displayed.

A *common error* is to forget to save the changes to your HTML document before going to the browser and reloading it. If you don't save the changes, the browser will be reloading the unchanged version of the document that still exists on the disk.

❑ If you haven't already, add several lines of text (with or without tags) to your HTML source document, save the document, and then view the results in the browser. Do the line breaks in the source document correspond with what you see on the screen? Record your answer on your web page itself.

❑ What happens if you leave out an ending tag so that you have an `<em>` tag without a corresponding `</em>`, or a `<strong>` without a `</strong>`? Record your answer on your web page itself.

Exercise 2.2: Lines and Paragraphs

❑ Add the necessary code to the source document you created in Lab Exercise 2.1 in order to make it an XHTML source document.

❑ Experiment briefly with the `<br />` tag and the `<p>` element, adding nice examples of each to the XHTML source document. *Make sure to save your document frequently so that you don't lose much work and time if your computer crashes or if the network goes down.* (These are infrequent events, but when they do occur they will be very discouraging if you have neglected to save your work recently.)

Exercise 2.3: Adding More Tags

❑ Add at least one example of each of the tags described in the section "Adding More Tags" to the XHTML source document you created in the previous exercises. Use headers, font size, blockquote, and comment elements. Use whatever text you would like to show the effects of the tags. The simplest text to use, of course, might be variations on the theme of "This is header 1 text", and so on, but feel free to be creative. *Make sure to save your document frequently so that you don't lose much work and time if your computer crashes or if the network goes down.*

Cascading Style Sheets

LEARNING OBJECTIVES

1. Learn how style sheets enable you to customize HTML elements and precisely control the formatting of a web page.

2. Learn how to specify font characteristics such as size, uppercase, lowercase, different weights of boldness, and font family and paragraph characteristics such as indentation and line spacing.

3. Learn how to create sub-styles called classes and use them, for example, to create multiple kinds of paragraphs in your document.

4. Learn how styles may be used in individual tags.

5. Learn how to create customized inline and block-level elements using <span> and <div>.

6. Learn how to use external style sheets to standardize the style for all pages in a website.

The Power of Styles

In Chapter 2 we learned about the distinction between, on the one hand, the structure and content of a web page and, on the other, its presentation. We use HTML elements like <h1>, <p>, <em>, and <strong> to classify the various sections of text on the page. The presentation or style of those sections, however, is not meant to be predetermined by the HTML elements. To be sure, the major personal computer browsers, Explorer and Navigator, display the text marked by these elements in certain default ways. The text in a header 1 element, for example, is displayed in 24-point, bold Times Roman typeface. Text marked by an <em> element is italicized, while text in a <strong> element is displayed in bold, and so on and so forth. But other browsers, designed for other types of devices, might not display these defaults. A browser for a handheld computer might display header 1 text in 14-point, all-caps typeface that is better suited for its smaller display. A special speech synthesis browser might display different elements using different inflections or other auditory clues.

We can change the presentation of Explorer and Navigator themselves. We don't have to be satisfied with <h1> elements that display in 24-point, bold Times Roman. We can instead use a different font, enlarge it to a different size, and display the text not only in boldface but also in small caps and in red if we desire. In this chapter we will learn how to do this by customizing the presentation rules for HTML elements via cascading style sheets, or simply, styles. If you have used style sheets in a word processing program like Microsoft Word, you will find that it's the same concept in HTML, although the implementation is different.

Creating an Internal Style Sheet

We'll start with a simple example. Imagine that we have been hired to design a web page for a business named Red Mountain Consulting. We know that a judicious amount of color can turn a web page (or any document) from so-so to striking. As we think about the design of the page, we decide that we will use <h2> elements for the main section headings and make them stand out by displaying them in red.

We can do this by creating an **internal style sheet** that redefines the presenta-tion rule, or the style, for the <h2> element. To create an internal style sheet, we use a <style> element that is placed in the <head> section of the HTML source document. Internal here refers to the fact that the style sheet is con-tained within the source document. Later in this chapter we will learn about external style sheets. (Keep in mind that we will just be scratching the surface of what can be done with styles, both in this chapter and in Chapter 6, when we consider web page layout.)

Because an HTML document may use different style sheet languages, the <style> element requires some special information in its beginning tag that specifies which language is being used. This information is supplied by a tag attribute. Remember that we first encountered attributes with the <meta> tag and that they allow us to specify additional information and/or various options for the tag. In this case, we use the type attribute and give it a value of "text/css" using the basic syntax nameofattribute = "valueofattribute":

```
<style type="text/css">
...
</style>
```

The value "text/css" indicates that the style sheet instructions in this <style> element are written in plain text format using the cascading style sheet language. We also need to specify a default style sheet language for the whole document, not just for any individual <style> element as we did here. To do so, we use a form of the <meta> element with the http-equiv and content attributes:

```
<meta http-equiv="Content-Style-Type" content="text/css" />
```

The "http-equiv" refers to "http equivalent" and is so named because HTTP web servers may make use of this information. Remember also that the <meta> element must be placed in the <head> element.

Although technically this <meta> element is required to use css styles in your document, you can get by without including it because the browser will assume that the default style language is css if none is specified. To save space in our examples, we will usually leave it out.

Now that we have the preliminaries out of the way, let's get down to how we use styles to customize the browser's presentation of a source document. In the <style> element we list the name of the tag we want to customize followed by a **style definition** enclosed in curly braces. The style definition consists of a **property** and a **value**, separated by a colon. In our example of the <h2> tag, the property is color and the value is red:

```
<head>
<title>Red Mountain Consulting Group</title>
<style type="text/css">
  h2 {color:red}
</style>
</head>
```

What this means in English is that we are telling the browser that text in all of the document's <h2> elements should be displayed in red, in addition to its usual boldface and enlarged format. Figure 3.1 shows how we put it all together. (To save space, we have left out the necessary XHTML information at the beginning of the document, as well as the <meta> element.)

Experimenting with Colors

HTML styles also allow the web designer to make quick and easy design changes. For example, if we decide that we don't like the red color, we can easily change it to another, such as blue, just by changing the style definition:

```
<head>
  <title>Red Mountain Consulting Group</title>
  <style type="text/css">
    h2 {color:blue}
  </style>
</head>
```

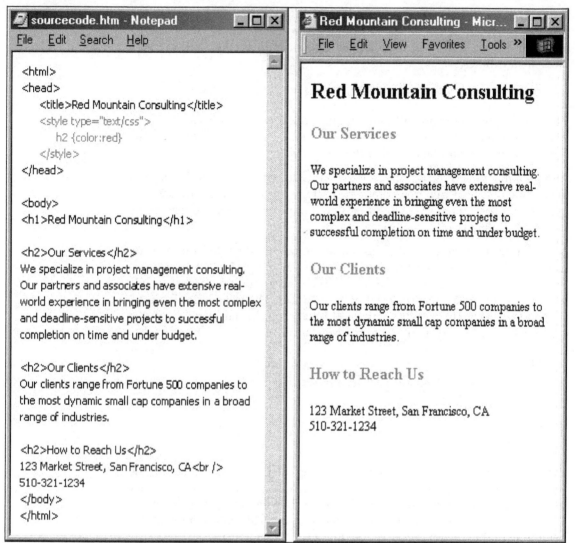

FIGURE 3.1. Customizing the <h2> tag

There are thousands of colors from which to choose, most of them specified by a six-digit **color number** or **color code**. Sixteen colors have predefined names as well as numbers. The values red and blue we used above are two of them; Table 3.1 lists all 16. (Note that the 0s are zeros, not uppercase Os.)

You probably notice that some of the color numbers shown in Table 3.1 have letters in them. The reason is that the numbering system used is based on the **hexadecimal (base 16) system**. This system uses the 10 symbols 0–9 plus the letters A–F to represent numbers. It's often used in computer science because it's easy to convert numbers between the hexadecimal system and the binary system on which computers are based. Also, the hexadecimal version of a

TABLE 3.1.   The Sixteen Predefined Color Names

Color	Number
black	000000
gray	808080
silver	C0C0C0
white	FFFFFF
red	FF0000
maroon	800000
magenta	FF00FF
purple	800080
blue	0000FF
navy	000080
cyan (or aqua)	00FFFF
teal	008080
green	008000
olive	808000
lime	00FF00
yellow	FFFF00

number is much more compactly written than the binary version. Our regular decimal number 214 (two hundred and fourteen), for example, is written as 11010110 in the binary system but as D6 in the hexadecimal system.

Behind the scenes, the six hexadecimal digits in the color code are actually divided into three pairs of two digits each. The first pair represents a red value, the second pair a green value, and the third pair a blue value. Red, green, and blue are the three primary colors used in various combinations by computer displays to generate all the other colors you see on the screen.

If we change our minds and decide to return to a red color for our headers but want a darker red than the predefined red, we can consult a color table and find the number for a darker red, such as D61130. We then simply rewrite the style definition for the h2 element as:

```
<style type="text/css">
    h2 {color:#D61130}
</style>
```

Note that when we use a color number, we must precede it with the # symbol.

Many websites exist that display various colors and their corresponding numbers. (To find them, search on hexadecimal color codes using your favorite search engine, such as www.google.com.) You should be aware, however, that certain colors do not display the same on all monitors. Some old monitors are only able to display 256 colors. Of these 256 colors, the operating system and the browser reserve 40 for their own use. The 216 colors that remain are called web safe or **browser safe colors** because they display correctly on all color monitors. Therefore, unless you absolutely have to have a certain color, you should stick with these 216 colors. For most purposes, these will give you far more choices than you need.

IMPORTANT

It is also important not to get too color-happy. The right amount of color, and the right combinations of colors, can spice up a page nicely. Too much color or the wrong color can make a page hard to read and confusing.

Changing the Alignment

As another example of using styles, we can use the text-align property to define the alignment of all header 2s in the document. Instead of accepting the default display of headers as aligned to the left, we can define the h2 style to be centered:

```
<style type="text/css">
  h2 {color:red; text-align:center}
</style>
```

A few syntax notes: We separate the two style definitions within the h2 style by a semicolon. The space between the semicolon and text-align is optional. The four possible values for the text-align property are left (which is the default alignment anyway), right, center, and justify (for even margins on both sides of the text). And finally, don't forget the hyphen in text-align!

In our Red Mountain Consulting example, we would like the main title to be centered. To do so, we add an h1 style definition to the style element:

```
<style type="text/css">
  h1 {text-align:center}
  h2 {color:red; text-align:center}
</style>
```

Figure 3.2 shows the result.

QuickCheck Questions

1. Create an internal style sheet that defines the style of the header 3 element to be right-aligned with yellow text.
2. What is the name of the property that you use to define the alignment of a header? What are its possible values?

Lab Exercise 3.1, "Basic Styles," may be done at this point.

FIGURE 3.2.   Using the text-align property to center headers

Formatting Fonts Using Styles

Imagine that after we have designed and coded our *Red Mountain Consulting* web page, we decide that we want the section headings to be bigger. What can we do? One solution would be to go over the whole source document and change all the pertinent <h2> elements to <h1> elements. We might speed up this process by using the automatic find-and-replace feature of our text editor. But this would not help much if we had used <h2> elements for other things as well as the headings. We seem to be faced with the tedious task of changing each element one by one. The font definition features of styles, however, make it a simple one-line, one-time change.

Font Size

Using the `font-size` property, we may change the size of all <h2> text to 24 points, the same size as <h1> text:

```
<style type="text/css">
  h1 {text-align:center}
  h2 {color:red; text-align:center; font-size:24pt}
</style>
```

Or, we can choose a size between the regular <h2> size (which is 18 points) and the <h1> size:

```
<style type="text/css">
  h1 {text-align:center}
  h2 {color:red; text-align:center; font-size:20pt}
</style>
```

Note that technically you should *not* put a space between the point size 20 and the letters pt (although some browsers will display the point size correctly despite the unwanted space).

It is also important to remember that the user has some control over what size of font is normally displayed by his or her browser. Just as the user can set the default variable width and fixed width fonts the browser is to use (as explained in Chapter 2), so too the user can set the default normal size of font to use. Navigator does this by allowing the user to set the size of the variable width and fixed width fonts (select Preferences under the Edit menu and then the Fonts option).

In Explorer, this is done via the Text Size option under the View menu by selecting Largest, Larger, Medium, Smaller, or Smallest. Selecting Medium, for example, sets the normal font size to 12 points and makes the regular header sizes 24 points for <h1>, 18 points for <h2>, 13.5 points for <h3>, 12 points for <h4>, 10 points for <h5>, and 7.5 points for <h6>. Selecting Smaller, however, will cause <h1> text to be displayed at 20 points, <h2> at 16, <h3> at 12, <h4> at 10, <h5> at 9, and <h6> at 7.

So the moral of this story for the web page designer is that if you use a style sheet to set <h2> header text at a size of 24 points, thinking that it will make the <h2> text the same size as any <h1> text in your document, it may not come out that way. If the user has set the browser's normal text size to Smaller, then <h1> text is displayed at 20 points, and your header 2s at 24 points will be displayed bigger than your header 1s!

The obvious solution is to use styles to set the exact font size for all the headers you use in the document. This allows you to have precise control over how your web page will be displayed, a control that most web designers appreciate and desire. The flip side, however, is that it takes control away from the user. A visually impaired person, for example, may set Explorer's Text Size option at

Largest, or Navigator's Preferences font size to a large point size, out of necessity. Web pages that override this setting by using styles to define absolute font sizes for various tags also override the needs and/or wishes of users.

There are also less obvious solutions to the problem of designing a website with consistently sized headers. The `font-size` property may be set to a percentage, e.g., `font-size:150%`, which would direct the browser to display the text 1.5 times its regular size for that tag. Or it may be set to `larger` or `smaller`, or even more precisely to the values `xx-small`, `x-small`, `small`, `medium`, `large`, `x-large`, or `xx-large`.

Bold and Italic Revisited

The `<b>` and `<i>` elements provide straightforward ways to generate bold and italic text in Navigator and Explorer. If we wanted, for example, to display our headers not only in bold (the default) but also in italic, we could simply nest an `<i>` element inside each `<h2>` element:

```
<body>
<h1>Red Mountain Consulting Group</h1>
<h2><i>Our Services</i></h2>
We specialize . . .
<h2><i>Our Clients</i></h2>
Our clients range from . . .
</body>
```

Straightforward, yes, but also a bit tedious if we have a number of headers. As you might guess, using styles lessens the pain via the use of the `font-style` property:

```
<style type="text/css">
   h2 {color:red; font-style:italic}
</style>
```

In addition to italic, the `font-style` property may be set to `normal` (no italic) or `oblique` (a slanted font style similar to italic).

But what if we want our headers to display in italic but not in bold? In other words, can we turn off the default bold display of headers? Using styles, the answer is yes. The relevant style property for bold text is `font-weight`. We may turn off the bold by setting `font-weight` to `normal`. Figure 3.3 shows how to set the h2 style so that all of the header 2s display aligned in the center with italic, red, non-bold text.

The `font-weight` property may also be used to define exactly how bold we want text to appear. It may be set to `normal` as above, and to `bold` when we want the standard bold text. It may also be set to `bolder` for a heavier look or to `lighter` for a lighter than normal look. Even more precisely, it may be set to one of the numeric values 100, 200, 300, . . . 900, where 400 represents the normal text and 700 represents the standard bold.

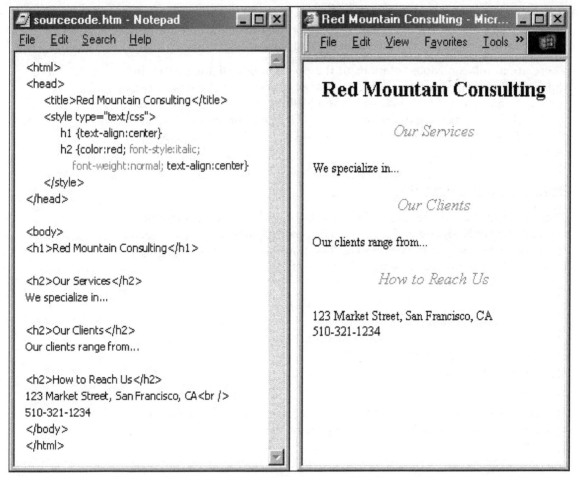

FIGURE 3.3.   Using the font-style property to control italic and the font-weight property to control boldness

Beyond Bold and Italic

As if the bold and italic options didn't give us enough from which to choose, HTML styles also provide four other major text properties that may be customized: text-decoration, text-transform, font-variant, and background.

Briefly summarized:

text-decoration

The text-decoration property controls underlines and the like, taking one of the following values: underline, overline, line-through, none, or blink. The last value, blink, is a tribute to the famous <blink> tag that was introduced in an early version of Netscape Navigator. But its gaudy character—as you might guess, it caused text to blink—and its overuse by amateur web designers quickly made it an object of derision. So use the blink value of the text-decoration property at your peril.

text-transform

The text-transform property takes the self-explanatory values capitalize, uppercase, lowercase, and none.

font-variant

The font-variant property may be set to small-caps or none.

background-color

The background-color property, which controls the color of the background behind the line of text, may be set to transparent or one of the color names or numbers.

Putting all this together can yield a very long style definition. For example, we might decide that we want our header 2s on the Red Mountain Consulting web page to be point size 20, extra bold, italicized, in small caps, underlined, red, and with a background color of silver. The code would be:

```
<style type="text/css">
  h2 {color:red; font-size:20pt; font-style:italic;
     font-weight:bolder; text-decoration:underline;
     font-variant:smallcaps; background-color:silver}
</style>
```

You may be wondering about the purpose of the none values for each of the above properties. In the case of headers and the font-weight property, we saw that setting font-weight to none allowed us to take away the default bold presentation of a header. But since no tags that we've learned about (and actually, no HTML tags at all) have a default small-caps setting, for example, why do we need a none value for the font-variant property? All in good time: The answer will become apparent when we consider style classes below.

Paragraph Styles

So far in our discussion of HTML styles we have focused on headers, as they provide an easy way to introduce the basic concepts and syntax of styles. But styles may be applied to any HTML element. They are especially useful with the paragraph element.

For example, if we wanted to have the text of our web page displayed in a larger than normal font, say 14 point, then we can define a paragraph style to implement it:

```
<style type="text/css">
  p {font-size:14pt}
</style>
```

Any text in our document that was placed inside a <p> element would then be displayed at the 14 point size. Note well, however, that for the paragraph style to work, all the text has to be in paragraph *elements*; using just <p> tags in your document with no ending </p> tags will not give the desired effect.

Using the <p> element also allows us to specify a first-line indent and the line height for our paragraphs by using the `text-indent` and `line-height` properties. The following paragraph style sets an indent of 25 points and a line height of 24 points (which corresponds to double spacing for a font size of 12 points):

```
<style type="text/css">
  p {text-indent:25pt; line-height:24pt}
</style>
```

Or we may use percentages, where the indent is a certain percentage of the paragraph width and the line height is a certain percentage of the font size:

```
<style type="text/css">
  p {text-indent:12%; line-height:150%}
</style>
```

Figure 3.4 shows an example.

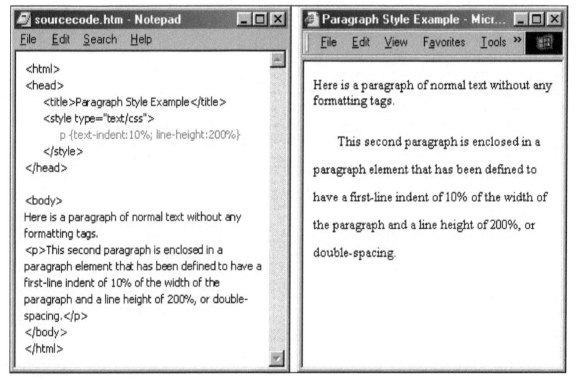

FIGURE 3.4.   Specifying paragraph indents and line height using styles

The values don't both have to be percentages, of course:

```
<style type="text/css">
  p {text-indent:25pt; line-height:150%}
</style>
```

You can get a hanging indent by using a negative number for the value of the text-indent property:

```
<style type="text/css">
  p {text-indent:-15pt}
</style>
```

For line height, we can also specify a number by which the font size is multiplied to get the desired line height. For example:

```
<style type="text/css">
  p {line-height:1.5}
</style>
```

This line-height value of 1.5 gives the same result as a line-height value of 150%, that is, line-and-a-half spacing.

We can even get down to the nitty-gritty details of how much space the browser should put between words and space between letters within words (this latter effect is known as kerning). For example:

```
<style type="text/css">
  p {word-spacing:3pt; letter-spacing:1pt}
</style>
```

Trying to specify this level of detail, however, often requires a lot of trial and error and does not give very satisfactory results. Moreover, word and letter spacing styles do not work in versions of Navigator before Version 6.

Font Families

We can use styles to change the font type or family that is displayed by using the font-family property followed by the name of the font in quotation marks. If, for example, we wanted all the paragraphs in our document to be displayed at normal size in the Lucida font, we would write the p style as:

```
<style type="text/css">
  p {font-family:"Lucida"}
</style>
```

One potential problem occurs when the font you choose is not installed on the user's computer. You therefore usually specify at least two font families, separated by a comma. If your first-choice font is an unusual one, it's prudent to make your second choice a more common style.

IMPORTANT

```
<style type="text/css">
  p {font-family:"Lucida","Arial"}
</style>
```

Be aware that different variable-width fonts of the same size (e.g., 12-point Times New Roman vs. 12-point Arial) often have very different letter sizes and spacing. A sentence displayed in one 12-point font, for example, may require more than one line, while the same sentence in another 12-point font may take less than one line. You should therefore view your page first using your first-choice font and then your second-choice font to see how the change affects the page's display.

If neither of your two specified choices is available on the user's system, the browser uses the default variable width font that the user has specified in the browser's preferences (usually Times New Roman for PCs and Times for Macintoshes). Although it's fun to design a web page that uses different and exotic fonts, the actual display the user sees may not be so appealing. Therefore it's best to stick to common fonts, if you change the font at all.

(If you really have to have a certain font for your web page, it's possible to embed the font family definition in your source document so that the font information is sent to the user's computer along with the source document. But this requires the font to be defined in a special type of file and also slows down the loading and display of the web page.)

We have now learned how to use styles to set all manner of aspects of text display including font-style (italic or oblique), font-weight (bold), font-variant (small-caps), font-size, line-height, and font-family. Putting these all together in one style definition makes for a rather long and awkward definition:

```
<style type="text/css">
  p {font-style:italic; font-weight:500;
     font-variant:small-caps; font-size:14pt;
     line-height:24pt; font-family:"Lucida","Arial"}
</style>
```

We can compact this, however, by using the font property:

```
<style type="text/css">
  p  {font: italic 500 small-caps 14pt/24pt "Lucida",
      "Arial"}
</style>
```

Note how we combined the font size and line height into one value, 14pt/24pt. You don't have to specify all these values. The following definition just sets the font weight and font size:

```
<style type="text/css">
  p {font: bold 20pt}
</style>
```

Although the order in which we wrote the properties in the first long example above does not matter, it does matter in the second case when we're using the shortened version with the `font` property. The official HTML specification as defined by the World Wide Web Consortium prescribes a certain order (the order we used above). Navigator follows the official specification, but Explorer does not. In Explorer, it doesn't matter what order you use.

QuickCheck Questions

1. What are some factors that must be taken into consideration when setting the font size of headers?
2. Write the HTML code for an internal style sheet that redefines the header 3 element to be displayed in normal (non-bold) text.
3. Write the HTML code for an internal style sheet that redefines the header 3 element to be displayed in both bold and italic text.
4. Which style property do you use for uppercase text?
5. Write the HTML code for an internal style sheet that redefines paragraphs to have a first-line indent of 15% of the line width and a line spacing of space-and-a-half.

Lab Exercise 3.2, "Specifying Presentation via Styles," may be done at this point.

Creating Tags with Multiple Styles

Although it's certainly helpful to use a paragraph style to change the display features of all the paragraphs in a source document, sometimes we want different types of paragraphs to be displayed in different ways. For example, if we had a web page with several sections and several paragraphs in each section, we might want to create a special style just for the introductory paragraphs. HTML allows us to do this by taking a given element and defining one or more **"classes" of styles** for it.

Here's how it works in the case of a special style for introductory paragraphs. We first define a style for regular paragraphs and then we specify a sub-style, or class, that is a modification of the primary style. As an example, we will define the regular paragraphs to have italic text with justified margins and the introductory paragraphs to have the same formatting, except be aligned in the center and have red text. To achieve this, we define a p style and a `p.intro` class (or sub-style), as follows:

```
<style type="text/css">
  p {text-align:justify; font-weight:bold}
  p.intro {text-align:center; color:red}
</style>
```

The p.intro class includes the complete set of styles that are defined for its **"parent" style** p, but then modifies it or adds to it in certain ways. In this case, the text-align property is changed from justify to center and the color property is added (red). The font-weight property (bold) will be the same for both the parent style and the class, since the class definition does not change it. (Note that "intro" is our name; we could have just as well named it something else, like p.introductory or p.first.)

When we want to specify the use of the p.intro class in our document, we add a class attribute to the <p> tag and specify its value as "intro" using the syntax:

```
<p class="intro">Paragraph text goes here . . . <p>
```

The full code is shown in Figure 3.5.

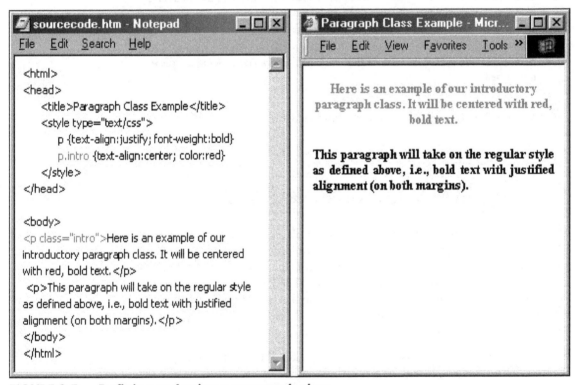

FIGURE 3.5.   Defining and using a paragraph class

Remember that an attribute is used in a tag to specify an option available for that tag. In this case, the name of the attribute is class and its value is "intro". In the next chapter we will learn to use a number of other attributes.

We are not limited to just one class, of course. We could define any number of <p> classes in the <style> element and specify their use with the class attribute in the <p> tag, using the class names we gave them.

We can now also answer the question we posed in the section "Beyond Bold and Italic" above: Why do we need a `none` value for the `font-variant` property or the `text-transform` property? If we define a basic paragraph style that sets the `text-transform` property to the value `uppercase`, for example, we might want to define a class of that paragraph style that does not have uppercase text. So we turn off the `uppercase` specification by using the `none` value, as follows:

```
<style type="text/css">
  p {font-style:italic; text-transform:uppercase}
  p.noupper {text-transform:none}
</style>
```

Figure 3.6 reviews some of the possibilities. Note how we set the value of the `class` attribute to different values, depending on which style we want to use for the paragraph.

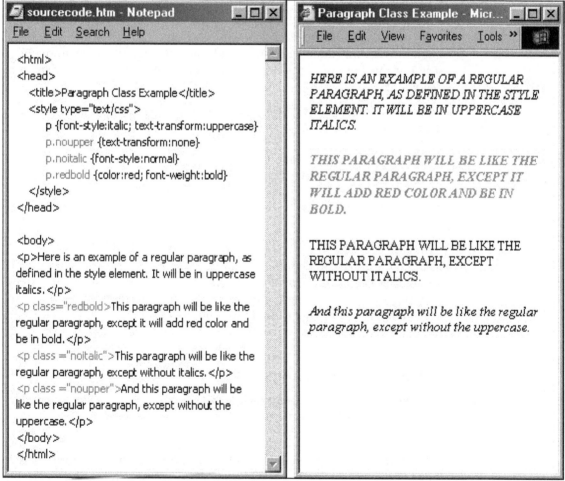

FIGURE 3.6.   Further use of styles and classes

QuickCheck Questions

1. What is a style class?
2. Write the HTML code for an internal style sheet that defines a paragraph class named "boldandblue," which will have its text displayed in bold and blue.
3. Given the style class definition in question 2, write the HTML code that would create a paragraph with that style. For the text of the paragraph, use "This is a sample paragraph displayed in bold and blue text."

Using Local Styles

It is occasionally useful to bypass the <style> element and insert a style definition directly into a tag. For example, if you had only one paragraph in your entire document that needed to be uppercase and red, defining a style for it would be overkill (the idea of styles and classes being, of course, to define a style once in the <style> element and then use it multiple times in your document).

Instead, you would add a style attribute to the tag with the intended style definitions.

```
<p style="text-transform:uppercase; color:red">This para-
graph will be uppercase and red (in addition to any other
style properties that may be defined for the regular para-
graph).</p>
```

This is known as a **local style**, because it only affects that individual tag.

Note that a local style definition takes precedence if there are any conflicts with a style definition for that type of tag in the <style> element. In our example, the local style definition of color:red overrides any other color definition that might exist in the p style definition in the <style> element. But the rest of the p style definition would be maintained.

QuickCheck Question

1. Write the HTML code for a local style that redefines a single header 2 element to be displayed in both bold and italic.

Lab Exercise 3.3, "Using Classes and Local Styles," may be done at this point.

Creating Custom Tags

We have seen how we can customize the presentation of existing HTML elements by using styles. It's also possible to create completely new elements. We do this by building on two generic tags, named <div> and <span>. The <div> tag is a generic block-level tag. (The div stands for division.) The <span> tag is a generic inline tag (span because it spans a series of characters).

What if, for example, we wanted to change the font size of selected individual words in our document. We could, of course, put each word in a <big> or <small> element. But that will not do if we want a bigger or smaller size than those elements provide. To satisfy this need, we can define a span style and use the <span> element to implement it.

```
<style type="text/css">
   span {font-size:18pt}
</style>
```

We would then enclose whatever text we wanted to enlarge in a <span> element:

```
Let me make one thing <span>perfectly</span> clear . . .
```

Or if you want to be able to change the background color of certain words or phrases to yellow in order to highlight them, you would write:

```
<style type="text/css">
   span {background-color:yellow}
</style>
```

If we need to change just the size of some words and change just the color of other words, we would define different span style classes, as in Figure 3.7.

Note that we can nest <span> elements within one another, as we did in the last sentence in Figure 3.7 to get large red text. Or, of course, we could get the same result with one <span> element by defining another span class with multiple properties:

```
<style type="text/css">
   span.largered {color:red; font-size:18pt}
</style>
```

The <div> element works the same way as <span>. If, for example, we want to change the background color of certain sections of our document to red but keep other sections the normal background color (presumably white), we can define a <div> tag with a redbkd class and use it in the normal way (Figure 3.8).

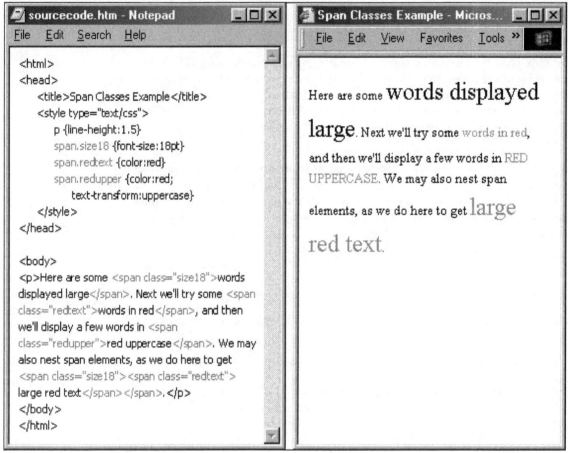

FIGURE 3.7.   Using the `<span>` element

Note that officially we could not use the inline `<span>` element to do what we did here with the block-level `<div>` element because there are several block-level elements included within it (i.e., the `<p>` elements). Nesting a block-level element inside an inline element goes against the rules of XHTML, although the browser may let you get away with it.

QuickCheck Questions

1. What is the difference between a `<span>` and a `<div>` element?
2. Write the HTML code that defines an inline custom element that can be used to format blue text with a yellow background and give an example of how it can be used to format the line of text, "This will appear in blue with a yellow background."

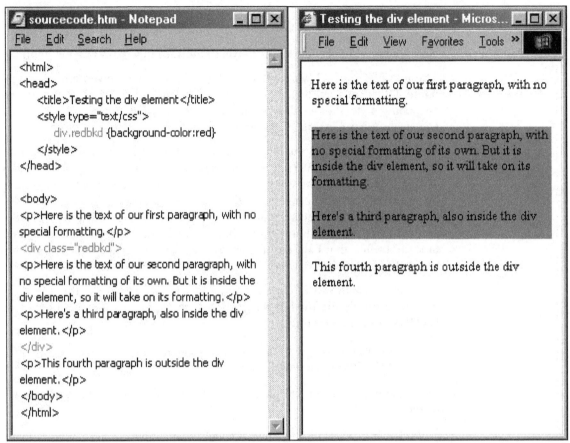

FIGURE 3.8.   Using the `<div>` **element**

External Style Sheets

In Chapter 5 we will learn how to use links to create a multiple-page website. In designing such a site, it's a good idea to have a standard "look and feel" for all the pages, which means using the same set of style definitions for each page. This might require a lot of retyping of style definitions, or at least cutting and pasting the style definitions between the source documents for the various pages. But fortunately HTML provides an easier way, known as external style sheets.

An **external style sheet** is simply a text-only file that contains nothing but a set of style definitions, such as:

```
h2 {color:red}
h3 {color:blue}
p {text-align:justify; font:12pt/16pt}
```

```
p.intro {text-align:center; color:red}
p.bigandbold {text-weight:900; font:20pt/30pt}
```

Note that we do *not* enclose these style definitions in a <style> element.

The text file in which we save these definitions may be given any legal file-name, but it must end in the three-letter extension .css. The css stands for **cascading style sheets**. This is the official name that the World Wide Web Consortium has given to HTML style sheets.

The cascading refers to the fact that there are three types of style sheets: local, internal, and external. We saw how to create a local style for a tag in the section "Using Local Styles." And what we have been doing in the rest of this chapter is using internal style sheets—styles that are defined using the <style> element. External style sheets are the subject of this section. The reason that these styles are cascading is that you may have all three in a document at the same time, and when that happens, the styles cascade: Any local styles override any internal style definitions, which in turn override any external style definitions.

In order to use the styles contained in an external style sheet (the .css document), we simply add the following <link> tag to the <head> element of an HTML source document:

```
<link rel="stylesheet" type="text/css"
    href="mystyles.css" />
```

where mystyles.css is the sample name of the text file where the definitions are stored.

When the browser sees this tag in the source document, it goes and looks for the mystyles.css document that contains the style definitions. It then uses those style definitions to display the source document. For this to work, the mystyles.css document *must be in the same folder as the source document.*

(Don't confuse the <link> tag with hypertext links, which we will learn about in Chapter 5.)

Although HTML style sheets give the web page designer more power and flex-ibility, they aren't without their drawbacks. The main one at present is that even the newest versions of Explorer and Navigator don't implement them completely. Navigator version 4 on the PC only recognizes about 33 percent of style commands and Explorer version 5 about 72 percent, although most of the basic styles work okay. Navigator 6 and Explorer 6 for the PC both imple-ment over 90% of styles. But older versions of browsers might not recognize styles at all. So we need some way to hide the HTML style instructions from these browsers, because they will ignore the <style> tag and treat the style instructions as regular text—they will be displayed on the web page.

This is where HTML comments have another use besides just annotating HTML code. By putting all the style instructions inside an HTML comment, older browsers will not display the instructions as text, and most newer browsers are set up so that they will still recognize the style instructions. That is:

```
<style type="text/css">
<!--
   h1 {text-align:center}
   h2 {color:red; text-align:center}
-->
</style>
```

Note that the comment tag goes inside the <style> element.

Unfortunately, the coming of XHTML has rendered this use of comments ineffective. The reason is that XML-based browsers are set up so that they completely ignore anything they find in the comments tag. So the only sure way to use style definitions but still keep them away from older browsers is to put them in an external .css file and access them via the <link> element as above. (Remember that this works because a browser ignores any tag it does not understand, so an older browser will ignore the <link> tag.)

IMPORTANT

Nevertheless, in our examples we will continue to use internal style sheets, and to save a little space we will usually omit the comment tag.

Finally, you may be wondering if style sheets enable you to display accented characters and other special symbols on a web page. You actually have to use a different method involving character codes to do this. See Appendix E for details.

QuickCheck Questions

1. What does cascading style sheets mean?
2. Where do you put the <link> tag?

Lab Exercise 3.4, "Using Custom Tags and External Styles," may be done at this point.

browser safe colors	hexadecimal (base 16) system	property
cascading style sheets	internal style sheet	property value
color number (or color code)	local style	style class
external style sheet	parent style	style definition

Key Terms

1. The Power of Styles

Defining the style sheet language for a `<style>` element as css (cascading style sheets):

```
<style type="text/css">
...
</style>
```

Using the `<meta>` element to define the default style sheet language for the whole document as css (placed in the `<head>` element):

```
<meta http-equiv="Content-Style-Type" content="text/css" />
```

Using the `<style>` element, placed within the `<head>` element, to create an internal style sheet (defining the color property of the `<h2>` and `<h3>` elements in this example):

```
<style type="text/css">
    h2 {color:red}
    h3 {color:#D61130}
</style>
```

2. Formatting Fonts Using Styles

Redefining the formatting of header tags, for example, using an internal style sheet (the `<style>` element goes in the `<head>` element):

```
<style type="text/css">
    h1 {text-align:center; font-style:italic; font-size:30pt}
    h2 {color:red; font-size:24pt; font-variant:small-caps}
</style>
```

Basic style properties and their possible values:

```
color:red (or other predefined color name or valid color number)
text-align:center (or right or left)
font-weight:bold (or normal, bolder, lighter, or the values 100, 200, . . . 900)
font-size:20pt (or other point value, or xx-small, x-small, smaller, small, medium, large,
    larger, x-large, xx-large, or a percentage of the "normal" size, e.g., 150%)
font-style:italic (or normal, oblique)
text-decoration:underline (or overline, line-through, none, blink)
text-transform:capitalize (or uppercase, lowercase, none)
font-variant:small-caps (or none)
background-color:red (or transparent or predefined color name or valid color number)
text-indent:25pt (or a percentage of the line width, e.g., 10%; negative for hanging indent)
line-height:20pt (or a percentage of the single-line height, e.g., 150%, or a multiplica-
    tion factor, e.g., 1.5)
font-family:"Lucida","Arial" (first-choice and second-choice font names)
```

Combining the font-style, font-weight, font-variant, font-size/line-height, font-family properties into one style definition (the order is important):

```
font: italic bolder small-caps 14pt/24pt "Lucida","Arial"
```

3. Creating Tags with Multiple Styles

Defining and using classes (sub-styles):

```
<html>
<head>
    <title>Class Example</title>
    <style type="text/css">
        p {text-align:justify; font-weight:bold}
        p.intro {text-align:center; color:red}
    </style>
```

```
</head>
<body>
<p class="intro">This paragraph will be centered with red, bold text.</p>
<p>This paragraph will be bold text with justified alignment.</p>
</body>
</html>
```

4. Using Local Styles

Creating a local style for a single instance of an element:

```
<p style="text-transform:uppercase; color:red">This paragraph will be uppercase and red (in addi-
tion to any other style properties that may be defined for the regular paragraph).</p>
```

5. Creating Custom Tags

Defining a custom inline element using `<span>` and a custom block-level element using `<div>` (classes of each may also be defined):

```
<style type="text/css">
   span {background-color:yellow}
   div {background-color:red}
</style>
```

6. External Style Sheets

Using an external style sheet saved in a file named mystyles.css (which contains style definitions *without* a `<style>` element):

```
<link rel="stylesheet" type="text/css" href="mystyles.css" />
```

When using hexadecimal color codes in a style definition (e.g., `h2 {color:#D61130}`), do not forget the # symbol.

When choosing colors for a web page, it's best to stick with the 216 browser safe colors.

It's easy to forget the hyphens that are part of many of the style properties (e.g., `font-size`, `text-align`).

Do not put a space between the number and "pt" when defining a font size value (for example, `font-size:20pt` is correct, `font-size:20 pt` is not).

Resist the temptation to create blinking text.

If you define a paragraph style, you must use a paragraph element, not the `<p>` tag by itself.

When specifying a font family in a style definition, list a first choice and a common second choice in case the first choice is not available on the surfer's computer. Also be aware that different fonts of the same point size do not necessarily display at the same size or with the same spacing.

If you use the font property to combine a number of font style definitions, remember that the order you list them matters (at least to Navigator).

Don't confuse the `<link>` tag (used with external style sheets) with hypertext links.

Although HTML comments have customarily been used to bracket style definitions so that non-styles-capable browsers do not display them as regular text, this is no longer guaranteed to work with XML-capable browsers, because the browser may ignore everything inside the comments.

Alerts and Advice

1. Which element is used to create an internal style sheet?
   a. `<internal>`
   b. `<style>`
   c. `<internalstyle>`
   d. `<stylesheet>`

2. A style definition consists of two things separated by a colon. What are they?

3. How many colors have predefined names?
   a. 10
   b. 12
   c. 16
   d. 32

4. How many browser safe colors are there?
   a. 32
   b. 64
   c. 128
   d. 216

5. Which of the following are properties used to define the style of text? What do each of them do?
   a. `font-weight`
   b. `text-style`
   c. `color`
   d. `font-align`
   e. `font-size`

6. Write a style definition for a paragraph with a first-line indent of 15 points.

7. Write a style definition for a paragraph class named greekletters with its font set to the Symbol font.

8. True or false: A local style definition always overrides any internal and external style definitions that might apply.

9. The _____ is a generic inline element and _____ is a generic block-level element that may be customized.

10. True or false: The best way to hide an internal style definition from older browsers that don't recognize styles is to enclose it in the comment tag.

1. Briefly define and/or explain the following terms: style definition, style property, style class.

2. Using a search engine, search the Web for sites with information on hexadecimal color numbers. Find the color numbers for five browser safe colors that you like plus the color numbers for three non–browser safe colors that you like. Write down the numbers along with a brief description (1 to 3 words) of each color.

3. Write the HTML code that would create a new style for header 1s, making them italic and bold.

4. Write the HTML code that would create a new style for header 3s, making them centered and upper-case.

5. Write the HTML code that would define a regular paragraph style with a hanging indent of 30 points and a first-choice font of Garamond and a second-choice font of Bookman.

6. Write the HTML code that would use the `font` property to define a paragraph style with 16-point italic text and a 32-point line height.

7. Write the HTML code that would define a paragraph class named doublespace that modified the regular paragraph style (however defined) to make it doublespaced. Also write the code for a sample paragraph of this class.

8. Write the HTML code that creates a local style of yellow text on a blue background for a header 1 element.

9. Write the HTML code to define a custom block-level element that will italicize all the text within it, and show how it may be used to italicize three paragraphs of text (as defined with paragraph elements).

10. Write the HTML code that creates an external style sheet with style definitions for the code in problems 6 and 7. Assuming that this style sheet has been saved in a file named teststyle.css, show how to write the HTML tag that you would place in the document where you wanted to apply the styles.

Debugging Exercise

1. Identify the errors in the following code and then sketch on paper how the browser would display it once the errors were corrected. (In this case, don't worry about adding the necessary XHTML code. Focus instead on the style code.)

```
<html>
<head>
    <title>Red Mountain Consulting</title>
<externalstyle>
    REL="stylesheet"
    TYPE="text/css"
    HREF="mystyles.css"
</externalstyle>
<internalstyle type="text/css">
    h2 {color:lightgreen; bgcolor:yellow}
    p {textalign:justify; text-weight:bold}
    p.intro {textalign:center; color:blue}
</internalstyle>
</head>
<body>
<h1>Red Mountain Consulting</h1>
<h2>Our Services</h2>
<p.intro>We specialize in project management consulting. Our partners and associates have
extensive real-world experience in bringing even the most complex and deadline-sensitive
projects to successful completion on time and under budget.</p>
<h2>Our Clients</h2>
<p>Our clients range from Fortune 500 companies to the most dynamic small cap companies
in a broad range of industries.</p>
<h2>How to Reach Us</h2>
<p localstyle="font-style:italics">123 Market Street, San Francisco, CA<br />
510-321-1234</p>
</body>
</html>
```

Note: Most of the exercises above may also be done as lab exercises.

Exercise 3.1: Basic Styles

❏ Create a simple HTML source document named styling.htm that demonstrates the color and text-align styles using the header elements <h1> through <h6>. Use whatever colors and text you like. Make sure to save your work.

Exercise 3.2: Specifying Presentation via Styles

❏ Using the document from Lab exercise 3.1, add various sample headers and paragraphs that demonstrate the use of the following style properties: font-size, font-style, font-weight, text-decoration, text-transform, font-variant, background-color, text-indent, line-height, font-family, and font. Include at least one example of each property. If you want to use more than one type of paragraph style, either comment out the previous definitions or use multiple source documents. Feel free to be creative. But also note that styles are very sensitive to spelling errors. If you leave off a hyphen or a curly bracket, or if you don't use the correct name (for example, using "text-style" instead of "font-style"), the browser will ignore the style.

Exercise 3.3: Using Classes and Local Styles

❏ Using the document from Lab exercises 3.1 and 3.2, add the HTML code that will create three different classes of the <h1> element: one with yellow text on a blue background, one with small caps text but not bold, and one with red text in the Arial font. Put at least one sample <h1> element of each style in the <body> element.

❏ Add code to your document that will define a regular paragraph style that uses italicized text (and the default font). Then define two classes of this paragraph that use space-and-half line spacing and double-space line spacing. Put at least one sample of each of these in the <body> element, making sure to include enough sample text so that the effects of the spacing can be seen.

❏ Add code to your document that will define a local style for an <h2> element in your document, making it red and giving it an indent of 25 points.

Exercise 3.4: Using Custom Tags and External Styles

❏ Add at least two examples of a <span> element and two examples of a <div> element to your document (your choice on what they do).

❏ Create a .css file named mystyles.css that contains the styles that you have been creating in the previous exercises. Then create a new HTML source document named externalstyles.htm that uses that external style sheet to define its styles. Include some code in the <body> element that demonstrates some (but not necessarily all) of the styles.

Attributes, Lists, and Tables

LEARNING OBJECTIVES

1. Learn about deprecated elements and the strict vs. transitional forms of XHTML.

2. Learn how to specify tag options by using attributes in various tags.

3. Learn the various ways in which HTML is used to structure ordered, unordered, and definition lists.

4. Learn how to display a table of information on a web page and the various options involved.

Extensions and Deprecations

Over the years both Navigator and Explorer have added a number of **extensions** of their own devising to the standard version of HTML. Although many of these HTML extensions let the web designer add cool and/or useful features to a web page, the drawback is that usually Navigator's extensions do not work in Explorer and Explorer's do not work in Navigator. For example, Navigator's `<blink>` element, which creates text that blinks, will not work in Explorer, nor will Explorer's `<marquee>` element, which displays moving text, work in Navigator.

Because one goal of any web designer should be to create a page that will display properly for all surfers who drop by, you should generally be cautious about using HTML features that have not yet been given official sanction or that work in only one browser. (You can find out what's official and what's not by consulting the World Wide Web Consortium's site at www.w3.org.) If for some reason you do need to use nonstandard HTML features, you should include a message at the beginning of your page informing surfers that "This page uses features that are best viewed using Netscape Navigator version 4.0 or greater [or Internet Explorer whatever]," or words to that effect.

A further complication is introduced by the W3C's practice of periodically "deprecating" certain elements. The **deprecated** label on an element means that it is on the way out and is no longer recommended for use, although it will still work in most browsers. Other elements are made **obsolete**, meaning that browsers that are in strict compliance with the new standard will not support their use. The W3C's primary motivation behind deprecating certain elements is the need to separate structure from presentation (see the section on "The <em> and <strong> elements" in Chapter 2). As previously discussed, the idea is to use the HTML source document to define the structure and classify the content of a web page and to use style sheets to define the presentation of the various content elements. Therefore, starting with HTML version 4 (when style sheets were introduced), many HTML elements that were used primarily for presentation were deprecated. Remember that deprecated does not necessarily mean eliminated. Most browsers will continue to recognize deprecated tags.

One of the more popular presentation elements that was deprecated was <font>. The <font> element is an inline element that defines the size, color, and fontstyle presentation of text via the `size`, `color`, and `face` attributes. Remember that an attribute is something we add to a tag that specifies an option available for that tag. To use an attribute in a tag, we specify the *name* of the attribute followed by an equal sign and then the *value* of the attribute enclosed in quotation marks. For example, the following <font> element directs the browser to display the enclosed text in red:

```
<font color="red">This is really red!</font>
```

By adding a `size` attribute and value, the display size of the font can also be defined:

```
<font size="5" color="red">This is really red!</font>
```

The values of the `size` attribute range from 1 to 7, with 1 being the smallest, 7 the largest, and 3 being normal size. The `color` attribute takes the usual color numbers or words for its value (with the # symbol before the color number, just as with styles), and the `face` attribute (signifying the face or look of the font) takes the name of the font desired. For example:

```
<font size="5" face="Garamond">This is the Garamond font
in slightly larger than normal text.</font>
```

The order of the attributes in the tag does not matter. We could have written the above as:

```
<font face="Garamond" size="5">This is the Garamond font
in slightly larger than normal text.</font>
```

You can also specify more than one font in case your first choice is not available on the user's computer:

```
<font face="Garamond,Arial" >Let's try Garamond, or Arial
if Garamond isn't available.</font>
```

In HTML 4 and before, the quotation marks around the attribute value are not always required (depending on the attribute used), but in XHTML they are. It's best to get in the habit of using them, even if you see other source documents where they are not used. You may also put spaces on either side of the equal sign, as below, although it's not required.

```
<font color = "red">This is really red!</font>
```

At this point you may be wondering why learn all this if it's on the way out? We're telling you about these elements and attributes not because we recommend you use them, but because in studying web pages you will often come across them and should know how they work.

Where does that leave XHTML? Because the W3C recognizes that the huge existing universe of web pages created under the older rules of HTML is not going to go away or be updated anytime soon and that surfers will continue to use older browsers that don't handle style sheets very well, it has defined multiple versions of XHTML. There is a **strict form of XHTML** that does not recognize deprecated tags and attributes. And there is a **transitional form of XHTML** that does. This is where we can return to the details of the Document Type Definition we put at the top of an XHTML document and understand it a little better. The DTD we used in Chapter 2 was:

```
<!DOCtype html PUBliC
   "-//W3C//dtD XHTML 1.0 Transitional//EN"
   "http://www/w3/org/tr/xhtml/11/dtD/xhtml1-
   transitional.dtd">
```

Note that the word "transitional" appears twice in this DTD. This indicates to the browser that the code in the document adheres to the transitional form of XHTML, with the last part of the DTD being a URL for a document at the W3C website that defines the details of the transitional form. If we instead replace "transitional" with "strict," we are telling the browser that the code is clean and pure XHTML:

```
<!DOCtype html PUBliC
   "-//W3C//dtD XHTML 1.0 Strict//EN"
   "http://www/w3/org/tr/xhtml/11/dtD/xhtml1-strict.dtd">
```

As a practical matter, for the next few years we will be in a transitional stage and so you should use the transitional DTD. If you were to write all web pages in strict XHTML, many surfers would not be able to view them as intended because their browsers do not handle XHTML and style sheets very well. Therefore you should prepare for the future by learning the philosophy and methods of XHTML and using it as much as possible in your web pages, if only to lessen the amount of changes you may have to make in the future. You also need to design your pages for the present, however, so that most surfers right now will be able to view them as intended. This means that sometimes you may decide it's best to use deprecated elements. Just try to keep their use to a minimum, and keep in mind the advantages of style sheets.

IMPORTANT

The <font> element, for example, is certainly a quick and easy way to change the color, size, or font of some text on a web page. But the advantage of styles becomes clear when you need to experiment with the overall look of a page. To change, for example, a highlight color from red to yellow only requires a single change in the style definition. In contrast, if you used <font> elements throughout your document, you would have to go through and change the color value for every single one of them.

As we proceed in our study of HTML, we will indicate which elements and attributes are deprecated. The table in Appendix B also lists deprecated elements.

QuickCheck Questions

1. What is the difference between a deprecated and an obsolete tag?
2. Is it possible to use a deprecated tag in a source document? Why or why not?
3. What is the difference between the strict form of XHTML and the transitional form?

More Tags and Attributes

Until styles were introduced with HTML version 4, tag attributes were the preferred way to specify the presentation of HTML elements. We will review a few of the most popular ones that you will see in HTML source documents.

The align Attribute

In Chapter 2 we learned about the six header elements <h1> . . . </h1>, <h2> . . . </h2>, and so on. The browser normally aligns the text of the header on the left margin of the browser window. We may instead use the align attribute with the value center to instruct the browser to center the header's text on the page:

```
<h2 align="center">Welcome to my Web page!</h2>
```

We may also specify its value as right or left, which will align the header along the right or left margin, respectively, as shown in Figure 4.1.

The align attribute may also be used in <p> elements. If the align attribute is not present in a tag, then align="left" is the default value.

An alternative way to center text on a page is to use the <center> element, as in Figure 4.2. Note that the browser automatically inserts a line break after the <center> element.

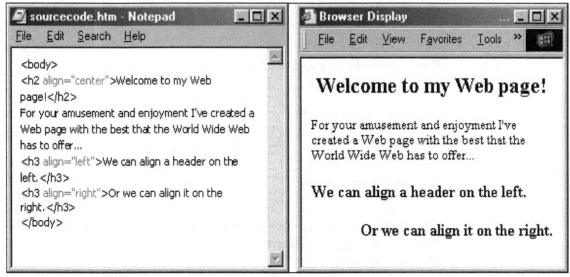

FIGURE 4.1.   Positioning a header using the align attribute

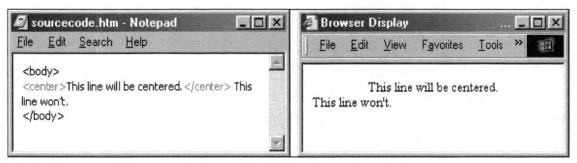

FIGURE 4.2.   Using the <center> element

The <center> element is a block-level element, so it may be used to center a header by nesting the header element inside it:

```
<center><h2>Welcome to my Web page!</h2></center>
```

Nevertheless, both the <center> element and the align attribute have been deprecated. You should therefore usually employ styles to specify the alignment of HTML elements. Remember that to center the header 2s in a document, we use the text-align property in a style definition:

```
<style type="text/css">
   h2 {text-align:center}
</style>
```

Or, if we didn't want all the header 2s to be centered, we would define a class for the ones we did want centered:

```
<style type="text/css">
   h2.centered {text-align:center}
</style>
```

The <h2> element would then be:

```
<h2 class="centered">This is the heading text</h2>
```

Note that when we define a style property there are no quotation marks involved. It's simply text-align:center. But we do put them around attribute values, as in <h2 align="center">.

Background Colors

As a more colorful example of the use of attributes to define presentation, consider the <body> element. By using the bgcolor attribute in the beginning <body> tag, we can change the color of the web page's background. The basic syntax is:

```
<body bgcolor="#$$$$$$">
```

where the $ signs are replaced by a color number (for example, FF0000 for red; see Table 3.1 for more). Or you may use one of the 16 predefined color names. For example:

```
<body bgcolor="#FF00FF">
```

Or the equivalent:

```
<body bgcolor="magenta">
```

Figure 4.3 shows the result (with an off-red color substituting for the real magenta).

We may also change the color of the page's text by using the text attribute in the <body> tag. The following code changes the background color to yellow and the text color to blue:

```
<body bgcolor="yellow" text="blue">
```

FIGURE 4.3.   Changing the background color of a web page

As usual with presentation-based attributes, however, the `bgcolor` and `text` attributes have been deprecated. So the preferred way to get the same results is to use a style sheet for the `<body>` element:

```
<style>
   body {background-color:yellow; color:blue}
</style>
```

Note that the name of the property for the background color is `background-color`, while the name of the attribute value for the background color is `bgcolor`.

Horizontal Rules

It often makes good design sense to separate sections in a web page using a horizontal line known as a "horizontal rule." The tag we use is the `<hr />` tag, which, like the `<br />` tag, is an empty element. By default, horizontal rules are centered on the page with a shadowed look. In the past, attributes were used to set the rule's size/thickness (measured in pixels—the individual dots or picture elements that comprise the screen display) and width (either in pixels or as a percentage of the page width), as shown in Figure 4.4.

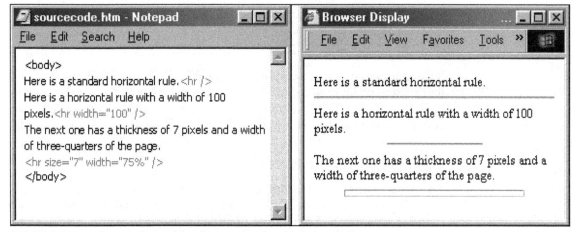

FIGURE 4.4.　Examples of horizontal rules using attributes

But the `size` and `width` attributes have been deprecated. Instead, we may define horizontal rule styles using the `height` and `width` properties. The style for the third horizontal rule in Figure 4.4 would be:

```
<style type="text/css">
   hr {height:7px; width:75%}
</style>
```

We may also change the color of the horizontal rule by using the `background-color` property, such as:

```
<style type="text/css">
   hr {height:7px; width:75%; background-color:red}
</style>
```

What Tags, Which Attributes?

How do you know what tags have which attributes, and which are deprecated and which not? You don't without an HTML reference. We provide a basic one in Appendix B. Further details are also easily available on the Web itself. We list a number of good sites in Appendix I.

QuickCheck Questions

1. Write the HTML code that creates a header 2 aligned in the center of the page, using first a style sheet and then an attribute. (Use whatever text you want for the header.)

2. Write the HTML code that creates a horizontal rule with a width of 200 pixels, using first a style sheet and then an attribute.

Lab Exercise 4.1, "Experimenting with Attributes," may be done at this point.

Displaying Lists

Sometimes you may want to display information on a web page in the form of a list or outline, with indentations for sub-items. HTML offers tags to create three kinds of lists. We will concentrate on the two most useful kinds—ordered lists and unordered lists—and say a few words about the third kind—definition lists.

Ordered and Unordered Lists

The items in an **ordered list** are listed by number or letter: 1, 2, 3 . . . or A, B, C. . . . The items in an unordered list are marked by a solid disc (bullet), open circle, or solid square. To create an ordered list, you use the <ol> element; for an **unordered list,** you use the <ul> element. Within the element you put the items in the list, each inside an <li> element. Figure 4.5 gives the basic examples. The browser automatically inserts a blank line before and after each list because <ol> and <ul> are block-level elements. It also indents each list slightly. Finally, note that in HTML 4 and before it was not required to include the </li> ending tag. But XHTML requires that all elements have ending tags.

Nested Lists

We may also nest lists so that a hierarchy is displayed. When you nest unordered lists, the top level uses solid discs to mark each item (as above), the

second level uses open circles, and the third level uses solid squares. Figure
4.6 shows the effect.

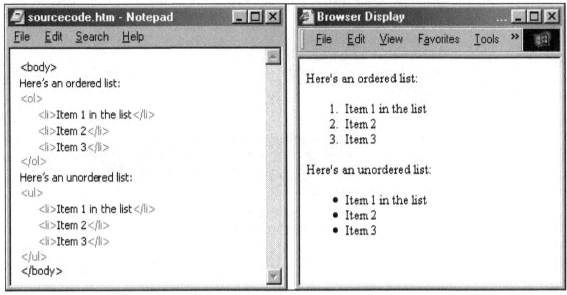

FIGURE 4.5.   Basic ordered and unordered lists

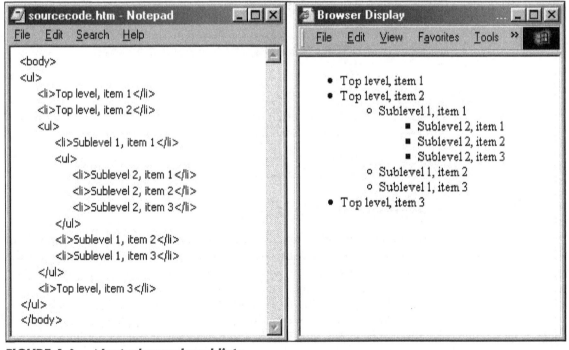

FIGURE 4.6.   Nested unordered lists

Note that in the source code we indented the nested lists to make the code easier to read. But the browser would have displayed it as shown whether or not we indented them. Different browsers may also display the discs, circles, and squares in slightly different sizes, so, if it matters to your page design, always check the display in both Explorer and Navigator.

A nested ordered list works the same way, except that all the levels use numbers to mark each item. Changing each <ul> . . . </ul> element in the source code of Figure 4.6 to <ol> . . . </ol> would yield the display in Figure 4.7.

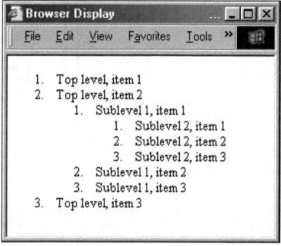

FIGURE 4.7.   **Display of a nested ordered list**

We can also nest lists of different types, such as unordered sublists within an ordered list. Figure 4.8 shows how.

Note that because the first unordered list is at the second level of the overall hierarchy, it uses open circles, not solid discs, to mark its items.

Customizing the List Display

If we don't like HTML's default choices for the list numbers or marks, HTML 4 (or transitional XHTML) allows us control over them. To override the default item mark used by an unordered list or sublist, we insert the type attribute in the <ul> tag. It may take one of three values: disc, circle, or square. The type attribute also works for ordered lists, using the values A, a, I, i, or 1 (corresponding to lists ordered A, B, C . . . , a, b, c . . . , I, II, III . . . , i, ii, iii . . . , or 1, 2, 3 . . .). Figure 4.9 shows a few of the possibilities.

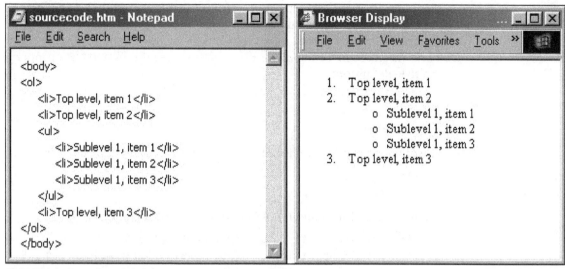

FIGURE 4.8.   Combining ordered and unordered lists

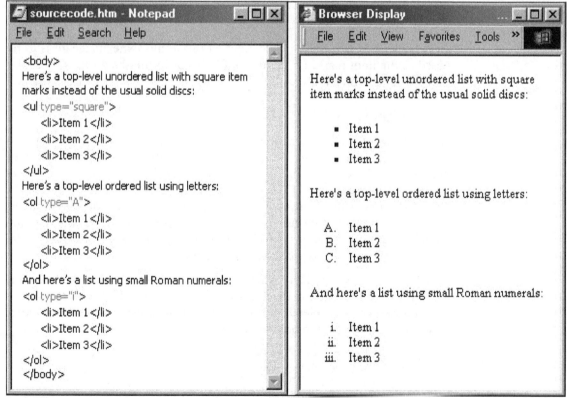

FIGURE 4.9.   Customizing the item marks of lists

The type attribute is yet another attribute that is deprecated. Defining the presentation of a list element using styles is straightforward, however. For example, to specify that all unordered lists in the document have square item marks (as in the first example in Figure 4.9) we use the list-style property in a style definition:

```
<style type="text/css">
  ul {list-style:square}
</style>
```

The other standard values for the list-style property of an unordered list are:

```
list-style:disc
list-style:circle
```

For an ordered list element, the following properties may be used:

```
list-style:decimal        (the numbers 1, 2, 3 . . . )
list-style:upper-alpha    (the uppercase letters A, B, C . . . )
list-style:lower-alpha    (the lowercase letters a, b, c . . . )
list-style:upper-roman    (the Roman numerals I, II, III . . . )
list-style:lower-roman    (the Roman numerals i, ii, iii . . . )
```

You may also use:

```
list-style:url(some_image.gif)
```

which specifies that the image contained in the file some_image.gif is to be used as the item mark. (If the image file is not in the same directory as the source document, a more complete path name must of course be provided.)

Definition Lists

A third type of list that sometimes may be of use is the **definition list**. You create a definition list using the <dl> element, within which you insert lines using the <dt> element for "definition terms" and lines using the <dd> element for "definition data." The contents of the <dd> elements are automatically indented by the browser. Figure 4.10 shows an example of how we might create a glossary of terms using these elements. (Remember that the indentation in the display comes from the browser's presentation of the <dd> elements, not from the indentations in the source code.)

Note how we have used the <strong> element to highlight the definition terms even more. The drawback is that we have to insert the <strong> element for every <dt> element. It would be much easier to define the style of the <dt> element to use bold text:

```
<style type="text/css">
  dt {font-weight:bold}
</style>
```

Like ordered and unordered lists, definition lists may also be nested. We will leave it up to the reader to experiment with the code to see the results.

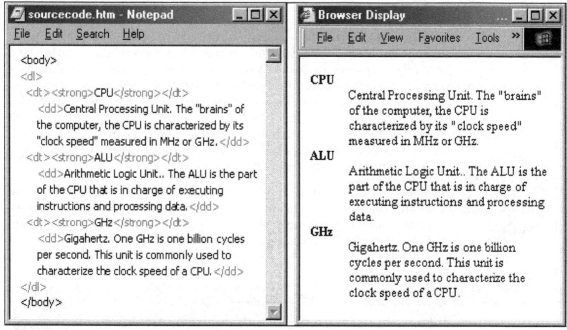

FIGURE 4.10.   Creating a definition list

QuickCheck Questions

1. Write the code that will create (a) an ordered list and (b) an unordered list using the following list items: pepperoni, salami, olives, mushrooms, extra cheese.

2. What are the three basic symbols that may be used as an item mark of an unordered list?

3. If you nest one ordered list within another ordered list, what numbering system is used for the top-level list and what is used for the sub-list: 1,2,3 . . . , A,B,C, . . . , a,b,c, . . . , or i,ii,iii, . . . ?

Lab Exercise 4.2, "More Practice with Tags," may be done at this point.

Turning to Tables

Sometimes you will want to present information on a web page in a tabular format. If you were designing a personal web page, for instance, you might create a table to display your class schedule. Or a website for a business might want to display a table listing store locations and hours. Starting with version 3.0, HTML added special tags to make table creation easy.

A Basic Table

A table in HTML consists of rows, and each row consists of rectangular boxes or cells. An HTML table definition is contained between the <table> and </table> tags. You define each row in the table separately using the <tr> and </tr> element, and then each cell within the row using the <td> and </td> element (where tr stands for table row and td for table data). Figure 4.11 gives a simple example of a table with four rows and three cells in each row to see how it works. (Note the indentations and comments that make it easier to read the code and see how the cells in each row are defined. The browser will of course ignore the indentations and comments.)

It is very important not to forget the ending </table> tag. HTML 4 and XHTML require it. Yet some browsers will ignore the fact that the tag is missing and display the table anyway, while others, such as Navigator pre-Version 6, follow the rules and display nothing.

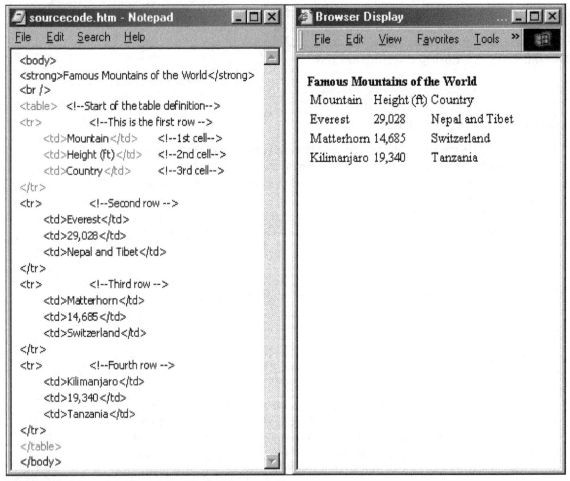

FIGURE 4.11.   Creating a basic table

Table Border Options

You can give 3D shadow borders to the table and its cells by including the border attribute in the <table> tag: <table border>. You can also set the width of the border. For example, <table border="4"> gives a border width of four pixels. If you don't specify the width, the default is a width of 1 pixel. Figure 4.12 shows the results of each of these border specifications.

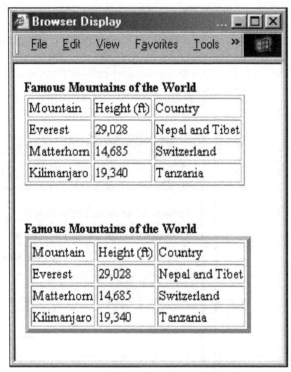

FIGURE 4.12. Tables with border="1" (top) and border="4"

Making the border visible also gives an indication as to how the browser formats a table. The text in each cell is automatically aligned to the left, and all the cells in a column have the same width. The width of the column is determined by the cell in it with the most text. In the first column of the Figure 4.12 tables, it's the "Matterhorn" cell, in the second column it's the "Height (ft)" cell, and in the third it's "Nepal and Tibet."

Table Headers and Captions

HTML has many other options for customizing the display of tables. In many tables, as in our example above, the first row consists of headings or labels for the table's columns. HTML provides a special cell tag, <th> (for "table header"), to create table headers. The <th> . . . </th> element works exactly like the <td> . . . </td> element for regular cells, but any text within the table header cell is automatically bold and centered.

Many tables also have captions, for which HTML provides the <caption> and </caption> tags. You place them just before the beginning <table> tag. The browser will normally center the caption at the top of the table. Unfortunately, different browsers display the caption differently, and sometimes not even correctly. So it's best to create a caption using a header element.

Adding these options to our sample table yields the code and display of Figure 4.13. We also have used this example to show what happens if you accidentally leave out a cell definition in a table row. In this case, we omitted the cell containing the height of the Matterhorn (i.e., the 14,685). The browser therefore reads the "Switzerland" cell as the second cell in the row and puts a blank space where the third cell would be.

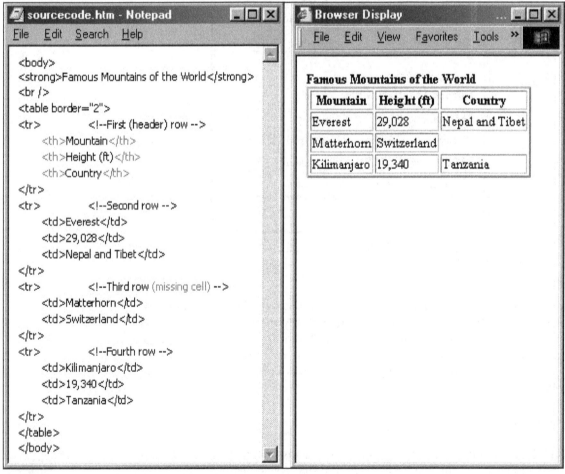

FIGURE 4.13.   Using the <th> element

Aligning Text in Table Cells

The text in a cell may be aligned horizontally either to the left, center, or right of the cell using the align="left" (or "right" or "center") attribute in the <td> tag. It can also be aligned vertically, either to the top, middle, or bottom using the valign="top" (or "middle" or "bottom") attribute. If align and valign are not specified, the default horizontal alignment is to the left of each cell and the default vertical alignment is to the middle of each cell.

The align and valign attributes are not deprecated, as long as you use them in a <td> element. (Previously it was legitimate to put them in a <tr> element to specify the alignment in all the cells in a row, but such a use is now deprecated.)

We may also adjust the **padding** within a cell and the **spacing** between cells. The padding is the amount of white space, measured in pixels, between the edges of the cell and the text inside the cell. It's analogous to the margin of a word processing document. You control it for the whole table by using the cellpadding attribute in the <table> tag. Cell spacing refers to the width of the dividers between the cells (whether made visible via the border attribute or left invisible). It's also measured in pixels and is set for the whole table by using the cellspacing attribute in the <table> tag.

Figure 4.14 demonstrates the use of the align attribute for several cells as well as the effects of the cellpadding and cellspacing attributes. Comparing the results of Figure 4.14 with those in Figure 4.13, we see that the use of the cellpadding attribute enlarges the size of each cell, and the cellspacing attribute puts more space between the cells.

Widening Cells

As noted previously, the browser automatically calculates the appropriate width for each column in a table, based on the cell with the most text in that column. We may set the width manually in pixels, however, with the width attribute. We use it in the <table> tag to set the overall width of the table (legitimately) and in the <td> tag to set the width of an individual cell (not so legitimately, since it's deprecated there). If the text in a cell is longer than the specified width, the browser automatically increases the height of the cell and wraps the text. In Chapter 6 we will learn how to create a magazine-style, multiple-column layout for a web page by using tables with the width attribute.

We can also format a single cell so that it spans a certain number of regular columns or rows. To do so, insert colspan="n" and/or rowspan="n" in the cell's <td> tag, where n is the number for how many columns or rows to span.

Figure 4.15 shows how to create a special top row that spans all three columns in order to put the table's title there. It also shows the use of the width attribute to give all the columns the same width (120 pixels in this case). Note how the text in the "Nepal and Tibet" cell is longer than 120 pixels and thus is

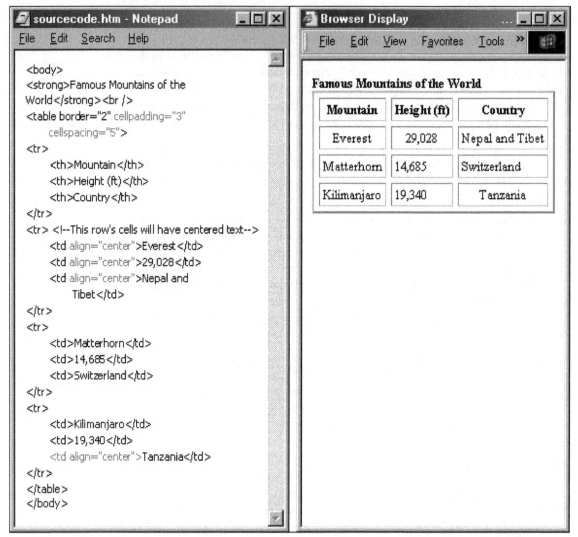

FIGURE 4.14.   Aligning table rows and individual cells and setting the cell padding and spacing

wrapped. (The table would look better if we also centered the text in each cell, but we didn't do so in order to give a clearer view of the effects of the width attribute. The "Famous Mountains of the World" title is centered because it's in a <th> element.)

Tables and Web Layout Design

So far we have just used the <table> element to create simple tables with a standard design. Many web designers, however, also use tables to create sophisticated layouts for their web pages. The <table> element and its various options make possible web pages with multiple columns of text and

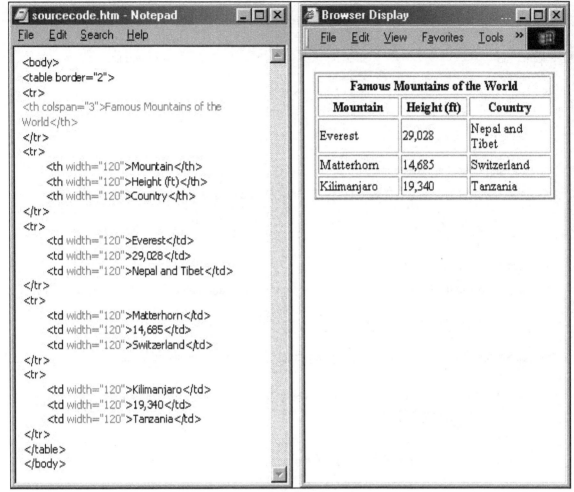

FIGURE 4.15. Spanning columns and setting cell widths

images, such as you see in magazines and newspapers. If, as you're browsing the Web, you take a look at the source code of such pages, you will probably see a good deal of `<tr>` and `<td>` tags. In Chapter 6 we will learn about more of the options available with the `<table>` element and how we can use them to create magazine-style web pages.

QuickCheck Questions

1. What are the three kinds of elements used to create a table?
2. What does the `<th>` element do?
3. What is the difference between cell spacing and cell padding?

Lab Exercise 4.3, "Experimenting with Tables," may be done at this point.

definition list
deprecated
extensions
obsolete

ordered list
padding
spacing
strict form of XHTML

transitional form of XHTML
unordered list

1. Extensions and Deprecations

Using the deprecated `<font>` element to specify the size, color, and/or font of a section of text:

```
<font size="5" color="red" face="Garamond, Arial">This will be displayed in the Garamond
font in slightly larger than normal size and in red. If Garamond isn't installed on the
surfer's computer, the Arial font will be substituted.</font>
```

2. More Tags and Attributes

Aligning a header in the center or on the right margin using the deprecated `align` attribute (default position is left):

```
<h2 align="center">Welcome to my Web page!</h2>
<h2 align="right">Welcome to my Web page!</h2>
```

The deprecated `<center>` element, used to center text or any element placed inside it:

```
<center>Welcome to my Web page!</center>
```

Specifying the background color of a web page using the `bgcolor` attribute (deprecated) and a predefined color or a hexadecimal color code:

```
<body bgcolor="magenta">
<body bgcolor="#FF00FF">
```

Specifying the color of a web page's text using the `text` attribute (deprecated):

```
<body text="blue">
```

Specifying the background color and text color on a web page using styles:

```
<style type="text/css">
   body {background-color:yellow; color:blue}
</style>
```

Creating varieties of horizontal rules using the deprecated `width` and `size` attributes:

```
<hr />
<hr width="150" />
<hr size="5" width="75%" />
```

Specifying the presentation of a horizontal rule using a style sheet:

```
<style type="text/css">
   hr {height:7px; width:75%; background-color:red}
</style>
```

3. Displaying Lists

A basic ordered list (for an unordered list, replace `<ol>` and `</ol>` with `<ul>` and `</ul>`):

```
<ol>
   <li>Item 1 in the list</li>
   <li>Item 2</li>
```

```
    <li>Item 3</li>
 </ol>
```

Customizing the item mark for an unordered list using the deprecated `type` attribute (default item mark is a disc):

```
<ul type="square">  <!-- type="circle" is the other option -->
   <li>Item 1</li>
   <li>Item 2</li>
   <li>Item 3</li>
</ul>
```

Customizing the style of the item mark for an unordered list:

```
<style type="text/css">
  ul {list-style:square}    <!-- disc and circle are the other possible values -->
</style>
```

Specifying that an image be used for the item mark of an unordered list:

```
<style type="text/css">
  ul { list-style:url(some_image.gif) }
</style>
```

Customizing the numbering for an ordered list using the deprecated `type` attribute (default numbering is 1,2,3 . . .):

```
<ol type="A">  <!-- Other options are type="a", type="I", or type="i" -->
   <li>Item 1</li>
   <li>Item 2</li>
   <li>Item 3</li>
</ol>
```

Creating a definition list (`<dd>` lines will be displayed as indented):

```
<dl>
<dt>First term to be defined</dt>
   <dd>Definition of first term</dd>
<dt>Second term to be defined</dt>
   <dd>Definition of second term</dd>
<dt>Third term to be defined</dt>
   <dd>Definition of third term</dd>
</dl>
```

4. Turning to Tables

Creating a basic table (2 rows with 3 cells in each row in this example):

```
<table>
<tr>
   <td>Row 1, cell 1</td>
   <td>Row 1, cell 2</td>
   <td>Row 1, cell 3</td>
</tr>
<tr>
   <td>Row 2, cell 1</td>
   <td>Row 2, cell 2</td>
   <td>Row 2, cell 3</td>
</tr>
</table>
```

Using the `border` attribute to set the size of the table border to 4 pixels (and make it visible):

```
<table border="4"> . . . </table>
```

Putting a header row in a table (centered, bold text):

```
<tr>
  <th>Row 1, cell 1</th>
  <th>Row 1, cell 2</th>
  <th>Row 1, cell 3</th>
</tr>
```

Centering text in each cell in a row:

```
<tr align="center"> . . . </tr>
```

Setting the cell padding and cell spacing for a table (in pixels):

```
<table cellpadding="3" cellspacing="5"> . . . </table>
```

Setting the width of a table or the width of an individual cell (in pixels):

```
<table width="500">...</table>
<td width="125"> . . . </td>
```

Use the transitional DTD for XHTML instead of the strict DTD in order to make your pages display well for the majority of surfers. But, as much as possible, avoid using deprecated tags and attributes.

Horizontal rules may be used to separate sections on a web page for a better design look.

Indenting and commenting code is always recommended, but it's especially important when creating tables.

Don't forget the `</table>` tag at the end of a table definition; some versions of Netscape Navigator will not display the table without it.

Don't leave out a cell definition within a table; the browser will display the table, but there will be a blank space at the end of that cell's row.

1. True or false: When a header tag does not have an `align` attribute specified, the default alignment is left.

2. Which attribute may be used in a `<body>` tag to specify the background color of a web page?
   a. `color`
   b. `bgcolor`
   c. `background`
   d. `backgroundcolor`

3. Which attribute may be used in a `<body>` tag to specify the color of text on a web page?
   a. `color`
   b. `textcolor`
   c. `text`
   d. `foregroundcolor`

4. True or false: The `<font>` element is the preferred way to change the font style and font size of a section of text on a web page.

5. The two most common kinds of lists are _____ and _____.

6. If you nest three ordered lists, what are the default number styles used for each level?
   a. Top level uses 1, 2, . . . ; second level uses 1, 2, . . . ; third level uses 1, 2,. . . .
   b. Top level uses A, B, . . . ; second level uses 1, 2, . . . ; third levels uses a, b,. . . .
   c. Top level uses I, II, . . . ; second level uses A, B, . . . ; third level uses 1, 2,. . . .
   d. Top level uses 1, 2, . . . ; second level uses a, b, . . . ; third level uses i, ii,....

7. The three types of item marks for an unordered list that may be specified using styles or the type attribute of the `<ul>` tag are: _____, _____, and _____.

8. True or false: When creating a table, the ending `</table>` tag may be omitted without any effect.

9. Which of the following attributes may be used in a `<td>` tag?
   a. `align`
   b. `valign`
   c. `cellpadding`
   d. `colspan`

10. True or false: The `<table>` element may be used to create multiple-column layouts for web pages.

1. Briefly define and/or explain the following terms: extensions, deprecated tags, cell padding.

2. Using first styles and then attributes, write two versions of HTML code that would create a web page with white text on a purple background.

3. Write three different ways to align a paragraph in the center of a page. Use the line "This text will be centered" for the contents of the paragraph.

4. Given the following code, show how you would comment out the third item in the list so that only the first two items are displayed.
```
<ul type="square">
    <li>Item 1</li>
    <li>Item 2</li>
    <li>Item 3</li>
</ul>
```

5. Using attributes, write the HTML code to create the following horizontal rules:
   a. One with a width of 50% of the window and a size of 7 pixels.
   b. One with a width of 350 pixels and centered.

6. Repeat Exercise 5, but this time use style classes to define the presentation of the horizontal rules. Part a should have the class name "halfsize" and part b should have the class name "centered350."

7. Write the HTML code that uses the `type` attribute to create the following nested ordered list:
   A. Major PC Manufacturers ca. 2000
      1. Dell
      2. IBM
      3. Apple
      4. Hewlett-Packard
      5. Compaq
   B. Personal Computer Operating Systems ca. 2000
      1. Microsoft Windows (various flavors)
      2. Mac OS
      3. Linux

8. Repeat Exercise 7, but this time use style classes to define the presentation of the list.

9. Write the HTML code for a table with three rows and four columns. The first row should contain the following headings for the table, centered and in bold: Name, Office Location, Phone, E-Mail. Give the table a border 3 pixels wide. Put whatever "Name" information you want in the second and third rows.

10. Write the HTML code for a table with six rows and three columns. The first row should contain a single cell that spans all three columns, with the contents of the cell being Great Places to Eat. The second row should contain the following headings for the table, centered and in bold: Restaurant, Type of Food, and Personal Rating. Center the text display for the cells in the middle column, and set a cellspacing of 5 pixels and a cellpadding of 3 pixels. Use the following restaurant information:

Strings	Italian	3 stars
Dos Coyotes	Fresh Mex	4 stars
Symposium	Greek	3 stars
The Graduate	Burgers	2 stars

Debugging Exercise

Identify the errors in the following code and then sketch on paper how the browser would display it once the errors were corrected. Assume that the transitional DTD for XHTML is being used.

```
<html>
<title>
Chapter 4 Debugging Challenge
</title>
<body bgcolor="FFFFFF">
<h2>Welcome to my Web page!</h2>
Here are some samples of my HTML expertise:<BR>
<ul type="box">                 <!-->Here's an unordered list.</--!>
   <li>Item 1</li>
   <li>Item 2</li>
   <li>Item 3</li>
</ul>
<ol>                            <!-->Here's an ordered list.</--!>
   <L1>Item 1</L1>
   <L2>Item 2</L2>
   <L3>Item 3</L3>
</ol>
<comment>Here's a horizontal rule</comment>
<hr width=60%>
<!--And here's a simple table:
<table border = "medium">
<tr>
   <td>Row 1, cell 1</td>
   <td>Row 1, cell 2</td>
   <td>Row 1, cell 3</td>
</tr>
<tr>
   <td>Row 2, cell 1</td>
   <td>Row 2, cell 2</td>
   <td>Row 2, cell 3</td>
</tr>
</body>
</html>
```

Note: Most of the Exercises above may also be done as lab exercises.

Exercise 4.1: Experimenting with Attributes

❑ Using an HTML source document you created in a previous exercise (or a new source document, if you prefer), experiment briefly with the `align` attribute in the header tags, with the `bgcolor` and `text` attributes in the `<body>` tag, and with the `<hr>` tag and its attributes. *As always, make sure to save your document frequently so that you don't lose much work and time if your computer crashes or if the network goes down.*

❑ Create a second source document with the same examples as the first, but use an internal style sheet to define the presentation.

Exercise 4.2: More Practice with Tags

❑ Add examples of ordered lists, unordered lists, and definition lists to one of your source documents from Lab Exercise 4.1. Use whatever text you would like to show the effects of the tags. Don't forget to save!

❑ Using either a style sheet or the type attribute, create an ordered list with the traditional outline numbering, as below:

I. Point Number 1
    A. Sub-item
        1. Sub-item
        2. Sub-item
    B. Sub-item
        1. Sub-item
            a. Sub-item
            b. Sub-item
            c. Sub-item
        2. Sub-item
            a. Sub-item
            b. Sub-item
    C. Sub-item
    D. Sub-item
II. Point Number 2
III. Point Number 3

Exercise 4.3: Experimenting with Tables

❑ Add a "Best of" table on a topic of your choice to the document you have been creating. For example, "The Five Best Local Places to Eat," "The Best Pizza in Town," "Great Places to Study," "The 10 Greatest Athletes Ever," "The Top 10 CEOs Today," and so forth. Your table should have at least three columns and four rows plus a title that spans the columns. The columns should have headings (for example, Name, Location, Price, Comments might be four columns for a table on "The Best Pizza in Town").

❑ What happens to your table display when you resize the browser window so that the table is wider than the window?

❑ Make two or more copies of your table code (in the same document) and experiment further with them by (a) commenting out some of the `<td>` elements to see what happens, and (b) adding `colspan` or `rowspan` attributes to various cells.

Images, Links, and |Multimedia|

LEARNING OBJECTIVES

1. Learn how to insert and display images in web pages.

2. Understand the three types of hypertext links and how they are used and coded.

3. Learn how to create image links and image maps.

4. Learn the potential and limitations of using multimedia elements on the Web and how to embed sound and video in a web page.

Displaying Images

Now that we know how to classify web page text in a variety of ways, the next step is to learn how to add some spice with images. You have of course noticed that many, if not most, of the documents you see on the World Wide Web have pictures or photos that appear on the page. The data that describe these images are contained in files, just as the data for a web page (its text and tags) are stored in the source document. To include an image as part of a web page, you use a tag in your source document that tells the web browser where to find the data source file for the image. When a surfer's web browser downloads and displays the source document that describes your web page, it also downloads the source files for any images referenced in your HTML document and displays those images.

Image Types and Files

Image files come in different types, depending on the process by which the image was converted into data. The most common types are the **Graphics Interchange Format** and the **Joint Photographic Experts Group** format, known by their abbreviations **GIF** and **JPEG.** The GIF format is usually used for things like logos and basic drawings while JPEG is designed for photographic images. A newer type of image file is **Portable Network Graphics (PNG)**, which is intended as a replacement for GIF files. (The disadvantage of the GIF format is that it's officially copyrighted. GIF, by the way, is variously pronounced "jiff" or "giff," although the inventor of it has said he intended it to be "jiff" like the peanut butter. JPEG is pronounced "jay-peg" and PNG is "ping.")

To signify which type of image it contains, an image data file will have a filename with an extension like .gif or .png or .jpeg (or .jpg). Most newer web browsers can automatically load, translate, and display these image formats, but may need a special add-on program, called an external viewer, to display other types of images.

Creating and Finding Images

You can create your own images using image editing programs like Adobe Illustrator or photo editing programs like Adobe Photoshop or Microsoft Picture It! Photo. Digital cameras often come with basic image editing software as well.

Another option is clip art—images that may be "clipped" and pasted into your documents or saved in one of the image file formats. Commercial clip art collections are available for purchase on CD-ROMs, although if you have the Microsoft Office suite of programs (or similar office suite) installed on your computer, you will probably find that the accompanying CD-ROMs contain a collection of clip art.

To access clip art in Microsoft Word:

1. Open a new blank document and then click on the Insert menu and select Picture: Clip Art. If the clip art has been installed, a window will open listing a number of art categories.

2. Browse through the images and, when you find one you like, right-click on it and choose the Insert option in the pop-up menu that appears. The image will be inserted into the active Word document at the position of the blinking vertical-line cursor (the insertion point cursor).

3. It would be nice if Word allowed you to save the image directly as a GIF file, but it doesn't. Instead, use the Save as Web Page command under the File menu to save the document (with image in it) as a .htm file, named "myimage.htm" (or whatever you want to name it). In the process of doing this, Word will not only save the myimage.htm file but will also create a new folder in the folder where the myimage.htm file is located. This new folder, which will be named "myimage_files," will contain a GIF file of the image named something like image001.gif. You may rename it to some-

thing more descriptive (but keep the .gif extension). This GIF file is the file you may use to add the image to your web page. (How to do this will be explained below.)

Collections of clip art and photos are also available on the Web. You will find two good archives of images at gallery.yahoo.com and multimedia.lycos.com. The search engine at www.google.com is also an excellent way to find images. (Click on the Images tab.) Be aware, however, that not all images on the Internet are in the public domain; that is, the legal right to use any given image may be prohibited or restricted under copyright or other law. If an image is not clearly marked as being in the public domain, you should assume it isn't and seek permission to publish it on your web page (unless you are just experimenting and never intend to put your page up on the Internet). Many copyrighted images also have visible watermarks inserted in them. To get the image without the watermark, you have to pay for the image.

The simplest way to get images, however, at least for purposes of experimentation, is to download and save an image you find right on the Web to your own computer.

To copy and save an image off a web page:

1. Right-click the mouse on the image as it is displayed in your web browser.

2. From the pop-up menu that appears, choose Save Picture as . . . (Explorer) or Save Image as . . . (Navigator).

3. Use the ensuing Save as . . . dialog box to save the image as a file on your computer. The type of the image file will automatically be listed in the dialog box, and the file will be saved as that type with the correct extension (such as, .jpg).

Adding an Image to an HTML Document

Once you have located or created the source file for an image that you would like to include in your web page, you must indicate the file's location by providing its URL. To do so, you use the image tag <img> with the source attribute src:

```
<img src="URL of the image file goes here" />
```

For example, the tag that tells the browser to retrieve and display an image called "earth2.jpg" located on the web server "www.nasa.gov" in the directory "images" would be:

```
<img src="http://www.nasa.gov/images/earth2.jpg" />
```

Note that the <img> tag is an empty element. To be XHTML-compliant, the end of the tag must be />, not just >. Note also that the attribute is src, not scr (it's easy to mistype it).

If you had created the image yourself, or had downloaded the image file in advance to your computer *so that the image file was in the same directory as your HTML document,* then you do not have to supply a full URL. Instead, you simply reference the name of the file:

```
<img src="earth2.jpg" />
```

If, however, the image file was located in a directory named astronomy, which in turn was a sub-directory of the source document's directory, then the code would be:

```
<img src="astronomy/earth2.jpg" />
```

Or, to go one more level, if the image file was in a directory named earth_photos, which was a sub-directory of the astronomy directory, then the code would be:

```
<img src="astronomy/earth_photos/earth2.jpg" />
```

In other words, you only have to give the path to the image file starting from the source document's directory (but not including the name of the source document's directory). This is known as relative addressing or a **relative path-name,** meaning that the pathname (the file's address) is specified relative to the location of the source document.

Before we see how we use the <img> element in an actual source document, we need to add an attribute to it that specifies alternative text.

Alternative Text for Images

Sometimes a browser cannot or will not display an image. It may have had trouble downloading the image, or it may not be able to handle an image of that particular type, or it may not be able to handle images, period (for example, the text-only web browser known as Lynx). In addition, the surfer may have disabled the show images option of the browser. If so, the browser will not display any images on a web page unless the surfer manually tells the browser to do so. Many surfers choose this option because loading and displaying images dramatically slows down the surfing process and, much of the time, they are looking for textual information and the images are a nice additional but unnecessary touch.

(In Explorer you can turn the show images option on and off by selecting Internet Option under the Tools menu and then clicking on the Advanced tab. Scroll down the resulting list of items to the section labeled Multimedia and click the checkbox labeled Show pictures on or off. In Navigator, look for Show images under the View menu.)

You should therefore always provide alternative textual information that will be displayed in lieu of the image. You do this using the alt attribute:

```
<img src="eiffel.gif" alt="Eiffel Tower Picture" />
```

If the image is not displayed by the browser, for whatever reason, the alternative text will be shown inside a generic picture frame (Figure 5.1).

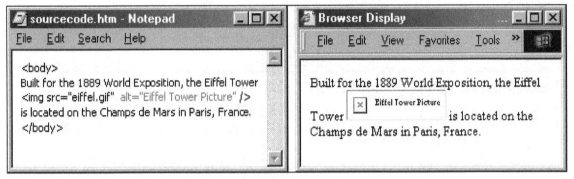

FIGURE 5.1. Alternative text for an image

Another good reason to use the alt attribute is that efforts are being made to make the Web more accessible to visually impaired people. Special browser software is available that can read and speak the text on a web page. Including the alternative text for an image allows the visually impaired user to hear a brief description of the image.

The final good reason to use the alt attribute is simple: With XHTML, it's required.

The Ins and Outs of Inline Images

The most common type of images that appear on a web page are called inline images, because you specify their location as if they were part of a line of text. That is, you place the <img> tag on a line in your HTML document, and the browser displays the image as part of that line. Of course, the browser will probably have to increase the height of the line to make room for the image, but it still treats the image as if it were one word of a line of text. Figure 5.2 shows an example.

You may also direct the browser to align the line of text with the middle or top of the image using a style definition for the img element. To specify that all the images on the web page are vertically aligned in the middle of their line, we set the vertical-align property to the value middle (or top to have the top of the image aligned with the top of the line):

```
<style type="text/css">
  img {vertical-align:middle}
</style>
```

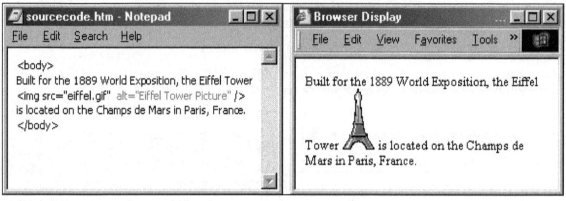

FIGURE 5.2.   Inserting an inline image

(If we wanted the alignment to apply just to certain images, we would use a style class.)

Alternatively, we may get the same results using the deprecated `align` attribute with the value `top`, `middle`, or `bottom`. Figure 5.3 shows the results (along with code that uses the `align` attribute).

We may get better looking results by specifying that the text wrap around the image, either to the left or to the right. We do so by using the `float` style property with the value `left` or `right`. The value specifies which way the image will be placed. A value of `left` means the image will float down to the next open line and be placed against the left margin, with the text flowing around its right side; a value of `right` means the image floats to the right margin and the text flows around its left side. Or, using the `align` attribute, we write `align="left"` or `align="right"` in the `<img>` tag. Figure 5.4 shows the results, with the code using two image style classes we have named `leftside` and `rightside`.

Given the use of `float:right` and `float:left`, it might seem logical that `float:center` (or `align="center"`) would center the image, with text flowing around it on both sides. HTML doesn't allow for this use, however. It is possible to center an image (without flowing text) using one of two methods.

To display a centered image without any associated text (for example, an organization's logo), put the `<img>` tag inside a paragraph element. You may then set the paragraph's style using the `text-align` property:

```
<style type="text/css">
  p.centered {text-align:center}
</style>
```

The code for the paragraph element is:

```
<p class="centered"><img src="eiffeltower.gif"
  alt="Eiffel Tower Picture" /></p>
```

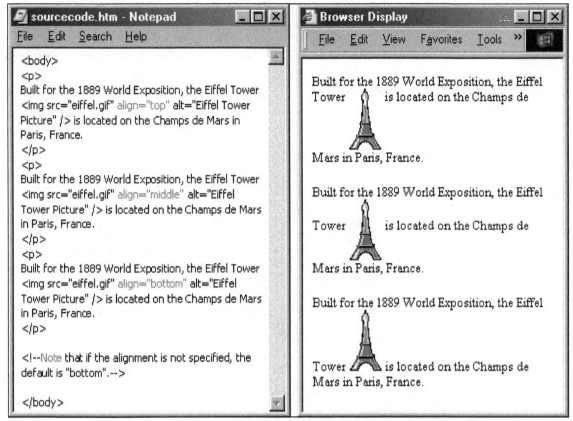

FIGURE 5.3. Aligning an image vertically (using either the align attribute as shown or the vertical-align style property)

Alternatively, you may use the align attribute in the paragraph tag:

```
<p align="center">
<img src="eiffeltower.gif" alt="Eiffel Tower Picture" />
</p>
```

Sizing Up an Image

Two other attributes that may be included in the <img> tag, height and width, tell the browser the exact size of the image in pixels. (For reference, the screen size of an average monitor circa the year 2002 is 1024 pixels across by 768 pixels down.) It is good practice to include these attributes, because then the browser can automatically reserve the appropriate space for the image as it downloads and displays the text first. If you do not include the image size, then the browser has to perform additional calculations in order to format the image and the rest of the page properly, which slows down the display process and thereby increases the frustration of the surfer who is waiting to see your web page.

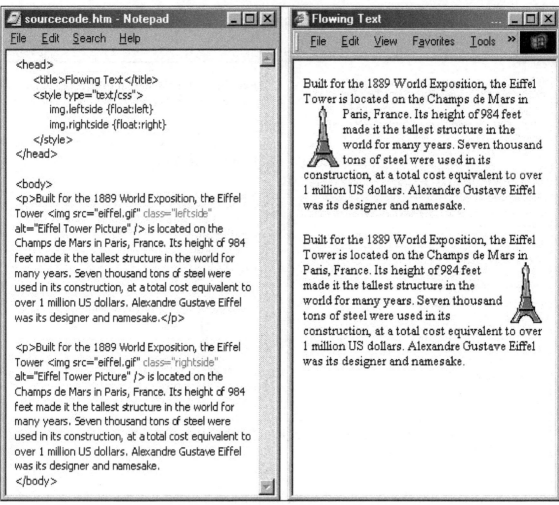

FIGURE 5.4.   **Wrapping text around an image**

The HTML syntax is:

```
<img src="eiffel.gif" alt="Eiffel Tower Picture"
    width="69" height="120" />
```

Note: The order of the width and height attributes does not matter (nor of any attribute in a tag).

You may find the exact pixel size of an image displayed on a web page (yours or someone else's) by using the pop-up menu that appears when you right-click on the image. When the menu appears, select View image (Navigator) or Properties (Explorer). In Navigator, a new window will open with just the image in it. The title bar of the window will say something like, "JPEG image 269x125 pixels–Netscape." The first number is the *width* of the image, the second the *height* of the image. In Explorer, the Properties dialog box will appear, with one of the properties being the dimensions of the image as width × height.

If the image file is on one of your computer's disks, you may open it directly using the Open command in your browser's File menu. When opened, Navigator will again display the image dimensions in the title bar, and Explorer will list the dimensions in the Properties dialog box (accessed via the File menu).

You may also use the `height` and `width` attributes to stretch or shrink an image. In other words, the browser will change the size of the image to fit the dimensions specified by `height` and `width`. The resulting display may be distorted, depending on the type of image. JPEG images usually resize relatively well, but if you need to shrink or enlarge other types of images and still maintain clarity, it's best to use a drawing program like Adobe Illustrator or a photo editing program like Adobe Photoshop to modify the original image.

QuickCheck Questions

1. What are the basic types of image file formats?
2. What does it mean for an image to be in the public domain?
3. What are the various attributes that may be used in an `<img>` tag and what purpose does each have?
4. What is an easy way to find the height and width of an image?
5. Why is it good to use the `alt` attribute?

Lab Exercise 5.1, "Adding Images," may be done at this point.

Creating Links

The real power of the World Wide Web comes in its ability to implement hypertext, whereby the surfer may click on a specially marked word or image on a web page and be automatically jumped or linked either to another web page or to another place in the same web page. Hypertext links work like electronic references or footnotes.

Imagine, for example, that you are creating a website devoted to marine mammals, in which you supply a picture and a paragraph or two of text for each species. If you use an existing web page on the subject of marine mammal physiology as a resource for your brief review of dolphins, you should of course reference it at the end of your review. Even if you do not use it as a resource, you might still want to direct the surfer to it for further information. Whatever the case, it would be more than just a normal citation. Using

HTML, you would be able to create a hypertext link from the citation on your page to the actual web page on marine mammal physiology so that by clicking on the citation, the surfer would be "transported" directly to the physiology web page (i.e., the surfer's browser would download and display the physiology page). This is known as an **external link,** because it links the surfer to an outside web page.

Web page designers make good use of HTML's hypertext capabilities in a second way by providing their pages with **internal links.** Clicking on an internal link on a web page will jump the surfer to another part of the same web page. Many web pages include a Back to Top link at the bottom of the page so that the surfer can quickly jump back to the top of the page instead of scrolling all the way back up.

Web page designers find another handy use for internal links in creating tables of contents. In your marine mammal web page, for instance, you might start out the page with a table of contents listing the marine mammals covered. By making each entry in the table of contents a hyperlink, the surfer could click on an entry and jump immediately to the corresponding section in your web page, instead of having to scroll down and look for it.

External and internal links look the same on a web page. In most cases, the surfer can tell the difference simply by the context. A piece of text that functions as a clickable hyperlink, whether external or internal, is signified by an underline and displayed in a different color than normal text (Figure 5.5).

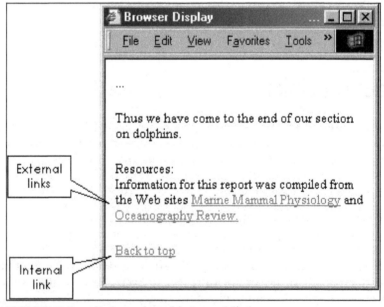

FIGURE 5.5.   External and internal links

The standard color for a link is blue, but the browser's user may customize the link color. Visited links—links that the surfer has previously clicked—are usually displayed in red. (All links shown in color in this textbook are simply colored red.)

Website Structure

This leads us to a brief but important word on website structure. (We will have more to say on this topic in Chapter 6.) The simplest design for a web page consists of a single web page (i.e., a single HTML source document). The more information the page contains, the longer it will be. To access the information, the surfer either scrolls down through the page or clicks on links, if they are provided, that jump to the various sections of information.

A more sophisticated structure for a website consists of multiple web pages. You set up each page as a separate HTML document and provide links for the surfer to navigate between them. In the example of the marine mammals website, you would create a web page for each mammal—one for dolphins, one for porpoises, and so on—plus an introductory page that offers the surfer a table of contents with hyperlinks. Figure 5.6 diagrams the structure.

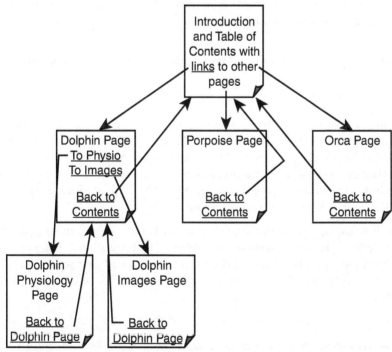

FIGURE 5.6   Link structure of a multiple-page website

Of course, more sophisticated designs that add links between the various pages are also possible. As a simple addition to the above design, we would probably want to add Back to Contents links to the Dolphin Physiology Page and the Dolphin Images Page so that the surfer could jump directly back to the Contents Page in one click, rather than first having to go back to the main Dolphin Page and then back to the Contents Page. A more complex design would make the Table of Contents links visible on every page, perhaps in a sidebar, so that the surfer would have instant access to all the main sections of the site. (One way to do this is to use frames—see Chapter 6.)

Another advantage to dividing a website, even small ones, into multiple pages is that web browsers retrieve and display smaller pages faster. This is especially true if a website contains a number of images. Although most web browsers utilize techniques that enable the surfer to start reading and navigating the text of a page before all its images have been downloaded and displayed, it is usually good form to divide a website into multiple pages so that each page only has one or a few images.

To summarize, we have three possible kinds of hyperlinks:

1. An external link that takes the surfer from one page to the beginning of a separate web page.

2. An internal link that takes the surfer from one part of a web page to another section in the same page.

3. A **combination external/internal link** that takes the surfer from one page to a certain section in a separate page (i.e., the combined actions of #1 and #2).

The following sections show how we code the HTML for each situation.

External Links

In order to create a link from one web page to another, we surround the hypertext link with the tags, `<a href="SomeURL">` and `</a>`. The `href` stands for hypertext reference. The `a` stands for anchor, because we are anchoring one side of the hypertext link in this document, and the other side of the link—the destination page—is given by the URL. As long as you know the URL for a web page, you can link to it.

To see how we put this together, consider an HTML source document for a web page for a history course on the American Revolution (History 170B). The document is named history170b.html and is stored on the Internet host www.ucdavis.edu in a directory named courses. The URL of this document is therefore:

```
http://www.ucdavis.edu/courses/history170b.html
```

If we want to create a link to this document using "Click here for information on the American Revolution" as the link text the surfer sees, then the HTML code is:

```
<a href = "http://www.ucdavis.edu/courses/history170b.html">
Click here for information on the American Revolution
course</a>
```

The web browser would display everything between the <a> and </a> tags as a link:

Click here for information on the American Revolution
course

When a surfer clicks on this link, the browser looks at the underlying URL that is specified in the <a> tag and downloads the corresponding HTML source document; it retrieves and displays the history170b.html source document from www.ucdavis.edu/courses.

As noted before, the underline and different color signify to the surfer that this text is a clickable hyperlink. Because the link is set apart from normal text in this way, it's usually not necessary to give the surfer such explicit directions as "Click here for . . .". You might, for instance, code something like this:

```
This quarter we will be offering special courses on the
<a href="http://www.ucdavis.edu/courses/history170b.html">
American Revolution</a> and the <a href="http://www.
ucdavis.edu/courses/history185b.html"> History of Technology
in America</a>, so don't miss these opportunities.
```

This code would display as:

This quarter we will be offering special courses on the American Revolution and the History of Technology in America, so don't miss these opportunities.

The underlined and different colored text would make it clear to the surfer that more information on each course could be had by clicking on each link.

If the HTML source document containing the above code with the <a> elements were stored in the same directory or folder as the history170b.html and history185b.html documents, we would not have to supply the full URL to code the links. Instead, we may use relative pathnames by supplying just the filenames in the <a> tags:

```
This quarter we will be offering special courses on the
<a href="history170b.html">American Revolution</a> and the
<a href="history185b.html"> History of Technology in
America</a>, so don't miss these opportunities.
```

To summarize: In the absence of a full URL in the <a> tag, the web browser assumes that it may find the linked document in the same folder as the source document that contains the <a> tag.

And just as in the similar situation with image files discussed above in the section "Adding an Image to an HTML Document," if the source document with the <a> elements were stored in the courses directory but the history170b.html and history185b.html documents were stored in a sub-directory of courses named "history," then the relative pathnames would be slightly longer:

```
This quarter we will be offering special courses on the
<a href="history/history170b.html">American Revolution</a>
and the <a href="history/history185b.html"> History of
Technology in America</a>, so don't miss this opportunity.
```

In other words, you only have to give the path to the linked document starting from the source document's directory (but not including the name of the source document's directory).

When you can, you should use relative addressing for links, because then you can move your linked documents from disk to disk without having to change all the URLs in your HTML code to reflect the new disk name. The key is to keep all the documents in the same directory (or folder), or to keep them in sub-directories of the same directory. (And then don't change their directory locations once you have coded the links.)

Sometimes you will want to include an external link to someone else's website on your web page. If, for example, you were creating a web page that provided news on the computer chip industry, you might want to have links to the websites of the major companies in the industry, such as Intel, Motorola, and Advanced Micro Devices (AMD). The code and display would be something like that in Figure 5.7.

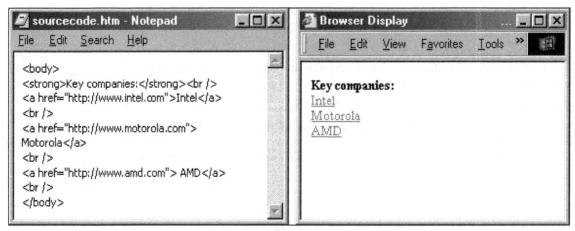

FIGURE 5.7.   External links without a source file

Note something strange in the code in Figure 5.7, however. There are no source document names in the URLs—nothing with a .html extension. Each href attribute simply lists the domain name of the company: www.intel.com, www.motorola.com, and www.amd.com. The href attribute tells the browser to make a "send document" request to the www.intel.com server, for instance, but it doesn't specify the document to request. So how does the browser know which source document to download?

The answer to this small mystery is that in the absence of a specified HTML source document, the server will send a source document named **index.html** to the browser. (This assumes, of course, that the index.html document actually exists and is stored on the server. Some servers alternatively use default.html as the name for the document involved in this default sending operation.)

What this means for you, the web page designer, is that when you create the home page source document for a multiple-page web site, you should get in the habit of naming it index.html (or index.htm). Then, when the time comes to upload the website files to the server and get the site up and running, you won't have to rename the home page document. All the other documents involved may be named whatever you want. (See Appendix H for a few more details on this process of actually making a web page available on the Internet.)

Internal Links

To create a link from one part of an HTML document to another part in the same document, we first must mark the location to which we want to jump. We do this by labeling it using a slightly different version of the anchor tag, containing the `id` attribute instead of the `href` attribute:

```
<a id="SomeLabel">
```

This attribute marks the location by specifying an identifying name. Note: Another attribute, the `name` attribute, is often used here instead of the `id` attribute. But the use of the `name` attribute in certain elements has been deprecated in XHTML. The main reason is that the `id` and `name` attributes serve similar purposes, so both weren't needed. In addition, the `name` attribute has other purposes in the elements used to create features like checkboxes and radio buttons.

Unfortunately, some older browsers don't recognize the `id` attribute in this context. So to be both XHTML-compliant and backward-compatible, you should use both the `id` and `name` attributes in the tag, set to the same value:

```
<a id="SomeLabel" name="SomeLabel">
```

In our examples, however, we will usually use just the `id` attribute.

Once we have the label established, we can link to it using the normal <a href> tag, but with one key difference. Instead of assigning a URL for the value of `href`, we put a # sign followed by the name of the label:

```
<a href="#SomeLabel"> Click here to go someplace else in
this document</a>
```

The # sign signifies that this is not an external link, but a link to a local label that we have defined someplace else in the source document. When the surfer clicks on the link, the browser will locate the position of the <a id="Some-Label"> tag in the document and display that section of the document. The following example shows how this works.

Ignoring our earlier advice on website structure using multiple pages, let's assume for the moment that we want to set up a marine mammals web page as a single page with a table of contents at the top and the various sections on the different marine mammals following after. We want the surfer to be able to click on an item in the table of contents and link to that section, i.e., have that section appear at the top of the browser window. In other words, we need internal links. The initial display seen by the surfer would look like Figure 5.8.

FIGURE 5.8.   Internal links for a table of contents

Each item in the table of contents is underlined and in a different color, indicating a link. Note that Sections 2 and 3 on Orcas and Dolphins, respectively, are not visible to the surfer.

When the surfer clicks on one of the links, the browser brings the corresponding section to the top of the browser window. As an example, Figure 5.9 shows the result when the link labeled <u>Dolphins</u> is clicked.

In order to write the HTML code for the link to "Section 3. All About Dolphins," we first use the <a> tag with the id attribute to define a label at the beginning of Section 3:

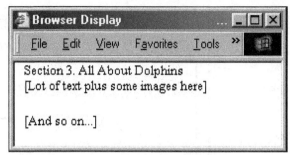

FIGURE 5.9.   Results of clicking an internal link

```
<a id="DolphinSection">Section 3. All About Dolphins</a>
```

Note that the section title, "Section 3. All About Dolphins," will not appear underlined when displayed because it is the destination point of a link, not the departure point. The departure point is in the table of contents and would be coded using an <a> tag with the href attribute:

```
<a href="#DolphinSection">Dolphins</a>
```

This line of code creates a link, displayed to the surfer as <u>Dolphins</u>. When the surfer clicks on this link, the browser will find the <a> tag with the id attribute that has the value DolphinSection.

Do not confuse the name of the label with the labeled text. The name of the label—DolphinSection, in this case—does not appear when the web page is displayed. It is the value of the id attribute in the <a> tag and remains invisible to the surfer. The labeled text—the text contained between the <a> and </a> tags, in this case, Section 3. All About Dolphins—is what does appear.

It's also easy to leave off or misplace the # sign. It does *not* go with the label name in the <a id> tag. Rather, it goes in the <a href> tag, inserted at the front of the label name to indicate that it is an internal link.

Putting all this together, the HTML code and corresponding display for the marine mammals page would be that shown in Figure 5.10.

Combining External and Internal Links

In order to link one web page to a specific point in another page, we simply combine the HTML syntax for external and internal links. The format is:

```
<a href="SomeURLForAWebPage#SomeLabelWithinThatWebPage">
Click here to go to a certain section within some web
page.</a>
```

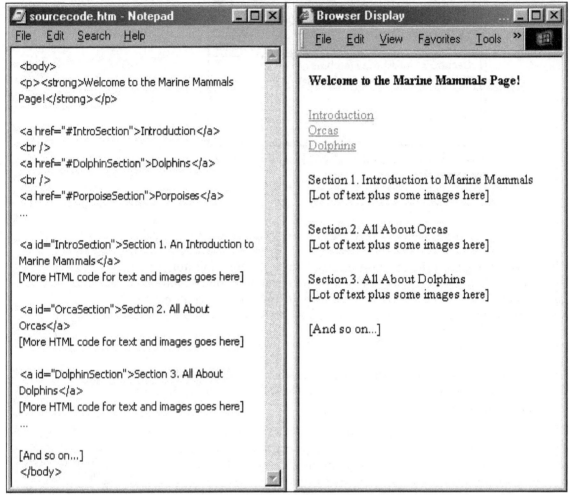

FIGURE 5.10.   Table of contents using internal links

The surfer would of course see:

Click here to go to a certain section within some web page

When the link was clicked, the web page referenced would be downloaded, but instead of the top of the page appearing in the browser as usual, the section of the page where the `<a id>` label was located would be displayed.

Note especially the syntax of the `href` value: You list the URL for the web page, then a # sign, and then the name of the label in question.

To give a more concrete example, let's assume that we are a big fan of dolphins, that we have learned about a Marine Mammals Web page at the URL http://www.marinebio.ucsandiego.edu/marinemammals.html (not an actual URL), and that we are creating our own personal web page and want to include a link to the dolphin section in the Marine Mammals page. But before we can link directly to the dolphin section in this page, we not only need to know the URL of the page, we also need to know the exact name of the label that the page's web designer used for the section on dolphins. But how do we find that? Contact the designer?

It's actually not as difficult as that. Remember that most web browsers allow the surfer to view the underlying HTML code for the currently displayed web page. To view the HTML code of a web page in Navigator, select "Page source" under the View menu. Navigator will open up a new window and show the source code, with tags displayed in a different color to help them stand out. In Explorer, select Source under the View menu. The contents of the source document will be displayed using Notepad.

Once you can see the HTML code for the Marine Mammals page, you can simply read through it and find out what <a id> or <a name> labels, if any, have been defined.

In our specific example of the Marine Mammals page, the URL for the source document is http://www.marinebio.ucsandiego.edu/marinemammals.html, and the <a id> label for the dolphin section inside the document is DolphinSection. The HTML code that you would add to your personal web page to create a link from it to this section is:

```
<a href="http://www.marinebio.ucsandiego.edu/marinemammals.
html#DolphinSection"> Click here to get even more
information on dolphins!</a>
```

The surfer would see:

Click here to get even more information on dolphins!

There's one potential flaw in this scheme, however. What do we do if the web designer of the Marine Mammals page had not included an <a id> label at the location of the Dolphin section? You might at first think: No problem, I can use my browser to see the source code for the Marine Mammals page, so I'll just add an <a id> label of my own at the needed location and save the revised document.

It's a nice idea, but it won't work. You cannot modify the HTML code because you are simply viewing a copy of the Marine Mammal source document, which the browser has downloaded to your computer. The original remains on the web server at www.marinebio.ucsandiego.edu. You can of course modify the copy of the source code all you want and even save the changed document to disk, but the original source document will not be affected. In this case, the best you could do is use the URL alone and link to the beginning of the Marine Mammals page.

QuickCheck Questions

1. Write the HTML code that creates an external link to the document http://www.marinemammals.com/bluewhales.html.
2. What two tags are used to create an internal link?
3. Where does the # symbol belong in the code for an internal link?
4. Under what conditions can you use just the name of the linked file for the value of an `href` attribute instead of the linked file's full URL?

Lab Exercise 5.2, "Creating a Multiple-Page Website," may be done at this point.

Making Images into Links

In all our link examples so far we have used text to display the link. For instance:

```
<a href="http://www.ucdavis.edu/courses/history170b.html">
Click here for information on the American Revolution
course</a>
```

with the browser displaying:

Click here for information on the American Revolution course

But HTML does not limit us to using text alone for links. We may also use images.

Simple Image Links

The method to create an image link is very simple: You replace the text Click here ... (or whatever) with an <img> tag. To be specific, if we wanted to use our Eiffel Tower image as the basis for a link to a French Travel website with the URL www.frenchtravel.com, the code would be:

```
<a href="http://www.frenchtravel.com"><img
src="eiffel.gif" alt="Eiffel Tower picture" /></a>
```

(This line of code of course assumes that the eiffel.gif file is in the same directory as the HTML source document that the code belongs to, otherwise we would have to supply a fuller URL in the <img> tag.)

In order to indicate to the surfer that a displayed image is also a clickable link, the browser displays a colored border around the image, using the same color as that used for a textual link (usually blue). The result is shown in Figure 5.11.

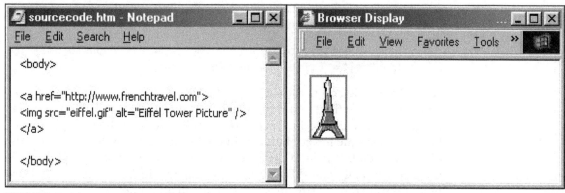

FIGURE 5.11.   An image link

Remember that not everyone sees the graphical web in all its glory. Some set their web browser to turn off the display of images, and others use the text-only Lynx browser. Using the `alt` attribute in the `<img>` tag helps, but it's also a good idea to include a textual link to supplement the image link (Figure 5.12).

IMPORTANT

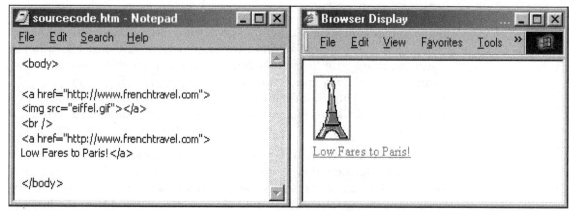

FIGURE 5.12.   Image link supplemented with text link

Image links are particularly useful when you want to display a number of photographs (JPEG images) on a web page. Because a large number of images on a page dramatically increases the download time, many web designers substitute small thumbnail pictures for the normal-sized images, and then make the thumbnail images links to the normal-sized images. Loading the smaller images takes less time, and the surfer is given the freedom to choose whether or not to see the full image, which may be done by clicking on the corresponding thumbnail image link.

Assuming that we had a JPEG photographic image of the Eiffel Tower named eiffelphoto.jpeg, and that we had created a thumbnail version named eiffelphoto_small.jpeg and stored in the same directory, the requisite code to display the thumbnail and use it as a link to the full-size image would be:

```
<a href="eiffelphoto.jpeg"><img src="eiffelphoto_small.
    jpeg" alt="Eiffel Image Link"></a>
```

Note what is going on in the <a> tag. The URL is simply the name of the original JPEG file: eiffelphoto.jpeg. When the surfer clicks on the thumbnail image and activates the link, the browser will download the eiffelphoto.jpeg file and display the image (by itself) in the browser window. So we see that the file referenced by the href attribute in the <a> tag may be a JPEG (or GIF) document as well as an HTML source document. (In Chapter 6 we will learn how to display the full-size image in a new, pop-up window.)

Creating thumbnail images requires the services of a drawing or image editing program that has the capability to reduce the size of a picture. You can of course use the height and width attributes in the <img> tag to shrink the display of an image. But that does not affect the download time, because the browser has to download the image file containing the full-size image before it can shrink it.

Image Maps

Some web designers find it useful to go beyond simple image links by implementing what is known as a **client-side image map**. This feature allows you to create an image with links embedded in various parts of the image. A real estate website, for example, might use an image map to display an image of a city map. By clicking on various parts of the city map, the surfer would activate links that would display documents with real estate information about the various areas of the city.

This type of map is called a client-side image map because the browser on the client computer determines where the surfer clicks and which map region corresponds to the click point. An earlier version of image maps involved server-side processing. The surfer would click on the map and then the browser would send the click information back to the server for processing. Because of the extra overhead involved in communicating with the server, server-side image maps run more slowly than client-side image maps. In addition, they require that the appropriate software is available on the server.

To define the map and its link areas, you use the <map> element in combination with the <area> tag:

```
<map id="myFirstMap" name="myFirstMap">
   <area shape="rect" coords="x1,y1,x2,y2"
      href="someURL" />
   <area shape="rect" coords="x3,y3,x4,y4"
      href="anotherURL" />
</map>
```

You give the map a name using the id attribute. Formerly the name attribute was used for this purpose. But, as with the <a> element, XHTML has deprecated it in the case of the <map> element. Because some older browsers do not recognize the id attribute, we have included both here for backward and forward compatibility.

The two <area> elements define the map as consisting of two rectangular areas. The coordinates of each rectangle are given in number of pixels as measured from the *left* side of the window (the x coordinates) and from the *top* of the window (the y coordinates). That is, the top of the window is at 0 and you measure down from there. The value x1 is the distance from the left side of the window to the left side of the first rectangle, and the value x2 is the distance from the *left* side of the window to the *right* side of the first rectangle. Similarly, the value y1 is the distance from the top of the window to the top of the rectangle, and the distance y2 is the distance from the top of the window to the *bottom* of the rectangle. (See Figure 5.13 below.)

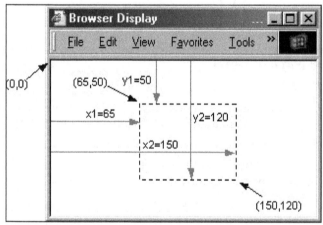

FIGURE 5.13.   Defining a rectangular area in the browser window

Another way to say this is that the (x1, y1) pair of the first rectangle represents its *top-left* corner, and the (x2, y2) pair its *bottom-right* corner. Similarly for the (x3, y3) and (x4, y4) pairs of the second rectangle.

For example:

```
<area shape="rect" coords="65,50,150,120"
   href="someURL" />
```

This would define a rectangular area with a height of 70 pixels (120–50) and a width of 85 pixels (150–65). Note that the x2 coordinate must always be greater than the x1 coordinate, and the y2 coordinate must always be greater than the y1 coordinate. Otherwise, the rectangle doesn't exist.

You may also use circles or polygons for the map areas. For circles, you use the attribute coords="x, y, r", where x and y are the coordinates of the center of the circle and r is its radius. For polygons, you use coords="x1, y1, x2, y2, x3, y3, x4, y4, etc.", where each (x,y) pair gives the coordinates of each corner of the polygon (Figure 5.14).

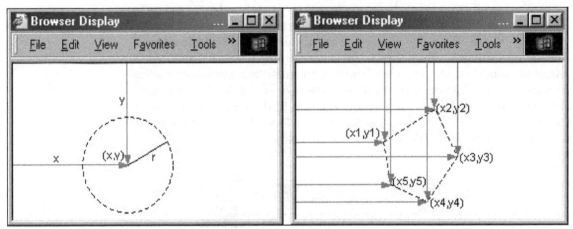

FIGURE 5.14. Defining a circle and a polygon

It usually takes some trial and error to get the coordinates and map areas defined correctly so that they work. (The services of an HTML editor may help here. See Appendix I for some suggestions.)

Once you have defined the clickable map areas using the <map> element, you lay an image over the map area using the <img> tag with the usemap attribute:

```
<img src="mapimage.gif" alt="Client-side map image"
usemap="#myFirstMap" width="250" height="376" />
```

Note that the value of the usemap attribute must correspond to the name that you gave the map in the <map> tag (with the id or name attribute). You also must insert a # symbol in front of it.

QuickCheck Questions

1. Write the HTML code that creates an image link to the document named bluewhales.html using the image file bluewhalephoto.jpeg. (Assume that all files are in the same directory.)
2. What is the difference between a client-side image map and a server-side image map?
3. What are the possible shapes for creating clickable regions in image maps?
4. What is the purpose of the usemap attribute in an <img> tag?

Lab Exercise 5.3, "Adding Image Links and Maps," may be done at this point.

Adding Multimedia Elements

Many web designers are taken with the idea of turning web pages into multimedia experiences by adding sound, animation, and even video. Many web surfers, however, do not find such web pages quite so appealing. The problem is twofold. First, in many cases the multimedia elements don't add much to a web page and often get in the way of the surfer's need to find some specific information. (The exceptions would be websites such as music sites, distance learning sites, news sites, and the like.) Second, sound and video files tend to be very large and thus take a long time to download via a standard 56K modem, and most surfers don't want to bother waiting around for the multimedia experience, no matter how slick. (It's possible to get around the download problem by using "streaming" audio or video, in which the sound or video starts playing as the browser continues to download the rest of the file. But the development and use of such features is beyond the scope of this book.)

The above problems notwithstanding, it is still useful to know how to add basic sound and video capabilities to a web page. To do so, the sound or video must be stored in a file of a certain format. In general, browsers do not know how to deal with sound and video files, but the major browsers do come with so-called plug-in software that is able to open certain audio and video files and play them. For audio, the basic file types are signified by the file extensions .au, .snd, .aif (or .aiff), and .wav. For video, the basic file types have the extensions .qt or .mov (both for the QuickTime format), .mpg (or .mpeg or .mpe), or .avi. (If a browser does not have the appropriate plug-in to open and play a multimedia file, it will usually direct the surfer to either its website or to another where it can be obtained.)

You may create files of these types if you have the appropriate software and hardware. Using a digital video camera and the appropriate software, for example, you may transfer videos you've shot to your computer. But for purposes of experimentation, it's easiest to visit one of the many websites that archive audio files and short video clips and download whatever looks or sounds interesting. (It's best to try short audio files at first, such as sound effects, because they are usually much smaller than video files.)

One tag that may be used to embed an audio or video file into a web page is the inline <embed> tag. Although this tag is not a part of official HTML or XHTML, both Explorer and Navigator support its use. We use it here because it provides the easiest example of adding audio or video to a web page. At its most basic, it takes the following form:

```
<embed src="URL of some audio or video file goes here" />
```

If the file was an audio file named samplesound.wav that was located in the same directory as the source document, the result would be as shown in Figure 5.15. We see that for an audio file the <embed> tag displays a console with audio controls. On the bottom left are play, pause, and stop buttons. On the bottom right is a sliding volume control. The slider bar on the top moves from left to right as the sound plays. The surfer may also click on it and drag it to move forward or backward in the sound. The other buttons are inactive for a basic audio file. (The console shown is that of Explorer. Other browsers have different versions.)

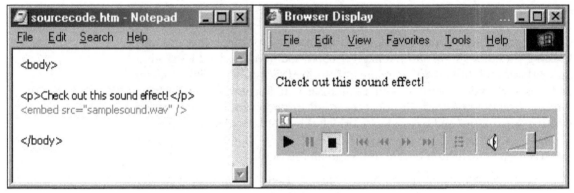

FIGURE 5.15.   Embedding a sound in a web page

When the browser loads a source document with an embedded sound, it automatically starts playing it. If we would rather give the surfer the option to start it, we add the autostart attribute to the <embed> tag and set it to false:

```
<embed src="samplesound.wav" autostart="false" />
```

(Some versions of Explorer do not recognize the autostart attribute and will start the sound clip even if autostart is false.)

We also may specify how the sound console will be displayed by using the height and width attributes in the <embed> tag. The console as shown has a height of 45 pixels and a width of 280 pixels (for Explorer). If, however, we set the width and height to 25 pixels each, only the play button is displayed. Increasing the width to 72 pixels displays the play, pause, and stop buttons. A width of 72 pixels and a height of 45 pixels displays the three basic buttons plus the slider bar at the top. The align attribute may also be used in an <embed> tag to align it on the right margin, just as is done with images. And adding loop="true" to the tag will cause the sound to be played in a continuous loop until the surfer clicks the stop button or leaves the page. Figure 5.16 shows a couple of the possibilities.

Embedding a video file in a web page works the same way, with a few minor differences. The width and height attributes specify the width and height of the video in pixels. And since the controls are not always displayed with the video image (depending on the browser), you should either add autostart="true" to the <embed> tag or instruct the surfer to click on the video image to start it.

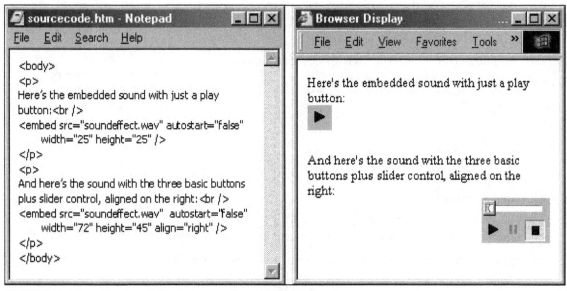

FIGURE 5.16. Customizing the audio console display

Another way to create simple animation on a web page is by using **animated GIF** files. The animated GIF format stores several GIF images in one .gif file. You place this image file in a source document using the normal <img> element just as if it were a regular GIF file. But when the file is loaded by the browser, the multiple images contained in it are displayed in sequence, giving an animated effect. All you need to create an animated GIF file is several GIF images and the software that puts them together into one file. Advanced image processing programs usually have an animated GIF option, but you may also create animated GIFs using various shareware or freeware programs available over the Internet at sites like www.download.com and www.tucows.com (search for "animated GIFs").

For more sophisticated animations, many web designers use a program called Flash, published by Macromedia (www.macromedia.com). Once created, **Flash animations** are embedded in HTML source documents. Most current browsers have Flash playback capabilities built into them, so the surfer doesn't need to acquire or download any extra software to view them.

QuickCheck Questions

1. List three of the file extensions for audio file types and two for video file types.

Lab Exercise 5.4, "Adding Sound and Video," may be done at this point.

animated GIF
client-site image map
combination external/internal
    link
external link

Flash animation
GIF (Graphics Interchange
    Format)
index.html
internal link

JPEG (Joint Photographic
    Experts Group)
PNG (Portable Network
    Graphics)
relative pathname

1. Displaying Images

Inserting an image using the full URL of the image file:

```
<img src="http://www.nasa.gov/images/earth2.jpg" />
```

Inserting an image when the image file is in the same directory as the code document:

```
<img src="earth2.jpg" />
```

Inserting an image using a relative pathname from the code document's directory:

```
<img src="astronomy/earth_photos/earth2.jpg" />
```

Specifying alternative text for an image:

```
<img src="eiffel.gif" alt="Eiffel Tower Picture" />
```

Aligning images vertically at the middle of the line of text using a style sheet (the value `top` may also be specified; default = `bottom`):

```
<style type="text/css">
   img {vertical-align:middle}
</style>
```

Aligning the image at the top or middle of the line of text using the deprecated `align` attribute (default = `bottom`):

```
<img src="eiffel.gif" align="top" alt="Eiffel Tower Picture" />
<img src="eiffel.gif" align="middle" alt="Eiffel Tower Picture" />
```

Defining an image style class to wrap text around the right side of an image (image on the left margin):

```
<style type="text/css">
   img.leftside {float:left}
</style>
```

Defining an image style class to wrap text around the left side of an image (image on the right margin):

```
<style type="text/css">
   img.rightside {float:right}
</style>
```

Wrapping text around the right side of an image using the deprecated `align` attribute (image on the left margin):

```
<img src="eiffel.gif" align="left" alt="Eiffel Tower Picture" />
```

Wrapping text around the left side of an image using the deprecated `align` attribute (image on the right margin):

```
<img src="eiffel.gif" align="right" alt="Eiffel Tower Picture" />
```

Centering images by defining a centered paragraph class and then placing the image tag within the paragraph element:

```
<style type="text/css">
  p.centered {text-align:center}
</style>
```

where:

```
<p class="centered"><img src="eiffeltower.gif" alt="Eiffel Tower Picture" /></p>
```

Specifying the width and height of an image (or specifying a different width and height to display the image at an altered size):

```
<img src="eiffel.gif" width="69" height="120" alt="Eiffel Tower Picture" />
```

2. Creating Links

Creating a link to an external file using a full URL (relative pathname also okay):

```
<a href = "http://www.ucdavis.edu/courses/history170b.html">Click here for information
on the American Revolution course</a>
```

Creating a link to a website using a domain name (index.html file assumed):

```
<a href="http://www.intel.com">Intel</a>
```

Creating the destination point for an internal link:

```
<a id="DolphinSection" name="DolphinSection">Section 3. All About Dolphins</a>
```

Creating the departure point for an internal link:

```
<a href="#DolphinSection">Dolphins</a>
```

Creating a combination link (combination of external and internal links):

```
<a href="http://www.marinebio.ucsandiego.edu/marinemammals.html#DolphinSection"> Click
here to get even more information on dolphins!</a>
```

3. Making Images into Links

Creating an image link:

```
<a href="http://www.frenchtravel.com"><img src="eiffel.gif"
   alt="Eiffel Tower Picture" /></a>
```

Creating clickable map regions (two rectangles, in this case):

```
<map id="myFirstMap" name="myFirstMap">
   <area shape="rect" coords="x1,y1,x2,y2" href="someURL" />
   <area shape="rect" coords="x3,y3,x4,y4" href="anotherURL" />
</map>
```

Overlaying an image on the clickable map regions to create an image map:

```
<img src="mapimage.gif" alt="Client-side map image"
   usemap="#myFirstMap" width="250" height="376" />
```

4. Adding Multimedia Elements

Embedding an audio (or video) file in a web page with the full console of controls:

```
<embed src="soundeffect.wav" autostart="false" width="280"
   height="45" align="right" />
```

Alerts and Advice

It's `src`, not `scr`, for the source attribute in the `<img>` tag.

For an internal link, don't confuse the name of a label (invisible to the surfer) with the labeled text (what the surfer sees).

Don't forget the # symbol in the `href` attribute value for internal links.

Supplement image links with text links.

If appropriate when displaying a series of images, use thumbnail images that are linked to the full-size images.

When defining rectangular clickable regions with the coordinates x1 ,y1, x2, y2, the x2 value must always be greater than the x1 value and the y2 value greater than the y1 value, otherwise the rectangle doesn't exist.

When creating an image map, the value of the `usemap` attribute in the `<img>` tag must correspond to the map name defined in the `<map>` tag, and a # symbol must be inserted at the beginning of the `usemap` value.

Review Questions

1. The two most common types of image files found on the Web are ——————— and ——————— .

2. In order to publish an image on a web page without the image creator's permission, which category must the image be in?
   a. Open access
   b. PNG
   c. Public domain
   d. Watermark

3. Which of the following `<img>` tags directs the browser to display an image using the image file mars28.jpg that is stored in a sub-directory of the source document's directory (where the sub-directory is named marsphotos)?
   a. `<img src="marsphotos.mars28.jpg" height=80 width=100 alt="Mars photo 28" />`
   b. `<img src="mars28/marsphotos" height=80 width=100 alt="Mars photo 28" />`
   c. `<img src="marsphotos/mars28" height=80 width=100 alt="Mars photo 28" />`
   d. `<img src="marsphotos/mars28.jpg" height=80 width=100 alt="Mars photo 28" />`

4. True or false: It is impossible to flow text around both sides of an image by using `align="center"` in an `<img>` tag.

5. True or false: In XHTML, the `alt` attribute is required in an `<img>` tag.

6. True or false: External and internal links usually display the same on a web page.

7. Which of the following creates an external link to a file named historyofpentium.htm at www.intel.com?
   a. `<a href="http://www.intel.com/historyofpentium.htm">All about the Pentium</a>`
   b. `<a href="http://www.intel.com" src="historyofpentium.htm">All about the Pentium</a>`
   c. `<a href="http://historyofpentium.htm/www.intel.com">All about the Pentium</a>`
   d. `<a src= "http://www.intel.com/historyofpentium.htm">All about the Pentium</a>`

8. Which of the following creates a label named "Section4" that may be used by an internal link?
   a. `<a href="Section4"> 4. Summary of Experimental Results</a>`
   b. `<a href="#Section4">4. Summary of Experimental Results</a>`
   c. `<a name="Section4"> 4. Summary of Experimental Results</a>`
   d. `<a name="#Section4"> 4. Summary of Experimental Results</a>`

9. Which of the following creates an internal link to a label named Section4 someplace else in the source document?

   a. `<a href="Section4">Click here to go to Section 4</a>`
   b. `<a href="#Section4">Click here to go to Section 4</a>`
   c. `<a name="Section4">Click here to go to Section 4</a>`
   d. `<a name="#Section4">Click here to go to Section 4</a>`

10. Which of the following creates an image link to a file named checkout.htm (in the same directory as the source document) using an image in a file named shoppingcart.gif (also in the same directory)?

    a. `<a href="checkout.htm"><img href="shoppingcart.gif" alt="the cart" /></a>`
    b. `<a href="checkout.htm" img="shoppingcart.gif" alt="the cart">`
    c. `<a href="checkout.htm"><img src="shoppingcart.gif" alt="the cart" /></a>`
    d. `<img ="shoppingcart.gif" alt="the cart" /><a href="checkout.htm"></a>`

11. True or false: The `<embed>` element is not part of the official HTML standard.

1. Briefly explain the following terms: external link, internal link, index.html file.

2. Write the HTML code that would display an image stored in the file rembrandt.jpg. The source document for the HTML code is named greatartists.htm and is in a directory named webfiles. Assume that the image has a width of 150 pixels and a height of 200 pixels and that the image file is in a directory named site_images, which itself is in the webfiles directory. Make sure that your code for the image is XHTML-compliant.

3. Write the HTML code that would display an image stored in the file companylogo.gif in the center of the page. Assume that the image has a width of 60 pixels and a height of 80 pixels. Show how to achieve the centered presentation using (a) a style sheet and (b) the `align` attribute. Make sure that your code for the image is XHTML-compliant.

4. Write the HTML code that would display an image stored in the file sunrise.jpg on the left margin of the page so that text flows around it. Assume that the image has a width of 120 pixels and a height of 90 pixels. Show how to achieve the text flow using (a) a style sheet and (b) the `align` attribute. Make sure that your code for the image is XHTML-compliant.

5. Explain how the following code works, despite the fact that the value of the `href` attribute does not specify an HTML source document:
   `<a href="http://www.yahoo.com">Click here for Yahoo</a>`

6. Consider an HTML source document named VirusInfo.htm that is stored in a directory named computer_security on a server named www.viruses911.com. Write the HTML code for a link from this document to a document named DestructiveViruses.htm, which is also in the computer_security directory. The link text that the surfer sees should be "Click here for an up-to-date list of destructive viruses."

7. Write the HTML code that would display an image in the VirusInfo.html document of Exercise 6. The image is contained in a file named VirusOutbreakMap.gif, which is stored in a sub-directory of computer_security named virus_images. The image has a height of 75 pixels and a width of 120 pixels. Include the alternative text "Map of Computer Virus Outbreaks", and use a style sheet to position the image so that its top is at the top of the line.

8. Using the VirusOutbreakMap.gif image of Exercise 7, write the code that would make it into an image link. Assume that the linked file has the name CurrentOutbreaks.html and that it is stored in the computer_security directory.

9. Write the HTML code that would create a Back to top link for a web page. Assume that the first line displayed on the web page is "Welcome to the Marine Mammals Page!"

10. Write the HTML code for an image map named quilt consisting of a large square divided into four equal-sized clickable squares. The large square should be 300x300 pixels, and its top right corner should be positioned 50 pixels in from the left side of the window and 80 pixels down from the top of the window. The image to be used for the map is named PatchworkQuilt.jpeg, and it's stored in the same directory as the code document. The upper left square should link to a document named doc1.htm. The upper right square should link to doc2.htm. The lower left square should link to doc3.htm, and the lower right square should link to doc4.htm. All four documents are in the same directory as the code document.

11. Write the HTML code that will embed an audio file named "trumpetfanfare.wav" in a web page with just the play, pause, and stop buttons showing in the console.

Identify the errors in the following `<body>` element code and then sketch on paper how the browser would display it once the errors were corrected. Also note how you would make the code XHTML-compliant.

```
<body>
<h2>All About The Eiffel Tower</h2>
<b>Outline<b><br>
<a href="Intro">Introduction</a><br>
<a href="Construction">Construction Details</a><br>
<a href="EiffelBio">The Life of the Designer</a><p>
<h3>Introduction</h3>
<a id="Intro">Built</a> for the 1889 World Exposition, the Eiffel Tower <img scr="eiffel.
gif" position="middle"> is located on the Champs de Mars in Paris, France.
    . . .
<h3><a id="#Construction">Construction Details</a></h3>
The tower's height of 984 feet made it the tallest structure in the world for many years.
Seven thousand tons of steel were used in its construction, at a total cost equivalent to
over 1 million US dollars.
    . . .
<h3>The Life of the Designer</h3>
<a id="EiffelBiography">Alexandre Gustave Eiffel</a> was the tower's designer and
namesake. He lived a fascinating life.
    . . .
</body>
```

Note: Most of the exercises above may also be done as lab exercises.

Exercise 5.1: Adding Images

❑ Experiment with adding some images to the web page(s) that you created in previous exercises (or make a new one). Use the `align` attribute(s) of your choice in the `<img>` tag. Make sure you also include the `width` and `height` attributes and alternative text with the `alt` attribute. To find some images, try gallery.yahoo.com, multimedia.lycos.com, www.google.com or similar websites with image archives. Or for experimentation purposes, simply find something you like on a website that you know. But remember the warning regarding public domain images.

Exercise 5.2: Creating a Multiple-Page Web Site

❏ In this exercise we will be creating a more sophisticated *website* that contains three HTML documents with links between them. The site's topic will be you—your interests and activities. The first of the three HTML documents will be an introduction/information page that displays a welcome message and your name, school (if appropriate), and field of study or work. It will also have a table of contents with links to the other two pages. The second page will be a *short* version of your resume and/or academic interests. The third page will describe your life outside the academic realm. You might include interesting information about your living situation, extracurricular interests, and/or personal opinions about things like courses, books, musical artists, TV shows, movies, and life in general.

❏ Use a text processor to create three HTML documents named WebSiteIntro.html, MyResume.html, and Extracurricular.html. (If you like, you may write the extensions as .htm instead of .html.) For now, leave them empty of any text or HTML code except the `<head>`, `<title>`, and `<body>` elements.

❏ In the WebSiteIntro.html document, put the HTML code for a Welcome message, personal information (name, school, major, year in school), and links to the other two pages. Don't waste any time making it fancy at this point.

❏ Add a brief line or two of text to the MyResume.html and Extracurricular.html documents for testing purposes and then add a link in each document that will link back to the WebSiteIntro.html document. Once you have the links working, then take a few minutes (but not too long) to fill in some of the rest of the text, images, and HTML code that you want to put in these two documents. Put enough text and/or images in one of the two documents so that the information extends beyond the bottom of the screen.

❏ In the long document (the one that extends beyond the bottom of the screen), add an internal link near the top that will jump the surfer to a section of text below that cannot be seen. Check to make sure the link works, then add a link to the WebSiteIntro.html document that will jump directly to that section of text in the long document.

Exercise 5.3: Adding Image Links

❏ Add to your WebSiteIntro.html document an external link to the home page of your school or organization.

❏ After making sure the link works, find an appropriate image and make it into an image link. (Remember: Once you have "traveled" from your page to that of your school or organization, you can get back via your browser's Back button.)

Exercise 5.4: Adding Sound and Video

❏ Experiment with the `<embed>` tag to add a sound effect and/or very short video clip to the WebSiteIntro.html document. Try an audio file first, and then if you get that to work, try a video file. (Get the audio or video file from a Web directory site like Yahoo or Lycos or from a specialized site like www.wavcentral.com.)

Sitebuilding Exercise 1 may be done at this point (see Appendix A).

Web Page Design and Layout

LEARNING OBJECTIVES

1. Learn how to create web pages with magazine-style layouts using the `<div>` element and the `position` style property.

2. Learn how to create web pages with magazine-style layouts using tables and nested tables.

3. Learn how to divide the browser window into frames and load different documents into them.

4. Learn how to use a link to open a new browser window and load a document into it.

Layout with Style

In the previous chapters we have learned much about HTML and how web pages work. But you may remember from the Lab Exercises in Chapter 1 that we also briefly considered another sense of how a web page works that's equally important: the layout and design of a web page. Consider Figure 6.1.

This "Technology Today" web page uses a magazine-style layout with a title that spans the top of the page, an image positioned underneath it on the left, and three columns of text. Such a layout may be created relatively easily by using HTML styles, especially if we take it one step at a time.

Magazine-Style Layouts

The first thing to do in designing such a layout is to set the overall height and width. The usual recommended value for web pages is 600 pixels (or so) for the width and 400–500 for the height. At this size, most monitors in use circa

143

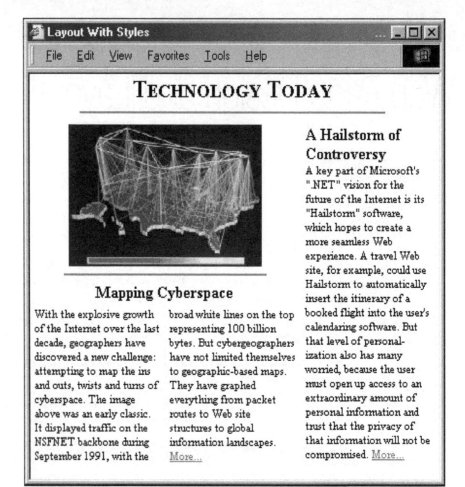

FIGURE 6.1.   Sample website with magazine-style layout

2002 will be able to display the whole layout without forcing the user to scroll horizontally or vertically. We then sketch the design on paper and figure out the sizes and positions of the various elements. (It's also possible to design layouts that use relative measurements instead of the absolute pixel measurements we use here, so that the page's layout automatically resizes as the browser window is resized. In actual practice, however, it doesn't always work very well. We will stick to the simpler method of setting the layout dimensions in exact pixels.)

In the case of Figure 6.1, we have five elements or sections: the title section, the image section, and the three columns. Making the columns all equal width, we have a width of 200 pixels for the columns, 400 pixels for the image, and the full 600 pixels for the headline section. We then estimate that 60 pixels would be a good height for the headline and 230 pixels for the image. (In general, the nature of the image itself will determine its best size, meaning either we have to design the layout around the image size or choose and/or edit the image to fit its spot in the layout.) This basic design structure is shown in Figure 6.2.

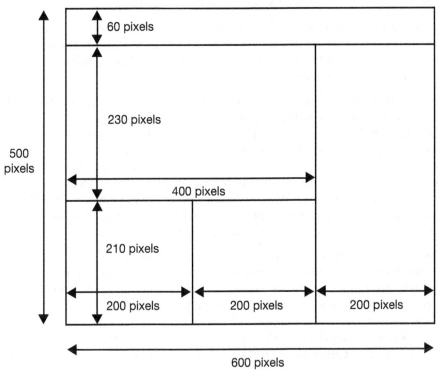

FIGURE 6.2.   Design specifications for a magazine-style layout

Positioning Web Page Elements

To create a magazine-style layout using HTML styles, we employ the <div> element that was introduced in Chapter 5. Recall that the <div> element enables us to create custom block-level elements by defining various classes of it. In one simple example, we defined a block-level division that had a red background by using the following style definition:

```
<style>
   div.redbkd {background-color:red}
</style>
```

We implemented this style in the <body> element with this code:

```
<div class="redbkd">
<p>This paragraph is inside the div container, so it will
take on its formatting.</p>
<p>Here's a second paragraph, also inside the div
container.</p>
</div>
```

(See Figure 3.8 for the full code and corresponding display.)

To create our magazine-style layout, we use <div> elements to define the properties of each of the divisions or sections of the layout, and then we fill in the text and/or images for each section by putting them inside the corresponding <div> element.

If we are going to do this, however, we need some way to specify the placement of the divisions on the web page. Every web page that we have created so far has loaded and displayed from top to bottom. Although we saw how we could wrap text around an image using the float style property or the align attribute in the <img> tag, in all other cases the browser has displayed the HTML elements in the order in which they appear in the <body> element of the source document. This is called the **normal flow** of the document—the HTML elements, tags, and text in the source document flow from the document into the browser's display in the normal top-to-bottom order.

The position property of HTML style sheets, however, gives us the capability to specify the exact position where we want a certain element to appear. If, for example, we wanted to display our Eiffel Tower image from Chapter 5 at a position 75 pixels down from the top of the page and 150 pixels in from the left, we would define an "eiffeltower" class for the <img> tag and specify its exact position using the position property in combination with the top and left properties. Figure 6.3 shows the details and the result.

Note the syntax in the style definition: We specify position:absolute and then the position for the top of the image, measured in pixels from the top of the browser window, and the position for the left side of the image, measured from the left edge of the browser window. The order does not matter: you may put the left value first and then the top value, if you choose. In addition, you should be aware that these position measurements are actually calculated from the edges of the element's **containing block**. In this case, the <img> element is inside the <body> element, which thus defines the containing block—the rectangular box of the browser window itself. But if we were to specify an absolute position for a paragraph class, and then place the <img> element within the <p> element, the containing block for the <img> element would now be the rectangular box that defines the borders of the <p> element. The top and left values for the image would thus be measured from the edges of the <p> element, not the window. In our examples we will avoid these nesting effects.

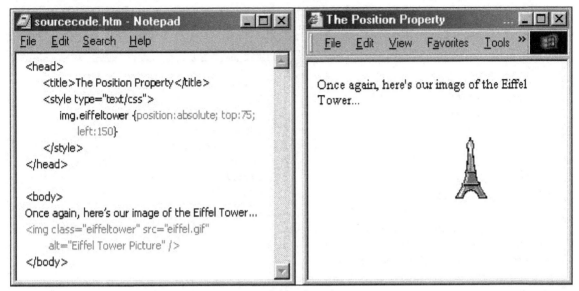

FIGURE 6.3.   Specifying the exact location of an image

Note also that this particular example would not be too useful by itself, because even though the image would be positioned exactly, the text on the page would still be positioned according to the normal flow. Figure 6.4 shows what happens if we add more text to the source document.

When we saw the Figure 6.4 code previously without the style and class definition (that is, using just a regular <img> tag—see Figure 5.2), the image was displayed after the word "Tower" and then the rest of the text, beginning with "is located on . . .", continued after the image.

In this case, however, we have defined an absolute position for the image, which takes it out of the normal flow. The document's text is therefore formatted and displayed as if the image wasn't there. As you can see, the result is less than satisfactory.

So if we are going to use the `position` property to specify the exact location of an element on a web page, in general we will need to do so for all the text and elements involved. This sounds more difficult than it is. In practice, all we need to do is define the positions of main sections of the layout using <div> elements and then add the other text and image elements to these elements, as previously mentioned.

Creating a Layout Using the <div> Element

To reproduce the "Technology Today" layout, we need to define five <div> elements (using classes) and specify their absolute locations on the page with

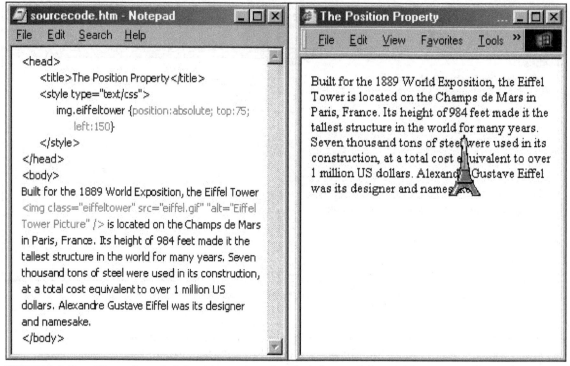

FIGURE 6.4.   The mismatch between an absolutely positioned image and text in the normal flow

the `position` property, using the layout dimensions of Figure 6.2. The "title" division will have a top position at 0 pixels, a width equal to 600 pixels, and a height equal to 60 pixels. For the width and height specifications we use the `width` and `height` properties, respectively. The "picture" division will have its top at 60 pixels, its height set to 230 pixels, and its width set to 400 pixels. The left bottom column (column 1) will have its top at 290, its left at 0, a height of 210 and a width of 200. The center bottom column (column 2) will have the same top, height, and width, but its left side will be positioned at 200 pixels. Finally, the right column (column 3) will have its top at 60, its left side at 400, a height of 440 and a width of 200.

IMPORTANT

Figure 6.5 shows the complete source document for the basic "Technology Today" layout, with sample text substituting for the actual text in the columns. (Designing a layout takes a certain amount of trial and error, and another useful technique is to give each division a different background color using the `background-color` property. The different colors make it easy to see the division boundaries. Here, however, we will just use sample text.) Note that we also made the title large and centered by adding the appropriate properties to the title division, and we centered the picture. Figure 6.6 displays the results (shown smaller than the actual size).

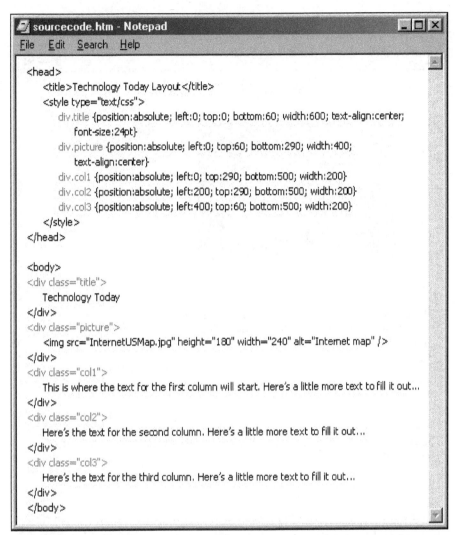

FIGURE 6.5.   Implementing a magazine-style layout with <div> elements

Although it is not apparent from Figure 6.6, if we add more text to each column we would find that the text would go past the bottom of the column, as defined by the value of the height property. In other words, the content of the <div> element overflows its containing block. The reason is that HTML uses the overflow property to specify whether content that overflows should be visible or not. The default value is visible. But if you want the overflow to be clipped, you add overflow:hidden to the element's style definition (<div>, in our case).

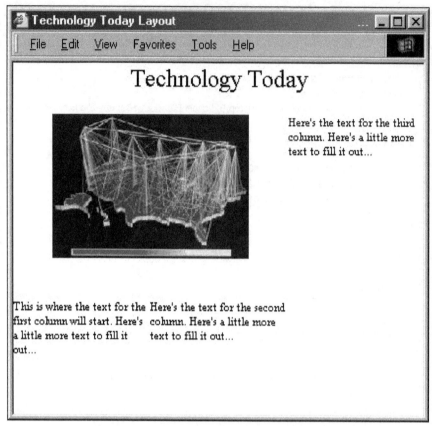

FIGURE 6.6.   Roughing out the Technology Today layout (not shown actual size)

One thing to notice in the Figure 6.6 display is that the text in the columns is displayed right up to the edges of the columns. We can adjust this problem by using the `padding` property, which lets us define a region around the inside edges of the division that will be left blank. That is, the text will be forced inward. We may define a padding of 10 pixels on all four sides of the first column like so:

```
div.col1 {position:absolute; left:0; top:340; bottom:500;
    width:200; padding:10}
```

But in our case, we would prefer to have no padding at the top and bottom of the columns and a padding of 5 pixels on the left and right sides. We also decide that a font size of 11 points would be good. So we specify:

```
div.col1 {position:absolute; left:0; top:340; bottom:500;
    width:200; font-size:11pt; padding:0 5}
```

And similarly for the second and third columns.

We also need to display the title in bold small caps, so we add the appropriate properties to the div.title definition:

```
div.title {position:absolute; left:0; top:0; bottom:60;
    width:600; text-align:center; font-size:24pt;
    font-variant:small-caps; font-weight:bold}
```

The final touch is to format the headings for each article. For the "Mapping Cyberspace" article, it's easiest to place the heading inside the div.picture division, because then it will end up centered across columns 1 and 2. The "Hailstorm of Controversy" heading is placed at the beginning of the div.col3 division. In order to enlarge the headings, we could place them in <h2> elements. But these block-level elements will give us unwanted blank lines before and after the headings. Instead, we will define a span.articleheading class that we use to display the headings in 18-point bold text. We also add a horizontal rule style with a width of 75%, height of 3 pixels, and a gray background to use below the main title and below the picture.

The final style definitions then are:

```
div.title {position:absolute; left:0; top:0; bottom:60;
    width:600; text-align:center; font-size:24pt;
    font-variant:small-caps; font-weight:bold}
div.picture {position:absolute; left:0; top:60;
    bottom:290; width:400; text-align:center}
div.col1 {position:absolute; left:0; top:290; bottom:500;
    width:200; font-size:11pt; padding:0 5}
div.col2 {position:absolute; left:200; top:290;
    bottom:500; width:200; font-size:11pt; padding:0 5}
div.col3 {position:absolute; left:400; top:60; bottom:500;
    width:200; font-size:11pt; padding:0 5}
span.articleheading {font-size:18pt; font-weight:bold}
hr {width:75%; height:3px; background:gray}
```

The completed version of the <body> element is shown in Figure 6.7 (with some of the text left out), which yields the original display of Figure 6.1. Remember, however, that even the latest browsers do not always display styles in the same way. You should always check a style-created layout in various browsers to make sure the layout appears as planned.

QuickCheck Questions

1. What is "normal flow"?
2. What does the padding style property do?
3. Write a style definition for a <div> class named "middlerow" that is positioned 150 pixels down from the top of the window and 0 pixels in from the left and that has a width of 600 pixels and a height of 75 pixels.

Lab Exercise 6.1, "Layout Using Styles," may be done at this point.

```
sourcecode.htm - Notepad                              _ □ X
File   Edit   Search   Help

<body>
<div class="title">
    Technology Today
    <hr />
</div>
<div class="picture">
    <img src="InternetUSMap.jpg" height="180" width="240" alt="Internet map" />
    <br />
    <hr />
    <span class="articleheading">Mapping Cyberspace</span>
</div>
<div class="col1">
    With the explosive growth of the Internet.... The image above was an early classic. It
    displayed traffic on the NSFNET backbone
</div>
<div class="col2">
    during September 1991, with the broad white lines on the top representing 100 billion
    bytes.... information landscapes. <a href="article1_continued.htm">More...</a>
</div>
<div class="col3">
    <span class="articleheading">A Hailstorm of Controversy</span>
    <p>A key part of Microsoft's ".NET" vision for the future of the Internet is its
    "Hailstorm" software.... trust that the privacy of that information will not be
    compromised. <a href="article2_continued.htm">More...</a></p>
</div>
</body>
```

FIGURE 6.7.   The <body> element for the Technology Today layout

The Return of Tables

Before HTML had the capability to do styles, web page designers did not have any easy way to create pages with sophisticated layouts. Early designers discovered, however, that with a little twiddling and by trial and error, they could use HTML's table capabilities to create magazine-style layouts. The key is to structure the layout using the table's cells.

We will start with a simple example, and then we'll expand on it to show how we can use tables to recreate the "Technology Today" layout. (Note that our code will use some deprecated attributes, so using tables in this way is not recommended. Nevertheless, many web pages still use tables for layout purposes. It is thus useful to understand how it works.)

Creating Layouts with Tables

Consider the basic layout in Figure 6.8 that has a small top row and a large bottom row, with the bottom row divided into two sections (columns) of equal width.

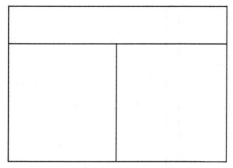

FIGURE 6.8.   Basic layout with three sections

For this example, we'll set the width at 600 pixels total, the height of the top row at 60 pixels, the height of the bottom columns at 440 pixels, and the width of the bottom columns at 300 pixels.

In order to recreate this layout using a table, we define a table with two rows. The second row will contain two cells for the two bottom columns, and the first row will use the `colspan` attribute to span across the two bottom cells and give an undivided top section. The code and display (in reduced size) are shown in Figure 6.9. Note that it's necessary to define the width of the cells such that their sum equals the width of the table. We also set the border of the table to 1 pixel for now because we want to see the boundaries of the cells. Eventually we will set it to 0.

We can refine the display in Figure 6.9 in several ways.

First, by adding the `cellspacing` attribute in the `<table>` tag and setting it to 0, we can get rid of the extra white space between the three table cells. (Again, we will keep `border=1` for the time being, in order to see the cell boundaries.)

We also will move the text 10 pixels away from the edge of the bottom cells by adjusting the padding for the cells using `cellpadding=10`. (Remember that the `cellpadding` attribute only works in the `<table>` tag, and thus sets the padding for all the cells in a table; we can't use it in a `<td>` tag to set the padding for a single cell.)

Finally, we will use `valign="top"` in the `<td>` elements for the bottom columns so that the text will be displayed at the top of the cell instead of in the middle (the default option, as can be seen in Figure 6.9).

Figure 6.10 shows the revised code and display.

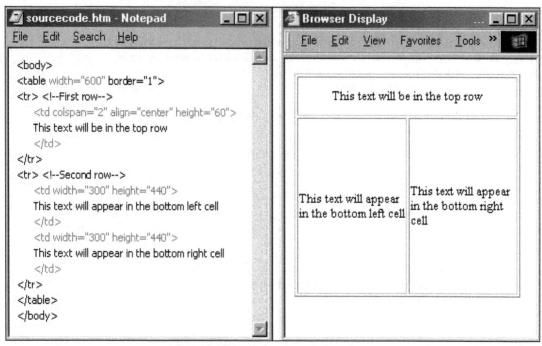

FIGURE 6.9.   Reproducing the basic layout of Figure 6.8 using tables (not shown actual size)

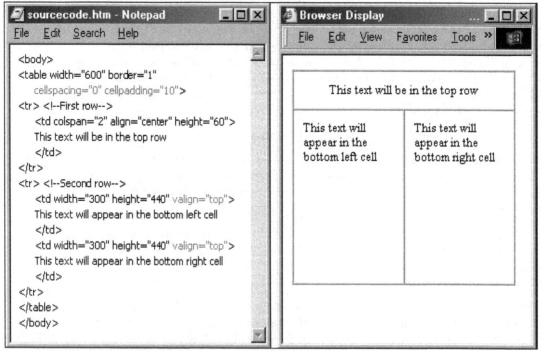

FIGURE 6.10.   Tweaking the table layout

Complex Layouts with Nested Tables

Now that we've seen how we can create a simple layout with tables, we want to reproduce the more complex "Technology Today" layout. Note that our simple layout above may be turned into the Technology Today layout by making two changes:

1. Shrink the width of the bottom-right cell so that it has a width of one-third of the total width, instead of one-half, while increasing the width of the bottom-left cell to two-thirds of the total width.

2. Divide the bottom-left cell into three cells, one to contain the picture and the other two to be the two bottom columns.

Change #1 is straightforward: we simply set the width in the <td> element for the bottom-right cell to 200 pixels, and the width in the bottom-left <td> element to 400 pixels.

Change #2 isn't quite so obvious, but it isn't much more difficult. The key is to create a second table that has the layout we need for the picture section and the two columns below it, and then insert that table into our first table. That is, we put another complete <table> definition inside the <td> element of the bottom-left cell, so that we have a **nested table**. This table will have a width that matches the width of the bottom-left cell (i.e., 400 pixels). The first row of the table will have a single cell with a width of 400 and a height of 230 pixels. This cell is where the image will go. The second row of the table will have two cells of equal width (200 pixels) and height (210 pixels). These two cells reproduce the bottom-left and bottom-center column of the Technology Today layout. Figure 6.11 gives the code details (showing just the key code for the nested table) and the resulting display.

Once we have recreated the general layout, it then is an easy matter to put the image and text in the appropriate cells in order to reproduce the Technology Today page. (It is at this point that we would change border=1 to border=0 in the two <table> tags to get rid of the lines between the cells. We also might have to fiddle a bit with the cell padding to get the look we want.)

QuickCheck Questions

1. How do you get rid of the white space between table cells?
2. What attribute do you use to set the vertical alignment of the contents in a table cell?
3. What is a nested table?

Lab Exercise 6.2, "Layout Using Tables," may be done at this point.

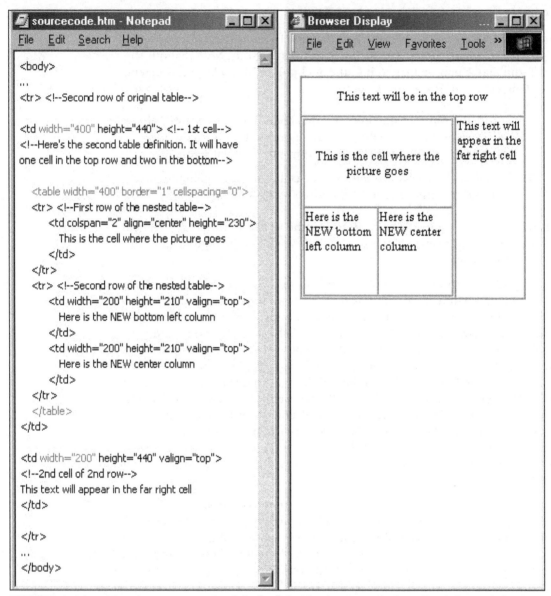

FIGURE 6.11.   Nesting a second table inside the bottom-left cell of the original table to recreate the Technology Today layout (not shown actual size)

Creating and Using Frames

In the first two sections of this chapter we learned how to create magazine-style layouts using either style sheets or tables. In this section we'll learn about a third method to create such layouts and do even more with them—**frames**.

Like the <div> element or table cells, frames allow the HTML coder to divide the browser window into different rectangular regions, like window panes. But with frames, each region may display the contents of a *different* HTML source document.

If the contents of a source document cannot be completely displayed within the given area of the frame, the frame may be given scroll bars. Frames are also resizeable: that is, if the surfer changes the size of the browser window, any frames will be resized automatically. (If necessary or desired, the HTML coder can also define frames that have the scrollbar and auto-resize options turned off.)

The Potential and Limitations of Frames

In designing our own websites, one possible use for frames is to implement a table of contents. Consider a multiple-page website (such as the one that you may have created in Lab Exercise 5.2 and that you may have modified in Lab Exercise 6.1). The introductory page generally has a table of contents with links to the other pages in the site. When the surfer clicks on a link, the browser leaves the table of contents and displays the appropriate page. To go back to the table of contents, the surfer clicks on a Back to the Contents page link (assuming one is provided) or clicks the Back button.

Using frames, we can make the Table of Contents links visible at all times and eliminate this back-and-forth surfing. We can divide the window into two frames: one will contain the table of contents and the other will display the contents of whatever link the surfer chooses from the table of contents. That is, when the surfer clicks on a link in the table of contents, the browser will retrieve the document for that link and display its contents in the second frame. The table of contents will still remain in view in the first frame.

The uses of frames are limited only by your imagination. For instance, consider an art history website that contains information on famous artists and images of some of their paintings. Because images usually take the browser a while to load and display, you might want to display the information on an artist without automatically displaying the corresponding image or images. Instead, you might give the surfer the option of seeing any given image by clicking on a link. To implement this scheme using frames, you can divide the browser window into three frames. One will display the table of contents (listing the artists covered, and so on), another the information on the currently selected artist, and a third the current image (if any).

On the other hand, frames have not always been a standard feature in HTML, and therefore they are not supported by all types of web browsers. Some surfers also think that frames don't add much of benefit to web page design, while others love them. In addition, frames are not the most robust feature of web browsers. So you may experience a little more frustration than usual trying to implement them, especially if you are trying a complex arrangement of frames. You must therefore weigh the pros and cons before designing a web page that implements frames.

IMPORTANT

It is not a good idea to design a page with more than three or four frames, because the resulting display will be cluttered and confusing.

The Layout Document: Using <frameset>

To implement frames, we first create a new type of HTML document, a **layout** or **frameset document**, with the following structure:

```
<html>
<head>
</head>
<frameset>
</frameset>
</html>
```

Note that there is no body element; it has been replaced with a <frameset> element. Note also something we do not show above: A frameset document that's XHTML-compatible needs a special Document Type Declaration named "frameset" instead of "strict" or "transitional." Therefore, to the above code we need to add the following DTD before the <html> (along with the other XML and namespace information—see "Creating an XHTML Source Document" in Chapter 2):

```
<!DOCTYPE html PUBLIC
    "-//W3C//DTD XHTML 1.0 Frameset//EN"
    "http://www/w3/org/TR/xhtml/11/DTD/xhtml1-frameset.dtd">
```

We will usually leave this DTD out of our code examples.

You define the layout structure of the frames—the size and location of each frame—using the <frameset> element and two of its attributes, rows and cols. You may set the sizes of the rows and columns in several ways: by exact number of pixels, by a percentage of the window size, or as a relative value whereby the row or column in question is assigned all the remaining space. The following examples show how this works.

Example 1

The <frameset> element below will divide the window into three rows, the first having a height of 25% of the window, the second having a height of 45%, and the third having a height of 30%:

```
<frameset rows="25%,45%,30%">
</frameset>
```

The result is displayed in Figure 6.12. Note: If the percentages don't add up to 100 percent, the browser will automatically scale the values up or down as appropriate.

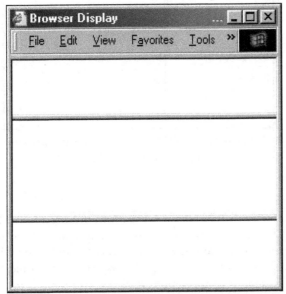

FIGURE 6.12. Dividing the browser window into three row frames (25%, 45%, 30%)

Example 2

This <frameset> element will divide the window into two columns, the first having a width of 40% of the window and the second having a width of 60%:

```
<frameset cols="40%,60%">
</frameset>
```

Figure 6.13 shows the results.

Example 3

We may also specify pixels instead of percentages. The following <frameset> element will divide the window into three columns, the first and third having widths of 80 pixels and the second having a relative width (signified by the asterisk) of whatever is left of the overall window width after the 160 pixels have been subtracted:

```
<frameset cols="80,*,80">
</frameset>
```

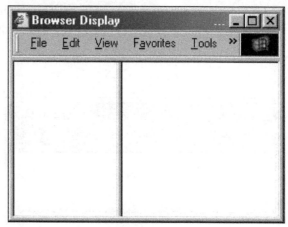

FIGURE 6.13.   Dividing the browser window into two column frames (40%, 60%)

Example 4

In order to create more complex combinations of rows and columns, you may create **nested frameset** elements. If, for instance, we wanted to quarter the window into four equal frames, we would first create two equal columns and then divide each column into two equal rows. The code would be:

```
<frameset cols="50%,50%">
  <frameset rows="50%,50%">
  </frameset>
  <frameset rows="50%,50%">
  </frameset>
</frameset>
```

The `<frameset cols="50%,50%">` tag divides the window into two equal columns, then the first `<frameset rows="50%,50%">` tag divides the *first* column into two equal rows and the second `<frameset rows="50%,50%">` tag divides the *second* column into two equal rows. (In this case we could also start with two equal rows and then divide each row into two equal columns.)

Note that the order matters. The first nested `<frameset>` acts on the first column of the outer `<frameset>`, and the second nested `<frameset>` acts on the second column of the outer `<frameset>`. If we wanted the second column divided into three instead of two rows, we would change the second `<frameset rows>` tag as below. (Note: Even though the three 33% figures add up to 99%, not 100%, it's okay; as mentioned above, the browser will automatically fill in the missing 1%.)

```
<frameset cols="50%,50%">
  <frameset rows="50%,50%">
  </frameset>
  <frameset rows="33%,33%,33%">
```

```
  </frameset>
</frameset>
```

The result would be a window divided as shown in Figure 6.14.

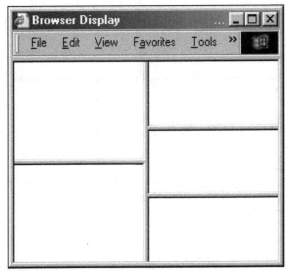

FIGURE 6.14.   The result of two row framesets nested inside a column frameset

Example 5

If we switched the rows and cols attributes in Example 4, we would have the following code, with the result being two rows, the first divided into two columns and the second into three columns (Figure 6.15).

```
<frameset rows="50%,50%">
  <frameset cols="50%,50%">
  </frameset>
  <frameset cols="33%,33%,33%">
  </frameset>
</frameset>
```

Giving Body to the Frame: The <frame> Tag

If you created an HTML layout document with any of the above <frameset> examples and loaded it in the browser, you would be disappointed to see a blank screen. Nothing appears because we have not specified any information to display in the frames. We specify the information to be displayed using the <frame> tag. A <frame> tag may have up to seven attributes:

1. The src attribute specifies the URL of the HTML document that will be loaded into the frame.

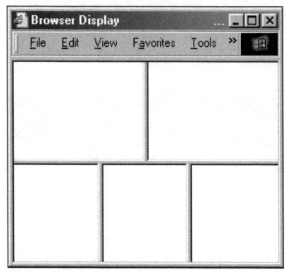

FIGURE 6.15.   The result of two column framesets nested inside a row frameset

2. The id attribute allows you optionally to assign an identifying name to the frame. You would do so if you wanted to create a link in another frame that, when clicked, would display something in the named frame. In other words, the frame in this case needs a name so that you can refer to it when needed. We will see how to do this in the section below on "Linking Between Frames."

    Note: As in the case of the <a> element, the name attribute has also often been used to assign this identifying name instead of the id attribute. But the name attribute has been deprecated for both the <a> and <frame> elements. To ensure backward compatibility with older browsers, you should use both the id and name attributes in the same <frame> element, giving each the same value. In our code samples, however, we will sometimes just use id.

3. and 4.   The marginwidth and marginheight attributes are optional attributes that allow you to control the size, in pixels, of the margins of the frame. The marginwidth attribute refers to the left and right margins; marginheight, the top and bottom margins. If these attributes are not specified, the browser decides the appropriate margin size.

5. The scrolling attribute indicates whether a frame should be given a scrollbar and has three values, yes, no, and auto, with auto being the default if nothing is indicated. Yes means that the frame will always have scrollbars. No means that the frame will never have scrollbars. Auto lets the browser decide, based on the length and width of the document in the frame, whether the frame should have scrollbars.

6. The `noresize` attribute has no associated value. If it is present in the `<frame>` tag, then the surfer will not be allowed to drag and resize the frame while viewing it. If it is absent, the surfer will be allowed to drag and resize the frame.

7. The `frameborder` attribute allows you to hide the frame's borders (that is, `frameborder=0` will make the frame's sculpted borders disappear). (Internet Explorer and Netscape Navigator each define several more attributes for the `<frame>` tag, but they aren't part of standard HTML version 4 or XHTML.)

The `<frame>` tag is an empty element, so don't forget to include the `/>` at the end. You normally include one `<frame>` tag for each frame. If a `<frameset>` element defines two columns, for example, it would have two `<frame>` tags within it. A simple example would be:

Error Alert!

```
<frameset cols="40%,60%">
   <frame id="leftframe" src="WelcomePage.htm"/>
   <frame id="rightframe" src="ContactsList.htm"/>
</frameset>
```

When the browser loads this frameset document, it will create two frames (columns) and load the "WelcomePage.htm" document into the left column and the "ContactsList.htm" document into the right column. We used the `id` attribute to name the frames `leftframe` and `rightframe`, respectively. These are not special names. We could have named them abc and xyz for all the browser cares. But it is good to use descriptive names.

Figure 6.16 shows a more complicated example of how it all fits together. In the frameset document we have defined three frames (two rows—a small row on top and a larger bottom row divided into two equal columns). In the first frame (the top row, with one column), the browser will load and display a "TableOfContents.htm" document. In the bottom-left frame, the browser will display an "Introduction.htm" document. And in the bottom-right frame, the browser will display a "ListOfPictures.htm" document. (Because the code only specifies a relative URL for each of these documents, they must all be located in the same directory as the frameset document.)

Because some web browsers do not support the use of frames, it is good practice to include the `<noframes>` element in an HTML layout document. The `<noframes>` element allows you to display a message to a surfer who is trying to view your framed web page with a browser that cannot display frames. The message might be something to the effect that, "This Web page uses frames and requires the use of a frames-capable browser, such as Netscape Navigator 2.0 or above or Microsoft Explorer 3.0 or above." The following HTML code shows how you implement this.

IMPORTANT

```
<frameset rows="25%,75%">
   <frame id="topframe" src="TableOfContents.htm"/>
   <frameset cols="50%,50%">
      <frame id="bottomleftframe" src="Introduction.htm"/>
```

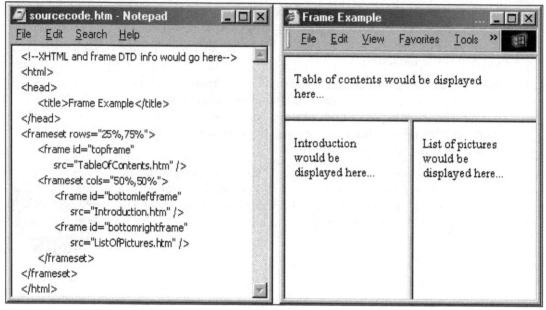

FIGURE 6.16.   Using the <frame> tag to load documents into frames

```
<frame id="bottomrightframe"
    src="ListOfPictures.htm"/>
  </frameset>
<noframes>This Web page uses frames and requires the use
of a frames-capable browser, such as Netscape Navigator
2.0 or above or Microsoft Internet Explorer 3.0 or
above.</noframes>
  </frameset>
```

If the surfer does have a frames-capable browser, the message and anything else in the <noframes> element will **not** be displayed.

In versions of Navigator *before* Version 6, clicking the Reload button reloads the source documents that make up the contents of each of the visible frames (as specified in the <frame> tags). It does *not* reload the HTML *layout* document that defines the <frameset>. Therefore, in order to experiment with different <frameset> combinations of rows and columns, you must actually open the layout document again using the Open command in the File menu. Navigator 6's Reload button and Explorer's Refresh button, on the other hand, do reload or refresh the layout document as well as the frames.

Also, if you forget to include the ending </frameset> tag of a <frameset> element, some versions of Navigator will display absolutely nothing when you load the frameset document, whereas Explorer will usually overlook this error. (The same thing happens if you leave off the ending </table> tag, as mentioned in Chapter 4.)

Note finally that if you select Page Source under the View menu in Navigator or Source under the View menu in Explorer, the code for the layout document will be displayed. In order to view the source document for any given frame (in the Windows operating system), right-click the mouse in the frame and then choose Frame source (in Navigator) or View source (in Explorer) from the pop-up menu that appears.

Linking between Frames

As previously mentioned, one reason frames are useful is because they allow the surfer to click on a link in a document that is displayed in one frame and see the results of that link displayed in another frame, without losing sight of the first document. In order to implement this kind of linking, we add the `target` attribute to the `<a>` tag. The `target` attribute tells the browser in what frame it should display the linked document. It does so by listing the name of the frame. (Remember that when we define a frame using the `<frame>` tag we may give it a name using the `id` attribute.)

Consider a simple example of a `<frameset>` with two side-by-side frames to see how the `target` attribute works:

```
<frameset cols="50%,50%">
  <frame id="leftframe" name="leftframe"
    src="ListOfLinks.htm" />
  <frame id="rightframe" name="rightframe"
    src="IntroMessage.htm" />
</frameset>
```

Within this `<frameset>` element, we have defined two frames using the `<frame>` tag. The first frame (i.e., the left column) is named `leftframe` and has the HTML document ListOfLinks.htm loaded into it. The second frame (the right column) is given the name `rightframe` and has the IntroMessage.htm document loaded into it. Note that for compatibility with older browsers we have used both the `id` and `name` attributes to specify the names.

The `<body>` code for the IntroMessage.htm document simply specifies a brief introductory message that will be displayed initially in the right frame:

```
<body>
Documents you select from the list of links at the left
  will be displayed here . . .
</body>
```

The ListOfLinks.htm document contains the HTML code for a list of links (two, in this case):

```
<body>
<p>Test of linking between frames:</p>
<p><a href="Doc1.htm" target="rightframe">Click here to
  view document 1</a></p>
```

```
<p><a href="Doc2.htm" target="rightframe">Click here to
    view document 2</a></p>
</body>
```

The first <a> element links to a document named Doc1.htm and the second to a document named Doc2.htm. The new addition to these <a> elements, which we haven't seen before, is the use of the target attribute. It tells the browser that when the surfer clicks on the first link, it should display Doc1.htm in the frame named rightframe. And similarly for the second link: Doc2.htm will be displayed in the frame named rightframe. (For testing purposes, the Doc1.htm and Doc2.htm documents each simply contain a line of text, "This is document 1" or "This is document 2.")

If you do not include the target attribute in the <a> element, the linked document will be displayed in the same frame that contains the link. In our example, the Doc1.htm and Doc2.htm documents would then be displayed in the left frame, erasing the list of links from view.

Figure 6.17 shows the display when the layout document has been opened in the browser. Figure 6.18 shows the display after the surfer has clicked on the "document 1" link. Note that the display in the left frame does not change (except that the link color might be different to indicate that it has been clicked).

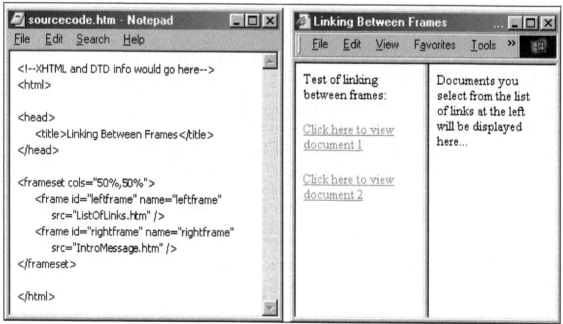

FIGURE 6.17.   Linking between frames

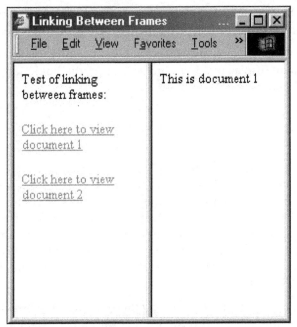

FIGURE 6.18. Result of clicking on the "document 1" link

Getting Out of a Frameset

Sometimes when you are designing a web page that uses frames, you will want to erase the frames and go back to a regular browser window. For example, when the surfer clicks on a certain link in a frame, you might want the resulting page to display in the entire window instead of inside the frame (which is what it will normally do).

One way to do this is to have the link reference a new layout document that simply defines a single frame (e.g., cols="100%" or rows="100%"). Then use the <frame> tag within that new layout document to load the document that is to be displayed. For example, the layout document would have the <frameset>:

```
<frameset rows="100%">
  <frame src="DocumentToDisplay.htm">
</frameset>
```

If this layout document had the name "fullwindow.htm," the code for the link would be:

```
<a href="fullwindow.htm">Click here to erase the frames
and see the document in the full window</a>
```

Clicking this link would cause the browser to first load the layout document with a single row, and then load DocumentToDisplay.htm into that row.

A more direct and elegant way, however, to get out of a frameset and have a linked document display in a full window is to set the link's target attribute to the special value "_top". The code is:

```
<a href="DocumentToDisplay.html" target="_top"> Click
here to erase the frames and see the document in the full
window </a>
```

The value "_top" refers to the "top" of the frameset, which is simply the browser window. The word "top" is used because the browser keeps track of the various framesets that are created by using a hierarchy. The browser window is at the top of the **frameset hierarchy**, and the first frameset to be defined in a layout document is the next level down. If there are any nested framesets within this first frameset, they are considered two levels down. (We will learn more about how this works when we combine frames with JavaScript in Chapter 17.)

Adding target="_top" to the <a> tag therefore tells the browser to display the linked document in the browser window without any frames.

Note: It's easy to forget the underscore character (_) in front of "top": it must be "_top" not "top".

QuickCheck Questions

1. Write the HTML code for a frameset that divides the browser window into two rows, the top one having a height of one-quarter of the window.
2. Write the HTML code that would name a frame "centerframe" and load a document named "TestPage.htm" into it.
3. What is the purpose of the target attribute?

Lab Exercise 6.3, "Layout Using Frames," may be done at this point.

Opening Multiple Windows

You may also have the browser display the document in a second browser window by using target="windowname" in the <a href> tag:

```
<a href="DocumentToDisplay.html" target="windowname"> Click
here to see the document displayed in a new window</a>
```

The name "windowname" is your choice. If a browser window with that name is not yet open, the browser will open a new window with that name and display the document in it. If the window already exists, the browser simply displays the document there. Note that the window name is an internal name for the browser's use only; the surfer never sees it.

Opening a new window is especially useful when you want to supply a link on your page to an outside website, but don't want the surfer to go there and forget all about your page. By opening up the new document in its own window, your page stays on the screen in the original window. (For now, we'll just open the window and let it appear wherever the browser puts it. Later, in Chapter 17, we'll learn how to specify its position and size using JavaScript.)

This feature is also useful if your website has an associated glossary. When the user clicks on a word or phrase to find out more information about it, the information appears in a new window, which may then be closed when the user has finished reading the information.

On the other hand, this new window feature has been overused by many websites, and some surfers do not take kindly to sites that open up new windows on their screen. Use it sparingly.

IMPORTANT

QuickCheck Questions

1. Write the HTML code for a link that, when clicked, would load the Microsoft home page (www.microsoft.com) in a new blank window.

Lab Exercise 6.4, "Implementing a Glossary Window," may be done at this point.

Key Terms

containing block	layout (frameset) document	normal flow
frame	nested frameset	
frameset hierarchy	nested table	

Code Summary

1. Layout with Style

Using a style definition to specify the absolute position of a web page element (an image, in this case):

```
<style type="text/css">
   img.eiffeltower {position:absolute; top:100; left:200}
</style>
```

Using a style definition to create three columns by specifying the absolute position of `<div>` elements:

```
div.col1 {position:absolute; left:0; top:290; bottom:500; width:200}
div.col2 {position:absolute; left:200; top:290; bottom:500; width:200}
div.col3 {position:absolute; left:400; top:60; bottom:500; width:200}
```

Adding equal padding around the inside of a `<div>` element (10 pixels worth, in this case):
```
div.col1 {position:absolute; left:0; top:340; bottom:500; width:200; padding:10}
```

Adding 5 pixels of padding at the top and bottom of a `<div>` element and 10 pixels of padding on the left and right sides:
```
div.col1 {position:absolute; left:0; top:340; bottom:500; width:200; padding:5 10}
```

2. The Return of Tables

Getting rid of the white space between table cells:
```
<table cellspacing="0"> . . . </table>
```

Setting the vertical alignment of a cell's contents (top, middle, or bottom):
```
<td valign="top">
```

Nesting a table inside the cell of another table (in this case the nested table has two rows with two cells in the top row and three in the bottom row):
```
<td width="400"> <!--A cell of the outer table-->
  <table width="400">
  <tr> <!--First row of the nested table-->
    <td> . . . </td>
    <td> . . . </td>
  </tr>
  <tr> <!--Second row of the nested table-->
    <td> . . . </td>
    <td> . . . </td>
    <td> . . . </td>
  </tr>
  </table>
</td>
```

3. Creating and Using Frames

Defining a frameset with rows (three, in this case):
```
<frameset rows="25%,45%,30%"> . . . </frameset>
```

Defining a frameset with columns (two, in this case):
```
<frameset cols="40%,60%"> . . . </frameset>
```

Defining a frameset using pixel measurements instead of window percentages (three columns, in this case, with the asterisk indicating that the middle column gets whatever's left after the 230 pixels of the other columns are subtracted from the window's width):
```
<frameset cols="80,*,150"> . . . </frameset>
```

Defining a nested frameset (two columns with two and three rows, respectively, in this case):
```
<frameset cols="50%,50%">
  <frameset rows="50%,50%">
  </frameset>
  <frameset rows="33%,33%,33%">
  </frameset>
</frameset>
```

Loading documents into a basic frameset (without giving names to the frames—see below):
```
<frameset cols="40%,60%">
  <frame src="WelcomePage.htm" />
  <frame src="ContactsList.htm" />
</frameset>
```

Loading documents into a nested frameset:

```
<frameset rows="25%,75%">
    <frame src="TableOfContents.htm" />
    <frameset cols="50%,50%">
        <frame src="Introduction.htm" />
        <frame src="ListOfPictures.htm" />
    </frameset>
</frameset>
```

Displaying a message to surfers who view a page without a frames-capable browser (the `<noframes>` element is placed inside a `<frameset>` element):

```
<noframes>This Web page uses frames and requires the use of a frames-capable browser,
such as Netscape Navigator 2.0 or above or Microsoft Internet Explorer 3.0 or
above.</noframes>
```

Giving identifying names to frames (for use with the `target` attribute in links—see next example; note that the `name` attribute is often used instead of or in addition to the `id` attribute, but the `name` attribute is now deprecated):

```
<frameset cols="50%,50%">
    <frame id="leftframe" src="ListOfLinks.htm" />
    <frame id="rightframe" src="IntroMessage.htm" />
</frameset>
```

Specifying that a linked document be displayed in a certain frame (`rightframe` in this case):

```
<a href="Doc1.htm" target="rightframe">Click here to view document 1</a>
```

Erasing a frameset and going back to a full-window display:

```
<a href="DocumentToDisplay.html" target="_top"> Click here to erase the frames and see
the document in the full window </a>
```

4. Opening Multiple Windows

Opening a new browser window (where you replace `"windowname"` with a name of your choice):

```
<a href="DocumentToDisplay.html" target="windowname">Click here to see the document
displayed in a new window</a>
```

When using the `position` property to specify the exact location of an element on a Web page, you must usually also specify the locations of all the other text and elements involved. (Solution: Use the `<div>` element to define the main sections of the layout.)

Designing a layout using `<div>` elements takes a certain amount of trial and error, and one useful technique is to give each division a different background color using the `background-color` property. The different colors make it easy to see the division boundaries.

When designing a layout using tables, make sure that you specify the cell widths and that they sum up to the width of the table.

Keep a frameset design clean and uncluttered by never using more than three or four frames.

The `<frame>` tag is an empty element, so don't forget the / at the end.

If you use frames, use the `<noframes>` element to display a warning message to surfers who are using a browser that can't display frames.

In order to experiment with different `<frameset>` combinations of rows and columns in older browsers, you must actually open the layout document again using the Open command in the File menu. Navigator 6's reload button and Explorer's refresh button, on the other hand, do reload or refresh the layout document as well as the frames.

If you forget to include the ending `</frameset>` tag of a `<frameset>` element, some versions of Navigator will display absolutely nothing when you load the frameset document.

To see the code for the layout document behind a web page with frames, select Page Source in Navigator's View menu or Source in Explorer's View menu. To see the source document behind the display in any given frame, right-click the mouse in the frame and then choose Frame source (in Navigator) or View source (in Explorer) from the pop-up menu that appears.

It's easy to forget the underscore character (_) in front of "top" when using it with the `target` attribute in an `<a>` tag: it must be "_top" not "top".

Don't overuse the capability to open up new browser windows.

Review Questions

1. Which element may we use to specify the location of the various sections in a magazine-style layout?
   a. `<div>`
   b. `<location>`
   c. `<position>`
   d. `<body>`
2. True or false: The key to creating a magazine-style layout is to keep all elements in their "normal flow" positions.
3. True or false: When specifying the top and bottom absolute position of an HTML element in the browser window, we specify the position for the top of the element measured in pixels from the top of the window and the position for the bottom of the element measured in pixels from the bottom of the window.
4. Which style property do you use to specify extra blank space around the inside of a `<div>` element so that the text displayed inside it does not run right up to the edges?
   a. `whitespace`
   b. `margin`
   c. `padding`
   d. `extraspace`
5. When designing a layout using a table, what attribute do you use in the `<table>` element to specify extra blank space around the inside edges of the table's cells?
   a. `padding`
   b. `cellpadding`
   c. `margin`
   d. `border`
6. To set the vertical alignment of text in a table cell, which attribute may we use?
   a. `valign`
   b. `vertical`
   c. `verticalalign`
   d. `verticaltext`
7. Which of the following `<frameset>` tags has the correct syntax to create a frameset with three columns of equal width?
   a. `<frameset columns="33,33,33">`
   b. `<frameset cols="1/3, 1/3, 1/3">`
   c. `<frameset columns="33%,33%,33%">`
   d. `<frameset cols="33%,33%,33%">`

8. True or false: The `<frame>` element is an empty element.

9. Which of the following elements do you use to display a message to a surfer who is trying to view your framed web page with a browser that cannot display frames?
   a. `<frame alt= "This page requires frames" />`
   b. `<frame noframes= "This page requires frames" />`
   c. `<noframes>This page requires frames</noframes>`
   d. `<plainpage>This page requires frames</plainpage>`

10. Which of the following elements creates a link that, when clicked, will load a document named paradeschedule.htm into a frame named `bottomframe`?
   a. `<a src="paradeschedule.htm" framename="bottomframe">Click here to see the parade schedule</a>`
   b. `<a href="paradeschedule.htm" framename="bottomframe">Click here to see the parade schedule</a>`
   c. `<a src="paradeschedule.htm" target="bottomframe">Click here to see the parade schedule</a>`
   d. `<a href="paradeschedule.htm" target="bottomframe">Click here to see the parade schedule</a>`

Exercises

1. Briefly define and/or explain the following terms: normal flow, nested table, frameset hierarchy.

2. Write the code for an HTML source document that would display an image contained in the file mydog.jpeg at a position 50 pixels down from the top of the browser window and 300 pixels in from the left.

3. Write the HTML code that would create a `<div>` element style class named `tableofcontents` to define a rectangular region on the web page that starts 0 pixels down from the top and 0 pixels in from the left, with a width of 75 pixels and a height of 150 pixels. Also write the line of HTML code that would display the text "Table of Contents" as a header 3 in this `<div>` element.

4. Write the HTML code that would use a `<div>` element style class named `centerstage` to define a rectangular region on the web page that starts 175 pixels down from the top and 100 pixels in from the left, with a width of 200 pixels and a height of 125 pixels. Put 5 pixels of padding at the top and bottom and 3 pixels of padding on the left and right. Also write the line of HTML code that would display the text "Pretty spectacular" in strongly emphasized text in this `<div>` element.

5. Write the HTML code for a `<table>` element that creates a layout with two columns, the left one having a width of 150 pixels and the right one having a width of 350 pixels. The left column should have text in a header 2 element that says "Presidential Portraits," aligned at the top of the column. The right column should display an image in a file named abelincoln.jpg.

6. Write the HTML code for a `<table>` element that creates a layout with two rows, the top one having a height of 350 pixels and the bottom one having a height of 75 pixels. The width of the table should be 600 pixels. The top row should also be divided into three equal columns. Display sample text in each part of the layout, such as "This is the top right section," "This is the top middle section," etc. The sample text should be aligned at the top of each section, and the table should have no border and no extra space between the cells.

7. Repeat Exercise 5, but this time use frames instead of a table. Load a document named presidents.htm into the left frame and the abelincoln.jpg file into the right frame. Make the left frame 40 percent of the window and the right frame 60 percent of the window.

8. Write the HTML code for a frameset document that divides the browser window into four frames: a left column with a width of one-third of the window and a right column with a width of two-thirds of the window, with the right column divided into three frames. The first frame in the right column should have a height of one-fourth of the window, the second frame should have a height of one-half

the window, and the third frame should have a height of one-fourth of the window. Load documents named Doc1.htm, Doc2.htm, Doc3.htm, and Doc4.htm into each of the four frames, respectively. (You don't have to write the code for these documents; assume they already exist.)

9. Write the HTML code to create a link that will display a document named LatestNews.htm in a frame named "newsframe." The text for the link should be: "Click here for the latest news."

10. Write the HTML code to create a link that will display a document named LatestNews.htm in a new window named "newswindow." The text for the link should be: "Click here for the latest news."

1. Identify the errors in the following code and then sketch on paper how the browser would display it once the errors were corrected. (It should also help you realize why it's a good idea to indent your code, even though the browser doesn't care.)

   - Frameset document

   ```
   <html>
   <head>
       <title>Linking Between Frames</title>
   </head>
   <frameset rows="25%,75%">
   <frameset cols="50%,50%">
   <frame src="TableOfContents.htm">id="topframe"</frame>
   <frame src="Introduction.htm">id="bottomleftframe"</frame>
   <frame src="ListOfPictures.htm">id="bottomrightframe"</frame>
   </frameset>
   </html>
   ```

   - TableOfContents.htm document

   ```
   <html>
   <head></head>
   <body>
   <p>Table of Contents:</p>
   <p><a href="Doc1.htm" target="rightframe">Click here to view document 1 in the bottom
       right frame</a></p>
   <p><a href="Doc2.htm" target="leftframe">Click here to view document 2 in the bottom left
       frame</a></p>
   </body>
   </html>
   ```

Note: Most of the exercises above may also be done as lab exercises.

Note also: Any one of Exercises 1, 2, and 3 could fill a two-hour lab period.

Exercise 6.1: Layout Using Styles

Many professional and commercial websites use a layout similar to the one shown below in Figure 6.19. On the left side it has a column that contains a navigation bar: a list of links that take the user to other pages or places within the website. The navigation bar thus serves as a table of contents for the site. The top right section often displays the heading for the site (and/or an advertisement). And the large bottom right section contains the main text and images for the page (and sometimes is also divided into two columns or some other more complex layout).

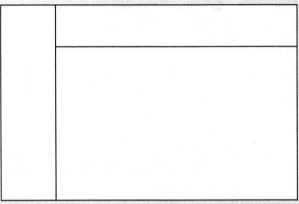

FIGURE 6.19.   Navigation bar layout for Lab Exercise 6.1

This layout then serves as the template for all the pages in the site. That is, every page has the navigation bar on the left and the heading section at the top. This type of design gives the surfer a good sense of where he/she is at all times and prevents surfers from getting lost among the links.

❑ Using styles, create a three-page (or more) website that uses a template like that shown above, or something similar. (For example, some sites put the navigation bar on the top.) Each page in the site should display the navigation bar. This means that every page will have the same style definitions in the <head> element, or you may define the styles in an external .css file and then reference it at the top of each page. The navigation bar should display links to each page in the site.

If you like, you may use the files that you created in Lab Exercise 5.2 for your multiple-page site. Or, design a template and test it with some skeleton files (files that just have a line or two of text) for the web project site you intend to create.

Exercise 6.2: Layout Using Tables

❑ Create another version of the website layout referred to in Lab Exercise 6.1, but this time use tables to specify the layout.

Exercise 6.3: Layout Using Frames

❑ Create another version of the website layout referred to in Lab Exercise 6.1, but this time use frames to specify the layout, as outlined below.

❑ As a start, create two simple HTML source documents named Doc1.htm and Doc2.htm. In the <body> element of each, put one or two brief sentences, e.g., "This is document 1". Also create another simple HTML source document, named PictureDoc.htm, that uses an <img> tag for an in-line image. (Use an image that you used in one of the Chapter 5 Lab Exercises, or find another one on the Web.)

❑ Create an HTML layout document that defines three frames according to the diagram in Exercise 6.1. Use <frame> tags to load Doc1.htm into the top right frame and Doc2.htm into the bottom right frame. Use the tags also to give the top right frame the name "topright" and the bottom right frame the name "bottomright." Then create one more HTML source document, named TOC.html, that will be a table of contents for your framed web page. It should use <a> tags with target attributes to offer the following hyperlink entries:

   "Click here to see document 1 in the top right frame"
   "Click here to see document 2 in the top right frame"

"Click here to see document 1 in the bottom right frame"
"Click here to see document 2 in the bottom right frame"
"Click here to see a picture in the bottom right frame"
(Use the PictureDoc.htm document for the last link.)

❑ If you still have time after you get the basic frame layout working, replace the skeleton files (Doc1.htm and Doc2.htm) with the files you created in Lab Exercise 5.2 for the multiple-page site, and revise the table of contents document accordingly.

Exercise 6.4: Implementing a Glossary Window

❑ Create a source document that contains the paragraph of text below (taken from the beginning of Chapter 2). Then, for each of the underlined terms, implement a link that, when clicked, displays the definition of that term in a new window.

In Chapter 1 we learned about the <u>client-server model</u> and how a web page works. To review: When you connect to a web page by entering its <u>URL</u> into the browser (or by clicking on a <u>hyperlink</u>), the browser instructs your computer to send a message out over the Internet to the computer specified by that URL and request that it send back a certain document. This document is the <u>HTML source document</u> for that Web page. The source document contains HTML "<u>source code</u>" that describes the content and layout of the page. When your computer receives the source document in reply, your browser software interprets the HTML code in the source document and displays the resulting Web page—its text, graphics, links, etc.—according to the HTML instructions.

Sitebuilding Exercise 1 may be done at this point (see Appendix A).

7

Introduction to Programming and JavaScript

LEARNING OBJECTIVES

1. Understand the nature and terminology of programming and programming languages, including the hierarchy of languages, object-oriented programming, algorithms, and control structures.

2. Understand the purpose of a scripting language and the differences between Java and JavaScript.

3. Learn how to insert JavaScript code into an HTML source document using the <script> element.

4. Learn about syntax errors and logic errors and how Explorer and Navigator report errors.

5. Learn how and why to annotate JavaScript code using single-line and multiple-line comments, and how to use HTML comments to hide JavaScript code from non-JavaScript browsers.

6. Understand the concept of events, and learn how to create click buttons and HTML links that use click, mouseover, and/or mouseout events.

Introduction to Programming

The brains of a computer is its microprocessor or central processing unit (CPU). The CPU is a computer chip that has millions or even billions of tiny transistors (electronic switches) and other circuit elements etched into it. This circuitry is designed to enable the CPU to process, calculate, and/or manipulate data and information. (Some computers have multiple CPUs wired together for extra computing power, but most personal computers have just one.)

177

A key part of the CPU's circuitry is a set of built-in instructions. This set of machine instructions is called the CPU's instruction set and may be likened to keys on a calculator. Just as a calculator has special keys to perform operations like addition, subtraction, etc., so too the CPU has special instructions to carry out those basic operations, plus many others. Most CPUs have several hundred or more instructions in their instruction set.

At its most basic, a computer program is simply a to-do list of these machine instructions for the CPU to carry out (or **execute**), one at a time and in the given order. Consider the example of a word processing program that allows the computer user to create text-based documents like reports or letters. The various instructions that constitute the word processing program are stored in a file on a hard disk or CD-ROM. When you open or **run** the word processing program, its instructions are copied into the computer's memory (RAM). The CPU then accesses and executes the instructions in the proper order as the user types and formats his or her text. (Because computers operate much faster than we do, in most cases the CPU actually spends most of its time waiting for the user to hit a key or make a menu choice so that it knows what instructions to execute next.)

The job of a computer programmer, therefore, is to write a to-do list of instructions for the CPU, choosing the appropriate instructions and putting them in the proper order to accomplish the desired result.

A Hierarchy of Languages

The CPU's built-in set of machine instructions is also known as its **machine language** or **machine code**. The machine language instructions are written in the form of binary numbers, consisting of 1s and 0s (which are ultimately represented by the on-off states of the CPU's transistors). For example, the following sequence of 1s and 0s represents an instruction in Intel's Pentium machine language:

1000111011011000

(If you really want to know, it tells the CPU to transfer the particular number stored in its AX register to its DS or data segment register.)

It's possible for a person to create a program using these machine language instructions, but as you might guess from the above example, it's not easy. A machine language, therefore, usually has a corresponding **assembly language** that puts each machine language instruction into a form that's more amenable to humans. Assembly language instructions take forms like:

```
ADD AX, 14  (i.e., add 14 to the contents of register AX)
MOV BX, 6   (i.e., move 6 into register BX, replacing whatever might be
             there)
CMP AX, BX  (i.e., compare the contents of registers AX and BX)
```

Although assembly language makes it easier to write computer programs, because we don't have to deal directly with the 1s and 0s of the machine language, it's still no picnic. Most computer programmers therefore use **high-level languages** to write programs. High-level in this sense means that the language's structure and syntax is closer to English than low-level assembly language, which corresponds closely to the very low-level machine language.

Since the 1950s, many different high-level languages have been developed. Some of the best-known include FORTRAN, BASIC, COBOL, Pascal, C++, and Java. Different languages have different purposes and strengths. For example, FORTRAN (short for Formula Translator) is a favorite language among scientists and engineers; COBOL (COmmon Business Oriented Language) was designed to make it easy to write data processing applications for business; BASIC and Pascal are good first languages to learn programming; C++ is a powerful general-purpose language and, with its relative C, perhaps the most widely used language today; and Java is a relatively new language designed especially for networked computing and the world of the Internet.

A typical instruction or command in a high-level language might look something like:

```
if (theLight == "red") {
   theBrake = "on"
}
```

Even though the syntax of this if-then statement might look strange to a non-programmer (the curly braces, the double-equal sign) its general meaning may be surmised: "if the light is red, then the brake is on," or perhaps, "if the light is red, then put the brake on." To write the equivalent in assembly language, however, might take five or ten lines of instructions that would be difficult for even an experienced programmer to decipher at first glance.

Interpreters and Compilers

Once a program has been created using a high-level language, it must then be translated into terms that the CPU can understand—machine language—so that the CPU can perform them. The translation process is done by another computer program, especially written for the task. This translator program takes the source code of the high-level language program (the instructions that the programmer wrote) and turns it into machine code (also called object code) that the CPU understands.

There are two basic ways that this translator program can work. The first method takes the programmer's source code and translates one line at a time into machine code and then executes the resulting machine code before moving on to the next high-level instruction to translate and execute. (As mentioned, one line or instruction of source code usually ends up being several machine code instructions.) This method is called interpreting the source code, and the special program that performs this process is an **interpreter**. For example, a software application that allows you to program in the BASIC language often contains a BASIC interpreter to run the program (translate and execute the program's instructions) once you're finished writing it.

The second method is known as compiling the source code, and the special program that does it is a **compiler**. A compiler takes the high-level source code of a program and translates all of it into machine language before executing or running any of it.

As an analogy, consider that you have written a speech in English but are then asked to give it in another language, say Chinese. (We'll assume you are fluent in both.) You have two options. Option 1 would be to translate it completely into Chinese first and then give the speech by reading from the Chinese text. Option 2 would be more daring. You would take the English version up to the podium and silently read the English while speaking it in Chinese. In other words, you would translate it line by line on the fly while talking. The first way corresponds to how a compiler translates source code (do all the translating before running the program); the second way corresponds to how an interpreter program does it (translate a line, then execute it, then translate another, and execute it, and so on and so forth).

Which way is best? It depends on the situation. Using an interpreter makes it easy to locate errors in the program, because it translates and executes one line at a time. If a line has an error in it, it will usually show up immediately and the program will stop running at that point. Interpreters are therefore excellent for introductory programming. They also find other uses, as we'll see when we talk more specifically about JavaScript. The main disadvantage of the interpreter's line-by-line translation process is that it may result in less efficient and slower programs. Going back to the English-Chinese analogy, if you attempted to translate from English to Chinese sentence by sentence on the fly, the result probably wouldn't be as eloquent or precise as you might hope.

A compiler, on the other hand, results in programs that execute faster, because by translating the whole program into a file before running it, the compiler can optimize how the machine code is organized. Again, in the English–Chinese example, if you sit down and translate your speech from English to Chinese in written form and then execute it by reading the Chinese text, the end result will be more eloquent and precise. The main drawback to using a compiler is that, because it often rearranges the source code for optimum results, it sometimes makes errors harder to track down. (Note: Some progamming languages are available in both compiled and interpreted versions; others, in just one or the other.)

Structured vs. Object-Oriented Programming

In addition to labeling languages as high-level vs. low-level and compiled vs. interpreted, there is one other significant way to categorize programming languages. In the 1960s some computer scientists became concerned that the early high-level programming languages were encouraging sloppy programming habits. They therefore started a movement to develop what became known as **structured programming** languages.

The difference between an unstructured language and a structured one is like the difference between writing an essay as one long rambling paragraph and writing an essay with paragraphs and a logical structure. Structured languages are designed so that programs may be built up out of smaller modules or sub-programs (also called subroutines, functions, and/or procedures). This modularization makes it easier to debug programs and/or modify them later, if need be.

Although structured programming resulted in better and more robust programs, computer scientists soon found that even a structured programming approach had problems dealing with very complex programs, where large numbers of programmers were involved. It was hard to keep track of who was doing what and how one part of the program affected another part. Out of these and other concerns a radically new programming paradigm emerged, called **object-oriented programming (OOP)**. In this approach, programmers build programs out of self-contained software objects. These objects in general are composed of two things: data and code (or, information and instructions). Prominent OOP languages include C++ and Java.

We will delve into some of the details of OOP a little later. For now, a simple example will suffice to give an idea of how it works. Anyone who has surfed the World Wide Web has at one time or another clicked on a button—for instance, to submit a search request. The button is itself a software object. It contains certain data or information about itself, such as its name or label (i.e., the text that is displayed on it), its color, its size, its shape, its location on the screen, and so on. It also contains certain instructions (programming code) that tell the computer what to do when the user clicks the button.

Algorithms and Control Structures

No matter what programming paradigm and programming language are being used, software development is not a simple task. Any reasonably complex program requires a lot of design work before a programmer sits down to actually write some code. Just as a home builder wouldn't start building a house by grabbing a hammer and some wood and nails without working out the blueprints and schematics, a programmer must first work out the outline and structure of a program.

An important early step is the development of an **algorithm** that outlines the logical flow of the program. An algorithm is like a recipe that is broken down into a number of steps and decisions for getting from point A to point B.

In order to see the nature of an algorithm, consider the case of an automated car (controlled by a computer program) that is approaching a traffic signal. The algorithm or recipe for this part of the program might be something like:

1. Check the traffic light.

2. If the light is green, continue on.

3. Otherwise, if it's red, activate the brakes and stop.

4. Otherwise (if it's not green or red), if it's yellow, make a decision about whether to stop or not based on speed, distance, and road conditions.

The Four Basic Control Structures

Besides illustrating the nature of an algorithm the above example also illustrates one of the four basic flow control structures that programs use: the if/then or conditional control structure. As the name control structure implies, these structures control and guide the flow of the program in determining what instructions to do and when to do them.

Structure 1: Sequence

The simplest **control structure** is **sequence**: the execution of a sequence of instructions in the order listed (Figure 7.1).

```
1. Do this
2. Do that
3. Do something else
4. Do that again
5. Do another thing
```

FIGURE 7.1.
A sequence of instructions

Structure 2: Conditional or if/then

The second control structure is the above-mentioned if/then or **conditional** or **branching** structure. This structure outlines a branch in the flow of the program. It's like a fork in the road. Depending on the condition of the situation, the program might follow one branch of instructions or the other branch, but not both. The traffic signal example above actually has three branches—one set of instructions in case the light is green, another set in case the light is red, and a third set in case the light is yellow. (And it should have other branches to take care of the cases when the light is blinking red or when it's not working.) Figure 7.2 outlines the conditional structure for three branches. Note that the branches can each have a different number of instructions and that each branch, at the end, returns to the main flow of program instructions, which continue on.

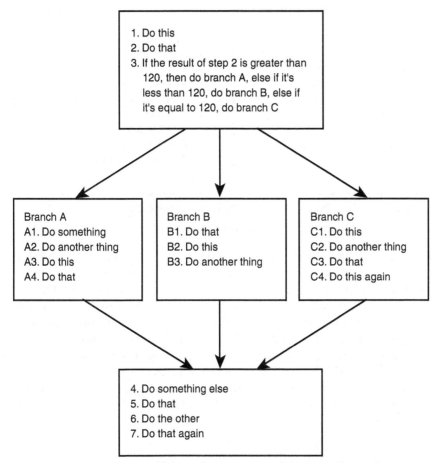

FIGURE 7.2.   The conditional structure with three branches

Structure 3: Looping

The third control structure is **looping** or **iteration**, which is where a program repeats the same series of instructions over and over until a certain condition is satisfied. A real-world example from the kitchen would be a recipe that directed the cook to add salt "to taste." The cook would add some salt, taste it, add some more salt, taste it, add some more salt, taste it, until the flavor was just right. We can also have a loop structure where the same series of instructions is repeated for a set number of times, after which the program moves on. Figure 7.3(a) diagrams this structure, and Figure 7.3(b) diagrams a loop that keeps repeating until a condition is satisfied.

Structure 4: Transfer

The fourth control structure is known as **transfer** or **go to** or **jump**. Instead of having a program execute its instructions in sequence, the programmer may design the program to use the transfer control structure to jump from

```
1. Do this
2. Do that
3. Do another thing
4. Do something else
5. Repeat steps 2-4 twelve times,
   then continue on
6. Do that
7. Do yet another thing


a.
```

```
1. Do this
2. Do that
3. Do another thing
4. Do something else
5. Repeat steps 2-4 until the result
   of Step 4 is less than 57, then
   continue on
6. Do that
7. Do yet another thing


b.
```

FIGURE 7.3.   Two examples of loop structures

one place in the program to another place, skipping the intervening instructions (Figure 7.4). You might think that this type of control structure would be very powerful and convenient, and you would be right. But it also leads to a serious malady known as spaghetti code, in which the logical flow of the program becomes so tangled from excessive jumping that even its own programmer may have trouble figuring out what's going on. Structured programming was developed, in part, to provide an antidote to spaghetti code. (Structured programming languages still include the transfer structure, but put strict limits on its use. When a program needs to execute a subprogram, or module of code, it temporarily transfers control to that module.)

```
 1. Do this
 2. Do that
 3. Jump to line 6 and continue from
    there
 4. Do something else
 5. Jump to line 37 and continue
    from there
 6. Do that
 7. Do yet another thing
 8. Jump to line 4 and continue from
    there
 9. Do this
10. etc.
```

FIGURE 7.4.   The transfer control structure

Once a rough algorithm has been created, programmers often use **flowchart** or **pseudocode** methods to refine it. A flowchart maps out the logical paths of the program using graphical symbols, making it easy to visualize the flow of the program. Figure 7.5 shows a simple example for a stoplight with just two colors, red and green.

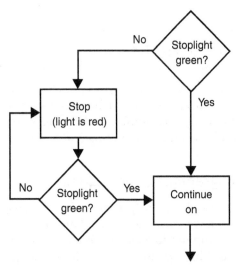

FIGURE 7.5. Flowchart for a red light, green light situation

Pseudocode, in contrast, is the method of writing an algorithm using half-programming-language and half-English (or other natural human language). We can demonstrate pseudocode using our traffic light example. One line of its algorithm is, "If it's red, activate the brakes and stop." In pseudocode, this might be written:

```
if the light is red then
   put the brake on
```

The final fully coded version might then be:

```
if (theLight == "red") {
   theBrake = "on"
}
```

We can see that the pseudocode version allows the programmer to get close to the final version without having to worry immediately about all the niceties of syntax—of making sure that all the programming i's are dotted and t's are crossed.

QuickCheck Questions

1. What are the three main levels in the hierarchy of languages?
2. What is the difference between an interpreter and a compiler?
3. What is an algorithm?

What is JavaScript?

In the first section we noted several ways to classify programming languages: interpreted vs. compiled languages, machine vs. assembly vs. high-level languages, and structured vs. object-oriented languages. Yet another way is to make the distinction between programming and **scripting languages**.

Scripting vs. Programming Languages

Sometimes when we use the term "programming" language, we mean it as a generic reference to any and all computer languages that allow us to write instructions for the computer to execute. Other times, however, it is used in a more restrictive sense that opposes it to "scripting language." Simply put, a programming language may be used to create stand-alone software programs, whereas a scripting language is usually built into a specific application, like a database or spreadsheet, and cannot be used outside that application. A scripting language allows the user of the software to automate certain tasks and increase the usefulness of that software using **scripts**: series of instructions for the computer to execute. A script is essentially a mini-program that runs within the confines of the application.

In 1995 Netscape decided to include a scripting language named JavaScript in its Navigator browser. Its primary motivation in doing so was to make it easier for a web page to check or validate information that a surfer had entered into a text box on the page. For example, JavaScript could be used to see if the entry was a valid number or if it was spelled correctly. But web designers soon found many other innovative uses for JavaScript, creating such things as image rollovers, online quizzes, and web page calculators. In general, they found that JavaScript was a great tool for adding interactivity to web pages. Web pages that responded in different ways depending on what the surfer did or didn't do, could now easily be designed.

The basic idea of JavaScript is simple: The web page designer adds JavaScript instructions directly into an HTML source document. On the browser side of things, a JavaScript interpreter is built into most current browsers, including Navigator and Explorer (although Microsoft officially calls its Explorer version of JavaScript "JScript"). When the source document is loaded by a browser, the browser translates the HTML code as usual, from top to bottom. If it also finds JavaScript instructions along the way, the built-in JavaScript interpreter translates and executes them line by line.

In the rest of this book we will learn how JavaScript works and explore how we may use it to create rollovers, quizzes, calculators, and much more.

Before we learn our first JavaScript, it should be noted that, despite the name, JavaScript is not Java, nor is it even officially related to Java. The 1990s saw a lot of attention given to Java, which was a new object-oriented programming language that was developed at Sun Microsystems. The attention came about because Java was optimized for use in a networked environment like the Internet, and the Internet was the hottest thing going.

When what became known as JavaScript was first being developed by Netscape, it was called LiveScript. But soon thereafter the Java hype began building, so Netscape quickly jumped on that bandwagon (with the blessing of Sun Microsystems) by renaming its browser scripting language "JavaScript." So, despite the name, JavaScript is not Java. Nor is it a stripped-down version of Java. Although it's easier to learn than Java, it has many complexities in its own right (some of which we will demystify). On the other hand, JavaScript is similar to Java in much of its structure and syntax. Learning to use JavaScript can help you later in learning Java, if you so desire.

Just as HTML has an official standard as defined and promoted by the World Wide Web Consortium, so too does JavaScript, although it's not the W3C that's involved. Instead, Netscape and Sun submitted JavaScript to a standards organization named ECMA, requesting that it establish an official standard. ECMA completed the first edition of what it called "ECMAScript" in 1997. (ECMA formerly stood for the European Computer Manufacturers Association, but now it is just named ECMA and pronounced "Eck-ma.") As of early 2002, the current ECMAScript edition is the third, established in 1999. The official specifications for ECMAScript, or "ECMA Standard #262," may be found on ECMA's website at www.ecma.ch. (ECMA headquarters are located in Switzerland, thus the top-level domain "ch," for "Confederation Helvetica.") Netscape also lists HTML and JavaScript resources at developer.netscape.com, while Microsoft provides a user's guide and language reference to JScript at msdn.microsoft.com. Appendix I lists other online resources.

Instructions/Code/Statements/Commands

As noted, a program or script consists of a series of **instructions**, or **code**, that the computer executes. Instructions may also be called **commands** or **statements**. They bear some similarity to sentences or phrases in a natural language like English. A simple example of a JavaScript instruction is the `alert` command, which allows the programmer to display an **alert box** on the screen with a message inside. The basic syntax is:

```
alert("Hello, world!")
```

The message displayed in the alert box will be whatever is between the quotation marks, or `Hello, world!` in this case, as shown in Figure 7.6. (Note that the quotation marks are not displayed, because they are part of the syntax of the alert command.)

FIGURE 7.6.   An alert box

(Instead of "Microsoft Internet Explorer" in the title bar, Navigator shows an alert box with the title "Alert" in version 6 and "[JavaScript Application]" in previous versions.)

Unlike HTML, but like XHTML, JavaScript is a **case-sensitive** language, which means that you have to spell its instructions correctly, including capitalization. So it must be `alert("Hello, world!")`, not `Alert("Hello, world!")`.

To use this JavaScript command, we would insert it into the HTML source document at an appropriate place. Then when the document was loaded by the browser, it would see the JavaScript command and execute it, displaying the alert box. But a JavaScript command can't just be inserted anywhere in the source document. HTML is not JavaScript and vice versa, so we have to indicate to the browser when we are using HTML in the source document and when we are using JavaScript, otherwise it won't be able to handle it. The next section shows how we distinguish JavaScript instructions from HTML instructions using the `<script>` element.

QuickCheck Questions

1. How does a scripting language differ from a general-purpose programming language?
2. Write the JavaScript command that will display an alert box with the message "Good to see you! Come back again."
3. What does it mean to say the JavaScript is a case-sensitive language? Is HTML case sensitive?

The <script> Element

In order to use the `alert` command or any JavaScript command on a web page, we must embed it in a <script> element:

```
<script>
  alert("Hello, world!")
</script>
```

Because it is possible to use other scripting languages in an HTML document, you usually specify JavaScript as the scripting language using the `type` attribute in the <script> tag:

```
<script type="text/javascript">
  alert("Hello, world!")
  [Additional JavaScript instructions would go here . . . ]
</script>
```

The `type` attribute specifies the type of content in the <script> element, with the "text" part of "text/javascript" indicating to the browser that the code is written in regular text characters. Although most recent browsers will assume that the script is written in JavaScript if you don't specify it, XHTML now requires the use of the `type` attribute in the <script> element, and Netscape 6+ (version 6 and beyond) and Explorer 5+ support it. In the past, many JavaScript programmers have used the `language` attribute instead of the `type` attribute to specify the language being used. For example:

```
<script language="JavaScript">
  [JavaScript instructions would go here . . . ]
</script>
```

The `language` attribute has the advantage that it allows the programmer to designate the version of JavaScript being used, such as `language="JavaScript1.2"`. (The most recent version is 1.5.) This becomes important if you are using a JavaScript feature that is not supported in some versions of the language. You only rarely need to do this in practice, however, because the newer browsers support all the features in the core of JavaScript (the things we will be learning). You may include both the `type` and `language` attributes in the <script> element, if desired or needed. In our examples, we will stick simply to the `type` attribute, mainly because the W3C has deprecated the `language` attribute.

The other primary scripting language for browsers is VBScript, which is based on Microsoft's Visual Basic programming language. It only works in Internet Explorer, however.

Note well that the <script> and </script> tags are part of IITML. But everything inside the <script> element must be a valid JavaScript statement or command. If you try to put an HTML tag inside the <script> element, you will usually get an error message from the browser when it tries to load the page, because it is expecting JavaScript commands there, not HTML commands.

Figure 7.7 shows a simple example of how we would use JavaScript's `alert` command in a complete HTML source document and the progression of the browser's display.

When the browser loads this source document, it will display the bold text, "This is a simple JavaScript test . . .", and then it will encounter the `<script>` element and the first instruction inside it—the first `alert` command. So it puts up the first alert box with "Hello, world!", as shown in the top Browser Display window of the figure. When the user clicks the OK button in the alert box, the first box disappears and a second alert box appears with the "Anybody out there?" message, as in the middle Browser Display. Finally, when the user clicks the OK button in the second alert box, the script is over and the browser moves on to loading and displaying the rest of the HTML document (the `<br />` tag and the bold "All done with the alert boxes" line). (Note: In some versions of Navigator, the alert boxes will appear before any text is displayed in the window.)

It's possible to have more than one `<script>` element, and they may be placed anywhere in the `<body>` or `<head>` elements, either before other HTML code, after other HTML code, or between HTML code. You would use multiple `<script>` elements when you want the browser to execute some JavaScript code (contained within one `<script>` element), then execute some regular HTML code, and then execute some more JavaScript code (contained in a second `<script>` element that followed the HTML code). Remember that the browser uses a "top-down" approach in translating and displaying HTML and JavaScript code. It starts at the top of the `<head>` element and proceeds down it, executing each line of HTML or JavaScript code in order.

As an example, we could add another `<script>` element after the "All done with the alert boxes" line in the Figure 7.7 code:

```
<body>
<strong>This is a simple JavaScript test . . . </strong>
<script type="text/javascript">
  alert("Hello, world!")
  alert("Anybody out there?")
</script>
<br /><strong>All done with the alert boxes.</strong>
<script type="text/javascript">
  alert("Oops, here's another one")
</script>
</body>
```

The `<script>` element may also be used to access JavaScript code that is stored in another file, known as an "external" file. This external file is a text file that has been saved with a .js extension, such as "testCode.js". The file must

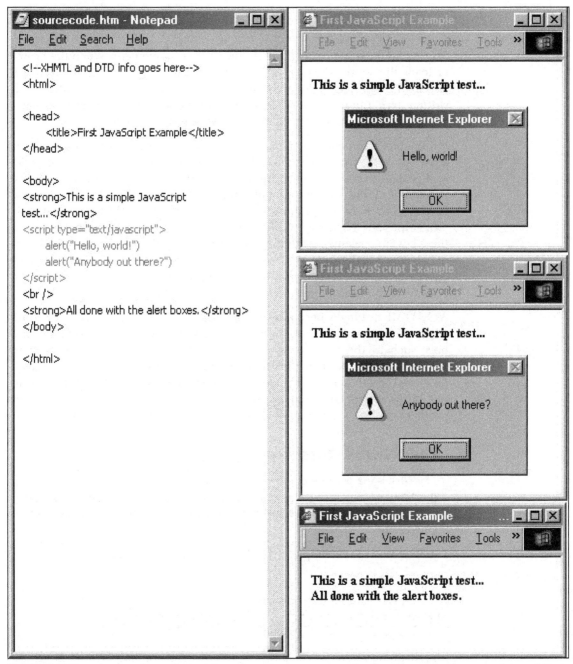

FIGURE 7.7. A simple script using the alert command, showing the progression of the browser display (top to bottom)

contain only JavaScript code—no HTML elements (including <script>). To use the code stored in an external file, you simply add a src attribute to the source document's <script> element:

```
<script src="testCode.js" type="text/javascript">
</script>
```

There's no need to put anything in the <script> element. When the browser loads the source document that contains this <script> element, it will also load the JavaScript code in the testCode.js file. (As the src attribute is written here, the testCode.js file must be in the same directory as the source document. If it isn't, then a fuller pathname must be supplied.)

Putting JavaScript code in an external file is particularly useful when you have a website with multiple pages, all of which use the same JavaScript code. Rather than typing (or copying and pasting) the code into all the documents, you can put it into one external file and use the <script> element to access it. Some JavaScript programmers also like to use external files to hide their JavaScript code from surfers. The browser's "View Source" option will show the <script> element with the src attribute and the reference to the external file, but not the code itself. A savvy surfer, however, can still see the code by checking the browser's cache, because that is where the browser stores the code from the external file.

As XHTML gradually becomes the standard, some JavaScript scripts will actually require the use of external files. The reason is that certain JavaScript symbols, such as the less-than symbol (<), are reserved for other uses in XHTML. So a browser that is strictly compatible with XHTML will not read a JavaScript less-than symbol correctly. The only way around this problem is to put any JavaScript code that uses the < symbol in an external file. (The other problem symbols are &, - -, and]]>, some of which we will encounter later.)

QuickCheck Questions

1. What is the purpose of the <script> element?
2. Write the code for a <script> element that displays two alert boxes, the first with the message "Hello!" and the second with the message "Good-bye!".

Lab Exercise 7.1, "A Simple Script," may be done at this point.

The Entomology of Programming

The first time you try to run any program or script you have written, there is a good chance that it will not work, because it will have one or more errors or "bugs" in it. Typically, the process of debugging software occupies 50 percent or more of a programmer's time. Even if you prepare the code beforehand using pencil and paper (an excellent idea, by the way), you will find that inevitably you have made some mistakes. The mistakes will come in two basic types: **syntax errors** and **logic errors**.

Syntax Errors and Logic Errors

A syntax error occurs when you misspell something or accidentally omit a required element of an instruction, such as leaving off the second quotation mark of a pair. Each of the three lines of JavaScript code below has a syntax error. Can you spot them? (Answers below.)

```
<script type="text/javascript">
  alert("My first JavaScript.)
  Alert("Too exciting for words.")
  alert["This is big time stuff."]
</script>
```

Answers: The first line is missing the second quotation mark. In the second line, it should be alert, not Alert. And the square brackets in the third line should be parentheses.

From these seemingly trivial yet show-stopping examples, it should be evident that programming languages are very picky about syntax. They need their instructions to be written in a certain manner and form, and the programmer must simply conform.

A logic error occurs when the programming code is written with the correct syntax, but its logic is wrong so that the code will not do what the programmer intended it to do. A programmer might, for example, intend for a message to be displayed whenever a certain value was greater than 50 *and* less than 100. But the actual program code might be written such that the message appears whenever the value was less than 100, period, so that a value of 40 would trigger the message. Logic errors are also known as **runtime errors**, because they show up when you run the program.

Logic errors can be very difficult to track down. The best cure is prevention, by carefully thinking through the program's logic and creating a well-designed algorithm before starting to write the actual code.

Some people like to point out yet a third type of error called **management errors**, which may occur even though your code is written correctly. Consider, for example, what may happen when you are revising and improving a website, perhaps adding some JavaScript features. You may have reached a point where you have eradicated all the syntax and logic errors and everything works perfectly in the new source document. The final step is to upload it to the web server, replacing the old version. But in the excitement (and sometimes haste) of doing so, it's not uncommon to upload the wrong file, such as a slightly outdated, still buggy version of the source document. It always pays to slow down and double-check everything.

Browser Error Messages

In the case of syntax errors, the browser will display an error message when it encounters the error. Figure 7.8 shows a typical error message from Internet

Explorer. (We generated it by misspelling the `alert` command as `Alert` instead of `alert` in a source document named alertbox.htm.) The bottom half of the box lists the location of the error by line number and character number within that line. (If you don't see the bottom half of the box, click on the Show Details button.) The browser counts the lines starting from the top of the source document. Blank lines are included in the count. Don't take the line number too literally. Sometimes the error is on the line above or below the line number listed. And the character number is even less exact.

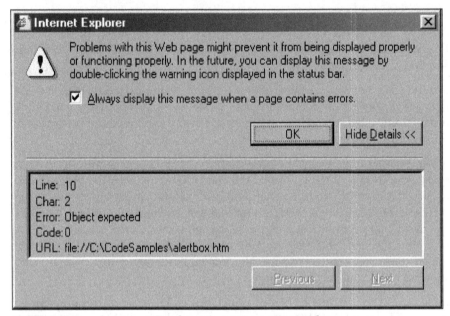

FIGURE 7.8.   **Internet Explorer's error message box**

If the error is way down in the source document so that the line number is large, it's usually not worth it to try to count the lines exactly to find the location of the error. But it does give you a general idea of the location. (Some text editors and specialized HTML editors, such as TextPad and HomeSite on Windows PCs, have a useful line numbering option that displays the number of each line of code on the left margin.)

The error message itself may also be more or less useful. In Figure 7.8 it's the mysterious (yet common) "Object expected." This means that the browser expected to find an object name (or other valid JavaScript name) but found something else. Often the problem is a simple misspelling, as in our example. When the browser encountered the command `Alert("Hello, world!")`, it didn't recognize `Alert` as a legitimate name.

You should also be aware that when Explorer encounters an error, it skips the incorrect line of code and all the rest of the code within that `<script>` element, and then continues displaying the rest of the source document. This means that if there are multiple errors in that `<script>` element, only the first will be flagged. Of course, once you have fixed the first error, reloading the source document in the browser will flag the next error, if it exists. If there are multiple `<script>` elements in the document, each with at least one error, then Explorer will display multiple error messages, one for each "first error" it finds in the individual `<script>` elements.

Early versions of Explorer displayed the error message box automatically. But because the appearance of the error message was disconcerting, not to mention incomprehensible, to the typical surfer, recent versions of Explorer only display error messages if the surfer has enabled them. To enable them, choose Internet Options under the Tools menu, click on the Advanced tab, and then select the checkbox labeled Display a notification about every script error. You may also see a check beside a checkbox labeled Disable script debugging. Though it's counter-intuitive, you may leave this checked, because as long as the Display a notification . . . option is checked, the error messages will appear. (The Disable script debugging refers to advanced debugging techniques that are beyond the scope of this course.) Web page programmers will always want error messages enabled, of course.

When the error message box is disabled, Explorer signifies that an error has occurred by displaying a small yellow "alert" triangle in the window status bar in the lower left corner of the window. (This icon doesn't always seem to appear, however, in some versions.) Clicking the icon will bring up the error message box.

When a JavaScript error occurs in Navigator 6, nothing seems to happen except that the browser skips the offending code. Navigator does announce the error, however, in a separate window named JavaScript Console. To open this window, select Tools underneath the Task menu and then select JavaScript Console in the submenu that appears. Figure 7.9 shows what it looks like in the case of our misspelling of the alert command. Note that its error message is more user-friendly and helpful: "Alert is not defined" compared to the "Object expected" of Explorer.

Like Explorer, the JavaScript Console will only display the first error it finds in each `<script>` element. But unlike Explorer, the Console will keep listing previous errors until the Clear option is clicked. For example, if a document has a single JavaScript error and you open the document several times in a row, the Console will display multiple copies of the same error message. So don't panic if, after you fix an error, you reload the document and still see an error message in the Console. It may simply be the previous message that hasn't been cleared.

Copies of Navigator version 4.07 and above (until version 6) do not have the JavaScript Console. Instead, they display an obscure error message in the sta-

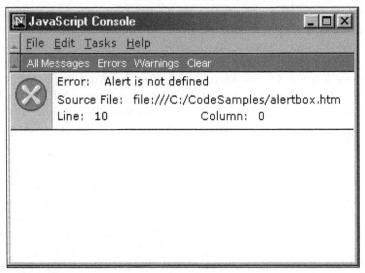

FIGURE 7.9.   The JavaScript Console window of Navigator 6

tus bar at the bottom left of the window, instructing the surfer to type "javascript:" in the location field (where the URL of the document normally is displayed). When you do so, an error window will come up that gives more detailed error messages. Note: Don't leave off the colon at the end—it's "javascript:" not "javascript". You may also select Open under the File menu and then type it in.

IMPORTANT

Unfortunately, whichever browser you're using, the error message will often be more enigmatic than helpful. In these cases, the best approach is trial and error: Change one thing in your code and try again. If that doesn't work, change something else. If that doesn't work, maybe even rewrite the section of code in question in a different way. Contrary to what you might think, most scripts can be written in many different ways, each correct in that it will give the intended result (although some versions will be better in the sense of being more clear and efficient).

Finally, in rare cases a bug will cause a catastrophic failure and the browser will crash or freeze. In such an event, usually the only remedy is to reboot the computer and hope that the last time you saved your work was not too long before.

QuickCheck Questions

1. Using the `alert` command as an example, show two different syntax errors.
2. When you get the error message "Object expected," what is one simple thing that might be wrong with the offending code?

Comments about Comments

Good programmers annotate their programs to clarify what the code does (or at least is supposed to do). In programming parlance, these annotations are called comments. Comments not only help other readers of the code figure out what's going on (the programmer's replacement, for example, when the programmer is promoted to bigger and better things), but the programmer as well. More often than one might think, it happens that a programmer will write some code, get it to work, and then come back a week or two or three later and have a hard time figuring out what exactly the code does.

Inserting Comments

In JavaScript there are two types of comments, single-line and multiple-line. Two consecutive slashes mark the beginning of a **single-line comment**. The browser will ignore everything from the two slashes until the end of the line.

```
<script type="text/javascript">
  //This is a single-line comment.
  //Here's another.
  //The browser ignores everything after the two slashes.
</script>
```

Single-line comments may be placed at the beginning of a line, or after JavaScript code on the same line.

```
<script type="text/javascript">
  alert("Hi!") //Display "Hi!" to the user.
</script>
```

To create a **multiple-line comment**, enclose the comment with /* and */. For instance:

```
<script type="text/javascript">
  /*This is a multiple-line comment in
  JavaScript. When you have a lot to say, this
  is what you use.*/
</script>
```

Multiple-line comments may also start on the same line as JavaScript code:

```
<script type="text/javascript">
  alert("Hi!") /*Display "Hi!" to the user.*/
  alert("Bye!") /*End our time together by displaying
          "Bye!" to the user. */
</script>
```

Note that the following would be incorrect, because the second `alert` command is actually inside the comment and therefore will be ignored:

```
<script type="text/javascript">
  alert("Hi!") /*Display "Hi!" to the user, and then
  alert("Bye!") display "Bye!" */
</script>
```

IMPORTANT

On the other hand, sometimes it's useful to "comment out" JavaScript commands when you are trying to debug some code. Instead of rewriting or deleting the code where you think the problem might be, first just put a single-line comment symbol (i.e., the //) at the beginning of the troublesome line of code (or enclose multiple lines of code with a multiple-line comment), save the file, and then open it in the browser to see if the problem has disappeared. When you're ready to put the code back into the script, simply delete the comment symbols and re-save the file.

Finally, don't confuse JavaScript comments with HTML comments. Remember that HTML uses a special tag that starts with <!-- and ends with --> for comments.

```
<!--Here is an html comment-->
<!--Here's another, using more than
one line-->
```

Everything inside the tag is ignored by the browser. Inside <script> elements you use JavaScript comments (with one exception, as detailed in the next section). Everywhere else in the HTML source document you use the HTML comment tag.

Making a Web Page Safe for Non-JavaScript Browsers

Early versions of web browsers do not recognize the <script> element and the JavaScript commands placed within it (e.g., Netscape Navigator, version 1.1). When a browser does not recognize an HTML tag, it ignores it. But although such a browser would ignore the <script> element, it would go ahead and display whatever is inside the element as regular text, i.e., the surfer will see the JavaScript code displayed on the web page. In order to prevent this undesirable occurrence, it became common practice to place all JavaScript commands inside HTML comment tags, like so:

```
<script type="text/javascript">
<!--
  JavaScript code goes here . . .
//-->
</script>
```

By doing this, browsers that are not JavaScript-enabled will ignore everything inside the <!-- and the -->. JavaScript-enabled browsers, for their part, know to ignore the <!-- that marks the beginning of the HTML comment tag, while the // (a single-line JavaScript comment) before the --> ensures that the browser doesn't try to interpret the --> as some kind of JavaScript command or symbol.

Unfortunately, browsers that follow the new XML and XHTML guidelines are set up to ignore everything inside the HTML comments tag, no matter what is inside. This means that the only certain way to make sure your JavaScript code (a) works on JavaScript-enabled browsers and (b) is not displayed by non-JavaScript browsers is to put it in an external file, as explained above in the section on "The <script> Element."

The <noscript> Element

It is also good practice to display a warning message to surfers who visit your JavaScript-powered web page using a non-JavaScript browser. To display such a message to just those surfers and not to those who have a JavaScript-capable browser, we use the <noscript> element:

IMPORTANT

```
<body>
<noscript>This Web page uses JavaScript. To get the full
effect, you must use a Web browser that implements
JavaScript and set the browser to have JavaScript
enabled.</noscript>
   .  .  .
</body>
```

Put this <noscript> element at or near the beginning of the <body> section of the source document. If the browser can handle JavaScript, then it will not display the contents of the <noscript> element. So only those surfers who are using a browser that can't handle JavaScript, or who have turned off JavaScript in their browser's settings, will see the message.

QuickCheck Questions

1. Write the code for a <script> element that displays two alert boxes, the first with the message "Hello!" and the second with the message "Good-bye!". Put an appropriate comment for each alert box, using a single-line comment for the first one and a multiple-line comment for the second.
2. Using the code in #1, add HTML comments so that non-JavaScript browsers won't display the JavaScript code.

Lab Exercise 7.2, "Getting the Bugs Out," may be done at this point.

Creating Interactive Web Pages

The real power of JavaScript lies in its ability to add interactivity to web pages. HTML, as we will learn, allows us to add elements like text input boxes, check boxes, and radio buttons to our web pages. Using JavaScript, we can program a web page to respond to the interactions of the user with these elements. For example, if we were designing a web page for a realtor, we might want to add a mortgage calculator to the page. The surfer would enter relevant information such as mortgage amount, interest rate, and length of loan into several textboxes, and then that information could be processed using JavaScript to calculate and display an answer regarding the monthly payment.

Click Buttons and Click Events

As a simple example to get started, we will learn how to create a click button that, when clicked, will display an alert box message.

A click button is one type of **input element** that may be added to a web page. Input elements allow the user to input information or otherwise interact with the page. Other common input elements, as mentioned above, include text boxes, where the surfer may enter text, and check boxes and radio buttons, where the surfer may make selections among one or more choices by clicking on the box or button. In order to create input elements on a web page, we use the <input> tag inside a <form> element. Figure 7.10 shows how we write the code for a simple click button and what the results look like.

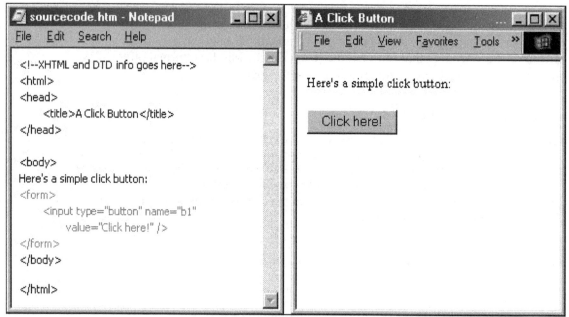

FIGURE 7.10.   Creating a click button

The value of the type attribute in the <input> tag tells the browser what type of input element to create. The value of the name attribute (b1 here) gives the input element an internal name (our choice) that the surfer does not see. In later chapters we will use this name when we learn how to use text boxes, check boxes, and other input elements. We don't really need it for a click button, and often you will see <input> tags that don't have a name attribute. But XHTML now requires its presence.

The value attribute of a click button tells the browser what text label to put on the button ("Click here!", in this case). The button will automatically be sized to contain the label; the longer the text label, the wider the button. The <input> tag is an empty element (it has no ending tag), so we must include the / at the end.

Note also that the <form> element is a block-level element, and thus automatically creates a blank line before (and after) its display. If we wanted the button to appear at the end of the "Here's a simple click button" line, then we would need to put the line of text inside the <form> element.

As it stands, our simple button may look nice, but it has one problem: It won't do anything when the surfer clicks on it. In order to get it to display an alert box when it's clicked, we need to learn about the concept of **events**.

Events are a central feature of object-oriented programming. An event is something that happens to an object or a specific element of an object. By "object," we mean for now a thing like a click button or text box. (We will learn more about software objects in general in Section 8.1.) For instance, if the surfer clicks the mouse on a button, that is a **click event**. Or if the surfer selects some text in a text box, a **select event** occurs. Or if the surfer moves the mouse pointer over a link, a **mouseover event** occurs for that link. The browser automatically keeps track of what the surfer is doing and generates the events; the web page programmer doesn't have to do anything to get them to occur.

The job of the programmer is needed in responding to an event. When an event occurs in an object, we can activate an **event handler** for that object, which will "handle" the event when it occurs and take appropriate action. JavaScript has a number of different kinds of events and event handlers. The event we will use most often is the click event, with its corresponding "onclick" event handler. (We will learn about other types of events later.)

For our simple "Click here!" button of Figure 7.10, we want to display an alert box when the surfer clicks on the button. The chain of action will be:

1. Surfer clicks on the button.

2. Browser automatically generates a click event for that button.

3. The button's click event handler is triggered, activating the appropriate JavaScript commands that display the alert box.

Once we have created a click button on a web page, steps 1 and 2 are out of our hands. It is step 3 that is missing from the code in Figure 7.10. To add a click event handler to our button, we use the onclick attribute in the button's `<input>` tag and set its value to whatever JavaScript code we want to be executed when the click event occurs. In other words:

```
<form>
  <input type="button" name="b1" value="Click here!"
    onclick="alert('Nice going!')" />
</form>
```

The `onclick` attribute is more commonly called the `onclick` event handler. Literally it means "on the occurrence of a click, execute the following JavaScript code." When the button is clicked in this example, the `onclick` event handler will be triggered and the `alert('Nice going!')` code is executed; that is, the alert box will appear with the message "Nice going!"

There are two important things to note about this event handler code. First, we see that we have JavaScript code (the `alert` command) embedded directly into an HTML tag. This is an exception to the rule that JavaScript instructions must be inside a `<script>` element. The `onclick` event handler provides a doorway between HTML and JavaScript. The `onclick` attribute itself is part of HTML, while its value—`alert('Nice going!')` in this case—consists of a JavaScript command.

Second, we see that we have two kinds of quotation marks: double quotation marks surrounding the complete value of the `onclick` attribute, and single quotation marks surrounding the 'Nice going!' message. The pair of single quotation marks is nested inside the pair of double quotation marks. We have to use two types of quotation marks in this case because if we used two pairs of double quotation marks, as below, the browser would get confused:

```
<input type="button" name="b1" value="Click here!"
  onclick="alert("Nice going!")" />
```

The reason for the confusion is that the browser would see the second quotation mark (the one just in front of the word `Nice`) and think it made a pair with the first quotation mark (the one in front of the word `alert`). It would thus interpret the second quotation mark as marking the end of the attribute's value, and it would not expect to see more characters after that. This confusion is avoided by using single quotation marks around the 'Nice going!'. It's also possible to use single quotation marks on the outside and double quotation marks around the alert message:

```
<input type="button" name="b1" value="Click here!"
  onclick='alert("Nice going!")' />
```

The key is that the two pairs of quotation marks must be of different types and that one pair must be nested inside the other.

Figure 7.11 shows the browser display before and after the surfer clicks the button. After the surfer clicks "OK" in the alert box, the alert box disappears and the "Click here!" button may be clicked again, triggering the alert box again.

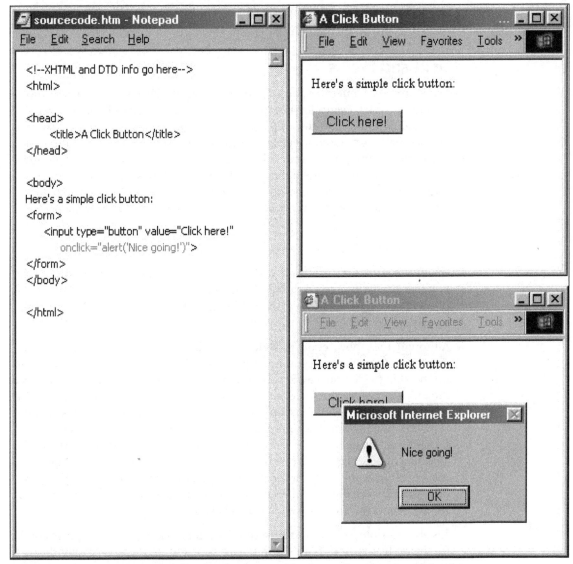

FIGURE 7.11.   Web page display before and after a button is clicked

It is also possible to put more than one JavaScript command into the value of the `onclick` attribute by separating the commands with semicolons. For instance:

```
<input type="button" name="b1" value="Click here!"
   onclick="alert('Nice going!'); alert('Keep up the good
   work!')" />
```

When the surfer clicks on the button, the `onclick` event handler will activate the JavaScript code: The "Nice going!" alert box will appear and then, after the surfer clicks the "OK" button in the alert box, the "Keep up the good work!" alert box will appear.

Links and Events

Events are not limited to special input elements like click buttons. The browser generates a click event, for instance, every time the surfer clicks on a regular HTML link. Links have two other types of events that occur with them as well: mouseover and mouseout events. A mouseover event occurs when the surfer moves the mouse pointer over the link text. A mouseout event occurs, in turn, when the surfer moves the pointer off the link. Each type of event has its corresponding event handler: `onmouseover` and `onmouseout`. To use a `mouseover` event with a link, we put an `onmouseover` event handler in its <a> tag:

```
<a href="photogallery.htm" onmouseover="alert('Are you
   sure?')">Click here to go to the photo gallery</a>
```

When the page with this code is displayed and the mouse is moved over the link text "Click here to go to the photo gallery", a mouseover event will occur, the `onmouseover` event handler will be activated, and an alert box with the message "Are you sure?" will appear.

Although the above code provides a simple example of the `onmouseover` event handler, it's not too useful in practice. The reason is that the surfer will not be able to click successfully on the link. As soon as the mouse passes over the link and before the surfer has a chance to click on it, the mouseover event will occur and the alert box will be displayed. The surfer next clicks on the alert box to get rid of it and moves the mouse back to the link to click on it. But before the click can occur, another mouseover event is generated and the alert box appears again. The only way out is to press the Enter key to get rid of the alert box, while keeping the mouse pointer over the link. Since the pointer is already over the link when the alert box disappears, no mouseover event will be generated and the link may be clicked.

It's also possible to add multiple event handlers to a tag. We can create a link, for example, that uses both the `onmouseover` and `onclick` event handlers:

```
<a href="photogallery.htm"
   onmouseover="alert('Are you sure?')"
   onclick="alert('Are you really sure?')">Photo
   gallery</a>
```

The "Are you sure?" alert box will appear whenever a mouseover event occurs for the link and the "Are you really sure?" alert box appears when a click event occurs. (The link itself will be activated after the surfer clicks OK in this second alert box.)

We will learn about better uses for mouseover and mouseout events in Chapter 9 when we consider image rollovers. In the meantime, one final syntax note.

Before XHTML, the convention was to write the event handler attributes in lowercase letters with the internal words capitalized: `onClick`, `onMouseover`, `onMouseout` (or sometimes `onMouseOver` and `onMouseOut`). But the XHTML requirement of lowercase tag and attribute names means that you should get in the habit of writing them as `onclick`, `onmouseover`, and so on.

QuickCheck Questions

1. What is an input element? Give two examples.
2. Write the HTML code that will create a click button with the label "Search".
3. To the click button code of #2, add an `onclick` event handler that will display an alert box with the message "Ready to initiate search?"
4. What is the difference between a mouseover and a mouseout event?

Lab Exercise 7.3, "An Eventful Web Page," may be done at this point.

Key Terms

alert box
algorithm
assembly language
case-sensitive
click event
compiler
conditional (branching)
control structures
event handler
events
execute
flowchart

high-level language
input element
instructions (code, statements, commands)
interpreter
logic error
looping (iteration)
machine language instructions
management error
mouseout event
mouseover event
multiple-line comment

object-oriented programming (OOP)
pseudocode
run
runtime error
script
scripting language
sequence
single-line comment
structured programming
syntax error
transfer (go to, jump)

Code Summary

1. The `<script>` Element

Using the `<script>` element to insert JavaScript code into a source document:

```
<script type="text/javascript">
   alert("Hello, world!")
[Additional JavaScript instructions would go here . . . ]
</script>
```

Multiple `<script>` elements:

```
<body>
<strong>This is a simple JavaScript test . . . </strong>
<script type="text/javascript">
```

```
   alert("Hello, world!")
   alert("Anybody out there?")
</script>
<br /><strong>All done with the alert boxes.</strong>
<script type="text/javascript">
   alert("Oops, here's another one")
</script>
</body>
```

2. Comments about Comments

Single-line comments using //:

```
<script type="text/javascript">
   //This is a single-line comment.
   alert("Hi!") //Display "Hi!" to the user.
   //The browser ignores everything after the two slashes.
</script>
```

Multiple-line comments using the pair /* and */:

```
<script type="text/javascript">
   /*This is a multiple-line comment in
   JavaScript. When you have a lot to say, this
   is what you use.*/
   alert("Hi!") /*Display "Hi!" to the user.*/
   alert("Bye!") /*End our time together by displaying
                "Bye!" to the user. */
</script>
```

Commenting out JavaScript code (using the HTML comment tag) so that non-JavaScript browsers don't display the code on the web page (but may not work with latest XML-complaint browsers):

```
<script type="text/javascript">
<!--
   JavaScript code goes here . . .
   //-->
</script>
```

Creating a warning message that will appear only in non-JavaScript browsers:

```
<body>
<noscript>This Web page uses JavaScript. To get the full effect, you must use a Web
browser that implements JavaScript and set the browser to have JavaScript
enabled.</noscript>
   . . .
</body>
```

3. Creating Interactive Web Pages

Creating a click button with an onclick event handler that calls the alert command:

```
<form>
   <input type="button" name="b1" value="Click here!" onclick="alert('Nice going!')" />
</form>
```

Adding event handlers to a link:

```
<a href="photogallery.htm" onmouseover="alert('Are you sure?')"
   onclick="alert('Are you really sure?')">Photo gallery</a>
```

Do not put HTML code inside a `<script>` element; only JavaScript code may go there.

Alerts and Advice

If debugging code using Navigator versions 4.07+ (up to but not including version 6), type "javascript:" in the Location field to see error messages, and don't forget the colon at the end of "javascript:".

Trial and error is often the most effective way to debug a script, especially if the error message is enigmatic.

When debugging code, instead of deleting the line(s) of code where the problem might be, comment them out and then save and load the source document to check the results.

Don't confuse JavaScript comments (the single-line `//` or the multiple-line `/*` and `*/`) with HTML comments (`<!--` and `-->`).

Use the `<noscript>` element to display a warning message to surfers who visit your JavaScript-powered web page using a non-JavaScript browser.

If it's necessary to use more than one set of quotation marks, such as when you have an alert command as part of an `onclick` event handler, alternate between sets of double and single quotation marks, nesting them.

Review Questions

1. At its most basic, a computer program may be likened to a _____ for the computer (or, more specifically, the CPU).

2. The three-level hierarchy of computer languages consists of _____, _____, and _____ .

3. The purpose of a compiler or an interpreter is to translate _____ into _____.

4. The four basic control structures are: _____, _____, _____, and _____.

5. True or false: The main purpose of a scripting language is to allow the programmer to create stand-alone programs that may be used independently of any other software program.

6. True or false: JavaScript is so-named because it was developed as a subset of the Java programming language.

7. True or false: JavaScript is a case-sensitive language.

8. The best cure for logic errors is prevention, by creating a well-designed _____ before starting to write the actual programming code.

9. Which of the following are used to mark comments in JavaScript?
   a. `<!--` and `-->`
   b. `//` (by itself)
   c. `/*` (by itself)
   d. `//` and `//` (i.e., a pair)
   e. `/*` and `*/` (a pair)
   f. `/*` and `/*` (a pair)

10. True or false: Although the `language` attribute in a `<script>` element is deprecated in favor of the `type` attribute, it is still useful for specifying the version of the JavaScript language that is being used by the document.

11. Which HTML element is used to create a click button?
   a. `<input>`
   b. `<click>`

    c. `<formtype>`
    d. `<clickbutton>`

12. True or false: When you have to put one pair of quotation marks inside another pair, as in the following code, both pairs must be double quotation marks.

```
<input type="button" name="b1" value="Click here!" onclick="alert("Nice going!")" />
```

13. When the surfer moves the mouse pointer over a link on a web page, the browser automatically generates a _____ event. This event may be handled, or connected with some JavaScript code, using the _____ event handler.

Exercises

1. Briefly define and/or explain the following terms: runtime error, event handler, interpreter, script.

2. List the four basic control structures and give a real-world example of each (different from the examples used in the text).

3. Write an algorithm for boiling water on a stove.

4. Write an algorithm for mowing a 50′ x 100′ patch of lawn.

5. Write an algorithm for sorting a set of five vocabulary flash cards into alphabetical order. Try to make your algorithm general enough so that it would work just as well for one thousand cards as for five.

6. Write the code for a `<script>` element that displays three alert boxes, the first with the message "Good to see you", the second with the message "Having a nice time?", and the third with the message "See you later." Include at least one comment in the code.

7. Write the code for a `<form>` element that creates a click button with an `onclick` event handler. The button should be labeled "Display an alert", and when clicked, an alert box should appear with the message "This is just a test."

8. Write the code for a `<form>` element that creates three click buttons in a row, each with `onclick` event handlers. The first button should be labeled "Door 1", the second "Door 2", and the third "Door 3." Also include a line of plain text at the beginning of the form that says, "Let's Make a Deal! Click on your choice." When the "Door 1" or "Door 3" button is clicked, an alert box should appear with the message "Sorry, you lose." When the "Door 2" button is clicked, an alert box should appear with the message "You are a winner!"

9. Write the code for a complete HTML source document that includes a link to a document named "finalpage.htm". The text of the link should be "Click here to go to the final page." When the surfer moves the mouse pointer over the link, an alert box should appear with the message "Leaving so soon?".

10. Write the code for a complete HTML source document that includes the following:

    a. Two `<script>` elements, one in the `<head>` element and one in the `<body>` element. The first should contain code to display the alert box message "Message Number 1" and "Message Number 2." The code in the second `<script>` element should display an alert box with the message "Message Number 3."

    b. A `<noscript>` element with an appropriate message.

    c. A click button with the label "Click here!" When clicked, an alert box with the message "Message Number 4" should appear.

Identify the errors in the following code and then sketch on paper how the browser would display it once the errors were corrected.

```
<html>
<head>
<title>Introduction to JavaScript</title>
</head>
<body>
<strong>This is a simple JavaScript test.</strong>
<script language="text/javascript">
   Alert("Hello, world!")
   Alert("Anybody out there?")
</script>
<form>
   <input type="clickbutton" value="Click here!" onclick="alert("Nice touch!")">
</form>
<script>
alert("Hi!") /*Display "Hi!" to the user, and then
alert("Bye!") display "Bye!" */
</script>
</body>
</html>
```

Note: Most of the exercises above may also be done as lab exercises.

Exercise 7.1: A Simple Script

❏ Create a simple web page using JavaScript's alert command. That is, put a `<script>` element in the `<body>` element of a new HTML source document. Within this `<script>` element, put *several* instances of the `alert` command. For example:

```
<script type="text/javascript">
   alert("My first JavaScript.")
   alert("Too exciting for words.")
   alert("This is big time stuff.")
</script>
```

❏ Try using more than one `<script>` element in the `<body>`, each with one or two `alert` commands in it. Put some regular HTML text and tags between the `<script>` elements. In other words, play around a little bit to get a feel for using JavaScript. Don't forget to give your HTML document a `<title>` element (with title inside, of course).

Exercise 7.2: Getting the Bugs Out

❏ Make a copy of your source document from Lab Exercise 7.1 and give it a new name, such as bugtest.htm. Using it, see how many different error messages you can generate. Make a list of each type of error and the error message each generates in both Explorer and Navigator.

Exercise 7.3: An Eventful Web Page

❏ Create a web page that uses at least one click button and at least one link to display alert box messages. Try at least two different kinds of event handlers. Include comments and a `<noscript>` element.

Objects and Variables

8

LEARNING OBJECTIVES

1. Learn the basic concepts, terminology, and syntax of object-oriented programming.

2. Learn what data types and variables are, how to create and initialize variables, and how to change their values.

3. Learn how a web browser is organized around objects like the document, location, and history objects, and how you may use JavaScript to access and change the properties of a web page such as its background color.

An Introduction to Objects

Before we can go further, we need to learn about a number of key JavaScript concepts and terms.

Chapter 7 introduced the concept of object-oriented programming languages. As we shall see, a web browser, including its built-in JavaScript language, is built around an object-oriented paradigm. Some people would therefore label JavaScript an OOP language. But because, as a scripting language, it doesn't implement all the features of a full-blown object-oriented language like Java, others prefer to call it object-based. In any event, an understanding of software objects is key to understanding JavaScript.

As mentioned briefly in Chapter 7, in the section "Structured vs. Object-Oriented Programming," an object in the software world consists of two things bundled together: (1) data (for example, text and numbers) and (2) code modules (sequences of instructions) that are usually related to or interact in some way with the bundled data.

Another way to say this is that every object has a **state** and certain **behaviors**. The state of an object is defined by its data, or—a new term—its **properties**, and the behavior of an object is defined by its code, or its instruction sequences, or—a new term—its **methods**. To sum up, an object consists of *properties* and *methods*. The properties define the object's state and the methods define how it acts, that is, its behavior.

A real-world example of an object can help make this clear. One reason for the invention of object-oriented programming (OOP) was that it made it easier for programmers to make software models of real-world objects. So real-world objects may serve as more familiar metaphors for how software objects work.

Consider as our "real-world" object an automatic coffee machine that we will call the "UltraJava 2000." It is so-called because when it is loaded with all its options and accessories, it can instantly make any kind of coffee you want.

State and Properties

Our UltraJava machine has certain settings or *properties* that define its *state* at any given time. To simplify things, we'll assume that we're using the base model of the UltraJava, which has three properties: power, bean, and grind. That is, the *state* of the UltraJava machine is given by the values of these three properties.

Power may have either the value "on" or "off"—the power property indicates whether the machine is on or off. Bean may have any number of values ("French Roast," "Colombian," "Decaf French Roast," for example). That is, the bean property indicates the currently selected type of bean. And grind indicates the grind setting, with the values "fine," "medium," or "coarse."

So the *state* of our UltraJava machine at any given time will be a combination of the three properties, such as "on, French Roast, medium" or "off, Colombian, fine." In more formal terms we write:

```
ultraJava.power has the value "on"
ultraJava.bean has the value "French Roast"
ultraJava.grind has the value "medium"
```

Note how we wrote these names. The general syntax of `ultraJava.power` or `ultraJava.bean` or `ultraJava.grind` is:

```
objectName.propertyName
```

This **dot notation** syntax shows that the indicated property belongs to the indicated object. When speaking this, we say "objectName-dot-propertyName," or "ultraJava-dot-grind." The period is pronounced as "dot."

If you are wondering about the use of a lowercase letter to start off each name, as in `ultraJava` or `propertyName`, it's simply a common convention among many programmers. When we start to name things, we may choose to capitalize the first letter or whatever. The important thing is to be consistent, however, because JavaScript is a case-sensitive language. This means that the name `ultraJava` is not the same as `ultrajava` or `UltraJava` or `ULTRAJAVA` or `uLTrAjaVa`.

Another important thing to note is the difference between the **name** of the property (e.g., `power`, `bean`, `grind`) and the **value** of the property (e.g., "on," "French Roast," "medium"). One way to visualize properties is as dials attached to the object, each dial having a label (the name) and some reading (the value).

Behavior and Methods

The other major characteristic of an object is its *behavior*, defined by its *methods*—the modules of code that it contains. The *behavior* of an object often leads to changes in its *state* or, in other words, its *methods* may change its *properties*.

Note that the term "method" is one of those English words that (a) has many meanings and (b) can be somewhat vague. Here we are adding to that list of meanings, but in a very precise manner. In the context of object-oriented programming, method means a module of code that belongs to a software object. If it helps, think of the definition of method as a procedure; that is, the bundle of code represents a method or procedure for performing some action.

The example of our UltraJava coffee machine again helps clarify this. One of its properties is `grind`—it has the value of either "fine," "medium," or "coarse." How do we change the grind setting? (For the purposes of our example, we are assuming that we operate our UltraJava coffee machine by remote control. With a less advanced machine, of course, we might just throw a switch.)

To change a property of an object, we **send a message** to the object telling it to execute the method—the sequence of instructions—that performs the change. Like properties, methods also have names, so let's assume the name of the method to change the grind setting is `changeGrind`. Now we just need to know how to address and send the message so that the object receives it. We address the message by giving the object name, followed by the name of the method to execute:

```
ultraJava.changeGrind
```

But this isn't quite enough, because we also need to tell the UltraJava machine which grind we want: "fine," "medium," or "coarse." We indicate our choice by including a **parameter** in our message, enclosing it in parentheses after the name of the method. Some methods require one parameter, some more than one, and some none. *The parameters are the means by which we send information to the object that it needs to execute the method.* Putting it all together in our change-the-grind example, we have:

```
ultraJava.changeGrind("coarse")
```

This command sends a message to the UltraJava, telling it to execute its `changeGrind` instructions and switch to a coarse grind setting. To change it to a fine grind, the command would be:

```
ultraJava.changeGrind("fine")
```

If we have a method that does not require any input information, then there are no parameters. For example, the UltraJava machine might have a power setting that can be toggled on or off using a method named `powerToggle`. The command to toggle the power on (if it was off) or off (if it was on) would be:

```
ultraJava.powerToggle()
```

Note that even though the `powerToggle` method doesn't take any parameters, we still include the pair of parentheses at the end. The parentheses indicate that `powerToggle` is a method of the `ultraJava` object, not a property.

When we refer to methods throughout the text of this book, we will usually append an empty pair of parentheses to their names to distinguish them visually from the names of object properties. For example, we might write "Now consider the `changeGrind()` method . . ." or "Be careful how you use `powerToggle()` in this situation . . ." or "The value of the `bean` property will then become . . ." (no parentheses after `bean` because it's a property, not a method).

Calling a Method and Sending It Parameters

We refer to this process of sending a message to the object to execute one of its methods by the terminology **calling a method**. That is, to execute the code contained in a method, we "call" it. The general syntax to call a method is:

```
objectName.methodName(parameter1, parameter2, . . . )
```

In summary, to send a message to an object telling it to execute a certain method, we "call" that method; to call that method, we simply write its full name with its parameters, if any, enclosed in parentheses.

If a method does not require any parameters (that is, it requires no extra information to be sent to it in order to execute its instructions), then as we saw in the `powerToggle()` example the parentheses remain as part of the method call, but with nothing inside them:

```
objectName.methodName()
```

A heads up: You may have noticed the presence of quotation marks around the parameters "coarse" and "fine" in our examples above, but their absence when we wrote:

```
objectName.methodName(parameter1, parameter2, . . . )
```

We will discuss the what, where, when, and how of quotation marks in JavaScript later when we discuss the concept of variables.

The Assignment Statement

In some cases, we don't need to call a method to change the value of a property of an object. Instead, we may directly *assign* the property a new value. We do this using an **assignment statement**. The syntax is simple:

```
objectName.propertyName = X
```

where X is the new value for the property (it might be a number or some text) and the equal sign is known as the **assignment operator**. "Operators" in programming languages are things that operate on, or do things to, values. When you see an assignment operator, you read the line of code from the left side to the right side. In this case, the code tells the browser to take the value of X and copy it into `objectName.propertyName`. Or "assign the value of X to the `propertyName` property of the `objectName` object."

To change the UltraJava to a fine grind, for instance, we could write:

```
ultraJava.grind = "fine"
```

Compare this syntax with the alternative of calling the `changeGrind()` method with "fine" as a parameter:

```
ultraJava.changeGrind("fine")
```

Don't misread the syntax of the assignment statement. It is not using the equal sign as it is used normally in mathematics, to indicate that the thing on the left side equals the thing on the right side. Instead, it uses an equal sign to indicate that the property on the left side is to be assigned the value on the right side. In other words, it is a dynamic statement rather than a static statement. The value of the property will be changed (unless, of course, the value of the property is already equal to X). We will talk more about assignment statements later in the section "Storing Things for Later Use: Variables."

Before we move on, let's list the key terms we have covered so far:

> *object*
> *state*
> *behavior*
> *property*
> *name vs. value of a property*
> *method*
> *parameter*
> *message*
> *calling a method*
> *assignment statement*

Make sure that you understand the definition of each of these terms and how we use them, because we will encounter them many more times as we continue with JavaScript.

A Hierarchy of Objects

The next thing to do is add an optional attachment to the base model of our UltraJava 2000. In particular, we're craving an automatic cappuccino maker. In the object-oriented analogy, the cappuccino maker is itself an object—we'll give it the name cappuccinoMaker—with its own properties and methods. For instance, our cappuccino maker attachment has a strength setting, so one of its properties would be strength, with the values of "single" or "double." And one of its methods might be changeStrength. To change the strength, we send a message to the cappuccinoMaker object telling it to execute its changeStrength() method. The syntax is the same as before, except that we have a longer address for the message, because the cappuccinoMaker object belongs to the ultraJava object. To change to double strength:

```
ultraJava.cappuccinoMaker.changeStrength("double")
```

What we see here is that a property of one object may itself be an object. That is, cappuccinoMaker is both an object in its own right and a property of the ultraJava object.

In general, we can have a whole hierarchy of objects and sub-objects (an **object hierarchy**) so that calling a method belonging to a particular sub-object becomes:

```
topLevelObject.secondLevelObject.thirdLevelObject.
    methodName(parm1, parm2, . . . )
```

where parm is a common abbreviation for parameter. And referring to a property attached to an object becomes:

```
topLevelObject.secondLevelObject.thirdLevelObject.
    propertyName
```

The topLevelObject is the **parent** of secondLevelObject, which is also a parent, that of thirdLevelObject. The objects below topLevelObject in the hierarchy—secondLevelObject and thirdLevelObject in this case—are the descendants of topLevelObject. We also may say that thirdLevelObject is the **child** of secondLevelObject, and secondLevelObject the child of topLevelObject. The objects above another object in the hierarchy are its ancestors: The ancestor of secondLevelObject is topLevelObject; the ancestors of thirdLevelObject are secondLevelObject and topLevelObject.

The object hierarchy may be complex, as each object may have several child objects, which in turn have several of their own, and so on. Each object may also, of course, have its own methods and properties. The whole hierarchy looks like a family tree (Figure 8.1).

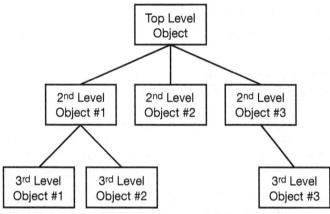

FIGURE 8.1. **A sample hierarchy of objects**

QuickCheck Questions

1. What does it mean to "call" a method?
2. Write the command that would execute the `powerToggle` method of the `ultraJava` object. (Remember that `powerToggle` has no parameters.)
3. Write an assignment statement that would change the value of the `grind` property of the `ultraJava` object to "medium".

Storing Things for Later Use: Variables

In the section "Calling a Method and Sending it Parameters" we learned how to change the `grind` setting on our UltraJava machine by calling the machine's `changeGrind()` method and sending it the parameter value "coarse":

```
ultraJava.changeGrind("coarse")
```

We can also imagine a situation where rather than changing the grind setting, we just want to find out what it is. Instead of sending a new grind value to the machine, we want to receive the current value of the grind setting. To do so, the UltraJava machine might have a `getGrind` method that gets the value of the current setting and sends it to us. To receive this value, we need to have something to catch and store it, whether "coarse", "medium", or "fine". This something that stores the value is known as a variable. In order to learn what variables are and how they work, we first need to consider the types of data that can be stored in JavaScript.

JavaScript's Three Types of Data

JavaScript has three main types of values, or **data types**: strings, numbers, and boolean.

The term **string** refers to a string of characters, that is, text. We indicate something is a string in JavaScript by enclosing it in either single or double quotation marks, such as "Greetings, earthling!" or 'Greetings!' or "472" or "530-762-1234" or "3.14159". All these are strings, even the numbers; that is, JavaScript stores them as text and they cannot be used in mathematical calculations. In the ultraJava examples we have been using, the values "coarse," "medium," and "fine" are all strings, as are "French Roast" and "Colombian."

If something is a number, we leave off the quotation marks. Numbers can be **integers** (positive or negative whole numbers) or real numbers with decimal points. Real numbers are also called **floating point numbers**, because the decimal point may float around, as in 43.587 or 75093.4 or 0.0582.

Boolean values are binary values, meaning that there are only two possible values: either *true* or *false*. (Think bicycle—two wheels—or binary stars—two stars orbiting around each other, etc.) The name boolean comes from George Boole, a 19th-century British mathematician who did pioneering work in binary mathematics. Our UltraJava machine provides a simple example of a boolean value. At any given time its power is either on or off, and the status of its power setting is stored in its power property. Previously we said that the value of the ultraJava.power property could be either "on" or "off." We just as well could have said that ultraJava.power either has the boolean value true (meaning the power is on) or the value false (meaning the power is off).

We will learn how boolean values may be used to good effect in later chapters, such as when we create check boxes on web pages. A check box is either checked or not checked at any given time, and so its checked status may be either true (it is checked) or false (it is not checked).

The Three Characteristics of a Variable

We store values, whether strings, numbers, or boolean, in things called **variables**. You may think of a variable as similar to a labeled storage box in which we store a value for later use. It is called a variable because its contents, or value, may vary while the script is running. For instance, if a given variable in a JavaScript program stores an answer to a Yes/No question, sometimes its value may be "Yes" and other times "No." Or we may have a variable that stores the numeric result of some calculation, such as the number 438.92. If the calculation is redone with different input numbers, then the variable would store a different number.

Variables are thus very similar to properties. Or, to look at it the other way around, we may also say that a property is simply a variable that is attached to a certain object. We use the storage box analogy for both variables and properties, where the storage box represents in reality a memory location in the computer where the value is stored. Figure 8.2 shows three variables, pictured as storage boxes, labeled `answer1`, `answer2`, and `answer3` with the contents 38.4, "George Washington," and false.

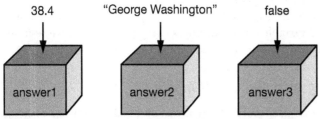

FIGURE 8.2. **Variables as storage boxes: Each has a label (a name) and some contents (a value)**

Every variable has three characteristics: type, name, and value.

1. *The type of a variable:* Every JavaScript variable stores a certain *type* of value at any given time: either a string, a number, or a boolean value. Unlike many programming languages, in JavaScript it is possible for a variable to contain a string at one point in time and later contain a real number. That is, a variable's type may change. In programming lingo, this makes JavaScript a **loosely typed** language. Many programming languages are more restrictive and **strongly typed**, meaning that any given variable can store only one type of **variable value**.

   To go back to our storage box analogy, variables in a loosely typed language are like storage boxes in which you're allowed to put anything. For example, you might put buttons in at first, then take the buttons out and put bows in, then later take the bows out and put socks in, and so on. Variables in a strongly typed language, on the other hand, are like storage boxes in which you're only permitted to put one kind of thing. If it's a box that holds buttons, you may change the buttons that are in it but you are not allowed to put bows or socks or anything else in it.

2. *The name of a variable:* Every JavaScript variable has a **variable name**. Each variable in a JavaScript program must be given a unique name or label to distinguish it from other variables and so that JavaScript knows how to refer to it and find it. As an example, consider an e-commerce web page for a small widget company where we need to store the prices of 20 products in order to use JavaScript to calculate the total amount of a customer's order. Our script would need 20 variables of the "number" type, one to store the price of each product. In order to keep track of which variable held which product's price, we would give each variable a name, such as BlueWidgetPrice,

LargeRedWidgetPrice, SmallRegularWidgetPrice, and so on. Or, in the analogy of variables as storage boxes, if we had 20 identical boxes to store shoes, we would probably write labels on them such as Running Shoes, Tennis Shoes, Black Dress Shoes, Brown Dress Shoes, and so on, in order to distinguish and keep track of them.

3. *The value of a variable:* Every JavaScript variable usually has a **variable value** (or is empty). That is, every variable has some contents. Number variables store numbers, string variables store text, and boolean variables store either the value `true` or the value `false`.

Declaring and Naming Variables

Before we can use a variable to store some value we want to keep around for later use, we must define or declare it. Declaring a variable means to specify its name using the `var` keyword. (JavaScript, like all programming languages, has certain special words it reserves for its own use, called **reserved words** or keywords. Appendix F lists them.)

To **declare a variable** with the name `answer` we write the following line of JavaScript code:

```
<script type="text/javascript">
  var answer
</script>
```

In the variable-as-box analogy, this code creates a storage box and gives the box the name `answer`. Or, in terms of the computer involved, when the browser executes this line of JavaScript code, it reserves a memory location that has a certain numeric address and associates the name `answer` with that address.

We can therefore make our storage box analogy a little more precise by thinking of the storage boxes as mailboxes in a post office. Each post office box has a certain number on its front, identifying its location in the wall of boxes. The same number appears also on the back of the box, of course, so that the post office employees know which box is which when they're putting mail in the boxes. When a box is rented by someone, the post office usually puts a label with the person's name on the back of the box as an extra identifier. In other words, the person's name is now associated with that box number. So the box is like the location in the computer's memory, the box number is like the address of that memory location, and the label with the person's name is like the variable name associated with that memory address.

So, going back to our code example, whenever the browser encounters the name `answer` in other lines of code in the source document, it knows that it refers to a certain memory location where some value is stored. (Getting values into variables is the subject of the next section.)

When creating more than one variable, we may list them on separate lines or, to save space, on the same line separated by commas. If on separate lines, we must use a `var` keyword for each line. If on the same line, only one `var` keyword is required. So we may write this:

```
<script type="text/javascript">
  var answer1
  var answer2
  var answer3
</script>
```

or this:

```
<script type="text/javascript">
  var answer1, answer2, answer3
</script>
```

You may not name a variable anything you like, but instead must follow JavaScript's naming rules, which are similar to HTML. Variable names must start with either a letter (A–Z or a–z) or an underscore character (_). After the first character, other characters may be letters, digits (0–9), or the underscore character. But do not use spaces or any other special symbols or punctuation marks.

IMPORTANT

When naming a variable, you should give it a name that is descriptive of its purpose. If you wanted to store three numbers (say, zip codes), you could name the three variables `a`, `b`, and `c`. But the names `number1`, `number2`, and `number3` would be more descriptive, and `zipCode1`, `zipCode2`, and `zipCode3` would be even better. You could also capitalize the names and use `ZipCode1`, `ZipCode2`, and `ZipCode3`. Some programmers instead prefer to separate the words in a multiple-word variable name using the underscore character: `zip_code_1`, `zip_code_2`, and so on. Still others simply write everything in lowercase with no separation mark: `zipcode1`, `zipcode2`, and so on. We will continue to follow the convention of starting names with lowercase letters and using uppercase letters to distinguish the words in multiple-word names. Whichever capitalization style you choose, try to use it consistently when defining variable names as it makes your code easier to read. Remember too that you must be consistent with the names themselves because JavaScript names are case sensitive. The name `FirstAnswer` is different from `firstAnswer`.

Although descriptive names are recommended, try not to make your variable names too long because it increases the chances of typographical errors and misspellings, which can be very frustrating to track down and fix. Finally, be aware that you cannot use any of JavaScript's reserved words (such as `var`) for your own variable names.

In our examples below, we will use a variety of names such as `answer`, `theAnswer`, `theResult`, `firstAnswer`, `secondAnswer`, `firstNumber`, `secondNumber`, `firstNum`, `secondNum`, `num1`, `num2`, and so on so that you remember there are many ways to name a variable.

Storing Values in Variables

It's good practice to **initialize a variable** when you create it, which means give it an initial or starting value. If you don't initialize it, then JavaScript gives it the value undefined, which may cause problems later in the code. We initialize a variable using an assignment statement in combination with the var keyword (leaving off the <script> tags to save space):

```
var answer = 42
```

This line of code uses the assignment operator to create a variable named answer and assign it a value of 42. In other words, the browser reserves a memory location, labels it with the name answer, and stores the value 42 in that location.

If we wanted to change the value of answer from 42 to 3.14, we would simply use another assignment statement:

```
answer = 3.14
```

Note that there is no var in front of answer here. The only time you put the var keyword with a variable is the first time, when you declare the variable.

We could also change the value of answer to a string:

```
answer = "George Washington"
```

After the browser had executed this last assignment statement, the variable named answer (or, to be precise, the memory location associated with that variable) would contain the text "George Washington".

Or we could change it to a boolean value:

```
answer = true
```

Note the absence of quotation marks around true. If we had enclosed it in quotation marks, the browser would think that you intended to store the *string* value "true" in the variable named answer. Without the quotation marks, it recognizes it as the *boolean* value true.

Just as we may declare more than one variable on the same line by separating them with commas, we may do the same when we both declare and initialize them:

```
var firstNumber=98, secondNumber=5.478, surferName="Fred"
```

What we have been doing so far is assigning a fixed or literal value to a variable, such as 42, 3.14, "George Washington", and true. We also may assign the value of one variable to another variable. For instance:

```
var presidentName, firstUser
presidentName = "George Washington"
firstUser = presidentName
```

Make sure that you are clear on what the last line of this code does and does not do. It does *not* take the *value* presidentName and assign it to be the new value of the variable named firstUser, so that firstUser ends up storing the string "presidentName". Rather, presidentName is the *name* of a variable, so the code takes the *value* of presidentName and assigns it to be the new value of the firstUser variable. If we had wanted to store the string value "presidentName" in firstUser, we would have written:

```
firstUser = "presidentName"
```

We can see this distinction between name and value in another way by using the alert command to display the value of the variable firstUser. Up to this point we've used the alert command to display brief messages, and each time we've enclosed the message string in quotation marks, as in alert("Hello, world!") or alert("Are you sure?"). When we do that we're telling the browser to send the literal string of characters to the alert method to be displayed in an alert box, just as they're written.

But we may also insert a variable name into the alert command:

```
alert(firstUser)
```

In this case, we don't want the alert command to display the string of characters f-i-r-s-t-U-s-e-r; instead we want it to display the *value* of the variable named firstUser. So we leave off the quotation marks. The absence of quotation marks tells the browser that firstUser is a variable name and that therefore it is to send the *value* of firstUser to the alert method, not the characters f-i-r-s-t-U-s-e-r. If firstUser had been assigned the value "George Washington", as in our code above, then the alert box would be displayed as shown in Figure 8.3.

FIGURE 8.3. Alert box displaying the value of the firstUser variable

If instead we had put quotation marks around firstUser, so that it was alert("firstUser"), then the alert box would treat firstUser as simply a string of characters and not a variable name. Figure 8.4 shows the result.

When we have two or more string values, we may combine them into one string by using the + operator. As previously mentioned when we introduced

FIGURE 8.4.   Alert box displaying the value "firstUser"

the assignment operator, operators are things that operate on, or do things to, values. In arithmetic we use operators like $+$, $-$, $*$, and $/$ to add, subtract, multiply, and divide values. (We will learn more about these and other mathematical operators in Chapter 11.) The following code takes the strings "Hello, " and "how are you?", combines them using the $+$ operator, and assigns the result (the combined string) to a variable named typicalGreeting:

```
var typicalGreeting
typicalGreeting = "Hello, " + "how are you?"
```

Note that we put a space at the end of "Hello, " (after the comma) so that the complete sentence displays properly.

The fancy word for this operation is **concatenation**: When we combine two or more strings into one longer string, we are concatenating them.

We may also concatenate the value of a string variable, such as userName, with a literal string value, such as "How are you, ":

```
var userName = "Jenny"
var greeting
greeting = "How are you, " + userName
```

After the browser executed the third line of code, the value of the greeting variable would be "How are you, Jenny". If we wanted to add a question mark at the end of this string, we would simply use two $+$ operators to put all three strings together:

```
var userName = "Jenny"
var greeting
greeting = "How are you, " + userName + "?"
```

Or, to put together two names stored in variables name firstName and lastName and add a space between them:

```
var fullName, firstName = "George", lastName = "Washington"
fullName = firstName + " " + lastName
```

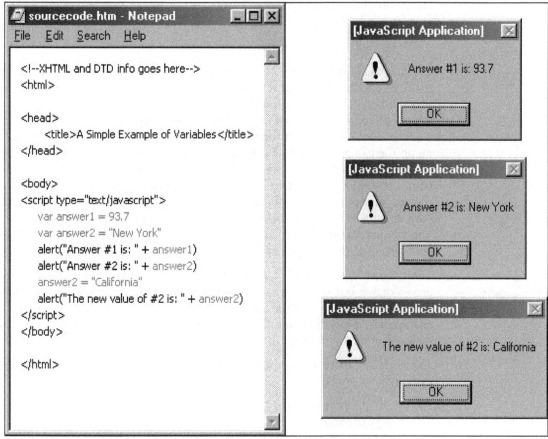

FIGURE 8.5. Declaring and using variables

Figure 8.5 shows the code for a simple script that declares and initializes two variables, displays their values using alert boxes, and then changes and displays the value of the second variable. (Note that we can use the + operator inside the alert command.)

Lab Exercise 8.1, "Practice with Variables," may be done at this point.

Returning a Value

We started the section "Storing Things for Later Use: Variables" by considering the situation where we wanted to get the current value of the grind property of the UltraJava machine. We will assume that the UltraJava machine has a getGrind() method that gets the value of the current setting and sends it to us. But, as previously mentioned, we need to have something to catch and store the value sent back from the machine, whether "coarse," "medium," or "fine." In other words, we need a variable.

Here's how we write the code to do this:

```
var grindSetting
grindSetting = ultraJava.getGrind()
```

The first line of code declares a new variable that we are naming `grindSetting`. In the second line, note that the code on the right side of the equal sign is simply a method call for the `getGrind()` method, with no parameters inside the parentheses because we don't need to send the machine any extra information for it to read the value of its `grind` property. The code on the left side of the equal sign is simply the name of our variable. Reading from right to left (as you should always do with an assignment statement), the full line of code sends a message to the UltraJava machine to execute its `getGrind()` method, which then checks the current value of the `grind` property ("coarse," "medium," or "fine") and sends it back or returns it. The returned value is stored in the variable `grindSetting`. This whole process is known as **returning a value**. We can see a real-world example by using a built-in JavaScript command named `prompt()`.

The `prompt()` command is similar to the `alert()` command in that it displays a dialog box on the screen with a message in it. But this **prompt box** also allows the surfer to enter some information into a textbox that's built into the prompt box. Thus the name: The message displayed in the box "prompts" the surfer to enter something.

The code to create a prompt box that requests the user to enter his or her name is:

```
<script type="text/javascript">
  var theName
  theName = prompt("Please enter your name:", "Enter name
    here")
</script>
```

The first parameter in the `prompt()` method call is the message to be displayed in the prompt box; the second parameter is text that will initially appear in the text box itself. The resulting display will be similar to Figure 8.6 (different browsers will display it with slight differences).

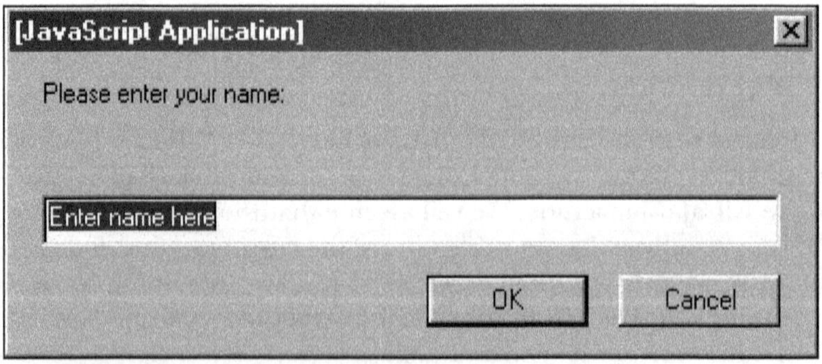

FIGURE 8.6.   A prompt box

Often we want to have the text box appear empty initially, in which case we write:

```
var theName
theName = prompt("Please enter your name:", "")
```

The second pair of quotation marks with nothing between them is required; it tells the `prompt()` command not to display anything in the prompt's textbox. If you leave them out completely, then the text "undefined" appears initially in the text box.

When the surfer enters something in the prompt's text box and clicks the OK button, `prompt()` returns the value of the text box. This is the reason that we use an assignment statement with `prompt()`, unlike with `alert()`, which returns nothing. In our example, the surfer's name (or whatever the surfer entered) will be returned and stored in the variable named `theName`. The following code may then use the value in `theName` in whatever way necessary. For example, we might just echo the surfer's entry with an alert box:

```
var theName
theName = prompt("Please enter your name:", "")
alert("Greetings, " + theName)
```

Putting this code into a `<script>` element in a source document, we would get the results shown in Figure 8.7.

If we simply need to get a Yes/No type of response from the user, there is another kind of box—the **confirm box**—that is better to use than a prompt box. The box displays a message or question to the surfer along with two buttons, OK and Cancel. The box and accompanying message are created using the `confirm()` command, with one parameter (the text of the message). If the surfer agrees with the message and confirms it by clicking the OK button, then `confirm()` will return a boolean value of `true`. If the surfer clicks the Cancel button, it returns a boolean value of `false`. For example:

```
var userAnswer
userAnswer = confirm("Are you sure you want to do that?")
alert("Your response was: " + userAnswer)
```

The confirm box generated by this code will appear as in Figure 8.8.

The confirm box is particularly useful in situations where it's best to ask the surfer's permission or give a warning before proceeding with something. There might be a link, for example, on a website that links to a very large audio or video file. If the surfer clicks the link, you would have the confirm box appear with the message "This is a very large file. Are you sure you want to download it?". If the surfer clicks OK, the download would proceed. (We don't yet know how to write the JavaScript code to do this, but by the end of Chapter 12, we will.)

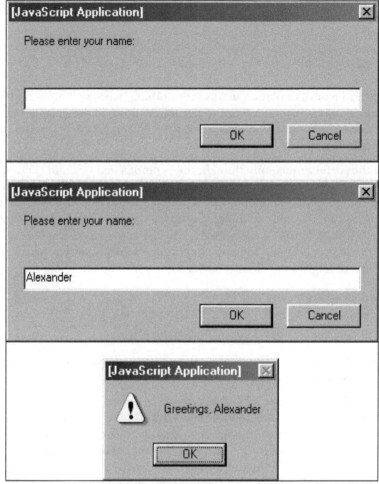

FIGURE 8.7.   Getting information using a prompt box and displaying it in an alert box (top to bottom)

QuickCheck Questions

1. Write the JavaScript code that declares three variables named `firstResult`, `secondResult`, and `thirdResult`. First do it on separate lines and then all on one line.

2. Repeat #2, but this time initialize `firstResult` to the value "Hello", `secondResult` to the boolean value `true`, and `thirdResult` to the value 18.

3. Write the code that displays a prompt box with the message "Please enter your age" and stores the user's answer in a variable named `userAge`.

Lab Exercise 8.2, "A Simple Online Quiz," may be done at this point.

FIGURE 8.8. Using a confirm box and displaying the response (assuming the surfer clicked OK)

The Object Structure of a Web Browser

Our next step is to learn how the concepts of object-oriented programming we introduced in the section "An Introduction to Objects" apply to a web browser. Current-day web browsers are constructed in an object-oriented fashion, with the top-level object being the browser window. Underneath the window object come three main objects: location, document, and history (Figure 8.9). These three types of **window objects** are the foundation for how the browser displays a source document as a web page, and the whole scheme is known as the **Document Object Model (DOM)**. (More recent browsers extend the DOM to include additional objects and sub-objects of their own design, but all except the most ancient browsers use the basic DOM at a minimum.)

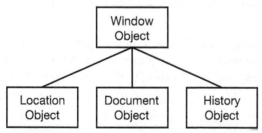

FIGURE 8.9. The basic objects of the Document Object Model

In addition to its three main child objects, the `window` object also has a number of other properties and methods attached to it. Several of these methods we have already seen and used: What we have been referring to as the "alert command," the "prompt command," and the "confirm command" are technically all methods belonging to the window object. From now on we will say the "`alert()` method," the "`prompt()` method," and the "`confirm()` method." Their full JavaScript names are therefore `window.alert()`, `window.prompt()`, and `window.confirm()`.

In OOP terminology we refer to the three key objects of the browser window as `window.location`, `window.history`, and `window.document`. In actual usage, however, we may leave off the reference to "window," because when you use `location`, `history`, or `document` as objects, the browser assumes that you are referring to those objects belonging to the current window. Similarly, we may write `alert("Message goes here")` instead of `window.alert("Message goes here")`, because the `window` reference is assumed.

We review the `document`, `location`, and `history` objects below.

The document Object

The `document` object, via its properties, contains information on the current document being displayed in the window and, via its methods, allows for the display of HTML code. The **document object** properties include:

- `URL` (stores the URL of the current document)
- `referrer` (stores the URL of the document from which the current document was linked; that is, it's the previous document that was displayed)
- `title` (stores the title of the document, as defined by the <title> element)
- `bgColor` (stores the number for the document's background color, as set by the `bgcolor` attribute or `background-color` style property of the document's <body> tag)
- `fgColor` (stores the number for the document's text color, as set by the `text` attribute or `color` style property of the <body> tag)

We will review some of the document object's other properties in later chapters, but it is useful to know that they include lists of all the links and forms in the document.

The most-used method of the document object is the `document.write()` (pronounced "document-dot-write") method, which in certain situations may be used to write text and HTML code to the window. An example would be:

```
document.write("This text will be
    <strong>displayed</strong> on the screen.")
```

The `document.write()` method will come in handy when we explore the combination of frames and JavaScript in Chapter 17.

The location Object

The `location` object stores information about the URL of the document currently displayed in the browser window. The **location object** has the property `location.href`, which contains the complete URL, plus it has a number of other properties that store the various parts of the URL separately, such as the property `hostname`. The `hostname` property stores the host and domain name of the URL, e.g., www.yahoo.com and socrates.berkeley.edu.

Note an important difference between the `location.href` property and the `URL` property of the `document` object. The `document.URL` property may not be changed; it is fixed. The properties of the `location` object, however, may be changed (and will change the document that is displayed in the window). For example, the following line of JavaScript code would tell the browser to load the home page of Yahoo, replacing the current document displayed:

```
<script type="text/javascript">
   location.href = "http://www.yahoo.com"
</script>
```

We will use this feature in Chapter 12 when we learn how to create pop-up menus and select-and-go navigation.

The history Object

The `history` object of the window stores the list of the previous URLs that the surfer has visited. The **history object** has three methods: `history.back()`, `history.forward()`, and `history.go()`. If you call the `history.back()` method, the document at the previous URL will be displayed. If you call the `history.forward()` method, you will move to the next URL forward on the history list (assuming that the surfer has moved back on the list, so that there's a page to move forward to.) In other words, these two methods work like the browser's Back and Forward buttons.

Finally, you may call the `history.go()` method with a negative or positive integer as a parameter to move that many clicks backward or forward, respectively, on the history list. For instance, `history.go(-4)` would move back and display the document from 4 clicks previously on the history list.

Accessing and Changing Object Properties

Some object properties are **read-only**, meaning that their values can only be read, not changed, using JavaScript. Others are **read-write** properties, meaning that we can use JavaScript not only to read their value, but also to change them to a new value. We have already mentioned one example of each of these: the `document.URL` property is read-only while the `location.href` property is read-write.

Among the document object's other properties that were listed above, `title` and `referrer` are read-only, while `fgColor` and `bgColor` are read-write (see the discussion below for a few exceptions). A simple way to access and read these properties is to use the `alert()` method. For instance, to display the value of `document.title` in an alert box, we write the code as shown in Figure 8.10. (Remember that the value of `document.title` is the title as defined in the `<title>` element of the document.)

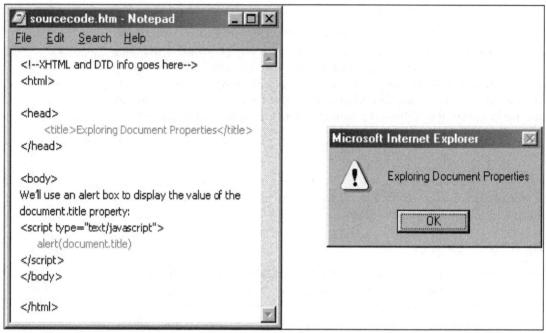

FIGURE 8.10.   Reading and displaying the value of the document.title property

Note again how we wrote the parameter in the call to the `alert()` method. It's `alert(document.title)`, not `alert("document.title")`, because we want the *value* of the property named `document.title` to be displayed.

We may improve the alert box display of the value of `document.title` by using the + operator:

```
alert("The title is: " + document.title)
```

Assuming the document's title is "Exploring Document Properties," the resulting alert box will be as shown in Figure 8.11.

More complex combinations may also be created, such as:

```
alert("The title is " + document.title + "\r and the
    background color is " + document.bgColor)
```

This message will display as shown in Figure 8.12. Note that we used the special **escape character combination** \r (backslash r) in the second string of

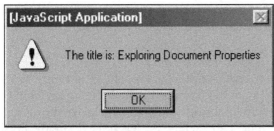

FIGURE 8.11.   Adding explanatory text to the display of document.title

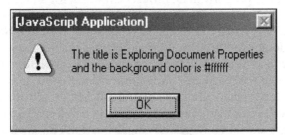

FIGURE 8.12.   Displaying multiple property values with a line break (the #ffffff is the color code for white)

text, i.e., `"\r and the background color is"`. The backslash indicates that the following character is not to be treated as a regular character but instead represents a special character. In this case, the combination `\r` represents the return key character; when the message is printed a line break will be inserted before the word "and." (The combination `\n` will also create a new line. If you want to actually print a backslash, you have to write it as a double backslash, `\\`.)

Although we can access and display the value of the `document.title` property, we cannot change it because it's read-only. In other words, we can't use a JavaScript assignment statement to try to change the value of the title:

```
document.title = "A Better Title"    //Not allowed
```

(Remember once again that an assignment statement, using the equal sign, means "take the value of the right side and assign it to whatever's on the left side.")

In contrast, the values of read-write properties may be changed. Consider the `document.bgColor` property. It stores the value of the web page's background color, as defined in the `<body>` tag using either the `bgcolor` attribute or the `background-color` style property. (See Chapter 3, "Experimenting with Colors," and remember that the value of the background color is stored in hexadecimal format, although we may specify certain basic colors using predefined names like red, yellow, cyan, and magenta.) We may change the background color using an assignment statement:

```
document.bgColor = "yellow"
```

When the browser executes this line of code, it not only changes the value of `document.bgColor` to yellow, it also changes the background color of the page itself. In other words, JavaScript enables us to change the background color of a web page at any time. Lab Exercise 8.2 lets you explore the possibilities of this.

IMPORTANT

Similarly, the foreground color of a web page (the color of the text) may be changed using the `document.fgColor` property. But it doesn't work as a read-write (changeable) property in all browsers. It works for all versions of Internet Explorer for Windows and the Macintosh, but only in versions 4 and above of Explorer for UNIX systems and only in version 6 of Netscape Navigator for all systems (Windows, Mac, UNIX). And although `document.bgColor` is a read-write property in all versions of Internet Explorer for Windows and the Macintosh and all versions of Netscape Navigator for Windows, it does not work properly in Navigator versions 2 and 3 for the Macintosh and for UNIX. So the bottom line is that it's nice (and instructive) to use JavaScript to play around with the background and foreground colors, but don't do so on a real web page unless you're sure that everyone visiting your page has an up-to-date browser.

Also be careful whenever you are typing things like `document.bgColor`. It's `document.bgColor`, not `document.bgcolor`! Being case-sensitive, JavaScript will not recognize the latter spelling.

Finally, you may be asking, "How do I know which document properties are read-only and which are read-write, or even what properties exist?" In Appendix F we list the major objects in the Document object model, along with their main methods and properties. To list and explain the methods and properties for all of the objects in the DOM, however, requires several hundred pages. You may find such a list in almost any good JavaScript reference book. Appendix I lists a number of JavaScript websites where documentation and other resources can be found. (To give you an idea of the complexity of the document object, it has over 60 properties, though many of them have only been added in recent years.)

QuickCheck Questions

1. What is the key difference between the `document.URL` and `location.href` properties?
2. Write the JavaScript command that would display the document's foreground color setting in an alert box.
3. Write the JavaScript command that would change the document's background color to blue.

Lab Exercise 8.3, "A Chameleon Web Page," may be done at this point.

assignment operator	floating point number	read-only
assignment statement	history object	read-write
boolean	initializing a variable	reserved word
calling a method	integer	returning a value
child object	location object	sending a message to an object
concatenation	loosely typed	state and behavior of an object
confirm box	name and value of a property	string
data type	object hierarchy	strongly typed
declaring a variable	parameter	variable
document object	parent object	variable name
Document Object Model (DOM)	prompt box	variable type
dot notation	properties and methods of an object	variable value
escape character		window object

1. An Introduction to Objects

Syntax for referring to a property of a software object:
```
objectName.propertyName
```

Syntax for calling (executing) a method of a software object when the method has no input parameters:
```
objectName.methodName()
ultraJava.powerToggle()    //Example from the imaginary ultraJava machine
```

Calling a method of a software object when the method has one or more parameters:
```
objectName.methodName(parameter1, parameter2, parameter3)
ultraJava.changeGrind("coarse")    //Imaginary ultraJava example
```

Using an assignment statement to assign a value to a property (read from right to left):
```
objectName.propertyName = X
ultraJava.grind = "fine"
```

Referring to a property of an object that is itself a child of one or more other objects:
```
topLevelObject.secondLevelObject.thirdLevelObject.propertyName
```

Calling a method of an object that is itself a child of one or more other objects:
```
topLevelObject.secondLevelObject.thirdLevelObject.methodName(parm1, parm2, . . . )
ultraJava.cappuccinoMaker.changeStrength("double")
```

2. Storing Things for Later Use: Variables

Declaring a variable named theResult:
```
var theResult
```

Declaring several variables named firstNum, secondNum, and thirdNum:
```
var firstNum
var secondNum
var thirdNum
```

Or:
```
var firstNum, secondNum, thirdNum
```

Declaring variables named `answer1`, `answer2`, and `answer3` and initializing them to a number value, a string value, and a boolean value, respectively:

```
var answer1 = 4.962
var answer2 = "Hello! How are you?"
var answer3 = true
```

Or:

```
var answer1 = 4.962, answer2 = "Hello! How are you?", answer3 = true
```

Concatenating several string values:

```
var userName = "Jenny"
var greeting
greeting = "How are you, " + userName + "?"
```

Basic syntax for calling a method that returns a value (the assignment statement stores the returned value in a variable named `grindSetting`):

```
var grindSetting
grindSetting = ultraJava.getGrind()
```

Displaying a prompt box with a prompt ("Please enter . . .") and an empty textbox for the user's entry:

```
var theName
theName = prompt("Please enter your name:", "")
```

Displaying a confirm box that will return a value of `true` or `false`, depending on whether the user clicks the OK or Cancel buttons in the box:

```
var userAnswer
userAnswer = confirm("Are you sure you want to do that?")
```

3. The Object Structure of a Web Browser

Using the `href` property of the `location` object to change the currently displayed web page by loading another one:

```
location.href = "http://www.yahoo.com"
```

Displaying the value of the `document.title` property in an alert box:

```
alert(document.title)
alert("The title is: " + document.title)
```

Displaying several property values in an alert box (and using the \r escape character to insert a line break):

```
alert("The title is " + document.title + "\r and the background color is " +
   document.bgColor)
```

Changing the values of the `bgColor` and `fgColor` properties of the document (and thus changing the background and foreground colors of the web page on the fly—but doesn't work with all browsers):

```
document.bgColor = "yellow"
document.fgColor = "blue"
```

As with HTML, names in JavaScript should never start with a numeral nor contain spaces.

More specifically, variable names must start with either a letter (A–Z or a–z) or an underscore character (_). After the first character, other characters may be letters, digits (0–9), or the underscore character. But do not use spaces or any other special symbols or punctuation marks.

When naming a variable, you should give it a name that is descriptive of its purpose. But don't make names too long or involved, because it increases the chances of typographical errors.

Don't use any of JavaScript's reserved words for your own variable names.

Remember that variable names are case sensitive.

Alerts and Advice

Only use the `var` keyword when you declare a variable.

Never enclose the boolean values `true` and `false` in quotation marks, otherwise they will be treated as strings.

When you want to use the `alert()` method to display the value of an object property, you do *not* enclose the property name in quotation marks.

Changing the background and text colors of a web page on the fly, by assigning new values to the `document.bgColor` and `document.fgColor` properties, does not work for all browsers.

Watch the spelling of object properties: for example, it's `document.bgColor`, not `document.bgcolor`.

1. A software object consists of two things bundled together: _____ and _____.
2. True or false: The phrase "call the method" means the same as "execute the code in the method."
3. Which of the following (one or more) is an assignment statement?
   a. `ultraJava.changeGrind("fine")`
   b. `ultraJava.bean`
   c. `ultraJava.bean = "French Roast"`
   d. `var lastBeanUsed`
4. The three main data types in JavaScript are: _____, _____, and _____.
5. The three characteristics of a variable are: _____, _____, and _____.
6. Which of the following terms refers to programming languages where only one type of data may be stored in any given variable?
   a. variable data language
   b. fixed data language
   c. loosely typed language
   d. strongly typed language
7. Which of the following declares a variable named `theResult` and initializes it to the value 3.14?
   a. `declare(theResult, 3.14)`
   b. `var theResult = 3.14`
   c. `var theResult, 3.14`
   d. `variable theResult = 3.14`
8. Which of the following are *not* legal variable names?
   a. `answer3`
   b. `answer 3`
   c. `3answer`
   d. `3Answer`
   e. `TheAnswer`
   f. `the_answer`
   g. `the-answer`
   h. `variable`
   i. `var`
9. What is the value of the variable named `theResult` after the following three lines of code are executed?
   ```
   var firstAnswer, theResult
   firstAnswer = "Hello"
   theResult = firstAnswer
   ```
   a. "Hello"
   b. "firstAnswer"

    c. "theResult"

    d. None of the above

10. Which of the following lines of code correctly displays a prompt box with the message "What is your name?" and an empty textbox where the user may type the name, and then stores the user's entry in a variable named `userName`. (Assume that the variable `userName` has already been properly declared.)

    a. `userName = prompt("What is your name?")`

    b. `userName = prompt("What is your name?", "")`

    c. `prompt("What is your name?", userName)`

    d. `prompt(userName, "What is your name?")`

11. Which of the following lines of code will, when executed, change the web page being displayed by the browser to Yahoo's home page?

    a. `location.href = "http://www.yahoo.com"`

    b. `document.change("http://www.yahoo.com")`

    c. `window.change("http://www.yahoo.com")`

    d. `document.URL = "http://www.yahoo.com"`

12. True or false: `document.title` is a read-only property.

13. True or false: When referring to the property of the `document` object that stores the background color of the current Web page, you may write it as any one of the following three variations: `document.bgcolor`, `document.bgColor`, or `document.BgColor`.

1. Briefly define and/or explain the following terms: state, behavior, property, method, parameter.

2. (a) Write an assignment statement that would change the `bean` property of the `ultraJava` object to the value "French Roast".

    (b) Assuming that the `ultraJava` object had a method named `changeBean()` that took a single parameter that was the value to change the `bean` setting to, write the code that would call this method and change the `bean` setting to "Decaf Colombian".

3. Assuming that the `ultraJava` object had a child object named `espressoMaker`, which had a method named `powerOn()` with no parameters, write the code that would call this method.

4. Assuming that the `espressoMaker` object mentioned in exercise 3 also has a method with the name `getPowerStatus()`, which returns a value of "on" or "off", write the code that would call this method and store the returned value in a variable named `espressoPower`.

5. In a `<script>` element, write the JavaScript code that would declare a number variable with the name `firstNum` and initialize it to the value 47.2, a string variable named `userName` and initialize it to the value "Abraham Lincoln", and a boolean variable named `matchFound` and initialize it to be false. Then write the code that would change the value of `firstNum` to 39.27, the value of `userName` to "Theodore Roosevelt", and the value of `matchFound` to `true`.

6. In a `<script>` element, write the JavaScript code that uses the `prompt()` method to ask the user to enter the name of their favorite movie. The code should store the movie name in a variable named `favoriteMovie`. After the user enters the movie name and clicks the OK button, an alert box should appear with the message, "That's mine, too."

7. In a `<script>` element, write the JavaScript code that uses the `confirm()` method to ask the user whether they want want to go through with their online purchase. The code should store the answer (either `true` or `false`) in a variable named `checkout`. After the user clicks the OK or Cancel button, an alert box should appear with the message, "Thank you."

8. Write the HTML code that creates a click button with the label "Click here to go to Yahoo." The code in the button's event handler should be an assignment statement that uses the `location.href` property to change the web page to the home page of www.yahoo.com (or other website of your choice).

9. Why can't you change the title of a web page by using an assignment statement to give the `document.title` property a new value?

10. **a.** Write the line of JavaScript code that would call the `alert()` method and display the value of the `document.URL` property.

   b. Write the line of JavaScript code that would call the `alert()` method and display the values of the `document.title` and `document.URL` properties in one alert box, so that the whole message is on one line using the format:

   "The title is [title is displayed here] and the URL is [URL goes here]."

   c. Show how to modify the code in part b so that the second part of the sentence starting with "and the URL is . . ." is displayed on a separate line in the alert box.

Debugging Exercise

1. Identify and correct the errors in the following `<body>` element code. (Assume that the corresponding `<head>` element was properly written—just focus on the code below.)

```
<body>
<script type="javascript">
   var last name
   var professionalTitle = Dr.
   prompt(Please enter your last name:)
   alert(Greetings, + professionalTitle + name)
   alert(For your information, the title of this document is: document.name)
</script>
</body>
```

Exercise 8.1: Practice with Variables

❏ Create an HTML source document with a `<script>` element in the `<head>` element that uses JavaScript to declare several variables as follows: a number variable named `testNumber` initialized to the value 109.4, three string variables named `name1`, `name2`, and `name3` (without initializing them), and two boolean variables named `cream` and `sugar` initialized to false and true, respectively. Display the value of `testNumber` in one alert box, the values of `name1`, `name2`, and `name3` in a second alert box, and the values of the boolean variables in a third alert box. What appears for the values of the string variables?

❏ Add code to the source document that will change the value of `testNumber` to 75, assign the values "Copernicus", "Galileo", and "Newton" to the three string variables and change the value of `sugar` to `false`. Display the new values in three new alert boxes, as before.

Exercise 8.2: A Simple Online Quiz

❏ Using the prompt, confirm, and alert boxes, it's possible to create a simple online quiz. We will use the three questions below as an example. Begin by creating a new source document named simplequiz. htm with a `<script>` element in the `<body>` element. In the `<script>` element write the code that will display a prompt box with Question 1 and a blank textbox where the surfer can enter the answer. Store the

Lab Exercises

surfer's answer in a variable named `firstAnswer`. Then have the code display an alert box with a two-line message: "You answered [surfer's answer goes here]" should be on the first line and "The correct answer is packet-switching" should be on the second line.

After the surfer clicks OK in the alert box, another prompt box should appear with Question 2. Store the surfer's answer in a variable named `secondAnswer` and then again display an alert box with the surfer's answer and the correct answer, (which is answer a).

Finally, for the third question, use a confirm box instead of a prompt box, storing the result (`true` or `false`) in a variable named `thirdAnswer`. Then display an alert box with the surfer's answer and correct answer (true).

The three questions:

1. The Internet uses a method of traffic control and flow known as _____.
2. Which checks for lost packets?
    a. Transmission Control Protocol (TCP)
    b. Internet Protocol (IP)
    c. Internet Error Checking Protocol (IECP)
3. True or false: XHTML tags are case sensitive (click OK for true, Cancel for false).

(Note: In Chapters 13 and 14 we will learn how to create more sophisticated quizzes using check boxes and radio buttons and have JavaScript automatically calculate the surfer's score.)

Exercise 8.3: A Chameleon Web Page

In this Exercise you will create a chameleon web page where the surfer can click various buttons and have the background and foreground colors change. But first we need to get some practice with document properties.

❑ Create an HTML source document with a `<script>` element in the `<body>` element. Using the `alert()` method, display the values of the `title`, `URL`, `bgColor`, and `fgColor` properties of the document object. Use a separate alert box for each, and make each message along the lines of "The document title is . . ." or "The background color of the document is . . ." (Don't forget to include a `<title>` element in the document.)

❑ At the beginning of the `<script>` element from the previous part, put an assignment statement that changes the background color of the page to a color of your choice. (Remember that the 16 predefined color names are black, white, silver, gray, maroon, red, magenta, purple, green, lime, olive, yellow, navy, blue, teal, and cyan.) At the end of the `<script>` element, after the alert commands, put an assignment statement that changes the background color back to white.

❑ Once you have the change in background color working, add an assignment statement at the beginning to change the foreground color to a color of your choice and an assignment statement at the end to change it back to black. (Note: In some versions of Navigator this will not work, but try it and see what happens.)

❑ Using a new source document, use a `<form>` element to create at least three click buttons. Label each button with the value Click for red, Click for blue, and so on (or just Red, Blue, and so on; also use whatever colors you like). Then put an assignment statement in the event handler of each button that will change the background color to whatever the button is labeled. When you're done, the background color should change when each button is clicked.

Functions and Parameters

LEARNING OBJECTIVES

1. Learn how to modularize JavaScript code by declaring and calling functions.

2. Learn how to send information to a function for processing.

3. Learn how to create image rollovers using the image object and mouseover and mouseout events.

Divide and Conquer: Using Functions

Once you have worked with JavaScript awhile, you will start wishing for methods that it doesn't have. To take a nonsensical but instructive example, imagine that you are writing some JavaScript code for a web page and you find yourself often using the following lines of code that put up three alert boxes, one after the other:

```
<script type="text/javascript">
  alert("Here is the first alert box")
  alert("Here is the second alert box")
  alert("Here is yet a third alert box")
</script>
```

You begin to think to yourself that it sure would be nice not to have to type the same lines of code again and again. You could copy and paste it each time, of course, but even that gets tiresome. Moreover, using the same three lines over and over in different places clutters up your code and makes it more difficult to read.

Or, consider the case where we would like the three alert boxes to be triggered by an `onclick` event handler in a click button. We would have to write:

241

```
<input type="button" value="Click here!"
  onclick="alert('Here is the first alert box');
  alert('Here is the second alert box'); alert('Here is
  yet a third alert box')">
```

You can see that it gets a little unwieldy trying to fit all that JavaScript code into the <input> tag, and that's only for three commands. Sometimes we will need to have 10 or 20 or more lines of JavaScript code triggered by an event handler.

It therefore would be convenient if we could give those specific lines of code some special name or label, and then just use the label instead of the lines wherever the lines occurred.

This idea is a fundamental concept in programming: that of **modularization**. You write your code in re-usable, self-contained modules, and then when you need to execute a certain module of code, you ask for it by name. Such modules not only reduce clutter, they also make it easier to find and eliminate errors in your program.

You may have realized that objects themselves, and their associated methods, reflect the concept of modularization. Each software object is a self-contained bundle of data (properties) and instructions (methods), and each method, in turn, is its own self-contained, re-usable module of code. So really our question is: How do we make our own methods? One way JavaScript allows us to do this is by defining our own functions.

Declaring and Calling Functions

In the general context of programming, a **function** is simply a module of code. In the specific context of JavaScript, a function is also a method that belongs to the window object. In other words, when we create a function in JavaScript, we are creating a new method for the window object.

The basic syntax for defining a function is:

```
function someName() {
  JavaScript instructions go here
}
```

To summarize: We write the word function, which is a reserved word in JavaScript. Remember that this means JavaScript reserves it for its own use and that programmers should not use that word in any other way. We follow the word function with some name we choose to give to it (which shouldn't be a JavaScript reserved word). In the example above, we used someName. Then we add a set of parentheses (about which more later—they concern the use of parameters, as you might guess) and a left curly brace. The left curly brace indicates the beginning of the section where we can place the function's instructions, in the order we want them executed. The right curly brace then signifies the end of the definition of the function.

Some programmers prefer to put the left curly brace on its own line, like so:

```
function someName()
{
   JavaScript instructions go here
}
```

Either position works. The only restriction is that the first thing the browser encounters after the parentheses must be the left curly brace.

The term usually given to this process of defining a function is declare—you define or **declare a function** by writing its sequence of instructions in the above format. Once you have declared the function—or, once you have written the **function declaration**—it is ready to receive a message to execute, i.e., it is ready to be called. You **call a function** the same way that you call a method, but without the necessity of listing all the method's ancestor objects. That is, you simply write the function's name. To call the `someName()` function in our example above, we would write:

```
someName()
```

You may also write `window.someName()`, because the function is technically a method of the `window` object. But normally the `window` reference is left off.

A reminder about naming: We start off the function name with a lowercase letter simply as a convention, and then use an uppercase letter at the beginning of each word within the name. You may also separate words within the name using the underscore (_) character, such as `some_name()`. What you may not do, however, is put spaces in a function name. Nor should you use any other characters besides letters and numbers. And finally, the first character in the name should be a letter, not a number.

Error Alert!

A Simple Example of a Function

Although technically not always necessary, it is good practice to declare functions in the <head> element of an HTML document. This ensures that the browser, as it loads the page from top to bottom, sees the functions before they can get activated by some event handler.

IMPORTANT

The first thing a web browser does when it accesses and displays an HTML source document is to check the <head> element for key information, such as the title of the web page. It also notes the existence of any function declarations and makes appropriate preparations for when they are called later. After it checks the <head> element, the web browser moves on to the HTML and JavaScript code in the <body> element. It starts at the top of the <body> element and works its way down line by line, translating the code it finds in each line into the web page display that the surfer will see.

The left box of Figure 9.1 shows how we declare a function with the name myFirstFunction() in the <head> element and call it from the <body> element. (The numbers in the left margin of the left box are referenced in the next section.)

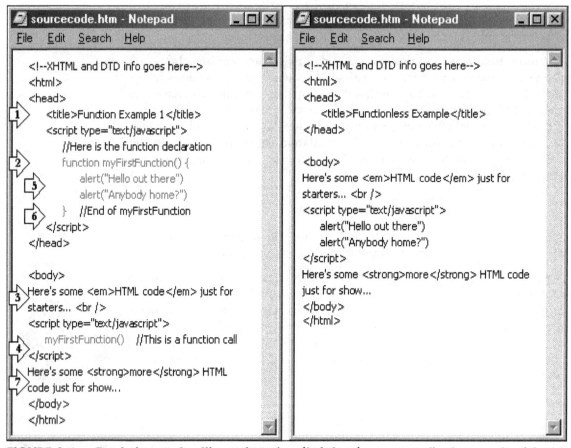

FIGURE 9.1. **Declaring and calling a function (left box) vs. same display result without using a function (right box). (The numbers in the left box margin are referenced in the section "Tracing the Browser's Execution of HTML and JavaScript Code.")**

When the browser loads this source document, it first reads the code in the <head> element. There it finds the <script> element with the function declaration. It inspects this function code but does not execute it, because a function's code is only executed when it is called. In other words, this is just the function definition.

When it comes to the <body> element, it displays the first line of text:

Here's some *HTML code* just for starters . . .

(Note: Because of a quirk in Navigator, it will display the alert boxes before anything else appears, even when the alert commands come after other things in the source document. So our description of what happens with the Figure 9.1 code pertains to Explorer.)

Then the browser comes to the <script> element with the function call to myFirstFunction(). This sends the browser to the code for myFirstFunction(), i.e., it goes up to the function declaration for myFirstFunction() and executes the code that if finds there. The first line of the function's code puts up an alert box with the message "Hello out there", followed by the second alert with the message "Anybody home?" (after the user clicks on the OK button of the first alert box). After the second alert box, the browser is at the end of the function, so it returns to the line of code where the function was called and continues on with whatever comes next. In this case, it's the last line of text:

Here's some **more** HTML code just for show . . .

We could have, of course, gotten the same result from the version shown in the right box of Figure 9.1. This source document is simpler and would normally be preferred. But we are using "Function Example 1" (the code in the left box) simply to show how we declare and call a function. Remember that the key principle behind all this is modularization, with the benefits it brings.

Tracing the Browser's Execution of HTML and JavaScript Code

Although the two HTML documents above give the same result, note the difference in the browser's execution of each. When the browser loads the functionless source document, it first executes the HTML instructions in the <head> element. In this case, it's simply the <title> element with the title "Functionless Example." It then goes on to translate the instructions in the <body> element, line by line, into the web page display, including the alert boxes in the <script> element.

We briefly traced the browser's execution of the "Function Example 1" source document above, but let's look at it in more detail. (The number of each step below is shown in Figure 9.1.)

1. It first executes the <title> instruction in the <head> and then goes on to the <script> element.

2. There it finds a declaration for a function named myFirstFunction(). It notes the name for future reference, in case later on it encounters a function call to myFirstFunction(). It also checks the function's code (the two alert commands, in this case) to make sure that it is legal code. For instance, if we had misspelled alert as dldrl, or if we had left off the right curly brace that signifies the end of the function, or if we had made some other syntactical mistake, the browser would generate an error message.

3. After finishing with the code in the `<head>` element, the browser moves on to the `<body>`, where it first translates and displays the line of HTML code `Here's some <em>HTML code</em> just for starters . . ..`

4. Then it finds the `<script>` element, within which is a single line of JavaScript code: the function call to `myFirstFunction()`.

5. It recognizes this function name from its previous encounter with its declaration in the `<head>` element, so it returns to the declaration and executes each line of code in the function in order. In this case, that means it executes the two alert commands.

6. When it comes to the end of the function declaration, signified by the right curly brace, it returns to the place where the function was called and continues on with the next instruction.

7. In this case, it returns to the `<script>` element where the call to `myFirstFunction()` is located, sees that the next instruction is the ending `</script>` tag, and continues on with the final line of HTML code.

Repeat: When the web browser comes to the end of a function that it has been executing (not checking, but actually executing its instructions), it returns to the line where the function was called and proceeds with whatever comes next. Many students fail to perceive this key point, and therefore fail to understand how JavaScript functions (or functions in almost any programming language) work.

Variations on the Function Theme

As we proceed with our study of JavaScript, we will create more complicated and useful examples of functions. But in order to get a better grasp of how functions work, we will review a few simple variations on the `myFirstFunction()` example, using the code shown in Figure 9.2.

First, you may declare any number of functions within a single `<script>` element, itself in the `<head>` element. So we might have the `<script>` element as shown in Figure 9.2. There is a lot going on in this code, but nothing we really haven't seen before, so we will take it slowly and break it down point by point.

IMPORTANT

Note that we have used single-line comments after each ending right curly brace to annotate the end of each function declaration. Although this practice doesn't add much right now and certainly is not required, later when you're working with longer functions and have more curly braces floating around in your code, you will find it very helpful in keeping track of what's what.

Now we have a question to ponder: In what order will the various alert instructions be executed and displayed by the web browser when it loads this source document? Try to trace it for yourself, and then we'll outline it below. Remem-

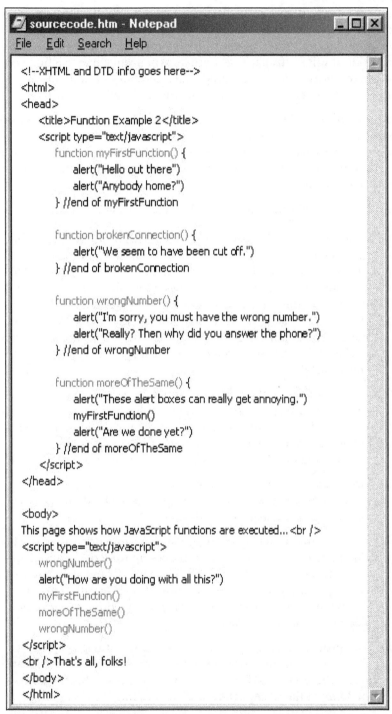

FIGURE 9.2. Variations on the function theme, Illustrating the order of execution and the fact that functions may be called from within other functions

ber that the key is to start at the beginning of the <head> element and work your way down. When you come to a function declaration, ignore it for the moment (unless you want to check for syntax errors). When you come to HTML code, it will be displayed as normal. When you come to a function call, go to where the function is declared, trace the lines of code in order, then return to the line of code that follows the function call and continue.

In tracing out the order of execution using the above guidelines, you should have discovered a very important point: *The order in which we declare functions is not necessarily the same as the order in which they are executed.* That is, the order in which they are executed is the order in which the functions *are called, not the order in which they are declared.*

Here's the outline of what happens in the Figure 9.2 code:

1. The browser first displays "This page shows how JavaScript functions are executed . . .", followed by a line break. Then it starts in on the JavaScript code in the <script> element. First it finds a call to the function wrongNumber(). So it goes up to where wrongNumber() is declared in the <head> element and executes the instructions it finds there. That is, it executes the two alert commands in order, displaying the first message "I'm sorry, you must have the wrong number" and then the second message "Really? Then why did you answer the phone?"

2. When it comes to the end of the function declaration for wrongNumber(), it follows the rule emphasized above and returns to the <script> element in the <body>, moving on to the line that follows the call to the wrongNumber() function. In this case, it is an alert command with the message "How are you doing with all this?"

3. After this alert command comes a function call to myFirst-Function(), so the browser goes up to its declaration and executes the two alert commands it finds there.

4. It then returns back down to find another function call to the function named moreOfTheSame(). It goes up to its declaration, executes the alert command there (displaying "These alert boxes can really get annoying"), and then finds a function call to myFirst-Function(). *It is perfectly legal, and often very useful, to call a function from within another function.*

5. The browser goes up and executes the instructions in myFirst-Function() again. When it's done there, it returns to the location from where myFirstFunction() was called—in this case, the second line of the moreOfTheSame() function.

6. It then continues on and executes the next line of code in moreOfTheSame(), i.e., the alert command that puts up the "Are we done yet?" message. After that, there are no more instructions in

moreOfTheSame(), so it returns to the location from where moreOfTheSame() was called—in this case, the fourth line of the <body>'s <script> element.

7. It then finds the next instruction to be another call to the myThirdFunction() function, so it goes back up and executes its instructions one more time.

8. When the browser returns from executing myThirdFunction() for the second time, it finds itself at the end of the <script> element, so it continues by executing and displaying the last two lines of HTML code in the document.

Make sure that you understand this process. You need to know how to look at HTML and JavaScript code and follow its line of execution step by step—especially function calls—so that you can see how the display will turn out. Conversely, given a display that you want to achieve, you need to know what HTML and JavaScript code to write. (This latter knowledge and skill will come gradually over time as you study JavaScript, but make sure that you are developing it as you go along.)

One final important point: Note that even though the function brokenConnection() was declared in the <head> element's <script> element, its instruction was never executed. That is, the alert box message "We seem to have been cut off" never appears. The reason is that brokenConnection() is not called anywhere in our code. We never tell the browser to execute it. Remember this, because it is easy when you are programming to declare a function but forget to call it, so that you're left wondering why the results of your carefully crafted code are not appearing on the screen when the browser loads the document.

QuickCheck Questions

1. What are the key syntax elements in a function declaration?
2. What is the basic syntax for calling a function?

Lab Exercise 9.1, "Adding Functions to the Chameleon Web Page," may be done at this point.

Adding a Delivery System: Parameters

We have one more major variation to add to our overview of functions, that of **parameters**. We briefly outlined the use of parameters when we first discussed methods and method calls. Parameters are simply the means by which we may send information to a method or function that it needs to use in the course of its instructions. (Another name for parameter that's sometimes used is **argument**.)

The Usefulness of Parameters

The changeGrind() method of the ultraJava object served as our basic example in Chapter 8. When we called the changeGrind() method, we had to tell it which grind setting we wanted ("fine," "medium," or "coarse"). So the method call was:

```
ultraJava.changeGrind("coarse")
```

In a similar manner, we would like to be able to implement parameters in the functions that we create and declare. For instance, we might want to create a function named printGreeting() that took someone's name—say, Fred—and used the alert method to display "Hello, Fred".

We could simply declare the printGreeting() function as follows:

```
function printGreeting() {
  alert("Hello, Fred")
}
```

Everytime we wanted to display "Hello, Fred" on the screen, we would call this function as follows:

```
printGreeting()
```

The resulting display would of course be an alert box with the message:

Hello, Fred

But if we wanted to print a greeting to someone else, say Ginger, we'd have to declare another function, which we'll name printGingerGreeting():

```
function printGingerGreeting() {
  alert("Hello, Ginger")
}
```

To display the "Hello, Ginger" alert box, we would call this function in our code:

```
printGingerGreeting()
```

But clearly, if we have to write a separate function for everyone to whom we want to say hello, this is not a very efficient or convenient way of programming. What we would like to have is a generic "printGreeting" function to which we could send anyone's name and have it print "Hello, [name]". In other words, we need to create a printGreeting() function that uses a parameter. Here's how we declare such a function:

```
function printGreeting(personName) {
  alert("Hello, " + personName)
}
```

In this example personName is the newly declared parameter of the function printGreeting(). We call our new printGreeting() function this way:

```
printGreeting("Fred")
```

Or:

```
printGreeting("Ginger")
```

When the web browser encounters a function call with a parameter involved, like these, it goes up to the function declaration and executes the instructions it finds there, as usual. But in doing so, it also takes the value "Fred" (or the value "Ginger", or whatever) up to the function declaration, where it inserts the value "Fred" into the parameter named personName.

In other words, the function call printGreeting("Fred") is telling the web browser: Go and execute the instructions in the function named print-Greeting(), and take along the value "Fred" and put it into the parameter you find in the function declaration because the function will need it to carry out its instructions.

Note also that really we have two parameters: one on the sending end (the value "Fred" in the function call) and one on the receiving end (personName in the function declaration). This whole process is called **passing a parameter**.

Let's look at the details in our example. When the web browser goes up to the printGreeting() declaration, it finds it has only one instruction:

```
alert("Hello, " + personName)
```

So it displays "Hello, " on the screen and then displays the *value* inside the personName parameter, i.e., the value "Fred" that was passed to it. The result in the alert box is:

Hello, Fred

Or, for the function call printGreeting("Ginger"):

Hello, Ginger

So now we have a generic function that can print a greeting to anyone, as long as we send it the person's name.

Three things to note: First, the comma in the alert command that comes immediately after "Hello" is within the quotation marks, so it's treated as part of the text to display.

Second, remember that the plus sign in alert("Hello, " + personName) is how we tell the browser to append the value of personName to the phrase "Hello, ", so that the combination "Hello, Fred" (or whoever) is displayed.

Third, remember that we don't put quotation marks around the name of the parameter, personName, because we want the *value* of the parameter displayed, not its *name*. In contrast, the following code:

```
alert("Hello, " + "personName")
```

would yield an alert box message of:

Hello, personName

And the code:

```
alert("Hello, + personName")
```

would yield:

Hello, + personName

Multiple Parameters

Functions are not limited to just one parameter. The basic format for a function declaration is:

```
function sampleFunction(a, b, c, d) {
   //JavaScript code that uses a, b, c, and d goes here
}
```

This `sampleFunction()` declaration has four parameters, named a, b, c, and d. (We could list more parameters, if needed.) The parameters are used in the function's code. For example:

```
function sampleFunction(a, b, c, d) {
   alert(a)
   alert(d)
   alert(c)
   alert(b)
}
```

To call this function, we would write:

```
sampleFunction("Bill", "Sarah", "Theresa", "John")
```

Note that the code in `sampleFunction()` doesn't necessarily have to use the parameters in the order in which they're listed: it starts with `alert(a)`, but then the second instruction is `alert(d)`. But the order does matter when we call the function. That is, when the browser executes the function call, the value "Bill" will be sent and placed in the parameter named a, the value "Sarah" will be put into the parameter named b, the value "Theresa" will be put into the parameter named c, and the value "John" will end up in the parameter named d (Figure 9.3). So "Bill" will appear in the first alert box, "John" in the second alert box, "Theresa" in the third alert box, and "Sarah" in the fourth alert box.

IMPORTANT

It's also a good idea to give descriptive names to the parameters, as we've done previously in our `printGreeting()` examples by using the parameter personName. If the parameters above were to store names, for example, we might name them name1, name2, name3, and name4 instead of a, b, c, and d.

Figure 9.4 puts all this together in a complete script. Note that the `printGreetings()` function is called twice: once in the `<script>` element that's in the `<body>` element and once using the `onclick` event handler in the `<input>` tag.

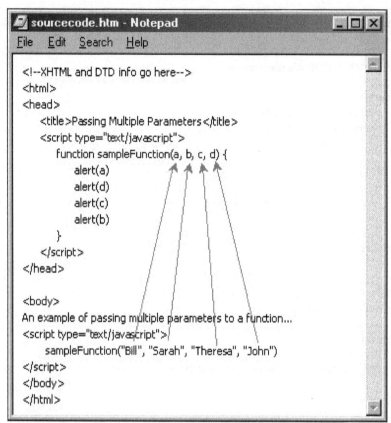

```
sourcecode.htm - Notepad                    _ □ ×

File   Edit   Search   Help

<!--XHTML and DTD info go here-->
<html>
<head>
    <title>Passing Multiple Parameters</title>
    <script type="text/javascript">
        function sampleFunction(a, b, c, d) {
            alert(a)
            alert(d)
            alert(c)
            alert(b)
        }
    </script>
</head>

<body>
An example of passing multiple parameters to a function...
<script type="text/javascript">
        sampleFunction("Bill", "Sarah", "Theresa", "John")
</script>
</body>
</html>
```

FIGURE 9.3.   Using multiple parameters

When the browser loads this source document, it will display the "This is a sample page . . ." line and then execute the JavaScript code in the <script> element; that is, it will call the printGreetings() function and send it the values "Brenda", "Bob", and "Barry." The four alert boxes will then appear, each in turn. After the surfer clicks the OK button in the last box, the browser returns to the <script> element in the <body> and finds that there's no more code to execute. So it continues on with the display of the rest of the HTML code, i.e., the click button that's defined in the <form> element. If and when the surfer clicks on this button, a click event will be generated and its onclick event handler will call the printGreetings() function and send it the values "Jim", "Jane", and "Jenell" to be displayed in the various alert boxes.

Make sure you also understand the code in each alert() method call in the printGreetings() function. The messages will display as follows (using "Brenda," "Bob," and "Barry" for the values of the parameters person1, person2, and person3):

```
sourcecode.htm - Notepad
File  Edit  Search  Help

<!--XHTML and DTD info goes here-->
<html>
<head>
    <title>Parameter Example</title>
    <script type="text/javascript">
        function printGreetings(person1, person2, person3) {
            alert("Hello, " + person3)
            alert(person1 + ", how are you?")
            alert("Nice to see you, " + person2 + "! Going my way?")
            alert("See you later, " + person3 + ", " + person1 + ", and " + person2)
        }
    </script>
</head>

<body>
This is a sample page that uses JavaScript functions and parameters.<br />
<script type="text/javascript">
    printGreetings("Brenda", "Bob", "Barry")
</script>
<form>
    <input type="button" value="Click here to see some more greetings"
        onclick="printGreetings('Jim', 'Jane', 'Jenell')">
</form>
</body>
</html>
```

FIGURE 9.4.   More with multiple parameters

First alert box:	*Hello, Barry*
Second alert box:	*Brenda, how are you?*
Third alert box:	*Nice to see you, Bob! Going my way?*
Fourth alert box:	*See you later, Barry, Brenda, and Bob*

QuickCheck Questions

1. Write a function declaration for a function named parametersTest with two parameters named firstName and lastName. (Don't put any code inside the function.)
2. Show how to call the function in #1, sending it the values "Bill" and "Smith".

Lab Exercise 9.2, "Practicing with Parameters," may be done at this point.

Creating Image Rollovers

We are now at the point where we can learn how to implement one of the most popular web page effects: **image rollovers**. An image rollover is often used in combination with an image link. When the surfer moves the mouse over the image link, the image changes. (Or, in the case of a regular link, an image elsewhere on the page may change.)

To understand how this works, we need to learn how the browser handles images. Recall that the HTML code to put an inline image on a web page is:

```
<img src="eiffel.gif" alt="Eiffel Tower picture"
   width="69" height="120" />
```

When the browser loads an image file and displays the image, behind the scenes it actually turns it into an **image object**. An image object is a child object of the `document` object and has a number of built-in properties, such as `height`, `width`, and `src`. The `height` property stores the height value of the image (in pixels), the width property stores its `width` value, and the `src` property stores the URL of the image file.

Because there may be many images on a web page, and therefore many image objects, the browser keeps track of them via a numbering system. The first image that is loaded is number 0 (!), the second is number 1, the third is number 2, and so on. We will have more to say about this numbering system when we talk about arrays in Chapter 14, but for now all we need to know is that for some mysterious reason it starts with 0. Also remember that the browser loads the HTML source document from top to bottom, so the image numbers go according to the order in which the <img> tags appear in the <body> element.

To refer to each of these image objects in JavaScript we use the object dot notation:

```
document.images[0]      //This refers to the first image
                        //object on the page
document.images[1]      //This refers to the second image
                        //object
document.images[7]      //This refers to the eighth image
                        //object (assuming it exists)
```

Note the meaning of this syntax: `images` refers to the list of image objects of the web page, with each image object belonging to (or being a child object of) the `document` object. Note also that the image number is enclosed in square brackets, which come immediately after `images` (no spaces between them). The square brackets are part of the syntax of the numbering system. You cannot substitute parentheses or curly braces.

Taking this further, we refer to the `height` or `width` property of any given image object as follows:

```
document.images[0].height        //This stores the height
                                 //value of the first image
document.images[0].width         //This stores the width
                                 //value of the first image
document.images[7].width         //This stores the width
                                 //value of the eighth image
document.images[4].src           //This stores the source
                                 //(URL) value of the fifth
                                 //image
```

This numbering system is a convenient way for the browser to label and keep track of the image objects of a web page, but it's not necessarily as convenient for the web page programmer. If we want to refer to a specific image object, we need to know its numbered position in the web page, which means we would have to look at the source document and manually count the images in the <body> element until we came to the one that interested us.

Fortunately, JavaScript provides an alternative: We may give an identifying name to an image object and then refer to that object using the name instead of its number. The simplest way to specify this name is to use the `id` attribute of the <img> tag:

```
<img src="eiffel.gif" alt="Eiffel Tower picture"
   width="69" height="120" id="eiffeltowerpic" />
```

If our Eiffel Tower picture were the third image on the web page, we could now refer to its `width` property in two ways:

```
document.images[2].width
document.eiffeltowerpic.width
```

The second way is obviously clearer to the human eye and mind.

Reminder: In the section on "Internal Links" in Chapter 5, we discussed how the `name` attribute has been deprecated in favor of the `id` attribute for certain elements in XHTML. Because some browsers don't recognize the `id` attribute, we may ensure backward compatibility by using both the `id` and `name` attributes:

```
<img src="eiffel.gif" alt="Eiffel Tower picture"
   width="69" height="120" id="eiffeltowerpic"
   name="eiffeltowerpic" />
```

In our examples, however, we will usually use just the `id` attribute.

Changing the Source of an Image Object

The height and width properties of an image object are read-only properties. Their values are set by the browser when it loads and displays the image, either using the values of the height and width attributes provided in the <img> tag, or using the actual height and width of the image as stored in the data contained in the image file. We therefore cannot use a JavaScript assignment statement to try to change the width of the Eiffel Tower image to, say, 95 pixels:

```
document.eiffeltowerpic.width = 95    //Not allowed
```

Although it's not possible to use the height and width properties of an image object to change the displayed height and width of the corresponding image, it *is* possible to change the image itself. To understand how this works, think of the image objects as rectangular placeholders in the web page layout. The height, width, and location of each placeholder are fixed when the web page loads, and the appropriate image is displayed in each placeholder. For a given placeholder/image object, the URL of its image file is stored in its src property. If we change the value of the src property to the URL of another image file, the browser will automatically load the new image into the placeholder.

To see how we do this, consider our usual Eiffel Tower image, stored in the file eiffel.gif. The HTML code to display it is:

```
<img src="eiffel.gif" alt="Eiffel Tower picture"
   width="69" height="120" id="eiffeltowerpic" />
```

We'll also assume again that it's the third image on the page, so we can refer to it either as document.eiffeltowerpic or as document.images[2].

Finally, we'll assume that we have another image of the Eiffel Tower as it's lit up at night. This image is stored in a file named eiffelnight.jpg and has the same height and width as the eiffel.gif image. The following code will change the displayed image from eiffel.gif to eiffelnight.jpg by changing the src property of the image object:

```
document.images[2].src = "eiffelnight.jpg"
```

We could also, of course, write this as:

```
document.eiffeltowerpic.src = "eiffelnight.jpg"
```

In either case, the image object's source file is being changed to eiffelnight.jpg, and the browser will automatically load and display that image, erasing the previous image (in this case, the eiffel.gif image).

So we see that the src property of an image object is a read/write property just like document.bgColor. Using JavaScript we not only can read its value, but we also can change it to a new value. And when we do so, a new image will appear (assuming that the new value for the src property is the URL of an image file).

When the browser displays the new image, however, it does not change the previously set height and width of the image object. So it's important to make the height and width of the replacement image the same as the original image, otherwise the replacement image may be distorted. (Starting with Explorer version 4 and above and Navigator version 6 and above, the browser can change the height and width on the fly. If the replacement image is a different size from the original, the browser will display it in its correct size and will reformat the page so that text flows around the new image properly.)

Implementing a Rollover

We now know enough to create an image rollover. There are two basic steps:

Step 1. Create an <img> tag in the source document that will load the original image. (We will use the eiffel.gif image.) Use the id attribute in the <img> tag to give the corresponding image object a name so that we don't have to use the image numbering system. (And, optionally, add the name attribute using the same value as the id attribute for backward compatibility with older browsers.) For our example, we will use the eiffel.gif image and give the image object the name eiffeltowerpic:

```
<img src="eiffel.gif" alt="Eiffel Tower picture"
    width="69" height="120" id="eiffeltowerpic" />
```

Step 2. Use an <a> element to create a link that uses the onmouseover and onmouseout event handlers. When a mouseover event occurs for the link, we want the original image to be replaced by the second image (eiffelnight.jpg in our case). So we will have the onmouseover event handler call a function that switches the images:

```
onmouseover = "switchImage()"
```

where the code for the switchImage() function consists of the appropriate assignment statement that loads the new image:

```
function switchImage() {
    document.eiffeltowerpic.src = "eiffelnight.jpg"
}
```

We actually could have written the whole assignment statement in the event handler:

```
onmouseover = "document.eiffeltowerpic.src =
    'eiffelnight.jpg'"
```

But once we put it inside the <a> tag where it belongs, it makes the tag rather long and hard to read.

When the surfer moves the mouse off the link, we want the original image to appear again. So we will have another function, named restoreImage(), that takes care of this case. The code for the onmouseout event handler will be:

```
onmouseout = "restoreImage()"
```

where the code for `restoreImage()` is:

```
function restoreImage() {
   document.eiffeltowerpic.src = "eiffel.gif"
}
```

Again, we could have put this all in the `onmouseout` event handler:

```
onmouseout = "document.eiffeltowerpic.src = 'eiffel.gif'"
```

But the code for the <a> tag would be extremely long at this point.

Figure 9.5 shows how we put it all together in the source document. When the surfer moves over the "Click here for nighttime festivities" link, the original image of the Eiffel Tower will be replaced by the night-time image. Then, when the mouse moves off the link, the original image is restored. Because the <a> tag with the event handlers is so long, we wrote it using multiple lines and indented the second line to make it easier to read. It could, of course, be written entirely on one line. But note that you should never break the event handler code itself over multiple lines; keep the whole `onmouseover =` " . . . " expression on one line.

Better Rollovers Using Precached Images

Before you can go out and add image rollovers to all your web pages, however, you need to know about some of the limitations in this example code. If the surfer is viewing this web page over a relatively slow dial-up connection, there may be an undesirable pause between the time the surfer moves the mouse over the link and the time the image changes. The reason is that the browser has to download the eiffelnight.jpg image before it can display it. The fix is relatively simple: Preload the eiffelnight.jpg image. Preloading, or **precaching**, an image means to instruct the browser to load the image into the browser's memory cache during the initial loading of the page. The image won't appear initially on the page, but once in the cache, the image is immediately available to the browser when it needs to be displayed.

To precache an image, we need to create a new image object in the browser's memory, where the image can be stored until ready for use. The following assignment statement creates a new image object and gives it the name `nightimage`:

```
var nightimage = new Image(69, 120)
```

Note the use of the special JavaScript keyword `new` to create the new object. The name `Image` refers to the image object "constructor," some special JavaScript code that creates an image object. The parameters shown (the 69 and 120) are the width and height of the image. So when we write the code `var nightimage = new Image(69, 120)`, it tells the browser to construct a new image object, give it the name `nightimage`, and set it up for an image

```
sourcecode.htm - Notepad                                    _ □ X
File   Edit   Search   Help

<!--XHTML and DTD info goes here-->
<html>
<head>
<title>Image Rollover Example</title>
<script type="text/javascript">
    function switchImage() {
        document.effeltowerpic.src = "eiffelnight.jpg"
    }

    function restoreImage() {
        document.effeltowerpic.src = "eiffel.gif"
    }
</script>
</head>

<body>
<p>Built for the 1889 World Exposition, the Eiffel Tower <img src="eiffel.gif"
alt="Eiffel Tower picture"  width="69" height="120" id="eiffeltowerpic" /> is located
on the Champs de Mars in Paris, France.</p>
<p><a href="nightschedule.htm" onmouseover = "switchImage()"
        onmouseout = "restoreImage()">Click here for a schedule of all
        the night-time festivities</a></p>
</body>

</html>
```

FIGURE 9.5.   Creating an image rollover using mouseover and mouseout events and the src property of the image object

with a width of 69 pixels and a height of 120 pixels. (Note: Specifying the width and height is optional.)

At this point the new image object is empty; it doesn't actually have an image in it. In order to load an image into the image object, we use an assignment statement to set its src property to the location of the actual image file, as we did above for the image rollover:

```
nightimage.src = "eiffelnight.jpg"
```

Remember that this line of code assumes that the eiffelnight.jpg file is in the same folder as the source document. If it were not, we would have to specify a longer pathname or even a full URL.

We put this all together inside a <script> element:

```
<script type="text/javascript">
  //Construct a new image object and name it
  var nightimage = new Image(69, 120)
  //Load an image into the image object
  nightimage.src = "eiffelnight.jpg"
</script>
```

We place this <script> element in the <head> element, because when the browser loads the page, it starts with the <head> element. This placement thus guarantees that the image will get loaded before the surfer has a chance to move the mouse around the page and generate any mouseover or other events. (It would also work fine if we placed the <script> element at the beginning of the <body> element, but convention is to put it in the <head>.)

Now that we've loaded the eiffelnight.jpg file into the nightimage image object, we need to change the line of code in the switchImage() function. Previously the code was:

```
document.eiffeltowerpic.src = "eiffelnight.jpg"
```

Now we write it:

```
document.eiffeltowerpic.src = nightimage.src
```

We should also create an image object for the original Eiffel Tower image (eiffel.jpg) and modify the onmouseout event handler accordingly, but we will leave that for one of the lab exercises.

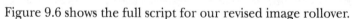

Finally, note that image rollovers as we have implemented them here do not work in older browsers, because image objects only became part of JavaScript in Navigator version 3 and Explorer version 4. Fortunately, however, very few surfers these days are using such old browsers.

Figure 9.6 shows the full script for our revised image rollover.

QuickCheck Questions

1. Assuming there were six images on a web page, write the full name of the JavaScript property that stores the width of the first image and the full name of the property that stores the URL of the image file of the sixth image.
2. What does it mean to "precache" an image?
3. Given an image object named testImage, write the line of JavaScript code that would change its source to the image stored in the file myportrait.jpg.

Lab Exercise 9.3, "Experimenting with Rollovers," may be done at this point.

```
sourcecode.htm - Notepad
File   Edit   Search   Help

<!--XHTML and DTD info goes here-->
<html>
<head>
    <title>Image Rollover Example</title>
    <script type="text/javascript">
        var nightimage = new Image(69, 120)   //Construct image object for rollover image
        nightimage.src = "eiffelnight.jpg"         //Load actual image into the image object

        function switchImage() {
            document.effeltowerpic.src = nightimage.src
        }

        function restoreImage() {
            document.effeltowerpic.src = "eiffel.gif"
        }

    </script>
</head>

<body>
<p>Built for the 1889 World Exposition, the Eiffel Tower <img src="eiffel.gif"
alt="Eiffel Tower picture"  width="69" height="120" id="eiffeltowerpic" /> is located
on the Champs de Mars in Paris, France.</p>
<p><a href="nightschedule.htm" onmouseover = "switchImage()"
        onmouseout = "restoreImage()">Click here for a schedule of all
        the night-time festivities</a></p>
</body>

</html>
```

FIGURE 9.6.   Revised code for image rollover utilizing the precaching of the rollover image

---

Key Terms

argument	function call	modularization
calling a function	function declaration	parameters
declaring a function	image object	passing a parameter
function	image rollover	precaching

Code Summary

1. Divide and Conquer: Using Functions

Basic syntax for declaring a function with no parameters:

```
function someName() {
    JavaScript instructions go here
}
function printGreeting() {
```

```
    alert("Hello, Fred")
  }
```

Basic syntax for calling a function with no parameters:

```
someName()
printGreeting()
```

2. Adding a Delivery System: Parameters

Declaring a function with parameters (four, in the first example):

```
function sampleFunction(a, b, c, d) {
  alert(a)
  alert(d)
  alert(c)
  alert(b)
}
function printGreeting(personName) {
  alert("Hello, " + personName)
}
```

Calling a function with parameters (passing the parameters):

```
sampleFunction("Bill", "Sarah", "Theresa", "John")
printGreeting("Fred")
```

3. Creating Image Rollovers

Using the image object numbering system to refer to the `height`, `width`, and `src` properties of various images on a web page:

```
document.images[0].height    //This stores the height value of the first image
document.images[0].width     //This stores the width value of the first image
document.images[7].width     //This stores the width value of the eighth image
document.images[4].src       //This stores the source (URL) value of the fifth image
```

Using the `id` attribute in an `<img>` tag to give a name to the image object underlying the image:

```
<img src="eiffel.gif" width="69" height="120" id="eiffeltowerpic" />
```

Referring to an image object property by object name instead of object number:

```
document.eiffeltowerpic.width
document.eiffeltowerpic.src
```

Displaying a new image in place of the original one:

```
document.images[2].src = "eiffelnight.jpg"
document.eiffeltowerpic.src = "eiffelnight.jpg"
```

Creating a basic image rollover, triggered when the surfer moves the mouse over a link and with the original image being restored when the mouse moves off the link (Note: This example puts the rollover code in the event handlers, whereas in the chapter we put the code in separate functions):

```
<a href="nightschedule.htm"
  onmouseover = "document.eiffeltowerpic.src = 'eiffelnight.jpg'"
  onmouseout = "document.eiffeltowerpic.src = 'eiffel.gif' ">Click here
  for a schedule of all the night-time festivities</a>
```

Precaching an image (place script in `<head>` element):

```
var nightimage = new Image(69, 120) //Construct a new image object and name it
nightimage.src = "eiffelnight.jpg"  //load an image into the image object
```

Creating a better image rollover using a precached image:

```
document.eiffeltowerpic.src = nightimage.src
```

Function names should never start with a numeral nor contain spaces.

Though not always necessary, it's good practice to put all function declarations in the `<head>` element (and in a `<script>` element, of course).

When tracing the execution of JavaScript code, remember that when the web browser comes to the end of a function that it has been executing (not checking, but actually executing its instructions), it returns to the line where the function was called and proceeds with whatever comes next.

It's useful to annotate the end of a function by putting a single-line comment after the ending right curly brace.

After writing a function declaration, don't forget to call it (in the appropriate manner and place), otherwise its code will never be executed.

When using a parameter name in an `alert` command (or similar command), don't put quotation marks around it. If you do, the parameter name will be displayed, not the parameter's value.

Give descriptive names to parameters in a function declaration.

The numbering system for a web page's image objects starts with 0, not 1; the syntax uses square brackets, e.g., `document.images[3].width`.

Remember that because some browsers don't recognize the `id` attribute in an `<img>` tag, we may ensure backward compatibility by using both the `id` and `name` attributes.

Although it's okay to write a long HTML tag over multiple lines, keep the code for any event handler all on one line—don't break it in the middle.

Image rollovers do not work in browsers before Navigator version 3 and Explorer version 4.

1. True or false: To declare a function means to execute the code contained within it.
2. True or false: To call a function means to have the browser check it for syntax errors.
3. True or false: It is okay to call one function from within another function.
4. Which of the following lines of code calls a function named `displayResult` (which has no parameters)?
   a. `displayResult()`
   b. `displayResult(none)`
   c. `function displayResult()`
   d. `call displayResult`
5. Which of the following lines of code is the correct beginning to a function *declaration* for a function named `displayResult` with no parameters?
   a. `displayResult()`
   b. `displayResult(none)`
   c. `function displayResult()`
   d. `declare displayResult`
6. Which of the following lines of code calls a function named `displayResult`, which has one parameter, and sends it the string value "Testing 1, 2, 3".
   a. `displayResult("Testing 1, 2, 3")`
   b. `displayResult = "Testing 1, 2, 3"`
   c. `function displayResult("Testing 1, 2, 3")`
   d. `call displayResult("Testing 1, 2, 3")`

7. Which of the following lines of code is the correct beginning to a function *declaration* for a function named `displayResult` with a parameter named `userName`?
   a. `displayResult(userName)`
   b. `displayResult("userName")`
   c. `function displayResult(userName)`
   d. `function displayResult("userName")`

8. Which of the following lines of code is the correct beginning to a function *declaration* for a function named `displayResult` with two parameters named `firstNum` and `secondNum`?
   a. `function displayResult(firstNum, secondNum)`
   b. `function displayResult("firstNum", "secondNum")`
   c. `function displayResult(firstNum + secondNum)`
   d. `function displayResult(var "firstNum", "secondNum")`

9. Which of the following lines of code refers to the first image object on a web page?
   a. `document.images[1]`
   b. `document.images[image1]`
   c. `document.images[0]`
   d. `document.images[first]`

10. Which of the following lines of code creates an image object named `africanSafari`?
    a. `new Image(africanSafari)`
    b. `Image = new africanSafari`
    c. `africanSafari.src = new Image()`
    d. `africanSafari = new Image()`

11. Which of the following lines of code assigns (or loads) an image stored in a file named elephant.jpg into an image object named `africanSafari`?
    a. `elephant.jpg = "africanSafari.src"`
    b. `africanSafari.src = "elephant.jpg"`
    c. `onmouseover = "africanSafari, elephant.jpg"`
    d. `africanSafari = elephant.jpg`

1. Briefly define and/or explain the following terms: calling a function, declaring a function, passing a parameter.

2. Write the JavaScript code for a `<script>` element with two function declarations. The first function, named `cheers`, should display two alert boxes with the messages "Way to go!" and "Fantastic!", respectively. The second function, named `encouragement`, should display an alert box with the message "Don't give up. You can do it!". Write a second `<script>` element that contains function calls for each of these functions. Where in the source document would you normally put each of these `<script>` elements?

3. Write an HTML source document with JavaScript code that declares three functions. The first two functions should be as specified in Exercise 2. The third function should have the name `displayAll` (with no parameters), and its code should first call the `encouragement()` function and then call the `cheers()` function. The `displayAll()` function should be called from a `<script>` element in the `<body>` element.

4. Assuming that the HTML source document in Exercise 3 exists, write the code that would add three click buttons to the document. The first click button, labeled "Cheers", should use its event handler to call the `cheers()` function. The second click button, labeled "Encouragement", should call the `encouragement()` function. And the third click button, labeled "Give me both", should call the `displayAll()` function.

5. Write an HTML source document with JavaScript code that declares a function named `customCheers` with two parameters named `firstCheer` and `secondCheer`. The code in the function should display the value of `firstCheer` in an alert box and the value of `secondCheer` in a second alert box. Also include code in a `<script>` element in the `<body>` element that calls this function and passes it the values "Way to go!" and "Fantastic!". (No click button needed.)

6. Write an HTML source document as described in Exercise 5. But instead of calling the `customCheers()` function when the browser loads the source document and sending it the values "Way to go!" and "Fantastic!", use a prompt box that asks the surfer to enter a cheer or message of their own and then a second prompt box that asks for a second cheer or message. Store the first message in a variable named `surferMessage1` and the second message in a variable named `surferMessage2`. Then send the values of these variables to the `customCheers()` function.

7. Write an HTML source document with JavaScript code that declares a function named `threeCheers` with three parameters named `cheer1`, `cheer2`, and `cheer3`. The code in the function should display the values of `cheer1`, `cheer2`, and `cheer3` in a single alert box (one message with all three cheers, one after another). Also include code in a `<script>` element in the `<body>` element that calls this function and passes it the three values "Hip", "Hip", and "Hooray". (No click button needed.)

8. Do Exercise 7, but instead of calling the `threeCheers()` function from within a `<script>` element, use a click button labeled "Three Cheers". The click button should use an event handler to call the `threeCheers()` function and pass it the three values "Hip", "Hip", and "Hooray".

9. Write an HTML source document that declares a function named `displayFullName` that has three parameters named `first`, `middle`, and `last`. The function's code should use an alert box to display the message "Your full name is: " followed by the the values of `first`, `middle`, and `last`. For example, if the values of `first`, `middle`, and `last` were "John", "Fitzgerald", and "Kennedy", respectively, then the message would be "Your full name is: John Fitzgerald Kennedy." Also include a `<script>` element in the `<body>` element with JavaScript code that uses three prompt boxes to get the surfer's first name, middle name, and last name, storing them in variables named `firstName`, `middleName`, and `lastName`, respectively. Then call the `displayFullName()` function and pass it the values of `firstName`, `middleName`, and `lastName`.

10. **a.** Write the JavaScript code that would create an image object named `vacationimage` and load an image file named "AtTheBeach.jpg" into it. Assume the beach image has a width of 200 pixels and a height of 150 pixels.

    b. Write the JavaScript code for a link that uses a mouseover event handler to load the beach image into an image object named `myphotos`. The link text should be: "Click here to see all my summer photos." Use summerphotos.htm for the linked document.

Debugging Exercise

1. Identify the errors in the following code and then describe how the page would work once the errors were corrected.

```
<html>
<head>
<title>Parameter Example</title>
<script type="text/javascript">
   function displayMessages(firstMsg, secondMsg, thirdMsg)
      alert(thirdMsg)
      alert("The first message is: firstMsg")
      alert(The second message is: "secondMsg")
   }
```

```
</script>
</head>
<body>
This is a sample page that uses JavaScript functions and parameters.<br />
<script type="text/javascript">
   displaymessages("Ready?", "Let's go", "Not yet")
</script>
<form>
   <input type="button" value="Click here to see some more messages"
      onclick="displaymessages("Here we go again", "What did you say?", "Time to go")" />
</form>
</body>
</html>
```

Exercise 9.1: Adding Functions to the Chamelon Web Page

❏ Create a new HTML source document named FunctionTest.htm (or something similar). Declare a function with the name `myFirstFunction()` in a `<script>` element in the `<head>` section and add an alert command or two to it. Then add a function call to `myFirstFunction()` in a `<script>` element in the `<body>` section.

❏ After checking to see if `myFirstFunction()` works, declare several more functions in the `<head>` element's `<script>` element, naming them whatever you want (if you're not inspired, names like `mySecondFunction`, `myThirdFunction`, etc. will work fine). Put some various (and different) alert commands in each of them. Then put calls to each of them, in turn, in the `<body>`'s `<script>` element.

❏ After you get that working, try calling the *same* function two or three times. What happens? Then try switching the order of the function calls. Do you notice a difference in the display? Then try switching the order of the function declarations but not the function calls (use the Copy and Paste commands so you don't have to retype everything). Any difference?

❏ Finally, open up your Chameleon Page document that you created in Lab Exercise 8.3. We want to rewrite it to use functions. First save it under the new name "ChameleonPageWithFunctions.htm" (or something similar, if not so long). Put a `<script>` element in the `<head>` section and declare a function named `changeToRed()` there, with one line of code: `document.bgColor = "red"`. (If you didn't have a Change to red button on your Chameleon page, then use one of the colors you did have.) Then put a function call to the `changeToRed()` function in the `onclick` event handler (i.e., replace the line of code, `document.bgColor = "red"`, that was previously there). Do the same for each of the other buttons and corresponding colors. Don't forget to save your work as you go along.

Exercise 9.2: Practicing with Parameters

❏ Create a new HTML source document named ParameterTest.htm (or something similar). Using the `printGreeting()` function and `personName` parameter as a model, write a `displayAnswer()` function with a parameter named `theAnswer`. This function should use the `alert` command to display "The answer is: " followed by a sample answer (whatever it might be). For instance, the function call `displayAnswer("red")` would display an alert box with the message "The answer is: red". Or `displayAnswer("46.8")` would display "The answer is: 46.8". Put several function calls to `displayAnswer()` in a `<script>` element in the `<body>` section, using different answers to see how it works.

❏ Add a function named `displayMoreAnswers()` that uses two or more parameters and add some sample function calls to it in the `<body>`'s `<script>` element.

❑ Finally, we want to modify our ChameleonPage code to use parameters. Open up your Chameleon-PageWithFunctions.htm document that you created in exercise 9.1 and save it under the new name "ChameleonPageWithParms.htm." Then rewrite the code so that instead of one function for each color change, it uses one function for *all* the color change possibilities. In other words, declare a function named `changeTheColor()` that uses a parameter named `newColor`. The function will have one line of code that assigns the value of `newColor` to `document.bgColor`. Then rewrite the `onclick` event handlers for each button to call this new function and send up the appropriate color for that button ("red," "blue," and so on) to the function.

Exercise 9.3: Experimenting with Rollovers

❑ For this exercise, you will need *two pairs* of images, each stored in a file (.gif or .jpeg). The two images in a pair should preferably have the same height and width, but it's not absolutely necessary. See the section in Chapter 5 on "Creating and Finding Images" for tips on getting images.

❑ Using a new source document, use the `<img>` tag to display one image from one of the pairs somewhere on the web page. Make sure to include the `id` attribute (and `name` attribute for backward compatibility) in the tag. Then create a link with `onmouseover` and `onmouseout` event handlers. (The link can link to any document or web page you want.) The `onmouseover` event handler should call a function that causes the displayed image to switch to its pair image, and the `onmouseout` event handler should call a function that switches it back to the original image. First get it to work without using new image objects, then save the source document, make a copy, and modify the copy so it uses new image objects and precached images to effect the rollover.

❑ Using the first image from the *second pair* of images, add an *image link* to the second source document you created in the previous paragraph. (See "Making Images into Links" in Chapter 5 for a review of image links.) Put `onmouseover` and `onmouseout` event handlers in the `<a>` tag of the image link so that the image of the image link changes to the second image of the pair when the mouse moves over the image link and then changes back to the original image when the mouse moves off the image link.

Exercise 9.4: Custom Buttons using Styles

As another example of rollovers and a nice additional touch for the Chameleon web page, we would like to make custom buttons that, when the mouse rolls over them, change color from white to whatever background color the button is being used for. For example, if the button was a Change to red button, the button would change to a red color when the mouse was moved over it, in order to give the surfer a preview of the background color before actually clicking the button.

We can do this via a combination of JavaScript and HTML style sheets. (See Chapter 3 for a review of how to use style sheets.)

Previously we created click buttons by using the `<input>` element inside a `<form>` element:

```
<input type="button" name="redButton" value="Click here for red!" />
```

But we can also use the `<button>` element (inside a `<form>` element) to do the same thing:

```
<button type="button" name="redButton">Click here for red!</button>
```

The advantage of the `<button>` element is that the button's label ("Click here!" in this case) goes between the `<button>` and `</button>` tags. This makes it possible to apply a style to this text using the style attribute. For example, we may define the background color of the button to be red instead of the normal silver-gray by using the `background-color` property:

```
<button type="button" name="redButton" style="background-color:red">Click here for
   red!</button>
```

Note that we are using a local style here. If we wanted all the buttons on the web page to have the same style, we would define a style for the button element using an internal or external style sheet:

```
button {background-color:red}
```

We could also change the color, font, and size of the "Click here!" text using the `color`, `font-style`, and `font-size` properties (or any of the other properties that may be used to define the display presentation of text). For example:

```
<button type="button" name="redButton" style="background-color:red; font-
    size:24pt">Click here for red!</button>
```

Or, for an internal or external style sheet:

```
button {background-color:red; font-size:24pt}
```

(Note: You may be wondering why we used the `name` attribute instead of the `id` attribute in the `<button>` element, seeing that we have said the `name` attribute is deprecated. This deprecation is not universal, however. Among the elements that we have used, it has been deprecated only in the cases of the `<a>`, `<form>`, `<img>`, and `<map>` elements. The other elements where it has been deprecated are the `<applet>`, `<frame>`, and `<iframe>` elements. The `name` attribute is therefore still a legitimate attribute for a number of elements.)

(Second Note: It is also possible to replace the "Click here!" text in the `<button>` element with an `<img>` element, so that the button displays an image inside itself.)

Being able to customize the background color and text style of buttons is certainly nice, but the real power for the web designer comes when we combine this use of styles with JavaScript. Using JavaScript we may access and change the style of any web page element. For example, if our button above were in a form named `chameleonForm`, then we would refer to the button as:

```
document.chameleonForm.redButton
```

And we can refer to the value of its `background-color` style property as:

```
document.chameleonForm.redButton.style.backgroundColor
```

If we had given it a font size using the `font-size` property (e.g., `style="font-size:24pt"`), we would refer to the value of this property as:

```
document.chameleonForm.redButton.style.fontSize
```

Note the difference in spelling between the name of the HTML style property (`font-size`) and the Document Object Model name of the property (`fontSize`). In general the DOM version of HTML style property names that use hyphens will have the hypen dropped and the first letter of the succeeding word capitalized. (Hyphens, remember, are not legal characters in JavaScript names.)

Now that we know how to reference the style properties of a given HTML element, it is a simple matter to change them using a JavaScript assignment statement. To change the color of the `redButton` button to blue, we write:

```
document.chameleonForm.redButton.style.backgroundColor = "blue"
```

When the browser executes this line of code, it will change the background color of the button's text (assuming it's not already blue) and redisplay the button with the new color.

Or to change its font size to 24 point, we write:

```
document.chameleonForm.redButton.style.fontSize = "24pt"
```

And so on for any of the style properties we define for the button. It should now be apparent how we change the color of the button when a mouseover event occurs on it. But if not, we outline the steps below. (Also note that combining styles and JavaScript in this way only works for more recent browsers, such as Explorer 5.5 and Navigator 6.)

❏ Make a copy of your source document for the Chameleon web page you created in Lab Exercise 9.1 and give it an appropriate name. (Note: It's possible to use the parameter version from Lab Exercise 9.2, but to do so requires the use of something called the elements array, which we haven't covered yet. See Chapter 14, "The Elements Array.") Replace the `<input type="button">` tags with `<button>` elements. Make sure to give each button a name. Add a style attribute for each button that defines the initial style to have a silver background (which is one of the 16 predefined color names and is usually close to the default color for buttons on a web page). If you wish, you may also specify a font size or other style properties. Leave out the `onmouseover` and `onmouseout` event handlers for now. Save your work and view the page to make sure that the buttons display as you want them.

❑ Next, add one function to the `<head>`'s `<script>` element for each button on the page. Each of these functions will use an assignment statement to change the `background-color` style property of its corresponding button, as outlined above. For example, if the page has a Change to red button, you will add a function named `redRollover()` (or something similar). The purpose of this function is to change the color of the button (not the whole page background) when the mouse rolls over the button. After you have added functions for each button, then add another function for each button that will change the button's color back to silver, naming them along the lines of `redToSilver()`, `blueToSilver()`, and so on. The code in these functions will change the color of the corresponding button back to silver.

❑ Add `onclick`, `onmouseover`, and `onmouseout` event handlers to each `<button>` tag that call the appropriate functions. The Change to red button, for example, will use a `changeToRed()` function, a `redRollover()` function, and a `redToSilver()` function. The `changeToRed()` function will be called by the button's `onclick` event handler; the `redRollover()` function will be called by the button's `onmouseover` handler; and the `redToSilver()` function will be called by the button's `onmouseout` handler.

Note: If you have three buttons, you will end up with a total of nine functions in the `<script>` element, three for each button. This is a lot of functions, especially since each just has one line of code. As mentioned above, it is possible to use parameters to write this code another way, on the model of Lab Exercise 9.2. Doing so reduces the number of functions needed from nine to three (or even fewer). But we don't yet know everything we need to know to do this. Alternatively, we could put each line of code in the appropriate event handler in the `<button>` element. But this makes for extremely long `<button>` tags, as each tag has three event handlers.

Forms and the Interactive Surfer

LEARNING OBJECTIVES

1. Learn how to use text fields (boxes) to access and respond to information the surfer enters.

2. Learn how to pass text box values, text box objects, and form objects to functions and access them within the function.

3. Understand the differences between focus, blur, and change events, and learn how to use an onchange event handler in a text box.

4. Learn how to have information that has been entered into a form e-mailed to a specified address.

Interactive Input/Output with Text Boxes

So far we have used click buttons to get some limited interaction with the surfer viewing our web page. Now we need to take that to the next level. As a simple example, we might like to ask the surfer his or her name and then reply with a personalized greeting:

Your web page asks: What is your name?

In reply, surfer types in: Odysseus

Web page responds by displaying: Greetings, Odysseus

We can do this by learning more about HTML forms. In Chapter 7 we saw how to create a click button using the <form> element and the <input> tag. But, as we've mentioned before, HTML allows us to create forms that contain any number of different **form elements** or **form fields** in which the surfer may enter information. Each information field in a form is of a certain type (for example, "text" for accepting textual information, "button" for click-ing) and often is given a name (for example, textBox1, surferName) so that we can refer to a field by its name.

Creating Text Boxes

In the case of a **text field**, or **text box**, we may give it a certain size in terms of the number of characters it can display. It may also have a default or initial value—some text that will be displayed in the text field when the field appears on the screen. This initial text is often used to prompt the surfer to enter the information desired, (for example, Please enter your name here).

To create a text box, we use the <input> tag with the type attribute set to the value of "text". (Note: It's not "textbox", just "text".) We also specify its name and size. Figure 10.1 shows the HTML code for a form with two text boxes and the resulting display.

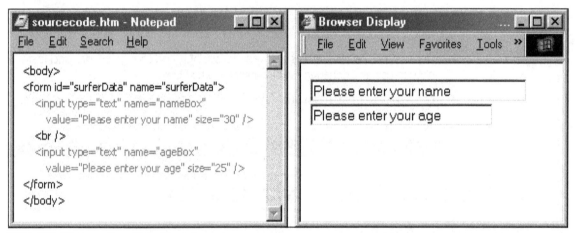

FIGURE 10.1.   Creating text boxes

Let's review the details of the syntax in Figure 10.1. Note first that we have added an id attribute to the <form> tag. We didn't use this attribute in Chapters 7 and 8 when we created click buttons using <form> elements because we didn't need the form to have a name. Now we do (as we'll discover in a lit-tle bit). We have given it the value surferData. We also have included a name attribute with the same value. As we have discussed previously, XHTML has deprecated the use of the name attribute for several elements, including <form>, with the id attribute taking its place. But although the id attribute in a <form> element works with Navigator 6, it does not work with Explorer 6. We will therefore include both attributes in our code samples, for both backward and forward compatibility.

The two text fields in the `surferData` form are `nameBox` and `ageBox`, of length 30 characters and 25 characters, respectively. The initial value of `nameBox` is "Please enter your name"; the initial value of `ageBox` is "Please enter your age."

If we wanted to place the two boxes on the same line, we would simply delete the `<br />` tag that is between the two `<input>` tags. We can also create blank text boxes by writing `value=""` (two quotation marks with nothing between them) in the `<input>` tag, or by leaving out the `value` attribute all together. If we choose to create blank text boxes, they will (usually) need some identifying label for the surfer to see, so we can use some regular HTML formatted text as in Figure 10.2. (Note that we did not put a `<br />` tag after the "Please enter your age" line so that the `ageBox` text field is displayed on the same line.)

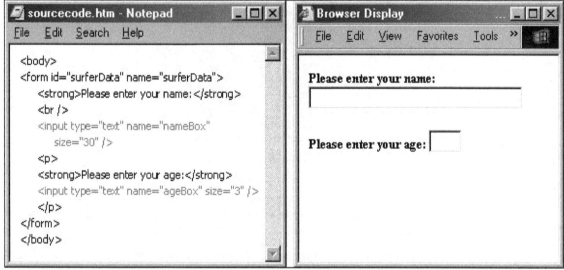

FIGURE 10.2. Labeling text boxes outside the box

The browser automatically handles the actual entry of text into the fields by the surfer. When the surfer clicks the mouse in a text field, the blinking cursor appears. If any text initially appears in the text box, the surfer may select it and replace it by typing something else.

The value Property

A form is a property of the document object and is also an object in its own right. Its child objects include each of its fields (referred to by name) and its length (the number of fields it has). The main property of each text field is named `value`, which stores the contents (value) of the field. In the case of `nameBox`, for instance, the `value` property would store the surfer's name (once he or she had entered it). We reference a field's `value` property in the normal way using dot notation. Since the `nameBox` text field is a child object of the `surferData` form, which in turn is a child object of the `document` object, we refer to the `value` property of `nameBox` by writing:

```
document.surferData.nameBox.value
```

We read this line as "document-dot-surferData-dot-nameBox-dot-value," meaning again the `value` property of the `nameBox` object, which belongs to the `surferData` form object, which belongs to the `document` object.

If the surfer had entered "Ryan" in the `nameBox` text box, then the following code:

```
alert(document.surferData.nameBox.value)
```

would display the alert message shown in Figure 10.3.

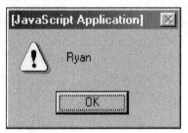

FIGURE 10.3.   Displaying the value of a text box

That is, the contents of `nameBox` are stored in its `value` property, and the `alert` method takes those contents and displays them. (We saw similar examples in Chapter 8 using properties like `document.title` and `document.bgColor`.)

As another variation, if the surfer entered "Linnea" into the `nameBox`, the following code:

```
alert("Good to see you, " + document.surferData.nameBox.
value)
```

would display the alert message in Figure 10.4.

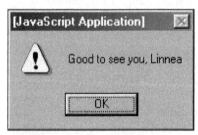

FIGURE 10.4.   Displaying a string plus the value of a text box

Retrieving and Processing Text Box Information

Now that we know how to create a simple text box that enables the surfer to enter information, we need to learn how to retrieve the information from the text box so that we can use it, process it, display it, or whatever. As a starting example, we would like to have the surfer enter his or her name in one text box (e.g., Odysseus) and then display a greeting in a second box (such as Greetings, Odysseus).

To set this up, consider the form layout of Figure 10.5, where we have two text boxes and a click button. The onclick event handler of the button calls a function named printGreeting(), the code of which remains to be written. When the surfer enters his or her name and clicks the button, we want the

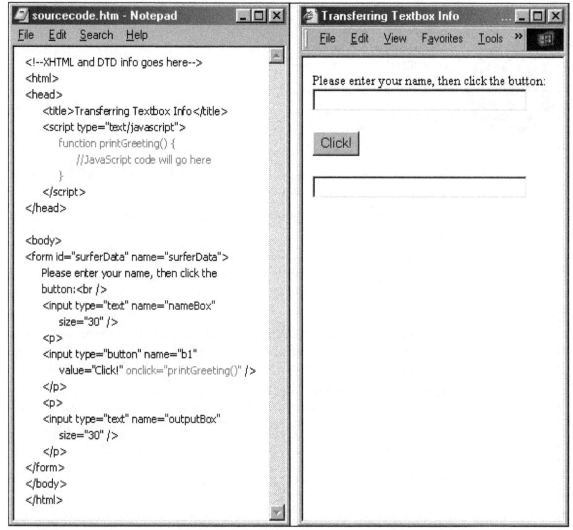

FIGURE 10.5. Form for transferring information from one text box to another

printGreeting() function to retrieve the surfer's name from the top box and display it in the bottom box.

In other words, we want it to take the surfer's name stored in document. surferData.nameBox.value and copy it over to the outputBox text field. It is actually very easy to do this using a basic assignment statement:

```
document.surferData.outputBox.value = document.surferData.
   nameBox.value
```

Remember that we read assignment statements from the right side to the left side. This assignment statement takes the value of the property named document.surferData.nameBox.value (the surfer's name in this case) and copies it into the property named document.surferData.outputBox. value. Once the surfer's name has been copied into document.surferData. outputBox.value, it will automatically appear on-screen in the outputBox ("automatically" means the browser does it for us).

Also note that a common error is to leave off the value property when writing code like this. For example:

```
document.surferData.outputBox = document.surferData.nameBox
```

Or:

```
alert("Good to see you, " + document.surferData.nameBox)
```

When you leave off the value name, the code refers to the text box object itself, not the value or contents of the text box.

So the code we need to put in the printGreeting() function is simply this assignment statement:

```
function printGreeting() {
   document.surferData.outputBox.value = document.
      surferData.nameBox.value
}
```

As written, however, this code does not quite do what we intended, which is to print a greeting with the surfer's name, such as "Greetings, Odysseus." Instead it just prints the surfer's name in the second text field with no greeting.

The fix for this is simple. We change the assignment statement in the print Greeting() function from:

```
document.surferData.outputBox.value = document.surferData.
   nameBox.value
```

to:

```
document.surferData.outputBox.value = "Greetings, " +
   document.surferData.nameBox.value
```

(Normally we would write this all on one line, but it's too long for the margins, and it's okay to break the line at a space as long as it's not in an event handler.)

Figure 10.6 shows the completed code and the display just before the surfer clicks the button and just after.

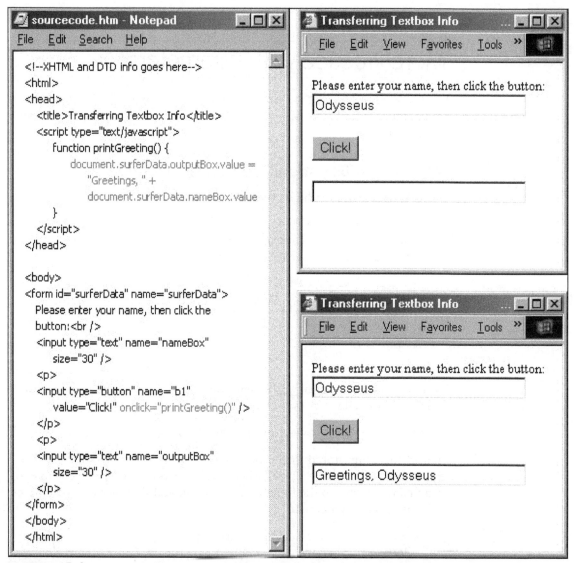

FIGURE 10.6. Greeting the surfer at the click of a button, showing the display just before and just after the click

QuickCheck Questions

1. Write an <input> tag that creates a text box named schoolName with a width of 30 characters and the initial value "Enter school name here".
2. Write the JavaScript code for an assignment statement that copies the contents of a text box named inputBox into a text box named outputBox, where both boxes belong to a form named messageTransfer.

Lab Exercise 10.1, "Greeting the Visitor," may be done at this point.

More Practice with Parameters

We now want to modify the Print Greeting code of Figure 10.6 so that it uses parameters. We will start with a simple example and then progressively add variations to it.

Sending Text Box Information via Parameters

Our original example, which used no parameters, was:

```
function printGreeting() {
  document.surferData.outputBox.value = "Greetings, " +
    document.surferData.nameBox.value
}
```

We called this function using the onclick event handler of the button:

```
onclick = "printGreeting()"
```

Variation 1
For our first modification, we will send the value of the nameBox to the function via a parameter. The event handler code to do this is:

```
onclick = "printGreeting(document.surferData.nameBox.value)"
```

That is, the value stored in the property document.surferData.nameBox.value will be sent to the printGreeting() function. On the receiving end, we add a parameter to the function declaration and then use that parameter in the assignment statement:

```
function printGreeting(theName) {
  document.surferData.outputBox.value = "Greetings, " +
    theName
}
```

Remember how this passing of the parameter works: When the surfer clicks the button, the event handler calls the `printGreeting()` function and sends it the value of the `document.surferData.nameBox.value` property. That is, it sends whatever name the surfer entered in the box. On the function's end, this value is received and stored in the parameter named `theName`. The value of `theName` is then used on the right side of the assignment statement, appending it to the phrase "Greetings, ". Finally, the whole phrase ("Greetings, " plus whatever name the surfer entered) is copied into the `document.surferData.outputBox.value` property, whereupon it automatically appears in the `outputBox` (the second text box).

In other words, `theName` serves as a temporary alias or placeholder for `document.surferData.nameBox.value`. Every place you see `theName` in the function's code, it really refers back to `document.surferData.nameBox.value`.

Variation 2

As our second variation, we will pass the textbox object (`document.surferData.nameBox`) instead of its value property (`document.surferData.nameBox.value`). The `onclick` event handler will be:

```
onclick = "printGreeting(document.surferData.nameBox)"
```

And the function declaration will be:

```
function printGreeting(theBox) {
   document.surferData.outputBox.value = "Greetings, " +
      theBox.value
}
```

Note that we write `theBox.value` in the assignment statement. Because the parameter `theBox` serves as an alias for `document.surferData.nameBox`, the browser understands `theBox.value` to refer to the `value` property of `document.surferData.nameBox`.

Variation 3

For our third variation we will pass two parameters: the `nameBox` and the `outputBox`. The event handler of the click button is:

```
onclick = "printGreeting(document.surferData.nameBox,
      document.surferData.outputBox)"
```

And the function declaration is:

```
function printGreeting(box1, box2) {
   box2.value = "Greetings, " + box1.value
}
```

We used `box1` and `box2` as parameter names, instead of more descriptive names, to remind us that we can make the parameter names whatever we want, as long as we obey the naming rules (although more descriptive names would usually be preferable.) Remember also that it's not the parameter names that matter so much as their order. In the code above, `document.surferData.nameBox` gets sent and stored in the `box1` parameter, and `document.surferData.outputBox` gets sent and stored in the `box2` parameter. We could just as easily switch the order of the boxes in the function call in the event handler:

```
onclick="printGreeting(document.surferData.outputBox,
    document.surferData.nameBox)"
```

as long as we adjust the assignment statement in the function declaration to reflect that the `box1` parameter now receives `document.surferData.outputBox` and the `box2` parameter receives `document.surferData.nameBox`:

```
function printGreeting(box1, box2) {
    box1.value = "Greetings, " + box2.value
}
```

Passing by Copy vs. Passing by Address

Variation 4

One variation that you might expect would work but that actually does not is to pass the `value` properties of both boxes:

```
onclick="printGreeting(document.surferData.nameBox.value,
    document.surferData.outputBox.value)"
```

The corresponding function declaration would be:

```
function printGreeting(theName, theMessage) {
    theMessage = "Greetings, " + theName
}
```

This code looks as if it would give the same result as our other variations, because the assignment statement would seem to be equivalent to:

```
document.surferData.outputBox.value = "Greetings, " +
    document.surferData.nameBox.value
```

But a technical detail in JavaScript prevents it from working. We are using the assignment statement in the function to change the `value` property of `outputBox`. But when we change the value of something inside a function via a parameter, the parameter cannot be a property of an object. Instead, it must be an object. The reason is that when JavaScript passes a property to a function, it sends a *copy* of that property to be stored in the appropriate parameter. So any changes that we make to the parameter inside the function only affect the copy, not the original value. When JavaScript passes an object to a function, on the other hand, it in effect sends the actual object to be stored in a parameter, not a copy of the object. So any changes made to the parameter get made to the actual object. (We'll have more to say in a minute about what "it in effect sends the actual object" actually means.)

In our example, we are passing `document.surferData.outputBox.value` to the parameter named `theMessage`. When the browser executes this code, it actually just sends a copy of `document.surferData.outputBox.value` to the parameter `theMessage`. So when we use this parameter on the left side of an assignment statement to try to change the value of the `outputBox` to `"Greetings, "` + `theName` (where the parameter `theName` has the value of the property `document.surferData.nameBox.value`), it doesn't work. It changes the value of `theMessage`, but not the value of the actual `outputBox`.

Note that it is okay to pass `document.surferData.nameBox.value` as a parameter, because it isn't changed inside the function.

These two different ways of passing parameters are known as passing by copy and passing by address. **Passing by copy** (also sometimes called **passing by value** in programming jargon) means that only a copy of `document.surferData.outputBox.value` (or whatever) is sent to the function and stored in a parameter.

To understand **passing by address**, we have to remember that all objects and their associated methods and properties are stored in the computer's memory while the browser is running. Passing by address means that the actual memory address of `document.surferData.outputBox` (or whatever) is sent to the function and stored in a parameter. When the function then manipulates that parameter, it's not just manipulating a copy of the original thing that was sent, it's manipulating the thing itself in its memory location. Any changes, therefore, that are made to the parameter inside the function are made directly to the actual value stored in memory, not just to a copy of the value.

So when we said above that "it in effect sends the actual object," what we really meant is that the address of the object is sent, so that the code in the function can access the object in its memory location directly.

The following analogy may help you get a handle on this. Imagine that you and a co-worker have been working on a project and that you have drafted a report on it for your manager. Before giving it to the manager, you want your co-worker, who lives across the country, to review it and make any necessary changes, additions, and deletions. You have saved the report document on your company's computer network.

You have two possibilities for getting the document to your co-worker. First, you can e-mail the network location of the document, essentially telling your co-worker "here's where you can find the report on the company network." Any changes the co-worker then makes are made to the original of the document. This situation is analogous to passing a parameter by address (where your co-worker is the function doing the processing and the document, or really its address, is being passed to the function).

The second possibility is that you e-mail your co-worker a copy of the document, while you retain the original on your computer. Then when the co-worker makes changes to it, only the copy is being altered, not the original. This situation is analogous to passing a parameter by value, because a copy of the document is being sent.

Error Alert!

As far as actual programming practice goes, the general rule to remember is: JavaScript objects are passed by address, but object properties are passed by copy. And the implication is: When you are sending something to a function via a parameter and the value of that something may be changed by the code inside that function, then you must pass it as an object, not as an object property.

Passing a Form as a Parameter

IMPORTANT

Our `printGreeting()` function is an example of a function that needs to access multiple elements within a form: the `nameBox` and the `outputBox`. When that's the case, it's often useful to pass the whole form object as a parameter. In this way we only need to use one parameter, but the function can access all the various items within the form. Here's how it works for our "Print Greeting" code.

The `onclick` event handler will call the `printGreeting()` function and send it the whole `surferData` form (or in actuality, because it's an object, send its memory address):

```
onclick = "printGreeting(document.surferData)"
```

The `printGreeting()` function will receive the address of `document.surferData` and store it in a parameter we'll name `f` (as shorthand for "form"). Then within the function the browser knows that any place `f` appears actually refers to `document.surferData`:

```
function printGreeting(f) {
    f.outputBox.value = "Greetings, " + f.nameBox.value
}
```

Note again that there is nothing special about `f` or any parameter name. It's just a temporary alias, only for use inside the function where it is defined. We could just as easily use `xyz`:

```
function printGreeting(xyz) {
    xyz.outputBox.value = "Greetings, " + xyz.nameBox.value
}
```

Nevertheless, `f` or something similar would be preferred, because it's good practice to make the name somewhat descriptive. We also see that parameters are useful for cutting down the length of our code. By using `f` as the parameter name, for example, the assignment statement becomes:

```
f.outputBox.value = "Greetings, " + f.nameBox.value
```

instead of our original version:

```
document.surferData.outputBox.value = "Greetings, " +
    document.surferData.nameBox.value
```

But more significantly, as we saw in the section "The Usefulness of Parameters" in Chapter 9 when we were printing greetings to Fred and Ginger, parameters allow us to create generic functions that can be used over and over again. To reiterate the point, but in the context of this chapter, by writing the printGreeting() function with a parameter named f (or whatever), we can send it any form that has an outputBox field and a nameBox field.

For instance, we might want to put not only a form named surferData on our web page but also several other similar forms, named perhaps surferData2, surferData3, and so on. We could then use the printGreeting() function to take information entered in the nameBox of surferData2 and print it in its outputBox, by using the onclick event handler for a button in the surfer Data2 form to call the printGreeting() function with surferData2 as its parameter:

```
onclick = "printGreeting(document.surferData2)"
```

Or, for a similar button in surferData3:

```
onclick = "printGreeting(document.surferData3)"
```

In each case, we don't need to make any changes to the printGreeting() function declaration as long as the surferData2 and surferData3 forms have text boxes named nameBox and outputBox. The function code remains as before:

```
function printGreeting(f) {
    f.outputBox.value = "Greetings, " + f.nameBox.value
}
```

A common mistake when sending forms as parameters is to confuse the parameter name with an actual form name. When we specify a form name like surferData2 or surferData3, we always indicate that the form belongs to the document object by preceding its name with document, e.g., document. surferData2, document.surferData3, and so on. We never precede the parameter name f with document, however, because being a parameter, f is a temporary alias for whatever sent to the function. It's not the name of a real form. So do not write something like:

```
function printGreeting(f) {
    document.f.outputBox.value = "Greetings, " + document.
        f.nameBox.value
}
```

The browser will not be able to execute this assignment statement because it will look for an actual form named f that has been defined using a <form id="f"> element in the <body> of the source document, and it will not find one.

Actual vs. Formal Parameters

You might have noticed in our examples above that we actually have two parameters involved in the parameter passing process. The first is the parameter in a function call, such as `document.surferData`:

```
printGreeting(document.surferData)
```

The second is the temporary or dummy parameter in a function declaration, such as f in the first line of the `printGreeting()` function:

```
function printGreeting(f) {
   //JavaScript code here
}
```

As mentioned previously, this dummy parameter serves as an alias.

To signify that there are these two kinds of parameters (one kind in function calls and the other kind in function declarations) and to keep them straight, we refer to them as **actual parameters** and **formal parameters** (where formal means dummy). In this case, `document.surferData` (or `document.surferData.nameBox` or `document.surferData.nameBox.value` or whatever) is the actual parameter and f (or `theName` or `box1` or whatever) is the formal parameter.

You may think of the actual and formal parameters as two ends of a pipeline connecting the function call and the function declaration. The actual parameter in the function call inserts its value (or address, if passing by address) into the pipeline and sends it to the formal parameter for use in the function.

As a service to our readers, we now provide a semi-useful mnemonic for remembering which is the actual and which is the formal parameter: The *actual* parameter is the one in the function *call,* and the first two letters of "actual" are the same, albeit reversed, as the first two letters of "call." Likewise, the *formal* parameter is the one in the function *declaration,* and, alphabetically, the first letter of "formal" comes right after the first two letters of "declaration."

Note: It is possible to give the formal parameter the same name as the actual parameter. We could, for instance, declare the `printGreeting()` function with `surferData2` instead of f as the formal parameter:

```
function printGreeting(surferData2) {
   surferData2.outputBox.value = surferData2.nameBox.value
}
```

The function call in the event handler would still be:

```
onclick = "printGreeting(document.surferData2)"
```

But even though the names of the actual and formal parameters look the same here, JavaScript treats them as two different things. That is, it creates a parameter named `surferData2` for use in the `printGreeting()` function. But this parameter is completely separate from the form object named `document.surferData2`. We can see this by considering the following function call to the printGreeting() function immediately above that uses surferData2 as its formal parameter:

```
onclick = "printGreeting(document.surferData3)"
```

This is a perfectly valid function call to printGreeting() (assuming a form named surferData3 exists in the document). In this case, the information in the actual parameter document.surferData3 would be sent to the formal parameter surferData2 of the printGreeting() function declaration. You can see how this might be confusing. It is therefore not recommended to give formal parameters the same name as something else that will be used as an actual parameter, because if you do, it's easy to forget that they are actually two different things.

IMPORTANT

The actual parameter also does not have to be a named property; it may simply be a literal value, as we saw when we discussed parameters in Chapter 9. Recall the simple printGreeting() function we considered then:

```
function printGreeting(personName) {
   alert("Hello, " + personName)
}
```

The formal parameter here is personName. We called this printGreeting() function using the string of text "Fred" as the actual parameter:

```
printGreeting("Fred")
```

That is, "Fred" is not a name of a property like document.surferData. nameBox.value; it is a literal value. In this case, the value "Fred" will be passed and inserted into personName, and then the alert command will be executed, displaying "Hello," plus the value of the personName parameter, i.e., "Hello, Fred".

QuickCheck Questions

1. Write the code for an onclick event handler that calls a function named messageDisplay and sends it the value of a text box named answerBox that belongs to a form named quiz.

2. If we have two text boxes and we want to use a function to transfer the value of one text box to the other, why can't we pass the values of both text boxes to the function and use them in an assignment statement to effect the transfer?

3. Write the code that declares a function named displayMessage with a formal parameter named theForm. When called, the function will receive a form object and store it in theForm. Assume that the form has, among other elements, two text boxes named myBox and yourBox. The code in the function should transfer the contents of myBox into yourBox.

4. Where do we find formal parameters and where do we find actual parameters?

Lab Exercise 10.2, "Greeting the Visitor Again, and Again, and Again," may be done at this point.

Focus, Blur, and Change Events

So far we have been using click buttons to trigger event handlers that activate JavaScript code (that is, call a function and execute the code in that function). There are other events that we may use, however, with text boxes. We will review three of them here: focus, blur, and change events.

We start with the concepts of a **focus event** and a **blur event**. When a surfer clicks the mouse in a text field, or tabs into the field via the keyboard (uses the tab key to move from field to field), then we say that the surfer has focused on that field, or that the field has received focus, or, most commonly, that a focus event has occurred in the field.

On the other hand, when the surfer moves on from the field currently in focus, either by clicking elsewhere or tabbing to another field, then we say that the field has lost focus and become blurred, or that a blur event has occurred. As you might guess, blur events are handled with the `onblur` event handler and focus events use the `onfocus` event handler.

We might use the fact that a blur event has occurred in a text field to activate its `onblur` event handler, which would call some JavaScript code to check that the entry in the text field has an appropriate value. If the surfer was supposed to enter a phone number, we would check that the entry actually was a number. (We will learn more about how to do this input validation in Chapter 15.)

We don't make use of focus events as often as blur events, but the concept of focus plays an important role in other events, such as **change events**. A change event occurs in a text field when the field loses focus *and* the value of the field has been changed. When a change event occurs, we can activate the `onchange` event handler to take appropriate action. In particular, when the change event occurs, we use the `onchange` event handler to call a function that will execute an appropriate series of instructions that we have written.

Let's see how we would use a change event in the "Print Greeting" example we have been working with in this chapter. Instead of creating a form with two text boxes and a click button as we did before, we will simply have two text boxes. Figure 10.7 shows the code and the display. (We changed the name of the function from `printGreeting` to simply `greet`, in order to save a little space. We also changed the function code to use a parameter.)

Note that in this code the `greet()` function is called via an `onchange` event handler in the first text box (`nameBox`), instead of an `onclick` event handler associated with a click button. You may think of this syntax as telling the browser that, *on* the occurrence of a *change* in the text field named `nameBox`, go and execute the instructions contained in the function `greet()`. As discussed above, a change event will occur when the text field loses focus (when the surfer tabs out of it or clicks someplace else) *and* the contents of the field have changed.

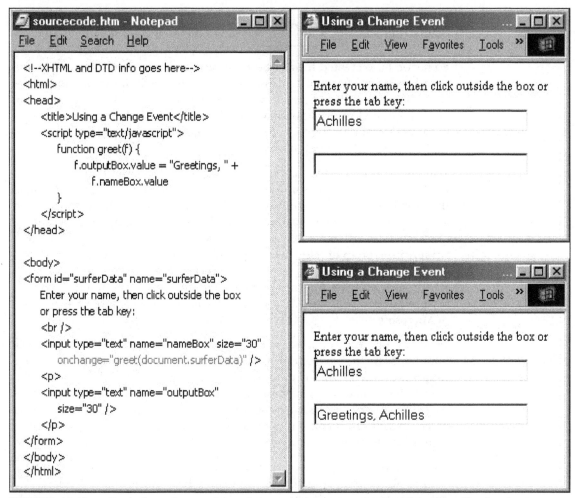

FIGURE 10.7. Greeting the surfer using a change event, showing the display just before and just after the change event occurs

QuickCheck Questions

1. What is the difference between a blur event and a change event?
2. Write the code for a text box named `userName` that uses an `onchange` event handler to display an alert box with the message "Are you sure you want to change that?"

Lab Exercise 10.3, "Working with Change Events," may be done at this point.

Submitting Form Information

So far we have created forms where the surfer enters some information and then JavaScript is used to process that information and display an immediate reply. But forms were originally designed to make it possible for the surfer to enter requested information and have it sent back to the web page designer/owner (or more precisely, the server where the web page is stored) by clicking a special submit button.

Writing the HTML code to create the form and the submit button is easy, as we'll see below. But that is only one side of the process. Once the surfer clicks the submit button and the browser sends the information, the web page's server must be set up correctly to receive it. The standard setup requires the use of so-called **CGI (Common Gateway Interface) scripts**. These scripts are often written in a programming language called **PERL (Practical Extraction and Report Language)**, which is well-suited to receive and process the information sent from the surfer. Another popular method by which to implement such server-side processing uses Active Server Pages (ASP), a technology developed by Microsoft.

You don't necessarily have to write your own CGI scripts or ASP documents, however. Many web page hosting services and/or Internet Service Providers supply prewritten CGI scripts on their servers for the use of their clients who want to implement form submission on their web pages. Unfortunately, CGI scripts, whether prewritten or not, are beyond the scope of this book. Fortunately, on the other hand, there is a simpler alternative: sending form information via electronic mail.

Although submitting forms via e-mail isn't part of the official HTML standard, both Explorer and Navigator allow it (with a few caveats detailed below). We only need to do two things:

1. Add certain attributes to the `<form>` tag that indicate how and where to send the form information:
   a. `method="post"`, which tells the browser what method to use in sending the information to the server.
   b. `enctype="text/plain"`, which tells the browser to put the information in the body of the e-mail message (`enctype` stands for encoding type).
   c. `action="mailto:mymail@somewhere.com"`, which tells the browser to e-mail the results and where to send them.

2. Add a special submit button to the form using an `<input>` tag with `type="submit"`:

   ```
   <input type="submit" value="Submit information" />
   ```

Figure 10.8 shows the code and display for such a form with two text boxes. We have also added a convenient reset button (using type="reset"), which gives the surfer an easy way to erase the entered information and start over. Note that no JavaScript code is required for the form submission. Also note that submit and reset buttons are exceptions to the XHTML rule that <input> elements must have a name attribute.

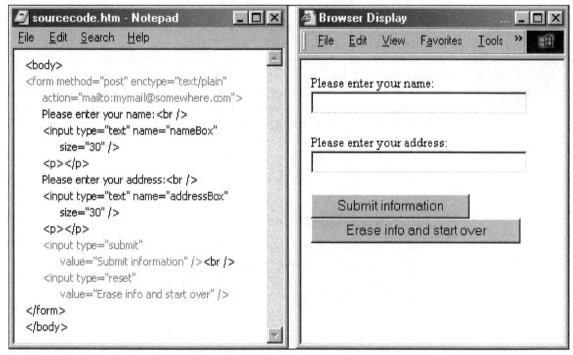

FIGURE 10.8. Submitting form information via e-mail

When the surfer clicks the submit button, the browser takes the information in each form element (two text boxes, in this case) and uses the default e-mail application on the surfer's computer to send the information to the indicated e-mail address. The information will appear in the body of the e-mail message in the general format:

NameOfFormElement=ValueOfInformationEntered

If, in our example, the surfer had entered "Abraham Lincoln" in the first text box (nameBox) and "1600 Pennsylvania Avenue" in the second text box (addressBox), the contents of the e-mail message would be:

nameBox=Abraham Lincoln

addressBox=1600 Pennsylvania Avenue

The From field of the e-mail message would contain the e-mail address of the surfer (at least as set in the properties of the surfer's e-mail program, which may or may not be the surfer's actual e-mail address).

So we see that using e-mail to submit form information can get the job done, although if we had many people submitting information we would end up with a lot of e-mail messages to be read one by one. (In contrast, CGI scripts can automate the collection and processing of form information submitted by multitudes of surfers.)

Several hangups may stall this e-mail process, however. First, e-mail form submission only works in Explorer and Navigator versions 4 and above. Second, when the surfer clicks the submit button, the browser may display a message warning that the transmitted information will not be encrypted and that the surfer's e-mail address will be included. It therefore gives the surfer the option to cancel the submission. Third, the surfer's e-mail program and/or firewall software may also display a warning message, because some viruses use behind-the-scenes e-mail transmissions to propagate. Therefore, in practice having a surfer submit form information to you via e-mail is uncertain at best.

QuickCheck Questions

1. Write the code that creates a submit button with the message "Place order".
2. Write the one line of HTML code for a $<form>$ tag (not a complete element) that instructs the browser to e-mail the form information to the address myaccount@yahoo.com when its submit button is clicked.

Lab Exercise 10.4, "Getting Visitor Contact Information," may be done at this point.

actual parameter	formal parameter	PERL (Practical Extraction and Report Language)
blur event	form elements	
CGI (Common Gateway Interface) scripts	form field	text box
	passing by address	text field
change event	passing by copy (passing by value)	
focus event		

1. Interactive Input/Output with Text boxes

Creating a text box with a width of 30 characters and text inside it:
```
<form id="surferData" name="surferData">
  <input type="text" name="nameBox" value="Please enter your name" size="30" />
</form>
```

Creating a blank text box (inside a `<form>` element, as above):
```
<input type="text" name="nameBox" size="30" />
```

Using JavaScript dot notation to refer to the contents, or value, of a text box:
```
document.surferData.nameBox.value
```

Changing the value of a text box using an assignment statement (in this example, copying the value of `nameBox` into `outputBox`):
```
document.surferData.outputBox.value = document.surferData.nameBox.value
```

2. More Practice with Parameters

Sending (passing) the value of a text box to a function via a parameter:

Function call (using an `onclick` event handler of a button):
```
onclick = "printGreeting(document.surferData.nameBox.value)"
```

Function declaration:
```
function printGreeting(theName) {
  document.surferData.outputBox.value = "Greetings, " + theName
}
```

Passing the textbox object itself to a function via a parameter:

Function call:
```
onclick="printGreeting(document.surferData.nameBox)"
```

Function declaration:
```
function printGreeting(theBox) {
  document.surferData.outputBox.value = "Greetings, " + theBox.value
}
```

Passing two textbox objects to a function:

Function call:
```
onclick="printGreeting(document.surferData.nameBox, document.surferData.outputBox)"
```

Function declaration:
```
function printGreeting(box1, box2) {
  box2.value = "Greetings, " + box1.value
}
```

Passing a whole form to a function:

Function call:
```
onclick = "printGreeting(document.surferData)"
```

Function declaration:
```
function printGreeting(f) {
  f.outputBox.value = "Greetings, " + f.nameBox.value
}
```

3. Focus, Blur, and Change Events

Using an `onchange` event handler of a text box to call a function:

```
<input type="text" name="nameBox" size="30" onchange="greet(document.surferData)" />
```

4. Submitting Form Information

Creating a form with a submit button that will e-mail the information entered in the form to some e-mail address (presumably that of the form's creator):

```
<form method="post" enctype="text/plain" action="mailto:mymail@somewhere.com">
    Please enter your name:<br />
    <p><input type="text" name="nameBox" size="30" /></p>
    Please enter your address:<br />
    <p><input type="text" name="addressBox" size="30" /></p>
    <input type="submit" value="Submit information" /><br />
    <input type="reset" value="Erase info and start over" />
</form>
```

When creating a text box using an `<input>` tag, remember that the value of the `type` attribute is `"text"`, not `"textbox"`.

When you want to refer to the contents of a text box, don't forget to put the `value` property at the end of the reference; for example, it's `document.surferData.nameBox.value`, not `document.surferData.nameBox` (the latter refers to the text box object, not its value).

When you send the contents of a text box to a function and the code in the function changes the value of that text box, you cannot pass the `value` property of the text box. You must either pass the text box object itself or the form object to which the text box belongs. This is a special case of the following general rule.

JavaScript objects are passed by address, but object properties are passed by copy. This means that when you are sending something to a function via a parameter and the value of that something may be changed by the code inside that function, then you must pass it as an object, not as an object property.

When a function needs to access multiple elements within a form, it's often useful to pass the whole form object as a parameter. In this way you only need to use one parameter, but the function can access all the various items within the form.

A common mistake when sending forms as parameters is to confuse the parameter name with an actual form name. Never precede the parameter name with `document`. That is, if the parameter name is `f`, never write things like `document.f.outputBox.value`.

A semi-useful mnemonic for remembering which is the actual and which is the formal parameter: The *actual* parameter is the one in the function *call,* and the first two letters of "actual" are the same, albeit reversed, as the first two letters of "call." Likewise, the *formal* parameter is the one in the function *declaration,* and, alphabetically, the first letter of "formal" comes right after the first two letters of "declaration."

Do not give formal parameters the same name as something else that will be used as an actual parameter because if you do, it's easy to forget that they are actually two different things.

Remember that several hangups may stall the process of having the surfer submit form information via e-mail. It's best not to rely on it.

1. Which of the following lines of HTML code creates an empty text box named `userAnswer` with a width of 45 characters?
   a. `<input type="textbox" name="userAnswer" width="45" />`
   b. `<input type="text" value="userAnswer" width="45" />`
   c. `<input type="textbox" name="userAnswer" size="45" />`
   d. `<input type="text" name="userAnswer" size="45" />`
   e. `<input type="text" value="userAnswer" width="45" />`
   f. `<input type="text" value="userAnswer" size="45" />`

2. Which of the following lines of JavaScript code is used to access text that the surfer has entered in a text box named `userAnswer`, defined in a form named `messageForm`?
   a. `document.messageForm.userAnswer.value`
   b. `document.messageForm.userAnswer`
   c. `messageForm.userAnswer`
   d. `userAnswer.value`

3. Assuming that the surfer has entered a city name in a text box named `city` and a state name in a text box named `state`, both of which belong to a form named `addressForm`, which of the following lines puts the city and state names together (with a comma between them) and displays the combined result in a text box named `cityState`, which belongs to a form named `mailingForm`?
   a. `document.mailingForm.cityState = document.addressForm.city + ", " +`
      `   document.addressForm.state`
   b. `document.mailingForm.cityState.value = document.addressForm.city.value + ", " +`
      `   document.addressForm.state.value`
   c. `mailingForm.cityState.value = addressForm.city + ", " + addressForm.state`
   d. `cityState = city + ", " + state`

4. True or false: When passing a parameter that is an object to a function, JavaScript passes the memory address of the object.

5. True or false: An object property that is passed to a function (for example, the `value` property of a text box) cannot be changed by code inside the function.

6. Parameters in a function declaration are known as _____ while those in a function call are _____.

7. If a form named `surveyForm` with two text boxes named `answer1Box` and `answer2Box` is passed to a function with a formal parameter `f`, which of the following lines of code in the function would copy the value of `answer1Box` into `answer2Box`?
   a. `f.answer1Box.value = f.answer2Box.value`
   b. `document.f.answer1Box.value = document.f.answer2Box.value`
   c. `f.answer2Box = f.answer1Box.value`
   d. `f.answer2Box.value = f.answer1Box.value`
   e. `document.f.answer2Box.value = document.f.answer1Box.value`

8. Which of the following lines of code correctly uses an `onclick` event handler to call a function named `calculateResult()` and passes it a text box object named `numberBox`, which belongs to a form named `dataForm`?
   a. `onclick = "calculateResult(document.dataForm.numberBox.value)"`
   b. `onclick = "calculateResult(dataForm.numberBox.value)"`
   c. `onclick = "calculateResult(document.dataForm.numberBox)"`
   d. `onclick = "calculateResult(numberBox)"`

9. Which of the following lines of code is the correct syntax for the first line of a function named `combine()` that uses two parameters to receive the *values* of two text boxes named `box1` and `box2` (and which belong to a form named `surferForm`):

   a. `function combine(b1value, b2value)`
   b. `function combine(document.surferForm.box1, document.surferForm.box2)`
   c. `function combine(surferForm.box1, surferForm.box2)`
   d. `function combine(document.surferForm.box1.value, document.surferForm.box2.value)`

10. True or false: A change event in a text field occurs when the user changes the contents of the field.

Exercises

1. Briefly define and/or explain the following terms: passing by address, formal parameter, blur event.

2. Write the HTML code that would create a form with four text boxes, displaying them with two on the first line and two on the second line. Give them each a width of 15 characters. Each box should initially appear with the text "Box 1" (or "Box 2", and so on) in it, except the last one, which should be empty.

3. Given a form named `testMessage` with two text boxes named `firstBox` and `secondBox`, write the line of JavaScript code that would take the contents of `secondBox` and display them in `firstBox` using the message: "The news from the second box is: [value of secondBox would be displayed here]". That is, if "pepperoni pizza" were displayed in the second box, then the display in the first box would become "The news from the second box is: pepperoni pizza". (Note: No parameters are involved here.)

4. Given a form named `question1` with two text boxes named `theQuestion` and `theAnswer`, write the code for an `onclick` event handler that would call a function named `checkTheAnswer`, for each of the following cases:

   a. Pass the values of the two text boxes to the function.
   b. Pass the text box objects themselves to the function.

5. Repeat Exercise 4 for the following cases:

   a. Pass the value of `theQuestion` box to the function while also passing `theAnswer` box itself to the function.
   b. Pass the `question1` form to the function.

6. For each of the following cases, write the code for a function named `processResults`:

   a. The function receives the value of a text box and stores it in a formal parameter named `theMessage`. The code in the function copies the value of the text box into another text box named `outputBox` that belongs to a form named `messageDisplay`.
   b. The function receives two text box objects themselves and stores them in formal parameters named `box1` and `box2`. The code in the function copies the value of `box1` into `box2`.

7. Repeat Exercise 6 for the following cases:

   a. The function receives the value of a text box and stores it in a formal parameter named `theMessage`. It also receives a text box object and stores it in a formal parameter named `theMessageBox`. The code in the function copies the value of `theMessage` into the text box represented by the parameter `theMessageBox`.
   b. The function receives a form and stores it in a formal parameter named `theForm`. The original form has two text boxes named `inputBox` and `outputBox`. The code in the function copies the value of `inputBox` into the `outputBox`.

8. What are the advantages of passing a form to a function instead of individual text boxes or individual text box values?

9. Write the HTML code for a form named `changeTest` that has two text boxes named `firstBox` and `secondBox`, each of size 40. The first box should also have an `onchange` event handler so that when

a change event occurs in the first box, the value of the first box is displayed in the second box. Note: You do not need to have the event handler call a function that does the transfer; remember that you can put an assignment statement directly into the event handler.

10. Write the HTML code for a form with three text boxes named ageBox, genderBox, and schoolyearBox, appropriately labeled. The form should use a submit button to e-mail the information in the boxes to the address studentsurvey@anonymouspollster.org. The form should also implement a reset button.

1. Identify the errors in the following code. Note that the page is designed to have two click buttons, each of which calls a different function via its event handler. Note also that there are two forms, named question1 and question2, each of which has a text box named messageBox. This is legitimate, because the two message boxes belong to different forms and therefore the browser can keep them straight. (It's like two people with the same first name but with different last names.)

```html
<html>
<head>
   <title>Questionnaire Page</title>
   <script type="text/javascript">
/*The first function will (supposedly) take the surfer's answer to the ice cream question,
e.g., "Mint chocolate chip" , and display "Mint chocolate chip is my favorite too!" in the
messageBox. The second function will (supposedly) take the surfer's answer to the movie
question, e.g., "Titanic", and display "Titanic, huh? I prefer the Marx Brothers." */
      function icecreamMessage(surferAnswer, theMessage) {
         theMessage = surferAnswer + " is my favorite too!"
      }
      function movieMessage(f). {
         document.f.messageBox.value = f.movieBox + ", huh? I prefer the Marx Brothers."
      }
   </script>
</head>
<body>
   <form id="question1">
      Please enter your favorite flavor of ice cream, then click the button:<br />
      <input type="text" name="icecreamBox" size="30" /><br />
      <input type="button" name="icBtn" value="Click!"
         onclick="icecreamMessage(icecreamBox.value,messageBox.value)" /><br />
      <input type="text" name="messageBox" size="30" />
   </form>
   <p>
   <form id="question2">
      Please enter your favorite movie of all time, then click the button:<br />
      <input type="text" name="movieBox" size="30" />
      <br />
      <input type="button" name="movieBtn" value="Click !"
         onclick="movieMessage(document. question1)">
      <br />
      <input type="text" name="messageBox" size="30" />
   </form>
</body>
</html>
```

Note: Most of the exercises above may also be done as lab exercises. If a problem involves a function, add a function call so that the function code is actually executed.

Exercise 10.1: Greeting the Visitor

❑ Create an HTML source document that has two text boxes, a click button, and a third text box underneath them. In the code, name the first text box `name1Box`, the second text box `name2Box`, and the third text box `messageBox`. Name the form `visitorInfo`. Surfers/visitors should be instructed to enter their first name in the first box and their last name in the second box, and then click the button. Use the button's `onclick` event handler to call a function named `hello()`. This function should use an assignment statement to display the following message in the third text box: "Hello, [first name last name]! Glad you could make it." That is, if the visitor enters "Isaac" in the first box and "Newton" in the second box, then the message will be: "Hello, Isaac Newton! Glad you could make it." Do not use any parameters for this exercise. (In addition to the material in the section "Interactive Input/Output with Text Boxes" you might want to review the section "Storing Values in Variables" in Chapter 8, where we talked about concatenating strings.)

Exercise 10.2: Greeting the Visitor Again, and Again, and Again

❑ Make a copy of your source document from Lab Exercise 10.1 and rename it by appending a "2" to the end of the name (if your original document was named Greeting.htm, this new copy will be Greeting2.htm). Then modify the code so that the `hello()` function has two formal parameters named `firstName` and `lastName`. Modify the function call in the event handler to pass the *values* of `name1Box` and `name2Box` to the function. And, of course, modify the function's assignment statement so that it uses the two parameters to display the message.

❑ Make a copy of the source document from the first part of this exercise (what you just did) and rename it by appending a "3" at the end of its name. Then modify the code so that instead of passing the two values of `name1Box` and `name2Box`, the text box objects themselves are passed in the function call. Name the formal parameters in the function declaration `firstBox` and `secondBox`. In addition, add a third parameter named `thirdBox`. This parameter should be used to pass the `messageBox` object. Modify the assignment statement in the function and the event handler code to use all three parameters.

❑ Make a copy of the source document from the second part of this exercise (what you just did) and rename it by appending a "4" at the end of its name. Then modify the code so that instead of passing the text boxes as individual objects, the whole `visitorInfo` form is passed to the function. Use `f` for the name of the parameter in the function declaration (i.e., the formal parameter).

Exercise 10.3: Working with Change Events

❑ Make a copy of the source document from the third part of this Lab Exercise 10.2 (or one of the other parts) and rename it appropriately. Then delete the click button from the code and modify it so that it uses a change event in the `name2Box` to trigger the display of the message.

Exercise 10.4: Getting Visitor Contact Information

❑ Create an HTML source document that allows the visitor to enter their contact information. Use eight text boxes, one each for first name, middle initial, last name, street address, city, state, zip code, and telephone number. Format the boxes as you might if the visitor were writing the information on a paper form (put the first name, middle initial, and last name boxes all on one line). Add submit and reset buttons to the form. Make the submit button so that, when clicked, it will e-mail the form information to your e-mail address. (To test this out, of course, you will need to be connected to the Internet and have access to your e-mail account.)

Sitebuilding Exercise 2 may be done at this point (see Appendix A).

11

Performing Calculations

LEARNING OBJECTIVES

1.   Understand the basic process of creating a calculator on a web page.

2.   Learn how to do addition, subtraction, multiplication, and division in JavaScript, as well as how to use the `Math` object to calculate square roots and generate random numbers and the `parseFloat` function to convert string values to number values.

3.   Learn how to write functions that do some calculating or processing and then return a result to the place where the function was called.

4.   Put all the above together to create a calculator that gets the height and width of a rectangle from the user and computes its area and width.

A Web Page Calculator

As a slightly more complicated example of how we may use JavaScript to implement interactivity in our web pages, we next will consider how to create a web page calculator. If we were designing a financial or real estate website, for instance, we might want to include a feature that allowed visitors to input interest rate and other information and receive back the amount that their monthly mortgage payment would be. Or if you were designing an e-commerce site, to take another example, you would need to have some way to calculate and display the total amount of a customer's order.

We will start with a less ambitious example: a simple calculator that, given the length and width of a rectangle (entered by the surfer), will compute and display its area and perimeter.

On the screen, we want it to look something like Figure 11.1.

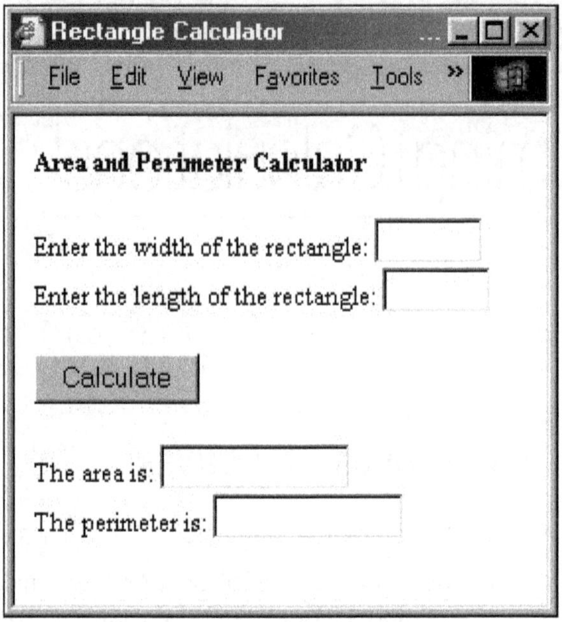

FIGURE 11.1.   A web page calculator

The surfer will enter the length and width of the rectangle in the two text fields at the top, then click the Calculate button, and the results for the area and perimeter will appear in the two text fields at the bottom. We know almost everything we need to know to do this:

1. Create a form with the two input text fields for length and width, with appropriate prompts.

2. In the same form, create the two output text fields, labeled "Area" and "Perimeter" on the screen as shown.

3. Still in the same form, create the Calculate button. Its onclick event handler will call a function that, using an assignment statement, will calculate the area of the rectangle from the values for the length and width entered by the surfer and then copy the result into the value property of the output field for the area. Using a second assignment statement, it will do the same for the perimeter.

Before we can proceed, however, we need to know a few more things that we have not yet covered. Clearly, we must learn how to add, multiply, etc. But we also need to learn how to turn a string (text) value into a number value. Because even though the surfer enters numbers into the length and width boxes, JavaScript stores those numbers as *text* values, and we obviously can't multiply two pieces of text together.

Basic Math with JavaScript

To perform basic arithmetic in JavaScript, such as adding two numbers together, we use an assignment statement with the standard **mathematical operators**: + and − for addition and subtraction and * and / for multiplication and division. For example:

```
var theResult, anotherResult, result3
theResult = 5.1 + 4.6 - 3
anotherResult = 7*3
result3 = 24 / 6
```

The assignment statements, of course, mean take the value that is on the right side and copy it over to the left side. When there are mathematical operations on the right side, the browser does them from left to right (with a few exceptions discussed below). So after the browser executes the above lines of code, the variable theResult will have the value 6.7, anotherResult will have the value 21, and result3 will have the value 4.

We may also perform mathematical operations with variables. For example:

```
var theResult, anotherResult, result3
theResult = 5.1 + 4.6 - 3
anotherResult = 7*3 + theResult
result3 = theResult / 10 - anotherResult
```

The third line of code here instructs the browser to multiply 7 by 3, add the value contained in the variable named theResult (6.7), and copy the whole result (27.7, in this case) into the variable named anotherResult. Similarly, the last line of code says to take the value of theResult, divide it by 10, subtract the value of anotherResult, and copy the final result (−27.03) into the variable named result3.

If you're thinking ahead, you might be wondering what happens when you use a variable in a calculation and then later change the value of that variable. Is the change retroactive? Does the browser automatically go back and redo the calculation with the new value? The answer is no. Consider the following code:

```
var firstNum, secondNum, theResult
firstNum = 12
secondNum = 7
theResult = firstNum + secondNum
firstNum = 10
alert("The value of theResult is: " + theResult)
```

The value of theResult that is displayed in the alert box will be 19, not 17, even though the value of firstNum has been changed from 12 to 10. The reason is that the line of code with the assignment statement (theResult = firstNum +

secondNum) is executed before the assignment statement that changes the value of firstNum (i.e., firstNum = 10). The calculation will be redone with the new value only if you the programmer include the necessary code to do so. In this example, you would add the line theResult = firstNum + secondNum someplace after the line firstNum = 10.

Another common question about how mathematical operations work in JavaScript is whether it matters when and where you use spaces. The answer again is no. Spaces are not required between variable names, numbers, and operators, although it's often helpful to put them in. All of the following lines of code are equivalent:

```
theResult=secondNum*3
theResult = secondNum*3
theResult = secondNum * 3
```

Keeping a Running Total

In programming we often come across a situation where we need to keep a running total of some value. For example, in Chapter 13 we will learn how to create an online, multiple-choice quiz. In order to total the user's score, we will check each answer against the correct answer in turn, and add one point to the user's score if they match.

To implement a running total like this, we define a variable with the name nmbrCorrect (or something similar) and initialize it to the value 0:

```
var nmbrCorrect = 0
```

Then every time the user's answer is correct, we add 1 to the nmbrCorrect variable as follows:

```
nmbrCorrect = nmbrCorrect + 1
```

At first glance, this line seems to be simply false. We know that in normal mathematics one number cannot equal the same number plus one: 5 does not equal 5 + 1, and in general a value A does not equal A + 1.

But this line is an assignment statement, not a mathematical equation. It is *not* nmbrCorrect equals nmbrCorrect + 1. Rather we read this line starting on the right side. It says to take the value of nmbrCorrect, add 1 to it, and then store the new result back into the same variable nmbrCorrect, replacing its previous value. If the value of nmbrCorrect was 0 before JavaScript executed this instruction, then afterward the value of nmbrCorrect would be 1.

We don't have to add just 1, of course. The following line adds 28 to the value of nmbrCorrect and makes the result the new value of nmbrCorrect:

```
nmbrCorrect = nmbrCorrect + 28
```

In similar fashion, we can decrement the value of nmbrCorrect by 1 or any number:

```
nmbrCorrect = nmbrCorrect - 1
```

Or:

```
nmbrCorrect = nmbrCorrect - 43
```

We can also multiply or divide:

```
nmbrCorrect = 15              //Set value of nmbrCorrect
                             //to 15
nmbrCorrect = 3*nmbrCorrect  //New value of nmbrCorrect
                             //will be 45
nmbrCorrect = 15             //Reset value of nmbrCorrect
                             //to 15
nmbrCorrect = nmbrCorrect/5  //New value of nmbrCorrect
                             //will be 3
```

Again, remember how this works: starting on the right side of the first line, the browser takes the value of nmbrCorrect, multiplies it by 3, and then stores the result back into the nmbrCorrect variable, thus changing it. The division works similarly. If we wanted to multiply nmbrCorrect by 3 but not change the value in nmbrCorrect, then we would store the result in a different variable (which we will name tripleScore):

```
var tripleScore
tripleScore = 3*nmbrCorrect
```

The Increment and Decrement Operators

Because incrementing or decrementing a number occurs often in programming, JavaScript has several special operators for these types of operations. The ++ and -- operators are the **increment** and **decrement operators**, respectively. Given a variable named nmbrCorrect, we can increment as above by writing:

```
nmbrCorrect = nmbrCorrect + 1
```

Or we can use the increment operator and write:

```
nmbrCorrect++
```

After this line of code is executed, the value of nmbrCorrect will be one more than before. The decrement operator works similarly, subtracting one from the value of nmbrCorrect:

```
nmbrCorrect--
```

It's also possible to put the increment and decrement operators in front of the variable name:

```
++nmbrCorrect
--nmbrCorrect
```

As written, these versions are equivalent to `nmbrCorrect++` and to `nmbrCorrect--`, respectively. But things get trickier if you use them in an assignment statement. Consider the following (where all variables have been previously declared):

```
firstNum = 7
result1 = firstNum++
secondNum = 7
result2 = ++secondNum
```

When the increment operator is placed after the variable name (as in the second line here), the browser does the incrementing *after* the assignment operator. In other words, it copies the value of `firstNum` into `result1`, giving `result1` the value 7, and then it increments `firstNum`, giving it the value 8. When, however, the increment operator is placed before the variable name (the fourth line), the browser does the incrementing first and then the assignment. So it increments `secondNum` by 1, making it 8, and then assigns the value of `secondNum` to `result2`, giving it also the value of 8. The decrement operator works similarly.

To liven things up even more, JavaScript also includes several combination versions of the assignment operator: $+=$, $-=$, $*=$, and $/=$ (the "plus-equals," "minus-equals," "times-equals," and "slash-equals" operators). The easiest way to see how these **combination assignment operators** work is via some simple examples. Given a variable named `theNum`, the following pairs of code are equivalent:

```
theNum+=7      //These two lines of code do the same thing
theNum = theNum + 7
theNum-=7      //These two lines of code do the same thing
theNum = theNum - 7
theNum*=7      //These two lines of code do the same thing
theNum = theNum*7
theNum/=7      //These two lines of code do the same thing
theNum = theNum/7
```

IMPORTANT

Although some experienced programmers like to use these combination operators to make their code as compact as possible, you should use them with caution. Compact code does not necessarily make very readable code; the more shortcuts you use, the easier it is to make mistakes.

In addition, there is a problem with the decrement operator in JavaScript. The double minus sign ($--$) is reserved for other uses in XHTML. This means that it cannot be used in JavaScript code if you want the source document to be in strict compliance with XHTML. If you still want to use the decrement operator, the only way to get around this problem is to put your JavaScript code in a separate text file, outside the source document. This file is known as an **external JavaScript file** and must have the extension .js, such as "testCode.js". The code in the file should be JavaScript only; do not include any <script> elements or other HTML code. To use the code stored in an external file in a source document, you simply add a src attribute to the source document's <script> element:

```
<script src="testCode.js" type="text/javascript">
</script>
```

There's no need to put anything in the <script> element. All its code is now in the testCode.js file. When the browser loads the source document, it will also load the JavaScript code in the testCode.js file. (As the src attribute is written here, the testCode.js file must be in the same directory as the source document. If it isn't, then a fuller pathname must be supplied. Also, some JavaScript programmers prefer to hide their code from the surfer, who can view the source document using the View source menu option. The code can be hidden by putting it in an external file. A savvy surfer, however, can still find it in the browser's cache.)

Precedence of Operations

Sometimes we will have more complicated mathematical expressions. For instance:

```
theAnswer = 9+2*4
```

After this line of code executes, what is the value of theAnswer? Is it 11*4, which is 44, or is it 9+8, which is 17? In other words, is the addition done first or is the multiplication done first?

Programming languages always have built-in **rules of precedence** that prescribe the order of mathematical operations in ambiguous cases like that above. The basic rules are:

1. Increment and decrement operations are done before addition, subtraction, multiplication, and division.

2. Multiplications and divisions are done next, from left to right.

3. Any additions and subtractions are done next, also from left to right.

4. Finally, any special combination operators (described in the previous section) are done last.

So 9+2*4 is calculated as 9+(2*4). The 2*4 is done first and then the 9 is added, giving the answer 17.

If you include parentheses in the mathematical expression, however, they take precedence over everything else. It's therefore always a good idea to use parentheses. They make it clearer for you and any other human readers of your code to understand what the code does so that it isn't misunderstood.

IMPORTANT

Consider the following examples with and without parentheses and make sure you understand how they work:

```
var firstNum = 2, secondNum = 5
var thirdNum = 3, fourthNum = 8
var theAnswer = 0
theAnswer = firstNum+secondNum*thirdNum-fourthNum
  //theAnswer will have a value of 9
theAnswer = firstNum+(secondNum*thirdNum)-fourthNum
  //theAnswer will have a value of 9
theAnswer = (firstNum+secondNum)*thirdNum-fourthNum
  //theAnswer will have a value of 13
theAnswer = (firstNum+secondNum)*(thirdNum-fourthNum)
  //theAnswer will have a value of -35
theAnswer = firstNum+secondNum*(thirdNum-fourthNum)
  //theAnswer will have a value of -23
```

Note that the combination assignment operators are almost designed to give trouble here. Consider the following code:

```
result = 7
result*=2 + 3
```

What is the final value of `result`? The rules of precedence state that multiplication comes before addition, so we might think the second line is equivalent to:

```
result = (result*2) + 3
```

This gives `result` a final value of 17. But remember that the rules of precedence also state that the combination assignment operators have a lower precedence than addition and subtraction. So the code `result*=2+3` is actually equivalent to:

```
result = result * (2 + 3)
```

The correct answer, therefore, is that `result` ends up having the value 35 (i.e., 7*5).

The Math Object

For the times when you need to do more complicated math than just the four basic operations, JavaScript provides the **Math object**. The `Math` object has a number of methods that enable operations such as square roots, logarithms, trigonometry, and so on. We will review a few examples here to show how the `Math` object is used. The basic syntax is:

```
theResult = Math.methodName(num1, num2, num3)
```

where `methodName` is the name of one of the methods included in the `Math` object (you can't just make up your own name for the method), `num1`, `num2`, and `num3` are variables containing numbers, and `theResult` is a previously declared variable. (There may be any number of actual parameters in the method call, not necessarily three as in this example.) When this line of code is executed, the browser calls the method named `methodName`, sends it the values of the numbers, does the calculations involved in the method, and returns a single result, which is then copied into the variable named `theResult`. You may recall that this is the syntax used when a method returns a value (see Chapter 8, "Returning a Value").

To take the square root of a number, for example, we use the `sqrt` method (note that it's `sqrt`, not `squrt`):

```
theResult = Math.sqrt(25)
```

After this line is executed, the value of `theResult` will be 5. Or, using a variable (`num1`) instead of a literal value (25) for the actual parameter in the method call:

```
var num1 = 36, theResult
theResult = Math.sqrt(num1)
```

After this line, the value of `theResult` will be the square root of the value of `num1` (6, in this case). The value of `num1` does not change, however. It remains at 36.

To square a number, such as $6^2 = 6*6 = 36$, we use the `pow()` method (meaning "power," as in raising one number to a certain power). The `pow()` method takes two parameters: The first is the value of the number and the second is the value of the power. So to square the value of `num1`, we write:

```
num1 = 6
theResult = Math.pow(num1, 2)
```

To take it to the third power, or "cube" it ($6^3 = 6*6*6 = 216$):

```
theResult = Math.pow(num1, 3)
```

To round a number to the nearest integer, we use the `round()` method of the Math object. When the decimal part of a number is greater than or equal to 0.5, then the number is rounded up; otherwise, it's rounded down. So 4.7, 4.613, and 4.5 would be rounded to the value 5, while 4.199, 4.01, and 4.499 would be rounded to the value 4. For example:

```
num1 = 4.49
theResult = Math.round(num1)   //Value of theResult will be 4
```

The value of `num1` remains at 4.49.

Sometimes we need to get rid of the decimal digits without rounding, so that 4.1, 4.499, and 4.99 all end up truncated to the value 4. To do so we use the `floor()` method:

```
num1 = 4.99
theResult = Math.floor(num1)   //Value of theResult will be 4
```

The `Math` object also has methods for trigonometric and logarithmic operations, as well as properties that store frequently used special numbers like π.

You may, of course, simply use the value 3.14 for π, but if precision is required the property `Math.PI` may be used. `Math.PI` stores the value of π to 18 decimal places (or, if you're interested, 3.141592653589793116). The circumference of a circle, for example, is π multiplied by the diameter. In JavaScript:

```
var diameter = 5
var circumference = Math.PI * diameter
```

We will mention just one more method here, the `random()` method. (See the `Math` object listing in Appendix F for the other methods. More descriptive information can be found at the JavaScript websites noted in the text of Appendix F.) The `random()` method takes no parameters and generates a random number between 0 and 1:

```
var theNumber = Math.random()   //Value of theNumber will be
                                //between 0 and 1
```

We can use this method to simulate the rolling of a six-sided die by (a) generating a random number between 0 and 1, (b) multiplying it by 6 so that it will then be a random number between 0 and 6, (c) using the `floor()` method to truncate the value to the nearest integer, which will be 0, 1, 2, 3, 4, or 5, and (d) adding 1, yielding a final value of 1, 2, 3, 4, 5, or 6. To give a specific example, assume that the first line of code below generates the random number 0.903:

```
var theNumber = Math.random()         //Assume theNumber has
                                      //the value 0.903
theNumber = theNumber * 6             //Now theNumber is 5.418
theNumber = Math.floor(theNumber)     //Now theNumber is 5
theNumber = theNumber + 1             //Now theNumber is 6
```

Note that the value generated by `Math.random()` will always be less than 1, so multiplying by 6 will always yield a number that's less than 6, and the final result of the above sequence will never be 7.

We can also put the whole sequence of operations in one line:

```
var theNumber = Math.floor(Math.random() * 6) + 1
```

In general, to generate a random number that is an integer from 1 to some given number N, the code is:

```
var theNumber = Math.floor(Math.random() * N) + 1
```

Converting Strings to Numbers

Now that we have learned about basic mathematical operations, we can return to the problem of how to turn a string or text value into a number value. Remember that our goal is to create a web page where the user enters values for the length and width of a rectangle into two text boxes, and then the web page will calculate and display the area and perimeter of the rectangle. The problem is that the text box values are stored by JavaScript as strings, and therefore before we can calculate the area and perimeter of the rectangle, we need to turn them into number values. Fortunately, JavaScript provides us with a built-in function that does the trick: parseFloat().

The parseFloat() function takes a string value, parses it, and converts it to a floating point number (real number) value. To show how parseFloat() works, let's declare four variables—firstEntry, secondEntry, length and width. We will assign firstEntry and secondEntry some initial *text* values. Then we call the parseFloat() function to turn them into number values and store them in the variables named length and width, respectively.

```
var firstEntry = "72.95", secondEntry = "43", length, width
length = parseFloat(firstEntry)
width = parseFloat(secondEntry)
```

After these three lines of code were executed, the variable named length would store the *number* 72.95 and the variable named width would store the *number* 43. The variables firstEntry and secondEntry would still contain the *string* values "72.95" and "43", respectively.

Note the syntax of calling the parseFloat() function using an assignment statement. Because it returns a value (i.e., a number), we put the method call on the right side of an assignment statement, just as we did with the methods of the Math object. As usual, we read it starting on the right side: in the case of length = parseFloat(firstEntry), JavaScript calls the parseFloat() function and passes it the string value stored in the firstEntry variable. After parseFloat() has converted the string value to a number value, it returns the number value and puts it into the variable named length, where we may use it.

(Sometimes we need the returned value to be an integer, not a floating point number. In that case, the parseInt() function may be used. It works similarly to the parseFloat() function.)

What happens if firstEntry cannot be converted to a number? For instance, what if firstEntry stored a telephone number like 987-1234? (The hyphen obviously cannot be converted to a number.) In that case, parseFloat() will convert the number characters until it reaches a character that is not 0–9 (in this case, the hyphen), whereupon it stops and just returns the value up to that point. So the string 987–1234 would become the number value 987.

You should also be aware that in certain situations JavaScript will automatically convert string values to number values if they are being used in a calculation, so that it's not always necessary to use parseFloat(). Nevertheless, it's good programming practice to make the conversion explicitly using the parseFloat() function rather than relying on JavaScript to do it implicitly.

QuickCheck Questions

1. Write a single line of JavaScript code that will add 3 and 8 together, subtract 2.6, divide the result by 7, and store it in a previously declared variable named doTheMath.

2. Write a single line of JavaScript code that will calculate the circumference of a circle using the formula $C = 2\pi r$, where r is the radius of the circle, and store it in a new global variable named circumference.

3. Write a single line of JavaScript code that will generate a random integer that is either 0 or 1, in order to simulate the flipping of a coin (0 for heads, 1 for tails).

Lab Exercise 11.1, "Practice with Math," may be done at this point.

Returning a Value from a Function

In the examples above using the parseFloat() function and the methods of the Math object, and previously using things like the prompt() method, we saw how to call a function that returns a value. You may think of this process of **returning a value** as complementary to the use of parameters. Using parameters, we are able to send information to a function, information that it needs to execute its instructions. We have used parameters numerous times already, using both built-in methods and our own functions that we have written. Now we need to learn how to write our own functions like parseFloat() that not only receive information but also return a result when done. You might think of this as setting up a two-way street, with information flowing first to the function and then back again, instead of just the one-way street of parameters alone.

Functions that return a value usually accept one or more values as input and process those values before returning the result. To carry out this processing, we often make use of variables to store intermediate values and then the final result itself. The use of variables within a function has a few twists, however. So in order to learn how to write functions that return values, we first need to learn a bit more about variables.

The Scope of a Variable: Local vs. Global

When we introduced variables in Chapter 8, we declared and used all the variables in a single <script> element. For example, Figure 8.5 used a <script> element in the <body> element to declare two variables named answer1 and answer2 and initialize and display their values:

```
<script type="text/javascript">
   var answer1 = 93.7
   var answer2 = "New York"
```

```
      alert("Answer #1 is: " + answer1)
      alert("Answer #2 is: " + answer2)
      answer2 = "California"
      alert("The new value of #2 is: " + answer2)
   </script>
```

We may also, however, declare a variable in one <script> element and use it in another. For example, we could rewrite the code to use two <script> elements, as in Figure 11.2. The variable named secondAnswer is declared in the first <script> element, used there, and then also used later in the second <script> element. Once a variable has been declared in a source document, you may use it anywhere in that document (with one exception detailed below).

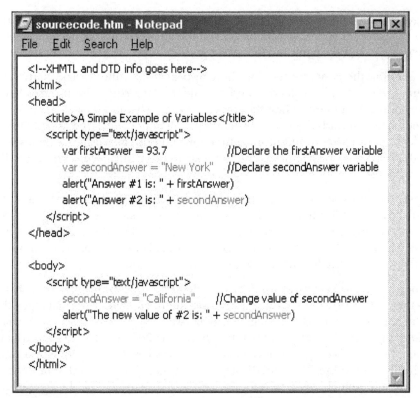

FIGURE 11.2. Using a variable throughout the source document

The exception to the rule that a variable may be used anywhere in a source document comes when we declare a variable in the code of a function. For example:

```
function testingVariables() {
   var result = 7.52
```

```
        alert("The value of the result is: " + result)
        result = "Texas"
        alert("Now the result is: " + result)
    }
```

In this case, the variable named result may only be used inside the function itself. It may not be used anywhere else in the source document to which the function belongs. If you try to do so, you'll get an error message. We call such a variable a **local variable** and we say that its **scope** is restricted to the code of that function. In contrast, when we declare a variable outside of a function, we refer to it as a **global variable**, or we say that it has global scope, meaning that it's okay to use it anywhere in the source document. The scope of a variable is a fourth key characteristic of a variable, in addition to its type, name, and value.

Figure 11.3 shows an example with both local and global variables. The question to consider is this: In what order will the alert boxes appear and what will they display? (Take a minute to make a guess at it before reading on.)

Examining the code, we see that there appear to be three variables involved named result, firstAnswer, and secondAnswer. When the browser loads this source document, it first sees the <script> element in the <head> element. There it finds firstAnswer and secondAnswer declared as global variables (because they aren't inside a function) and initialized to the values 93.7 and "New York," respectively. The two calls to the alert() method then display the values of firstAnswer and secondAnswer.

Next the browser finds a declaration for a function named testing Variables(). Within it there is a variable named result, and secondAnswer appears again. But because this is a function declaration, the browser does not execute this code yet. (We will discuss the details of this code in a minute, when we get to the line of code that calls this function.)

When the browser gets to the <body> element, it finds another <script> element. The first line of code is an assignment statement that changes the value of secondAnswer, which originally was "New York", to "California". Then the testingVariables() function is called. In it, a local variable named result is declared (local, because it's declared inside a function), initialized to the value 7.52, and displayed in an alert box. The value of secondAnswer is next changed to "Florida" and also displayed. That being the end of the function, the browser returns to the point where it was called and continues from there. In other words, it comes to the line of code:

```
    alert("The new value of #2 is: " + secondAnswer)
```

And this is where it gets tricky. The question is this: What is displayed in this alert box? Tracing what happens to the variable named secondAnswer, it would seem that the alert box would display "The new value of #2 is: Florida." Originally secondAnswer had the value "New York," then it was changed to "California" in the first line of the second <script> element, and finally,

```
 sourcecode.htm - Notepad                      _ □ X
File   Edit   Search   Help

<!--XHTML and DTD info goes here-->
<html>
<head>
    <title>A Simple Example of Variables</title>
    <script type="text/javascript">
        var firstAnswer = 93.7
        var secondAnswer = "New York"      //This declares a global variable
        alert("Answer #1 is: " + firstAnswer)
        alert("Answer #2 is: " + secondAnswer)

        function testingVariables() {
            var result = 7.52
            alert("The value of the result is: " + result)
            var secondAnswer = "Florida"    //This declares a local variable
            alert("The value of answer #2 is: " + secondAnswer)
        } //end of testingVariables
    </script>
</head>

<body>
    <script type="text/javascript">
        secondAnswer = "California"    //Is this the local or global variable?
        testingVariables()
        alert("The new value of #2 is: " + secondAnswer)
    </script>
</body>
</html>
```

FIGURE 11.3.   Using both local and global variables

when the function was called, the code in the function changed it to the value "Florida" before using the alert box to display the value.

But there's a catch here that we glossed over in our description above. The assignment statement in the function that changes the value of secondAnswer to "Florida" is preceded by a var keyword:

```
function testingVariables() {
   var result = 7.52
   alert("The value of the result is: " + result)
   var secondAnswer = "Florida"  //This declares a local
                                 //variable named secondAnswer
```

```
    alert("The value of answer #2 is: " + secondAnswer)
} //end of testingVariables
```

The presence of `var` makes this line a variable declaration for a variable named `secondAnswer`. Moreover, it is a declaration for a local variable. But, you might say, we already have a variable named `secondAnswer`, declared as a global variable in the first `<script>` element. So how does the browser resolve this conflict?

The answer is that the browser creates two separate variables, one global and one local, stored in different memory locations but both with the same name. It's like taking two identical storage boxes on your closet shelf and labeling them with the same name. Even though they have the same name, they are separate boxes and their contents will be different.

Although creating two variables with the same name resolves the conflict, it introduces another problem: When the browser encounters the name `secondAnswer` in a line of code, how does it know which variable it is? The rule it uses is simple. Inside that single function, the name `secondAnswer` refers to the local variable. Anywhere else in the document (including any other functions that may exist), `secondAnswer` refers to the global variable.

So now we can fully decipher the code of Figure 11.3 and answer the question as to what the last `alert` command in the second `<script>` element displays. At the beginning of the second `<script>` element we have the line:

```
secondAnswer = "California"
```

This line, being outside the function, refers to the global variable named `secondAnswer`, so it changes its value to "California." Then comes the function call to `testingVariables()`. The first two lines of code in it deal with the local variable named `result`. The third line declares a local variable named `secondAnswer` and assigns it the value "Florida." Note that at this point the global variable named `secondAnswer` still has the value "California" in it. The fourth line then displays the value of the local variable named `secondAnswer`—it displays "The value of answer #2 is: Florida".

Finally, the function's code being at an end, the browser returns to the second `<script>` element and finds the line:

```
alert("The new value of #2 is: " + secondAnswer)
```

The `secondAnswer` in this line refers to the global variable, so the alert box displays "The new value of #2 is: California".

Although the browser doesn't get confused in all this, it's obviously very easy for us humans to lose track of which variable is which. So the moral of the story is be careful how you use the `var` keyword, and never give the same name to both a local variable and a global variable.

At this point you might be thinking why use local variables at all? Why not just make all variables global variables, so that they may be used anywhere in the source document? The reason to use local variables is that in long scripts and programs they help minimize the number of programming bugs. In large complex programs, where there are hundreds or thousands or even millions of lines of code written by teams of programmers, it's very easy for one team of programmers to do something to a global variable in their section of code that messes up something another team is doing with the global variable in their section of code. Minimizing the use of global variables reduces the possibility of this sort of error.

In using JavaScript in HTML source documents we rarely have scripts that are over 100 lines of code, so using local variables is not quite as critical. Nevertheless, as you will see them used in other people's code, you need to know how they work. And it's simply good programming practice to use them yourself. The basic rule of practice is that if you know you are only going to use a variable within a certain function, then you should use the var keyword to declare it as a local variable within that function. Otherwise, make it a global variable. It is also good form to declare all the global variables used in the source document at the beginning of a <script> element in the <head> element, right before you declare any functions you will be using.

IMPORTANT

You should always declare a variable using the var keyword. But if you forget to use the var keyword when declaring a variable, JavaScript overlooks the omission. For example, consider the following assignment statement:

```
thirdAnswer = 3.14
```

If a variable named thirdAnswer does not already exist when the browser gets to this line of code, a new variable named thirdAnswer will automatically be created and assigned the value 3.14. This behavior of JavaScript is very different from most programming languages. In most languages if you try to assign a value to a variable name that has not previously been properly declared, an error message is generated. But not in the case of JavaScript: It simply assumes that since the name thirdAnswer is used, it should create such a variable if one doesn't already exist. This new variable created will *always* be a *global* variable, even if the line of code (thirdAnswer = 3.14, in this case) is inside a function.

Although this automatic creation of a variable seems convenient, it can lead to tricky programming errors. It also only works when the new variable is on the left side of an assignment statement. So it's always best to declare your variables explicitly by using the var keyword appropriately, whether for a global or a local variable.

One final note on the limits of variables: When the browser replaces the document by loading a new document, all the variables used in the original document are deleted from memory and are no longer available for use. So if you have a multiple-page website, you can't declare a variable in one source document, store a value in it, and then try to access that value in another document of the same website. (One way to get around this limitation is to use cookies,

one of the subjects of Chapter 15. Another way is to use JavaScript in combination with frames, the subject of Chapter 17.)

Lab Exercise 11.2, "Practice with Global and Local Variables," may be done at this point.

Returning a Value

As an example of a function that returns a value, we will calculate the average of three numbers. We might write a function to perform this calculation as follows:

```
function calculateAverage(num1,num2,num3) {
  var average
  average = (num1+num2+num3)/3
  alert("The average is " + average)
}
```

This function has three formal parameters (num1, num2, and num3) and one local variable (average). To call this function we would write:

```
calculateAverage(8, 3, 12)
```

Or perhaps something like:

```
var firstNum = 8, secondNum = 3, thirdNum = 12
calculateAverage(firstNum, secondNum, thirdNum)
```

The function will receive the three numbers, calculate their average and store the result in a local variable named average, and then display the result in an alert box.

Now we will rewrite this function so that instead of displaying the result in an alert box, it will return the result to the place where it is called. In other words, we want the code where we call the function to be:

```
var theResult
theResult = calculateAverage(8, 3, 12)
alert("The average is " + theResult)
```

The second line in this code will call the calculateAverage() function and send it the values 8, 3, and 12. The function will calculate their average and return the result, whereupon it will be stored in the variable named theResult. The third line will then display the average in an alert box.

Now we need to rewrite the calculateAverage() function so that it returns the average value. The key is to use the JavaScript reserved word return, followed by the name of the variable whose value we want returned:

```
function calculateAverage(num1,num2,num3) {
  var average
  average = (num1+num2+num3)/3
  return average
}
```

When the browser encounters a `return` keyword in a function, it immediately exits the function and goes back to where the function was called, sending back the value indicated after the `return` keyword (in this case, the value contained in the `average` variable). This means that usually the return line of code should be the last line in the function, because anything after it will not be executed. For example, the `alert` command in the following version of the function will never occur:

Error Alert!

```
function calculateAverage(num1,num2,num3) {
  var average
  average = (num1+num2+num3)/3
  return average
  alert("The average is " + average)
}
```

We do not have to use a variable after the keyword `return`; any valid JavaScript expression that evaluates to a single value will do. We may therefore write:

```
return (num1+num2+num3)/3
```

instead of:

```
return average
```

This has the advantage of shortening the code in our function:

```
function calculateAverage(num1,num2,num3) {
  return (num1+num2+num3)/3
}
```

QuickCheck Questions

1. What are local variables? Why is it good to use them?
2. Write the code that declares a function named `ratio` with two parameters named `num1` and `num2`. The function should divide `num1` by `num2` and return the result.
3. Write the line of code that will call the function in #1 and send it the values 8 and 3.

Lab Exercise 11.3, "Returning a Value from a Function," may be done at this point.

Implementing a Simple Calculator

Finally, now, we're ready to write the code to calculate the area and perimeter of a rectangle. In summary, here is what we need to do:

1. Create a form, named `calcForm` (or whatever), with the two input text fields for length and width (we'll name them `widthBox` and `lengthBox`, respectively), with appropriate labels so the surfer knows which box is which and what to do.

2. In the same form, create the two output text fields, named `areaBox` and `perimeterBox` and labeled Area and Perimeter.

3. Still in the same form, create the Calculate button. Its `onclick` event handler will call a function named `calc()` and send it the whole form as a parameter. This function will use the `parseFloat()` function and appropriate assignment statements to convert the entered values for the length and width from text to numbers and then calculate the area and perimeter of the rectangle using these numbers. Finally, the results for the area and perimeter will be put into the `value` property of the output fields for the area and perimeter (`areaBox.value` and `perimeterBox.value`).

The Calculator Code

Putting all this together, the code for the Calculate button will be:

```
<input type="button" name="calcButton" value="Calculate"
    onclick="calc(document.calcForm)" />
```

where the function referred to in the `onclick` event handler is:

```
function calc(f) {
    var width = parseFloat(f.widthBox.value)
    var length = parseFloat(f.lengthBox.value)
    f.areaBox.value = length*width
    f.perimeterBox.value = 2*(length+width)
}
```

Review how this works: When the surfer clicks on the Calculate button, the information in the form named `calcForm` (referred to by its full name, `document.calcForm`) is passed to the function named `calc()`, where it is put into the formal parameter named `f`. The first two lines in the function take the values that the surfer has entered into the `widthBox` and `lengthBox` and convert them from text to numbers using the `parseFloat()` function. The numbers are stored in the local variables named `width` and `length`, respectively. Finally, the area of the rectangle is calculated and displayed in the `areaBox` text box, and the perimeter is calculated and displayed in the `perimeterBox` text box.

Figure 11.4 shows the complete source document for the rectangle calculator and the display before and after the button is clicked.

Revising the Calculator Code

In our Rectangle Calculator we are performing a very simple calculation and therefore the `calc()` function only has a few lines of code. Sometimes, how-

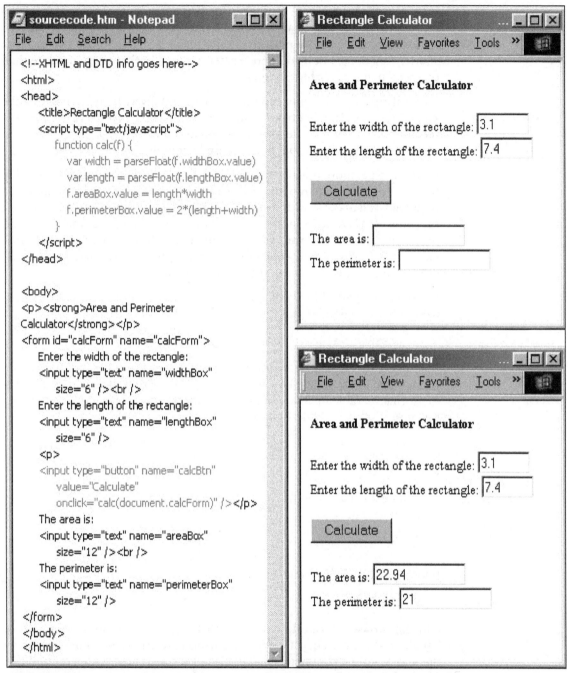

FIGURE 11.4. The code for the Rectangle Calculator web page and the display before and after the surfer clicks the Calculate button

ever, we have more complicated calculations and/or information processing to perform, and the function we write to do those calculations may grow very long. At a certain size, it is good practice to break a long function into two or more shorter functions. This makes for better readability and easier debugging, because any bugs may be isolated and identified more readily. There is no set limit at which you must or should divide a function into two or more shorter functions, but if you have written a function that takes up more than one screen, it is probably too long.

To break up a function into two functions, we usually write them such that the second function is called from within the first. In doing so, we often want the second function to execute its instructions and then return a value to the first function, which the first function will use in completing the calculations.

In order to get more practice returning a value from a function, we will divide the `calc()` function into three functions: Instead of doing the area and perimeter calculations within the `calc()` function, we will declare two new functions—`calcArea()` and `calcPerim()`—that calculate the area and perimeter, respectively. Each of these functions will be called from our original `calc()` function and, when done executing, will return their result to the `calc()` function so that it can display the overall results.

Consider one part of how this works, the calculation of the area. In the original `calc()` function, we did it this way:

```
f.areaBox.value = length*width
```

This line of code calculates the area (length times width) and assigns the result to the `areaBox` text box, where it will be displayed. (Remember that f is the formal parameter that contains the form that was passed to the `calc()` function.) Now we will do it this way:

```
f.areaBox.value = calcArea(length, width)
```

where we declare our own `calcArea()` function as follows:

```
function calcArea(l, w) {
  var area = l*w
  return area
}
```

In other words, the line of code

```
f.areaBox.value = calcArea(length, width)
```

tells the browser to call the `calcArea()` function and send it the values of `length` and `width`. The `calcArea()` function receives these values and stores them in its formal parameters, named l and w. The function then multiplies l and w and stores the result in a local variable named `area`. Finally, it uses the `return` keyword to signify that the result now stored in the variable named `area` should be returned to where the function was called. In this case, the function was called from the line of code:

```
f.areaBox.value = calcArea(length, width)
```

So the value that is returned is assigned to the value of the areaBox text box and thus displayed.

Similarly, we write a function named calcPerim() to calculate and return the perimeter value. The complete <script> element, revised to use the return feature, is shown in Figure 11.5.

```
sourcecode.htm - Notepad                        _ □ ×
File   Edit   Search   Help

<script type="text/javascript">
    function calcArea(l, w) {
        var area = l*w
        return area
    }

    function calcPerim(l, w) {
        var perimeter = 2*(l+w)
        return perimeter
    }

    function calc(f) {
        var width = parseFloat(f.widthBox.value)
        var length = parseFloat(f.lengthBox.value)
        f.areaBox.value  = calcArea(length, width)
        f.perimeterBox.value = calcPerim(length, width)
    }
</script>
```

FIGURE 11.5.   The script for the Rectangle Calculator, revised to use multiple functions and the return feature

This revised version is obviously more complicated than our first version without any real benefit. But it is a simple example that demonstrates how to use the return keyword as well as how, when necessary, you might divide a long function into several shorter functions.

QuickCheck Question

1. Rewrite the calcArea() function of Figure 11.5 so that it doesn't use a local variable.

Lab Exercise 11.4, "A Sales Tax Calculator," may be done at this point.

Key Terms

combination assignment
    operators (+=, −=, *=, and
    /=)
decrement operator (−−)
external JavaScript file

global variables
increment operator (++)
local variables
Math object

mathematical operators
returning a value from a function
rules of precedence
scope

Code Summary

1 Basic Math with JavaScript

Using the +, −, *, and / operators to add, subtract, multiply, or divide:

```
result = firstNum + secondNum - thirdNum
result = firstNum * secondNum
result = firstNum / secondNum
```

Incrementing the value of a number variable by 1:

```
firstNum = firstNum +1
```

Using the increment operator to increase the value of a number variable by 1:

```
firstNum++
```

Decrementing the value of a number variable by 1:

```
firstNum = firstNum - 1
```

Using the decrement operator to decrease the value of a number variable by 1:

```
firstNum--
```

Using combination assignment operators:

```
theNum+=7              //These two lines of code do the same thing
theNum = theNum + 7
theNum-=7              //These two lines of code do the same thing
theNum = theNum -7
theNum*=7              //These two lines of code do the same thing
theNum = theNum*7
theNum/=7              //These two lines of code do the same thing
theNum = theNum/7
```

Using parentheses to specify the order of mathematical operations:

```
theAnswer = (firstNum+secondNum)*thirdNum-fourthNum
theAnswer = firstNum+secondNum*(thirdNum-fourthNum)
```

Using the Math object to calculate a square root:

```
num1 = 36
theResult = Math.sqrt(num1)
```

Calculating the square and the cube of a number:

```
theNum = 6
firstResult = Math.pow(theNum, 2)
secondResult = Math.pow(theNum, 3)
```

Rounding a number to the nearest integer:

```
theResult = Math.round(theNum)
```

Truncating a number to the next lowest integer:
```
theResult = Math.floor(theNum)
```

Generating a random number between 0 and 1:
```
theNum = Math.random()
```

Generating a random *integer* from 1 to N (i.e., 1, 2, 3, . . . N):
```
theNum = Math.floor(Math.random() * N) + 1
```

Converting a string value to a number value using the `parseFloat()` function:
```
theStr = "72.95"
theNum = parseFloat(theStr)
```

2 Returning a Value from a Function

Declaring a local variable named `theResult`:
```
function someName() {
   var theResult
   //etc.
}
```

Declaring a function so that it returns a value:
```
function calculateAverage(num1,num2,num3) {
   var average = (num1+num2+num3)/3
   return average
}
```

Calling a function that returns a value:
```
var theResult
theResult = calculateAverage(8, 3, 12)
```

Or:
```
var firstNum = 8, secondNum = 3, thirdNum = 12
calculateAverage(firstNum, secondNum, thirdNum)
```

Use special operators like ++, −−, +=, *=, etc. with caution. They can make your code nice and compact, but that compactness can make it hard to read and understand. They also tend to lead to more programming errors, especially when you use them in combination with other operators in a mathematical expression.

The double-minus symbol for the decrement operator (−−) is reserved for other uses in XHTML. If you want to use it in a script, you should therefore put the script in an external file.

Use parentheses in mathematical expressions.

Even though JavaScript will automatically convert strings to numbers in certain calculations, it's good practice to make the conversion explicitly using `parseFloat()`.

Never give the same name to both a local variable and a global variable.

When using global variables, it's good to declare them at the beginning of a <script> element in the <head> element.

Use the `var` keyword to declare variables (don't rely on JavaScript's automatic capabilities) and use local variables as much as possible.

Alerts and Advice

All variables associated with a document are deleted from memory and are no longer available for use when the browser loads a new document. (Exceptions to this rule occur when using frames or multiple windows—see Chapter 17.)

The line of code in a function that uses a `return` keyword should usually be the last line in the function.

Break up long functions into two or more functions when possible.

Review Questions

1. What is the value of the variable named `anotherResult` after the following lines of code are executed?
```
var theResult, anotherResult
theResult = 12 - 7 + 2
anotherResult = 4 + theResult
```
   a. 4
   b. 7
   c. 11
   d. undefined (because the code has an error in it)

2. What is the value of the variable named `answer` after the following lines of code are executed?
```
var num1,num2, answer
num1 = 15
num2 = 3
answer = num1/num2
num1 = 12
alert("The value of answer is: " + answer)
```
   a. 4
   b. 5
   c. 9
   d. 15

3. What is the value of the variable named `theAnswer` after the following lines of code are executed?
```
theAnswer = 8 - 2 * 3 + 6 / 2
```
   a. 12
   b. 4
   c. 5
   d. 27

4. Which line(s) of code below assign(s) the numeric value 9 to the variable named `finalResult`?
   a. `finalResult = 9`
   b. `finalResult = parseFloat("9")`
   c. `finalResult = Math.sqrt(81)`
   d. `finalResult = Math.pow(3,2)`
   e. `finalResult = Math.round(9.7)`

5. Which of the following lines of code will generate a random number between 0 and 10 and store it in a variable named `randomNum`?
   a. `randomNum = random(0, 10)`
   b. `randomNum = random(0-10)`
   c. `randomNum = Math.random(0, 10)`
   d. `randomNum = 10*Math.random()`

6. Which of the following lines of code calculates the area of a circle, using the formula $A = \pi r^2$ (where r is the radius of the circle), and stores it in a variable named `theArea`?
   a. `theArea = (Math.PI)*(Math.pow(r, 2))`
   b. `theArea = pi*r_squared`

    c. `theArea = pi*Math.pow(r, 2)`

    d. `theArea = (Math.PI)*r_squared`

7. True or false: The first time you use a variable in a source document, you always have to use the `var` keyword to declare it, otherwise the browser will generate an error message.

8. True or false: If you have a multiple-page website that doesn't use frames or multiple windows, you can't declare a variable in the source document for one page and then try to use it in a source document for one of the other pages.

9. Assuming that each of the following lines of code was in a function, which would declare a local variable named `result` and initialize it to 0?

    a. `result = 0`

    b. `var result`

    c. `var result = 0`

    d. `var result(0)`

10. Assuming that the following lines of code were in a function, which would be used to send back the value of a variable named `theResult`?

    a. `return theResult`

    b. `pass theResult`

    c. `return = theResult`

    d. `theResult = back`

1. Briefly define and/or explain the following terms: loosely typed, boolean, variable scope.

2. What is the difference between a local variable and a global variable? What are the advantages and disadvantages of each?

3. Write the following expression in JavaScript code: Take the value of a variable named `firstNum`, add 3 to it, then multiply by 5, then subtract 12, and finally divide by 4. Store the result in a variable named `finalAnswer`.

4. In a `<script>` element, write the JavaScript code for a function named `testingVariables` that declares the following local variables: a number variable named `num1` that is initialized to the value 19.54, a string variable named `name3` that is initialized to the value "Theodore Roosevelt", and a boolean variable named `matchFound` that is initialized to be true. Then write the code that would change the value of `num1` to 29.1, the value of `name3` to "Abraham Lincoln", and the value of `matchFound` to false.

5. In a `<script>` element, write the JavaScript code that declares a global variable named `theNumber` and gives it the value 7. Add a single line of code that subtracts 4 from `theNumber`, multiplies the result by 5, and stores it in a new global variable named `answer`. Finally, write a line of code that adds 4 to `answer` (so that `answer` ends up with a value of 19).

6. In a `<script>` element, write the JavaScript code that declares a global variable named `theNumber` and gives it the value 7. Add a line of code that takes the square root of `theNumber`, multiplies the result by 5, and stores it in a new global variable named `answer`. Finally, write a line of code that rounds the value of `answer` to the nearest integer and stores it in a new global variable named `finalAnswer`.

7. In a `<script>` element, write the JavaScript code that declares a global variable named `luckyNumber` and gives it a random value between 0 and 10. (It doesn't matter whether the random value is an integer or not.) Then declare a global variable named `luckyNumber2` and give it a random integer value from 1 to 100 (that is, it can only be 1, 2, 3, . . . 100, not any numbers in between).

8. In a `<script>` element, write the JavaScript code that generates two random integers, each from 1 to 6, to represent two rolls of a single die. Store the random values in new global variables named `roll1` and `roll2`. Then add the values of the two rolls and display the total in a text box named `document.diceForm.rollBox`.

9. In a `<script>` element, write the JavaScript code that declares a global variable named `finalAnswer` and initializes it to 0. Then the code should take a number that the surfer has entered in a text box named `document.answerForm.box3`, add 100 to it, and store it in `finalAnswer`.

10. In a `<script>` element, write the JavaScript code that declares a function named `fullName()` with two parameters named `firstName` and `lastName`. The code in `fullName()` should put the values of `firstName` and `lastName` together, with a space between them, store them in a local variable named `theName`, and then return the value of `theName`. After the code for the function declaration, write the code that will pass the values "Babe" and "Ruth" to the function and store the returned result in a global variable named `hallOfFamer`. The `hallOfFamer` variable should be declared before the function declaration.

1. Identify and correct the errors in the following code for the rectangle calculator.

```html
<html>
<head>
    <title>Rectangle Calculator</title>
    <script type="text/javascript">
        function calcArea(l, w) {
            var area = l*w
        }
        function calcPerim(l, w) {
            var perimeter = 2*(l+w)
        }
        function calc(f) {
            var width = parseFloat(widthBox)
            var length = parseFloat(lengthBox)
            area = calcArea(length.value, width.value)
            areaBox.value = area
            perimeterBox.value = calcPerim(length.value, width.value)
        }
    </script>
</head>
<body>
<p><strong>Area and Perimeter Calculator</strong></p>
<form id="calcForm">
    Enter the width of the rectangle:
    <input type="text" name="widthBox" size="6" /><br />
    Enter the length of the rectangle:
    <input type="text" name="lengthBox" size="6" />
    <p><input type="button" name="calcBtn" value="Calculate"
        onclick="calc(document.calculatorForm)" /></p>
    The area is: <input type="text" name="areaBox" size="12" /><br />
    The perimeter is: <input type="text" name="perimeterBox" size="12" />
</form>
</body>
</html>
```

Note: Most of the exercises above may also be done as lab exercises. When a problem involves the creation and manipulation of variables, simply add some alert boxes to the code to display the ending values of the variables. If a problem involves a function, add a function call so that the function code is actually executed.

Exercise 11.1: Practice with Math

❑ Create a new HTML source document that has a form named `mathForm` with a text box named `inputBox`, a click button labeled Calculate, and three more text boxes named `result1Box`, `result2Box`, and `result3Box`. The `inputBox` text box should have a prompt (either next to it or inside it) that asks the surfer to enter a number and then click the button. The `result1Box` should have a label next to it that says "Twice the number is: ", the `result2Box` should have the label "One half the number is: ", and the `result3Box` should have the label "The square root of the number is: ". The button should have an `onclick` event handler that calls a function named `sampleCalculations()`, with no parameters. The code in the `sampleCalculations()` function should convert the value in the `inputBox` from a string to a number and store it in a local variable named `theNum`. It should then multiply `theNum` by 2 and display the result in `result1Box`, divide `theNum` by 2 and display the result in `result2Box`, and take the square root of `theNum` and display the result in `result3Box`.

Exercise 11.2: Practice with Global and Local Variables

❑ Create an HTML source document with a `<script>` element in the `<head>` element that uses JavaScript to declare three global variables named `name1`, `name2`, and `name3` and initialize them to the string values "Copernicus", "Galileo", and "Newton", respectively. Using a separate `<script>` element in the `<body>` element, use the `alert()` method to display the values of `name1`, `name2`, and `name3` (one alert box for all three values).

❑ Declare a function named `testVariables` (with no parameters) in the `<script>` element that is in the `<head>` element. The function's code should declare a local variable named `name4`, initialize it to the value "Einstein", and display the value of `name4` in an alert box. In the `<script>` element in the `<body>` element, add the code that calls this function.

❑ After the line of code that calls the function, add another call to the `alert()` method and use it to display the value of `name3` only. Then change the name of the variable in the `testVariables()` function from `name4` to `name3`, so that `name3` will be given the value "Einstein". What value does this final alert box display, and why?

Exercise 11.3: Returning a Value from a Function

❑ Make a new source document named MeterConversion.htm (or something similar). In a `<script>` element in the `<head>` element, declare a function named `metersToFeet()` with one parameter named `meters` (assumed to be a number). The code in the function should multiply `meters` by 3.281 (the conversion factor for changing meters into feet), store it in a local variable named `feet`, and return the value of `feet`. In a `<script>` element in the `<body>` element, call this function and send it the value 30. Store the returned value in a variable named `numberFeet` and display its value in an alert box (with the message "The number of feet in 30 meters is . . .").

Exercise 11.4: A Sales Tax Calculator

❑ Use the Save As menu option to save a copy of your source document from Lab Exercise 11.1 and rename it "SalesTaxCalculator.htm". Also change the contents of the `<title>` element to "Sales Tax Calculator".

❑ Change the name of the form to `taxForm` and the name of the first text box to `saleAmountBox`. Also change the prompt for the box to "Enter amount of sale (e.g., 19.95, without a dollar sign):". Change the name of the `result1Box` to `taxBox` and the name of `result2Box` to `totalAmountBox`. Also change the labels next to the boxes to "Sales tax due" and "Total amount due". Delete the code for `result3Box`. Save your work!

❑ Rename the `sampleCalculations()` function to `calculateTax()` and modify it to:

   a. Convert the amount of sale the surfer has entered from a text value to a number, stored in an appropriately named variable.

   b. Multiply that number by 0.075 to calculate the sales tax due (assuming a 7.5% tax), and then display that sales tax amount in the appropriate output textbox.

   c. Add the amount of sale and the sales tax due to yield the total amount due, which is then displayed in its textbox.

Note: When you get your sales tax calculator working, you will find that the browser will often display the result to a large number of decimal places. Obviously we would rather have the result displayed to two decimal places, so it's dollars and cents. Navigator version 6 and Explorer version 5.5 provide a built-in method named `toFixed()` to accomplish this formatting. It takes one parameter, which specifies the number of decimal places to display. Variables that contain numbers are treated as objects, and this method automatically belongs to these number objects. The following code shows how you round a number to two decimal places:

```
var result = 394.2445
var roundedNumber = result.toFixed(2)    //roundedNumber will be 394.24
```

Unfortunately, browser versions before Navigator 6 and Explorer 5.5 do not include the `toFixed()` method. But it's not too hard to write our own function that will do the job. We have provided two versions below. The first version, named `round2Places()`, will round a number to two decimal places. The second, named `roundXPlaces()`, will round a number to a specified number of decimal places.

The first version accepts a number and stores it in a parameter named `numToRound`. It then multiplies the value in `numToRound` by 100, rounds the result, and finally divides that result by 100. To see what happens during this process, consider the number 46.3872. Multiplying it by 100 gives 4638.72. Rounding it to the nearest integer gives 4639. And dividing this result by 100 gives 46.39, which is the desired result.

The second version not only accepts the number to round but also an integer that specifies how many decimal places to round it to (e.g., 1, 2, 3, 4, and so on). This integer is stored in a parameter named `numberPlaces`. The key is that to round to one place, we use 10 instead of 100; to round to three places, we use 1000; to round to four places, we use 10000, and so on. So we simply replace the 100 in the first version with 10*numberPlaces.

First version:

```
function round2Places(numToRound) {
  var theResult
  theResult = numToRound*100
  theResult = Math.round(theResult)
  theResult = theResult/100
  return theResult
}
```

We have written this code so that the calculations are done step by step. But it's possible to shorten it considerably by doing the whole calculation in one line:

```
function round2Places(numToRound) {
  return (Math.round(numToRound*100))/100
}
```

To call this function and get the rounded value back, we write:

```
theRoundedNumber = round2Places(46.3872)
```

where `theRoundedNumber` is a variable previously declared.

Or:

```
theRoundedNumber = round2Places(theNum)
```

where `theNum` is a variable that stores a number.

The second version of this function, in step-by-step form, is:

```
function roundXPlaces(numToRound, numberPlaces) {
  var theResult
  theResult = numToRound*10*numberPlaces
  theResult = Math.round(theResult)
  theResult = theResult/100
  return theResult
}
```

The shortened version is:

```
function roundXPlaces(numToRound, numberPlaces) {
  return (Math.round(numToRound*10*numberPlaces))/100
}
```

To call this function and get the rounded value back, we send it two parameters, the number to round and the number of places to round it to:

```
theRoundedNumber = roundXPlaces(46.3872, 1)
```

After this line of code executes, `theRoundedNumber` will contain the value 46.4.

Or, to round a value stored in a variable named `theNum` to three decimal places:

```
theRoundedNumber = roundXPlaces(theNum, 3)
```

❑ Once you have the sales tax calculator working, make a copy of your source document and give it the name SalesTaxCalculator2.htm (use the Save As command). Using this new document, add a feature such that the surfer may enter the sales tax rate into a text box (instead of the script assuming that it's 0.075). Note that the surfer should enter the tax rate as 6 or 4.5 or 5.75 or whatever (without the % sign), and then the script will need to divide the entered value by 100 to put the rate in decimal form before doing the other calculations.

❑ Optional: Make a copy of your SalesTaxCalculator2.htm document and rename it SalesTaxCalculator3.htm. Using the new copy, divide the `calculateTax()` function into two functions, the second of which will calculate the sales tax and return the result to the first function using the `return` keyword. The first function will then display the results as before.

Increasing the Interactivity

LEARNING OBJECTIVES

1. Learn how JavaScript can make decisions to execute one set of instructions or another set of instructions based on whether a certain condition is true or false.

2. Learn how to create check boxes on a web page and read and respond to the check boxes the surfer selects.

3. Learn how to create a set of radio buttons on a web page and read and respond to which radio button the surfer selects.

4. Learn how to create a pop-up menu on a web page and read and respond to which option the surfer selects.

The Conditional Statement

So far in our quest to create interactive web pages we have learned how to (1) allow the surfer to enter a value (e.g., a name) and then parrot it back, as in "Greetings, [surfer's name here]!" and (2) take some information entered by the surfer and process it, returning an answer, as in our rectangle calculator.

Now we would like to take it to the next level by learning how to respond to the surfer's input in different ways depending on what the surfer entered. For instance, you might ask the surfer a Yes or No question, such as "Do you take sugar in your coffee?" If the surfer answered "Yes," you might then have JavaScript respond, "One lump or two?" If the surfer answered "No," you'd have it respond, "Would you like cream?"

This kind of programming logic may be implemented via the conditional control structure (also known as a branching or if . . . else structure; see Chapter 7, "The Four Basic Control Structures" section). The names come from the fact that you have JavaScript test some condition; if the condition is true, then you do one thing, else if it is false, you branch another way and do something else. It's like a fork in the road. Which path the program takes depends on whether the condition is true or not.

if . . . else Statements

The basic syntax of a **conditional statement** (in pseudocode format) is:

```
if (some condition is true) {
    //first JavaScript statement or block of statements to
    //be executed
}
else {
    //second statement or block of statements to be executed
}
//Continue with the code that comes next . . .
```

If the condition is true, then the first block of statements will be executed, otherwise (else) the second block will be. So either the first block of statements or the second block of statements will be executed, but not both. After one of the two blocks is executed, the browser continues with whatever comes next. The pairs of curly braces—one for the **if clause** and one for the **else clause**—define the beginning and end of each block of statements.

The else clause, with its block of code, is optional. In other words, you might have:

```
if (some condition is true) {
    //JavaScript statements to be executed if condition is
    //true
}
//Continue with what comes next . . .
```

In this case, if the condition is true, the statements inside the if statement are executed and then the browser continues with what comes next. If the condition is false, then the browser skips the statements inside the if statement and just continues with whatever is next.

A third possibility is to have a series of mutually exclusive else if clauses in what is sometimes called a **compound conditional statement**:

```
if (some condition is true) {
    //first JavaScript statement or group of statements to
    //be executed
}
else if (another condition is true) {
    //second statement or group of statements to be executed
}
else if (yet another condition is true) {
    //third statement or group of statements to be executed
```

```
}
else {
    //fourth statement or group of statements to be executed
}
//Continue with the code that comes next . . .
```

The logical flow of this series of conditional statements is as follows: If the first condition is true, the browser executes the first group of statements and then skips the rest of the else clauses and continues with the code that comes after the last else clause. If the first condition is false, the browser moves to the next else if condition and checks it. If it's true, the browser executes the second group of statements and then skips the rest of the else clauses and continues on. And so on for any other else if clauses.

Note that in our example the last else clause does not have an if condition. If the browser reaches this clause (meaning that none of the conditions above it were true), then it will execute the fourth group of statements. By including this else clause at the end of a compound conditional statement, we guarantee that one of the groups of statements will be executed. This last else clause in effect acts as a last resort option. It's sometimes used to display a warning message when at least one of the previous conditions is supposed to be true but none are (indicating that an error has occurred). It's not necessary, however, to include it. If it's not present, and none of the conditions are true, then the browser will skip the code in all the clauses.

Another key point to grasp here is that at most only one of the clauses in a compound conditional statement will be executed, even if more than one of the conditions is true. The reason is that once the browser comes to a condition that is true, it executes the corresponding code and then doesn't even look at any of the following else if and/or else clauses. It jumps to the end of the compound conditional statement and continues with whatever code comes next.

The Equality Operator

The following example, using our coffee question above and something called the equality operator, will reveal the basic details of using a conditional statement. Later in this chapter we will learn how to create web page check boxes, radio buttons, and pop-up menus. They will provide opportunities to use the more extended forms of compound conditional statements.

For this example, we will assume that we are using a text field named document.myForm.questionBox to ask the question (i.e., a text field named questionBox that belongs to a form named myForm), and a text field named document.myForm.answerBox in which the surfer will type an answer to the question. We will also assume that the surfer has just entered an answer to the first question, "Do you take sugar in your coffee?" The conditional statement for checking the surfer's answer against the two possibilities, "Yes" and "No", would be:

```
if (document.myForm.answerBox.value == "Yes") {
   document.myForm.questionBox.value = "One lump or two?"
}
else {
   document.myForm.questionBox.value = "Would you like
   cream?"
}
```

Note the use of the double equal sign (==) in the code for the condition. The == is one of JavaScript's **comparison** or **relational operators**. They get their name because they are used to check the relation of one value to another value. In this case, it is the **equality operator**, and it tells JavaScript to compare the values of the two things on either side of itself (in this case, document.myForm.answerBox.value and "Yes"). If they are equal, then the condition is true, and the statements in the if block of code are executed. If they are not equal, then the condition is false, and the statements in the else block of code are executed.

Here are a few more simple examples using the equality operator:

```
var result = 12
if (result == 12) {
   alert("The result is equal to 12")
}
else {
   alert("The result is not equal to 12")
}
```

Because the variable named result was assigned the value 12, the condition (result == 12) is true and the browser will display the first alert box but not the second. If result had been given a value other than 12, the condition would be false and the second alert box would be displayed.

Note that the following version is not correct:

```
var result = 12
if (result == 12) {
   alert("The result is equal to 12")
}
alert("The result is not equal to 12")
```

The reason is that the second alert box will be displayed whether or not result is equal to 12, because the alert command is not part of the conditional statement. So you will see both alert boxes in this case.

We can also compare the value of one variable with the value of another variable:

```
var firstResult = 12, secondResult = 7
if (firstResult == secondResult) {
   alert("The two results are equal")
```

```
  }
  else {
    alert("The two results are not equal")
  }
```

Because the value of `firstResult` (12) is not the same as the value of `second Result` (7), the condition (`firstResult == secondResult`) is false and the browser will execute the code in the `else` clause, displaying the alert box with the "not equal" message.

Do not confuse the use of the double equal sign in JavaScript with that of the equal sign, which is the assignment operator. The latter is used in assignment statements where the value of the right side is being copied into a variable on the left side. In contrast, the double equal sign indicates that JavaScript is to test whether something equals something else. No variable values are being changed.

A common mistake is to use a single equal sign instead of the double equal sign to check a condition, such as:

Error Alert!

```
  if (document.myForm.answerBox.value = "Yes") {
    document.myForm.questionBox.value = "One lump or two?"
  }
  else {
    document.myForm.questionBox.value = "Would you like
    cream?"
  }
```

Even if you know better than to do this, your fingers may not cooperate as you type it, because in your mind you are likely saying, "if the value of the `answerBox` equals Yes." It's helpful, therefore, to get in the habit of saying and thinking "equals-equals," as in "if the value of the `answerBox` equals-equals Yes."

IMPORTANT

Forgetting to use a double equal sign in a conditional test leads to an error that is very difficult to debug. Consider the following code:

```
  var firstNum = 4, secondNum = 7
  if (firstNum = secondNum) {
    alert("They're equal!")
  }
  else {
    alert("Not equal")
  }
```

This code seems to be straightforward. If `firstNum` and `secondNum` are equal, then an alert box with that message will appear, otherwise the "Not equal" message will appear. In this case, `firstNum` and `secondNum` are obviously not equal, so the "Not equal" message should appear. But if you type this code into a `<script>` element and load the source document in a browser, you would instead find that the "They're equal" message appears. So what's going on?

The problem is that we used a single equal sign instead of a double equal sign in the conditional test. We should have written: `if (firstNum == secondNum)`, not `if (firstNum = secondNum)`. Our mistake is compounded, moreover, by the fact that the browser treats the single equals version as perfectly legitimate JavaScript code and does not generate an error message. Instead, it takes `firstNum = secondNum` as the assignment statement it is, and copies the value of `secondNum` into `firstNum`. Then, since this is a legitimate operation, it treats the result as a true result, meaning the condition is true and it executes the first alert statement rather than the one in the `else` clause.

We can also use this code example to note three other syntax points about conditional statements. First, the parentheses around the condition are required. We can't write:

```
if firstNum == secondNum {
   alert("They're equal!") }
else {
   alert("Not equal")
}
```

Fortunately, this error does generate an error message.

Second, when an `if` or `else` block of code only has a single statement in it, we can dispense with the curly braces:

```
if (firstNum == secondNum)
   alert("They're equal!")
else
   alert("Not equal")
//Following JavaScript code goes here
```

IMPORTANT

Nevertheless, it's recommended to use the curly braces anyway, because if you later decide to add more lines of code in one of the clauses, it's easy to forget to add the necessary braces.

Third, it's not necessary to indent the code in the various clauses of a conditional statement. But not indenting the code makes it more difficult to read:

```
if (firstNum == secondNum) {
alert("They're equal!")
}
else {
alert("Not equal")
}
//Following JavaScript code goes here
```

You may also save some space by writing it as follows:

```
if (firstNum == secondNum) {alert("They're equal!")}
else {alert("Not equal")}
//Following JavaScript code goes here
```

Note that, reading from left to right and top to bottom, everything comes in the same order as before, so the browser treats both versions identically. But, in general, it is better to use a few extra lines along with indenting to make the code easier to read.

Relational Operators and Nested Conditions

The double equal sign is just one of a number of relational operators. The other relational operators that JavaScript uses are listed in Table 12.1, along with snippets of conditional statements with a variable named theAnswer showing how they are used.

TABLE 12.1.   The Relational Operators

Symbol	Meaning	Code Sample
<	less than	if (theAnswer < 12)
>	greater than	if (theAnswer > 12)
<=	less than or equal to	if (theAnswer <= 34)
>=	greater than or equal to	if (theAnswer >= 34)
!=	not equal	if (theAnswer != 21)

In Chapter 11 we noted that because the double-minus sign symbol for the decrement operator is reserved for other purposes in XHTML, it was necessary to put JavaScript code that used it in an external file. Unfortunately, the same is true of the < symbol. Code that uses the decrement operator can always be rewritten without it. Doing so for the less-than operator is more awkward, however. The bottom line is that it is good to get in the habit of putting your JavaScript code in external .js files and using the src attribute in a <script> element to load the code along with the source document. (In our examples, we will continue to put the code in <script> elements so that the whole combination of HTML elements and JavaScript code in a source document may be seen.)

Sometimes it's necessary for more than one condition to be true before a certain block of code is executed. In such a case, we may use a **nested conditional statement**. For example, imagine that we want to check the value of a variable named firstNum to see if it is greater than 12 and less than 25. If it is, we'll display an alert box with the message "The number is between 12 and 25." We would write the code to do this using two conditional statements, one nested inside the other:

```
if (firstNum > 12) {
  if (firstNum < 25) {
    alert("The number is between 12 and 25")
  }
}
```

If firstNum is greater than 12, the first condition is true, so the browser will execute the following code, that is, it comes to the second conditional statement. If firstNum is then found to be less than 25, the alert message appears. So clearly firstNum must be both greater than 12 and less than 25 for the message to appear.

Although nested conditional statements are useful, their logical flow can be tricky to figure out and write correctly. For example, imagine now that we want to modify the nested conditional statement so that when the value of firstNum is not between 12 and 25 the message "The number is out of bounds" is displayed. We might write the code by adding an else clause to the nested conditional statement above:

```
if (firstNum > 12) {
  if (firstNum < 25) {
    alert("The number is between 12 and 25")
  }
}
else {
    alert("The number is out of bounds")
}
```

At first glance this code looks as if it will do the job. As before, if firstNum is greater than 12, the first condition is true, so the browser will get to the second conditional statement. If firstNum is then found to be less than 25, the alert message appears.

Now let's check the code for the case when firstNum is less than 12. When firstNum is less than 12, the first condition is false, so the browser skips the following code and instead executes the code in the else clause. So the alert box with the message "The number is out of bounds" appears, which is what we want.

Finally, let's check the code for the case when firstNum is greater than 25 (say, 27, to pick a specific number). The value 27 is greater than 12, so the first condition is true and the browser executes the following code, i.e., it comes to the second conditional statement. But 27 is not less than 25, so the second condition is false and the alert command will not be executed. There is no else clause associated with this inner conditional statement, so the browser continues with whatever comes *after* the outer if . . . else statement and therefore does not display the "out of bounds" message. The reason is that the else clause with the "out of bounds" alert box belongs to the *first* if condition. But when firstNum is 27, the first if condition is true (i.e., 27 is greater than 12). So the browser will skip its associated else clause.

Error Alert!

IMPORTANT

One lesson we learn here is that when you work with conditional statements it is crucial to check the logic of all the possibilities. Once the code is written, you should test it with actual values that represent the different possibilities. In our example, you might set the value of firstNum to 10 and run the code, then 15 and run it, and finally 27 and run it. You should also pay careful attention to the endpoints of the range involved (12 and 25 in this case). We wrote the code so that the values of 12 and 25 were out of bounds. If they were supposed to be "in bounds," then we would have to use the >= and <= operators instead of > and <.

Note also how easy it would be to drop or misplace one of the curly braces in this code. The brace immediately above the else is particularly easy to leave out. It's always a good idea to count the braces and make sure that they pair up correctly after you have written a complicated conditional statement like the one above.

To fix our code so that the "out of bounds" message appears when firstNum is greater than 25, we could add an else clause to the inner conditional statement:

```
if (firstNum > 12) {
  if (firstNum < 25) {
    alert("The number is between 12 and 25")
  }
  else {
    alert("The number is out of bounds")
  }
}
else {
  alert("The number is out of bounds")
}
```

This code is getting a bit unwieldy, however, and JavaScript provides an alternative way to write it using a logical operator.

The "and" and "or" Logical Operators

The **logical operators and** and **or** allow us to combine two (or more) conditions in a single if statement. The "and" operator is represented by back-to-back ampersands (&&). The "or" operator is represented by back-to-back vertical bars (||). A single vertical bar is usually typed by pressing shift-backslash on a computer keyboard. Note that the backslash key may show a broken vertical bar as the shift option; however it's pictured, it's the one you want. Also note that the & symbol is yet a third instance of a JavaScript symbol that is used in XHTML. Code that uses it should therefore be placed in an external file.

For example:

```
if ((firstNum > 12) && (firstNum < 25)) {
  alert("The number is between 12 and 25")
}
else {
  alert("The number is out of bounds")
}
```

We read this as: "If the value of firstNum is less than 12 *and* the value of firstNum is greater than 25, then display the alert box." For the alert box to appear, *both* of the conditions (firstNum > 12 *and* firstNum < 25) must be true. If either one *or* the other is false, such as when firstNum has the value 7 or when firstNum has the value 27, then the combined "and" condition is not true and the browser will skip the code block of the if clause and execute instead the code block of the else clause, i.e., the "out of bounds" message will appear.

This code is obviously much cleaner and easier to follow than the equivalent code of the last section, where we used a nested conditional statement.

If both conditions in an "and" combination are false, then of course the combined condition is false. We see this when we have more than one variable involved:

```
if ((firstNum > 5) && (secondNum > 9)) {
    alert("The first number is greater than 5 and the second
        number is greater than 9")
}
```

In this example, if firstNum has the value 3 and secondNum has the value 8, then both conditions are false, and the combined "and" condition is false. Table 12.2 shows the possible combinations and results.

TABLE 12.2.   Results of the Condition: if ((firstNum > 5) && (secondNum > 9))

firstNum	secondNum	Does the alert box appear?
7	12	Yes
7	5	No
3	12	No
3	5	No

We may also create a general **truth table** for an "and" operator that combines two conditions (Table 12.3). From it we see that the only case in which the combined condition is true is when both the first condition and the second condition are true.

The "or" operator is less restrictive than the "and" operator. It yields a true result when one of the conditions is true or both of them are true. The only time the combined condition ends up being false is when *both* of the conditions connected by the "or" operator are false. For example:

TABLE 12.3. Truth Table for the "and" Operator

1st condition (1)	2nd condition (2)	Combined condition (1 "and" 2)
True	True	True
True	False	False
False	True	False
False	False	False

```
if ((firstNum > 5) || (secondNum > 9)) {
    alert("Either the first number is > 5 or the second
        number is > 9, or both")
}
```

Table 12.4 shows a range of sample results for this conditional statement.

TABLE 12.4. Results of the Condition: if ((firstNum > 5) || (secondNum > 9))

firstNum	secondNum	Does the alert box appear?
7	12	Yes
7	5	Yes
3	12	Yes
3	5	No

Table 12.5 gives a general truth table for an "or" operator that combines two conditions. From it we see that the only case where the combined condition is *false* is when both the first condition and the second condition are false.

TABLE 12.5. Truth Table for the "or" Operator

1st condition (1)	2nd condition (2)	Combined condition (1 "or" 2)
True	True	True
True	False	True
False	True	True
False	False	False

As a final syntax point regarding the "and" and "or" operators, note that in all the "and" and "or" examples we placed parentheses around each of the conditions to separate them better visually, and then another pair around the whole condition. The outer pair is required; the two inner pairs are not, although they are helpful.

There is a third logical operator that is occasionally useful with boolean variables: the **not operator**. Its symbol is an exclamation point. To see how it works, imagine that we are searching an address book database for someone's name. (We will learn how to create and search a database using JavaScript in Chapter 16.) If we find the name in the database, then we will set the value of a boolean variable named found to the value true. Otherwise, the value of found will remain false, indicating that no match was found. In such a case, we want to display an alert box with the message, "Sorry. No match found." The code to do so might be something like the following:

```
var found = false //Initialize a boolean variable named
                       //found
/*Code to search database goes here. If match is found, then
the value of the found variable will be changed to true.*/
if (! found) {
   alert("Sorry. No match found.")
}
```

We read this conditional statement as "If not found, then display the alert message." The "not" operator (the exclamation point) turns true into false and false into true. Remember that the code in the if statement code will be executed if the condition is true. So if the found variable has the value false, the condition will be true, and the alert box will be displayed. If the found variable has the value true, the condition will be false, and the alert box will not be displayed.

You can see that the logic involved when using the "not" operator can be a little difficult to decipher, so it's usually best to avoid it unless you're sure of the logic. It's clearer, if not so compact, to use the double equal operator or the not equal operator. The conditional statement above, for example, can be written using the equality operator as:

```
if (found == false) {
   alert("Sorry. No match found.")
}
```

Or it can be written using the not equal operator as:

```
if (found != true) {
   alert("Sorry. No match found.")
}
```

QuickCheck Questions

1. Write a conditional statement that checks whether the value of a variable named examScore is greater than 100. If it is, display an alert box with the message "Greater than 100!".
2. Modify the code in #1 so that if the condition is not true, the message "It's 100 or less" is displayed in an alert box.
3. Write a conditional statement that checks whether the value of a variable named luckyNum equals 7 or 77. If the condition is true, display the message "You win!" in an alert box.

Lab Exercise 12.1, "A Guess-the-Number Game," may be done at this point.

More HTML Forms: Check Boxes

The conditional statement is particularly useful when combined with three types of form elements we have yet to cover: check boxes, radio buttons, and pop-up menus.

Creating Check Boxes

A **check box** allows the surfer to respond to a Yes/No or True/False situation. A questionnaire implemented on a web page, for instance, might give a list of choices, each preceded by a small check box, and instruct the surfer to "check all boxes that apply." When the surfer clicks the box, the browser puts a checkmark in it. If the surfer clicks a check box that already has a checkmark in it, then the browser erases the checkmark. Figure 12.1 shows an example that uses several check boxes, along with the <form> element code used to create them.

We see that, as with text fields and click buttons, we use the <input> tag in a <form> element to create a check box.

```
<input type="checkbox" name="perlCB" />
```

The value of the type attribute is checkbox (but remember that for a text box it's text, not textbox). As with text boxes, we give a check box a name using the name attribute. In order to recognize check box names when we see them, we will usually give them names that end in "CB." (This is not required, however.)

IMPORTANT

The check box's name is an internal name, used only by HTML and JavaScript and invisible to the surfer. To label a check box, therefore, we must add some appropriate text *after* the <input> tag:

```
<input type="checkbox" name="perlCB" />PERL
```

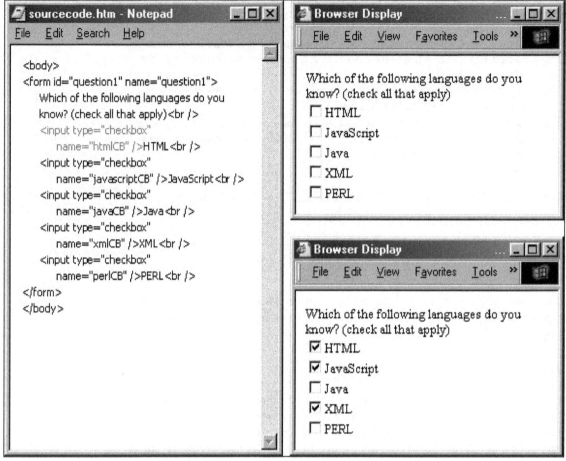

FIGURE 12.1.   Creating check boxes

If we want the check box to have a checkmark in it when initially displayed, we add the `checked` attribute with a value of `"checked"` to the `<input>` tag:

```
<input type="checkbox" name="perlCB"
    checked="checked" />PERL
```

Note: In versions of HTML before XHTML it's okay to write the `checked` attribute without a value, so that it's simply the word `checked` in the tag:

```
<input type="checkbox" name="perlCB" checked />PERL
```

When you look at other people's JavaScript code you will often see this. But XHTML now requires that every attribute be given an explicit value.

Testing the Status of a Check Box

We can tell whether the surfer has selected a check box via the `checked` property of the check box. Remember that an HTML form is an object belonging to the `document` object, and each element in the form is itself an object with its own properties. In this case, each check box in the form is an object, and one of its properties is `checked`. As an example, consider a web page for an online automobile dealership that allows the surfer to choose the desired options for a car (Figure 12.2).

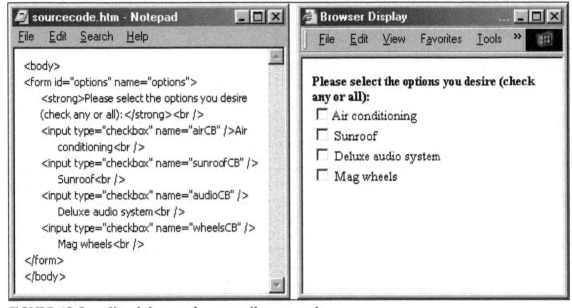

FIGURE 12.2.   Check boxes for an online car sale

The name of the form is `options` and the name of the air conditioning check box is `airCB`, so `document.options.airCB.checked` would store whether the air conditioning option was checked. Similarly, the property `document.options.sunroofCB.checked` would store whether the sunroof option was checked, and so on. The `checked` property is a boolean property, meaning that it either has the value `true` or `false` (the box is either checked or unchecked).

Reading the status of a check box (checked or unchecked) provides a perfect opportunity to use a conditional statement. For instance, if the sunroof check box were checked, then we might want to display an alert box message lauding the surfer for their excellent choice. The following conditional statement would do the job:

```
if (document.options.sunroofCB.checked == true) {
  alert("Excellent choice! But don't forget the sunscreen.")
}
else {
  alert("Are you sure you wouldn't like a sunroof?")
}
```

Remember that we don't use quotation marks around the boolean values `true` and `false`, because if we do they become string values. We also don't need to include the `== true` in the conditional statement. Instead, we may simply write:

```
if (document.options.sunroofCB.checked) {
  alert("Excellent choice! But don't forget the sunscreen.")
}
else {
  alert("Are you sure you wouldn't like a sunroof?")
}
```

You may read the first line of this code in your mind as, "If `document.options.sunroofCB` is checked, then . . .".

When the surfer clicks a check box the browser generates a click event for that check box, and therefore you may use an `onclick` event handler to respond to the click. The sunroof code above provides a nice example of how this works. When the surfer clicks on the sunroof check box, we want to display one of two alert messages. If the surfer clicks the check box so that it's checked, then we want the "Excellent choice!" message displayed. But if the surfer is clicking the sunroof check box to uncheck it, then we want the "Are you sure . . ." message displayed. To implement this, the `<input>` tag for the sunroof check box would have an event handler that passed the `options` form to a function named `sunRoofMessage`:

```
<input type="checkbox" name="sunroof"
  onclick="sunRoofMessage(document.options)" />Sunroof
  <br />
```

where the function `sunRoofMessage()` is declared as:

```
function sunRoofMessage(f) {
  if (f.sunroofCB.checked) {
    alert("Excellent choice! But don't forget the
      sunscreen.")
  }
  else {
    alert("Are you sure you wouldn't like a sunroof?")
  }
}
```

Alternatively, we might wait until the surfer has checked all of his/her option choices and then use a "Click here when you're done" click button to activate a displayMessage() function.

```
<input type="button" name="b1"
  value="Click here when you're done"
  onclick="displayMessage(document.options)" />
```

In the displayMessage() function we would use a series of conditional statements to test each check box and print appropriate messages in a series of corresponding text boxes (one for each check box), such as:

```
function displayMessage(f) {
  if (f.airCB.checked) {
    f.airMessageBox.value = "Keep it cool!"
  }
  if (f.sunroofCB.checked){
    f.sunroofMessageBox.value = "Feel the fresh air!"
  }
  if (f.audioCB.checked){
    f.audioMessageBox.value = "Crank it up!"
  }
  if (f.wheelsCB.checked){
    f.wheelsMessageBox.value = "Looking good!"
  }
}
```

Remember that the f in the function is a formal parameter standing for the document.options form in this case, so the series of conditional statements is, in effect, the following:

```
if (document.options.airCB.checked) {
  document.options.airMessageBox.value = "Keep it cool!"
}
if (document.options.sunroofCB.checked){
  document.options.sunroofMessageBox.value = "Feel the
  fresh air!"
}
if (document.options.audioCB.checked){
  document.options.audioMessageBox.value = "Crank it up!"
}
if (document.options.wheelsCB.checked){
  document.options.wheelsMessageBox.value = "Looking
  good!"
}
```

Note that each of these conditional statements is separate from the others; they are not connected via else if clauses. We must use an independent

conditional statement for each check box because more than one of the boxes may be checked, and therefore we need to test each box. We will get some practice with check boxes in our next exercise. But first, we need to learn about radio buttons.

QuickCheck Questions

1. Write an <input> tag that creates a check box named partTimeCB and put a label next to it that says "Employment status: Part-time".
2. Write a conditional statement that tests whether the check box in #1 is checked. If it is, then display an alert box with the message "You selected part-time status."

More HTML Forms: Radio Buttons

In contrast to a set of checkboxes, a set of **radio buttons** allows the surfer to choose one, and only one, of several options. The name radio buttons comes from the old pushbutton car radios, where you could assign a radio station to each of four or five buttons. Pushing in a button tuned the radio to its station; when you pushed in another button to change stations, the first popped out, so that only one button (and, obviously, only one station) was selected at any given time. So you use a set of web page radio buttons when you want to give the surfer a choice of mutually exclusive options. Radio buttons therefore nearly always come in sets.

A radio button is displayed as a hollow circle; when the surfer clicks it, the browser fills it with a black dot. When one button is selected and the surfer clicks another button, the browser automatically erases the dot in the first button and puts a dot in the second button.

Creating Radio Buttons

As with a set of check boxes, you use a series of <input> tags to create a set of radio buttons. If you want one of the radio buttons to be checked initially, you include checked="checked" at the end of the <input> tag, just as you do with a check box.

One key difference between radio buttons and check boxes, however, is that because the radio buttons in a set are all connected (that is, if one is selected, the others are not), all the radio buttons in a set must have the same name. For instance, if you wanted the surfer to indicate a favorite soft drink from a list of choices, you might code it as in Figure 12.3. We've named the radio buttons sodaRB, using the RB at the end to indicate that they're radio buttons. (The RB is not required.) The form is named survey.

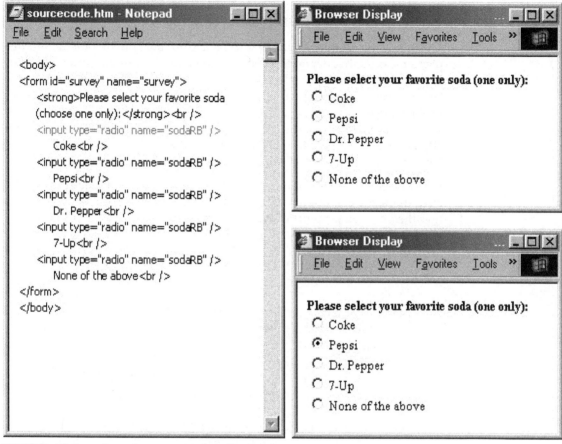

FIGURE 12.3.   Creating a set of radio buttons

Testing the Status of a Radio Button

Since, unlike check boxes, the radio buttons don't have individual names, how do we refer to an individual radio button in the set? The answer is that we use the same type of numbering system as we did with image objects (Chapter 9, "Creating Image Rollovers"). Each radio button in a set of buttons is automatically given a number, with 0 indicating the first button in the set. The name of a button is the name of the set followed by the number of the button enclosed in *square* brackets. For instance, the "Coke" button in Figure 12.3 is sodaRB[0], the "Pepsi" button sodaRB[1], and so on. Their full names, of course, are document.survey.sodaRB[0] and document.survey.sodaRB[1]. Remember that the square brackets are part of the syntax of the numbering system. You cannot substitute parentheses or curly braces.

Note that it's also possible to define a set of check boxes by giving them all the same name and using the same syntax and numbering convention as with radio buttons. But, despite having identical names, the check boxes will still be independent of each other; that is, if the surfer checks or unchecks one of the check boxes, it has no effect on any of the others.

To see how we use radio buttons with JavaScript, imagine that we want to display a message that depends on which soda radio button the surfer selects in Figure 12.3. If the surfer selects the "Coke" button, we'll display the message "It's the real thing!" in a text box named `document.survey.messageBox` (we'll assume that we have added such a text box to the survey form). If the "Pepsi" button is chosen, the message will be "Join the Pepsi Generation!" The "Dr. Pepper" message will be "Be a Pepper!", the "7-Up" message will be "The Uncola!", and the "None of the above" message will be "None at all?"

Radio buttons have the same `checked` property that check buttons do. To code the messages, therefore, we use a *compound* conditional statement that tests the `checked` property of each radio button:

```
if (document.survey.sodaRB[0].checked) {
   document.survey.messageBox.value = "It's the real
      thing!"
}
else if (document.survey.sodaRB[1].checked){
   document.survey.messageBox.value = "Join the Pepsi
      Generation!"
}
else if (document.survey.sodaRB[2].checked){
   document.survey.messageBox.value = "Be a Pepper!"
}
else if (document.survey.sodaRB[3].checked){
   document.survey.messageBox.value = "The Uncola!"
}
else if (document.survey.sodaRB[4].checked){
   document.survey.messageBox.value = "None at all?"
}
```

Remember how the logic of a compound conditional statement works: If the first box is checked, the browser will write the first message and *skip the rest* of the `else if` conditions. If the first box is not checked, the browser will skip the first message and go to the `else if` clause to see if the second box is checked. If it is, its message will be displayed, and then the rest of the `else if` conditions will be skipped. And so on and so forth.

The reason we use a compound conditional statement (one with a series of `else if` clauses) for radio buttons is that we know in advance that, at most, only one radio button can be checked. Once we find that one is checked, therefore, there's no need to try the rest of the buttons.

In contrast, remember that when we have a series of check boxes we *cannot* use a compound conditional statement, because more than one box might be checked. Instead, we must use a separate conditional statement for each check box, as we saw at the end of the section "Testing the Status of a Check Box."

QuickCheck Questions

1. Write the <input> tags for a set of three radio buttons named salary RangeRB. Label the first button "Below $50,000", the second button "$50,000–100,000", and the third button "Above $100,000".

2. Write a conditional statement that tests which radio button in #1 is selected and displays an appropriate message in an alert box (e.g., "You selected: Below $50,000").

Lab Exercise 12.2, "The CyberPizza Page," may be done at this point.

More HTML Forms: Pop-up Menus

We use radio buttons when we want the surfer to choose one option from among several possibilities. An alternative way to do this involves another HTML form element: **pop-up menus**. The list of options within a menu only appears when the surfer clicks on the menu, so pop-up menus don't take up as much space on a web page as would the same list implemented as radio buttons. One popular use for a pop-up menu is to provide a Quick Links list for a large website. The menu contains a list of key pages within the site. A surfer can use the menu to select one of the listed pages and then click on a Go click button. The click button's event handler activates the necessary code to load the page selected.

Creating a Pop-Up Menu

We will start with a simpler example to illustrate the essential details of implementing a pop up menu. Figure 12.4 shows the HTML code to create a menu that lists the favorite soda choices we used in the last section, plus two views of the menu. The first view is before the surfer clicks on the menu; the second view is after the menu pops up (or, actually, down). Once the surfer makes a menu selection and clicks the button, the corresponding message will be displayed in the text box. (We'll add the JavaScript code for the displayMessage() function below.)

The HTML code to create the menu uses a <form> element, but instead of using an <input> tag, we use a special <select> element. Inside the <select> element, we use one <option> element for each item in the menu. The name that will actually appear in the menu goes in the <option> element.

The onclick event handler of the click button calls a function we have named displayMessage() and passes it the whole form (document.survey) as a parameter. This function will use a conditional statement to check which menu option the surfer selected and then print the corresponding message in the

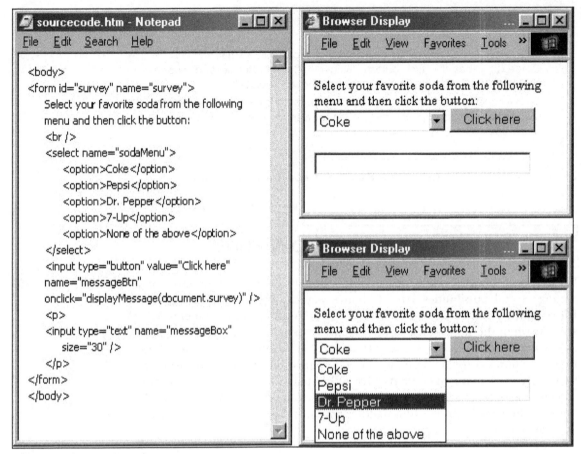

FIGURE 12.4.   Creating a pop-up menu

text box named `messageBox`. The number of the option that the surfer selected is automatically stored in a property of the menu object that is named `selectedIndex`. The full name of this property in our example above would therefore be `document.survey.sodaMenu.selectedIndex`. As with radio buttons, the numbering system starts with 0. So the number of the first option (Coke, in this case) is 0, the number of the second option (Pepsi) is 1, and so on.

Now we can write the code for the `displayMessage()` function, using f as the name of the formal parameter. Figure 12.5 shows the function code plus the display when the surfer has chosen "Dr. Pepper" from the menu before clicking the Click here button and then after clicking the button. The button click activates the `onclick="displayMessage(document.survey)"` event handler, which calls the `displayMessage()` function and sends it the `document.survey` form. The function checks which radio button is selected and displays the corresponding message in the `messageBox` texbox. (The `<script>` element containing the function code would of course go in the `<head>` element of the source document.)

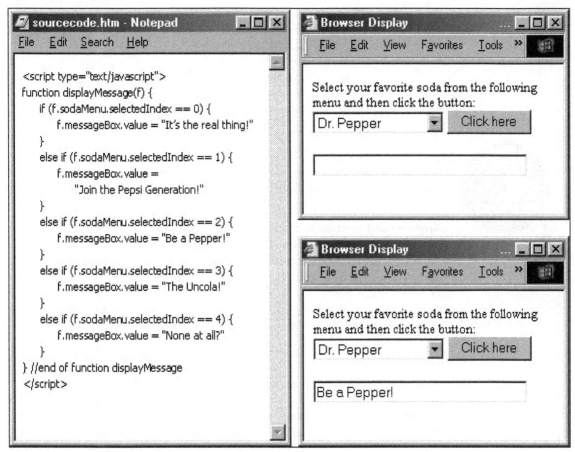

FIGURE 12.5.   Checking the value of the menu selection and displaying a corresponding message (after the button is clicked)

Note that we chose to send the whole survey form to the function, although we could have simply sent the value of the selectedIndex property itself, because that's all the function needs to know.

Revising the Pop-Up Menu Code

The displayMessage() function in the previous section uses the fact that the number of the surfer's selected menu option is stored in the selectedIndex property. The conditional statement then tests the value of selectedIndex and displays the appropriate message. It turns out that it's possible to simplify this code by embedding the various messages in the menu itself.

We embed the messages by using the value attribute of the <option> tag. This attribute lets us associate a value with each menu option. The revised code for the menu is:

```
<select name="sodaMenu">
  <option value="It's the real thing!">Coke</option>
  <option value="Join the Pepsi
    generation!">Pepsi</option>
  <option value="Be a Pepper!">Dr. Pepper</option>
  <option value="The Uncola!">7-Up</option>
  <option value="None at all?">None of the
    above</option>
</select>
```

Remember that the text in the <option> element is what the surfer sees; the value of the value attribute is for HTML/JavaScript use only and remains hidden.

Now we need to know how to access these values using JavaScript. In the previous section we described how the browser numbers the menu options starting with 0, just as is done with radio buttons. A second similarity with radio buttons is the syntax we use to refer to each menu option. Remember that if we have a form named survey with a set of radio buttons all named sodaRB, then we refer to the first button in the set as document.survey.sodaRB[0], the second button as document.survey.sodaRB[1], and so on.

We use the same syntax for the set of menu options, except for two minor differences: (1) The name for the set of menu options is preset to options so we don't have to choose our own name, and (2) the options belong to the menu object (named sodaMenu in this case), which belongs to the form named survey. In contrast, the set of radio buttons belongs to the form object itself. So the name for the first menu option is document.survey.sodaMenu.options[0], the name for the second option is document.survey.sodaMenu.options[1], and so on. The name for the value of the first menu option (as set by the value attribute) is document.survey.sodaMenu.options[0].value, the name for the value of the second option is document.survey.sodaMenu.options[1].value, and so on. In other words, the message "It's the real thing!" is stored in document.survey.sodaMenu.options[0].value, the message "Join the Pepsi Generation!" is stored in document.survey.sodaMenu.options[1].value, and so on.

This setup enables us to rewrite the displayMessage() function and get rid of the conditional statement, as follows:

```
function displayMessage(f) {
  var menuChoice = f.sodaMenu.selectedIndex
  f.messageBox.value = f.sodaMenu.options[menuChoice].value
}
```

Let's take this code line by line to figure out what's going on. Remember that the function call in the onclick event handler is displayMessage(document.survey). So the formal parameter f in the displayMessage() function is an alias for document.survey. The first line of code in the function declares a local variable named menuChoice and takes the value of the pop-up menu's selected Index property and copies it into menuChoice. So now menuChoice stores the number of the menu option that the surfer selected. If the surfer chose Coke from the menu, menuChoice would have the value 0; if the surfer chose Pepsi, menuChoice would have the value 1; and so on.

The second line in the function is where all the action is. To make it easier to decipher, let's assume that the surfer has chosen 7-Up from the menu. This means that the selectedIndex property of the sodaMenu has the value 3, as does the variable menuChoice. So the second line of code, in this case, is really:

```
f.messageBox.value = f.sodaMenu.options[3].value
```

Or, replacing the f with document.survey, it is:

```
document.survey.messageBox.value = document.survey.
   sodaMenu.options[3].value
```

This assignment statement tells the browser to take the value of option 3 of the sodaMenu and copy it over to the textbox named messageBox, where the value of option 3 is set by the value attribute of the *fourth* <option> tag in the <select> element (the one for 7-Up). In other words, the browser takes the value "The Uncola!" and copies it into messageBox, where it's displayed.

There are two more revisions we could make to this pop-up menu code. First, it's possible to make the displayMessage() code even more compact. We really don't need the menuChoice variable. Instead of

```
function displayMessage(f) {
  var menuChoice = f.sodaMenu.selectedIndex
  f.messageBox.value = f.sodaMenu.options[menuChoice].value
}
```

we could write:

```
function displayMessage(f) {
  f.messageBox.value = f.sodaMenu.options[f.sodaMenu.
    selectedIndex].value
}
```

On the other hand, declaring the menuChoice variable and making one line of code into two makes it a little easier to see what's going on.

The other revision we will make concerns how the pop-up menu is displayed. As we initially created it, the value "Coke" appears at the top of the menu and is visible to the surfer while the rest of the menu options are still hidden. Web page designers often prefer to give all the options equal billing by making the value of the first menu option something that describes the menu or gives instructions to the surfer, such as "Soda choices":

```
<select name="sodaMenu">
  <option value="">Soda choices . . . </option>
  <option value="It's the real thing!">Coke</option>
  <option value="Join the Pepsi
    generation!">Pepsi</option>
  <option value="Be a Pepper!">Dr. Pepper</option>
  <option value="The Uncola!">7-Up</option>
  <option value="None at all?">None of the
    above</option>
</select>
```

Figure 12.6 shows the new display.

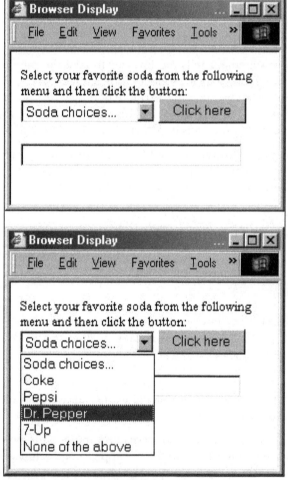

FIGURE 12.6.   Making the first option in the menu a descriptive title

Note that in the code we leave the value of the "Soda choices . . ." option blank. Note also that by making this change the index numbers of the various options have also changed; that is, the Coke option is now `document.survey.sodaMenu.options[1]` instead of `document.survey.sodaMenu.options[0]`, and similarly for the other menu options. In our original version of the `displayMessage()` function, where we used the conditional statement (Figure 12.5), we would have to make corresponding changes to the series of `if...else if` statements. But no changes are necessary for our revised version without the conditional statement, because nowhere in the code do we refer to any of the specific index numbers.

It's also possible to specify which menu option appears when the menu is first displayed. In other words, we don't have to have the first menu option be the one that appears when the menu is displayed. Including the `selected` attribute in an `<option>` tag with the value `"selected"` will make that option the one that first appears. For example, if we wanted the Dr. Pepper option to appear when the menu is first displayed, then the code would be:

```
<select name="sodaMenu">
  <option value="It's the real thing!">Coke</option>
  <option value="Join the Pepsi
    generation!">Pepsi</option>
  <option value="Be a Pepper!" selected="selected">Dr.
    Pepper</option>
  <option value="The Uncola!">7-Up</option>
  <option value="None at all?">None of the
    above</option>
</select>
```

If none of the `<option>` tags has a `selected` attribute, then the first one is initially selected by default.

Creating a Quick Links Menu

We mentioned above that a popular use of pop-up menus is to provide a **Quick Links** list for a large website so that surfers can choose from the menu and jump immediately to the page they're looking for. With a few modifications to the menu code developed in the previous section we can implement our own Quick Links menu.

Imagine that we are designing a website for a college or university. A Quick Links list for such a website might include the following pages: Academic Departments, Athletics, Bookstore, Library, Registrar, and Schedule of Classes. We would create the pop-up menu as usual, except that we put the URL for each page into the `value` attribute (we will see why in a minute) and we insert an `onchange` event handler in the `<select>` tag:

```
<form id="siteNav">
<select name="linksMenu"
    onchange="jumpToPage(document.siteNav)">
  <option value="">Quick Links</option>
  <option value="departments.htm">Academic
    Departments</option>
  <option value="athletics.htm">Athletics</option>
  <option value="bookstore.htm">Bookstore</option>
  <option value="library.htm">Library</option>
  <option value="registrar.htm">Registrar</option>
  <option value="classes.htm">Schedule of
    Classes</option>
</select>
</form >
```

In this example we used the names of the various source documents (depart-ments.htm, athletics.htm, etc.) for the URLs, which of course means that they must be stored in the same folder as the pop-up menu's source document. We may also use full URLs, such as http://www.collegename.edu/library.htm.

The `onchange` event handler in the `<select>` tag is activated when a change occurs in the menu, that is, when the surfer selects one of the options from the menu. It calls a function named `jumpToPage()` and passes it the `siteNav` form (standing for "siteNavigation") as a parameter. The `jumpToPage()` function will use the `selectedIndex` property of the menu to find out which option the surfer selected and then retrieve the value of that option, that is, the name of the source document to jump to. For example, if the surfer chose the Library option, the value of `document.siteNav.linksMenu.selectedIndex` would be 4. The corresponding option value, stored in `document.siteNav.linksMenu.options[4].value`, would be library.htm.

In order to jump to the library.htm page, we employ a little trick we mentioned in Chapter 8 concerning the `location` object. Remember that, like the `docu-ment` object, the `location` object belongs to the `window` object. One of the properties of the `location` object is `href`, which stores the URL of the brows-er's currently loaded document. The `href` property is a read-write property, and therefore we may use an assignment statement to change the value of `href` to another URL, thereby causing the browser to load the document at that URL. For example, the following line of JavaScript code would tell the browser to load the home page of Intel, replacing the current document displayed:

```
<script type="text/javascript">
  location.href = "http://www.intel.com"
</script>
```

(It's also possible to write this assignment statement as `window.location.href = "http://www.intel.com"` or even simply as `location = "http://www.intel.com"`. Any of these variations works.)

So to jump to the library.htm page in our example, we could write:

```
location.href = "library.htm"
```

Or we could write:

```
location.href = document.siteNav.linksMenu.options[4].value
```

Suitably modified, this line of code forms the basis of our `jumpToPage()` function:

```
function jumpToPage(f) {
   var menuChoice = f.linksMenu.selectedIndex
   location.href = f.linksMenu.options[menuChoice].value
}
```

where the formal parameter f is passed the form `document.siteNav`.

As written, however, this function has one small problem. If the surfer selects the first option in the menu (Quick Links) instead of one of the other options, there's no URL stored in the `value` attribute of the first `<option>` tag. So the last line in the `jumpToPage()` code translates into:

```
location.href = ""
```

The result of this line of code is that the browser displays a list of the files in the current document's folder, which is not something we normally want displayed.

We could fix this by making the `value` attribute of the first `<option>` tag equal to the URL of the source document that contains the pop-up menu code. Then, if the surfer selects the Quick Links option, the `jumpToPage()` function code will simply reload the pop-up menu's source document.

But reloading the page might take a few seconds, so a better solution would be to prevent the code from executing when the surfer selects Quick Links. We can do this using a conditional statement with the not-equal operator (!=):

```
function jumpToPage(f) {
   var menuChoice = f.linksMenu.selectedIndex
   if (f.linksMenu.options[menuChoice].value != "") {
      location.href = f.linksMenu.options[menuChoice].value
   }
}
```

If the value of `f.linksMenu.options[menuChoice].value` is not equal to `""` (that is, if the `value` property is not blank but stores something—a URL in this case), then the line of code will be executed. Otherwise, it will be skipped and the `jumpToPage()` function ends up doing nothing.

More on Submitting Form Information

In Chapter 10 in the section on "Submitting Form Information," we learned how to have information that is entered into a form sent back to us via e-mail.

At that time the only form elements we covered were click buttons and text boxes. Now we have added radio buttons, check boxes, and pop-up menus to our repertoire. The form submission procedure is exactly the same, however. We add the `method`, `enctype`, and `action` attributes to the `<form>` tag:

```
<form method="post" enctype="text/plain"
  action="mailto:mymail@somewhere.com">
```

And we add special submit and reset buttons to the form:

```
<input type="submit" value="Submit information" />
<input type="reset" value="Erase info and start over" />
```

We did not include a name attribute in these tags because, unlike the other input elements (text boxes, click buttons, check boxes, radio buttons, and pop-up menus), submit and reset buttons do not require one.

The form information will appear in the body of the e-mail message in the general format:

NameOfFormElement=ValueOfInformationEntered

The right side of this message will be the value of the `value` attribute of the form element. When we introduced check boxes and radio buttons earlier in this chapter, we didn't include `value` attributes in their `<input>` tags, because we didn't need them. When we want to have the form information submitted back to us (whether by e-mail or another method like CGI scripts), we do need them. For example, we might write the code for the sunroof checkbox as:

```
<input type="checkbox" name="sunroofCB"
  value="Yes" /> Sunroof
```

If the surfer selected the sunroof checkbox and submitted the form, the e-mail message would contain the line:

sunroofCB=Yes

Similarly for the Pepsi radio button (the second in the set in our soda example), if we wrote:

```
<input type="radio" name="sodaRB"
  value="Pepsi-Cola" />Pepsi
```

then the message would contain the line:

sodaRB=Pepsi-Cola

If the check box and/or radio button that the surfer selects does not have its `value` attribute set to some value, then the e-mail message becomes:

sunroofCB=on
sodaRB=on

In the case of the sunroof check box, this conveys enough information. But all this tells us in the case of the set of soda radio buttons is that one of them is selected.

For our pop-up menu named sodaMenu, one of the <option> elements was:

```
<option value="Be a Pepper!">Dr. Pepper</option>
```

If the surfer selects this option from the menu and submits the form, then the message received would be:

sodaMenu=Be a Pepper!

If the <option> tag of a pop-up menu option does not have a value attribute, however, then the browser will send the value that comes in the given <option> element, which is the phrase "Dr. Pepper" in this case:

sodaMenu=Dr. Pepper

QuickCheck Questions

1. Write the code that creates a pop-up menu named salaryMenu, with the first option being "Below $50,000", the second option being "$50,000–100,000", and the third option being "Above $100,000".

2. Write a conditional statement that tests which menu option in #1 is selected and displays an appropriate message in an alert box (e.g., "You selected: Below $50,000").

Lab Exercise 12.3, "The CyberPizza Page, Continued," may be done at this point.

check box	equality operator	Quick Links menu
comparison operator	if clause	radio button
compound conditional statement	logical operators and, or, not	relational operator
conditional statement	nested conditional statement	truth table
else clause	pop-up menu	

1. The Conditional Statement

Basic form of an if...else conditional statement (the else clause is optional):

```
if (some condition is true) {
    //first JavaScript statement or block of statements to be executed
}
else {
    //second statement or block of statements to be executed
}
```

Using the double-equal operator to check for equality:

```
if (document.myForm.answerBox.value == "Yes") {
   document.myForm.questionBox.value = "One lump or two?"
}
else {
   document.myForm.questionBox.value = "Would you like cream?"
}
```

Nesting one conditional statement inside another:

```
if (firstNum > 12) {
   if (firstNum < 25) {
      alert("The number is between 12 and 25")
   }
}
```

Using the logical "and" operator (&&):

```
if ((firstNum > 12) && (firstNum < 25)) {
   alert("The number is between 12 and 25")
}
else {
   alert("The number is out of bounds")
}
```

Using the logical "or" operator (||):

```
if ((firstNum > 5) || (secondNum > 9)) {
   alert("Either the first number is > 5 or the second number is > 9, or both")
}
```

Using the logical not operator (!):

```
var found = false //Initialize a boolean variable named found
/*Code to search database goes here. If match is found, then
the value of the found variable will be changed to true.*/
if (!found) {
   alert("Sorry. No match found.")
}
```

2. More HTML Forms: Check Boxes

Creating a check box (inside a `<form>` element):

```
<input type="checkbox" name="sunroofCB" />Sunroof
```

Testing whether a check box that belongs to a form named `options` is checked:

```
if (document.options.sunroofCB.checked == true) {
   alert("Excellent choice! But don't forget the sunscreen.")
}
else {
   alert("Are you sure you wouldn't like a sunroof?")
}
```

3. More HTML Forms: Radio Buttons

Creating a set of radio buttons (inside a `<form>` element):

```
<input type="radio" name="sodaRB" />Coke<br />
<input type="radio" name="sodaRB" />Pepsi<br />
<input type="radio" name="sodaRB" />Dr. Pepper<br />
```

Testing a set of radio buttons (belonging to a form named `survey`) to see which is selected:

```
if (document.survey.sodaRB[0].checked) {
    document.survey.messageBox.value="It's the real thing!"
}
else if (document.survey.sodaRB[1].checked){
    document.survey.messageBox.value="Join the Pepsi Generation!"
}
else if (document.survey.sodaRB[2].checked){
    document.survey.messageBox.value="Be a Pepper!"
}
```

4. More HTML Forms: Pop-up Menus

Creating a pop-up menu (inside a `<form>` element):

```
<select name="sodaMenu">
    <option value="It's the real thing!">Coke</option>
    <option value="Join the Pepsi generation!">Pepsi</option>
    <option value="Be a Pepper!">Dr. Pepper</option>
</select>
```

Testing the `selectedIndex` property of a pop-up menu (belonging to a form named `survey`) to see which option is selected, and then copying the value of the selected option into a text box named `messageBox`:

```
if (document.survey.sodaMenu.selectedIndex == 0) {
    document.survey.messageBox.value = document.survey.sodaMenu.options[0].value
}
else if (document.survey.sodaMenu.selectedIndex == 1){
    document.survey.messageBox.value = document.survey.sodaMenu.options[1].value
}
else if (document.survey.sodaMenu.selectedIndex == 2){
    document.survey.messageBox.value = document.survey.sodaMenu.options[2].value
}
```

Creating a Quick Links pop-up menu using a function that takes as its parameter the pop-up menu's form (the value of each website menu option must be the URL of the website):

```
function jumpToPage(f) {
    var menuChoice = f.linksMenu.selectedIndex
    location.href = f.linksMenu.options[menuChoice].value
}
```

A common mistake is to use a single equal sign instead of the double equal sign to check a condition for equality in a conditional statement. It's helpful, therefore, to get in the habit of saying and thinking "equals-equals," as in "if the value of the `answerBox` equals-equals Yes."

You must use at least one set of parentheses around the condition in a conditional statement.

When a block of code for an `if` or `else` clause only has a single statement in it, the curly braces around the code are not necessary, but it's recommended to use them anyway because it's easy to forget to put them in later if you add more code.

Like the double-minus symbol of the decrement operator, the less-than symbol (<) is reserved for other uses in XHTML, so code that uses it should be placed in an external .js file.

Although it's not necessary, it's recommended to indent the code in the various clauses of a conditional statement for the sake of readability.

When writing nested conditional statements, be careful about which `else` clause belongs to which `if` statement.

When using complex logical structures such as nested conditional statements, it's important to test the code with actual values that represent the different possibilities and branches of the conditional statement. (It's actually good to do this no matter how simple or complex the code is.)

It's easy to drop or misplace curly braces when writing nested conditional statements or other complex code.

It's helpful, but not required, to put parentheses around each condition in a multiple-condition conditional statement (where the conditions are connected by logical operators like "and" and "or"). The outer pair of parentheses is required.

It's useful for recognition purposes to give check boxes names that end in "CB" (or something similar) and sets of radio buttons names that end in "RB".

When creating a set of radio buttons, you must give all the radiio buttons the same name.

The `checked` attribute in an `<input>` tag that creates a pre-checked check box must be given a value in order to be XHTML-compatible.

When using a conditional statement to check whether the `checked` property of a check box or radio button is true or false, the `==true` or `==false` may be left off, such as, `if (document.options.sunroofCB. checked)`. . . .

To test a series of check boxes, you must use a series of independent conditional statements, one for each check box. To test a set of radio buttons, it's best to use a compound conditional statement (an `else if` clause for each button), because at most only one radio button can be checked.

When creating a pop-up menu, the text after the `<option>` tag is what the surfer sees; the `value` of the value attribute is for HTML/JavaScript use only and remains hidden.

1. True or false: When the code below is executed, the alert message "The number is also greater than 40" will *not* appear.

```
var theNum 5 45  //Initialize the value of theNum to 45
if(theNum . 30){
alert("The number is greater than 30")
}
else if (theNum . 40){
alert("The number is also greater than 40")
}
else if (theNum . 50){
alert("The number is even bigger than 50")
}
```

2. The equality operator is represented with the symbol _____, and the assignment operator is represented with the symbol _____.

3. True or false: The parentheses around the condition in a conditional statement are required. (For example, the parentheses in `if (firstNum == secondNum) ....`)

4. If the value of `num1` is 8 and the value of `num2` is 15, is the condition `((num1 >= 8) && (num2 > 15))` true or false?

5. If the value of `num1` is 8 and the value of `num2` is 15, is the condition `((num1 >= 8) || (num2 > 15))` true or false?

6. If the value of `num1` is 8 and the value of `num2` is 13, is the condition `((num1 >= 8) || (num2 > 15))` true or false?

7. Given a boolean variable named `married`, which of the following conditional statements are equivalent (i.e., give the same answer)?

   a. `if (married == true)` ...
   b. `if (married != false)` ...
   c. `if (married)` ...
   d. `if (!married)` ...

8. Which of the following lines of HTML code create a check box labeled "Window seat" (the label is what the surfer will see next to the check box)?

   a. `<input type="checkbox" name="Window seat" />`
   b. `<input type="checkbox" name="windowseatCB" value="Window seat" />`
   c. `<input type="checkbox" name="windowseat" />Window seat`
   d. `<input type="checkbox" value="Window seat" />`

9. Given a set of 10 radio buttons named `favoritefoodRB` in a form named `foodSurvey`, which of the following conditional statements would test if the last radio button was selected?

   a. `if (document.foodSurvey.favoritefoodRB.checked == true)` ...
   b. `if (document.foodSurvey.favoritefoodRB.9.checked == true)` ...
   c. `if (document.foodSurvey.favoritefoodRB.10.checked == true)` ...
   d. `if (document.foodSurvey.favoritefoodRB[9].checked == true)` ...
   e. `if (document.foodSurvey.favoritefoodRB[10].checked == true)` ...

10. Given a pop-up menu named `foodMenu` in a form named `cafeteria`, which of the following stores the number of the menu option selected by the surfer?

    a. `document.foodMenu.cafeteria.menuChoice`
    b. `document.cafeteria.foodMenu.menuChoice`
    c. `document.foodMenu.cafeteria.selected`
    d. `document.cafeteria.foodMenu.selected`
    e. `document.foodMenu.cafeteria.selectedIndex`
    f. `document.cafeteria.foodMenu.selectedIndex`

1. Briefly define and/or explain the following terms: compound conditional statement, nested conditional statement, logical operator.

2. Write the JavaScript code that will test whether a previously declared variable named `userGuess` is less than 50. If it is, display an alert box with the message "You guessed a number that is less than 50"; otherwise display an alert box with the message "You guessed a number greater than or equal to 50."

3. Write a compound conditional statement that tests whether a previously declared variable named `finalScore` is greater than or equal to 90, less than 90 but greater than or equal to 80, less than 80 but greater than or equal to 70, or less than 70. Do not use any logical operators (`&&` or `//`). Depending on which condition is satisfied, the code should display an alert box message with an appropriate message ("Final score is in the 80s" or "Final score is below 70").

4. Repeat exercise 3, but this time use logical operators (either the && or the // operator) in the conditions that test whether the finalScore value is in the 80s or 70s.

5. Write the HTML code for a form named questionForm with four check boxes named movieCB, televisionCB, amradioCB, and fmradioCB. The purpose of the form is to ask the surfer to check which activities he or she did in the previous week: went to a movie, watched television, listened to AM radio, listened to FM radio (checking all that apply).

6. Write the JavaScript code that will test whether the check box named movieCB in Exercise 5 is checked. If it is checked, display an alert box with the message "Hope you enjoyed it"; otherwise display an alert box with the message "Anything good playing this week?"

7. Write the HTML code for a form named actorQuestion with a set of radio buttons named actorsRB. The purpose of the form is to ask the surfer to indicate his or her favorite male actor: Arnold Schwarzenegger, Tom Hanks, Sylvester Stallone, Tom Cruise, John Wayne, Harrison Ford, Robert Redford, Brad Pitt, or Other. The set of radio buttons should be displayed in a vertical column.

8. Write the JavaScript code that will test which radio button in Exercise 7 is checked and display the message "You chose Schwarzenegger" or "You chose Redford" (or whatever) in a text box named outputBox belonging to the same form.

9. Repeat Exercise 7, but this time use a pop-up menu named actorsMenu. (It's not necessary to specify the value attribute in the <option> elements.)

10. Write the JavaScript code that uses a compound conditional statement to test which menu option in Exercise 9 is selected and display the message "You chose Schwarzenegger" or "You chose Redford" (or whatever) in a text box named outputBox belonging to the same form.

Debugging Exercise

Identify the errors in the following code. The page presents the user with various choices via check boxes, radio buttons, and a pop-up menu. After making the choices, the user clicks a button. The event handler belonging to this button then calls a function named displayMessage(), which is supposed to display various alert boxes corresponding to the user's choices.

```html
<html>
  <head>
    <title>Check boxes and Radio buttons</title>
    <script type="text/javascript">
      function displayMessage(f) {
        //Check the check boxes
        if (f.airCB[0].checked) {
          alert("Keep it cool!")
        }
        else if (f.sunroofCB[1].checked){
          alert("Feel the fresh air!")
        }
        else if (f.audioCB[2].checked){
          alert("Crank it up!")
        }
        //Check the radio buttons
        if (f.colorRB[0].checked == true) {
          alert("Nice and cool!")
        }
        else if (f.colorRB[1].checked == true){
          alert("Refreshing!")
```

```
                    }
                    else if (f.colorRB[2].checked == true){
                       alert("Who likes it hot?")
                    }
                    //Check the popup menu
                    if (f.selectedIndex.checked == 0) {
                       alert("Go for the caffeine!")
                    }
                    else if (f.selectedIndex.checked == 1){
                       alert("Who needs cola?")
                    }
                    else if (f.selectedIndex.checked == 2){
                       alert("Goes down smooth!")
                    }
         </script>
      </head>
      <body>
      <form id="survey" name="survey">
         <strong>Please select the options you desire (check any or all):</strong><br />
         <input type="checkbox" name="airCB" />Air conditioning<br />
         <input type="checkbox" name="sunroofCB" />Sunroof<br />
         <input type="checkbox" name="audioCB" />Deluxe audio system<br />
         <strong>Select your favorite color:</strong><br />
         <input type="radio" name="color[0]RB" />Blue<br />
         <input type="radio" name="color[1]RB" />Green<br />
         <input type="radio" name="color[2]RB" />Red<p>
         <strong>Select your favorite soft drink type:</strong><br />
         <input name="sodaMenu">
            <option>Cola
            <option>Lemon-lime
            <option>Root beer
         </input>
         <input type="button" name="b1" value="Click when finished"
         onclick="displayMessage(document.survey)" />
      </form>
      </body>
      </html>
```

Note: Most of the exercises above may also be done as lab exercises. If a problem involves a function, add a function call so that the function code is actually executed.

Exercise 12.1: A Guess-the-Number Game

❏ Create an HTML source document named GuessingGame.htm that has a text box, a click button, and another text box in a form named guessForm. The surfer should be instructed to guess a whole number from 1 to 10 by entering it in the first box and then clicking the button. The onclick event handler in the button should call a function named checkTheNumber() that accepts the guessForm as a parameter, converts the entry in the text box from a string to a number, and checks to see if it equals 7 (or whatever number from 1 to 10 you want to make the lucky number). If the surfer's guess matches the lucky number, then a "You win!" message should appear in the second text box; otherwise, a "Sorry, try again" message should appear.

❑ Save a copy of the "guess-the-number" source document, renamed as GuessingGame2.htm, and then modify the new version so that instead of using a preset number as the lucky number, it uses the `Math.random()` method (covered in Chapter in the section "The Math Object") to pick a random number from 1 to 10 and store it in a global variable named `luckyNumber`. Note that this code must be outside the `checkTheNumber()` function, otherwise the lucky number will get changed every time the surfer clicks the button.

❑ Optional: Save a copy of the GuessingGame2.htm document and rename it GuessingGame3.htm. Modify the code so that it counts how many guesses it takes the surfer to guess the number and then displays that number in the "You win" message (e.g., "You win! It took you 4 guesses."). Also add a click button labeled "Play again with a new lucky number" that the surfer can use to generate a new random number. (In the GuessingGame2.htm version, the surfer has to open the document again to generate a new random number.) Finally, when the surfer's guess is only one away from the lucky number, display the message "Close, but not quite. Try again." in the second text box; when the guess is two or three away from the lucky number, display the message "You're getting warmer. Try again."; and when the guess is more than three away from the lucky number, display the message "You're cold as ice. Try again."

Exercise 12.2: The CyberPizza Page

❑ Create a source document, named CyberPizza.htm, that is designed to be a pizza order web page. The page will ask the surfer to indicate what kind of pizza toppings and pizza crust he or she desires. Offer pepperoni, sausage, tomatoes, olives, mushrooms, and anchovies for toppings and thin, thick white, or thick wheat as the crust choices. Use a set of check boxes for the toppings and a set of radio buttons for the crust choices. Also implement a Place Order Now click button for the surfer to click when he or she is ready to place the order, and two text fields where you can output messages to the surfer once the order has been placed. Put all of these elements in the same form, named `pizzaForm`.

❑ When the surfer clicks on the Place Order Now button, use its `onclick` event handler to call a function named `respondToOrder()` that has `f` as its formal parameter. When calling the function, send it `document.pizzaForm` as the actual parameter. The `respondToOrder()` function should use a conditional statement to check if the surfer has selected anchovies. If so, display a message in the *first* text box that says, "Anchovies?!? Count me out!" If not, display a message in the first text box that says, "Excellent choices! I can't wait to eat!" Declare the function in a `<script>` element within the `<head>` element.

❑ Once you have the above working, add a third condition to the conditional statement in the `respondToOrder()` function: check to see if the user has selected pepperoni *or* sausage and, if so, display a message in the first text field that says, "Ugh! Too much fat! I'm on a diet." That is, the conditional statement will have the following structure (where the text in square brackets is to be replaced by the appropriate JavaScript code):

```
if [anchovies box is checked] {
   [write appropriate message to first textbox]
}
else if [pepperoni box or sausage box is checked] {
   [write appropriate message to first textbox]
}
else {
   [write "Excellent choices" message to first textbox]
}
```

❑ Finally, add a *separate* conditional statement to the `respondToOrder()` function that checks the radio buttons for the crust choices. If the crust choice is thin, print a message in the *second* text field that says "Crisp and crunchy!" Else, if the crust choice is thick white, print a message in the second text field that says "Nice and chewy!" And else, if the crust choice is thick wheat, print a message that says "Sounds healthy!"

Exercise 12.3: The CyberPizza Page, Continued

❑ Save a copy of the CyberPizza.htm document and rename it CyberPizza2.htm. Add a pop-up menu that allows the surfer to choose a store location: Midtown, North, South, East, or West. Also add a third text box to the bottom of the page and appropriate code in the `respondToOrder()` function so that the store location selected will be displayed in the third text box. The message should be: "Your order will be delivered from our South location" (or whatever location was chosen).

❑ Optional: Using a search site like Google or Yahoo, spend a few minutes looking for interesting pizza-related sites. Once you have found three or four, add a Quick Links menu to the CyberPizza2.htm document that enables the surfer to jump directly to these sites.

Putting It All Together: Online Quizzes and Slide Shows

LEARNING OBJECTIVES

1. Learn how to use radio buttons to create an online quiz and use conditional statements to score the quiz.

2. Learn how to implement write-in questions for a quiz and check the surfer's answers.

3. Learn how to use the image object and a built-in JavaScript timing function to create an automatic slide show.

Implementing an Online Quiz

In this chapter we will take a number of things we learned in the past few chapters and put them together to create first an interactive quiz and second an automatic slide show.

We will implement the interactive quiz using radio buttons and text boxes. (The same format could be used for an online questionnaire.) Such a quiz provides a good exercise in reviewing and putting together key concepts such as functions, parameters, the return statement, and form elements.

The quiz will present the surfer/student with a series of multiple-choice questions. The answers for each question will be displayed as a set of radio buttons. When done selecting the answers, the student will click a "Grade my answers!" button, whereupon the `onclick` event handler will call a function that processes and displays the student's score.

For a sample quiz, we'll use three questions on the topic of the first Apollo moon mission. Figure 13.1 shows the key parts of the code to create the multiple-choice questions and the resulting display. (We'll add the JavaScript below.)

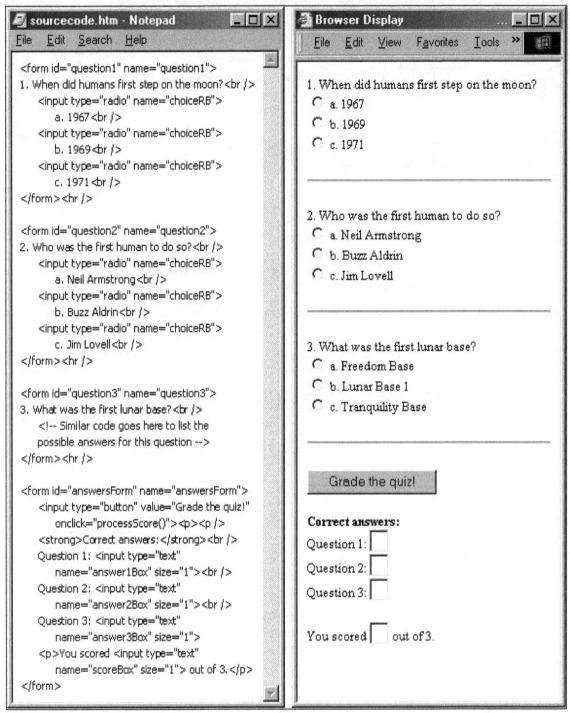

FIGURE 13.1.   The Apollo Mission Quiz

Note that although we could use one long form that includes all the questions and answers shown, we instead use one form for each question, plus a form named `answersForm` that defines the click button, the text boxes to display the correct answers, and the text box to display the student's score. Using a separate form for each question makes the radio button code a little simpler to write.

We also used the same name for each question's set of radio buttons, `choiceRB`, to label the possible choices for each question. We can do this without the browser getting confused because each set of radio buttons belongs to a different form, so the complete name for each radio button is unique. For example, `document.question1.choiceRB[0]` refers to the first radio button for the *first* question, while `document.question2.choiceRB[0]` refers to the first radio button for the *second* question. If we had put all the questions in one form, then we would have to use different names for each set of radio buttons.

Grading the Quiz

The `onclick` event handler of the click button in the `answersForm` calls a function named `processScore()`. This function will check the student's radio button answer against the correct answer for each question and tally the total number of correct answers. In our previous examples using functions to check form elements like radio buttons, we sent the form to the function as a parameter. In this case, we have no parameter at all involved. Why not?

The reason is that we are dealing with multiple forms—one for each question, plus the `answersForm`—all of which the function needs to access. We would therefore have to pass each form as a parameter to the function. The function call would be:

```
onclick = "processScore(question1, question2, question3,
    answersForm)"
```

The first line of the function declaration that matches this call would be something like:

```
function processScore(q1, q2, q3, ansForm) {
    //etc.
}
```

This isn't too bad for a three-question quiz, but what if we had 20 or 50 or 100 questions?

Another option is to pass the whole document to the function:

```
onclick = "processScore(document)"
```

where the function declaration would be:

```
function processScore(d) {
    //etc.
}
```

In this case, the formal parameter d becomes an alias for document. This solves the problem of having to have one parameter for every question. To make the code as simple as possible for our quiz, however, we will write the processScore() function using no parameters and leave the above for Exercise 5.

The processScore() function will do three things:

1. Declare a local variable named score and initialize it to 0. This variable will keep track of the student's score.

2. Use a series of conditional statements to check the student's answer for each question (as recorded by the radio button the student checked) against the correct answer. If they match, one point is added to the score variable.

3. Display the student's total score and the correct answers for each question.

The code that implements these steps is shown below. The comments throughout the code will help you identify each part (although they also make the code look longer than it really is). Note that because we didn't use any parameters, we have to use the full names for the radio buttons and text boxes involved (for example, document.question1.choiceRB[1]).

```javascript
function processScore() {
  var score = 0     //Initialize a variable to keep track
                    //of the score
  //Next, check each answer the user gave and add 1 to
  //score if correct
  //The correct answer for Question 1 is radio button 1
  //(i.e., answer b)
  if (document.question1.choiceRB[1].checked) {
    score = score + 1
  }

  //The correct answer for Question 2 is radio button 0
  //(i.e., answer a)
  if (document.question2.choiceRB[0].checked) {
    score = score + 1
  }
  //The correct answer for Question 3 is radio button 2
  //(i.e., answer c)
  if (document.question3.choiceRB[2].checked) {
    score = score + 1
  }
  //Display the resulting value of score in the score box
  document.answersForm.scoreBox.value = score
```

```
    //Display the correct answers
    document.answersForm.answer1Box.value = "b"
    document.answersForm.answer2Box.value = "a"
    document.answersForm.answer3Box.value = "c"
  } //end of function processScore
```

Make sure that you understand how the score is tallied. The value of the score variable starts out as 0. If the student gets the first question correct, then the assignment statement score = score + 1 takes the current value of score (i.e., 0), adds 1 to it, and makes it the new value of score. So now score has the value 1. If the student gets the second question correct, then the assignment statement score = score + 1 takes the current value of score (i.e., 1), adds 1 to it, and makes it the new value of score. So now score has the value 2. And so on.

Revising the Grading Code

The code in the previous section for the processScore() function works fine. But, if we had a much longer quiz, we would end up with a very long series of conditional statements. It would be useful, therefore, to put the answer-checking code in a function. Such a function would also be handy if we were creating a number of different quizzes, because then we could easily reuse the answer-checking code for each quiz we made.

We will name this answer-checking function multipleChoicePoint(). It will be called from within the processScore() function and will receive two parameters: the form corresponding to the question to be graded and the radio button *number* for the correct answer for that question. It will check that correct answer against the radio button the student checked (which is stored in the question form). If the student is correct, the function will return a value of 1—the student gets 1 point for a correct answer. Otherwise, it will return a value of 0. In other words, it determines whether or not the student receives a point for a given multiple-choice question; thus the name we chose for it: multipleChoicePoint(). All that said, the code will be:

```
    function multipleChoicePoint(theQuestion, correctAnswer) {
      if (theQuestion.choiceRB[correctAnswer].checked) {
        return 1
      }
      else {
        return 0
      }
    } //end of function multipleChoicePoint
```

In order to check the first question, we would call this function as follows:

```
    score = multipleChoicePoint(document.question1, 1)
```

This line of code calls the function and sends it the form named `document.question1` along with the number of the radio button that is the correct answer for that question (1, corresponding to answer b). The function will check whether the student clicked radio button 1 in the `document.question1` form. If so, the value 1 is returned and stored in the variable named `score`. If not, the value 0 is returned and stored in `score`.

This syntax for the function call would be fine for the first question. But for the subsequent questions we of course need to add the returned value to the current value of the score variable (that is, we need to keep a running tally of the score as each question is checked). So we really need to write:

```
score = score + multipleChoicePoint(document.question1, 1)
```

This line is the revised version of the line `score = score + 1` in our original code. The code for checking questions 2 and 3 will be:

```
score = score + multipleChoicePoint(document.question2, 0)
score = score + multipleChoicePoint(document.question3, 2)
```

Putting it all together, Figure 13.2 shows the complete revised script.

QuickCheck Questions

1. Write the HTML code for a form named `sampleQuestion` that creates a multiple-choice question with radio buttons. (Make up your own question and possible answers.)

2. If the question in #1 was worth 3 points and the student's score was tallied in a variable named `studentScore`, write the single line of JavaScript code that would check the question and add 3 points to the student's score if correct.

Lab Exercise 13.1, "Getting a Feel for the Quiz Code," may be done at this point.

Adding a Write-In Question

Now we'd like to add another question to our quiz, but instead of giving the user the luxury of multiple-choice, we want it to be a write-in question. The question will be: "What was the name of the first lunar module that landed on the moon (one word)?" (The answer is "Eagle", as in the famous first words spoken from the moon: "Houston, Tranquility Base here. The Eagle has landed.")

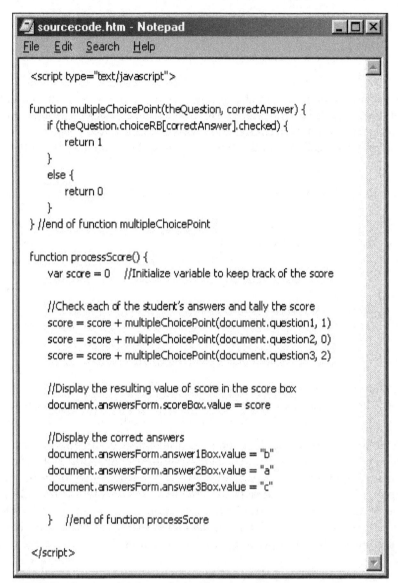

```
sourcecode.htm - Notepad

File  Edit  Search  Help

<script type="text/javascript">

function multipleChoicePoint(theQuestion, correctAnswer) {
    if (theQuestion.choiceRB[correctAnswer].checked) {
        return 1
    }
    else {
        return 0
    }
} //end of function multipleChoicePoint

function processScore() {
    var score = 0    //Initialize variable to keep track of the score

    //Check each of the student's answers and tally the score
    score = score + multipleChoicePoint(document.question1, 1)
    score = score + multipleChoicePoint(document.question2, 0)
    score = score + multipleChoicePoint(document.question3, 2)

    //Display the resulting value of score in the score box
    document.answersForm.scoreBox.value = score

    //Display the correct answers
    document.answersForm.answer1Box.value = "b"
    document.answersForm.answer2Box.value = "a"
    document.answersForm.answer3Box.value = "c"

    } //end of function processScore

</script>
```

FIGURE 13.2.   Final version of the script that scores the quiz

Checking a Write-In Question

In the case of a write-in question, we have to think carefully about how the program is going to check whether the surfer entered the correct answer. The first part is straightforward, because we can use the double-equal sign (==) in a conditional statement to check strings for equality, just as we do for numbers. For instance, if we had a variable named studentName, we could check to see if its value was "Fred" like so:

```
if (studentName=="Fred") {
  document.myForm.messageBox.value="Did you dance with
     Ginger?"
}
```

But what do we do if instead of entering "Eagle" for the write-in answer, the student enters "eagle" or "EAGLE"? Assuming we want to accept all these answers as correct, we could use a combination conditional statement, with one if statement for each possibility. In the "Fred" example above, the code would be:

```
if (studentName=="Fred") {
  document.myForm.messageBox.value="Did you dance with
     Ginger?"
}
else if (studentName=="fred") {
  document.myForm.messageBox.value="Did you dance with
     Ginger?"
}
else if (studentName=="FRED") {
  document.myForm.messageBox.value="Did you dance with
     Ginger?"
}
```

Note that we used else if clauses because if the value of studentName is "Fred" there is no need to check the other two possibilities, and if it's not "Fred" but is "fred", there is no need to check whether it's "FRED."

This code is more redundant than we would like, however, since every if statement has the same "Did you dance" line of code. And, in fact, we can compact it by using the logical operator "or" that we introduced in the last chapter. The logic we need is: If the value of studentName is "Fred" OR if the value of studentName is "fred" OR if the value of studentName is "FRED" then display the message "Did you dance with Ginger?" Remembering that the symbol for the "or" operator is two vertical lines, | | , we therefore write:

```
if ((studentName=="Fred") || (studentName=="fred") ||
   (studentName=="FRED")) {
  document.myForm.messageBox.value="Did you dance with
     Ginger?"
}
```

Note that in addition to enclosing each equality condition in parentheses—(studentName=="fred")—we also enclosed the whole set of three in an outer pair of parentheses. If we leave off the outer pair, JavaScript generates an error message.

Lab Exercise 13.2, "Adding a Write-In Question," may be done at this point.

Improving the Write-In Code

Although the conditional statements that check the surfer's write-in answers work fine, it would be better if we could check the write-in answers in the same way that the script checks the multiple-choice answers and increments the `score` variable. That is, we check the multiple-choice answers and increment `score` using the `multipleChoicePoint()` function:

```
score = score + multipleChoicePoint(document.question3, 2)
```

So for the "Eagle" question, we would like to write something like:

```
score = score + writeinPoint(document.question5, "Eagle")
```

The `writeinPoint()` function has two parameters passed to it: the form for a given write-in question and the correct answer for that question. The code for the `writeinPoint()` function will be similar to the `multipleChoicePoint()` function, in that it will return a 1 if the answer is correct and a 0 if it isn't. The format of the conditional statement will of course be a little different. Instead of checking if the correct radio button was selected, it will check whether the value of the `writeinAnswer` text box matches the correct answer.

A slight problem occurs, however, because as mentioned in the last section the correct answer for the "Eagle" question is not just "Eagle," but also "eagle" or "EAGLE". We could take this into account by passing all three answers to the `writeinPoint()` function:

```
score = score + writeinPoint(document.question5, "Eagle",
    "eagle", "EAGLE")
```

Instead of doing that, however, we will use a built-in feature of JavaScript that enables us to convert any string value to either all uppercase or all lowercase characters. For example, we can take the surfer's write-in answer to the "Eagle" question, which is stored in `document.question5.writeinAnswer.value`, and convert it to all lowercase letters before we check it with the conditional statement. By doing this, we don't have to check the answer against "Eagle", "eagle", and "EAGLE", but just against "eagle".

IMPORTANT

The key to doing this is that when a string variable is declared, JavaScript actually makes it a **string object**, and every string object has a built-in method named `toLowerCase()` and a method named `toUpperCase()`. As the names imply, the `toLowerCase()` string method converts a string to all lowercase characters and the `toUpperCase()` method converts a string to all uppercase characters. We use them like this:

```
var stringA, stringB
var myString = "Hello, Fred!"
```

```
stringA = myString.toLowerCase()     //Converts the value of
                                     //myString to lowercase
                                     //and stores it in the
                                     //variable named stringA
stringB = myString.toUpperCase()     //Converts the value of
                                     //myString to uppercase
                                     //and stores it in the
                                     //variable named stringB
```

After these lines of code are executed, the value of StringA will be "hello, fred!" and the value of StringB will be "HELLO, FRED!". But myString will still have its original value of "Hello, Fred!".

If we were converting the value of a text box named userNameBox that belonged to a form named myForm, the code would be:

```
stringA = document.myForm.userNameBox.value.toLowerCase()
stringB = document.myForm.userNameBox.value.toUpperCase()
```

Don't forget the value property here!

Lab Exercise 13.3 asks you to improve the code of Lab Exercise 13.2 by adding string conversion code to the checking of the "Eagle" question.

QuickCheck Questions

1. Write a conditional statement that checks whether a variable named firstName has the value "Fred" <u>and</u> a variable named lastName has the value "Astaire". If both conditions are true, then display the message "How is Ginger?" in a text box named outputBox belonging to a form named danceForm. (Don't worry about checking whether firstName may be "fred" or "FRED" and lastName may be "astaire" or "ASTAIRE".)

2. Write a conditional statement that converts the value of a variable named firstName to lowercase characters and checks whether it has the value "fred". Do the same for a variable named lastName with the value "astaire". If both conditions are true, then display the message "How is Ginger?" in a text box named outputBox belonging to a form named danceForm.

Lab Exercise 13.3, "Improving the Code," may be done at this point.

An Automatic Slide Show

In Chapter 9, in the section "Creating Image Rollovers," we learned how to use image objects to change an image when a mouseover event occurs. Now we will see how we can use a conditional statement with an image object to create an automatic, repeating slide show.

Here are the key things we will need:

1. An image object, plus several image files that will be loaded into the object at two-second intervals to create the slide show. For this example, we'll use three image files, named firstimage.jpg, secondimage.jpg, and thirdimage.jpg. We will name the image object slideShow.

2. A variable named currentImage to keep track of which image is currently being displayed (image 1, 2, or 3). When it's time to display a new image, currentImage will be incremented by 1, except when it has the value 3. In that case, it should be changed back to the value 1 so that the slide show will automatically repeat.

3. A conditional statement that checks the value of the currentImage variable and executes the code to display the corresponding image.

4. A timing mechanism to indicate when the next image should be displayed.

We have learned how to do all of this except the timing mechanism. For the timing mechanism, we use a special JavaScript function named setTimeout(). This function acts like an alarm clock. We can set it to go off at a certain time in the future, and when it goes off, it calls a function that we specify. It therefore takes two parameters: the first is a *string* that specifies the name of the function to call, and the second is a *number* that specifies the value of the time interval, in milliseconds (*thousandths* of seconds).

Applying this to our slide show, we will use the setTimeout() function to call a function named changeImage() every two seconds (or 2000 milliseconds). The necessary code is:

```
setTimeout("changeImage()", 2000)
```

The core of the changeImage() function will be steps 2 and 3 above, written as two conditional statements (Figure 13.3). The first conditional statement checks the value of currentImage. If it's less than 3 (i.e., if it's 1 or 2), then it increments it by 1 for the next image. The other possibility is that it equals 3, in which case the else clause resets it to the value 1. The second conditional statement then checks the value of currentImage and loads the corresponding image file into the image object. And finally the setTimeout() function is called to reset the timer for another two seconds.

Note that once the setTimeout() function sets the timer, the function ends so that the browser can move on to whatever code comes next. Contrast this behavior with the alert method. When the alert method is called and the alert box appears, the alert method does not end until the surfer clicks the OK button. So the browser doesn't do anything else until that happens—it just sits and waits.

When we covered image rollovers in Chapter 8 we noted that they only work in Navigator version 3 and Explorer version 4 or later. At that time we had not

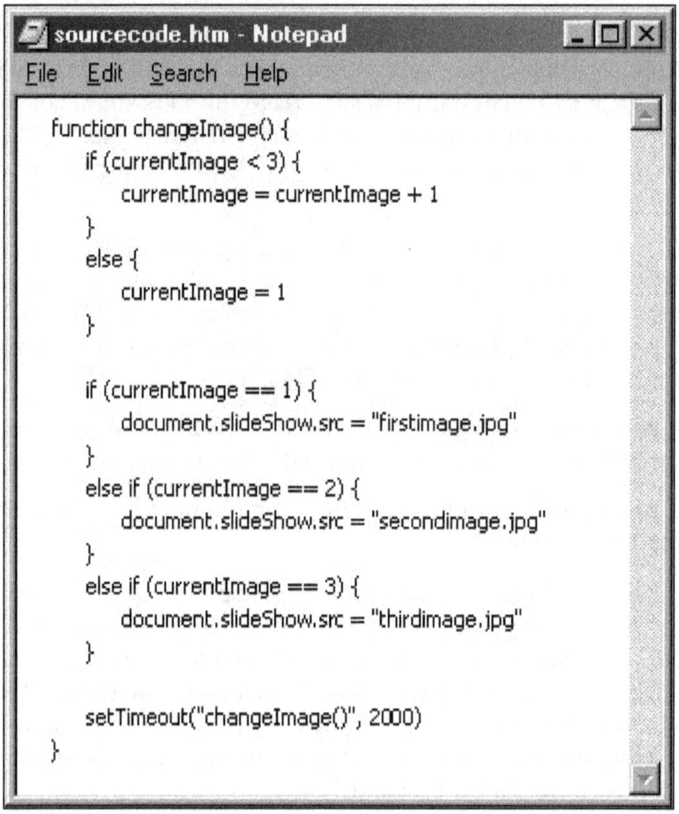

```
sourcecode.htm - Notepad

File   Edit   Search   Help

function changeImage() {
    if (currentImage < 3) {
        currentImage = currentImage + 1
    }
    else {
        currentImage = 1
    }

    if (currentImage == 1) {
        document.slideShow.src = "firstimage.jpg"
    }
    else if (currentImage == 2) {
        document.slideShow.src = "secondimage.jpg"
    }
    else if (currentImage == 3) {
        document.slideShow.src = "thirdimage.jpg"
    }

    setTimeout("changeImage()", 2000)
}
```

FIGURE 13.3.   Basic code for changing to the next image in the slide show

learned about conditional statements. But now that we know about them, we can use one to make sure that the image rollover code does not "break" in older browsers and generate an error message. The problem comes in the assignment statements that reference the image object, such as:

```
document.slideShow.src = "thirdimage.jpg"
```

Older browsers that don't know about image objects do not recognize `document.slideShow.src` as valid, and thus they will generate an error message. We fix this problem by enclosing the code in the `changeImage()` function body in another conditional statement that checks whether the browser knows about image objects. To check this, we look at the `images` property of the `document` object. If this property has the value `true` (i.e., the browser knows about image objects), then the image rollover proceeds and the `setTimeout()` function is set. If this property has the value `false`, then the image rollover code is skipped and the `setTimeout()` function is never set. The key conditional statement is simply `if (document.images==true)`, as in:

```
if (document.images==true) {
  if (currentImage < 3) {
```

```
        currentImage = currentImage + 1
    }
    else {
        currentImage = 1
    }

    if (currentImage == 1) {
        document.slideShow.src = "firstimage.jpg"
    }
    else if (currentImage == 2) {
        document.slideShow.src = "secondimage.jpg"
    }
    else if (currentImage == 3) {
        document.slideShow.src = "thirdimage.jpg"
    }
    setTimeout("changeImage()", 2000)
}
```

Note that we could also write the conditional statement as:

```
if (document.images) { //etc. }
```

The only things left to get the slide show up and running are: (1) include an <img> tag in the <body> container that displays the first image in the slide show and also specifies the name of the image object (slideShow); (2) initialize the currentImage variable to have the value 0 (it will be changed to 1 the first time the changeImage() function is executed); and (3) call the changeImage() function for the first time to get the slide show rolling.

The <img> tag that displays the image for the first time and associates it with an image object named slideShow will be:

```
<img src="firstimage.jpg" alt="Slide Show" width="200"
    height="150" id="slideShow" />
```

(Note: For backward compatibility, we might also want to include a name attribute in this tag, i.e., name="slideShow".)

We declare and initialize the currentImage variable to 0 in the <script> container just before the changeImage() function declaration. The browser will therefore initialize it when the page is loaded. (Note that we can't make it a local variable and initialize it inside the function, because then it would get reset to 0 every time the function executed, thus ruining the counting of the images.)

```
<script type="text/javascript")
    var currentImage = 0
    function changeImage() {
        //etc.
    }
</script>
```

Finally, we call the `changeImage()` function for the first time immediately after the `<img>` tag has created the image object:

```
<img src="firstimage.jpg" alt="Slide Show" width="200"
  height="150" id="slideShow" />
<script type="text/javascript">
  changeImage()
</script>
```

Although this code works fine, we can also employ a more sophisticated way to call the `changeImage()` function the first time. The key is to use an `onload` event handler in the `<body>` tag. When the browser finishes loading a web page, it generates a **load event** that is associated with the `<body>` container (that is, the load event indicates that the body of the source document is now completely loaded). We may therefore use the `onload` event handler in the `<body>` tag to do some JavaScript when the page is loaded and ready to go. In this case, we simply want to call the `changeImage()` function. The key code is shown below. Note that we still have to declare the `currentImage` variable and initialize it to 0 at the beginning of the `<script>` container. The only code that the `onload` code replaces is the line that calls the `changeImage()` function.

```
<body onload="changeImage()">
  <p>Check out our slide show . . . </p>
  <img src="firstimage.jpg" alt="Slide Show" width="200"
    height="150" id="slideShow" />
  <script type="text/javascript">
    //The changeImage() function call here was deleted
  </script>
</body>
```

Figure 13.4 shows the complete code for the slide show. To summarize, here are the key things that happen when the browser loads this code, from top to bottom:

1. In the `<head>` container, the `currentImage` variable is initialized to 0 and the `changeImage()` function declaration is checked (but not executed).

2. In the `<body>` container, the firstimage.jpg image is displayed (after the initial line of text) and associated with an image object named `slideShow`.

3. The browser finishes loading the document (whatever else is in the `<body>` container) and then generates a load event, activating the `onload` event handler of the `<body>` container.

4. The `onload` event handler calls the `changeImage()` function, where the value of `currentImage` is incremented by 1 (so now it has the value 1). The conditional statement then tests the value of `currentImage`

```
sourcecode.htm - Notepad                              _ □ ×
File   Edit   Search   Help

<!--XHTML and DTD info goes here-->
<html>
<head>
   <script type="text/javascript")
      var currentImage = 0

      function changeImage() {
         if (document.images==true) {
            if (currentImage < 3) {
               currentImage = currentImage + 1
            }
            else {
               currentImage = 1
            }

            if (currentImage == 1) {
               document.slideShow.src = "firstimage.jpg"
            }
            else if (currentImage == 2) {
               document.slideShow.src = "secondimage.jpg"
            }
            else if (currentImage == 3) {
               document.slideShow.src = "thirdimage.jpg"
            }

            setTimeout("changeImage()", 2000)
         } //end of if (document.images==true) code
      } //end of function changeImage
   </script>
</head>

<body onload="changeImage()">
   <p>Check out our slide show...</p>
   <img src="firstimage.jpg" alt="Slide Show" width="200"
      height="150" id="slideShow" name="slideShow" />
</body>
</html>
```

FIGURE 13.4.   Complete code for the slide show

and loads firstimage.jpg into the slideShow image object. (In other words, the image doesn't change this first time, because the <img> tag already loaded the first image.) The setTimeout() function is set to wake up in two seconds and call the changeImage() function again.

5. Two seconds later, the setTimeout() function goes off and calls the changeImage() function, which increments currentImage (so now

it has the value 2). The conditional statement tests the value of currentImage and loads secondimage.jpg into the slideShow image object, thus changing the displayed image. Finally, the setTimeout() function is reset for two seconds.

6. Two seconds later, the setTimeout() function goes off and the process repeats itself, incrementing currentImage to 3 and loading the third image.

7. Two seconds later, the setTimeout() function goes off and the process repeats, but this time currentImage is reset to 1 and the first image is loaded.

And so on and so forth.

QuickCheck Questions

1. Write the code that will set the timer to one minute, at which time it will call a function named displayWarning().

2. Write the code that uses a load event to call a function named displayWarning() when the browser finishes loading the page.

Lab Exercise 13.4, "Adding a Slide Show," may be done at this point.

Key Terms

load event
string object

Code Summary

1. Implementing an Online Quiz

Tallying the quiz score by initializing a variable named score to 0 and then incrementing it for each correct answer:

```
score = score + 1
```

Declaring a function that accepts two parameters, a form with a set of radio buttons named choiceRB and a number value that indicates which radio button is the correct choice, and then returns a 1 if the user's choice matches the correct choice and a 0 if not:

```
function multipleChoicePoint(theQuestion, correctAnswer) {
    if (theQuestion.choiceRB[correctAnswer].checked) {
        return 1
    }
    else {
```

```
        return 0
    }
}
```

Calling the above function for a question with the first radio button (number 0) as the correct answer:

```
score = score + multipleChoicePoint(document.question2, 0)
```

2. Adding a Write-In Question

Converting a string to all lowercase letters or all uppercase letters:

```
var stringA, stringB
var myString = "Hello, Fred!"
stringA = myString.toLowerCase()    //Converts the value of myString to lowercase
                                    // and stores it in the variable named stringA
stringB = myString.toUpperCase()    //Converts the value of myString to uppercase
                                    // and stores it in the variable named stringB
```

Converting the contents of a text box to all lowercase letters or all uppercase letters:

```
stringA = document.myForm.userNameBox.value.toLowerCase()
stringB = document.myForm.userNameBox.value.toUpperCase()
```

3. An Automatic Slide Show

Setting an alarm clock timer to go off N milliseconds (where 1 millisecond is 1/1000 of a second) in the future and call a function named someFunction():

```
setTimeout("someFunction()", N)
```

Remember that when testing multiple conditions using logical operators like "and" and "or" in a conditional statement, you must enclose the whole set in parentheses.

When checking a string value for equality with another string, it's good first to change it to all uppercase or all lowercase letters (assuming that the case of the letters doesn't matter).

Alerts and Advice

1. Which of the following increments a variable named score?
   a. document.increment(score)
   b. increment(score)
   c. score = score + 1
   d. score = 1
   e. score++

2. True or false: When using a conditional statement to check whether a radio button named document.someform.choiceRB[3] has the value true or not, it is okay to write it either of the two following ways. Either:
```
if(document.someForm.choicesRB[3].checked==true){
   //more code here
}
```

Review Questions

Or:

```
if (document.someForm.choicesRB[3].checked){
    //more code here
}
```

3. True or false: The following conditional statement checks whether the fourth radio button in a set of radio buttons named `document.someForm.choicesRB` has the value true.

```
if (document.someForm.choicesRB[4].checked==true){
    //more code here
}
```

4. Which of the following lines of code, when placed as the last executed line in a function, will return the value 12?
   a. `return 12`
   b. `function return 12`
   c. `var return 12`
   d. `return = 12`

5. True or false: The following code correctly checks whether a variable named `studentName` has the value "Marilyn" or the value "MARILYN".

```
if ((studentName=="Marilyn") or (studentName=="MARILYN")){
    //more code goes here
}
```

6. Which of the following lines of code converts the value of a string variable named `userAnswer` to all lowercase characters and stores it in a variable named `modifiedAnswer`?
   a. `modifiedAnswer = userAnswer.toLowerCase()`
   b. `toLowerCase(modifiedAnswer, userAnswer)`
   c. `modifiedAnswer = toLowerCase(userAnswer)`
   d. `userAnswer.toLowerCase() = modifiedAnswer`

7. Which of the following lines of code sets a timer for 3 seconds, at which time a function named `displayMessage()` is called?
   a. `setTimer("displayMessage()", 3)`
   b. `setAlarm("displayMessage()", 3)`
   c. `setTimeout("displayMessage()", 3000)`
   d. `setAlarm("displayMessage()", 3000)`

8. Which of the following lines of code takes the images stored in the image file `eiffeltower.jpg` and loads it into an image object named `parisSights`?
   a. `document.parisSights = "eiffeltower.jpg"`
   b. `document.parisSights.src = "eiffeltower.jpg"`
   c. `"eiffeltower.jpg" = document.parisSights`
   d. `load(parisSights, "eiffeltower.jpg")`

Exercises

1. Briefly define and/or explain the following terms: string object, load event, the `setTimeout()` function.

2. Write the HTML code for a form named `vpQuestion` that creates a multiple-choice question that may have more than one correct answer, so the student has to choose one or more of the answers to get it correct. The question will be: Which of the following presidents also served as vice president of the United States? The possible answers, which will be implemented with check boxes, are: Theodore Roosevelt, Franklin Roosevelt, Harry Truman, John F. Kennedy, Richard Nixon, and Ronald Reagan. Name the check boxes `trooseveltCB`, `frooseveltCB`, `trumanCB`, `kennedyCB`, `nixonCB`, and `reaganCB` and display them in a vertical column.

3. Write a single conditional statement that will check the student's answers to the question in exercise 2 and add five points to a previously declared variable named `quizScore` if the student answers correctly. (The correct answer is Theodore Roosevelt, Harry Truman, and Richard Nixon. Note that, to be correct, the student should have checked all three of these answers and not have checked any of the other answers.)

4. Write JavaScript code that will check the student's answers to the question in exercise 2 and add points to or subtracts points from a previously declared variable named `quizScore` as follows: For every correct name selected, the student gets one point, but for every incorrect name selected the student loses one point. (The correct names are Theodore Roosevelt, Harry Truman, and Richard Nixon.)

5. The section "Grading the Quiz" presented a basic way to write a `processScore()` function for a multiple-choice quiz without using parameters. Rewrite the code for the `processScore()` function and the code for the `onclick` event handler that calls it, so that the whole `document` object is passed as a parameter to the function.

6. Write the code that will take the value of a text box named `document.infoForm.userNameBox`, convert it to uppercase characters, and store it in a global variable named `allcapsName`. Then use a conditional statement to check whether the value of `allcapsName` is "JAMES". If it is, display the message "Good to see you again, Mr. Bond" in a textbox named `document.infoForm.greetingBox`.

7. Write the code for a source document that, once the browser loads it, will display an alert box every five seconds with the message "Are we having fun yet?"

8. Write the code for a source document that, once the browser loads it, will display a random image every two seconds. The random image should be chosen from a set of 10 images stored in the files image1.jpg, image2.jpg, ... image10.jpg, respectively. Use JavaScript's random number generator (see "The Math Object" in Chapter 11) to generate a number between 1 and 10 and then use a compound conditional statement to pick the image that should be shown each time. When the page first loads, display image1.jpg as the starting image. Assume all the images have a height of 75 pixels and a width of 125 pixels.

9. There is a way to dramatically shorten the code for Exercise 8 by using JavaScript's capability to convert numbers to strings automatically. We know that we can use the + operator to concatenate strings, such as:

```
var userName = "Jennifer"
var greeting = "Hello," + name + "!"      //greeting will have the value "Hello, Jennifer!"
```

If, however, we replace the `userName` variable with a variable that stores a number, JavaScript will automatically convert the number to a string value and then put the whole string together. For example:

```
var someNumber = 34.7
var message = "The number is: " + someNumber + "!"
```

This assignment statement takes the value of `someNumber` (34.7) and converts it to the string "34.7" and concatenates it with the other strings, so that the value of the message variable will be: "The number is 34.7!". But the value of `someNumber` itself remains the number 34.7. (This number-to-string conversion only works if the number is on the right side of the + operator and a string is on the left side. For more details, see the section in Chapter 17 on "Screen Width and Number-To-String Conversions.")

Do Exercise 8, but without using a conditional statement. Hint: The key is to get the random number from 1 to 10 and then use this number in an assignment statement that constructs a string with the value of the name of the corresponding image file. For example, if the random number has the value 7, then the string will be the value "image7.jpg", which may then be used to change the image.

Debugging Exercise

Identify and correct the errors in the following JavaScript code. The document in question has three forms named `q1Form`, `q2Form`, and `q3Form` that implement three multiple-choice questions, each with a set of three radio buttons named `answerRB`. The `processScore()` function below is called by an `onclick` event handler with the syntax: `onclick = "processScore()"`. The code should be set up so that each correct answer is worth 2 points, but each time the student gets an incorrect answer he or she loses 1 point.

```
<script type="text/javascript">
   function multipleChoicePoint(Q, A) {
      if (q1Form.answerRB[Q, A].checked)
         return 2
      else
         return 0
   } //end of function multipleChoicePoint

   function processScore() {
      //The correct answers for the three questions are radio buttons 1, 0, and 2
      score = score + multipleChoicePoint(q1Form, 1)
      score = score + multipleChoicePoint(q2Form, 0)
      score = score + multipleChoicePoint(q3Form, 2)
      //Display the resulting value of score in an alert box
      alert("You scored " + score + " points.")
   } //end of function processScore
</script>
```

Lab Exercises

Note: Most of the exercises above may also be done as lab exercises. If a problem involves a function, add a function call so that the function code is actually executed.

Exercise 13.1: Getting a Feel for the Quiz Code

❏ Create a source document that implements an online quiz using the Apollo Quiz questions from the text. In order to make sure you understand how the code for the interactive quiz works, add a fourth question to the quiz: "What mission was the first moon landing?" The possible answers will be: "a. Apollo 8 b. Apollo 11 c. Apollo 13" (the correct answer is b).

Exercise 13.2: Adding a Write-In Question

❏ After the form for the last multiple-choice question in the `<body>` container of your quiz document, create a new form for the write-in question, using a text box for the surfer to enter the answer. Name the form `question5` and the text box `writeinBox`.

❏ After the lines in the `processScore()` function that check the surfer's multiple-choice answers and calculate the total score (the `score = score + multipleChoicePoint( . . . )` lines), put a single conditional statement that checks the surfer's write-in answer. If the surfer entered "Eagle" or "eagle" or "EAGLE", then add 1 point to the `score` variable. (Note that you won't want to use the `multipleChoicePoint()` function to do this, because that function was designed for use with the multiple-choice questions.)

❏ Don't forget to modify the `answersForm` appropriately so that it will display the correct answer to the write-in question in addition to the multiple-choice answers.

❏ Add a second write-in question to the quiz that asks: "What was the last name of the president of the United States when the first moon landing too place?" (The answer is "Nixon".) Name the form `question6` and the text box `writeinBox`.

Exercise 13.3: Improving the Code

❏ Enclose in a JavaScript comment the conditional statements that you wrote in Lab Exercise 13.2 to check the two write-in answers. (That is, don't delete them, just deactivate them by putting them inside a comment.) Replace them with the code:

```
score = score + writeinPoint(document.question5, "Eagle")
score = score + writeinPoint(document.question6, "Nixon")
```

❏ Write the function declaration for the `writeinPoint()` function, with two formal parameters named `theQuestion` and `correctAnswer`. Use a conditional statement to check whether the value the surfer entered in the `writeinBox` text box equals `correctAnswer`. But before the conditional statement is executed, convert the surfer's answer stored in `theQuestion.writeinBox` to lowercase and the value of `correctAnswer` to lowercase as well. Then use the conditional statement to compare the two lowercase versions and see if they are equal.

Note: Instead of converting the value of the `correctAnswer` formal parameter to lowercase, we could simply write "Eagle" as "eagle" and "Nixon" as "nixon" in the function calls to the `writeinPoint()` function. But it is good practice to do the conversion in the function anyway, because it makes the function more robust. That is, it doesn't matter how the value of the correct answer is written in the function call, the function will still be able to check it correctly.

Exercise 13.4: Adding a Slide Show

❏ Create a new source document named SlideShow.htm that implements a simple slide show with three or four images. The images should preferably have the same height and width, but it's not absolutely necessary. See the section on "Creating and Finding Images" in Chapter 5 for tips on getting images.

❏ Optional: Save a copy of your slide show source document and rename it ManualSlideShow.htm. Create two click buttons labeled "Next" and "Previous". The "Next" button should call a function that displays the next image in the sequence, and the "Previous" button should call a function that displays the previous image in the sequence. Each function should change the value of the global variable that keeps track of the current image accordingly. Once you have the "Next" and "Previous" buttons working, add a "Home" button that will go back to the first image of the slide show. Finally, try to replace the three functions that take care of the "Next", "Previous", and "Home" buttons with one function. The new function should use a parameter that tells it which operation it should perform.

Loops and Arrays

LEARNING OBJECTIVES

1. Consider how JavaScript may be used to create and score a personality-type quiz.

2. Learn how to implement looping structures using for loops, while loops, and do-while loops and how to avoid common loop errors.

3. Learn how to create compound variables, known as arrays, and store various values in them.

4. Learn how to refer to form elements such as text boxes, radio buttons, and check boxes by number instead of by name.

5. Learn how to calculate the average of a set of numbers using an array and a loop and how to create a personality-type quiz using the forms array.

A Different Kind of Quiz

The online quiz we created in Chapter 13 was a standard multiple-choice quiz, where each question had one and only one correct answer. Because there is no pattern to the a, b, or c answers for such a quiz, our code had to check each question individually. The more questions in the quiz, the more lines of code we have to write.

Not all quizzes have this drawback, however. Consider, for example, the ubiquitous personality tests found online and offline. They range from the academic, such as the Meyers-Briggs personality test, to the whimsical, such as tests that purport to reveal which cartoon character you are most like. This type of test is often set up so that the "a" answers all correspond to a certain trait, the "b" answers to another, and so on. To score the test results, therefore, we just need to tally how many times the test-taker chose "a", how many times "b", and so on.

The following conditional statement would do the job for a question with three possible answers, represented by a set of three radio buttons named `choiceRB` in a form named `question1`:

```
var scoreA = 0, scoreB = 0, scoreC = 0
if (document.question1.choiceRB[0].checked) {
  scoreA = scoreA + 1
}
else if (document.question1.choiceRB[1].checked) {
  scoreB = scoreB + 1
}
else if (document.question1.choiceRB[2].checked) {
  scoreC = scoreC + 1
}
```

The variable `scoreA` keeps track of how many times the first answer (a) is checked for the series of questions in the test, `scoreB` keeps track of how many times the second answer (b) is checked, and `scoreC` keeps track of how many times the third answer (c) is checked. If the surfer had chosen answer (b) on the first question (represented by the second radio button), then the above code increments the value of `scoreB` by 1 while the values of `scoreA` and `scoreC` remain at 0.

The conditional statement for the second question would be:

```
if (document.question2.choiceRB[0].checked) {
  scoreA = scoreA + 1
}
else if (document.question2.choiceRB[1].checked) {
  scoreB = scoreB + 1
}
else if (document.question2.choiceRB[2].checked) {
  scoreC = scoreC + 1
}
```

If the surfer had chosen answer (b) again, then `scoreB` would be incremented again and have a value of 2, while `scoreA` and `scoreC` would still be at 0. And so on and so forth for the remaining questions in the test. For each question, only one of the three variables `scoreA`, `scoreB`, and `scoreC` gets incremented. At the end, the values of `scoreA`, `scoreB`, and `scoreC` would tell us how many times the surfer chose answer (a), answer (b), and answer (c), respectively.

If there were 25 questions in the test, then there would be 25 conditional statements like those above, one to check each question. But if we look at the code above for the first and second questions, we see that the two conditional statements are nearly identical. The only difference is the name of the form involved: The first conditional statement references the `question1` form and the second references the `question2` form. The conditional statements for the rest of the questions would also be almost identical, except that they would reference the forms named `question3`, `question4`, and so on.

When we have a situation where the same block of code is repeated over and over, with minor variations, we can often replace the repetitions with a programming loop. We introduced the idea of loops in Chapter 7 in the section "The Four Basic Control Structures." Now it's time to learn how we use them in JavaScript and eventually how we can use a loop for our quiz example above.

Three Types of Loops

We use programming loops to repeat one or several instructions over and over again. Computers excel at this repetitive work because they can do it much faster than humans, and they never get bored. JavaScript has three main types of loops, the first one being the `for` loop.

The for Loop

The **for loop** repeats the instruction(s) contained in its loop *for* a fixed number of times (thus the name). The basic syntax in pseudocode format is:

```
for (some number of times) {
   //Execute a sequence of instructions here . . .
}
```

Consider a simple example. If we wanted to put up five alert boxes, one after the other, all with the message "I deserve an A+!", we could program it as five `alert()` method calls in sequence:

```
alert("I deserve an A+!")
alert("I deserve an A+!")
alert("I deserve an A+!")
alert("I deserve an A+!")
alert("I deserve an A+!")
```

This certainly works, although it's not very elegant. And if we wanted to do it 20, or 50, or 100 times, this technique would really clutter up our program (and you definitely would not get an A+ for programming style).

But by using a `for` loop, we can make this code very compact:

```
for (5 times) {
   alert("I deserve an A+!")
}
```

This code tells the browser to repeat the `alert` command five times in a row. (The "5 times" part is still in pseudocode format.) If we put several lines of code inside the body of the `for` loop (delineated by the pair of curly braces), the browser repeats the lines as a set. For example, the `for` loop:

```
for (3 times) {
   alert("Hello!")
   alert("Good-bye!")
}
```

would display six alert boxes with alternating messages: first "Hello!", then "Good-bye!", then "Hello!" again, and then "Good-bye!", "Hello!", and finally "Good-bye!". Each time around the loop the browser executes each individual line of code in the body of the loop in order.

Now we just need to write the "5 times" or "3 times" part in JavaScript. In this part we use a counter variable to tell the browser three things: what number to start the loop at, how long to keep looping, and how to increment the counter each time around the loop. For example, if we want to start the counter at 1, end the counter at 5, and add 1 to the counter each time around the loop, we would write:

```
var ctr
for (ctr = 1; ctr <= 5; ctr = ctr + 1) {
   alert("I deserve an A+!")
}
```

The expression in parentheses after the `for` on the first line has the JavaScript syntax for telling the browser the three things it needs to know. The first part of the expression is the assignment statement `ctr = 1`. This sets the starting value of the counter variable (which we named `ctr` in this case). The second part of the expression is the condition `ctr <= 5`. This defines the "continuing" condition for the loop. It tells the browser to keep looping as long as the value of `ctr` is less than or equal to 5. The third part of the expression is the assignment statement `ctr = ctr+1`, which tells the browser to increment the value of `ctr` by 1 each time around the loop. Note also the use of semicolons to separate the three items within the parentheses. Do not use commas!

To get a better idea of how a `for` loop works and what happens to the `ctr` variable as the loop executes, consider the following `for` loop step by step:

```
for (ctr = 1; ctr <= 3; ctr = ctr + 1) {
   alert("The value of ctr is: " + ctr)
}
```

Step 1 (Start): The browser starts executing the loop and sets the value of `ctr` to 1. It also checks the continuing condition (`ctr <= 3`) to see if it should continue with the body of the loop code. In this case the condition is true, because 1 is less than or equal to 3, so it proceeds into the loop.

Step 2 (Execute body of loop): The browser displays the alert box with the message "The value of ctr is: 1". If there were other lines of code following the `alert` command, the browser would execute them as well, in order.

Step 3 (Increment counter variable and check if should continue with loop): Then the browser comes to the end of the loop body (marked by the right curly brace). At that point it returns to the first `for` line and does two things. First, it executes the incrementing instruction, i.e., the `ctr=ctr+1`, so now `ctr` has the value 2. Second, it checks the continuing condition using the new value of `ctr` to see if it should continue with the loop. In this case the condition is true, because 2 is less than or equal to 3, so it proceeds into the loop again.

Steps 4 and 5: The browser repeats steps 2 and 3, but this time with `ctr` having the value 2. So the alert box displays the message "The value of ctr is: 2". Back at the top again, the incrementing instruction adds 1 to `ctr`, making it 3. The continuing condition is true (3 is less than or equal to 3), so it proceeds into the loop again.

Steps 5 and 6: The browser repeats steps 2 and 3, but this time with `ctr` having the value 3. So the alert message is "The value of ctr is: 3". Back at the top again, the incrementing instruction adds 1 to `ctr`, making it 4. And now the continuing condition is no longer true (4 is not less than or equal to 3). So the browser does not continue into the loop, but instead goes on to whatever code comes after the loop.

All this action is going on behind the scenes. The result that the surfer sees is simply three alert boxes, the first with the message:

The value of ctr is: 1

The second with the message:

The value of ctr is: 2

And the third:

The value of ctr is: 3

The convenience and power of `for` loops becomes clear if we decide we want to count to 100 instead of to 3. All we have to do is change the 3 to a 100:

```
for (ctr = 1; ctr <= 100; ctr = ctr + 1) {
    alert("The value of ctr is: " + ctr)
}
```

We change the incrementing condition if we want to count by some other number than 1. To increment the `ctr` variable by 2 each time, we write:

```
for (ctr = 1; ctr <= 100; ctr = ctr + 2) {
    alert("The value of ctr is: " + ctr)
}
```

The alert box messages in this case would be: "The value of ctr is: 1", "The value of ctr is: 3", "The value of ctr is: 5", and so on up to "The value of ctr is: 99". Note that even though the continuing condition says to continue as long as `ctr` is less than or equal to 100, the message "The value of ctr is: 100" will not appear. So you can't just look at the 100 in the continuing condition and assume that it will be the last value displayed. The last value displayed also depends on the incrementing instruction.

To display even numbers instead of odd numbers, we change the starting condition from 1 to 0:

```
for (ctr = 0; ctr <= 100; ctr = ctr + 2) {
    alert("The value of ctr is: " + ctr)
}
```

The alert box messages now would be: "The value of ctr is: 0", "The value of ctr is: 2", "The value of ctr is: 4", and so on up to "The value of ctr is: 100".

It's also possible to use a `for` loop to count backward. We simply write the incrementing assignment statement as a decrementing assignment statement. Instead of `ctr = ctr +1`, or `ctr = ctr + 2`, or whatever, we write `ctr = ctr -1` or `ctr = ctr - 2`, or whatever decrementing amount we want. The following loop displays alert box messages that count down from 100 to 0:

```
for (ctr = 100; ctr >= 0; ctr = ctr - 1) {
    alert("The value of ctr is: " + ctr)
}
```

The starting value of the counter variable for this loop is 100. The continuing condition is `ctr >= 0` (not less than or equal, as before). And the decrementing instruction is `ctr = ctr - 1`.

Most times, however, we need to count forward and increment the `ctr` variable by 1 each time. Many programmers like to use the increment or `++` operator in a `for` loop. You simply write: `ctr++`. Remember that this tells the browser to increment the value of `ctr` by 1 (see the section on "The Increment and Decrement Operators" in Chapter 11 for details). Used in a `for` loop, it looks like:

```
for (ctr = 1; ctr <= 100; ctr++) {
    alert("The value of ctr is: " + ctr)
}
```

Remember also that the increment operator may be used on a line by itself, as an alternative to `ctr = ctr + 1`:

```
var ctr = 5
ctr++
alert("The value of ctr is now: " + ctr)
```

Similarly, we may use the decrement operator (`--`) and write `ctr` as a substitute for `ctr = ctr - 1`.

A few syntax and error alerts regarding `for` loops: First, we have already mentioned that you must use semicolons between the starting and continuing conditions in a `for` loop and between the continuing condition and the incrementing instruction. The reason is that JavaScript uses semicolons to separate instructions that appear on the same line. Usually we write each JavaScript instruction on its own line, so we don't need to use a semicolon. But here we do, and they must be semicolons, not commas.

Second, the case-sensitive nature of JavaScript requires that in a for loop it's for, not For.

Third, in our examples above we used the variable name ctr for the counter variable. This is not a special name, however. It's simply the name we chose to use; we just as easily could have used count or counter or i or xyz or whatever (as long as it's a legal variable name). Many programmers use i or j for the name of the loop counter variable.

Fourth, although it's good practice to use the var keyword to officially declare the counter variable someplace in the code before the loop, it's not necessary. As discussed in the section "The Scope of a Variable" in Chapter 11, when the browser encounters an assignment statement like the starting condition in a for loop (e.g., ctr = 1), and the variable has not been declared previously, it automatically creates a new global variable with the given name.

Finally, note that the value of the counter variable after the for loop concludes is not necessarily the "stop" value of the continuing condition. In our step-by-step example above, we examined the following loop with a stop value of 3 (i.e., ctr <= 3):

```
for (ctr = 1; ctr <= 3; ctr = ctr + 1) {
   alert("The value of ctr is: " + ctr)
}
```

We saw that the last alert box is displayed when ctr has the value 3. Then ctr is incremented by 1 to make it 4, at which point the browser checks the continuing condition and finds it is false, so the loop ends. We can check the value of ctr after the loop is over by adding an alert method call after the loop:

```
for (ctr = 1; ctr <= 3; ctr = ctr + 1) {
   alert("The value of ctr is: " + ctr)}
alert("The post-loop value of ctr is: " + ctr)
```

When this code is executed the final message is "The post-loop value of ctr is: 4".

The while Loop

Unlike the for loop, the **while loop** iterates an indefinite number of times, which makes it the loop of choice in situations when you don't know in advance how many times to loop but want to keep looping until something happens, such as the value of a variable being changed. The basic form is:

```
while (some condition is true) {
   //Execute instructions listed here...
}
```

In loose English terms, a `while` loop says: as long as some test condition is true ("while" some test condition is true), keep executing the instructions within the loop. This test condition is therefore like the continuing condition of a `for` loop. But unlike a `for` loop, the `while` loop has no starting condition or incrementing instruction.

To demonstrate a simple but practical use of a `while` loop, we will use a prompt box to ask the surfer to guess a number from 1 to 10. If the surfer enters 7, then we will display an alert message "You win!". Otherwise, we will ask the surfer to guess again. (We considered a variation of this "guess-the-number" game in Lab Exercise 12.1, but without using the prompt box.)

We clearly have a situation here where we need to repeat the same code over and over again (the prompt box), so a loop would be recommended. But we don't know in advance how many times the loop will need to repeat, because we don't know how long it will take for the surfer to guess 7. We therefore can't use a `for` loop. A `while` loop, on the other hand, works perfectly. Here's one way to write the code with a `while` loop:

```
var theGuess, theNumber
theGuess = prompt("Enter a number from 1 to 10 and click
   OK:", "")
theNumber = parseFloat(theGuess)        //Convert string to
                                        //number
while (theNumber != 7) {
   theGuess = prompt("Enter a number from 1 to 10 and click
      OK:", "")
   theNumber = parseFloat(theGuess)
}
alert("You guessed it! It was 7.")
```

Breaking this down line by line, we first declare variables named `theGuess` and `theNumber` and prompt the surfer to enter a number from 1 to 10. The number the surfer enters is stored in `theGuess`. But because it came from a text box, it is stored as a string value. We therefore use the `parseFloat()` function to convert it to a number value and store it in the variable named `theNumber`. The test condition of the `while` loop then checks to see if `theNumber` is not equal to 7. If it is not 7, the condition is true and the code in the `while` loop is executed. That is, the prompt box is displayed again, the surfer enters another number, the number is converted from a string value to a number value, and we're back at the test condition of the loop again. If, at the test condition step, the number is equal to 7, then the test condition is false and the loop stops. The `alert()` command then displays the "You guessed it" message.

Note that the `while` loop may never be executed in this code. If the surfer enters 7 as the first guess, then the test condition of the `while` loop is false the first time, and the loop is skipped completely. Note also that the code seems a little redundant. We have two lines of code—the two assignment statements—

that are repeated. When you see something repeated like that, it's often possible to write it more compactly. In this case, we could write:

```
var theGuess, theNumber = 0
while (theNumber != 7) {
   theGuess = prompt("Enter a number from 1 to 10 and click
      OK:", "")
   theNumber = parseFloat(theGuess)
}
alert("You guessed it! It was 7.")
```

The key in this revised code is that we initialized the value of theNumber to 0 so that the while loop test condition is guaranteed to be true the first time. Then the body of the loop executes and the prompt box will appear, and so on.

It is also possible to write while loops that count like for loops, executing a set number of times. Although normally we would use a for loop in such a situation, we will show how to do so using a while loop, because it illustrates a key point concerning how while loops work.

In the last section we used a for loop to count 1, 2, 3 with the numbers appearing in successive alert boxes:

```
var ctr
for (ctr = 1; ctr <= 3; ctr++) {
   alert("The value of ctr is: " + ctr)
}
```

Here's the while loop version of that code:

```
var ctr = 1
while (ctr <= 3) {
   alert("The value of ctr is: " + ctr)
   ctr = ctr + 1
}
```

Because a while loop does not have a starting condition and an incrementing instruction built into it, we must supply them separately. The first line, var ctr = 1, sets the initial value of ctr. The last line in the body of the loop, ctr = ctr + 1, increments the value of ctr.

We may also get the same result by putting the incrementing line at the beginning of the loop and modifying the initializing line and the continue test condition:

```
var ctr = 0
while (ctr < 3) {
   ctr = ctr + 1
   alert("The value of ctr is: " + ctr)
}
```

We have to initialize the value of `ctr` to 0, because once inside the loop it first gets incremented by 1 before being displayed in the alert message. We also have to change the continue test condition from `ctr <= 3` in the previous code to `ctr < 3` in this code. To see why, let's look at how the browser executes this code step by step.

Step 1 (Initialization):

1. A variable named `ctr` is declared and assigned the value of 0.

Steps 2–5 (First time through the loop):

2. Check to see if `ctr` is less than 3. It is (it's equal to 0), so proceed with instructions in loop.

3. Add 1 to `ctr`, so now its value is 1.

4. Display value of `ctr` in an alert box (i.e., "The value of ctr is: 1").

5. End of loop, so go back to the beginning (i.e., the `while` line with the continue test condition).

Steps 6–9 (Second time through the loop):

Steps 2–5 are repeated, incrementing `ctr` by 1 and displaying the message "The value of ctr is: 2".

Steps 10–13 (Third time through the loop):

10. Check to see if `ctr` is less than 3. It is (it's equal to 2 at this point), so proceed with loop instructions.

11. Add 1 to `ctr`, so now it equals 3.

12. Display value of `ctr` in an alert box (i.e., "The value of ctr is: 3").

13. End of loop, so go back to the beginning (the `while` line).

Step 14 (Fourth time at the top of the loop):

14. Check to see if `ctr` is less than 3. It is not (it now equals 3), so skip the loop's instructions and continue on with whatever comes after the loop.

This loop therefore iterates three times, and displays three alert boxes with the messages "The value of ctr is: 1", "The value of ctr is: 2", and "The value of ctr is: 3."

We now can see the key point about `while` loops that we wanted to illustrate with this example. In step 11, note that `ctr` is no longer less than 3. In other words, the continue test condition of the loop (`ctr < 3`) is no longer true. But the loop does not end, because the browser doesn't "know" this yet: It hasn't come to the test condition line where it checks the value of `ctr`. It is only when it gets to step 14 that it performs the test and stops the loop.

We can draw another moral from this story as well. If you were to look at the `while` loop above and ask yourself what the screen output would look like

and, in particular, whether the message "The value of ctr is: 3" would be printed, you would probably think not. For is not the test condition "while (ctr < 3)"? But the message "The value of ctr is: 3" does get printed because of the lag between when ctr becomes 3 and when the browser gets back to checking the condition at the beginning of the loop.

You therefore have to be very careful when writing while loops that have a counter variable involved. It's very easy to write a loop that you think will iterate 10 times but that actually iterates 9 times or 11 times. This type of error is so common that it has a special name: an **off-by-one error**.

An incorrectly written while loop can also result in a so-called **infinite loop**. For instance (using a variable named counter this time):

```
counter = 0
while (counter < 2) {
   alert("The count is: " + counter)
   counter = counter − 2
}
```

The variable counter starts out with a value of 0, which satisfies the counter < 2 condition. Then in the loop we subtract 2 from its value every time around, so it will always be less than 2, and the alert() method will be executed over and over again.

Here's another example of an infinite loop:

```
counter = 1
while (counter <= 4) {
   alert("The count is: " + counter)
}
counter = counter + 1
```

This loop iterates endlessly because the counter = counter + 1 statement is not part of the while loop. As written, the while loop just contains the one alert statement. So counter will always be <= 4, the loop will never end, and the counter = counter + 1 line will never be executed. To make the counter = counter + 1 line part of the while loop, we of course have to put it inside the curly braces defining the statements belonging to the loop.

An infinite loop can also be generated with a for loop by changing the value of the counter variable inside the loop. For example:

```
for (ctr = 1; ctr <= 7; ctr++) {
   alert("The value of ctr is: " + ctr)
   ctr = 4
}
```

This code will display an alert box with the message "The value of ctr is: 1", but then the value of ctr is changed to 4. The browser will go back to the top of the for loop, where it increments ctr to 5, tests it and finds it is less than or equal to 7, and continues with the loop code. So next the message "The value

of ctr is: 5" will be displayed. But immediately after, the value of ctr is changed back to 4 and the whole process starts over. The value of ctr will therefore oscillate between 4 and 5, and the loop's continue condition will always be true. The result is an infinite loop. For these and other reasons, you should never change the value of a for loop's counter variable inside the loop.

The do-while Loop

The third type of JavaScript loop is the **do-while loop** (sometimes simply called the do loop). It works analogously to the while loop, except that the continue test condition is at the end of the loop instead of the beginning. The basic syntax is:

```
do {
   // JavaScript instructions go here...
} while (some condition is true)
```

The code inside the body of the loop (delineated by the curly braces) will continue to be executed until the condition is found to be false.

Our "guess-the-number" example using a while loop was:

```
var theGuess, theNumber = 0
while (theNumber != 7) {
   theGuess = prompt("Enter a number from 1 to 10 and click
     OK:", "")
   theNumber = parseFloat(theGuess)
}
alert("You guessed it! It was 7.")
```

We can equally well write this using a do-while loop:

```
var theGuess, theNumber
do {
   theGuess = prompt("Enter a number from 1 to 10 and click
     OK:", "")
   theNumber = parseFloat(theGuess)
} while (theNumber != 7)
alert("You guessed it! It was 7.")
```

The only difference, besides the loop itself, is that we don't need to initialize theNumber to 0, because it's not tested until the end of the loop.

We may use a counter variable with do-while loops as well. The following code displays 1, 2, and 3 in successive alert boxes:

```
var ctr = 1
do {
   alert("The value of ctr is: " + ctr)
```

```
    ctr = ctr + 1
  } while (ctr <= 3)
```

For comparison, the `while` loop version was:

```
  var ctr = 1
  while (ctr <= 3) {
    alert("The value of ctr is: " + ctr)
    ctr = ctr + 1
  }
```

QuickCheck **Questions**

1. Write a `for` loop that displays the integers 2 through 9 in successive alert boxes (the first alert message will be "The number is 2", the second will be "The number is 3", and so on).
2. Repeat #1, but using first a `while` loop and then a `do-while` loop.
3. Write the code that will display a prompt box with the message "Yes or No?" and store the user's response in a variable named `theAnswer`.
4. How many iterations will the following loops perform (i.e., how many times will the alert box appear)? What's the last number that will appear in the alert box?

Loop 1

```
var ctr = 0
while (ctr < 3) {
  ctr = ctr + 1
  alert(ctr)
}
```

Loop 2

```
var ctr
for (ctr = 0; ctr < 3;
ctr ++){
  alert(ctr)
}
```

Loop 3

```
var ctr = 0
while (ctr < 3) {
  alert(ctr)
  ctr = ctr + 1
}
```

Lab Exercise 14.1, "Going Around in Circles," may be done at this point.

Arrays

A very useful programming concept that is often used in concert with a loop is that of an **array**. Sometimes in a JavaScript program we need to store a series of variables. For instance, we might want to store the names of 20 students, or the answers to a series of 30 true–false questions. We could simply declare 20 separate string variables to store the student names and 30 separate boolean variables for the true–false answers, and so on. But JavaScript and most high-level programming languages provide a better way: a type of compound variable called an array.

Arrays as Cubbyholes

An array is an ordered collection of data. If a single variable is like a storage box, then an array is like a series of numbered boxes or cubbyholes, each of which stores one value. Instead of giving each cubbyhole a name (as we do with individual variables), we give the whole series of cubbyholes (the whole array) a name, and we refer to each individual cubbyhole, or **array element**, by a number starting with 0 (0, 1, 2, 3, 4, etc.). We then may store number, string, or boolean values in each element (Figure 14.1). We have actually already encountered this concept several times before: with image objects, radio buttons, and pop-up menus. Each of these uses a special type of array that's built in to JavaScript. Now, however, we want to create our own arrays.

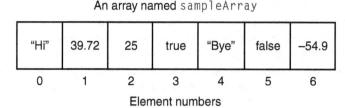

An array named `sampleArray`

"Hi"	39.72	25	true	"Bye"	false	−54.9
0	1	2	3	4	5	6

Element numbers

FIGURE 14.1. An array as a series of numbered cubbyholes or elements

Creating Arrays

Like image objects, we create arrays by calling a special **array constructor function** using the reserved word `new`. In this case, the constructor function is named `Array` instead of `Image`, and we send it the number of elements the array should have rather than the width and height of the image. We also of course have to give the array a variable name. Using the name `sampleArray` for the array, the code for a seven-element array like the one in Figure 14.1 is:

```
var sampleArray = new Array(7)
```

Three things about the syntax of this code: (a) the constructor function name `Array` on the right side must be capitalized; (b) they are parentheses, not square brackets, after the function name `Array`; and (c) we don't have to use the name `Array` in the variable name (we could have named it just `sample` instead of `sampleArray`).

We assign values to each element or cubbyhole of the array by referring to each element by its number, where the numbering system starts at 0. So the seven elements of our `sampleArray` are numbered from 0 to 6. As before, we put the number in square brackets immediately after the name.

```
sampleArray[0] = "Hi"
sampleArray[1] = 39.72
sampleArray[2] = 25
sampleArray[3] = true
sampleArray[4] = "Bye"
sampleArray[5] = false
sampleArray[6] = -54.9
```

When speaking, you say "The value of sampleArray sub 2 is 25" or "The value of sampleArray sub 4 is the word 'Bye'." That is, you use the word "sub" to indicate that it's an array element. (Some programmers use the word "index" instead of "sub," as in "The value of sampleArray index 2 is 25.")

We don't have to assign the values for each element in order. We could have filled the array equally as well by writing:

```
sampleArray[4] = "Bye"
sampleArray[6] = -54.9
sampleArray[3] = true
sampleArray[1] = 39.72
sampleArray[2] = 25
sampleArray[0] = "Hi"
sampleArray[5] = false
```

Note that, although in many cases all the elements of an array will be of the same variable type (that is, string, number, or boolean), they may also be of different types, as our example above shows. Many programming languages do not allow this diversity—they restrict an array's contents to values of all the same type.

JavaScript also allows you to increase the size of an array on the fly. For example, even though our sampleArray only has seven elements, numbered 0 through 6, we may write:

```
sampleArray[7] = 37
```

Most programming languages would choke at this point. They would not let you assign a value to an array element that did not exist or change the size of an array after it had been created. This restriction is not without good reason, because it sometimes works to keep you, the programmer, out of trouble. But in the case of JavaScript, it simply increases the size of the array on the fly, creating a new *eighth* element and assigning the value 37 to it. This goes by the fancy name of dynamic array addressing, with dynamic referring to the fact that the size of the array may be increased at any time.

If the array we need is not too large, JavaScript provides two other convenient ways to create and fill an array. Consider an array, for example, in which we want to store the abbreviated names of weekdays. We could use the array constructor to create it and then fill it using assignment statements:

```
var daysOfWeek = new Array(7)
daysOfWeek[0] = "Sun"
daysOfWeek[1] = "Mon"
daysOfWeek[2] = "Tue"
//etc.
```

The result would be an array as diagramed in Figure 14.2.

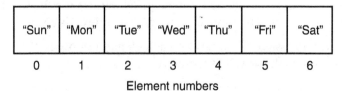

FIGURE 14.2. An array filled with the abbreviations for days of the week

But we can also create this array by passing the values of the array elements directly to the array constructor:

```
var daysOfWeek = new Array("Sun", "Mon", "Tue", "Wed",
    "Thu", "Fri", "Sat")
```

This line of code creates the `daysOfWeek` array and puts the value "Sun" into `daysOfWeek[0]`, the value "Mon" into `daysOfWeek[1]`, and so on.

Even better, we can dispense with the explicit call to the array constructor and simply list the array element values inside a pair of square brackets:

```
var daysOfWeek = ["Sun", "Mon", "Tue", "Wed", "Thu",
    "Fri", "Sat"]
```

These last two methods of creating and filling an array are, however, only available in JavaScript version 1.2 (or later), which was first included in Navigator version 4 and Explorer version 4.

Using Arrays with Loops

We can now see how arrays and loops work well together. If we wanted, for example, to write the value of each element of our previously created `sampleArray` in a series of alert boxes, we might do it with seven `alert()` commands:

```
alert(sampleArray[0])
alert(sampleArray[1])
alert(sampleArray[2])
```

```
alert(sampleArray[3])
alert(sampleArray[4])
alert(sampleArray[5])
alert(sampleArray[6])
```

But a for loop allows us to write this much more compactly:

```
var ctr
for (ctr = 0; ctr <= 6; ctr++) {
   alert(sampleArray[ctr])
}
```

Note how we use the variable ctr to refer to the array element; the first time through the loop ctr will have the value 0, and the value of sampleArray[0] will be displayed; the second time ctr will have the value 1, and the value of sampleArray[1] will be displayed, and so on until ctr is 6.

Loops are also often used to fill an array with its initial values. The following code will assign the value "Hello" to each of the seven elements of sampleArray:

```
var ctr
for (ctr = 0; ctr <= 6; ctr++) {
   sampleArray[ctr] = "Hello"
}
```

We also can initialize all the array values to 0 using a loop:

```
var ctr
for (ctr = 0; ctr <= 6; ctr++) {
   sampleArray[ctr] = 0
}
```

Sometimes we need to fill an array with numbers that follow a certain pattern, such as 0, 1, 2, 3, 4, and so on. A loop makes this easy. In order to fill sampleArray with the integers 0 through 6, we write:

```
var ctr
for (ctr = 0; ctr <= 6; ctr++) {
   sampleArray[ctr] = ctr
}
```

Note how the assignment statement works. For the first loop iteration, when the value of ctr is 0, it will be:

```
sampleArray[0] = 0
```

In other words, the value 0 will be assigned to the 0th element of the array. The next iteration the assignment statement will put the value 1 into the 1st element of the array:

```
sampleArray[1] = 1
```

And so on and so forth. The resulting array is shown in Figure 14.3.

The `sampleArray` array

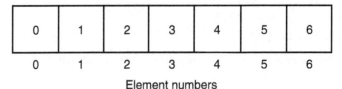

Element numbers

FIGURE 14.3.   An array filled with the numbers 0 through 6

If we wanted to fill the array with the integer values 1 through 7 instead of 0 through 6, we would write:

```
var ctr
for (ctr = 0; ctr <= 6; ctr++) {
    sampleArray[ctr] = ctr + 1
}
```

This loop is equivalent to the seven assignment statements:

```
sampleArray[0] = 1
sampleArray[1] = 2
sampleArray[2] = 3
sampleArray[3] = 4
sampleArray[4] = 5
sampleArray[5] = 6
sampleArray[6] = 7
```

When programmers use `for` loops like these, they sometimes prefer to write the continuing condition as `ctr < 7` instead of `ctr <= 6`:

```
var ctr
for (ctr = 0; ctr < 7; ctr++) {
    sampleArray[ctr] = ctr + 1
}
```

Both conditions give the same results, but the 7 is a visual reminder that the loop will iterate seven times.

QuickCheck Questions

1.   Show two ways to write the code that creates an array named `colors` and fills it with the values "blue", "red", "yellow", "green", "purple", and "orange".

2.   Write the code that creates a 10-element array named `someNumbers` and then uses a loop to fill the array with the numbers 10, 20, 30, 40, . . . 90, 100.

3.   Write a line of code that changes the value of the last element of the `someNumbers` array in #2 to 101.

Lab Exercise 14.2, "An Array of Greetings," may be done at this point.

The elements Array

Lab Exercise 14.2 gives some practice in the use of arrays and loops by using two arrays—one that stores five greetings and one that stores five names—to display personalized greetings in alert boxes. Now we want to improve this "Greetings" code by allowing the surfer to enter four names and four greetings in text boxes and then, when the surfer clicks a "Display!" button, we'll have JavaScript display the complete greetings in four output text boxes. (We use four instead of five greetings just to save a little space.) Figure 14.4 shows the <body> container code to implement this (minus the necessary JavaScript code, which we'll add below), and Figure 14.5 shows the corresponding display before and after the button has been clicked.

Note that we have used three different forms: one for the name text boxes (a form named namesForm with boxes n1Box, n2Box, and so on), one for the greetings text boxes (greetingsForm with g1Box, g2Box,...), and one for the output textboxes (outputForm with o1Box, o2Box,...). We'll see why that's useful in a minute. Note also that the onclick event handler for the button calls a function named displayGreetings() and passes it the document object as a parameter. This function will take the information stored in the first two forms (namesForm and greetingsForm), combine it together, and display it in the outputForm text boxes.

The code for this function will be:

```
function displayGreetings(d) {
    d.outputForm.o1Box.value = d.greetingsForm.g1Box.value
        + " " + d.namesForm.n1Box.value
    d.outputForm.o2Box.value = d.greetingsForm.g2Box.value
        + " " + d.namesForm.n2Box.value
    d.outputForm.o3Box.value = d.greetingsForm.g3Box.value
        + " " + d.namesForm.n3Box.value
    d.outputForm.o4Box.value = d.greetingsForm.g4Box.value
        + " " + d.namesForm.n4Box.value
}
```

Let's explore what's going on here. We declare the displayGreetings() function with a single formal parameter named d. This parameter will act as an alias for the document object, which is what is passed in the displayGreetings() function call in the onclick event handler. The first line of code in the function is an assignment statement that combines the value of the g1Box with the value of the n1Box, with a space between them, and puts the result in the o1Box:

```
d.outputForm.o1Box.value = d.greetingsForm.g1Box.value
    + " " + d.namesForm.n1Box.value
```

The rest of the code in the displayGreetings() function simply does the same thing for the second through fourth greetings and names.

```
sourcecode.htm - Notepad                    _ □ ×
File  Edit  Search  Help

<body>
<form id="namesForm" name="namesForm">
    Please enter four names in the boxes below: <br />
    <input type="text" name="n1Box" size="15">
    <input type="text" name="n2Box" size="15">
    <br />
    <input type="text" name="n3Box" size="15">
    <input type="text" name="n4Box" size="15">
</form>

<form id="greetingsForm" name="greetingsForm">
    Please enter four short greetings below: <br />
    <input type="text" name="g1Box" size="15">
    <input type="text" name="g2Box" size="15">
    <br />
    <input type="text" name="g3Box" size="15">
    <input type="text" name="g4Box" size="15">
    <p>
    <input type="button" value="Display!"
        onclick="displayGreetings(document)">
    </p>
</form>

<form id="outputForm" name="outputForm">
    <input type="text" name="o1Box" size="30">
    <br />
    <input type="text" name="o2Box" size="30">
    <br />
    <input type="text" name="o3Box" size="30">
    <br />
    <input type="text" name="o4Box" size="30">
</form>
</body>
```

**FIGURE 14.4.   HTML <body> code for the
Display Greetings web page**

You might think that this could get very tedious if we had a lot of greetings and names to display, and you'd be correct. Fortunately, JavaScript provides a way to make things a little more compact via its built-in **elements array**.

If you think about it, an HTML form is like an array. It has a certain number of input elements that store information (for example, five text boxes, three

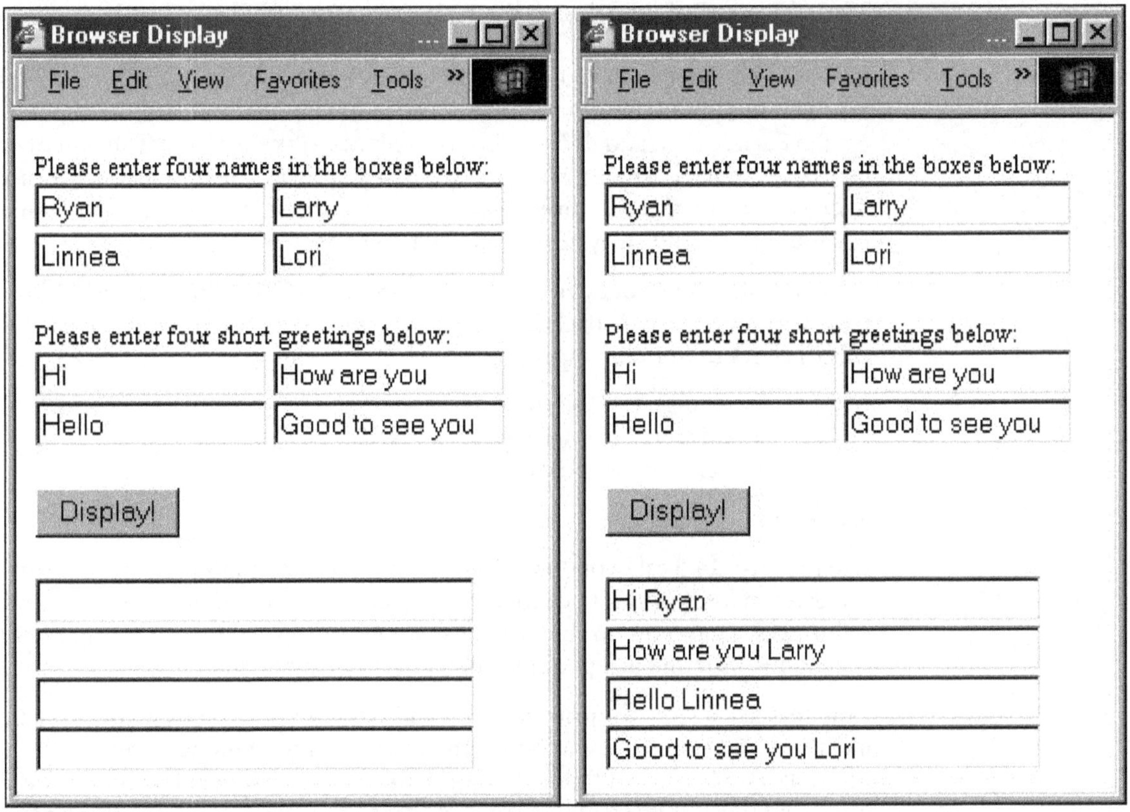

FIGURE 14.5. **The Display Greetings web page before and after the button has been clicked**

radio buttons, etc.). And, in fact, JavaScript treats forms like arrays. In particular, instead of referring to a given form element by its name, we can refer to it by a number—its position in the form.

That is, when we create a form, JavaScript creates an array of the elements in the form: The first input element defined within a `<form>` container is the 0th element of the so-called `elements` array, the second is the 1st element of the `elements` array, and so on. This is exactly analogous to how radio buttons work, except that it's the form elements that are being numbered, not the radio buttons. As with all arrays in JavaScript, the numbering system begins with 0, not 1. An example shows how this works. Instead of writing, as we did above,

```
d.outputForm.o1Box.value = d.greetingsForm.g1Box.value + " "
    + d.namesForm.n1Box.value
```

we can write:

```
d.outputForm.elements[0].value =
  d.greetingsForm.elements[0].value + " "
    + d.namesForm.elements[0].value
```

That is, instead of referring to the o1Box element of outputForm by its given name, we can refer to it by d.outputForm.elements[0], i.e., the o1Box text box is the 0th element in outputForm. (Remember that d is the formal parameter representing the document object; the actual names are document. outputForm.o1Box and document.outputForm.elements[0].) The other two text boxes may be written using the elements array for their respective forms: d.greetingsForm.g1Box may be written d.greetingsForm.elements[0] and d.namesForm.n1Box may be written d.namesForm.elements[0].

Similarly, the references in the function's second line of code to o2Box, g2Box, and n2Box may each be replaced with elements[1], because each is the *1st* element in their respective forms:

```
d.outputForm.elements[1].value =
   d.greetingsForm.elements[1].value + " "
   + d.namesForm.elements[1].value
```

And so on.

Lab Exercise 14.3 asks you to finish rewriting the function's code by replacing the given names of the text boxes with their corresponding elements array references. Once you do that, the next step is to replace the four assignment statements with one assignment statement inside a for loop.

Note that the elements array numbers and references all the elements within a form, not just text boxes. If a form named testForm was used to a create a check box, followed by a set of three radio buttons and then two text boxes, the check box could be referenced as document.testForm.elements[0]; the three radio buttons could be referenced as document.testForm.elements[1], document. testForm.elements[2], and document.testForm.elements[3]; and the text boxes would be document.testForm.elements[4] and document.testForm. elements[5].

Do not confuse the elements array with the term "array element." Array element is a general term that applies to all arrays. It refers to the array's cubby-holes and their contents. The elements array is a special JavaScript array that indexes the elements in an HTML form.

QuickCheck Questions

1. Consider a form named outputForm with five text boxes in it. Using the elements array, write the code that would assign the value "Hello" to the first text box and the value "Good-bye" to the last text box.

2. Consider a form named messageForm with 10 text boxes in it. Using the elements array and a for loop, write the code that would assign the value 1 to the first text box, 2 to the second text box, and so on up to 10 to the tenth text box.

3. What is the difference between an array element and the elements array?

Lab Exercise 14.3, "Revising the Array of Greetings," may be done at this point.

More with Loops and Arrays

In Chapter 11, in the section "Implementing a Simple Calculator," we wrote a function that received three numbers as input, calculated their average, and then returned the result. One version of the function was:

```
function calculateAverage(num1,num2,num3) {
  var average
  average = (num1+num2+num3)/3
  return average
}
```

A second, shorter version was:

```
function calculateAverage(num1,num2,num3) {
  return (num1+num2+num3)/3
}
```

Whichever version we use, however, the function has a major shortcoming: It can only calculate an average for three numbers. We can fix this problem by using an array and a loop. Instead of sending the numbers to be averaged to the function separately, we will first store them in an array and then send the whole array to the function. We will also send the number of numbers to be averaged to the function as a second parameter. The function will use a `for` loop to sum the numbers in the array, after which it will divide the sum by the number of numbers to get the average.

Improving the calculateAverage() Function

The code below shows the function. The first parameter, `theNumbers`, receives the array of numbers; the second parameter, `numNumbers`, receives the value for how many numbers are in the array:

```
function calculateAverage(theNumbers, numNumbers) {
  var sum = 0, ctr, average
  for (ctr=0; ctr<=numNumbers-1; ctr++) {
    sum = sum + theNumbers[ctr]
  }
  average = sum/numNumbers
  return average
}
```

If we had an array named `examScores` filled with 5 numbers (the exam scores), then we would call this function as follows:

```
var averageScore
averageScore = calculateAverage(examScores, 5)
```

Note two things about the `for` loop in the function. First, the continuing condition is `ctr <= numNumbers - 1`. The end point is not `numNumbers` but

one less than `numNumbers` because of course the array numbering system starts at 0. So if there were five numbers in the array (making `numNumbers` equal to 5), then the `ctr` variable in the loop would go from 0 to 4. That is, the five numbers are stored in cubbyholes 0 through 4 in the array.

Second, the assignment statement

```
sum = sum + theNumbers[ctr]
```

in the body of the loop shows how we sum up the values in an array. To see how this works, imagine that the array holds the three numbers 5, 9, and 2, as shown in Figure 14.6. (Elements 3 through 6 in the array are empty.)

The `theNumbers` array

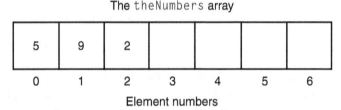

Element numbers

FIGURE 14.6.　A seven-element array with three numbers stored in it

The purpose of the variable named `sum`, which is initialized to 0 in the function, is to hold a running total of the sum of the array's values.

The first time through the loop, when `ctr = 0` (and `sum = 0`), the right side of the `sum` assignment statement will be `0 + theNumbers[0]`, or `0 + 5`. So the new value of `sum` will be 5.

The second time through the loop, when `ctr = 1`, the right side of the assignment statement will be `5 + theNumbers[1]`, or `5 + 9`. So the new value of `sum` will be 14.

The third time through the loop, when `ctr = 2`, the right side of the assignment statement will be `14 + theNumbers[2]`, or `14 + 2`. So the new value of `sum` is 16, and then the loop stops.

The forms Array

We started this chapter by considering how we might create a multiple-choice test that either is, or works like, a personality test. To score such a test, we tally the number of times the test-taker chose each of the three possible answers, (a), (b), and (c). Assuming that the three answers were represented by a set of three radio buttons named `choiceRB` and that each question was coded in a separate form, named `question1`, `question2`, etc., then the conditional statement to check the first question is:

```
var scoreA = 0, scoreB = 0, scoreC = 0
if (document.question1.choiceRB[0].checked) {
   scoreA = scoreA + 1
}
else if (document.question1.choiceRB[1].checked) {
   scoreB = scoreB + 1
}
else if (document.question1.choiceRB[2].checked) {
   scoreC = scoreC + 1
}
```

And the conditional statement to check the second question is:

```
if (document.question2.choiceRB[0].checked) {
   scoreA = scoreA + 1
}
else if (document.question2.choiceRB[1].checked) {
   scoreB = scoreB + 1
}
else if (document.question2.choiceRB[2].checked) {
   scoreC = scoreC + 1
}
```

Similar conditional statements would be used to check the questions that followed. The more questions, the more conditional statements. We noted before, however, that these conditional statements are very similar, the only difference being the name of the form (question1 vs. question2 vs. question3 vs. etc.). With the help of another built-in JavaScript array—the **forms array**—we can replace the whole series of conditional statements with one conditional statement inside a for loop.

The forms array works as does the elements array, except that it numbers all the forms in the document rather than all the elements in an individual form. As an example, we may refer to the question1 form in our example using its given name: document.question1. But, assuming this form is the first form in the source document, we may also refer to it using the forms array: document.forms[0]. The full name of the last (of three) radio buttons in the first form may then be written: document.forms[0]. choiceRB[2]. Similarly, assuming that the question2 form is the second form listed in the source document, we may refer to it as document. forms[1], and its first radio button would be document.forms[1]. choiceRB[0]. And so on and so forth for all of the question forms.

We may also use references to both the forms array and the elements array in referring to a form element. If the first form in the document defined two text boxes and then two check boxes, the text boxes would have the names document.forms[0].elements[0] and document.forms[0].elements[1] and the check boxes would be document.forms[0].elements[2] and `document.forms[0].elements[3]`. In other words, we don't need to know the given names of the form or the input elements in the form. All we need to know is the number of the form within the document and the number of the input element within that form. On the other hand, don't overdo the use of the `forms` and `elements` arrays because, in the absence of the given names, the code is often harder to read and understand. The `forms` and `elements` arrays are best used when you need their numbering systems to employ a loop.

Exercise 11 asks you to rewrite the above conditional statements for `question1` and `question2` using the forms array, and Lab Exercise 14.4 provides practice creating a simple (and simplistic) personality test.

QuickCheck Questions

1. Consider a 50-element array named `examPoints`, which stores the number of points a student received on each of 50 questions. Write the code that would sum the total number of points and store it in a variable named `totalPoints`.

2. Consider a document with five forms in it, each of which has a text box named `messageBox`. Using the `forms` array, write the code that would assign the value "Hello" to the `messageBox` belonging to the first form and the value "Good-bye" to the `messageBox` belonging to the last form.

Lab Exercise 14.4, "A Personality Test," may be done at this point.

Key Terms

array	elements array	off-by-one error
array constructor function	for loop	while loop
array elements	forms array	
do-while loop	infinite loop	

Code Summary

1. Three Types of Loops

A basic `for` loop that displays the numbers 1, 2, and 3 in successive alert boxes:

```
var ctr
for (ctr = 1; ctr <= 3; ctr=ctr+1) {
    alert("The value of ctr is: " + ctr)
}
```

A `for` loop that counts to 100 and uses the increment operator (ctr++):

```
for (ctr = 1; ctr <= 100; ctr++) {
    alert("The value of ctr is: " + ctr)
}
```

A `for` loop that counts by 2s:

```
for (ctr = 0; ctr <= 100; ctr=ctr+2) {
   alert("The value of ctr is: " + ctr)
}
```

A `for` loop that counts backwards from 100 to 0:

```
for (ctr = 100; ctr >= 0; ctr=ctr-1) {
   alert("The value of ctr is: " + ctr)
}
```

Using a `while` loop to count to 3:

```
var ctr = 1
while (ctr <= 3) {
   alert("The value of ctr is: " + ctr)
   ctr = ctr + 1
}
```

Using a prompt box and a `while` loop to code a simple "Guess the Number" game:

```
var theGuess, theNumber = 0
while (theNumber != 7) {
   theGuess = prompt("Enter a number from 1 to 10 and click OK:", "")
   theNumber = parseFloat(theGuess)
}
alert("You guessed it! It was 7.")
```

Using a `do-while` loop to count to 3:

```
var ctr = 1
do {
   alert("The value of ctr is: " + ctr)
   ctr = ctr + 1
} while (ctr <= 3)
```

2. Arrays

Creating an array named `sampleArray` with five elements:

```
var sampleArray = new Array(5)
```

Assigning values to the five array elements (in no particular order):

```
sampleArray[0] = "Hi there!"
sampleArray[4] = 26.3
sampleArray[3] = false
sampleArray[1] = "Fred"
sampleArray[2] = 12
```

Creating an array by sending the array values directly to the array constructor:

```
var daysOfWeek = new Array("Sun", "Mon", "Tue", "Wed", "Thu", "Fri", "Sat")
```

Creating an array without using the array constructor at all:

```
var daysOfWeek = ["Sun", "Mon", "Tue", "Wed", "Thu", "Fri", "Sat"]
```

Using a `for` loop to assign the same value "Hello" to the five elements of `sampleArray`:

```
var ctr
for (ctr = 0; ctr <= 4; ctr++) {
   sampleArray[ctr] = "Hello"
}
```

Using a `for` loop to assign the values 0, 1, 2, 3, and 4 to the five elements of `sampleArray`:

```
var ctr
for (ctr = 0; ctr <= 4; ctr++) {
```

```
        sampleArray[ctr] = ctr
    }
```

3. The elements Array

Referring to the third element (e.g., a text box) in a form named `outputForm` using the built-in `elements` array instead of the element's given name:

```
document.outputForm.elements[2].value = "You win!"
```

4. More with Loops and Arrays

Summing number values stored in an array, where `numNumbers` is the number of array values and `theNumbers` is the name of the array:

```
for (ctr=0; ctr<=numNumbers-1; ctr++) {
    sum = sum + theNumbers[ctr]
}
```

Referring to the fourth form in a document using the built-in `forms` array instead of the form's given name:

```
document.forms[3].messageBox.value = "You win!"
```

Use semi-colons, not commas, to separate the three items within the parentheses of a `for` loop (the starting condition, the continuing condition, and the incrementing statement).

Remember that JavaScript is case sensitive, so it's `for` not `For` in a `for` loop.

After a loop has finished executing, the value of the loop counter variable is not necessarily the stop value of the loop's continuing condition.

Just because the counter variable in a loop has a value that makes the loop's continuing condition false (i.e., it's time to stop iterating), the loop does not necessarily stop immediately. It only stops when the condition is checked (at the top of a loop for a `while` loop and at the end of a loop for a `do-while` loop).

Watch out for off-by-one errors in writing loops and reading them in your mind.

Watch out for infinite loops, such as when the incrementing condition in a `while` (or `do-while`) loop is not in the body of the loop.

Never change the value of a `for` loop's counter variable inside the loop.

In using the array constructor, make sure to capitalize `Array` and use parentheses (not square brackets) correctly.

Do not confuse the `elements` array with the term array element. Array element is a general term that applies to all arrays. The `elements` array is a special JavaScript array that indexes the elements in an HTML form.

When using a loop to cycle through the values of an array, remember that the numbering system starts at 0, not 1.

1. Which of the following are types of loops in JavaScript?
    a. `while`
    b. `repeat`
    c. `iterate`
    d. `do-while`

2. Which of the following loops is guaranteed to always execute its code at least once?
   a. for
   b. repeat
   c. do-while

3. How many times will the alert box in the following loop appear?
```
for (ctr=0; ctr<4; ctr++){
    alert("Anybody home?")
}
```
   a. 0
   b. 3
   c. 4
   d. infinite

4. How many times will the alert box in the following loop appear?
```
while (ctr<=5){
    ctr=0
    alert("Anybody home?")
}
```
   a. 0
   b. 3
   c. 4
   d. infinite

5. How many times will the alert box in the following loop appear?
```
for (ctr-0; ctr<5; ctr=ctr+3){
    alert("Anybody home?")
}
```
   a. 0
   b. 2
   c. 3
   d. 4

6. Which of the following lines of code creates an array named phoneNumbers with 50 elements?
   a. var phoneNumbers = array(50)
   b. var phoneNumbers[50] = array
   c. var phoneNumbers = new Array(50)
   d. var phoneNumbers = new Array[49]
   e. var phoneNumbers = newarray(50)

7. Which of the following lines of code assigns the value 51.9 to the seventh element of an array named theResults?
   a. theResults[6] = 51.9
   b. theResults.value[6] = 51.9
   c. theResults[6].value = 51.9
   d. theResults[7].value = 51.9
   e. theResults[7] = 51.9
   f. theResults(7) = 51.9

8. True or false: In JavaScript, all the values in an array must be of the same type (either all numbers, all strings, or all booleans).

9. Consider a form named messageForm with three textboxes named box1, box2, and box3. Which of the following lines of code assigns the value "Good decision" to box3? (More than one may be correct)
   a. document.box3.value = "Good decision"
   b. document.messageForm.elements[2].value = "Good decision"
   c. document.element[3].value = "Good decision"
   d. document.messageForm.elements[3].value = "Good decision"

10. Consider a source document with three unnamed forms. The second form has four textboxes named `firstBox`, `secondBox`, `thirdBox`, and `fourthBox`. Which of the following lines of code assigns the value "Nice choice" to `fourthBox`? (More than one may be correct.)

   a. `document.secondform.fourthBox.value = "Nice choice"`

   b. `document.forms[1].elements[3].value = "Nice choice"`

   c. `document.forms[1].fourthBox.value = "Nice choice"`

   d. `document.forms[2].elements[4].value = "Nice choice"`

   e. `document.forms[2].fourthBox.value = "Nice choice"`

1. Briefly define and/or explain the following terms: decrement operator, off-by-one error, array constructor.

2. Write the code for a `for` loop that displays a number of alert boxes in sequence, with the first box containing the message "Counting by fives: 5", the second containing the message "Counting by fives: 10", and so on up to the last box containing the message "Counting by fives: 50". Then use another `for` loop to display another sequence of alert boxes, but counting backward by 10s from 50 to 0. The first message in the new sequence should be "Counting backward by tens: 50", then "Counting backward by tens: 40", and so on to the last message, "Counting backward by tens: 0".

3. Repeat Exercise 2 using a `while` loop.

4. Repeat Exercise 2 using a `do-while` loop.

5. Describe what the following loops will display:

Loop A:
```
var ctr
for (ctr = 1; ctr <= 6; ctr = ctr + 2) {
   alert("The count is: " + ctr)
}
```

Loop B:
```
var counter = 1
while (counter < 5) {
   alert("The count is: " + counter)
}
```

Loop C:
```
var count = 1
do {
   alert("The count is: " + count)
} while (count == 5)
```

6. Write the JavaScript code that creates three arrays, each with 100 elements. Name the arrays `countingNumbers`, `evenNumbers`, and `oddNumbers`. Then use a `for` loop to fill the `countingNumbers` array with the numbers 1 to 100, another `for` loop to fill the `evenNumbers` array with the numbers 2 to 200, and a third `for` loop to fill the `oddNumbers` array with the numbers 1 to 199.

7. Write the JavaScript code that uses a prompt box to ask the surfer to enter a number from 2 to 10. Then create an array with that number of elements (that is, whatever number the surfer entered) and use a `for` loop to fill the array completely with random numbers between 0 and 1. (Use the random number function covered in Chapter 11.)

8. Modify the code in Exercise 7 so that the array is filled with random numbers equal to either 0 or 1. Taking 0 to represent heads and 1 to represent tails, the array of values then represents the flipping of a coin for a certain number of times (as specified by the surfer). Use a loop and a conditional statement to count how many times heads (0) appears in the array and display the total number of flips (the number of elements in the array) and the number of heads in an alert box.

9. Consider a form named `infoForm` that defines three check boxes, then a click button, and finally two text boxes. Using the `elements` array, write the code for a conditional statement that tests if the third check box is checked. If it is, the message "Good choice!" should be displayed in the first text box. If it isn't checked, the message "What about choice 3?" should be displayed in the *second* text box.

10. Write the code for a function named `maxValue()` with two parameters, named `theArray` and `numValues`. The function should use a loop and a conditional statement to find the maximum value in the array and then return that value.

11. Rewrite the `question1` and `question2` conditional statements at the beginning of the section "The forms Array" so that they use the `forms` array. Then rewrite them again using a `for` loop so that the code only has one conditional statement (inside the loop). Show the change you would make to the loop if there were 25 questions instead of just 2.

Debugging Exercise

Identify and correct the errors in the following code. The page is designed to have the surfer enter four numbers, one in each text box, and then click the button. The `calculate()` function is then supposed to calculate the sum and average of the four numbers, using a `for` loop in combination with the `elements` array to calculate the sum. Finally, it displays the results in two text boxes.

```
<html>
<head>
<script type="text/javascript">
   function calculate(f) {
      var sum, ctr
      for (ctr = 0, ctr <= 4, ctr++) {
         sum = elementsArray[ctr].value
      }
      f.sumBox.value = sum
      f.averageBox.value = sum/4
   }
</script>
</head>

<body>
Please enter four numbers in the boxes below:<br />
<form id="numbersForm" name="numbersForm">
   <input type="text" name="num1Box" size="5"><br />
   <input type="text" name="num2Box" size="5"><br />
   <input type="text" name="num3Box" size="5"><br />
   <input type="text" name="num4Box" size="5">
   <p>
   <input type="button" value="Calculate Sum and Average"
      onclick ="calculate(document)">
   <p>
   The sum is: <input type="text" name="sumBox" size="6"><br />
   The average is; <input type="text" name="averageBox" size="6"><br />
</form>
</body>
</html>
```

Note: Most of the exercises above may also be done as lab exercises. If a problem involves a function, add a function call so that the function code is actually executed.

Exercise 14.1: Going Around in Circles

❏ Create a source document that implements a "Guess my Birthday" game, as follows. Define two global variables, one named `birthMonth` and one named `birthDate`, and assign a month (in all lowercase letters) to the first and a date to the second (for example, for a birthday on September 15, the value of `birthMonth` would be set to "september" and the value of `birthDate` would be set to 15). Using a prompt box, the surfer should first be asked to enter a month of the year. The code should use a `while` loop to keep asking the surfer to enter a month until it matches the preset month. (Tip: You will want to use the `toLowerCase()` method to change the entered month to all lowercase letters before the code checks it for a match.)

❏ Once the surfer guesses the correct month, use a second prompt box and loop to ask the surfer to enter the day of the month (from 1 to 31; assume that the surfer knows how many days each month has—don't worry about reminding the surfer how many days the month in question has).

❏ Add a global variable named `guessCounter` to the code that keeps track of how many guesses it takes the surfer to guess the correct birthday. Display this number in an alert box with an appropriate message at the end.

❏ Optional: Add a conditional statement to the code that will give the surfer hints when he or she is trying to guess the day of the month. If the guess is too high, display an alert box that says "Too high. Try again.", and similarly for a guess that is too low. If you like, do the same for guessing the month.

Exercise 14.2: An Array of Greetings

❏ As a beginning exercise that combines arrays and loops, consider the following code for a `<body>` element (note the comments):

```
<body>
<strong>Greetings to Friends!</strong><br />
<script type="text/javascript">
/*The following instructions create an array named greetings with five elements and store
various greetings in elements 0 to 4 of the array*/
   var greetings = new Array(5)
   greetings[0] = "Hi "
   greetings[1] = "Hello "
   greetings[2] = "How are you, "
   greetings[3] = "Good to see you, "
   greetings[4] = "Have a good day, "
/*The following instructions create an array named names with five elements and store var-
ious names in elements 0 to 4 of the array*/
   var names = new Array(5)
   names[0] = "John"
   names[1] = "Jack"
   names[2] = "Jenny"
   names[3] = "Jill"
   names[4] = "Jake"
/*The following instructions write the first greeting and then the first name in an alert
box, then the second greeting and the second name in the next alert box, and so on*/
   alert(greetings[0] + names[0])
   alert(greetings[1] + names[1])
   alert(greetings[2] + names[2])
   alert(greetings[3] + names[3])
   alert(greetings[4] + names[4])
</script>
</body>
```

❑ Create a source document named GreetingsArray.htm with the code above and load it into the browser to see how it works (and catch any errors you may have made).

❑ Replace the five alert commands in the code with a `for` loop.

❑ Add a sixth greeting and a sixth name to the script (that is, change the arrays and the `for` loop so that they work with six names and greetings).

Exercise 14.3: Revising the Array of Greetings

❑ Create a source document named ImprovedGreetings.htm with the `<body>` element code from Figure 14.3 and the declaration for the corresponding `displayGreetings()` function in the `<head>` element (the version that uses the `elements` array).

❑ Once you have the ImprovedGreetings.htm document working, comment out the four lines of code in the `displayGreetings()` function. (Don't delete them; just comment them out using `/*` and `*/`.) Replace the original four lines of code with a `for` loop.

❑ Optional: To get further practice with loops and arrays, add the appropriate input and output text boxes and change the code so that the surfer can type in five greetings and five names and have five complete greetings displayed, instead of just four.

Exercise 14.4: A Personality Test

❑ Create a source document named PersonalityTest.htm that implements a simplistic personality test using the three questions below. (To save typing, you may wish to save a copy of the Apollo Quiz document you worked on in Lab Exercise 13.1 and rename it PersonalityTest.htm. Just make sure that you change all the form and element names appropriately.) Include a "Score my answers" click button that, when clicked, calls a function that uses a `for` loop and the `forms` array to total the number of (a) answers, (b) answers, (c) answers, and (d) answers and then displays the totals in four text boxes. The text box displaying the total for the (a) answers should be labeled "Your Spring Personality score (out of 3) is:"; the (b) answers total should be labeled "Your Summer Personality score (out of 3) is:"; the (c) answers total should be labeled "Your Fall Personality score (out of 3) is:"; and the (d) answers total should be labeled "Your Winter Personality score (out of 3) is:".

Question 1: Which of the following colors do you like best?

    a. Green

    b. Yellow

    c. Red

    d. Blue

Question 2: What is your favorite mealtime?

    a. Breakfast

    b. Lunch

    c. Dinner

    d. Midnight snack

Question 3: Which of the following sports do you like best (either to watch or to participate)?

    a. Golf

    b. Baseball

    c. Football

    d. Skiing

Strings, Dates, and Cookies

LEARNING OBJECTIVES

1. Understand the difference between validating and verifying input information and how JavaScript is well-suited for validation.

2. Learn how the `length` property and `substring()` and `charAt()` methods of string objects may be used to validate a surfer's identification number.

3. Learn how to find and display the current time using the `Date` object.

4. Learn how to use cookies to store information for later use.

Validation vs. Verification

There are often times in designing an interactive web page when we need to validate and/or verify a surfer's input. Consider the case of a password-protected site where passwords must be between four and ten characters long and must contain at least one character other than a letter of the alphabet. (Such restrictions are common in order to make it harder for someone else to guess what a password might be.) When a user enters a password into a text box, the password is usually first **validated**—it is checked to see if it meets the restrictions. Then, if the password entered by the user is a valid entry, it must be **verified**—it must be checked to see whether it is an actual password, usually by looking it up in a database of current passwords.

Verifying a password requires that it be sent back to the web page's server, where the database resides. Although it is possible to use JavaScript for such server-side transactions, they also require more sophisticated programming techniques and other programming languages (for example, so-called CGI scripts) that are beyond the scope of this book. JavaScript is well-suited, however, for the process of validating a password, because all the necessary computing can take place solely on the user's computer (the client).

Validating an Identification Number

In order to investigate how JavaScript may be used to validate a surfer's entry and as a final touch to the interactive quiz we developed in Chapter 13, we will add two text boxes at the beginning of the quiz for the surfer to enter his or her name and a student identification (SID) number.

In the case of the student identification number, we want to make sure that the surfer enters a valid SID number, which we will assume is eight digits, with no alphabetical or other characters. So what we need to do is (a) check the length of the string containing the SID to see if it's eight characters long, and (b) check each character in the surfer's entry to see if it is a number between 0 and 9.

Strings as Objects

Fortunately, JavaScript provides several helps for us to do this. As we saw in Chapter 13, in the section "Improving the Write-in Code", a string variable in JavaScript is actually a string object, and this object has a number of attached methods plus a single property. There are 30 string methods, allowing the programmer not only to do such things as change the case of the string but also search through a string for a given character and/or replace it with another character. (See the table of JavaScript objects in Appendix F for a complete list.)

The one property of a string object is `length`, which stores the number of characters in the string. The following code would display an alert box with the message "The length of the string is 12":

```
var numberCharacters
var myString = "Hello, Fred!"
numberCharacters = myString.length
alert("The length of the string is " + numberCharacters)
```

Note that each space and punctuation mark or other special character counts as one character.

If, in the case of the SID number, we have a text box named `SIDBox` that belongs to a form named `surferInfo`, then `document.surferInfo.SIDBox.value.length` contains the length of whatever is in the `SIDBox`, that is, the number of characters it has. So we can see that it is easy to check if the entered SID has the correct number of characters: We use a conditional statement to check if `document.surferInfo.SIDBox.value.length` equals 8.

The substring() and charAt() Methods

Every string object also has a method named `substring()`, which will extract a given character, or sequence of characters, from a string. This is exactly what we need to check each individual digit in the user's SID to see if it is between 0 and 9, inclusive. The idea is to extract each individual character in turn and check to see if it is a number between 0 and 9. If one of them isn't, then we will display a warning message and ask the surfer to enter the SID number again. Let's look first at how we use the `substring()` method to extract a character from a string.

Assuming that we have a string variable named `myString` and another string variable named `theChar`, then the syntax for extracting the first character of `myString` and storing it in `theChar` is:

```
theChar = myString.substring(0,1)
```

In English this says: Use the `substring()` method to pull out the character in the 0th position of `myString` (i.e., the first character in the string—as usual, JavaScript starts numbering with 0, not 1) and store it in the variable named `theChar`. Note also that the method's name is `substring`, not `subString`.

If we wanted to pull out the first two characters of `myString` and store them in a variable named `moreChars`, the code would be:

```
moreChars = myString.substring(0,2)
```

So if `myString` contained the value "How are you?", then this line of code would result in `moreChars` having the value "Ho".

Another example: If we wanted to pull out the third through seventh characters of `myString` and store them in `moreChars`, the code would be:

```
moreChars = myString.substring(2,7)
```

And, assuming again that `myString` contained the value "How are you?", `moreChars` would have the value "w are".

To summarize: in the `substring(x,y)` method the first parameter (x) tells the starting position of the substring to extract from the string (counting from 0), and the second parameter (y) gives the ending position *plus one* of the substring. A quick way to tell how many characters the `substring()` method will extract is to subtract x from y. For instance, `myString.substring(2,5)` will start at position 2 in the string (the third character) and extract $5 - 2 = 3$ characters.

INFORMATION

If we only need to extract one character from a string, we may also use the `charAt()` method of the string object. To pull out the third character in a string (at position 2) and store it in a variable named `theChar`, we write:

```
theChar = myString.charAt(2)
```

Note that when we say we are "extracting" or "pulling out" a character or characters from a string, we really mean that we are pulling out a copy and storing it someplace else. That is, using the substring() and charAt() methods does not reduce the number of characters in a string.

Validating the Surfer's Identification Number

Now let's see how we can apply the substring() method to validate the surfer's student identification number (SID). (We equally well could use the charAt() method.) We will assume that we've defined a form named surferInfo at the beginning of our ApolloQuiz.html source document and that this form contains two text boxes named nameBox and SIDBox. The SID will therefore be stored in document.surferInfo.SIDBox.value.

We want to use the substring() method to extract the first character in the SID string, check to see if it's a number from 0 to 9, and then, if it isn't, put an alert box on the screen asking the surfer to enter a valid SID. If the first character is okay, then we want to check the second character, and so on, up until the eighth and last character.

We extract the first character of the SID string by applying the substring() method to the value property of the text box (which of course is a string):

```
theChar = document.surferInfo.SIDBox.value.substring(0, 1)
```

After we have extracted the character and stored it in theChar, we use a conditional statement to check if it's a character between "0" and "9". Note that we put quotation marks around the digits here, because these are characters, not regular numbers. So the conditional statement, with the alert() method, looks like:

```
if ((theChar < "0") || (theChar > "9")) {
   alert("Invalid SID! No non-number characters allowed.")
}
```

This conditional statement checks to see if the value of theChar is less than "0" *or* greater than "9". If either of those conditions is true, then theChar cannot be one of the values "0", "1", . . . "9", and the alert() method is called to put the warning message on the screen.

You might be wondering how one character can be "less than" another character. The answer is that JavaScript is actually comparing the **ASCII numbers** of the characters. ASCII (pronounced "ask-kee", and standing for the American Standard Code for Information Interchange) assigns every character a number in an organized fashion, and it is set up so that the character "0" has a lower ASCII number than the character "1", which has a lower ASCII number than the character "2", and so on.

Similarly, the ASCII numbers of the characters "A", "B", "C", etc. go in order, from lower to higher ASCII values, as do the lowercase characters "a", "b", "c", etc. (The actual numbers for the uppercase characters "A" through "Z" are 65 through 90, while the lowercase letters "a" through "z" are 97 through 122. The ASCII numbers for the digits "0" through "9" are 48 through 57.) This system makes it possible, among other things, to use JavaScript to sort values alphabetically. If we had the last names of two people stored in the variables lastName1 and lastName2, we could extract the first character of each name using the substring() method or the charAt() method and then compare these characters to see which came before the other in the alphabet.

Getting back to the SID number, once we've checked the first character of the SID string to see if it's between "0" and "9" inclusive, we simply repeat the process for the second through eighth characters. Remember that to extract the second character in a string, we would use substring(1,2); for the third character, use substring(2,3), and so on. So to extract each character in turn, we would first do the above assignment statement with substring(0,1), then do another assignment with substring(1,2), then substring(2,3), and so on through substring(7,8) for the last character. You should be able to see a pattern here that you can exploit with an appropriate for loop. That is, in pseudo-JavaScript code the algorithm is:

```
for (charNumber goes from 0 to 7) {
   Extract character number charNumber (i.e., 0, 1, 2,
      3, . . . or 7) from the string
   Use conditional statement to check if its value is <
      "0" or > "9", and if it's not, call "alert" method to
      put up warning message
}
```

Lab Exercise 15.1 (at the end of the next section) asks you to write this algorithm in JavaScript.

Using the break Statement to Stop a Loop

Sometimes it is useful to be able to stop a loop before it finishes its complete number of iterations. In the example immediately above, once it is discovered that one of the digits in the SID is invalid, it is a waste of time to check the rest. So there's no need to continue with the for (charNumber goes from 0 to 7) loop. JavaScript provides a nice, simple way to stop the execution of the loop: the break statement. When the browser encounters the break command, it breaks out of the loop and continues with whatever code comes after the loop.

For example, the following for loop searches an array of 10 radio buttons named drinkChoice (and belonging to a form named myForm) to see which one is checked. Once it finds a radio button that is checked, there's no need to continue because only one button in the set can be checked at any one time:

```
for (counter = 0; counter <= 9; counter++) {
   if (document.myForm.drinkChoice[counter].checked) {
```

```
        alert("Button number " + counter + " is checked.")
        break
    }
}
```

Note that when the `break` statement breaks out of the loop, the `counter` variable contains the number of the radio button that is checked. So we could also write the above code as:

```
for (counter = 0; counter <= 9; counter++) {
    if (document.myForm.drinkChoice[counter].checked) {
        break
    }
}
alert("Button number " + counter + " is checked.")
```

QuickCheck Questions

1. What will be the values of `chars1` and `chars2` after the following code is executed?

    ```
    var chars1, chars2, userName
    userName = "George Washington"
    chars1 = userName.charAt(3)
    chars2 = userName.substring(4, 8)
    ```

2. What does it mean to check if one character is "less than" another? Why can we say that "Z" is less than "a"?

Lab Exercise 15.1, "Validating an Identification Number," may be done at this point.

Accessing the Date Object

Some websites display different information depending on the day of the week or even the time of day. To do so, the web page being displayed needs to read the date and time as stored by the system clock of the surfer's computer. JavaScript makes it easy to do this via the **Date object**. We create a new `Date` object using the normal syntax with the keyword `new` and no parameters:

```
var timeAndDate = new Date()
```

The resulting object stores the time and date at the moment it was created, according to the system clock of the surfer's computer. (So you cannot necessarily assume that the time and date are accurate.) We then may access the time and date information using various methods of the `Date` object. We'll cover a number of them in this section and introduce a few more in the next section on cookies. (There are nearly 50 methods in all; we list them in Appendix F.)

We may retrieve the year, month (numbered 0–11), date within the month (1–31), day of the week (numbered 0–6 starting with Sunday), the hour (0–23), the minute (0–59), and seconds (0–59) from a Date object with the following methods:

```
var timeAndDate = new Date()              //Create a Date
                                          //object
var theYear = timeAndDate.getFullYear()   //Four digit
                                          //year, e.g., 2002
var theMonth = timeAndDate.getMonth()     //Months are
                                          //numbered 0-11
var dateOfMonth = timeAndDate.getDate()   //Date of month
                                          //numbered 1-31
var dayOfWeek = timeAndDate.getDay()      //Day of week
                                          //numbered 0-6
var theHour = timeAndDate.getHours()      //Hours numbered
                                          //0-23
var theMinute = timeAndDate.getMinutes()  //Minutes
                                          //numbered 0-59
var theSecond = timeAndDate.getSeconds()  //Seconds
                                          //numbered 0-59
```

As a simple example of using the time information, consider how we may display the current hours, minutes, and seconds in text boxes named hoursBox, minutesBox, and secondsBox (belonging to a form named timeForm) when the surfer clicks a button. We'll have the button's event handler call the following function:

```
function displayTime() {
    var currentTime, hour, minute, second
    currentTime = new Date()
    document.timeForm.hoursBox.value = currentTime.getHours()
    document.timeForm.minutesBox.value = currentTime.
      getMinutes()
    document.timeForm.secondsBox.value = currentTime.
      getSeconds()
}
```

We could display the whole time in a single text box in the format "hours:minutes:seconds" (e.g., 11:49:03). But that would require a little more code. When the minutes value or the seconds value was a single digit (0–9), we would have to add a leading 0, otherwise times such as 11:49:03 would display as 11:49:3. We'll leave the coding of this for Lab Exercise 15.2.

In the next section we'll also learn how to change the time and date contained in a Date object. But note that changing the time and date of a Date object

does not affect the actual system clock. A `Date` object simply stores a static time and date.

QuickCheck Questions

1. Write the code that creates a new `Date` object named `currentTime`.
2. Write the code that will get the hours value as stored in `currentTime` and store it in a variable named `currentHours`.

Lab Exercise 15.2, "Using the Date Object," may be done at this point.

Creating and Reading Cookies

In programming it is often useful to store values past the time a program stops running. Typically we do so by writing the values to a file on a disk. The user can then come back at a later time and use the program to open the file and add to or edit the stored data. JavaScript, however, is prevented from writing to a user's disk because of security reasons. If a web page that a surfer had downloaded contained JavaScript code that could access the surfer's hard disk, it could be used maliciously to spy on and/or modify the surfer's system and data files without the surfer's knowledge.

The one exception to this security roadblock occurs with **cookies**. A web page (or sometimes, the web page's server) is allowed to store a limited amount of information in a special file on the surfer's computer known as a **cookie file**. When, at a later date, the surfer downloads the web page again, the page can access the cookie file, read the information previously stored there, and store new information if necessary. (The origin of the name "cookie" is obscure, although it probably came from the UNIX programming jargon "magic cookies," which referred to small pieces of data that tracked a program's or user's progress.)

Introduction to Cookies

As an example of how cookies may be used, on the surfer's first visit to a web page the page might store the surfer's name (after the surfer entered it in a text box) in a cookie. Then when the surfer downloaded the page the next time, the page could check the previous cookie and display a personal greeting to the surfer. Members-only websites often store a member's login name and password as a cookie on the member's computer so that the member doesn't have to enter the login name and password every time he or she visits the site. Instead, when the member downloads the site's home page, the page's server checks the cookie file and retrieves the login name and password stored there from the member's first visit, matching it with the name and password stored in a database attached to the server. (Such actions require server-side processing, which is beyond the scope of this text. But in Lab Exercise 15.3 we will implement a simple client-side password system using cookies.)

Electronic commerce sites often use cookies for temporary purposes while the surfer is browsing the site and filling a shopping cart. Remember that JavaScript variables are associated with a particular page and, therefore, when another page is loaded all the variable values normally disappear. (Exceptions to this rule occur when using frames or multiple windows—see Chapter 17.) This means that any information stored by one page cannot be carried over to another. In programming terminology, the values of variables do not **persist** beyond the time the page is actually loaded into the browser. This presents a problem for a commerce site, because an online shopper often travels through several pages when shopping, selecting various items to put in the shopping cart. In order to get around this persistence problem and remember which items the user has selected, the website stores the item information in a cookie. Then when the shopper is ready to check out, the item information is retrieved from the cookie.

Although the cookie file may contain cookies from many different web pages, only the web page that created a cookie is allowed to access it, or alternatively a web page from the same server or same Internet domain (e.g., netscape.com, microsoft.com, yahoo.com). This enables a multiple-page website like an e-commerce site to access any and all cookies created by its many different web pages.

There is a limit, however, as to how much information may be stored in a cookie. Depending on how the cookie is put together, the maximum number of characters ranges from 2,000 to 4,000. And the total number of cookies that have been created by web pages from a certain Internet domain may not exceed 4,000 characters in total. There may also be a limit on the total number of cookies allowed in the cookie file. Some versions of Navigator, for example, have a maximum limit of 300 cookies. Most cookies therefore have expiration dates (of which more below), so that the browser can automatically delete old cookies.

The cookie file is named and located differently depending on the combination of the browser (Explorer, Navigator, etc.) and operating system (Windows, Mac, Linux, etc.) being used. If you want to find it on a given computer, either consult a good Internet reference book or try using the operating system's search function to look for files or folders containing the word "cookie." But be warned: You should never try to edit the original version of the cookie file—because doing so might impair how your browser works with certain websites.

The full use and deployment of cookies requires an advanced knowledge of JavaScript and/or server-side programming. In addition, you should be aware that the use of cookies is controversial in some quarters, because some websites use them to track surfers' browsing habits and gain other information

IMPORTANT

about surfers, thus violating their privacy. Some surfers therefore set the preferences on their browser to prevent the use of cookies on their system. The World Wide Web Consortium has also been working on the **Platform for Privacy Preferences Project (P3P)**, in the hopes of standardizing privacy practices among websites and making it possible for surfers to specify their privacy preferences in advance as they interact with sites. More information on P3P may be found at http://www.w3.org/P3P/p3pfaq.html.

Used judiciously, however, cookies can be an effective tool in designing interactive websites, and learning how to use JavaScript to create and read simple cookies is relatively easy.

Creating a Simple Cookie

At its most basic, a cookie is simply a string of text arranged in a special format. A **cookie string** contains information such as the domain of the server or page that created the cookie, the expiration date of the cookie, the name of the cookie, and a string of text that stores the value of the cookie (for example, a login name or password or shopping cart item).

To create a cookie using JavaScript, we assign a string value to the `cookie` property of the `document` object, or `document.cookie`. The format of the string value is precisely prescribed. It may contain up to five parts, in the following order:

1. The cookie name and cookie value.
2. The cookie's expiration date.
3. The pathname of the web page creating the cookie.
4. The domain name of the server creating the cookie.
5. A security parameter that may be used to restrict access to the cookie.

When creating simple cookies, parts 3, 4, and 5 of the cookie string are usually not specified, leaving the browser to fill in default values.

We may create a cookie using only the first part, the cookie's name and value. If, for example, we wanted to create a cookie named `userName` and store the name "Heidi" in it, we would write the following assignment statement:

```
document.cookie = "userName=Heidi"
```

This line of code takes the string of text `userName=Heidi` and stores it in the cookie file. The equal sign is required: It is used to separate the cookie name (`userName` in this case) from the cookie value (`Heidi`).

If the surfer had entered his or her name into a text box named `document.someForm.nameBox`, the code would be:

```
var theName = document.someForm.nameBox.value
document.cookie = "userName=" + theName
```

Or:

```
document.cookie = "userName=" + document.someForm.
    nameBox.value
```

Don't get confused with the two equal signs in this line of code. The first equal sign is the assignment operator, meaning that the browser will take the value of the left side and copy it into `document.cookie`. The second equal sign is inside the quotation marks and is therefore part of the cookie string. It is used to separate the cookie name and the cookie value.

IMPORTANT

Error Alert!

Note also that even though `userName` is the name of the cookie, and we talk about it having the value `Heidi` (or whatever), it is not a variable name. It simply is the first part of the string of text that makes up the cookie.

To summarize: The general procedure for creating a simple cookie is to construct a string in the format `"cookieName=cookieValue"` and then assign it to `document.cookie`. As another example, we might want to store a password that the surfer had entered in a text box named `document.someForm.pwdBox`. The cookie name might be `password` and the cookie value would be `document.someForm.pwdBox.value`. The code to create the cookie would be:

```
document.cookie = "password=" + document.someForm.pwdBox.
    value
```

Setting an Expiration Date

In order to add an expiration date to a cookie, we simply construct a longer string that contains the date information after the cookie's name and value. The date must be specified in Greenwich Mean Time (GMT), but fortunately JavaScript provides an easy way to do so. If, for example, we wanted to set an expiration date 30 days from now, we would start by creating a new `Date` object:

```
var expDate = new Date()
```

By default, this new `Date` object will store the time and date of its creation. The next step is to advance its stored date ahead 30 days. One way to do so is by using the `setTime()` method of the `Date` object. This method will set a `Date` object to any time and date we want, as long as we specify the time and date in terms of the number of milliseconds since January 1, 1970(!), because that's how the browser stores time and date information. (There are one thousand milliseconds in one second; that is, a millisecond is a thousandth of a second.) So to add 30 days to the current date, we need to calculate the number of milliseconds in 30 days. The calculation is simply 30 days times 24 hours per day times 60 minutes per hour times 60 seconds per minute times 1,000 milliseconds per second:

```
var thirtyDaysInMilliseconds = 30*24*60*60*1000
```

We get the current date (in milliseconds format) using the `getTime()` method of the `expDate` object:

```
var currentDateInMilliseconds = expDate.getTime()
```

So 30 days from now in milliseconds format would be:

```
var thirtyDaysFromNow = currentDateInMilliseconds +
    thirtyDaysInMilliseconds
```

The variable `thirtyDaysFromNow` stores the time, in milliseconds, from January 1, 1970, to the day 30 days in the future.

Finally, we pass the value of `thirtyDaysFromNow` to the `setTime()` method of the `expDate` object (which all `Date` objects have):

```
expDate.setTime(thirtyDaysFromNow)
```

The `expDate` object now stores a date 30 days in the future. All together the code is:

```
var expDate = new Date()
var thirtyDaysInMilliseconds = 30*24*60*60*1000
var currentDateInMilliseconds = expDate.getTime()
var thirtyDaysFromNow = currentDateInMilliseconds +
    thirtyDaysInMilliseconds
expDate.setTime(thirtyDaysFromNow)
```

We could also write this in more compact fashion:

```
var expDate = new Date()
expDate.setTime(expDate.getTime() + 30*24*60*60*1000)
```

Although doing such a calculation using milliseconds is somewhat tedious, now that we know how it works we can set the expiration date to any future time we want. Nevertheless, it is useful to know that JavaScript provides another, more elegant way to specify an expiration date a month hence (or two or three or however many months) by using the `getMonth()` and `setMonth()` methods of a date object.

The code, with comments, is:

```
var expDate = new Date()                        //Create a new
                                                //date object
var currentMonth = expDate.getMonth()           //Get the current
                                                //month
expDate.setMonth(currentMonth + 1)              //Add 1 to the
                                                //current month
                                                //and set expDate
                                                //to that month
                                                //(1 month ahead)
```

Once we have set the expiration date, we can change it to a GMT time string using the `toGMTString()` method of the `Date` object:

```
expDate.toGMTString()
```

Finally, to add this expiration date to the cookie string, we append a semicolon, the word `expires`, and an equal sign immediately after the cookie's `name=value` part, followed by the value of the GMT string:

```
var theName = document.someForm.nameBox.value
document.cookie = "userName=" + theName + ";expires=" +
    expDate.toGMTString()
```

So the first part of a cookie string with a name, value, and expiration date is `"cookieName=cookieValue;expires="`, followed by the expiration date in GMT syntax (the details of which we don't need to know). Note that there are no spaces in this string.

When a cookie is created the browser does not immediately store it in the cookie file. Instead it keeps its value in memory. Only when the surfer quits the browser does it actually write the cookie to the cookie file. Moreover, if we do not specify an expiration date when creating a cookie, the browser never writes the cookie to the cookie file. The cookie disappears when the surfer exits the browser. Although you might think this makes the cookie worthless, it's actually a common method for the shopping cart case mentioned above. A cookie that stores shopping cart information as the shopper moves from page to page does not need to keep the information once the shopper checks out. (The exception would be if the website wanted to save the information in an "abandoned" shopping cart in case the shopper came back at a later date to finish shopping.)

Reading a Cookie

As the purpose of a cookie is to store information for later use, we need to know how to read the contents of a previously created cookie. JavaScript is limited to reading only the name and value of a cookie. It cannot read the expiration date or any of the other information that may be in the cookie, such as the pathname or domain.

To read the contents of a cookie string, we split it apart into its name and its value by using the `split()` method. The `split()` method is part of all string objects. You use it by passing it a character as a parameter. It then looks for that character in the string and splits the string anyplace the character occurs, breaking the string into multiple pieces and storing each piece in an array. Each piece is referenced by number, starting from 0 as usual. A simple example makes it easier to see how this works:

```
var testStr = "alpha&beta&gamma"
var thePieces = testStr.split("&")
```

The variable named `thePieces` is now an array of strings, the value of `thePieces[0]` being "alpha", the value of `thePieces[1]` being "beta", and the value of `thePieces[2]` being "gamma" (Figure 15.1). Note that the specified split character (&, in this case) is not included in these string pieces.

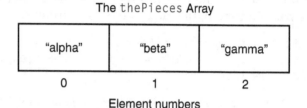

The `thePieces` Array

"alpha"	"beta"	"gamma"
0	1	2

Element numbers

FIGURE 15.1.   The array that is created when the string "alpha&beta&gamma" is split at the &s

The `split()` method often comes in handy when you are manipulating and processing string information. For example, if you have someone's full name (first name, middle name, and last name, with a space between each) stored in a string variable named `customerName`, you can separate the three names by specifying the space as the split character:

```
var namePieces, firstName, middleName, lastName
var customerName = "John William Smith"
namePieces = customerName.split(" ")      //Split the string at
                                          //the space characters
firstName = namePieces[0]                 //firstName will have
                                          //the value "John"
middleName = namePieces[1]                //middleName will
                                          //have the value
                                          //"William"
lastName = namePieces[2]                  //lastName will have
                                          //the value "Smith"
```

We may get rid of the `namePieces` variable and shorten this code by putting the array element reference (i.e., the number in the square brackets) immediately after the reference to the `split()` method:

```
var firstName, middleName, lastName
var customerName = "John William Smith"
firstName = customerName.split(" ")[0]    //firstName will
                                          //have the value
                                          //"John"
middleName = customerName.split(" ")[1]   //middleName
                                          //will have the
                                          //value "William"
```

```
lastName = customerName.split(" ")[2]     //lastName will
                                          //have the value
                                          //"Smith"
```

Another common example uses the split() method to break an e-mail address into its component parts, the user name and domain name:

```
var emailName, domainName
var emailAddress = "jwsmith@someorganization.com"
emailName = emailAddress.split("@")[0]
domainName = emailAddress.split("@")[1]
```

After the browser executes this code, emailName will store the value "jwsmith" and domainName will store "someorganization.com".

In the case of a cookie, we extract its name and value by splitting the document.cookie string at the equal sign:

```
var theCookieName, theCookieValue
theCookieName = document.cookie.split("=")[0]
   //Retrieves the cookie's name
theCookieValue = document.cookie.split("=")[1]
   //Retrieves the cookie's value
```

If we had created this cookie with the code from one of our previous examples:

```
var theName = document.someForm.nameBox.value
document.cookie = "userName=" + theName
```

and if the user had entered "Roy" in the nameBox, then the variable named theCookieName would have the value "userName" and the variable named theCookieValue would have the value "Roy".

Creating and Reading Multiple Cookies

We often need to store more than one value in the cookie file by creating multiple cookies. The process of creating multiple cookies follows the same format as creating a single cookie, but the process of reading multiple cookies adds a new wrinkle.

To store a user name and password as separate cookies, for example, we simply write two assignment statements for document.cookie (assuming that the expDate has already been created and set):

```
var theName = document.someForm.nameBox.value
var thePwd = document.someForm.pwdBox.value
document.cookie = "userName=" + theName + ";expires=" +
   expDate.toGMTString()
document.cookie = "password=" + thePwd + ";expires=" +
   expDate.toGMTString()
```

Although the last line in this code looks like it takes the `document.cookie` string and replaces the `userName` value stored in the previous line with the password value, it actually directs the browser to add a new cookie to the cookie file with the password value. In other words, every time your code uses `document.cookie` in an assignment statement, the browser simply *appends* the data for the new cookie to the cookies file. Previously created cookies are not erased.

In order to read the values of multiple cookies, JavaScript does not treat the multiple cookies as separate entities but as if they were part of one long cookie string stored in `document.cookie`. The `"cookieName=cookieValue"` strings of the individual cookies are combined into the one string, with a semicolon and a space separating each individual `"cookieName=cookieValue"` string. If we have three cookies in the cookie file, the combined string of the three cookies has the general format:

```
cookie1Name=cookie1Value; cookie2Name=cookie2Value;
   cookie3Name=cookie3value
```

To take a specific example, imagine that we create three cookies named `"userName"`, `"userEmail"`, and `"userZip"` (for the user's zip code), respectively. Assuming that the `expDate` object had already been created and that the user had entered "Meg", "technophile@somecompany.com", and "10014" in the appropriate text boxes, the code would be:

```
var name = document.someForm.nameBox.value
var emailAddress = document.someForm.emailBox.value
var zipCode = document.someForm.zipBox.value
document.cookie = "userName=" + name + ";expires=" +
   expDate.toGMTString()
document.cookie = "userEmail=" + emailAddress +
   ";expires=" + expDate.toGMTString()
document.cookie = "userZip=" + zipCode + ";expires=" +
   expDate.toGMTString()
```

Although these are separate cookies, JavaScript accesses them as if they consisted of one long string stored in `document.cookie`. Moreover, JavaScript only sees the name and value information, not the date information. In other words, to JavaScript `document.cookie` has the value:

```
userName=Meg; userEmail=technophile@somecompany.com;
   userZip=10014
```

To break apart this string and extract the individual cookie values, we apply the `split()` method twice. We first split the combined string using the split characters "; " (a semicolon followed by a space):

```
var theCookies = document.cookie.split("; ")
```

After this line of code executes, theCookies[0] will have the value "user Name=Meg", theCookies[1] will have the value "userEmail=technophile@ somecompany.com", and theCookies[2] will have the value "userZip= 10014".

We then use the split() method with an equal sign on any one of these elements to extract the desired value. For example, to extract the *value* of the third cookie:

```
var valueOfCookie3 = theCookies[2].split("=")[1]
    //The result will be "10014"
```

Or to extract the *name* of the third cookie:

```
var nameOfCookie3 = theCookies[2].split("=")[0]
    //The result will be "userZip"
```

To take one more example, consider the userName and password example we started with above. If the user had entered the name "Theresa" and the password "zyx", the combined string would have the form:

```
userName=Theresa; password=zyx
```

To extract the *values* of the userName and password cookies, we split the overall string at the "; " "(the semi-colon and space)" in order to separate the multiple name/value pairs, and then split the name/value pairs at their equal signs:

```
var theUserName, theUserPwd
var theCookies = document.cookie.split("; ")
theUserName = theCookies[0].split("=")[1]    //The result
                                             //will be
                                             //"Theresa"
theUserPwd = theCookies[1].split("=")[1]     //The result
                                             //will be
                                             "zyx"
```

QuickCheck Questions

1. Write the code that creates a cookie with the name lastName and the value Washington.
2. Rewrite the code in #1 so that the cookie has an expiration date three months in the future.
3. Write the code that will read the cookie in #2 and display its value in a text box named document.outputForm.messageBox.

Lab Exercise 15.3, "Creating a Simple Password System," may be done at this point.

ASCII numbers

cookie

cookie file

cookie string

Date object

persistence of variables

Platform for Privacy Preferences
Project (P3P)

validation

verification

1. Validating an Identification Number

Finding the number of characters contained in a string named `testString` (that is, the string's length) by using the `length` property of a string object:

```
var numberChars = testString.length
```

Extracting a substring from a string using the `substring()` method of a string object:

```
var secretWord= "gigabyte"
var slangTerm = secretWord.substring(0,3)    //slangTerm will have the value "gig"
var anotherTerm = secretWord.substring(4,8)  //anotherTerm will be "byte"
var thirdTerm = secretWord.substring(2,5)    //thirdTerm will be "gab"
var firstLetter = secretWord.substring(0,1)  //firstLetter will be "g"
```

Extracting a single character from a string using the `charAt()` method of a string object:

```
var secretWord= "gigabyte"
var firstLetter = secretWord.charAt(0)     //firstLetter will have the value "g"
var anotherLetter = secretWord.charAt(4)   //anotherLetter will be "b"
```

Checking whether one character is "less than" another character (based on its ASCII number):

```
if (theChar < "0") {
  alert("Invalid entry!")
}
```

Using the `break` statement to break out of a loop before it has completed all its iterations (using the example of looping through a set of radio buttons named `drinkChoice` to see which one is checked):

```
for (counter = 0; counter <= 9; counter++) {
  if (document.myForm.drinkChoice[counter].checked) {
    alert("Button number " + counter + " is checked.")
    break
  }
}
```

2. Accessing the Date Object

Creating a new `Date` object and using some of its built-in methods to access the time and date information stored in it:

```
var timeAndDate = new Date()                //Create a Date object
var theYear = timeAndDate.getFullYear()     //Four digit year, e.g., 2002
var theMonth = timeAndDate.getMonth()       //Months are numbered 0-11
var dateOfMonth = timeAndDate.getDate()     //Date of month numbered 1-31
var dayOfWeek = timeAndDate.getDay()        //Day of week numbered 0-6
```

```
var theHour = timeAndDate.getHours()       //Hours numbered 0-23
var theMinute = timeAndDate.getMinutes()   //Minutes numbered 0-59
var theSecond = timeAndDate.getSeconds()   //Seconds numbered 0-59
```

3. Creating and Reading Cookies

Creating a cookie named `userName` with the value `Heidi`:
```
document.cookie = "userName=Heidi"
```

Creating a cookie named `password` with the value of whatever is stored in a text box named `document.someForm.pwdBox`:
```
document.cookie = "password=" + document.someForm.pwdBox.value
```

Using the `getTime()` and `setTime()` methods of a `Date` object to set it to a time a certain number of milliseconds in the future (30 days, in this example):
```
var theDate = new Date()
var currentTime = theDate.getTime()
theDate.setTime(currentTime + 30*24*60*60*1000)
```

Using the `getMonth()` and `setMonth()` methods of a `Date` object to set it to a time a certain number of months in the future (6 months, in this example):
```
var theDate = new Date()
var currentMonth = theDate.getMonth()
theDate.setMonth(currentMonth + 6)
```

Creating an expiration date 12 months in the future, converting it to a GMT (Greenwich Mean Time) string, and putting it into the cookie string:
```
var expDate = new Date()
expDate.setMonth(expDate.getMonth() + 12)
var theName = document.someForm.nameBox.value
document.cookie = "userName=" + theName + ";expires=" + expDate.toGMTString()
```

Using the `split()` method of a string object to split a string into pieces:
```
var firstName, middleName, lastName
var customerName = "John William Smith"
firstName = customerName.split(" ")[0]    //firstName will have the value "John"
middleName = customerName.split(" ")[1]   //middleName will have the value "William"
lastName = customerName.split(" ")[2]     //lastName will have the value "Smith"
```

Using the `split()` method to read the name and value of a single cookie:
```
theCookieName = document.cookie.split("=")[0]    //Retrieves the cookie's name
theCookieValue = document.cookie.split("=")[1]   //Retrieves the cookie's value
```

Creating multiple cookies:
```
var theName = document.someForm.nameBox.value
var thePwd = document.someForm.pwdBox.value
document.cookie = "userName=" + theName + ";expires=" + expDate.toGMTString()
document.cookie = "password=" + thePwd + ";expires=" + expDate.toGMTString()
```

Reading multiple cookies (JavaScript retrieves multiple cookies as one long string of cookie name/value pairs, each pair separated by a semicolon and space, e.g., `userName=Theresa; password=zyx`):
```
var theUserName, theUserPwd
var theCookies = document.cookie.split("; ")   //Split into separate cookies
theUserName = theCookies[0].split("=")[1]      //The value will be "Theresa"
theUserPwd = theCookies[1].split("=")[1]       //The value will be "zyx"
```

Alerts and Advice

The name of the `substring()` method is not `subString()`.

A quick way to tell how many characters the `substring(x,y)` method will extract is to subtract x from y.

The time and date information stored in a `Date` object are based on the system clock of the surfer's computer at the moment the `Date` object is created. So don't assume that the information in a `Date` object is accurate.

A `Date` object stores a static time and date. It's possible to change the information in a `Date` object, but doing so has no effect on the system clock.

Cookies are controversial because of privacy issues, so use them judiciously.

Don't confuse the meaning of the two equal signs in an assignment statement involving `document.cookie`. The first one is the assignment operator; the second is part of the cookie string and is used as a divider.

Though we talk about the name and value of a cookie, the cookie name is not a regular variable name. It simply is the first part of the string that makes up the cookie.

The browser only saves a cookie to disk when the surfer exits the browser, and if the cookie has no expiration date, the cookie is never saved to disk.

Review Questions

1. True or false: JavaScript is well-suited to verify user input data, such as verifying a user's membership identification number for entry into a website.

2. Consider a text box named `userNameBox` that belongs to a form named `userData`. Assuming that the user has entered his/her name into `userNameBox`, which of the following stores the number of characters in the name?
   a. `document.userData.userNameBox.characters`
   b. `document.userData.userNameBox.length`
   c. `document.userData.userNameBox.value.characters`
   d. `document.userData.userNameBox.value.length`
   e. `characters(document.userData.userNameBox)`
   f. `length(document.userData.userNameBox)`

3. Given a string named `userAnswer`, which of the following extracts the second, third, and fourth characters from the string and stores them in a previously declared variable named `someChars`?
   a. `someChars = userAnswer.substring(2,5)`
   b. `someChars = userAnswer.substring(1,4)`
   c. `someChars = userAnswer.substring(2,4)`
   d. `someChars = userAnswer.substring(1,3)`
   e. `userAnswer.substring(2,5).someChars`
   f. `userAnswer.substring(1,4).someChars`
   g. `userAnswer.substring(2,4).someChars`
   h. `userAnswer.substring(1,3).someChars`

4. Given a string named `customerName`, which of the following (one or more) extracts the first character from the string and stores it in a variable named `firstLetter`?
   a. `firstLetter = customerName.substring(0,1)`
   b. `firstLetter = customerName.substring(1,1)`
   c. `firstLetter = customerName.substring(1,2)`
   d. `firstLetter = customerName.charAt(0)`
   e. `firstLetter = customerName.charAt(1)`

5. Given the following code, will the alert box appear or not?
```
var letter1 = "B"
var letter2 = "b"
if (letter1 < letter2){
   alert("The character B is less than the character b.")
}
```

6. True or false: The `break` statement is used to stop the execution of a loop prematurely.

7. Given a date object named `currentDate` that stores the current date and time, which of the following lines of code will retrieve the current hours value and store it in a variable named `theHour`?
   a. `var theHour = getHours(currentDate)`
   b. `var theHour = getHours()`
   c. `var theHour = currentDate.getHours()`
   d. `currentDate.getHours(theHour)`

8. Which of the following lines of code creates a cookie named `state` and stores the value `California` in it?
   a. `document.cookie = "state=California"`
   b. `document.cookie(state,"California")`
   c. `document.cookie.name = "state", document.cookie.value = "California"`
   d. `cookieName = "State", cookieValue = "California"`

9. Given a date object named `expirationDate` that stores the current date and time, which of the following lines of code will change the date value of `expirationDate` to 9 months from now?
   a. `expirationDate.setMonth(9)`
   b. `expirationDate.setMonth(expirationDate.getMonth() + 9)`
   c. `expirationDate.currentMonth = expirationDate.currentMonth + 9`
   d. `expirationDate.getMonth() + 9`

10. Given the cookie referred to in question 8, which of the following lines of code will retrieve its value (i.e., California) and store it in a variable named `userState`?
    a. `var userState = document.cookie.value`
    b. `var userState = document.cookie.split("=")[0]`
    c. `var userState = document.cookie.split("=")[1]`
    d. `var userState = document.cookie.split("=")`

1. Briefly define and/or explain the following terms: validation, variable persistence, ASCII number.

2. Write the code that tests the value of a text box named `document.inputForm.nameBox` to see how many characters it has. If it has more than 10 characters, display an alert box with the message "Do you have a nickname?"

3. Write the code that extracts the first character of a variable named `customer1` and the first character of a variable named `customer2` and stores them in variables named `firstLetter1` and `firstLetter2`, respectively. Compare the two characters and display the names of the two customers in alphabetical order in a text box named `document.resultsForm.sortBox`. If the two characters are the same, display instead the message "Both customers names start with the same letter."

4. Repeat Exercise 3, but this time for three customer names. Assume that all three names start with different letters.

5. The Date object methods `getUTCDay()`, `getUTCHours()` and `getUTCMinutes()` do the same thing as `getDay()`, `getHours()` and `getMinutes()`, except that they return the time in Coordinated Universal Time, which is another way of saying Greenwich Mean Time, which is another way of saying the time

in London. Write code that will display the current day of the week and time in London (hours and minutes) when the surfer clicks a button labeled London Time. Use separate text boxes for the display (day, hours, minutes).

6. Imagine a variable named `userInfo` that contains a string with the user's name, street address, city, state, and zip code, each separated by a comma. So, for example, its contents might be something like the following:

> Thomas Edison,123 Main Street,Menlo Park,New Jersey,08837

Write the JavaScript code that will split this string into its component parts and save them in variables named `userName`, `userAddress`, `city`, `state`, and `zip`. Then also take the `userName` variable, split it, and store the results in variables named `firstName` and `lastName`.

7. Write the code for a function named `setTimeCookie()` that creates a cookie named `timeOfVisit` and stores the value of the current hour of the day in it. The function should be called by an `onLoad` event handler in the `<body>` tag of the source document. Give the cookie an expiration date 12 months from the present.

8. Write the code that would read the value of the cookie set in Exercise 7 and display its value in a text box named `timeOfVisitBox` that belongs to a form named `timeForm`.

9. Write the code for a function named `setDateCookie()` that (a) creates a cookie named `lastVisitMonth` and stores the value of the current month in it, and (b) creates a second cookie named `lastVisitDate` and stores the value of the current date of the month (1–31) in it. Give the cookies expiration dates nine months from the present.

10. Write the code that would read the values of the cookies set in Exercise 9 and display their values in text boxes named `monthOfVisitBox` and `dateOfVisitBox` that belong to a form named `timeForm`.

Debugging Exercise

Identify and correct the errors in the following JavaScript code. The code is supposed to create a cookie named `userName` and give it the value stored in a text box named `nameBox` that belongs to a form named `someForm`. The cookie should have an expiration date of nine months from the present. The code is also then supposed to read the value of the cookie and display it in an alert box.

```
<script type="text/javascript">
    var expDate = new date()
    var expDate.setMonth(getMonth() + 9)
    var theName = document.someForm.nameBox.value
    document.cookie[0] = "userName=" + theName + ";expDate" + expDate.toGMTString()
    var theUserName = theCookies.substring("=")[0]
    alert("The value of the cookie is " + theUserName)
</script>
```

Note: Most of the exercises above may also be done as lab exercises. If a problem involves a function, add a function call so that the function code is actually executed.

Exercise 15.1: Validating an Identification Number

❏ Using the sample code and algorithms in the section "Validating an Identification Number" as guidelines, add two textboxes to your Apollo Quiz web page (Lab Exercises 13.1–13.3) that instruct the surfer to enter his or her name and 8-digit identification number. Also add code to the beginning of the `processScore()` function of the Quiz program that checks whether the surfer has entered a valid SID. That is, first check to see if the length of the SID string has 8 characters and then, if it does, check each character in turn to make sure each is between 0 and 9, inclusive. Written in pseduo-JavaScript, your code will have the following format:

```
if (the length does not equal 8) {
    Use alert box to display message "SID must be 8
    numbers long. Please re-enter your SID."
}
else {
    The SID length is correct, so now check each of the
    characters in the SID string to make sure they're
    between "0" and "9". In other words, the for loop
    outlined at the end of the section on "Validating the Surfer's Identification Num-
    ber" goes here.
}
```

Remember that the length of the SID string is stored in `document.surferInfo.SIDBox.value.length`. Check your code by entering various SID numbers to see what happens.

❏ Once you have the above code working, try leaving out the `break` statement in the `for` loop and write down what happens when you enter an SID with several bad characters (for example, letters instead of numbers). Then put the `break` statement back in.

❏ Finally, we need to make one more adjustment. You might note that, as your code is currently written, even if the surfer enters a bad SID (and gets the appropriate warning message), the `processScore()` function goes ahead and scores the surfer's quiz answers. We'd rather not have this done until the surfer has entered a valid SID. In other words, if the surfer enters a bad SID, we want to skip the rest of the instructions in the `processScore()` function.

The basic algorithm would be:

```
Check the SID number at the beginning of the processScore() function
If the SID number is good then
    continue on with the processScore() instructions
```

One common way to implement this algorithm uses a flag variable. A flag variable is a boolean variable that indicates whether something has happened or not, or whether something is true or not. (The name comes from the old-style mailboxes that have red metal flags on them. When the flag is up, it indicates to the mail carrier that there is outgoing mail in the box to pick up. When the flag is down, there is no outgoing mail.)

❏ Declare a variable named `validSID` at the beginning of the `processScore()` function and initialize it to the value `true`. This flag variable will indicate whether or not the form of the SID number (length of 8, only digits) is valid. If and when the code finds that the SID number is invalid and displays an alert message, add a line of code after the `alert` command that sets the value of `validSID` to false. Then add a conditional statement after the code that checks the SID but before the rest of the code in the `processScore()` function. This conditional statement should check whether the value of `validSID` is true. If it is, then the rest of the `processScore()` instructions should be executed. In other words, the body of this conditional statement must contain all the rest of the code that tests the surfer's answers and displays the results.

Exercise 15.2: Using the Date Object

❑ Rewrite the `displayTime()` function, described in the text, so that it displays the time in a single text box in the format hours:minutes:seconds (e.g., 11:49:03). Also make it so that the hours display from 1–12 (A.M. or P.M.) instead of 0–23.

❑ Optional: Create a web page that displays different images depending on the time when the page is loaded. To do so, use one image object and three image files that store images of approximately the same height and width. Use an `<img>` tag in the `<body>` element to load a blank image with the same height and width of the three images (to display a blank image, use `src=""` for the value of the `src` attribute). Use the `id` attribute to give the image the name `randomImage`. Precache the three image files in `Image` objects named `picture1`, `picture2`, and `picture3` (see the section "Better Rollovers using Precached Images" in Chapter 9). If you did Lab Exercise 13.4 in Chapter 13 (the slide show), use the images you used for it. Otherwise, find three new images (any will do—see the section "Creating and Finding Images" in Chapter 5 for tips on getting images).

Then use an `onLoad` event handler in the `<body>` tag that calls a function named `chooseImage()`. The `chooseImage()` function should create a new `Date` object and check the current seconds value. Using a conditional statement, if the value is from 0 to 19, load the first image (`picture1.src`) into the `src` property of the `randomImage` object; if it's from 20 to 39, load the second image (`picture2.src`) into `randomImage`; and if it's from 40 to 59, load the third image (`picture3.src`) into `randomImage`. (The `onLoad` event handler is covered in Chapter 13 in the section "An Automatic Slide Show".) Note: This code could easily be modified so that the different images were displayed at different times of the day (morning, afternoon, night) or different seasons of the year (fall, winter, spring, summer), thus enabling you to automatically customize the web page look for different times or seasons.

Exercise 15.3: Creating a Simple Password System

❑ Create a source document named SetPassword.htm that displays "Welcome First-Time Visitor" and prompts the surfer to set a password by entering it into a text box and clicking a button. The `onclick` event handler of the click button should call a function that creates a cookie named `password`, storing the surfer's password in it and setting an expiration date of 12 months.

❑ Create a second source document named CheckPassword.htm that uses a text box to prompt the surfer to enter his or her password and then click a button labeled Security Check. The button's `onclick` event handler should call a function that retrieves the password stored in the cookie file (the result of running the script in the SetPassword.htm document) and compares it with the surfer's entry. If they match, display an alert box with the message "Valid password", followed by a line of code that uses the `window.location` property to load a document named MainPage.htm. That is:

```
window.location = MainPage.htm
```

The MainPage.htm document should simply display the text "Welcome to the main page" in an `<h2>` element. If the password doesn't match, then just display the alert message "Invalid password. Please reenter it."

❑ As we wrote the code above for the SetPassword.htm and CheckPassword.htm documents, the surfer must know to load SetPassword.htm first so the password can be set. It would be better if the browser automatically routed the surfer to the correct page: SetPassword.htm if no password had been set yet and

CheckPassword.htm if a password had already been set. You can do so by adding the following conditional statement to the `<script>` element in CheckPassword.htm:

```
if (document.cookie == "") {
    window.location = SetPassword.htm
}
```

This conditional statement checks whether the cookie string for the page is blank. If it is, then it loads the SetPassword.htm document. Otherwise, the code in the CheckPassword.htm document continues on. Note that the conditional statement should not be inside a function declaration, because we want the browser to execute it as the page is loading.

Important Security Note: Do not rely too much on a password system like the one in this exercise. It provides only minimal security, because a clever (or even half-clever) surfer can find the URL for the main page (MainPage.htm) by viewing the source code for CheckPassword.htm and then go directly to the page by typing the URL into the Location field of the browser. A more secure system would require server-side processing of the password.

Custom Objects: Creating and Searching a Database

LEARNING OBJECTIVES

1. Understand the basic concepts and terminology of databases, such as records and fields, and how you may create a database using objects.

2. Learn how to create your own objects with custom-designed properties.

3. Learn how a database may be implemented in JavaScript as an array of objects.

4. Learn how to use conditional statements and a loop to search a database for specified information.

The Basics of Databases

Sometimes in writing a JavaScript program, we need to create groups of associated variables. This is often the case when we are making a database.

For example, consider how we might create a database that stores names, addresses, and phone numbers. We would store the information in the form of a simple tabular database as shown in Table 16.1, consisting of **fields** (the column headings) and **records** (the rows of information). Fields and records are standard database terminology. A simple tabular database is known as a flat file database.

The database in Table 16.1 has three fields—Name, Address, and Phone—and six records—storing information about Bill, Theresa, Emily, Clyde, John, and Sarah. (We might include any number of other fields, such as City, State, Zip Code, Cell Phone, etc., but we limit it to three here to save space.)

So how can we implement such a database in JavaScript? The answer is "objects." If we think about it, an object and its associated properties are similar to a record and its fields in a database. We might have an object, for instance,

TABLE 16.1.   A Simple Database

Name	Address	Phone
Bill	123 Main Street	321-4567
Theresa	456 Elm Place	987-1234
Emily	65 Oriole Drive	487-0246
Clyde	1003 Court Street	357-9087
John	294 Amherst Avenue	732-7457
Sarah	98 Stanford Place	487-3123

that had three properties: name, address, and phone. If we could create a number of copies of this object, perhaps naming them Object1, Object2, etc., then we could store the information in each record of our database in one of the objects. That is, each object would be equivalent to a record in our database. The name property of Object1 would store "Bill", its address property would store "123 Main Street", and its phone property would store "321-4567". The name property of Object2 would store "Theresa", its address property would store "456 Elm Place", and so on. The database of Table 16.1 would require six such objects.

QuickCheck Questions

1. What is the difference between a database record and a database field?
2. If you had a database that stored customer information under the field headings Name, Date, and Purchase Amount, describe how you would implement a record in that database as an object.

Creating Custom Objects

The next question is, How do we define and create our own objects in JavaScript? In the past we have created objects that were already defined in JavaScript, such as image objects (Chapter 9) and date objects (Chapter 15). To create an image object, we called the constructor function for image objects (Image) using the new keyword and assigning the resulting Image object to a variable name:

```
var someImage = new Image(69, 120)
```

(Remember that the two parameters are values for the width and height of the image, stored in an image file, that will be associated with the Image object at a later point in the code. These parameters are optional.)

In the terminology of object-oriented programming, this line of code creates an **instance** of the Image object. That is, we may think of the Image object constructor as defining the basic template, or blueprint, for an Image object. By calling the constructor, we are creating an actual Image object based on the template. An imaginary muffin-maker machine provides a good analogy to the constructor. The machine stores the recipe, or blueprint, for a muffin, but not actual muffins. A muffin is produced when we tell the machine to do so (by pressing a button or something). Each muffin that comes out of the machine is an "instance" of the muffin blueprint/recipe.

We may define and create our own custom-designed objects using a two-step process. First, we write a **constructor function** that defines the template for the object by specifying the properties and methods that the object is to have. Second, we create an actual object (or technically, an "instance" of the object) by calling the constructor function using the new keyword with the syntax above.

For a JavaScript database, we only need to create objects with properties, but not methods. Let's see how this works by creating a template for an object that will have three properties: named name, address, and phone. The code for the constructor function defines this template in the following manner:

```
function addressEntry(nm, adr, ph) {
   this.name = nm
   this.address = adr
   this.phone = ph
}
```

We have named the constructor function addressEntry() and given it three assignment statements: this.name = nm, this.address = adr, and this. phone = ph. Note the use of the keyword this. It is JavaScript shorthand for "this object." When we write this.name, therefore, it means "the name property of this object." So, in English, the assignment statement this.name = nm means to take the value of the formal parameter nm and copy it into the name property of the new object. Similarly, the value of adr is copied into the address property, and the value of ph is copied into the phone property.

It's easier to understand how this works when we consider how we call the constructor function. To create a new object based on the addressEntry() template and store the string values "Bill", "123 Main Street", and "321-4567" in its name, address, and phone properties, we write:

```
var firstAddress = new addressEntry("Bill", "123 Main
   Street", "321-4567")
```

When the browser executes this line of code, the value "Bill" is passed to the formal parameter nm in the addressEntry() function, the value "123 Main Street" is passed to the formal parameter adr, and the value "321-4567" is passed to the formal parameter ph. From there these values are copied into the name, address, and phone properties of the object via the assignment statements in the constructor function. The new object is thereby created, and the left side of the assignment statement above assigns it the name firstAddress. (We could, of course, choose some other name.) We may then reference these values using normal dot notation for objects. For example, `firstAddress.name` has the value "Bill", `firstAddress.address` has the value "123 Main Street", and `firstAddress.phone` has the value "321-4567".

Don't forget to include the keyword `new` in the line of code that creates the object; it's easy to leave out. Note also that `nm`, `adr`, and `ph` are simply formal parameters that perform the service of transferring the values into the object's properties. The actual names of the object's properties are `name`, `address`, and `phone`. So we may refer to `firstAddress.name` or `firstAddress.address` or `firstAddress.phone`, but not to `firstAddress.nm`, `firstAddress.adr`, or `firstAddress.ph`.

Similarly, we may create separate objects to store the information for the other entries in our sample address database:

```
var secondAddress = new addressEntry("Theresa", "456 Elm
   Place", "987-1234")
var thirdAddress = new addressEntry("Emily", "65 Oriole
   Drive", "487-0246")
//And so on . . .
```

Each assignment statement here creates a new instance of the `addressEntry` object with the name `secondAddress`, or `thirdAddress`, and so on, and with the indicated information stored in its properties. In other words, each row or record in the database is defined as a separate object. The complete database exists as a set of objects. The information for any given entry in the database may then be accessed by its object name and particular property. To display Theresa's phone number in an alert box, for example, we would write:

```
alert("The phone number for Theresa is: " +
   secondAddress.phone)
```

QuickCheck Questions

1. Using the `addressEntry()` constructor function, write the code that creates an object named `myAddress` and stores your name, address, and phone number in its properties.
2. Write an assignment statement that would display your address, as stored in the `myAddress` object in #1, in a text box named `outputBox` that belongs to a form named `someForm`.

A Database as an Array of Objects

Although we have now seen how we can create a database in JavaScript by making an object for each record in the database, we have a problem: It is very difficult to search the database for information. If, for example, we wanted to search the database for Emily's phone number, we would have to check the `name` property of each object separately until we found Emily's name, and then we could get and display the phone number. The code to do this would be:

```
if (firstAddress.name == "Emily") {
   alert("The number for Emily is: " + firstAddress.phone)
}
if (secondAddress.name == "Emily") {
   alert("The number for Emily is: " + secondAddress.phone)
}
if (thirdAddress.name == "Emily") {
   alert("The number for Emily is: " + thirdAddress.phone)
}
//And so on for all six (or however many) addressEntry
//objects
```

To solve this inconvenience, we will turn our set of `addressEntry` objects, each with the separate names `firstAddress`, `secondAddress`, and so on, into an *array* of `addressEntry` objects with a single name and numbering system. Here's how we do it, using the name `addresses` for the array. First we declare our array as usual, and then we use our constructor function to define each element of the array as an object with specific information stored in each of its properties. That is, to create an array that can store the information for the six entries in our address book database, we write:

```
var addresses = new Array(6)   //Create a 6-element array
                               //named addresses
addresses[0] = new addressEntry("Bill", "123 Main Street",
   "321-4567")
addresses[1] = new addressEntry("Theresa", "456 Elm
   Place", "987-1234")
addresses[2] = new addressEntry("Emily", "65 Oriole
   Drive", "487-0246")
//And so on through addresses[5]
```

If you compare this code with the previous non-array version in the section "Creating Custom Objects" you will see that the only difference is the names of the variables. The variable `firstAddress` has become `addresses[0]`, `secondAddress` has become `addresses[1]`, and so on.

We now may refer to each object in the array by its subscript, such as `addresses[0]`, `addresses[1]`, `addresses[2]`, and so on (corresponding to what we previously named `firstAddress`, `secondAddress`, and `thirdAddress`). The series of conditional statements above would then become:

```
if (addresses[0].name == "Emily") {
   alert("The number for Emily is: " + addresses[0].phone)
}
if (addresses[1].name == "Emily") {
```

```
      alert("The number for Emily is: " + addresses[1].phone)
   }
   if (addresses[2].name == "Emily") {
      alert("The number for Emily is: " + addresses[2].phone)
   }
   //And so on for all six (or however many) addressEntry
   //objects
```

At first glance it doesn't seem we have gained much with this substitition. But then we see the number pattern and remember that we can use a loop. All six conditional statements may be replaced by the following for loop:

```
   var ctr
   for (ctr = 0; ctr < 6; ctr++){
      if (addresses[ctr].name == "Emily") {
         alert("The number for Emily is: " +
         addresses[ctr].phone)
      }
   }
```

IMPORTANT

It is important to understand the limitations of using JavaScript to create a web page database. Because of security reasons, JavaScript cannot be used to save information to a disk (with the limited exception of cookies). This restriction means that the database only exists in the code of the source document itself, which cannot be changed by the surfer. Therefore it's impossible to give the surfer the option of adding new records to a JavaScript database or modifying the existing ones, which are common operations with databases. Nor would you want to use JavaScript to create a very large database, because it would take the browser too long to download the source document that contained the database code and information (as well as the regular HTML code).

When web page designers need to add database capabilities to a website, they typically create and store the database on the server (or on a computer connected to the server). Any interactions with the database therefore require communication between the surfer's client machine and the server. When, for example, you enter a word or phrase into a search text box on a web page and click a Search button, the information you typed in the text box is sent back to the server and its database for processing (which involves CGI programming, Active Server Pages or other similar technologies). The results are then sent from the server back to the client machine, where the browser displays them for you.

But even with these limitations JavaScript databases can serve a useful purpose. A medium-sized organization with several hundred employees, for example, may want to include contact information for its employees on its website. It might simply create a page that listed all the employees alphabetically, but it could also store the employee information as an array of objects in the source document. Each object in the array of objects would contain the contact information for one employee. Including a search text box on the page (plus the necessary JavaScript code to do the search) would enable the surfer to jump right to the contact information being sought. (How to implement a search function is the subject of the next section.)

It would require approximately 100 bytes to store a single record in an employee database like this one. (This figure comes from the fact that the line of code that creates an object is usually anywhere from 60–150 characters long, and each character in a text document takes up 1 byte of storage space.) A database with 200 records typed into a source document's <script> element would thus increase the size of the source document by approximately 20,000 bytes. This size is equivalent to that of a medium-size image file, so it usually would not significantly affect the download time for the source document. (Although initially typing all the JavaScript code to create each record in the database would take a while.)

QuickCheck Questions

1. Write the line of code that will create a sixth object in the addressess array of objects and store the contact information for Sarah in it (as listed in Table 16.1).

2. Write a conditional statement that checks the "Sarah" object in #1 to see if the phone number stored in it has the value "123-4567".

Lab Exercise 16.1, "Creating a Database," may be done at this point.

Searching a Database

In Lab Exercise 16.1 we take you through the steps of creating a database for a "Great Physics Discoveries" web page. One of the fields in this database stores the physicist's nationality. As an example of searching a database, we will consider how to search the physics database for all physicists of a certain nationality. The web page will prompt the surfer to enter a nationality and then the page will return a list of all physicists of that nationality in the database.

The algorithm to implement such a search function would be:

1. Prompt user to enter nationality for which to search (i.e., a text box plus a click button labeled Search).

2. When the surfer clicks the Search button, use its onclick event handler to call a function named searchForNationality() and send the function the name of the nationality as a parameter.

3. The searchForNationality() function will go through the database's array of objects one object at a time, using a conditional statement to check if the nationality stored in the nationality property of the object matches the nationality for which we are looking (stored in the parameter in step 2).

4. If and when a match is found, use an assignment statement to store the name of the scientist in a string named searchResults. Once JavaScript is done with the search, we'll display the contents of searchResults in a text box or text area.

5. Keep going until the end of the array of objects is reached, in case the nationality is represented more than once in the database.

Lab Exercise 16.2, which may be done at this point, guides you through the process of implementing this algorithm in JavaScript code.

Key Terms

constructor function	instance of an object	record
field		

Code Summary

1. Creating Custom Objects

Declaring a constructor function that defines an object with three properties named name, address, and phone:

```
function addressEntry(nm, adr, ph) {
    this.name = nm
    this.address = adr
    this.phone = ph
}
```

Creating a new instance of an object by calling the constructor function and passing it values to store in the new object's properties (the object will be named firstAddress):

```
var firstAddress = new addressEntry("Bill", "123 Main Street", "321-4567")
```

Displaying the value stored in the phone property of the firstAddress object:

```
alert("The phone number for Bill is: " + firstAddress.phone)
```

Using a conditional statement to check the value stored in the name property of the firstAddress object:

```
if (firstAddress.name == "Emily") {
    alert("The number for Emily is: " + firstAddress.phone)
}
```

2. A Database as an Array of Objects

Creating an array of objects named addresses using the addressEntry() constructor:

```
var addresses = new Array(6)
addresses[0] = new addressEntry("Bill", "123 Main Street", "321-4567")
addresses[1] = new addressEntry("Theresa", "456 Elm Place", "987-1234")
addresses[2] = new addressEntry("Emily", "65 Oriole Drive", "487-0246")
//And so on through addresses[5]
```

Using a conditional statement to check the value stored in the `name` property of the first object in the `addresses` array of objects:

```
if (addresses[0].name == "Emily") {
   alert("The number for Emily is: " + addresses[0].phone)
}
```

Using a conditional statement inside a `for` loop to check the value of the `name` property for all objects in the array:

```
var ctr
for (ctr = 0; ctr < 6; ctr++){
   if (addresses[ctr].name == "Emily") {
      alert("The number for Emily is: " + addresses[ctr].phone)
   }
}
```

Do not forget to include the keyword `new` when calling a constructor function to create a new object.

Do not confuse the names of the formal parameters in a constructor function with the actual names of the properties of the object that is to be constructed. The property names are specified using the `this.propertyName` syntax.

JavaScript is not suitable for creating large databases or databases that provide the user with the option to add or modify database records. But small- to medium-size databases (up to several hundred records) can work well.

Alerts and Advice

1. True or false: In a simple tabular (flat file) database consisting of rows of information with various column headings (such as Table 16.1), the columns correspond to database records and the rows correspond to database fields.

2. True or false: A constructor function defines the blueprint for an object.

3. Assuming that a constructor function named `dvdInfo()` exists, and that it creates an object with three properties named `title`, `artist`, and `year` (corresponding to the title, artist name, and year of composition for a DVD recording), which of the following lines of code creates an instance of `dvdInfo` named `beethoven5` with the values "Fifth Symphony", "Beethoven", and "1808"?
   a. `var beethoven5.dvdInfo = "Fifth Symphony", "Beethoven", "1808"`
   b. `var beethoven5 = dvdInfo("Fifth Symphony", "Beethoven", "1808")`
   c. `var beethoven5 = new dvdInfo("Fifth Symphony", "Beethoven", "1808")`
   d. `dvdInfo("Fifth Symphony", "Beethoven", "1808") = beethoven5`

4. Given the `beethoven5` object from Review Question 3, which of the following stores the value "Beethoven"?
   a. `beethoven5`
   b. `dvdInfo.artist`
   c. `beethoven5.artist`
   d. `dvdInfo`

5. Given the `beethoven5` object from Review Question 3, which of the following gives the value "1808" to a variable named `famousYear`?
   a. `var famousYear = beethoven5.year`
   b. `var famousYear = beethoven5("1808")`

Review Questions

c. `var famousYear = dvdInfo("1808")`
d. `var famousYear = new dvdInfo("1808")`

6. Which of the following lines of code creates an array of 500 objects named `beethovenWorks`?
   a. `var beethovenWorks = array(500)`
   b. `var beethovenWorks = array[500]`
   c. `var beethovenWorks = Array(500)`
   d. `var beethovenWorks = Array[500]`
   e. `var beethovenWorks = new array(500)`
   f. `var beethovenWorks = new array[500]`
   g. `var beethovenWorks = new Array(500)`
   h. `var beethovenWorks = new Array[500]`

7. Which of the following lines of code uses the `dvdInfo()` constructor function from Review Question 3 to create an object with the values "Fifth Symphony", "Beethoven", and "1808" and store it in the fifth element of the array from Review Question 6?
   a. `beethovenWorks[4].dvdInfo = "Fifth Symphony", "Beethoven", "1808"`
   b. `beethovenWorks[5].dvdInfo = "Fifth Symphony", "Beethoven", "1808"`
   c. `beethovenWorks[5] = dvdInfo("Fifth Symphony", "Beethoven", "1808")`
   d. `beethovenWorks[4] = new dvdInfo("Fifth Symphony", "Beethoven", "1808")`

8. Which of the following conditional statements checks whether the value of the `year` property of the tenth element of the `beethovenWorks` array is equal to "1801"?
   a. `if (beethovenWorks[9].year == "1801") { . . . }`
   b. `if (beethovenWorks[10].year == "1801") { . . . }`
   c. `if (beethovenWorks.year[9] == "1801") { . . . }`
   d. `if (beethovenWorks.year[10] == "1801") { . . . }`

Exercises

1. Give brief explanations of the following terms: record, field, instance.

2. Write the code for a constructor function named `restaurantRecord` that defines an object with five properties named `name`, `address`, `phone`, `priceCategory`, and `rating`.

3. Write the code that calls the constructor function defined in Exercise 2 to create a new object named `firstRestaurant` with the string values "Gina's Grill", "123 Main Street", "555-123-4567", "moderate", and "2 stars".

4. Write the code that creates an array named `restaurants` with 100 elements for use on a web page that provides information on local restaurants. Then, using the constructor function defined in Exercise 2, write code that creates and stores three new objects in the first three elements in the array. The property values of the first object should be "Carlo's Cafe", "456 A Street", "555-765-4321", "inexpensive", and "2 stars". The property values of the second object should be "Gina's Grill", "123 Main Street", "555-123-4567", "moderate", and "2 stars". And the third object's values should be "Billie's Bistro", "789 6th Street", "555-321-7654", "pricey", and "3 stars".

5. Given the array of objects named `restaurants` described in Exercise 4, write the code for a `for` loop that searches for a restaurant with the name "Sam's Steakhouse". If the restaurant is found, the code should display the restaurant name, address, phone number, price category, and rating in a text box named `document.searchForm.resultsBox`. If the restaurant is not found, the code should display a "Not found" message in the text box. Assume that there is only one restaurant with that name in the database (one entry in the array). Due to this last assumption, the code should stop searching the array if and when the restaurant is found.

6. Given the array of objects named `restaurants` described in Exercise 4, write the code for a `for` loop that tallies how many restaurants are listed as "moderate" in the price category. Store the running tally in a variable named `moderateCount`. When the tally is finished, display the result in a text box named `document.searchForm.tallyBox`.

7. Given the array of objects named `restaurants` described in Exercise 4, write the code for a `for` loop that tallies how many restaurants satisfy both of the following criteria: a price category of "moderate" and a rating of "3 stars". Store the running tally in a variable named `moderate3starCount`. When the tally is finished, display the result in a text box named `document.searchForm.tallyBox`.

8. Given the array of objects named `restaurants` described in Exercise 4, write the code for a `for` loop that tallies how many restaurants are located in the 530 area code. (Hint: You will need to use the `substring()` method discussed in Chapter 15.) Store the running tally in a variable named `areacodeCount`. When the tally is finished, display the result in a text box named `document.searchForm.tallyBox`.

9. Consider an array named `diceRolls` with 100 elements. The array is filled with random numbers from 2 through 12 that represent the roll of two dice. Write the code for a `for` loop that tallies how many times the number 7 appears in the array. Store the running tally in a variable named `nmbrOfSevens`. When the tally is finished, display the result in a text box named `document.resultsForm.sevensBox`.

10. Consider an array named `monthlySales` that stores a company's sales results for each month, January through December (that is, the array has 12 elements). Write the code for a `for` loop that finds the month with the highest sales figure. When the search is finished, display the number of the month (1 = January, 2 = February, etc.) and the sales figure in a text box named `highMonthBox` that belongs to a form named `salesResults`. (Assume that all the months have different sales figures.)

Identify and correct the errors in the following `<script>` element. The code is supposed to define an array of four objects that represent an address book database. The address book object has three properties named `name`, `address`, and `phone`. The code uses a `for` loop to search the database for the name "Clyde" and display Clyde's phone number.

```
<script type="text/javascript">
   var addresses = new Array(3)
   addresses[0] = addressEntry("Bill", "123 Main Street", "321-4567")
   addresses[1] = addressEntry("Theresa", "456 Elm Place', "987-1234")
   addresses[2] = addressEntry("Emily", "65 Oriole Drive", "487-0246")
   addresses[3] = addressEntry("Clyde", "1003 Court Street", "357-9087")
   var ctr
   for (ctr = 0; ctr < 3; ctr++){
      if (addressEntry[0] = "Clyde") {
         alert("The number for Clyde is: " + addresses.phone)
      }
   }
</script>
```

Note: Most of the exercises above may also be done as lab exercises. If a problem involves a function, add a function call so that the function code is actually executed.

Exercise 16.1: Creating a Database

In this exercise we will create a web page on "Great Discoveries in Physics" that has an underlying database containing information on those great discoveries. When the page loads, the information in the database will not be visible. Instead, the page will prompt the surfer to enter a nationality, and then the web page will search the database and display a list of the physicists of that nationality. (Obviously, the web page should also have options to search for physicists by name and to search for discoveries by name or by year, but we'll leave those complications out.) First, we need to set up the database.

❑ Create a source document named PhysicsDatabase.htm that implements the following database.

Discovery/Event	Approx. Year	Scientist	Nationality
Theory of Gravity	1687	Isaac Newton	British
Conservation of Energy	1850	William Thomson	British
X Rays	1895	Wilhelm Roentgen	German
Radioactivity	1896	Henri Becquerel	French
Electron	1897	J.J. Thomson	British
Radium	1898	Marie Curie	French
Theory of Relativity	1905	Albert Einstein	Swiss
Unit of Electric Charge	1910	Robert Millikan	American

To do so, write a constructor function named `scientificDiscovery()` that defines an object with four properties, named `name`, `year`, `scientist`, and `nationality`. Then write the code that uses that function to create an array, named `discoveries`, of eight objects (one object for each of the eight records in the database). All this code should go in a `<script>` element in the `<head>` element.

In the `<body>`, create a form named `searchForm` that has the text "Please enter a nationality" followed by a text box named `nationalityBox` and then a click button labeled Search. Underneath the click button create a text area box with 8 rows and a width of 60 characters, as so:

```
<textarea name="resultsDisplay" rows="8" cols="60" wrap="wrap">Search results displayed
here . . . </textarea>
```

(A text area is like a text box, except it has more than one row. The full name of this text area is `document.searchForm.resultsDisplay` and its contents are stored in `document.searchForm.resultsDisplay.value`.)

We will add the necessary search code to this document in Lab Exercise 16.2.

Exercise 16.2: Searching a Database

❑ Using your source document from Lab Exercise 16.1, declare a function named `searchForNationality()` with a parameter named `n` (for nationality). This function will contain the code that will search the database. The `onclick` event handler of the Search click button should call this function and send it the value that the surfer has entered in the `nationalityBox` text box. Write the search code without a `for` loop at first. That is, `searchForNationality()` will have eight conditional statements, one for each object/record in the database. Note the hints and explanations that follow.

The first conditional statement, for example, will check to see if `discoveries[0].nationality` equals `n` (which has been passed the value the surfer entered in the text box). Note that you don't need to use the `substring()` method to see if `n` matches the `nationality` property of each `discoveries` object. A simple conditional statement checking to see whether `n` equals the nationality stored in each object will work fine. In addition, don't worry at this point about whether the user typed the nationality with a beginning upper-case letter. Just use it as typed.

If the value of `discoveries[0].nationality` equals the value of `n`, then use an assignment statement to store the name of the scientist in a string named `searchResults`. But you need to write this assignment statement carefully. The next conditional statement will check `discoveries[1].nationality` and, if it equals `n`, will also store the name of that scientist in the string variable `searchResults`. So you have to be careful here not to erase the names of any preceding matches. That is, we don't just want to store the second name in `searchResults`, we want to *append* it to anything that's already in `searchResults`. We do it with an assignment statement like this:

```
searchResults = searchResults + discoveries[0].scientist + "/r"
```

Or, for the second name (assuming that the nationality matches):

```
searchResults = searchResults + discoveries[1].scientist + "/r"
```

In other words, the right side of this assignment statement tells the browser to take the current value of `searchResults` and add, or append, the value of `discoveries[1].scientist` to it. The "/r" at the end is a special character combination that represents a return character. In other words, when the whole `searchResults` string is displayed in the text area, there will be a line break after each scientist's name. At the very beginning of the `searchForNationality()` function we should also put a line initializing `searchResults` to an empty string:

```
searchResults = ""
```

❑ After you have written the eight conditional statements, put an assignment statement that displays the contents of `searchResults` in the text area. Don't forget to save your work periodically!

❑ Once you have the `searchForNationality()` function working with the eight conditional statements, you should be able to see how you can replace them with a `for` loop, so do that now. Hint: We wrote a similar `for` loop in the section "A Database as an Array of Objects." (Don't delete the nine conditional statements; just comment them out of the code using /* and */.)

❑ Optional: Instead of just displaying the name of the scientist in the text area, rewrite the code so that it displays the name of the scientist, the name of the discovery, and the year of the discovery, followed by a line break. (You will have to make the text area box wider, of course.)

❑ Optional: Add a second search option that allows the user to enter two years, a beginning year and an ending year, and then searches the database and displays all the discoveries that occurred between those two years.

JavaScript with Frames and Windows

LEARNING OBJECTIVES

1. Learn how to use JavaScript with frames so as to be able to test a surfer's input and respond on the fly with a customized display.

2. Learn how to use JavaScript to open new browser windows and write content into them.

Dynamic Content with Frames

In Chapter 6 we learned how to create magazine-style layouts for web pages using frames and how to create links in one frame that load a source document into another frame. Such links between frames make for more elegant and interactive web pages, but limitations still exist. Each link is static—that is, selecting a given link will always load the same document in the same frame, resulting in the same display. It would be nice if we could vary the display depending on some input from the surfer. Consider, for instance, our Great Discoveries database of the last chapter. We might like to redesign it so that it used two side-by-side frames. The left frame would display the text box that prompted the user to enter a nationality for which to search. Once the surfer entered a nationality and clicked the Search database function, the database would be searched (using the code developed in Lab Exercise 16.2). But instead of displaying the results in a text area, we will use JavaScript to display them in the right frame. In doing so, we will be able to use HTML elements and tags to format the display in almost any way we desire. For example, we might display the results in an ordered list or in a table format. The result is a more visually attractive design, as shown in Figure 17.1 (using a table format with <th> tags to make the headings Discovery, Year, etc., display in bold).

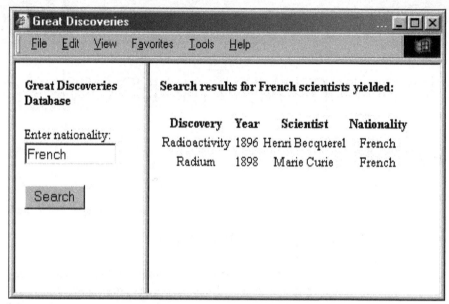

FIGURE 17.1. "Great Discoveries" page redesigned to use frames and dynamically display the search results as an HTML table

Implementing interactive frames using our Great Discoveries database is an optional part of Lab Exercise 17.1. Here we'll start with a simpler example to learn how JavaScript works with frames.

The CyberPizza Web Page

For our example of a web page that combines frames with JavaScript, we will return to the CyberPizza page of Lab Exercises 12.2 and 12.3 in Chapter 12 and spruce it up by dividing the page into two side-by-side frames. The left frame will contain the checkboxes, radio buttons, and click button that allow the surfer to select the pizza toppings and crust, and the right frame will display the surfer's choices after he or she has clicked the Submit Pizza Order button. The basic display is shown in Figure 17.2, just after the page has been loaded.

This revised CyberPizza web page uses three documents: CyberPizza.htm as the frameset document, SelectPizza.htm as the document that contains the code for the left frame, and DisplayChoices.htm as the document that contains the code for the initial display in the right frame. This latter document is the simplest of the three. It just displays the line "Your pizza choice will be displayed here . . ." in bold type. The complete document is:

```
<!--XHTML and DTD info goes here-->
<html>
```

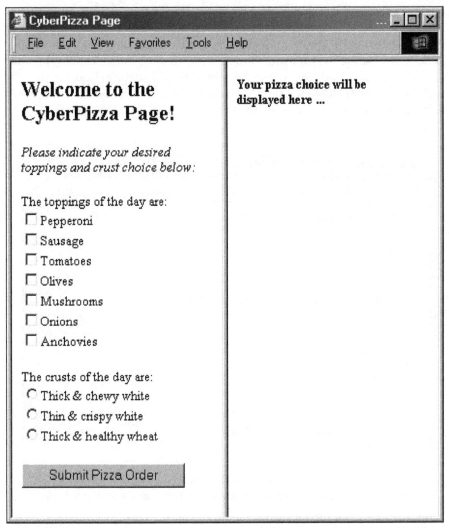

FIGURE 17.2. The CyberPizza page redesigned as two side-by-side frames

```
<head>
  <title>Choices Display</title>
</head>
<body>
  <strong>Your pizza choice will be displayed
  here ...</strong>
</body>
</html>
```

We will look at each of the other two documents in turn.

The CyberPizza <frameset> Code

The CyberPizza.htm frameset document contains the code shown in Figure 17.3. It divides the browser into two column frames, named `leftFrame` and `rightFrame`, and loads the source document SelectPizza.htm into `leftFrame` and the document DisplayChoices.htm into `rightFrame`. For the moment, we'll ignore the purpose and contents of the `displayOrder()` function.

```
sourcecode.htm - Notepad
File  Edit  Search  Help

<!--XHTML and frameset DTD info goes here-->
<html>
<head>
    <title>CyberPizza Page</title>
    <script type="text/javascript">
        function displayOrder(tpgForm,crustForm) {
            //Code to be discussed later goes here...
        }
    </script>
</head>

<frameset cols="50%,50%">
    <frame id="leftFrame" name="leftFrame" src="SelectPizza.htm" />
    <frame id="rightFrame" name="rightFrame" src="DisplayChoices.htm" />
</frameset>
</html>
```

FIGURE 17.3. The frameset document for the CyberPizza page

The SelectPizza.htm Code (Left Frame)

Figure 17.4 has the code for the SelectPizza.htm document, which is loaded into the left frame.

A cursory examination of the SelectPizza.htm code reveals that it uses check boxes and radio buttons to offer the surfer a choice of pizza toppings and crusts. We also note that the code specifies a `value` for each check box and radio button. We will use these values later to display the surfer's choices in the right frame. When the surfer has chosen the toppings and crust desired and clicks the Submit Pizza Order button, the button's event handler calls a function by the name of `parent.displayOrder()` and passes it two parameters (the `toppings` form and the `crusts` form).

To understand what is going on here, consider how we want the CyberPizza page to work. We get the surfer's pizza order using the forms in the left

```
sourcecode.htm - Notepad
File   Edit   Search   Help

<!--XHTML and DTD information goes here-->
<html>
<head>
    <title>Pizza Selection Page</title>
</head>

<body>
<h2>Welcome to the CyberPizza Page!</h2>
<em>Please indicate your desired toppings and crust choice below:</em>
<form id="toppings" name="toppings">
    The toppings of the day are: <br />
    <input type="checkbox" name="pepCB" value="Pepperoni" />Pepperoni<br />
    <input type="checkbox" name="ssgCB" value="Sausage" />Sausage<br />
    <input type="checkbox" name="tomCB" value="Tomatoes" />Tomatoes<br />
    <input type="checkbox" name="olvCB" value="Olives" />Olives<br />
    <input type="checkbox" name="mrCB" value="Mushrooms" />Mushrooms<br />
    <input type="checkbox" name="onCB value="Onions" />Onions<br />
    <input type="checkbox" name="anchCB" value="Anchovies" />Anchovies<br />
</form>
<p></p>
<form id="crusts" name="crusts">
    The crusts of the day are: <br />
    <input type="radio" name="crustRB" value="Thick & chewy white" />Thick &
        chewy white<br />
    <input type="radio" name="crustRB" value="Thin & crispy white" />Thin & crispy
        white<br />
    <input type="radio" name="crustRB" value="Thick & healthy wheat" />Thick &
        healthy wheat<br />
</form>
<p></p>
<form id="placeOrder" name="placeOrder">
    <input type="button" name="b1" value="Submit Pizza Order"
        onclick="parent.displayOrder(document.toppings, document.crusts)" />
</form>
</body>
</html>
```

FIGURE 17.4.   The SelectPizza.htm code for the left frame of the CyberPizza page

frame, and we want to display the order in the right frame. But the left
frame and the right frame involve two separate documents. The SelectPiz-
za.htm document is loaded into the left frame, and any functions we declare

and call in this document will act only in that frame. So how can we call a `displayOrder()` function from the left frame but have it act in the right frame? The answer is that when we are using frames, we may have a function call in one document that refers to a function declared in an entirely different document, as long as both documents are simultaneously present in different frames in the frameset.

How do we call a function from one document that exists in another document? We do it the same way as we've always done: We write its name so that JavaScript knows to go and execute that function. But now, in order to find the function, JavaScript needs a more complete address. It's similar to the difference between telling someone that a friend lives at 123 Main Street and telling someone that the friend lives at 123 Main Street, San Francisco, CA. In the first case, presumably you are having the conversation in San Francisco and therefore it's not necessary to mention the city and state. But if you were having the conversation in Chicago, you would mention the more complete address.

The complete address for calling the `displayOrder()` function is:

```
parent.displayOrder(document.toppings, document.crusts)
```

This simply indicates to the browser that it will not find the function `displayOrder()` in the current document, but in its **parent document**. The word `parent` is a reserved word in JavaScript and refers to the frameset document of a document. That is, a frameset document that creates one or more frames is known as the parent of those frames. In this case, the parent or frameset document of SelectPizza.htm is CyberPizza.htm, because the CyberPizza.htm document is the frameset document that creates the frames and loads SelectPizza.htm into the left frame. So by writing the function call as `parent.displayOrder()` we tell the browser that it will find the `displayOrder()` function in the CyberPizza.htm document.

Figure 17.5 diagrams the hierarchical relationship between the parent frameset document and the two child documents in the left and right frames (which are SelectPizza.htm and DisplayChoices.htm in this example).

The displayOrder() Function

Now let's look at the details of the `displayOrder()` function, which is declared in the <head> element of the CyberPizza.htm document and is shown in Figure 17.6.

The first strange thing that you will probably notice in the `displayOrder()` code is all the references to `rightFrame.document.write()`. We'll explain the `document.write()` part first.

The `document.write()` method (pronounced document-dot-write, meaning the `write()` method belonging to the `document` object) is a JavaScript

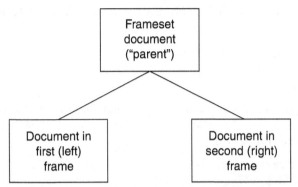

FIGURE 17.5. The frameset hierarchy for a basic two-frame frameset

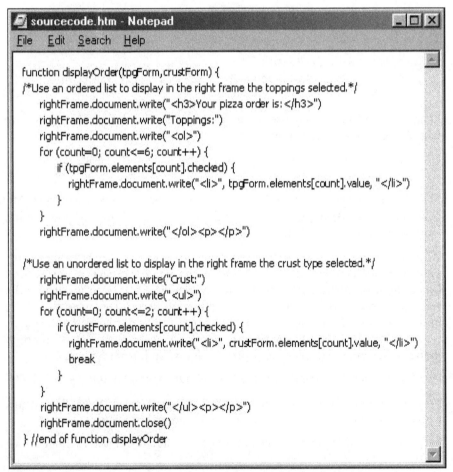

```
function displayOrder(tpgForm,crustForm) {
/*Use an ordered list to display in the right frame the toppings selected.*/
    rightFrame.document.write("<h3>Your pizza order is:</h3>")
    rightFrame.document.write("Toppings:")
    rightFrame.document.write("<ol>")
    for (count=0; count<=6; count++) {
        if (tpgForm.elements[count].checked) {
            rightFrame.document.write("<li>", tpgForm.elements[count].value, "</li>")
        }
    }
    rightFrame.document.write("</ol><p></p>")

/*Use an unordered list to display in the right frame the crust type selected.*/
    rightFrame.document.write("Crust:")
    rightFrame.document.write("<ul>")
    for (count=0; count<=2; count++) {
        if (crustForm.elements[count].checked) {
            rightFrame.document.write("<li>", crustForm.elements[count].value, "</li>")
            break
        }
    }
    rightFrame.document.write("</ul><p></p>")
    rightFrame.document.close()
} //end of function displayOrder
```

FIGURE 17.6. The code for the displayOrder() function, which displays the surfer's pizza choices in the right frame

method that takes a line of HTML code and writes the result on the screen. For example:

```
<script type="text/javascript">
   document.write("Testing, testing, 1, 2, 3...")
</script>
```

This line of JavaScript code will simply display the line of HTML code "Testing, testing, 1, 2, 3 . . ." in the browser window. In this example, the HTML code is just text. But we can also include tags:

```
document.write("<strong>Testing,</strong> Testing<br />
   <em>1, 2, 3...</em>")
```

The displayed result would be:

Testing Testing

1, 2, 3...

Variables also may be used as parameters in the document.write() method. The following code would display the value of firstName:

```
var firstName = "Jamie"
document.write("<strong>The surfer's first name is:
   </strong> " + firstName)
```

As an alternative, we may use a comma instead of a plus sign when we are combining two or more things to write:

```
document.write("<strong>The surfer's first name is:
   </strong> ", firstName)
```

In sum, the document.write() method gives us the power of creating HTML code on the fly. (Although before you get too excited about the possibilities, read the next section to learn about its limitations.)

What about the rightFrame reference in the code rightFrame.document. write()? Remember that rightFrame is the name we gave to the second frame when we defined it in the frameset document. We need to include the references to it in the displayOrder() function because we need to tell the browser in which frame we want the pizza order results displayed. For instance, the line of code below tells the browser to use the document.write() method in the right frame to display "Your pizza order is:" in header 3 format:

```
rightFrame.document.write("<h3>Your pizza order is:</h3>")
```

Note: If this line of code were in the leftFrame document (SelectPizza.htm), we would have to add a parent reference before rightFrame:

```
parent.rightFrame.document.write("<h3>Your pizza order is:
   </h3>")
```

The reason is that the reference to rightFrame does not make sense in the context of the leftFrame document. The leftFrame document literally has no `rightFrame`. Rather, it's the parent document where `rightFrame` is defined. The `parent` reference tells the browser: "Go back up to the parent document and then go to 'rightFrame', as defined by the parent document." In our CyberPizza example, however, the code for the `displayOrder()` function is in the parent document (CyberPizza.htm), not in the `leftFrame` document (SelectPizza.htm), so the reference to `rightFrame` alone suffices.

The final thing to note in the `displayOrder()` code is how we use a `for` loop, a conditional statement, and the `document.write()` method to display the surfer's topping choices using an ordered list and the crust choice using an unordered list. A sample of the displayed results is shown in Figure 17.7.

FIGURE 17.7.   The CyberPizza page after the Submit button has been clicked, displaying the surfer's choices in the right frame as an ordered list for the toppings and an unordered list for the crust

Let's analyze the code for the display of the ordered list:

```
rightFrame.document.write("<ol>")
for (count=0; count<=6; count++) {
  if (tpgForm.elements[count].checked) {
    rightFrame.document.write("<li>", tpgForm.
      elements[count].value, "</li>")
  }
}
rightFrame.document.write("</ol><p></p>")
```

The basic idea behind this code is to write the HTML commands for an ordered list to the right frame, where each item in the list will be one of the toppings that the surfer has selected. If, for example, the surfer had chosen pepperoni, olives, and mushrooms, the HTML code would be:

```
<ol>
<li>Pepperoni</li>
<li>Olives</li>
<li>Mushrooms</li>
</ol>
```

It's not quite as simple as that, however, because we don't know in advance which toppings the surfer is going to select. If the surfer selects two toppings, then we'll need to write two <li> lines. If three toppings, then there will be three <li> lines, and so on. And no matter how many toppings, we need to know which ones they are. We determine all this by using a for loop and a conditional statement.

The first line of code above, rightFrame.document.write("<ol>"), writes the <ol> tag to the right frame. Then we come to the for loop and the conditional statement, which use the elements array to cycle through all the check boxes and test which ones are checked. This loop code is equivalent to seven conditional statements:

```
if (tpgForm.elements[0].checked) {
  rightFrame.document.write("<li>", tpgForm.elements[0].
    value, "</li>")
}
if (tpgForm.elements[1].checked) {
  rightFrame.document.write("<li>", tpgForm.elements[1].
    value, "</li>")
}
//etc. etc.
if (tpgForm.elements[6].checked) {
  rightFrame.document.write("<li>", tpgForm.elements[6].
    value, "</li>")
}
```

Remember that tpgForm is the name of the first formal parameter in the displayOrder() function and refers back to the toppings form in SelectPizza.htm. So tpgForm.elements[2], for example, refers to the third input element in the toppings form, which in this case is the third checkbox.

When the browser finds that a check box is checked, it uses the document.write() method to write an <li> element to the right frame, with the topping value corresponding to that check box. If you go back and look at the forms in SelectPizza.htm (Figure 17.4), you will note that we used the value attribute in each check box to store the name of the associated topping in its value property, precisely so we could display it here when necessary.

After the for loop finishes cycling through all the check boxes and writing the <li> lines, the next line of JavaScript code writes the ending </ol> tag to complete the ordered list (it also adds a <p> element with nothing in it to generate a blank line):

```
rightFrame.document.write("</ol><p></p>")
```

The code then continues with a similar for loop that tests the radio buttons in the crusts form (represented by the formal parameter crustForm) and creates an unordered list:

```
rightFrame.document.write("Crust:")
rightFrame.document.write("<ul>")
for (count=0; count<=2; count++) {
  if (crustForm.elements[count].checked) {
    rightFrame.document.write("<li>",crustForm.
      elements[count].value, "</ul>")
    break
  }
}
rightFrame.document.write("</ul><p></p>")
```

The only significant difference between this code and the code for the ordered list (besides the fact that there are only three radio buttons) is the presence of the break command in the conditional statement. We include it because once the browser has found that one of the radio buttons is checked, there's no need to check the rest. So the break command stops the loop.

The final line of code in the displayOrder() function calls the close() method of the document object:

```
rightFrame.document.close()
```

This method takes the necessary steps to properly finish the writing process by closing the document output stream (see the next section) and completing the document display in the right frame. (There is a corresponding document.open() method that opens a document for receiving HTML code via the document.write() method, but its use is optional because the document.write() method itself will automatically open the document if it isn't already open.)

The Document Output Stream

There is one important limitation on using the `document.write()` method. It only works while the web browser is actively loading an HTML source document, either into a window or into a frame. When a web browser retrieves an HTML source document and starts translating the HTML code for display on the screen, it opens something called the **document output stream**.

You may think of this in almost literal terms that conjure up an image of avant garde art: the web browser takes the HTML code, translates it, and "sprays" the results on the screen, starting at the top and working its way down to the bottom. Once the document has finished loading and the display has been sprayed or written to the screen, this output stream of code is closed and no more writing can take place for that document. In Navigator, the closing of the output stream is signaled by the "Document: Done" message you see at the bottom left of the Navigator window in the status bar. In Explorer, the message is simply "Done".

The `document.write()` method may therefore not normally be used in conjunction with `<input>` tag elements like click buttons, radio buttons, and check boxes. You cannot, for example, use a conditional statement to check some radio buttons and then use `document.write()` to display something in the same window that contains the radio buttons, because the radio buttons aren't ready to be used until the document has been loaded and the document output stream is closed, at which point `document.write()` will not work for that document. If you attempt to use `document.write()` after the document has been loaded, the browser will open a new document output stream and replace the current document with whatever content is specified by the `document.write()` method.

Now that we know about frames, however, we can use the `document.write()` method to display something in a separate frame from that in which the radio buttons (or whatever) reside, as demonstrated in the `displayOrder()` function above.

QuickCheck Questions

1. Consider a frameset document that defines three row frames (named `topFrame`, `middleFrame`, and `bottomFrame`) and loads the documents Doc1.htm, Doc2.htm, and Doc3.htm into each frame, respectively. Assuming the frameset document contained a function named `calculateResults()`, with no parameters, write the line of code that would call this function from within the Doc3.htm document (that is, the line of code is in a `<script>` element in Doc3.htm).

2. Considering the `calculateResults()` function from #1, write a line of code to put in it that would display the text "The results are: " in italic in the middle frame.

Lab Exercise 17.1, "Using JavaScript with Frames," may be done at this point.

Manipulating Windows

In Chapter 6 in the section "Opening Multiple Windows" we learned a simple way to have the browser display a document in an entirely new window when the surfer clicked on a link. The trick is to set the `target` attribute in the `<a>` tag to some name, such as `"windowname"`:

```
<a href="DocumentToDisplay.htm" target="windowname">Click
here to see the document displayed in a new window</a>
```

The name `windowname` is your choice. If a browser window with that name is not yet open, the browser will open a new window with that name and display the document in it. If the window already exists, the browser simply displays the document there. Remember that the surfer does not see the window name, as it is an internal name for the browser's use only. What the surfer does see is the title bar of the window, which will display the contents of the `<title>` element in the DocumentToDisplay.htm document. This technique, however, will only open the window. JavaScript gives us the capability to do much more.

Creating Custom Windows

To start, we may open a window by using the `open()` method of the `window` object. The code is:

```
var sampleWindow = window.open("DocumentToDisplay.htm",
    "testWin", "width=250,height=200,left=110,top=60")
```

We see that the `open()` method takes three string parameters. The first string gives the name of the source document to display in the newly opened window; the second string specifies a name that a `target` attribute may use for the window; and the third string specifies various features of the window, such as its width, height, and top and left position on the screen, measured in pixels. The `top` value specifies the position of the top of the new window in terms of the number of pixels down from the top of the screen; the left value specifies the position of the `left` edge of the window in terms of the number of pixels from the left side of the screen. (As written, this specification of the `left` and `top` values only works in Explorer. We will discuss the Navigator version below.)

When the `window.open()` method is executed, the browser creates a new window object. The variable name on the left side of the assignment statement—`sampleWindow`, in this case—is the name that is given to the new window object. It is used to refer to the window in later JavaScript code. For example, we may close the window by calling its `close()` method:

```
sampleWindow.close()
```

The surfer, of course, can always close the window by clicking its close box. Because of this possibility, it's good practice before you call the `close()` method to check whether the window is still open. We do so by checking the `closed` property of the window:

```
if (sampleWindow.closed == false) {
   sampleWindow.close()
}
```

Another useful method of a window object is the `focus()` method. When called, this method brings the specified window to the front of all other open windows:

```
sampleWindow.focus()
```

Overall, a window object has in excess of 40 methods, plus over 50 properties. We list the basic ones in Appendix F. More detailed information about them may be found at the JavaScript websites cited in that appendix. (Sometimes the window object and its associated sub-objects, methods, and properties go by the name of the **Browser Object Model**, just as we refer to the Document Object Model when speaking of the document object and its sub-objects, methods, and properties. Because the document object is a child of the window object—see Figure 8.9—the Document Object Model is technically a part of the Browser Object Model.)

Note the difference between the window object name (`sampleWindow`) and the name we used in the second parameter (`testWin`):

```
var sampleWindow = window.open("DocumentToDisplay.htm",
   "testWin", "width=250,height=200,left=110,top=60")
```

The `testWin` name is only used when the window is the subject of a `target` attribute reference. The following line of HTML code would display the listed source document in the new window (assuming it was open):

```
<a href="DocumentToDisplay.htm" target="testWin">Click
here to see the document displayed in a new window</a>
```

If you don't plan on writing such code, you may leave the name blank when creating the window:

```
var sampleWindow = window.open("DocumentToDisplay.htm", "",
   "width=250,height=200,left=110,top=60")
```

You may also leave out the other parameters and simply write:

```
var sampleWindow = window.open()
```

In such a case the browser opens a new window and gives it a default size and location (usually in the upper left of the screen).

There are over 25 possible **window features** that may be specified in the third parameter string. The most common ones besides `height`, `width`, `top`, and `left` are three boolean values: `toolbar`, `scrollbars`, and `resizable`. You include them in the parameter string when you want the window to have a toolbar and/or have scrollbars and/or be resizable (by the surfer dragging the resize box in the bottom-right corner of the window). The following code creates a resizable window with a toolbar and scrollbars:

```
var secondWindow = window.open("DocumentToDisplay.htm", "",
   "toolbar,scrollbars,resizable,width=250,height=200,
   left=110,top=60")
```

If you leave out the third parameter, then the browser creates a default window with all the normal window features. But when you use the third parameter to specify any one of the window features, then the others are automatically turned off. In other words, once you specify one feature, you have to specify all the other features you want the window to have as well.

As mentioned above, the `top` and `left` features only work in Explorer. To set the window position in Navigator, you must use `screenX` and `screenY` for the left and top positions of the window on the screen. Fortunately, it's okay to include both `top` and `screenY`, and `left` and `screenX`, references in the third parameter. If the browser doesn't recognize any of them, it ignores them. So the code to open and position a basic window (without the toolbar, etc.) that works in both Explorer and Navigator would be:

```
var secondWindow = window.open("DocumentToDisplay.htm", "",
   "width=250,height=200,left=110,top=60,screenX=110,
   screenY=60")
```

You might note that we did not put spaces between any of the values in the third parameter string. Technically, we may add spaces, but it turns out that some browsers do not give good results when they're there. The order of the features listed in the third parameter also does not matter.

Screen Width and Number-to-String Conversions

By themselves, the `left` and `top` values (or `screenX` and `screenY` values) cannot be used to center a window in the middle of the screen or position a window on the right edge of the screen. To do so, we need to know the width and height of the user's screen. Fortunately, version 4 of both Explorer and Navigator introduced the `screen` object as a child object of the `window` object. Among the `screen` object's properties are `height` and `width`, which store the height and width of the user's screen in pixels. These values may be accessed via `window.screen.height` and `window.screen.width`, or simply `screen.height` and `screen.width`, because the `window` reference is assumed.

In order to position a window on the right edge of the screen, we first need to decide how wide the window should be. We then subtract this width from the total screen width, as stored in `screen.width`. The resulting value will be the left position for the window. For example, if we want the window to be 300 pixels wide, then the left position of the window will be:

```
var leftPosition = screen.width - 300
```

If the screen width were 1024 pixels, then the variable `leftPosition` would have the value 1024 − 300, or 724. This would be where we want the left edge of the window. The right edge of the window would be at 724 + 300 = 1024, i.e., the right edge of the screen.

There's one other tricky part to making this work. Remember that the third parameter in the `window.open()` method, which specifies the window features (width, height, scrollbars, etc.), is a string. So we can't just use the `leftPosition` number as is. We need to do a **number-to-string conversion** so that we can insert it in the proper place in the window features string. Fortunately, JavaScript will do the conversion automatically if we use the concatenation (+) operator (see Chapter 8, the section "Storing Values in Variables"). Here's how it works in a simple example:

```
var sampleString1, sampleString2, theNum, result1, result2
sampleString1 = "The answer is: "
sampleString2 = "George Washington"
firstNum = 59
result1 = sampleString1 + sampleString2
result2 = sampleString1 + firstNum
```

When the browser executes this code, the value of `result1` will be the concatenated string "The answer is: George Washington". But the assignment statement involving `result2` looks as if it would yield an error message, because how can you add a string and a number? In actual fact, however, when the variable on the left side of the + operator contains a string (`sampleString1`, in this case) and the variable on the right side of the + operator contains a number (`firstNum`, in this case), then the rules of JavaScript prescribe that the number value on the right side be converted to a string and then concatenated with the left-side string variable. The final result is a string. So in our example, the value of `firstNum` is turned into the string value "59" and appended onto `sampleString1`. The value of `result2` will therefore be the string "The answer is: 59".

(Note: If the number comes first, then the + operator, and then a string, JavaScript attempts to convert the string to a number and do a normal arithmetic addition. But, as discussed in in Chapter 11, in the section "Converting Strings to Numbers" it's best to do string-to-number conversions explicitly using the `parseFloat()` function.)

Now we can write the code to create a window with a width of 300 pixels that is positioned on the right edge of the screen. We'll assume that we want a window height of 180 pixels, with the top edge of the window 75 pixels down from the top of the screen. The code will be:

```
var leftPosition = screen.width - 300
var featuresString = "width=300,height=180,left=" +
   leftPosition + ",top=75"
var rightedgeWindow = window.open("DocumentToDisplay.htm",
   "", featuresString)
```

When the browser executes the assignment statement for featuresString, it will convert the numeric value of leftPosition to a string value, append it to the string "width=300,height=180,left=", and then append the string ",top=75" to the end of that. So, assuming that the width of the screen is 1024 pixels, the value of featuresString will be:

```
"width=300,height=180,left=724,top=75"
```

We left out the Navigator screenX and screenY values in this example, but they could be included in the same fashion. We also don't need to use the featuresString variable. Instead, we can put everything in the window.open() method:

```
var rightedgeWindow = window.open("DocumentToDisplay.htm",
    "","width=300,height=180,left=" + leftPosition +
    ",top=75")
```

Exercise 10 provides the challenge of writing the code to center a window on the screen.

Although designing a website that opens and uses multiple windows is a nice JavaScript exercise, be aware that they tend to be error-prone. For example, it's possible to use the document.write() method to write HTML text and tags to a newly opened window just as we do with frames. The code would be:

IMPORTANT

```
var secondWindow = window.open("blank.htm", "",
    "width=250,height=200,left=110,top=60,screenX=110,
    screenY=60")
secondWindow.document.write("<strong>This will appear in
    the new window</strong>")
```

But Explorer, in particular, has trouble with this sequence of commands. It may not have finished opening the window when it tries to execute the document.write() code, and therefore generates an error message.

Also remember from our discussion in Chapter 6, in the section "Opening Multiple Windows," that some websites overuse pop-up windows, and therefore many surfers have grown to dislike them. So both from a design perspective and a code perspective, it's best not to get too enamored with multiple windows.

QuickCheck Questions

1. Write the JavaScript code that would open a new window with a height of 100 pixels and a width of 150 pixels, positioned 50 pixels down from the top of the screen and 50 pixels in from the left. Also give the window scrollbars.

2. Modify the code that creates the rightedgeWindow so that it includes screenX and screenY values for Navigator.

Lab Exercise 17.2, "A Custom Alert Box," may be done at this point.

Key Terms

Browser Object Model

document output stream

number-to-string conversion

parent document

window features

Code Summary

1. Dynamic Content with Frames

Consider a function named `displayOrder()`, with no parameters, that is declared in a frameset document. To call it from a document that is loaded into one of the frameset's frames, write:

```
parent.displayOrder()
```

Using JavaScript to write HTML text and tags (as the page is loading):

```
<script type="text/javascript">
   var firstName = "Jamie"
   document.write("<strong>The surfer's first name is:</strong> " + firstName)
</script>
```

Writing HTML text and tags into a frame named `rightFrame` (this line of code must be in the parent document of the `rightFrame` document):

```
rightFrame.document.write("<h3>Your pizza order is:</h3>")
```

Closing the document output stream after one or more `document.write()` statements have written HTML code to a frame:

```
rightFrame.document.close()
```

Writing HTML text and tags into a frame named `rightFrame` when the line of code is in a document in another frame of the frameset (the frameset must not have nested frames):

```
parent.rightFrame.document.write("<h3>Your pizza order is:</h3>")
```

2. Manipulating Windows

Opening a new window and setting its height, width, and position, and the document that will be displayed in it:

```
var secondWindow = window.open("DocumentToDisplay.htm", "win2",
   "width=250,height=200,left=110,top=60,screenX=110,screenY=60")
```

Closing a window (and checking the `closed` property of the window to make sure it's currently open before closing it):

```
if (secondWindow.closed == false) {
   secondWindow.close()
}
```

Bringing a window to the front of all other windows:

```
secondWindow.focus()
```

Creating a window that has a toolbar and scrollbars and is resizable:

```
var secondWindow = window.open("DocumentToDisplay.htm", "",
   "toolbar,scrollbars,resizable,width=250,height=200")
```

Converting a number to a string using the concatenation (+) operator:

```
var sampleString = "The answer is: "
var firstNum = 59
var result = sampleString1 + firstNum    //firstNum will be converted to "59"
```

Accessing the height and width (in pixels) of the surfer's screen using the window.screen object:

```
var heightOfScreen = screen.height
var widthOfScreen = screen.width
```

Writing HTML code into a new window:

```
secondWindow.document.write("<strong>This will appear in the new window</strong>")
```

The document.write() method may not normally be used in conjunction with <input> elements like click buttons, radio buttons, and check boxes, because the input elements aren't ready to be used until the document has been loaded and the document output stream is closed, at which point the use of document.write() is invalid. (The exception is when multiple frames or windows are used.)

When creating a new window, do not confuse the name of the window object (referenced by a JavaScript variable on the left side of the assignment statement that creates the window) and the name specified in the second parameter in the window.open() method (which relates to the use of the target attribute in an HTML <a> tag).

When using the third parameter in the window.open() method to specify a window's features such as height, width, scrollbars, and so on, you must specify each feature you want; there are no default features. (If you leave out the third parameter, the window will appear with its default features.)

When using the third parameter in the window.open() method to specify a window's features such as height, width, scrollbars, etc., do not put spaces between the feature specifications, because some browsers do not handle them well.

Creating and manipulating multiple browser windows using JavaScript tends to generate more errors than normal in browsers, so use them only when you have a good reason to do so. (Some users also find them annoying.)

1. Which of the following lines of code correctly calls the document.write() method so that it displays the message "Anybody home?" in bold text?
   a. document.write(<b> + "Anybody home?" + </b>)
   b. document.write("<b> + Anybody home? + </b>")
   c. document.write("<b>Anybody home?</b>")
   d. document.write(<b>, "Anybody home?", + </b>)

2. Which of the following lines of code correctly calls the document.write() method so that it displays the message "The answer is: " followed by the value of a variable named theResult?
   a. document.write("The answer is: " + theResult)
   b. document.write("The answer is: ", theResult)
   c. document.write("The answer is: theResult")
   d. document.write("The answer is: " + "theResult")

3. True or false: The document.write() method may only be used to display text in the browser window during the time the browser is loading a document.

4. Consider a web page that uses three frames named `topFrame`, `middleFrame`, and `bottomFrame`. The frame-set document has a function named `calculateResults()` that takes no parameters. A document named middleTest.htm is loaded into the `middleFrame`. Which of the following lines of code uses an `onclick` event handler to call the `calculateResults()` function from within the middleTest.htm document? (That is, the code to call the function is contained in the middleTest.htm document.)
   a. `onclick = "calculateResults()"`
   b. `onclick = "frameset.calculateResults()"`
   c. `onclick = "middleFrame.calculateResults()"`
   d. `onclick = "parent.calculateResults()"`

5. Given the web page from Review Question 4, which of the following lines of code could be used in the `calculateResults()` function to write the message "You're right!" in the `bottomFrame`?
   a. `document.write("You're right!")`
   b. `document.bottomFrame.write("You're right!")`
   c. `bottomFrame.document.write("You're right!")`
   d. `parent.document.write("You're right!")`

6. If the `calculateResults()` function mentioned in Review Question 4 was declared in the mid-dleTest.htm document instead of the frameset document, which of the following lines of code could be used in the `calculateResults()` function to display the message "Good job!" in the `bottomFrame`?
   a. `parent.document.write("Good job!")`
   b. `parent.document.bottomFrame.write("Good job!")`
   c. `parent.bottomFrame.document.write("Good job!")`
   d. `bottomFrame.document.write("Good job!")`

7. Which of the following lines of code opens a new browser window with a default size and location?
   a. `var secondWindow = new window`
   b. `var secondWindow = window.open()`
   c. `var secondWindow = openNewWindow()`
   d. `var secondWindow = defaultWindow`

8. Which of the following lines of code brings the window created in Review Question 7 to the front of all other windows?
   a. `secondWindow.focus()`
   b. `secondWindow.bringToFront()`
   c. `secondWindow = window.bringToFront()`
   d. `focus.secondWindow`

9. Which of the following lines of code opens a new browser window with a default size and location and that has scrollbars? The window is also resizable and displays a document with the name productInformation.htm.
   a. `var productInformation = new window("scrollbars,resizable")`
   b. `var secondWindow = openNewWindow("productInformation.htm", "scrollbars,resizable")`
   c. `var secondWindow = window.open("productInformation.htm", "w2", "scrollbars,resizable")`
   d. `var secondWindow = resizablewindow("productInformation.htm", "scrollbars,resizable")`

10. After the following code executes, what will be the value of the variable named `result`?
```
var firstNum = "7"
var secondNum = 5
var result = firstNum + secondNum
```
   a. 7
   b. 5

c. 12

d. 75

e. An error message will be displayed

1. Give brief explanations of the following terms: parent document, document output stream.

2. Write the JavaScript code that uses the `document.write()` method (in a `<script>` element placed in a `<body>` element) to display the line "Welcome to my web page" as a header 1, followed by the line "Here is the *Table of Contents*" in regular size type (where, as shown, *Table of Contents* is italicized).

3. Write the JavaScript code that uses a `for` loop and the `document.write()` method (in a `<script>` element placed in a `<body>` element) to display the numbers 1 through 20 in bold type. Each number should be on a separate line.

4. Write the HTML code for a frameset document that divides the browser window into three column frames named `leftFrame`, `middleFrame`, and `rightFrame`. The first column should be 20 percent of the window and the other two should each be 40 percent. Load a document named contents.htm into the left frame, one named userinfo.htm into the middle frame, and one named userportrait.htm into the right frame.

5. Given the frameset document outlined in Exercise 4, write the code that declares a function named `displayMessage()` in a `<script>` element in the frameset document's `<head>` element. The function should have one parameter, named `f`, that receives a form with a text box named `userNameBox`. The function's code should take the value of `userNameBox` and display it in the middle frame as a header 2 in the format "Greetings, User!" (where User is replaced by the actual value of the `userNameBox`).

6. Do Exercise 5, but this time assume that the `displayMessage()` function is declared in the contents.htm document that is loaded into the left frame. What change(s) do you need to make to the `displayMessage()` code?

7. Assuming that the contents.htm document mentioned in exercise 4 has a click button, write the code for its `onclick` event handler that will call the `displayMessage()` function in exercise 5 and pass it a form named `infoForm` (which has a text box named `userNameBox`).

8. Do Exercise 7, but this time assume that the `displayMessage()` function is declared in the userinfo.htm document (in the middle frame).

9. Write the JavaScript code that would open a new, non-resizable window with scrollbars and a height of 200 pixels and a width of 325 pixels, positioned in the upper-left corner of the screen. Display a document named SpecialOffer.htm in the window.

10. Write the JavaScript code that would open a new window with a height of 200 pixels and a width of 325 pixels, positioned in the center of the screen both horizontally and vertically. Don't assume that the screen has a certain height and width; use the `screen.height` and `screen.width` properties instead. Display a document named SpecialOffer.htm in the window. The window should have no toolbar and no scrollbars and should not be resizable.

11. Write the JavaScript code that would open a new, resizable window with a height of 125 pixels and a width of 200 pixels, positioned 100 pixels down from the top of the screen and 100 pixels in from the left. Then display the word "Glossary" in a header 2 format and the line of text "DOM: Document Object Model" in bold type below it, before closing the document output stream.

Debugging Exercise

Identify and correct the errors in the following function. The function is declared in a frameset document that defines two frames, named `topFrame` and `bottomFrame`. When the function is called, a form is passed to it that has four text boxes (and no other input elements). The formal parameter representing this form is named `f`. The purpose of the function is to use the `elements` array to display the values of the four text boxes as an ordered list.

```
function displayBoxInfo(f) {
    document.topFrame.write("<h3>Contents of the four textboxes</h3>")
    for (count=0; count<=4; count) {
        document.topFrame.write("<ol>")
        document.topFrame.write("<li> elements[count].value")
        document.topFrame.write("</ol>")
    }
} //end of function displayBoxInfo
```

Note: Most of the exercises above may also be done as lab exercises. If a problem involves a function, add a function call so that the function code is actually executed.

Exercise 17.1: Using JavaScript with Frames

Lab Exercises

In this exercise, we will create a web page with two side-by-side frames. On the left side, we'll prompt the surfer to enter his or her name and then click a button. When the surfer clicks the button, we will use its `onclick` event handler to call a function that is in the frameset (or parent) document. This function will display a reply to the user in large-size type in the right frame.

❑ Create an HTML frameset document named JSFramesTest.htm with two side-by-side columns. Use `<frame>` tags to load a document named GetUserName.htm into the left frame and a document named BigReply.htm in the right frame. Use the `id` and `name` attributes in each `<frame>` tag to give appropriate names to the frames as well.

❑ Create the GetUserName.htm and BigReply.htm documents. The GetUserName.htm document should prompt the user to enter his or her name into a text box and then click a button. That is, you will need to create a form with a text box and a click button. The BigReply.htm document should simply display the message "Your name will appear here in big type . . .".

❑ In the `<head>` container of JSFramesTest.htm, declare a function named `displayBigReply()` that has one parameter named `theName`. For its instructions, use the `document.write()` method to display `theName` as a level-1 header (i.e., the `<h1>` . . . `</h1>` container) in the *right frame*.

❑ Finally, note that we left out the function call for the button's `onclick` event handler in GetUserName.htm. This event handler should call the `displayBigReply()` function and send it the user's name as stored in the form's text box. Fill this in, using the appropriate `parent` syntax.

❑ Optional: Rewrite the code developed for the "Great Physics Discoveries" page in Lab Exercises 16.1 and 16.2 so that the page consists of two side-by-side frames (as in the CyberPizza page). The left frame should display the text box that prompts the user to enter a nationality for which to search. When the surfer clicks the Search button, the database should be searched as before, but instead of displaying the results in a text area, use JavaScript to display them in the right frame in an HTML table format as shown in Figure 17.1. That is, use the `document.write()` method to write HTML table code to the right frame, similarly to how we wrote the ordered list code for the CyberPizza page. Tip 1: Put the code that creates the database, as well as the code for the `searchForNationality()` function, in a `<script>` element in the `<head>` element of the frameset document. Tip 2: This optional exercise is not short.

Exercise 17.2: A Custom Alert Box

One potential problem with the CyberPizza page (and similar pages) comes up if the surfer clicks the Submit Pizza Order button without selecting one of the crust choices. To take this situation into account, it's a good idea to have the `displayOrder()` function display an alert box if no crust choice has been selected, telling the surfer to please select a type of crust. We could certainly use a regular alert box to do this, but JavaScript's window commands give us the capability to create custom alert boxes with formatted text. (We could also simply mark one of the crust choice radio buttons as checked when they're first displayed by adding the `checked="checked"` value to one of their `<input>` tags. But then we might get complaints from customers who didn't realize they needed to check another option if they didn't want the default checked crust choice.)

❑ To test a custom alert box, create a simple non-frames document that has three crust choices radio buttons, a Submit Pizza Order click button, and a function named `displayOrder()`. At the beginning of the `displayOrder()` function, write the code that will test the radio buttons and, if none of them are checked, will display a new window centered in the middle of the screen (approximately). This new window should display a document named CrustAlert.htm, which has the line of text "Please enter a crust choice before submitting your order" (formatted nicely using some HTML tags). The CrustAlert.htm document should also have a click button labeled "Close window". The event handler for this click button should call a function named `closeTheWindow()`, with no parameters. The function's code should simply be the line: `self.close()`. The keyword `self` in this case refers, as you might guess, to the current window. So this line of code closes the CrustAlert window. (The surfer can also, of course, click the window's close box to close it.) Note: Because the purpose of this exercise is to practice creating a window using JavaScript, there's no need to put any code in the `displayOrder()` function other than the code that tests the radio buttons and generates the custom alert box. Normally, of course, you would fill out the rest of the function with the code that tested the radio buttons and displayed the surfer's choice.

Sitebuilding Exercises

Sitebuilding Exercise 1: Basic Site Structure

This is the first of a series of five exercises on building a website. Their purpose is to guide you through the process of building a sophisticated, JavaScript-powered website from the ground up. You may either do these exercises as they are cited in the text (at the end of various chapters), thus gradually assembling the website over the course of your study, or you may wait until all the pertinent material has been covered and then focus solely on the sitebuilding exercises as an end-of-term programing project. (Your instructor, of course, will have something to say about which method you use.)

Your first task is to choose the type of site you would like to design:

1. A Company or Organization Information Site

2. A Distance Learning Site

3. An Electronic Commerce Site

Each sitebuilding exercise will suggest certain features to add to the site, based on the material covered and the type of site chosen.

Developing a full-fledged electronic commerce site, or any of these sites, is of course beyond the scope of this sitebuilding project. Most commercial or professional sites these days require server-side processing, a topic for another book or course. But these exercises will introduce you to many of the issues involved in designing and coding the client-side front end of a professional site.

The purpose of this first sitebuilding exercise is to design the skeleton structure and navigation pathways of the website.

Note: If you wish, you may put off this first exercise until you have finished Chapter 6, which covers how to create columns and other magazine-style layout features.

Step 1

Choose the type of site you would like to create from among the three choices above. Once you have decided, or at least have an idea, use a web catalog site or search engine to find some sites of that type. Examine how they are designed. What kind of features are included? What works well? What doesn't work? What do you like? What don't you like? For further insights and tips, check out one or more sites that specialize in website design, such as www.useit.com or www.webpagesthatsuck.com.

Step 2

Review Figure 5.6 (the structure of a multiple-page website) and the corresponding discussion. On a single sheet of paper, sketch out a basic design for your site along the lines of Figure 5.6. Think especially about the main sections of the site and how to implement a table of contents on the introduction page. If you have covered Chapter 6, think about how you might use a multiple-column layout or frames. On the other hand, be wary of getting too ambitious or fancy. Simple is better at this point.

Step 3

Take each page represented in the step 2 diagram and sketch out its details on a separate piece of paper. (In the movie business, this is known as storyboarding—creating a series of sketches that lay out the sequence of the story or, in our case, the site design.)

Step 4

Create the HTML source documents for the basic structure and navigation pathways of your site design. Leave out most of the details of each page. It's enough to put a brief heading and/or description on each page, plus the necessary links to navigate to other pages of the site. The goal is to create a skeleton site, where the navigation works but little else is included.

Sitebuilding Exercise 2: Basic User Input

If you are doing this exercise after Chapter 10, most of what you have learned so far in JavaScript is preparing you for the next several chapters, where we will learn how to do things such as create an online calculator and an online quiz. But text boxes, in combination with form submission (Chapter 10, in the section "Submitting Form Information"), now allow you to add something practical to the site you are building.

Taking the skeleton site you created in Sitebuilding Exercise 1, add one or more of the following options to one of its pages. (We suggest one option for each type of site.)

Option 1 (for a Company or Organization Information Site)

Add a page to your site that lets the visitor request information about your organization and be put on its mailing list. You will need text boxes for first name, last name, street address, and so on, plus submit and reset buttons. Use your own e-mail address for the submission destination.

Option 2 (for a Distance Learning Site)

Add a page to your site that lets the visitor submit the answers to a short quiz via text boxes. Each text box should be labeled with one of the quiz questions. (Make up a few sample questions on whatever topic you wish.) Include submit and reset buttons, of course, and use your own e-mail address for the submission destination.

Option 3 (for an Electronic Commerce Site)

Add a page to your site that lets the visitor submit a request for more information about a certain product. List several sample products with their product numbers on the page and instruct the visitor to write the product number in a text box. (You might also add several more text boxes to allow the visitor to enter several product numbers, as there should be only one product number entered per box.) Also include, of course, text boxes for first name, last name, street address, and so on, plus submit and reset buttons. Use your own e-mail address for the submission destination. (Note: When you learn about the other kinds of HTML form elements, such as check boxes and pop-up menus, you will be able to improve upon this user interface. As it stands, it's a little tedious for visitors to have to enter the product numbers themselves.)

Sitebuilding Exercise 3: Interactive Features

Taking the site you worked on in Sitebuilding Exercises 1 and 2, add one or more of the following interactive options to one of its pages. (We suggest one option for each type of site.)

Option 1 (for a Company or Organization Information Site)

Add a customer survey with multiple-choice questions to the site. Use a submit button to e-mail the results back to your e-mail address. You might also redesign the information request code from Sitebuilding Exercise 2 so that the visitor can use check boxes to select various documents or brochures to receive.

Option 2 (for a Distance Learning Site)

Add a page to your site that implements one or more multiple-choice quizzes. Each quiz can be either a self-test option for the student's practice or an actual quiz in which the results are submitted back to you (via e-mail).

Option 3 (for an Electronic Commerce Site)

Use check boxes to add an order form to the site, in which each check box represents a certain product (with price listed). Each product should also have a text box next to it that allows the visitor to indicate the quantity desired. Add a Calculate Total button that calculates and displays the total amount of the planned purchase, plus tax, plus some kind of shipping and handling fee. You might also redesign the information request procedure from Sitebuilding Exercise 2 so that it uses check boxes and/or pop-up menus instead of text boxes for the product entry.

Sitebuilding Exercise 4: Validating and Storing Information

Taking the site you worked on in previous sitebuilding exercises, add one or more of the following options.

User-proofing the Interface

If your site uses text boxes for user input, add input validation code to ensure that the user enters the information correctly. For example, if the user is asked to enter an e-mail address, the entered address should be checked to make sure that it has the correct form for an e-mail address (use of @ character and a domain name with a valid ending such as .com, .edu, .org, .net, .mil, or .gov).

Storing Information

Add a basic password system to your site and/or simple data storage capabilities. For example, a company site might have a page where salespeople can enter their weekly (or monthly) sales results and have them stored in a cookie (one cookie for each salesperson). Another page on the site would read the cookies and display recent sales results. A distance learning site might store and display results from online quizzes that each student had completed so that students could track their results (one cookie for each student). And an electronic commerce site needs a shopping cart feature that stores the shopper's choices until checkout. (Note that the value of a cookie can be a long series of results all put together in one string. Four quiz results, for example, could be a string like "13,24,18,19". The `split()` method can then be used to split the string at the commas in order to extract the individual scores.)

Sitebuilding Exercise 5: Searchable Database

Taking the site you worked on in previous sitebuilding exercises, add a page that offers a searchable database and displays the results in a list or table format using frames and the `document.write()` method. You might consider an employee contact list for a company site, a product information database or a store location list for an electronic commerce site, and an everchanging quiz for a distance learning site. (For the quiz, each record in the database would store a quiz question, possible answers, and the correct answer. The code would then randomly choose and display a set number of quiz questions when the student clicked a Take quiz button.)

HTML and XHTML Elements

B

This appendix does not cover every possible variation of HTML tags and attributes that have been implemented in Internet Explorer and Netscape Navigator, but rather lists the elements in XHTML version 1.0. The Status line in each element's listing indicates whether the element is part of XHTML 1.0 strict, XHML 1.0 transitional, or XHTML 1.0 frameset. All elements in XHTML 1.0 strict are included in the transitional version, and the combination of the transitional and frameset DTDs essentially constitutes the older HTML 4. For a discussion of the differences between HTML 4, XHTML 1.0 strict, XHTML 1.0 transitional, and XHTML 1.0 frameset, see the sections "HTML, XML, and XHTML" in Chapter 2 and "Extensions and Deprecations" in Chapter 4. Also see the note regarding XHTML 1.1 below.

Each element entry in the table below includes information on the element's attributes, divided into five categories: core, required, other, deprecated, and event handlers.

Core attributes are four basic attributes that are available for use with most elements. They are:

1. class (specifies a class name for an element)
2. id (specifies a unique identifying name for an element)
3. style (specifies a style for an element)
4. title (specifies advisory information about an element)

Required attributes are attributes that must be present in an element if it is to be in compliance with the XHTML standard. (Most current-day browsers are more lax than the standard, but that may not be true in the future.)

Other attributes are optional attributes that may be used with the element.

Deprecated attributes are attributes that were included in the HTML 4 standard (and in XHTML 1.0 transitional) but marked as being on the way out. These attributes have now been removed from XHTML 1.0 strict. The most common reason for their deprecation and removal is that they specified the presentation of the document, and the preferred method for specifying presentation is now style sheets (as discussed in Chapter 3, in the section "The Power of Styles"). You should avoid the use of deprecated attributes (and deprecated elements), although most browsers will continue to support them for the foreseeable future in order to maintain backward compatibility.

Event handler attributes (event handlers) provide support for handling events. The 10 event handlers `onclick`, `ondblclick`, `onmousedown`, `onmouseup`, `onmousemove`, `onmouseover`, `onmouseout`, `onkeypress`, `onkeydown`, and `onkeyup` may be used in most elements (as indicated in each element listing below). Others, such as `onchange`, `onload`, `onunload`, `onfocus`, and `onblur`, may be used only in certain elements.

A sixth category of attributes, **internationalization attributes**, is not included in the listings. This category consists of the `lang` and `dir` attributes. The `lang` attribute specifies the base natural language used in the document, such as `"en"` for English, `"fr"` for French, `"de"` for German, `"es"` for Spanish, `"zh"` for Chinese, and so on. The `dir` attribute specifies the directionality of the language used, either `"ltr"` for left-to-right or `"rtl"` for right to left. The `lang` and `dir` attributes may be used in all elements except `<applet>`, `<base>`, `<basefont>`, `<bdo>`, `<br>`, `<frame>`, `<frameset>`, `<iframe>`, `<param>`, and `<script>`. (As noted below, the `lang` attribute has been replaced in XHTML 1.1 by the `xml:lang` attribute. Note also that the abbreviation "i18n" is used in HTML circles for "internationalization.")

Brief descriptions of what each attribute does are included in the listings below. More detailed information may be found at the World Wide Web Consortium site: www.w3.org. In particular, documentation on all the elements in HTML 4 (most of which still exist in XHTML) is at www.w3.org/TR/REC-html40. Links to detailed information on each element may be found in the comprehensive table of the elements at www.w3.org/TR/REC-html40/index/elements.html (all elements in this table are included in the list below). A table of attributes is at www.w3.org/TR/REC-html40/index/attributes.html.

The latest version of XHTML as of Spring 2002 is XHTML 1.1. It is based on XHTML 1.0 strict, with a few differences. These differences are:

1. The `lang` attribute has been replaced with the `xml:lang` attribute.

2. The name attribute for the `<a>` and `<map>` elements has been replaced with the `id` attribute. Although the `name` attribute was officially deprecated in XHTML 1.0 strict for use in the `<a>` and `<map>` elements, it still was included in the specifications. In XHTML 1.1, however, the `name` attribute does not exist for these elements.

If keeping all that straight is confusing, the bottom line is that any element listed below as belonging to XHTML 1.0 strict is safe to use, as are any non-deprecated attributes listed.

<!-- --> element

Status: XHTML 1.0 strict.

Purpose: Insert comments in the source document.

Core attributes: Not applicable.

Required attributes: None.

Other attributes: None.

Deprecated attributes: None.

Event handler attributes: None.

<!DOCTYPE> element

Status: XHTML 1.0 strict.

Purpose: Indicates the document type definition (DTD) used by the document.

Core attributes: Not applicable.

Required attributes: None.

Other attributes: None.

Deprecated attributes: None.

Event handler attributes: None.

<?xml> element

Status: XHTML 1.0 strict.

Purpose: Indicates the version of XML being used.

Core attributes: Not applicable.

Required attributes: None.

Other attributes: None.

Deprecated attributes: None.

Event handler attributes: None.

<a> . . . </a> element

Status: XHTML 1.0 strict (target attribute defined in the XHTML 1.0 frameset DTD).

Purpose: Create links and anchors.

Core attributes: May be used (class, id, style, title).

Required attributes: None.

Other attributes:

accesskey	(adds a keyboard shortcut for the link)
href	(specifies URL of web page or name of anchor to link to)
name	(specifies a name for an anchor; deprecated in XHTML 1.1 in favor of the id attribute)
tabindex	(defines the order in which the user may tab through elements on the page)
target	(specifies window or frame in which to load linked document)

Deprecated attributes:

charset	(specifies character encoding for the linked document)
coords	(used with client-side image maps)
hreflang	(specifies the base language of the linked document)
rel	(specifies the type of relationship between the current document and the linked document)
rev	(specifies the reverse relationship between the linked document and the current document)
shape	(used with client-side image maps)

Event handler attributes:

onclick, ondblclick, onmousedown, onmouseup, onmousemove, onmouseover, onmouseout, onkeypress, onkeydown, onkeyup, onfocus, onblur

\<abbr\> . . . \</abbr\> element

Status: XHTML 1.0 strict.

Purpose: Specify an abbreviation (useful for automated spell checkers).

Core attributes: May be used (class, id, style, title).

Required attributes: None.

Other attributes: None.

Deprecated attributes: None.

Event handler attributes:

onclick, ondblclick, onmousedown, onmouseup, onmousemove, onmouseover, onmouseout, onkeypress, onkeydown, onkeyup

<acronym> . . . </acronym> element

Status: XHTML 1.0 strict.

Purpose: Specify an acronym (useful for automated spell checkers).

Core attributes: May be used (class, id, style, title).

Required attributes: None.

Other attributes: None.

Deprecated attributes: None.

Event handler attributes:

```
onclick, ondblclick, onmousedown, onmouseup, onmousemove,
onmouseover, onmouseout, onkeypress, onkeydown, onkeyup
```

<address> . . . </address> element

Status: XHTML 1.0 strict.

Purpose: Specify e-mail address of the web page designer.

Core attributes: May be used (class, id, style, title).

Required attributes: None.

Other attributes: None.

Deprecated attributes: None.

Event handler attributes:

```
onclick, ondblclick, onmousedown, onmouseup, onmousemove,
onmouseover, onmouseout, onkeypress, onkeydown, onkeyup
```

<applet> . . . </applet> element

Status: XHTML 1.0 transitional (deprecated).

Purpose: Insert an applet.

Core attributes: May be used (class, id, style, title).

Required attributes:

height	(specifies height of applet's display)
width	(specifies width of applet's display)

Other attributes:

align	(specifies alignment of applet on page)
alt	(specifies alternative text to describe applet)

archive	(specifies URLs for files to preload that applet uses)
code	(specifies the name of the applet file)
codebase	(specifies the base URL for the applet)
hspace	(specifies amount of whitespace on left and right of applet display)
name	(specifies a name for the applet to use within the source document)
object	(specifies information about the applet's code)
vspace	(specifies amount of whitespace on top and bottom of applet display)

Deprecated attributes: Not applicable (entire element is deprecated).

Event handler attributes: None.

\<area /\> element

Status: XHTML 1.0 strict (target attribute defined in XHTML 1.0 frameset DTD).

Purpose: Specifies the coordinates and link destination of part of an image map.

Core attributes: May be used (class, id, style, title).

Required attributes:

alt	(specifies alternative text for the image)

Other attributes:

accesskey	(adds a keyboard shortcut for the link)
coords	(specifies the coordinates of the image map area)
href	(specifies the URL for the link destination)
shape	(specifies the shape of the area—a rectangle, circle, or polygon)
tabindex	(defines the order in which the user may tab through elements on the page)
target	(specifies window or frame in which to load linked document)

Deprecated attributes: None.

Event handler attributes:

onclick, ondblclick, onmousedown, onmouseup, onmousemove, onmouseover, onmouseout, onkeypress, onkeydown, onkeyup, onfocus, onblur

<b> ... </b> element

Status: XHTML 1.0 strict.

Purpose: Marks text as bold.

Core attributes: May be used (`class`, `id`, `style`, `title`).

Required attributes: None.

Other attributes: None.

Deprecated attributes: None.

Event handler attributes:

> `onclick, ondblclick, onmousedown, onmouseup, onmousemove,`
> `onmouseover, onmouseout, onkeypress, onkeydown, onkeyup`

Notes: Although not deprecated, it is encouraged to use elements like
<`strong`> instead.

<base /> element

Status: XHTML 1.0 strict.

Purpose: Specifies a base URL for generating relative URL addresses and a
default target for links.

Core attributes: Not available.

Required attributes: None.

Other attributes:

> `href`   (specifies a base URL to be used with any relative URLs in
>   the document)
>
> `target`   (specifies default window or frame in which to load linked
>   documents, if not otherwise specified via a target attribute
>   in an <`a`> element)

Deprecated attributes: None.

Event handler attributes: None.

<basefont /> element

Status: XHTML 1.0 transitional (deprecated).

Purpose: Specifies the default font for an entire web page.

Core attributes: Not available, with the exception of `id`.

Required attributes: None.

Other attributes:

color	(specifies the default font color)
face	(specifies the default font face)
size	(specifies the default font size)

Deprecated attributes: Not applicable (entire element is deprecated).

Event handler attributes: None.

`<bdo> ... </bdo>` element

Status: XHTML 1.0 strict

Purpose: Overrides the default direction of text display.

Core attributes: May be used (`class`, `id`, `style`, `title`).

Required attributes:

dir	(specifies direction of text, either `ltr` or `rtl`—left to right or right to left)

Other attributes:

lang	(specifies natural language code)

Deprecated attributes: None.

Event handler attributes:

```
onclick, ondblclick, onmousedown, onmouseup, onmousemove,
onmouseover, onmouseout, onkeypress, onkeydown, onkeyup
```

`<big> ... </big>` element

Status: XHTML 1.0 strict.

Purpose: Specifies larger than normal text.

Core attributes: May be used (`class`, `id`, `style`, `title`).

Required attributes: None.

Other attributes: None.

Deprecated attributes: None.

Event handler attributes:

```
onclick, ondblclick, onmousedown, onmouseup, onmousemove,
onmouseover, onmouseout, onkeypress, onkeydown, onkeyup
```

`<blockquote> ... </blockquote>` element

Status: XHTML 1.0 strict.

Purpose: Specifies a block quotation.

Core attributes: May be used (`class`, `id`, `style`, `title`).

Required attributes: None.

Other attributes:

`cite`   (specifies URL for the block quotation reference)

Deprecated attributes: None.

Event handler attributes:

```
onclick, ondblclick, onmousedown, onmouseup, onmousemove,
onmouseover, onmouseout, onkeypress, onkeydown, onkeyup
```

`<body>` ... `</body>` element

Status: XHTML 1.0 strict.

Purpose: Defines the main section for the page contents.

Core attributes: May be used (`class`, `id`, `style`, `title`).

Required attributes: None.

Other attributes: None.

Deprecated attributes:

`alink, link, vlink`	(specify colors of active links, new links, and visited links)
`background`	(specifies a background image via URL of the image file)
`bgcolor`	(specifies a background color of the page)
`text`	(specifies color of text on the page)

Event handler attributes:

```
onclick, ondblclick, onmousedown, onmouseup, onmousemove,
onmouseover, onmouseout, onkeypress, onkeydown, onkeyup,
onload, onunload
```

`<br />` element

Status: XHTML 1.0 strict.

Purpose: Specifies a line break.

Core attributes: May be used (`class`, `id`, `style`, `title`).

Required attributes: None.

Other attributes: None.

Deprecated attributes:

    clear   (used to stop text wrapping around an image)

Event handler attributes: None.

\<button\> . . . \</button\> element

Status: XHTML 1.0 strict.

Purpose: Creates a click button.

Core attributes: May be used (class, id, style, title).

Required attributes: None.

Other attributes:

    accesskey   (adds a keyboard shortcut for the link)

    disabled   (marks the button as disabled)

    name   (specifies an internal name for the button for scripting use)

    type   (specifies type of button: button, submit, or reset)

    tabindex   (defines the order in which the user may tab through elements on the page)

    value   (specifies an initial value for the button)

Deprecated attributes: None.

Event handler attributes:

    onclick, ondblclick, onmousedown, onmouseup, onmousemove, onmouseover, onmouseout, onkeypress, onkeydown, onkeyup, onfocus, onblur

\<caption\> . . . \</caption\> element

Status: XHTML 1.0 strict.

Purpose: Specifies a caption for a table.

Core attributes: May be used (class, id, style, title).

Required attributes: None.

Other attributes: None.

Deprecated attributes:

    align   (specifies alignment of caption with respect to the table)

Event handler attributes:

    onclick, ondblclick, onmousedown, onmouseup, onmousemove, onmouseover, onmouseout, onkeypress, onkeydown, onkeyup

Notes: Must be placed immediately after the beginning \<table\> tag.

<center> . . . </center> element

Status: XHTML 1.0 transitional (deprecated).

Purpose: Used to center text or images on the page.

Core attributes: May be used (class, id, style, title).

Required attributes: None.

Other attributes: None.

Deprecated attributes: None.

Event handler attributes:

```
onclick, ondblclick, onmousedown, onmouseup, onmousemove,
onmouseover, onmouseout, onkeypress, onkeydown, onkeyup
```

<cite> . . . </cite> element

Status: XHTML 1.0 strict.

Purpose: Marks text as a citation or reference (usually displayed in italic).

Core attributes: May be used (class, id, style, title).

Required attributes: None.

Other attributes: None.

Deprecated attributes: None.

Event handler attributes:

```
onclick, ondblclick, onmousedown, onmouseup, onmousemove,
onmouseover, onmouseout, onkeypress, onkeydown, onkeyup
```

<code> . . . </code> element

Status: XHTML 1.0 strict.

Purpose: Marks text as computer code (usually displayed in a fixed width font).

Core attributes: May be used (class, id, style, title).

Required attributes: None.

Other attributes: None.

Deprecated attributes: None.

Event handler attributes:

```
onclick, ondblclick, onmousedown, onmouseup, onmousemove,
onmouseover, onmouseout, onkeypress, onkeydown, onkeyup
```

<col> . . . </col> element

Status: XHTML 1.0 strict.

Purpose: Used to group columns in a table into a single unit.

Core attributes: May be used (`class`, `id`, `style`, `title`).

Required attributes: None.

Other attributes:

`align`	(specifies horizontal alignment of data in columns)
`char`	(specifies a single character to align around, such as a decimal point)
`charoff`	(specifies an offset to the alignment character)
`span`	(specifies number of columns spanned)
`valign`	(specifies vertical alignment of data in columns)
`width`	(specifies width of columns)

Deprecated attributes: None.

Event handler attributes:

```
onclick, ondblclick, onmousedown, onmouseup, onmousemove,
onmouseover, onmouseout, onkeypress, onkeydown, onkeyup
```

<colgroup> . . . </colgroup> element

Status: XHTML 1.0 strict.

Purpose: Used to join columns in a table into a single unit.

Core attributes: May be used (`class`, `id`, `style`, `title`).

Required attributes: None.

`align`	(specifies horizontal alignment of data in columns)
`char`	(specifies a single character to align around, such as a decimal point)
`charoff`	(specifies an offset to the alignment character)
`span`	(specifies number of columns spanned)
`valign`	(specifies vertical alignment of data in columns)
`width`	(specifies width of columns)

Deprecated attributes: None.

Event handler attributes:

```
onclick, ondblclick, onmousedown, onmouseup, onmousemove,
onmouseover, onmouseout, onkeypress, onkeydown, onkeyup
```

\<dd> . . . \</dd> element

Status: XHTML 1.0 strict.

Purpose: Marks a definition in a definition list.

Core attributes: May be used (`class`, `id`, `style`, `title`).

Required attributes: None.

Other attributes: None.

Deprecated attributes: None.

Event handler attributes:

```
onclick, ondblclick, onmousedown, onmouseup, onmousemove,
onmouseover, onmouseout, onkeypress, onkeydown, onkeyup
```

\<del> . . . \</del> element

Status: XHTML 1.0 strict.

Purpose: Marks deleted text (usually displayed with a strikethrough line).

Core attributes: May be used (`class`, `id`, `style`, `title`).

Required attributes: None.

Other attributes:

`cite`	(specifies a URL for a document that explains why the text was deleted)
`datetime`	(specifies the date and time when the deletion was made)

Deprecated attributes: None.

Event handler attributes:

```
onclick, ondblclick, onmousedown, onmouseup, onmousemove,
onmouseover, onmouseout, onkeypress, onkeydown, onkeyup
```

\<dfn> . . . \</dfn> element

Status: XHTML 1.0 strict.

Purpose: Marks text as the definition of a term used on the page.

Core attributes: May be used (`class`, `id`, `style`, `title`).

Required attributes: None.

Other attributes: None.

Deprecated attributes: None.

Event handler attributes:

```
onclick, ondblclick, onmousedown, onmouseup, onmousemove,
onmouseover, onmouseout, onkeypress, onkeydown, onkeyup
```

\<dir\> . . . \</dir\> element

Status: XHTML 1.0 transitional (deprecated).

Purpose: Used to create a multiple column directory list.

Core attributes: May be used (class, id, style, title).

Required attributes: None.

Other attributes:

compact   (specifies reduced spacing between list items, but many browsers don't support its use)

Deprecated attributes: None.

Event handler attributes:

```
onclick, ondblclick, onmousedown, onmouseup, onmousemove,
onmouseover, onmouseout, onkeypress, onkeydown, onkeyup
```

\<div\> . . . \</div\> element

Status: XHTML 1.0 strict.

Purpose: Used to divide a web page into sections (often for layout or style purposes).

Core attributes: May be used (class, id, style, title).

Required attributes: None.

Other attributes: None (the core attributes class and id are often used with \<div\>).

Deprecated attributes:

align   (specifies horizontal alignment of left, center, or right)

Event handler attributes:

```
onclick, ondblclick, onmousedown, onmouseup, onmousemove,
onmouseover, onmouseout, onkeypress, onkeydown, onkeyup
```

\<dl\> . . . \</dl\> element

Status: XHTML 1.0 strict.

Purpose: Specifies a definition list.

Core attributes: May be used (class, id, style, title).

Required attributes: None.

Other attributes: None.

Deprecated attributes:

compact   (specifies reduced spacing between list items, but many browsers don't support its use)

Event handler attributes:

onclick, ondblclick, onmousedown, onmouseup, onmousemove, onmouseover, onmouseout, onkeypress, onkeydown, onkeyup

<dt> . . . </dt> element

Status: XHTML 1.0 strict.

Purpose: Marks a definition term within a definition list.

Core attributes: May be used (class, id, style, title).

Required attributes: None.

Other attributes: None.

Deprecated attributes: None.

Event handler attributes:

onclick, ondblclick, onmousedown, onmouseup, onmousemove, onmouseover, onmouseout, onkeypress, onkeydown, onkeyup

<em> . . . </em> element

Status: XHTML 1.0 strict.

Purpose: Marks emphasized text (usually displayed as italics by personal computer browsers).

Core attributes: May be used (class, id, style, title).

Required attributes: None.

Other attributes: None.

Deprecated attributes: None.

Event handler attributes:

onclick, ondblclick, onmousedown, onmouseup, onmousemove, onmouseover, onmouseout, onkeypress, onkeydown, onkeyup

<embed> . . . </embed> element

Status: Not official HTML, but more or less supported by Explorer and Navigator.

Purpose: Used to embed multimedia elements in a web page, such as sounds.

Core attributes: Not applicable.

Required attributes: None.

Other attributes:

align	(horizontal alignment of left, center, or right for the controls)
autostart	(whether multimedia effect should start automatically when page loads)
controls	(display of control buttons, such as play, pause, etc.)
loop	(whether the effect should play more than once, in a loop)
src	(URL for the multimedia file)
width, height	(width and height for the control button console)

Deprecated attributes: Not applicable (never had official HTML status).

Event handler attributes: None.

\<fieldset\> . . . \</fieldset\> element

Status: XHTML 1.0 strict.

Purpose: Creates a group out of separate form fields.

Core attributes: May be used (class, id, style, title).

Required attributes: None.

Other attributes: None.

Deprecated attributes: None.

Event handler attributes:

onclick, ondblclick, onmousedown, onmouseup, onmousemove, onmouseover, onmouseout, onkeypress, onkeydown, onkeyup

Notes: Used with the \<legend\> element.

\<font\> . . . \</font\> element

Status: XHTML 1.0 transitional (deprecated).

Purpose: Used to specify font display information for text.

Required attributes: None.

Other attributes:

color	(specifies font color)

`face`   (specifies font typeface)

`size`   (specifies font size)

Deprecated attributes: Not applicable (entire element is deprecated).

Event handler attributes: None.

`<form>` . . . `</form>` element

Status: XHTML 1.0 strict.

Purpose: Used to create forms for user input.

Core attributes: May be used (`class`, `id`, `style`, `title`).

Required attributes:

`action`   (specifies URL of server-side script used to process form; not applicable when using a form solely with client-side JavaScript code)

Other attributes:

`method`   (specifies method to be used in submitting form information)

`enctype`   (specifies content type of the form)

`accept`   (list of MIME types the server can handle for file upload)

`accept-charset`   (list of character sets accepted by the server)

Deprecated attributes:

`name`   (specifies a name for a form for use with scripts; deprecated in favor of the `id` attribute)

Event handler attributes:

`onclick, ondblclick, onmousedown, onmouseup, onmousemove, onmouseover, onmouseout, onkeypress, onkeydown, onkeyup, onsubmit, onreset`

Notes: For backward and forward compatibility, use both the `name` and `id` attributes (set to the same value).

`<frame />` element

Status: XHTML 1.0 frameset.

Purpose: Specifies properties of a frame, including the source document.

Core attributes: May be used (`class`, `id`, `style`, `title`).

Required attributes: None.

Other attributes:

frameborder	(specifies whether to hide or display frame border)
longdesc	(specifies a URL for a file where a long description of the frame is available)
marginheight	(specifies height of frame margin in pixels)
marginwidth	(specifies width of frame margin in pixels)
noresize	(prevents user from resizing a frame)
scrolling	(specifies whether or not to use scrollbars)
src	(specifies source document to load into the frame)

Deprecated attributes:

name	(specifies a name for the frame; deprecated in favor of the id attribute)

Event handler attributes: None.

Notes: For backward and forward compatibility, use both the name and id attributes (set to the same value).

`<frameset>` ... `</frameset>` element

Status: XHTML 1.0 frameset.

Purpose: Specifies properties of a frame, including the source document.

Core attributes: May be used (class, id, style, title).

Required attributes: None.

Other attributes:

rows	(specifies number and size of rows for the frameset)
cols	(specifies number and size of columns for the frameset)

Deprecated attributes: None.

Event handler attributes: onload, onunload.

`<hn>` ... `</hn>` element (where *n* = 1, 2, 3, 4, 5, or 6)

Status: XHTML 1.0 strict.

Purpose: Marks text as one of the six levels of headers.

Core attributes: May be used (class, id, style, title).

Required attributes: None.

Other attributes: None.

Deprecated attributes:

> `align`   (specifies horizontal alignment of header)

Event handler attributes:

> `onclick, ondblclick, onmousedown, onmouseup, onmousemove, onmouseover, onmouseout, onkeypress, onkeydown, onkeyup`

`<head> ... </head>` element

Status: XHTML 1.0 strict.

Purpose: Creates the head section of the web page.

Core attributes: Not available.

Required attributes: None.

Other attributes:

> `profile`   (specifies URL of a meta data profile with information about the document)

Deprecated attributes: None.

Event handler attributes: None.

`<hr />` element

Status: XHTML 1.0 strict.

Purpose: Creates a horizontal rule.

Core attributes: May be used (`class`, `id`, `style`, `title`).

Required attributes: None.

Other attributes: None.

Deprecated attributes:

> `align`   (specifies alignment of rule—`left`, `center`, or `right`)
>
> `noshade`   (specifies a solid color with no shading)
>
> `size`   (specifies height in pixels)

Event handler attributes:

> `onclick, ondblclick, onmousedown, onmouseup, onmousemove, onmouseover, onmouseout, onkeypress, onkeydown, onkeyup`

`<html> ... </html>` element

Status: XHTML 1.0 strict.

Purpose: Defines a document as an HTML source document.

Core attributes: Not available.

Required attributes: None.

Other attributes:

xmlns   (specifies XML namespace for the document; is required in XHTML 1.1)

Deprecated attributes:

version   (specifies version of DTD; now replaced by DTD declaration)

Event handler attributes: None.

\<i> . . . \</i> element

Status: XHTML 1.0 strict.

Purpose: Marks text as italicized.

Core attributes: May be used (class, id, style, title).

Required attributes: None.

Other attributes: None.

Deprecated attributes: None.

Event handler attributes:

onclick, ondblclick, onmousedown, onmouseup, onmousemove, onmouseover, onmouseout, onkeypress, onkeydown, onkeyup

Notes: Although not deprecated, it is encouraged to use elements like \<em> instead.

\<iframe> . . . \</iframe> element

Status: XHTML 1.0 frameset.

Purpose: Creates an inline frame.

Core attributes: May be used (class, id, style, title).

Required attributes: None.

Other attributes:

align   (specifies alignment of frame: top, middle, bottom, left, right)

frameborder   (specifies whether to hide or display frame border)

height, width   (specify size of floating frame)

longdesc   (specifies a URL for a file where a long description of the frame is available)

`marginheight`	(specifies height of frame margin in pixels)
`marginwidth`	(specifies width of frame margin in pixels)
`scrolling`	(specifies whether or not to use scrollbars)
`src`	(specifies source document to load into the frame)

Deprecated attributes:

`name`	(specifies a name for the frame; deprecated in favor of the `id` attribute)

Event handler attributes: None.

Notes: For backward and forward compatibility, use both the `name` and `id` attributes (set to the same value).

`<img />` element

Status: XHTML 1.0 strict.

Purpose: Specifies the placement of an image on a web page.

Core attributes: May be used (`class`, `id`, `style`, `title`).

Required attributes:

`alt`	(specifies alternative text that describes the image)
`src`	(specifies the URL of the image file)

Other attributes:

`height, width`	(specify height and width of image in pixels)
`ismap`	(specifies use of a server-side image map)
`longdesc`	(URL to document with long description of image)
`usemap`	(specifies use of a client-side image map)

Deprecated attributes:

`align`	(specifies alignment of image: `top`, `middle`, `bottom`, `left`, `right`)
`border`	(specifies width of border around image)
`hspace, vspace`	(specify amount of space on top, bottom, and sides of image)
`name`	(specifies a name for an image; deprecated in favor of the `id` attribute)

Event handler attributes:

`onclick`, `ondblclick`, `onmousedown`, `onmouseup`, `onmousemove`, `onmouseover`, `onmouseout`, `onkeypress`, `onkeydown`, `onkeyup`

<input /> element

Status: XHTML 1.0 strict.

Purpose: Used to create form components (such as text boxes, radio buttons, etc.)

Core attributes: May be used (`class`, `id`, `style`, `title`).

Required attributes:

`name`	(except for `submit` and `reset` input elements)

Other attributes:

`accept`	(list of MIME types the server can handle for file upload)
`accesskey`	(adds a keyboard shortcut for the link)
`alt`	(provides an alternative short description)
`checked`	(specifies whether a radio button or check box is checked by default)
`disabled`	(disables a form component)
`maxlength`	(specifies maximum number of characters for a text field)
`name`	(specifies a name for a form component)
`readonly`	(makes a text field or password field read-only, so user can't change it)
`size`	(specifies size of a text field)
`src`	(specifies image source file for graphical submit buttons)
`tabindex`	(specifies component's position in the tabbing order)
`type`	(specifies type of form component)
`usemap`	(specifies map to use for client-side image map)
`value`	(specifies a value associated with a component)

Deprecated attributes: None.

Event handler attributes:

`onclick, ondblclick, onmousedown, onmouseup, onmousemove, onmouseover, onmouseout, onkeypress, onkeydown, onkeyup, onfocus, onblur, onselect, onchange`

<ins> ... </ins> element

Status: XHTML 1.0 strict.

Purpose: Marks text that has been inserted into a previous version of a document (usually displayed as underlined; used especially in legal documents).

Core attributes: May be used (`class`, `id`, `style`, `title`).

Required attributes: None.

Other attributes:

    `cite`   (specifies a URL for a document that explains why the text
                         was deleted)

    `datetime`   (specifies the date and time when the deletion was made)

Deprecated attributes: None.

Event handler attributes:

    `onclick, ondblclick, onmousedown, onmouseup, onmousemove,`
    `onmouseover, onmouseout, onkeypress, onkeydown, onkeyup`

`<isindex />` element

Status: XHTML 1.0 transitional (deprecated).

Purpose: Creates a single-line input text field.

Core attributes: May be used (`class`, `id`, `style`, `title`).

Required attributes: None.

Other attributes:

    `prompt`   (specifies prompt for the input field)

Deprecated attributes: None.

Event handler attributes: None.

Notes: Instead of `<isindex />`, use the `<input>` element within a form to create an input text box.

`<kbd>` . . . `</kbd>` element

Status: XHTML 1.0 strict.

Purpose: Marks text that represents keyboard entries (usually displayed using a fixed width font).

Core attributes: May be used (`class`, `id`, `style`, `title`).

Required attributes: None.

Other attributes: None.

Deprecated attributes: None.

Event handler attributes:

    `onclick, ondblclick, onmousedown, onmouseup, onmousemove,`
    `onmouseover, onmouseout, onkeypress, onkeydown, onkeyup`

`<label>` . . . `</label>` element

Status: XHTML 1.0 strict.

Purpose: Used to provide a visible label for a form element.

Core attributes: May be used (`class`, `id`, `style`, `title`).

Required attributes: None.

Other attributes:

    `accesskey`   (adds a keyboard shortcut for the label)

    `for`   (indicates the `id` of the form element to label)

Deprecated attributes: None.

Event handler attributes:

    `onclick, ondblclick, onmousedown, onmouseup, onmousemove, onmouseover, onmouseout, onkeypress, onkeydown, onkeyup`

`<legend>` . . . `</legend>` element

Status: XHTML 1.0 strict.

Purpose: Used for labeling a fieldset.

Core attributes: May be used (`class`, `id`, `style`, `title`).

Required attributes: None.

Other attributes:

    `accesskey`   (adds a keyboard shortcut for the legend)

Deprecated attributes:

    `align`   (alignment of legend—`top`, `bottom`, `left`, or `right`)

Event handler attributes:

    `onclick, ondblclick, onmousedown, onmouseup, onmousemove, onmouseover, onmouseout, onkeypress, onkeydown, onkeyup`

`<li>` . . . `</li>` element

Status: XHTML 1.0 strict.

Purpose: Creates a list item.

Core attributes: May be used (`class`, `id`, `style`, `title`).

Required attributes: None.

Other attributes: None.

Deprecated attributes:

type   (specifies the style of a list item)

value   (sets the number of the list item)

Event handler attributes:

onclick, ondblclick, onmousedown, onmouseup, onmousemove,
onmouseover, onmouseout, onkeypress, onkeydown, onkeyup

`<link />` element

Status: XHTML 1.0 strict (XHTML 1.0 frameset required for target attribute)

Purpose: Specifies a media independent link (main use is to specify an external style sheet for the document).

Core attributes: May be used (class, id, style, title).

Required attributes: None.

Other attributes:

charset   (specifies character encoding for the linked document)

href   (specifies URL for linked document)

hreflang   (specifies the base language of the linked document)

media   (specifies type of media used for display, such as "screen")

rel   (specifies a forward link between the current document and the linked document)

rev   (specifies a backward link between the linked document and the current document)

target   (specifies frame for the linked document)

type   (specifies MIME type of linked document)

Deprecated attributes: None.

Event handler attributes:

onclick, ondblclick, onmousedown, onmouseup, onmousemove,
onmouseover, onmouseout, onkeypress, onkeydown, onkeyup

Notes: May only be used in the `<head>` element.

`<map>` . . . `</map>` element

Status: XHTML 1.0 strict.

Purpose: Used to create a client-side image map.

Core attributes: May be used (class, id, style, title).

Required attributes:

   id   (specifies an identifying name for the map; see note below)

Other attributes: None.

Deprecated attributes:

   name   (specifies a name for the map; deprecated in XHTML 1.1 in favor of the id attribute)

Event handler attributes:

   onclick, ondblclick, onmousedown, onmouseup, onmousemove, onmouseover, onmouseout, onkeypress, onkeydown, onkeyup

Notes: For backward and forward compatibility, use both the name and id attributes (set to the same value).

\<menu> . . . \</menu> element

Status: XHTML 1.0 transitional (deprecated).

Purpose: Used to create a single column menu list.

Core attributes: May be used (class, id, style, title).

Required attributes: None.

Other attributes:

   compact   (specifies reduced spacing between list items, but many browsers don't support its use)

Deprecated attributes: None.

Event handler attributes:

   onclick, ondblclick, onmousedown, onmouseup, onmousemove, onmouseover, onmouseout, onkeypress, onkeydown, onkeyup

\<meta /> element

Status: XHTML 1.0 strict.

Purpose: Provides information about the web page.

Core attributes: Not available.

Required attributes:

   content   (specifies value for the meta-information)

Other attributes:

   http-equiv   (used by HTTP servers to generate a response)

   name   (specifies a name for the meta-information)

`scheme`   (used to interpret the content value)

Deprecated attributes: None.

Event handler attributes: None.

<noframes> . . . </noframes> element

Status: XHTML 1.0 frameset.

Purpose: Marks text to be displayed if the web page uses frames but the browser cannot display them.

Core attributes: May be used (`class`, `id`, `style`, `title`).

Required attributes: None.

Other attributes: None.

Deprecated attributes: None.

Event handler attributes:

```
onclick, ondblclick, onmousedown, onmouseup, onmousemove,
onmouseover, onmouseout, onkeypress, onkeydown, onkeyup
```

<noscript> . . . </noscript> element

Status: XHTML 1.0 strict.

Purpose: Marks text to be displayed if the web page uses scripts but the browser is not script-capable.

Core attributes: May be used (`class`, `id`, `style`, `title`).

Required attributes: None.

Other attributes: None.

Deprecated attributes: None.

Event handler attributes:

```
onclick, ondblclick, onmousedown, onmouseup, onmousemove,
onmouseover, onmouseout, onkeypress, onkeydown, onkeyup
```

<object> . . . </object> element

Status: XHTML 1.0 strict.

Purpose: Used to embed objects, such as Java applets, in a web page.

Core attributes: May be used (`class`, `id`, `style`, `title`).

Required attributes: None.

Other attributes:

archive	(specifies one or more URLs of archives containing resources that the object uses)
classid	(specifies URL for the object's implementation)
codebase	(specifies base path for relative URLs used)
codetype	(specifies content type of object's data)
data	(specifies URL for location of object's data)
declare	(specifies that the object element is a declaration only, not an instantiation)
height	(specifies height for object, overriding the default height)
name	(specifies a name for the object)
standby	(specifies a standby message to display while the object is loading)
tabindex	(specifies position in the tab order)
type	(specifies content type of object's data)
usemap	(specifies use with client-side image map)
width	(specifies width for object, overriding the default width)

Deprecated attributes: None.

Event handler attributes:

onclick, ondblclick, onmousedown, onmouseup, onmousemove, onmouseover, onmouseout, onkeypress, onkeydown, onkeyup

`<ol>` ... `</ol>` element

Status: XHTML 1.0 strict.

Purpose: Creates an ordered list.

Core attributes: May be used (class, id, style, title).

Required attributes: None.

Other attributes: None.

Deprecated attributes:

compact	(specifies reduced spacing between list items, but many browsers don't support its use)
start	(specifies the starting number of the first item in the list)
type	(specifies the style of the list items)

Event handler attributes:

```
onclick, ondblclick, onmousedown, onmouseup, onmousemove,
onmouseover, onmouseout, onkeypress, onkeydown, onkeyup
```

<optgroup> . . . </optgroup> element

Status: XHTML 1.0 strict.

Purpose: Used to create a pop-up menu with submenus.

Core attributes: May be used (`class`, `id`, `style`, `title`).

Required attributes:

```
label          (specifies label for option group)
```

Other attributes:

```
disabled       (disables the submenu)
```

Deprecated attributes: None.

Event handler attributes:

```
onclick, ondblclick, onmousedown, onmouseup, onmousemove,
onmouseover, onmouseout, onkeypress, onkeydown, onkeyup
```

<option> . . . </option> element

Status: XHTML 1.0 strict.

Purpose: Used to specify pop-up menu options.

Core attributes: May be used (`class`, `id`, `style`, `title`).

Required attributes: None.

Other attributes:

```
disabled       (disables the menu option)
label          (provides a shorter label for the menu option than the
                contents of the element itself)
selected       (specifies that the option should be selected by default)
value          (specifies the initial value of the menu option)
```

Deprecated attributes: None.

Event handler attributes:

```
onclick, ondblclick, onmousedown, onmouseup, onmousemove,
onmouseover, onmouseout, onkeypress, onkeydown, onkeyup
```

<p> ... </p> element

Status: XHTML 1.0 strict.

Purpose: Marks a paragraph.

Core attributes: May be used (`class`, `id`, `style`, `title`).

Required attributes: None.

Other attributes: None.

Deprecated attributes:

> `align`   (specifies alignment of paragraph—`left`, `center`, `right`, `justify`)

Event handler attributes:

> `onclick, ondblclick, onmousedown, onmouseup, onmousemove, onmouseover, onmouseout, onkeypress, onkeydown, onkeyup`

<param /> element

Status: XHTML 1.0 strict.

Purpose: Used within an `<object>` or `<applet>` element to specify parameter values.

Core attributes: Only `id` may be used.

Required attributes:

> `name`   (specifies name of parameter)

Other attributes:

> `value`   (specifies the value of the parameter)
>
> `valuetype`   (specifies the type of the parameter value)

Deprecated attributes: None.

Event handler attributes:

> `onclick, ondblclick, onmousedown, onmouseup, onmousemove, onmouseover, onmouseout, onkeypress, onkeydown, onkeyup`

<pre> ... </pre> element

Status: XHTML 1.0 strict.

Purpose: Marks text to be formatted exactly as typed in the source document (in fixed width font).

Core attributes: May be used (`class`, `id`, `style`, `title`).

Required attributes: None.

Other attributes:

xml:space (specifies whether whitespace in the element is to be considered significant)

Deprecated attributes:

width (specifies width of text to be formatted; not supported by most browsers)

Event handler attributes:

onclick, ondblclick, onmousedown, onmouseup, onmousemove, onmouseover, onmouseout, onkeypress, onkeydown, onkeyup

\<q> . . . \</q> element

Status: XHTML 1.0 strict.

Purpose: Marks text that is a short quotation.

Core attributes: May be used (class, id, style, title).

Required attributes: None.

Other attributes:

cite (specifies URL for the quotation reference)

Deprecated attributes: None.

Event handler attributes:

onclick, ondblclick, onmousedown, onmouseup, onmousemove, onmouseover, onmouseout, onkeypress, onkeydown, onkeyup

\<s> . . . \</s> element

Status: XHTML 1.0 transitional (deprecated).

Purpose: Marks strikethrough text (usually displayed with a line through it).

Core attributes: May be used (class, id, style, title).

Required attributes: None.

Other attributes: None.

Deprecated attributes: None.

Event handler attributes:

onclick, ondblclick, onmousedown, onmouseup, onmousemove, onmouseover, onmouseout, onkeypress, onkeydown, onkeyup

Notes: Same as \<strike> element.

<samp> . . . </samp> element

Status: XHTML 1.0 strict.

Purpose: Marks text as sample program/script output (usually displayed in a fixed width font).

Core attributes: May be used (`class`, `id`, `style`, `title`).

Required attributes: None.

Other attributes: None.

Deprecated attributes: None.

Event handler attributes:

> `onclick`, `ondblclick`, `onmousedown`, `onmouseup`, `onmousemove`, `onmouseover`, `onmouseout`, `onkeypress`, `onkeydown`, `onkeyup`

<script> . . . </script> element

Status: XHTML 1.0 strict.

Purpose: Used to include scripts in a web page.

Core attributes: May be used (`class`, `id`, `style`, `title`).

Required attributes:

> `type`   (specifies the scripting language)

Other attributes:

> `charset`   (specifies character encoding for the external script document)
>
> `defer`   (specifies that the browser defer execution of the script)
>
> `src`   (specifies URL for an external script)
>
> `xml:space`   (specifies whether whitespace in the element is to be considered significant)

Deprecated attributes:

> `language`   (specifies the scripting language; deprecated in favor of the `type` attribute)

Event handler attributes: None.

<select> . . . </select> element

Status: XHTML 1.0 strict.

Purpose: Creates pop-up menu.

Core attributes: May be used (`class`, `id`, `style`, `title`).

Required attributes: None.

Other attributes:

disabled	(disables the menu)
multiple	(allows user to make multiple selections from menu options)
name	(specifies a name for the menu)
size	(specifies number of rows visible in the menu)
tabindex	(specifies position of menu within the tab order)

Deprecated attributes: None.

Event handler attributes:

```
onclick, ondblclick, onmousedown, onmouseup, onmousemove,
onmouseover, onmouseout, onkeypress, onkeydown, onkeyup,
onfocus, onblur, onchange
```

\<small> . . . \</small> element

Status: XHTML 1.0 strict.

Purpose: Specifies smaller than normal text.

Core attributes: May be used (class, id, style, title).

Required attributes: None.

Other attributes: None.

Deprecated attributes: None.

Event handler attributes:

```
onclick, ondblclick, onmousedown, onmouseup, onmousemove,
onmouseover, onmouseout, onkeypress, onkeydown, onkeyup
```

\<span> . . . \</span> element

Status: XHTML 1.0 strict.

Purpose: Customizable inline element for use with styles.

Core attributes: May be used (class, id, style, title).

Required attributes: None.

Other attributes: None.

Deprecated attributes: None.

Event handler attributes:

```
onclick, ondblclick, onmousedown, onmouseup, onmousemove,
onmouseover, onmouseout, onkeypress, onkeydown, onkeyup
```

\<strike\> . . . \</strike\> element

Status: XHTML 1.0 transitional (deprecated).

Purpose: Marks strikethrough text (usually displayed with a line through it).

Core attributes: May be used (`class`, `id`, `style`, `title`).

Required attributes: None.

Other attributes: None.

Deprecated attributes: None.

Event handler attributes:

> `onclick, ondblclick, onmousedown, onmouseup, onmousemove, onmouseover, onmouseout, onkeypress, onkeydown, onkeyup`

Notes: Same as \<s\> element.

\<strong\> . . . \</strong\> element

Status: XHTML 1.0 strict.

Purpose: Marks strongly emphasized text (usually displayed as bold by personal computer browsers).

Core attributes: May be used (`class`, `id`, `style`, `title`).

Required attributes: None.

Other attributes: None.

Deprecated attributes: None.

Event handler attributes:

> `onclick, ondblclick, onmousedown, onmouseup, onmousemove, onmouseover, onmouseout, onkeypress, onkeydown, onkeyup`

\<style\> . . . \</style\> element

Status: XHTML 1.0 strict.

Purpose: Used to define style sheet information.

Core attributes: Not available.

Required attributes:

> `type`   (specifies style sheet language)

Other attributes:

> `media`   (specifies intended destination medium for the style; default = "screen")

title   (specifies an advisory title for the style)

xml:space   (specifies whether whitespace in the element is to be considered significant)

Deprecated attributes: None.

Event handler attributes: None.

\<sub\> . . . \</sub\> element

Status: XHTML 1.0 strict.

Purpose: Marks subscript text.

Core attributes: May be used (class, id, style, title).

Required attributes: None.

Other attributes: None.

Deprecated attributes: None.

Event handler attributes:

    onclick, ondblclick, onmousedown, onmouseup, onmousemove,
    onmouseover, onmouseout, onkeypress, onkeydown, onkeyup

\<sup\> . . . \</sup\> element

Status: XHTML 1.0 strict.

Purpose: Marks superscript text.

Core attributes: May be used (class, id, style, title).

Required attributes: None.

Other attributes: None.

Deprecated attributes: None.

Event handler attributes:

    onclick, ondblclick, onmousedown, onmouseup, onmousemove,
    onmouseover, onmouseout, onkeypress, onkeydown, onkeyup

\<table\> . . . \</table\> element

Status: XHTML 1.0 strict.

Purpose: Creates a table.

Core attributes: May be used (class, id, style, title).

Required attributes: None.

Other attributes:

border	(specifies width of table border)
cellpadding	(specifies whitespace margins within table cells)
cellspacing	(specifies spacing between table cells)
frame	(specifies which parts of the outer border are visible)
rules	(specifies which "rules"—the dividers between cells—are visible)
summary	(provides summary of table's purpose and contents)
width	(specifies table width)

Deprecated attributes:

align	(specifies alignment of table—left, center, right—within the document)
bgcolor	(specifies background color for cells)

Event handler attributes:

onclick, ondblclick, onmousedown, onmouseup, onmousemove, onmouseover, onmouseout, onkeypress, onkeydown, onkeyup

<tbody> . . . </tbody> element

Status: XHTML 1.0 strict.

Purpose: Defines the body of a table (used to specify the style for part of a table).

Core attributes: May be used (class, id, style, title).

Required attributes: None.

Other attributes:

align	(specifies horizontal alignment—left, center, right, justify, char)
char	(specifies a single character to align around, such as a decimal point)
charoff	(specifies an offset to the alignment character)
valign	(specifies the vertical alignment—top, middle, bottom, baseline)

Deprecated attributes: None.

Event handler attributes:

onclick, ondblclick, onmousedown, onmouseup, onmousemove, onmouseover, onmouseout, onkeypress, onkeydown, onkeyup

`<td>` . . . `</td>` element

Status: XHTML 1.0 strict.

Purpose: Specifies the content (data) for a cell of a table.

Core attributes: May be used (`class`, `id`, `style`, `title`).

Required attributes: None.

Other attributes:

`abbr`	(specifies an abbreviation for the header cell)
`align`	(specifies horizontal alignment—`left`, `center`, `right`, `justify`, `char`)
`axis`	(specifies a conceptual category for the cell)
`char`	(specifies a single character to align around, such as a decimal point)
`charoff`	(specifies an offset to the alignment character)
`colspan`	(specifies number of columns spanned by the cell)
`headers`	(specifies list of header cells that provide header information for this cell)
`rowspan`	(specifies number of rows spanned by the cell)
`scope`	(specifies a set of data cells for which a header provides information)
`valign`	(specifies vertical alignment—`top`, `middle`, `bottom`, `baseline`)

Deprecated attributes:

`bgcolor`	(specifies background color of cell)
`nowrap`	(disables text wrapping for the cell)
`width`, `height`	(specify cell width and height)

Event handler attributes:

`onclick`, `ondblclick`, `onmousedown`, `onmouseup`, `onmousemove`, `onmouseover`, `onmouseout`, `onkeypress`, `onkeydown`, `onkeyup`

`<textarea>` . . . `</textarea>` element

Status: XHTML 1.0 strict.

Purpose: Creates a multiple-line text field within a form.

Core attributes: May be used (`class`, `id`, `style`, `title`).

Required attributes: None.

Other attributes:

`accesskey`	(adds a keyboard shortcut for the link)
`cols`	(specifies number of columns for the text area, i.e., its width)
`disabled`	(disables the text area)
`name`	(specifies a name for the text area)
`readonly`	(makes a text area read-only, so the user can't change its contents)
`rows`	(specifies number of rows in the text area)
`tabindex`	(specifies position of the text area in the tab order)

Deprecated attributes: None.

Event handler attributes:

onclick, ondblclick, onmousedown, onmouseup, onmousemove, onmouseover, onmouseout, onkeypress, onkeydown, onkeyup, onblur, onselect, onchange

<tfoot> . . . </tfoot> element

Status: XHTML 1.0 strict.

Purpose: Defines the footer of a table (used to specify the style for part of a table).

Core attributes: May be used (class, id, style, title).

Required attributes: None.

Other attributes:

`align`	(specifies horizontal alignment—left, center, right, justify, char)
`char`	(specifies a single character to align around, such as a decimal point)
`charoff`	(specifies an offset to the alignment character)
`valign`	(specifies the vertical alignment—top, middle, bottom, baseline)

Deprecated attributes: None.

Event handler attributes:

onclick, ondblclick, onmousedown, onmouseup, onmousemove, onmouseover, onmouseout, onkeypress, onkeydown, onkeyup

<th> . . . </th> element

Status: XHTML 1.0 strict.

Purpose: Specifies a header cell of a table.

Core attributes: May be used (`class`, `id`, `style`, `title`).

Required attributes: None.

Other attributes:

`align`	(specifies horizontal alignment—`left`, `center`, `right`, `justify`, `char`)
`axis`	(specifies a conceptual category for the cell)
`char`	(specifies a single character to align around, such as a decimal point)
`charoff`	(specifies an offset to the alignment character)
`colspan`	(specifies number of columns spanned by the cell)
`headers`	(specifies list of header cells that provide header information for this cell)
`rowspan`	(specifies number of rows spanned by the cell)
`scope`	(specifies a set of data cells for which a header provides information)
`valign`	(specifies vertical alignment—`top`, `middle`, `bottom`, `baseline`)

Deprecated attributes:

`bgcolor`	(specifies background color of cell)
`nowrap`	(disables text wrapping for the cell)
`width, height`	(specify cell width and height)

Event handler attributes:

`onclick`, `ondblclick`, `onmousedown`, `onmouseup`, `onmousemove`, `onmouseover`, `onmouseout`, `onkeypress`, `onkeydown`, `onkeyup`

<thead> . . . </thead> element

Status: XHTML 1.0 strict.

Purpose: Defines the header of a table (used to specify the style for part of a table).

Core attributes: May be used (`class`, `id`, `style`, `title`).

Required attributes: None.

Other attributes:

align	(specifies horizontal alignment—left, center, right, justify, char)
char	(specifies a single character to align around, such as a decimal point)
charoff	(specifies an offset to the alignment character)
valign	(specifies vertical alignment—top, middle, bottom, baseline)

Deprecated attributes: None.

Event handler attributes:

onclick, ondblclick, onmousedown, onmouseup, onmousemove, onmouseover, onmouseout, onkeypress, onkeydown, onkeyup

\<title> . . . \</title> **element**

Status: XHTML 1.0 strict.

Purpose: Defines the title for the web page (required).

Core attributes: Not available.

Required attributes: None.

Other attributes: None.

Deprecated attributes: None.

Event handler attributes: None.

\<tr> . . . \</tr> **element**

Status: XHTML 1.0 strict.

Purpose: Creates a row in a table.

Core attributes: May be used (class, id, style, title).

Required attributes: None.

Other attributes:

align	(specifies horizontal alignment—left, center, right, justify, char)
char	(specifies a single character to align around, such as a decimal point)
charoff	(specifies an offset to the alignment character)
valign	(specifies the vertical alignment—top, middle, bottom, baseline)

Deprecated attributes:

> `bgcolor`   (specifies background color of table row)

Event handler attributes:

> `onclick, ondblclick, onmousedown, onmouseup, onmousemove,`
> `onmouseover, onmouseout, onkeypress, onkeydown, onkeyup`

`<tt> ... </tt>` element

Status: XHTML 1.0 strict.

Purpose: Marks text for display in a fixed width font ("teletype").

Core attributes: May be used (`class, id, style, title`).

Required attributes: None.

Other attributes: None.

Deprecated attributes: None.

Event handler attributes:

> `onclick, ondblclick, onmousedown, onmouseup, onmousemove,`
> `onmouseover, onmouseout, onkeypress, onkeydown, onkeyup`

`<u> ... </u>` element

Status: XHTML 1.0 transitional (deprecated).

Purpose: Marks text as underlined.

Core attributes: May be used (`class, id, style, title`).

Required attributes: None.

Other attributes: None.

Deprecated attributes: None.

Event handler attributes:

> `onclick, ondblclick, onmousedown, onmouseup, onmousemove,`
> `onmouseover, onmouseout, onkeypress, onkeydown, onkeyup`

Notes: Not recommended for use because (a) links are usually shown as underlined and (b) styles should be used for textual presentation.

`<ul> ... </ul>` element

Status: XHTML 1.0 strict.

Purpose: Creates an unordered list.

Core attributes: May be used (`class, id, style, title`).

Required attributes: None.

Other attributes: None.

Deprecated attributes:

> compact   (specifies reduced spacing between list items, but many browsers don't support its use)
>
> type   (specifies the style of the list items)

Event handler attributes:

> onclick, ondblclick, onmousedown, onmouseup, onmousemove, onmouseover, onmouseout, onkeypress, onkeydown, onkeyup

\<var\> . . . \</var\> element

Status: XHTML 1.0 strict.

Purpose: Marks text as a variable name.

Core attributes: May be used (class, id, style, title).

Required attributes: None.

Other attributes: None.

Deprecated attributes: None.

Event handler attributes:

> onclick, ondblclick, onmousedown, onmouseup, onmousemove, onmouseover, onmouseout, onkeypress, onkeydown, onkeyup

Converting HTML to XHTML

This appendix reviews the changes that need to be made to convert an HTML source document into a valid XHTML document. The World Wide Web Consortium has a handy software tool to help you make most of these conversions automatically and clean up your HTML code. It's called HTML Tidy, and it's available free for downloading at www.w3.org.

1. Add the following two tags at the beginning of the HTML source document:

```
<?xml version="1.0"?>
<!DOCTYPE html PUBLIC
    "-//W3C//DTD XHTML 1.0 Strict//EN"
        "http://www/w3/org/TR/xhtml/11/DTD/xhtml1-
        strict.dtd">
```

The first tag is an XML declaration, which declares that the document conforms to version 1.0 of XML (Extensible Markup Language). The second tag is a Document Type Definition (DTD), which specifies the version of XHTML being used. The words "Strict" and "strict" within it indicate that the document conforms to the strict version of XHTML. If the document uses an older version of HTML, such as version 4, with deprecated elements, "Strict" and "strict" should be replaced with "Transitional" and "transitional". If the document is a frameset document or uses the `target` attribute to link between frames, the two words should be "Frameset" and "frameset". For more information on these matters, see Chapter 2, the section "Creating an XHTML Source Document" and Chapter 4, the section "Extensions and Deprecations."

2. Add the `xmlns` (XML namespace) attribute to the `<html>` tag as follows:

```
<html xmlns="http://www.w3.org/1999/xhtml">
```

This attribute tells the browser that all tags contained within the `<html>` element belong to the XHTML namespace as defined by

537

the World Wide Web Consortium and located at the given URL. Although this attribute is not officially required, it's helpful to include it. (In XHTML 1.1 it is required. See the section "Creating an XHTML Source Document" in Chapter 2, for more information on the purpose of a namespace.)

3. All element names, attribute names, and style property names must be in lowercase letters.

4. All elements must have closing tags. For example, in the past the `<li>` element in lists was often written without a closing `</li>` tag. Similarly, many web page designers used the `<p>` tag without an ending `</p>` tag. In XHTML the `</li>` and `</p>`, respectively, must be present. The only exceptions are single-tag, empty elements—but see #5.

5. Add / to all empty elements (elements that, as officially defined, do not have an ending tag). For example:

```
<br> becomes <br />
<hr> becomes <hr />
```

The empty elements are `<area />`, `<base />`, `<basefont />` (but it's deprecated), `<br />`, `<hr />`, `<img />`, `<input />`, `<isindex />` (deprecated), `<link />`, `<meta />`, and `<param />`. It's also possible to write the examples above as `<br></br>` and `<hr></hr>`, but some existing browsers have trouble with this syntax.

On the other hand, this / syntax should not be used with non-empty elements that may have no contents. For example, a paragraph element with nothing inside should be written

```
<p></p>
```

not

```
<p />
```

6. All attribute values must be enclosed in quotation marks. The first example below is correct. The second is not.

```
<input type="text" name="usernameBox" size="25" />
<input type="text" name="usernameBox" size=25 />
```

7. Any attributes that do not have values must be given values. Consider, for example, an `<input>` element that creates a check box that is already checked when it appears. Previously this code was often written as:

```
<input type="checkbox" name="sunroofCB" checked />
```

But now the `checked` attribute must have a value specified, so write it as:

```
<input type="checkbox" name="sunroofCB"
  checked="checked" />
```

The following attributes are involved: `compact`, `nowrap`, `ismap`, `declare`, `noshade`, `checked`, `disabled`, `readonly`, `multiple`, `selected`, `noresize`, and `defer`.

8. If an attribute value contains an ampersand (&) character, the & must be replaced with its character code:

```
&amp;
```

In other words, tack on an a-m-p and semicolon to the lone & character. The reason for this substitution is that the & character has a special meaning in XML. (Attribute values with & characters will be a rare occurrence unless the source document involves the use of CGI scripts. Appendix E provides more information about character codes.)

9. All elements should be nested correctly. No elements should overlap each other, as shown below.

```
<!--Incorrect-->
<p><strong>Here is some sample text.</p></strong>
<!--Correct-->
<p><strong>Here is some sample text.</strong></p>
```

Nor should certain elements be nested. These restrictions are:

An `<a>` element cannot contain any other `<a>` elements.

A `<button>` element cannot contain an `<input>`, `<select>`, `<textarea>`, `<label>`, `<button>`, `<form>`, `<fieldset>`, `<iframe>`, or `<isindex>` element.

A `<form>` element cannot contain any other `<form>` elements.

A `<label>` element cannot contain any other `<label>` elements.

A `<pre>` element cannot contain an `<img>`, `<object>`, `<big>`, `<small>`, `<sub>`, or `<sup>` element.

10. If you use the `name` attribute in any of the following elements, add the `id` element set to the same value. The elements are: `<a>`, `<applet>`, `<form>`, `<frame>`, `<iframe>`, `<img>`, and `<map>`. The `name` attribute for these elements has been deprecated in favor of the `id` attribute. Note that the `name` element is not deprecated, however, for elements like `<input>`.

11. If any element uses the `lang` attribute, add the `xml:lang` attribute set to the same value. (The `lang` attribute has been deprecated in favor of the `xml:lang` attribute.)

12. Check that tags with required attributes do in fact have them. The following attributes are required:

<area> and <img> elements must have an alt attribute

<img> elements must also have a src attribute

<input> and <param> elements must have a name attribute (except for submit and reset buttons in the case of the <input> element)

<script> and <style> elements must have a type attribute

<meta> elements must have a content attribute

<optgroup> elements must have a label attribute

<map> elements must have an id attribute

13. If the document contains a style sheet or a script, check for the presence of the following characters in the style definitions or script code. These characters have special meanings in XML (and thus XHTML) and so the browser will treat them differently than expected:

```
<
&
]]>
--
```

If any are present, then you should use an external style sheet and/or an external script. Alternatively, you may enclose the style definitions or script code between the hieroglyphics <![CDATA[and]]>, as shown below:

```
<script type="text/javascript">
<![CDATA[
  //script goes here
]]>
</script>
```

Note also that the common practice of using the HTML comments tag to hide styles and scripts from older, noncompatible browsers is not guaranteed to work in new browsers that follow the XHTML rules, because the browser may completely ignore the contents inside the comments tag.

14. Eliminate any line breaks and back-to-back spaces (or other white-space characters) inside attribute values. Not all browsers, whether new or old, handle them well. For example:

```
<input type="button" name="b1" value="Click here!"
    onclick="displayMsg(document.someForm.userBox)" />
```

It's better to break the line, if necessary, between attributes:

```
<input type="button" name="b1" value="Click here!"
    onclick="displayMsg(document.someForm.userBox)" />
```

Basic Style Properties and Values

The following table lists the basic style properties covered in the text, plus a few others. A complete list of styles and their accompanying documentation may be found at www.w3.org/TR/REC-CSS2. Note: In recent versions of Explorer and Navigator (Explorer 5.5 or later and Navigator 6.0), JavaScript may access and change the style of any HTML element via the `style` property of that element's underlying object. See for example, Lab Exercise 4 in Chapter 9, which shows how to create a red click button and then change its color style when a mouseover event occurs.

Styles for Formatting Text

Property	Purpose	Values	Examples

`background-color`	Specifies the background color of an element	Color name or color number, or the value `transparent`	`background-color:red`
			`background-color:transparent`
			`background-color:#A23F14`

`background-image`	Specifies an image to use for the background of an element	URL of the image file, or the value `none`	`background-image:` `  url(mydog.gif)`

`background-repeat`	Specifies whether a background image should be tiled	`repeat`
		`repeat-x` (tile only in horiz. direction)
		`repeat-y` (tile only in vert. direction)
		`no-repeat`
			`background-repeat:repeat-x`

Continued

Property	Purpose	Values	Examples
background-position	Specifies position for a background image relative to the element	Number of pixels over from left and down from top (x,y) of element, or % values over and down, or one of following: top, center, or bottom for x value and left, center, or right for y	background-position:50,30 background-position:10%,15% background-position:center, center background-position:top,left
color	Specifies foreground color of text or other element	Color name or color number	color:red color:#FF358E
font	*See note at end of table		
font-family	Specifies font type	One or more font names (quotation marks not required but recommended, expecially for multiple-word font names)	font-family:"Arial" font-family:"Arial","Lucida"
font-size	Specifies font size	Point value, or a % of the normal size, or one of the following: xx-small x-small smaller small medium large larger x-large xx-large	font-size:24pt font-size:150% font-size:x-small
font-style	Specifies italic	italic normal oblique	font-style:italic
font-variant	Specifies small-caps	small-caps none	font-variant:small-caps

Continued

Property	Purpose	Values	Examples
font-weight	Specifies lightness/boldness	One of the values 100, 200, . . . , 900 (900 being the boldest), or one of the following: bold normal bolder lighter	font-weight:800 font-weight:bold
line-height	Specifies line spacing	Point value, or a % of the single-line height, or a multiplication factor	line-height:20pt line-height:150% line-height:1.5
text-align	Specifies alignment	center left right	text-align:center
text-decoration	Specifies underline, etc.	underline overline line-through none blink	text-decoration:underline
text-indent	Specifies indentation	Point value, or a % of the line width; negative for a hanging indent	text-indent:30pt text-indent:10% text-indent:-30pt text-indent:-10%
text-transform	Specifies capitalization	capitalize uppercase lowercase none	text-transform:capitalize

*The font-style, font-weight, font-variant, font-size/line-height, and font-family properties may be combined into one style definition using the font property. For example (where the order must be as shown):

```
font: italic bolder small-caps 14pt/24pt "Lucida","Arial"
```

Formatting Lists

The style of the item marks for an unordered list may be specified via the list-style property:

```
list-style:square
list-style:disc
list-style:circle
```

For an ordered list element the following properties may be used:

list-style:decimal	(the numbers 1, 2, 3...)
list-style:upper-alpha	(the uppercase letters A, B, C...)
list-style:lower-alpha	(the lowercase letters a, b, c...)
list-style:upper-roman	(the Roman numerals I, II, III...)
list-style:lower-roman	(the Roman numerals i, ii, iii...)

You may also use:

```
list-style:url(some_image.gif)
```

which specifies that the image contained in the file some_image.gif is to be used as the item mark. (If the image file is not in the same directory as the source document, a more complete pathname must of course be provided.)

Formatting Links

The style for links on a page may be specified by using a:link for regular links, a:visited for visited links (links the surfer has clicked on), a:action for links in the process of being clicked, and a:hover for links when the mouse hovers over them. For example, to specify that the text of regular links should be displayed in red with no underlining, the style definition is:

```
a:link {color:red; text-decoration:none}
```

Or to specify that all links should change to bold text when the mouse hovers over them:

```
a:hover {font-weight:bold}
```

And similarly for a:visited and a:action.

Styles for Specifying Layout

Property	Purpose	Values	Examples

`border`	Creates border around an element and specifies its width, style, and color (all three must be specified, in that order; to specify individual aspects, see below)	`thin`, `medium`, `thick`, or number of pixels for width
		
		`none`, `dotted`, `dashed`, `solid`, `double`, `groove`, `ridge`, `inset`, `outset`
		
		color name or number for color
			`border:thick double green`
			`border:thin inset #FA14E3`
			`border:8px solid yellow`

`border-width`	Specifies just the width of the border	`thin`, `medium`, `thick`, or number of pixels (`medium` is default)	`border-width:thick` `border-width:12px`
`border-style`	Specifies just the style of the border	`none`, `dotted`, `dashed`, `solid`, `double`, `groove`, `ridge`, `inset`, `outset` (`solid` is default)	`border-style:dotted` `border-style:ridge`
`border-color`	Specifies just the color of the border	color name or number	`border-color:red` `border-color:#35F2E8`
`border-top`	Same as `border`, but just specifies style for the top edge of the border	See values for `border`	`border-top:thick double blue`
`border-bottom`	Same as `border`, but just specifies style for the bottom edge of the border	See values for `border`	`border-bottom:thin inset red`
`border-left`	Same as `border`, but just specifies style for the left edge of the border	See values for `border`	`border-left:thick groove red`
`border-right`	Same as `border`, but just specifies style for the right edge of the border	See values for `border`	`border-right:thin ridge blue`

Continued

Property	Purpose	Values	Examples
border-top-width	Specifies width of top edge of border	Same as border-width	border-top-width:thin border-top-width:5px
border-top-style	Specifies style of top edge of border	Same as border-style	border-top-style:groove
border-top-color	Specifies color of top edge of border	Same as border-color	border-top-color:blue
(and similarly for other border combinations)			
float	Specifies how text should flow around an element	left (specifies element on the left, text flow on the right) or right	float:left float:right
margin	Specifies size of margin around an element (the transparent space around the element); does not apply to absolutely positioned elements	Number of pixels, or % of the width of the parent element (the element that contains the margin element)	margin:30 (sets it to 30 pixels for all sides) margin:20 30 (sets top and bottom to 20, right and left to 30) margin:10 12 20 12 (sets top, right, bottom, left in that order)
padding	Specifies padding (blank space) between border of the element and its contents	Number of pixels, or % of the parent element	padding:10 padding:12% padding:7 10 (sets top, bottom to 7, right and left to 10) padding:5 8 5 3 (sets top, right, bottom, left in that order)
padding-top	Specifies padding at top	Same as padding	padding-top:12
padding-bottom	Specifies bottom padding		padding-bottom:7
padding-left	Specifies left-side padding		padding-left:4
padding-right	Specifies right-side padding		padding-right:6

Continued

Property	Purpose	Values	Examples
`position:absolute`	Specifies absolute positioning of an element, relative to its parent element (the element it is inside of)	Specify `top`, `bottom`, `left`, or `right` values in pixels or as % offset from parent element	`position:absolute; top:20; left:50` `position:absolute; top:8%; left:11%`

`vertical-align`	Specifies vertical alignment of an element relative to its parent element	`baseline`
		`middle`
		`sub`
		`super`
		`text-top`
		`text-bottom`
		`top`
		`bottom`
			`vertical-align:middle`

Color and Character Codes

Color Codes

The hexadecimal color codes used to specify colors on web pages, as well as the concept of browser-safe colors, are explained in Chapter 3, in the section "Experimenting with Colors." Here we list the 16 basic colors that also have defined names. Remember that when using a color number as the value of an attribute or style property it must be preceded with the # symbol, such as:

```
<style type="text/css">
    h2 {color:#D61130}
</style>
```

For more colors and color codes, check out the HTML-oriented websites listed in Appendix I. The one at www.webmonkey.com has a particularly nice table of the 216 browser-safe colors (click on Color Codes in the Quick Reference list). Starting with version 4, Explorer added a number of other color names, such as darkseagreen, lemonchiffon, and cornflowerblue. Navigator has similar, but not always identical names. Because of these incompatibilities, you should stick with the color numbers for colors other than the 16 with predefined names.

Color	Number
black	#000000
gray	#808080
silver	#C0C0C0
whIte	#FFFFFF
red	#FF0000
maroon	#800000

Continued

Color	Number
magenta	#FF00FF
purple	#800080
blue	#0000FF
navy	#000080
cyan (or aqua)	#00FFFF
teal	#008080
green	#008000
olive	#808000
lime	#00FF00
yellow	#FFFF00

Character Codes

Sometimes you may need to use special characters on a web page. For example, you might want to put a copyright notice on your page using the copyright symbol ©, or use the registered symbol ® to specify a registered trademark. Or, if your page has some foreign expressions, you may need to use accented characters. These characters do not appear on a regular computer keyboard, so you can't type them into your source document directly.

In addition, some symbols have special meanings in HTML, such as < and > in tags. If you had a math tutorial web page, you would need to use these symbols to represent the less-than and greater-than signs. But if you type them directly into your HTML code, the browser will try to interpret them according to their special HTML meaning.

To get around these problems, HTML implements numeric character codes and sometimes abbreviated character names for special symbols. In order to place the © symbol on a web page, for example, you type © where you want it to appear. (That's an ampersand, the numeral symbol, the digits 1, 6, 9, and finally a semicolon.) Or you may type © (an ampersand, the word copy and then a semicolon). For a less-than sign you type < or < (the lt standing for less than). Similarly, the greater-than sign is either > or >. If, for example, you wanted to display the sentence "Do the following problem to answer whether the value of A is > the value of B.", you would write:

```
Do the following problem to answer whether the value of A
is &#62; the value of B.
```

Or:

```
Do the following problem to answer whether the value of A
is &gt; the value of B.
```

In general it's best to use the abbreviated names, such as > and ©, because when you see the character code in a source document it's easier to figure out what it is. On the other hand, however, outdated browser versions sometimes only recognize the number not the name.

One character that many web page designers used in the past is the non-breaking space, which has the code   or . They employed it to force the browser to put in white space where otherwise it wouldn't (because it ignores any extra regular space characters and tabs that are in the source document). So you will sometimes see this character number in the source code of web pages. But you should only rarely, if ever, use it that way yourself. The preferred way to define such formatting is by using style sheets.

The following table lists the character codes and names of the symbols you are most likely to need. A full list may be found at http://www.w3.org/TR/REC-html40/sgml/entities.html. The official W3C name for the character codes is "character entity references." Many of the websites listed in Appendix I also post full or partial lists. Note that some characters that had numbers in the 128 to 156 range have been renumbered in order to avoid conflicts due to the fact that some computer operating systems displayed differing characters for them. For example, the number for Ÿ was 159, but the preferred number is now 376. Be aware, however, that these new numbers, as well as some of the more established numbers may not work on older browsers. If you use character codes, you should check how they display in different browser versions.

Character/Symbol	Number Code	Name Code
"	&#34;	&quot;
'	&#8216;	&lsquo;
'	&#8217;	&rsquo;
"	&#8220;	&ldquo;
"	&#8221;	&rdquo;
&	&#38;	&amp;
<	&#60;	&lt;
>	&#62;	&gt;
(non-breaking space)		

Continued

Character/Symbol	Number Code	Name Code
– (en-dash)	&#8211;	&ndash;
— (em-dash)	&#8212;	&mdash;
¡	&#161;	&iexcl;
¢	&#162;	&cent;
£	&#163;	&pound;
¥	&#165;	&yen;
€	&#8364;	&euro;
§	&#167;	&sect;
©	&#169;	&copy;
«	&#171;	&laquo;
»	&#187;	&raquo;
®	&#174;	&reg;
°	&#176;	&deg;
±	&#177;	&plusmn;
µ	&#181;	&micro;
¶	&#182;	&para;
·	&#183;	&middot;
¿	&#191;	&iquest;
÷	&#247;	&divide;
×	&#215;	&times;
−	&#8722;	&minus;
≠	&#8800;	&ne;
¼	&#188;	&frac14;
½	&#189;	&frac12;
¾	&#190;	&frac34;
√	&#8730;	&radic;
À	&#192;	&Agrave;
à	&#224;	&agrave;
Á	&#193;	&Aacute;
á	&#225;	&aacute;

Continued

Character/Symbol	Number Code	Name Code
Â	&#194;	&Acirc;
â	&#226;	&acirc;
Ã	&#195;	&Atilde;
ã	&#227;	&atilde;
Ä	&#196;	&Auml;
ä	&#228;	&auml;
Å	&#197;	&Aring;
å	&#229;	&aring;
Æ	&#198;	&AElig;
æ	&#230;	&aelig;
È	&#200;	&Egrave;
è	&#232;	&egrave;
É	&#201;	&Eacute;
é	&#233;	&eacute;
Ê	&#202;	&Ecirc;
ê	&#234;	&ecirc;
Ë	&#203;	&Euml;
ë	&#235;	&euml;
Ì	&#204;	&Igrave;
ì	&#236;	&igrave;
Í	&#205;	&Iacute;
í	&#237;	&iacute;
Î	&#206;	&Icirc;
î	&#238;	&icirc;
Ï	&#207;	&Iuml;
ï	&#239;	&iuml;
Ò	&#210;	&Ograve;
ò	&#242;	&ograve;
Ó	&#211;	&Oacute;
ó	&#243;	&oacute;
Ô	&#212;	&Ocirc;

Continued

Character/Symbol	Number Code	Name Code
ô	&#244;	&ocirc;
Õ	&#213;	&Otilde;
õ	&#245;	&otilde;
Ö	&#214;	&Ouml;
ö	&#246;	&ouml;
Ø	&#216;	&Oslash;
ø	&#248;	&oslash;
Œ	&#338;	&OElig;
œ	&#339;	&oelig;
Ù	&#217;	&Ugrave;
ù	&#249;	&ugrave;
Ú	&#218;	&Uacute;
ú	&#250;	&uacute;
Û	&#219;	&Ucirc;
û	&#251;	&ucirc;
Ü	&#220;	&Uuml;
ü	&#252;	&uuml;
Ÿ	&#376;	&Yuml;
ÿ	&#255;	&yuml;
Ç	&#199;	&Ccedil;
ç	&#231;	&ccedil;
ß	&#223;	&szlig;
Ñ	&#209;	&Ntilde;
ñ	&#241;	&ntilde;
A	&#913;	&Alpha;
B	&#914;	&Beta;
Γ	&#915;	&Gamma;
Δ	&#916;	&Delta;
E	&#917;	&Epsilon;
Z	&#918;	&Zeta;

Continued

Character/Symbol	Number Code	Name Code
H	&#919;	&Eta;
Θ	&#920;	&Theta;
I	&#921;	&Iota;
K	&#922;	&Kappa;
Λ	&#923;	&Lambda;
M	&#924;	&Mu;
N	&#925;	&Nu;
Ξ	&#926;	&Xi;
O	&#927;	&Omicron;
Π	&#928;	&Pi;
P	&#929;	&Rho;
Σ	&#930;	&Sigma;
T	&#931;	&Tau;
Υ	&#932;	&Upsilon;
Φ	&#933;	&Phi;
X	&#934;	&Chi;
Ψ	&#935;	&Psi;
Ω	&#936;	&Omega;
α	&#945;	&alpha;
β	&#946;	&beta;
γ	&#947;	&gamma;
δ	&#948;	&delta;
ε	&#949;	&epsilon;
ζ	&#950;	&zeta;
η	&#951;	&eta;
θ	&#952;	&theta;
ι	&#953;	&iota;
κ	&#954;	&kappa;
λ	&#955;	&lambda;
μ	&#956;	&mu;

Continued

Character/Symbol	Number Code	Name Code
ν	&#957;	&nu;
ξ	&#958;	&xi;
o	&#959;	&omicron;
π	&#960;	&pi;
ρ	&#961;	&rho;
ς	&#962;	&sigmaf;
σ	&#963;	&sigma;
τ	&#964;	&tau;
υ	&#965;	&upsilon;
φ	&#966;	&phi;
χ	&#967;	&chi;
ψ	&#968;	&psi;
ω	&#969;	&omega;

The codes and names for the following symbols work in Navigator 6 but not in Explorer 6.

≤	&#8804;	&le;
≥	&#8805;	&ge;
∞	&#8734;	&infin;
†	&#8224;	&dagger;
‡	&#8225;	&Dagger;
♠	&#9824;	&spades;
♣	&#9827;	&clubs;
♥	&#9829;	&hearts;
♦	&#9830;	&diams;

JavaScript Versions, Objects, and Reserved Words

Overview of JavaScript Development

Key Versions of JavaScript	Browser Version	Date
JavaScript 1.0	Navigator 2.0	March 1996
JavaScript 1.1	Navigator 3.0	August 1996
JavaScript 1.2	Navigator 4.0-4.05	June 1997
JavaScript 1.3	Navigator 4.06-4.7	November 1998
JavaScript 1.4	—	
JavaScript 1.5	Navigator 6.0 and	November 2000
	Mozilla (open source	
	browser on which	
	Navigator 6 is based)	

Key Versions of JScript	Browser Version	Date
JScript 1.0	Explorer 3.0	August 1996
JScript 3.0	Explorer 4.0	October 1997
JScript 5.0	Explorer 5.0	March 1999
JScript 6.0	Explorer 6.0	October 2001

Latest Version of ECMAScript

ECMAScript, third edition, is roughly equivalent to JavaScript 1.5. As of spring 2002, work is proceeding on a fourth edition.

JavaScript Reserved Words

JavaScript has a number of words it reserves for its own use, meaning that you should never use them for your own variable or function names. Some of the reserved words in the list below are used explicitly by JavaScript (or JScript). Others are words that appear in the Java programming language and are reserved by JavaScript to prevent possible confusion on the part of the browser. And some are words that have been reserved for possible future use. In addition, you should avoid using any JavaScript object, property, or function name for your own objects, functions, and variables. These names include words like `button`, `checkbox`, `radio`, `Array`, `array`, `form`, `document`, `element`, `elements`, `frame`, `Image`, `image`, `Date`, `date`, `String`, `string`, `link`, `self`, `top`, `parseFloat`, `alert`, `confirm`, `prompt`, and so on and so forth. Because most of these names are single whole words, if you make your names either two-word combinations or abbreviations (for example, `ctr`, `nmbr`, `num`, etc.) you are less likely to run into trouble.

```
abstract
as
asset
boolean
break
byte
case
catch
char
class
const
continue
debugger
default
delete
do
double
else
enum
export
extends
event
false
final
finally
float
for
function
```

```
goto
if
implements
import
in
instanceof
insure
int
interface
internal
is
long
namespace
native
new
null
package
private
protected
public
require
return
sbyte
set
short
static
super
switch
synchronized
this
throw
throws
transient
true
try
typeof
unint
ulong
use
ushort
var
void
volatile
while
with
```

Table of JavaScript Objects, Methods, and Properties

JavaScript has grown enormously over the last few years, to the point where the versions in Explorer 6 and Navigator 6 implement close to 100 objects with over 600 methods and properties total. Any HTML element on a web page may now be accessed and manipulated via JavaScript. To understand and use these objects and their methods and properties, however, takes us into advanced JavaScript programming. In addition, some of these methods and properties work only in Explorer or only in Navigator. We have limited the contents of the following table, therefore, to the core JavaScript objects that we have covered plus those that are implemented in most browsers from 1997 on. (For Explorer and Navigator, this means versions 4 and beyond.) In some cases, such as the Date object, we have covered only a few of the methods involved, but we give a full list anyway. More information about the various objects may be found at the websites listed in the next paragraph or from one of the several good JavaScript reference books. In addition, sometimes you can figure out how a method works simply by trying it out in a source document and using an alert box to display the results.

Complete documentation for Internet Explorer's version of JavaScript (JScript) may be found at msdn.microsoft.com/library. (In the table of contents on the left side of the screen, click on Web Development and then Scripting.) Documentation for Navigator's (and now Mozilla's) version of JavaScript may be accessed at http://www.mozilla.org/docs/web-developer (scroll down to the section on Scripting). The documentation for ECMAScript is not very user friendly, but may be found at http://www.ecma.ch/ecma1/STAND/ECMA-262.HTM. The third edition of ECMAScript is essentially contained in JavaScript 1.5 and JScript 6.0, although JavaScript and JScript each go beyond it in many ways. Information on the World Wide Web Consortium's work to standardize the Document Object Model may be found at www.w3.org (click on the link for DOM in the index on the left side of the page).

Figure F.1 shows a hierarchical diagram of the objects that make up the basic Document Object Model (implemented in Navigator 2 and Explorer 3). All of them are covered in the text in greater or lesser detail except the link and anchor objects. The link object lies behind any <a href> elements in the source document, and the anchor object lies behind any <a id> (or <a name>) elements used. The methods and properties of both are listed in the table that starts on page 562. Note also that the same diagram applies to the case of a frame, with the frame object taking the place of the window object at the top of the hierarchy.

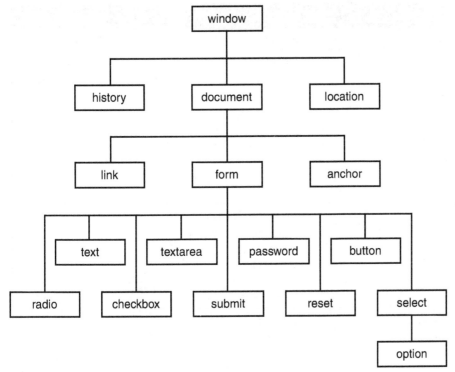

FIGURE F.1   Hierarchy of the basic Document Object Model

Table Notes:

Parameters (in italic) are shown for the methods that take them. For example, the write() method of the document object takes a string as a parameter, so it's listed as write("*string*"). Optional parameters are shown within square brackets, such as open([mimetype]) for the open() method of the document object. Properties that are arrays are shown with an *i* inside square brackets (the *i* standing for the index number of an array element), such as the elements array belonging to the form object: elements[*i*]. For detailed information on each object, property, method, and event handler, see the web references listed above. And again note that this table represents the core of JavaScript implemented in all (or nearly all) browsers since 1997. Many more objects, properties, methods, and event handlers have been added by the two major browsers since then.

Object	Properties	Methods	Event handlers
anchor	name	(none)	(none)
area	hash host hostname href pathname port protocol search target	(none)	onmouseout onmouseover
Array	length	concat(*anotherArray*) join("*separatorChar*") reverse() slice(*i*) sort(*compareFunction*) toString()	(none)
button	checked form name type value	click()	onclick onmousedown onmouseup
checkbox	checked defaultChecked form name type value	click()	onclick onmousedown onmouseup
Date	(none)	getFullYear() getYear() getMonth() getDate() getDay() getHours() getMinutes() getSeconds() getTime() getMilliseconds() getUTCFullYear() getUTCMonth() getUTCDate() getUTCDay()	(none)

Continued

Object	Properties	Methods	Event handlers
		getUTCHours()	
		getUTCMinutes()	
		getUTCSeconds()	
		getUTCTime()	
		getUTCMilliseconds()	
		setFullYear(*datevalue*)	
		setYear(*datevalue*)	
		setMonth(*datevalue*)	
		setDate(*datevalue*)	
		setDay(*datevalue*)	
		setHours(*datevalue*)	
		setMinutes(*datevalue*)	
		setSeconds(*datevalue*)	
		setTime(*datevalue*)	
		setMilliseconds(*datevalue*)	
		setUTCFullYear(*datevalue*)	
		setUTCMonth(*datevalue*)	
		setUTCDate(*datevalue*)	
		setUTCDay(*datevalue*)	
		setUTCHours(*datevalue*)	
		setUTCMinutes(*datevalue*)	
		setUTCSeconds(*datevalue*)	
		setUTCTime(*datevalue*)	
		setUTCMilliseconds(*datevalue*)	
		getTimezoneOffset()	
		toGMTString()	
		toLocaleString()	
		toString()	
		toUTCString()	
		parse("*datestring*")	
		UTC(*datevalue*)	
document	alinkColor	clear()	
	anchors[*i*]	close()	
	applets[*i*]	open([*mimetype*])	
	bgColor	write("*string*")	
	cookie	writeln("*string*")	
	domain		
	embeds[*i*]		
	fgColor		
	forms[*i*]		
	images[*i*]		
	lastModified		

Continued

Object	Properties	Methods	Event handlers
	linkColor		
	links[*i*]		
	location		
	referrer		
	title		
	URL		
	vlinkColor		
form	action	reset()	onreset
	elements[*i*]	submit()	onsubmit
	encoding		
	length		
	method		
	name		
	target		
hidden	defaultValue	blur()	onblur
	form	focus()	onchange
	name	select()	onfocus
	type		onkeydown
	value		onkeypress
			onkeyup
			onselect
history	length	back()	(none)
	current	forward()	
	next	go(*integer*) or go("*URL*")	
	previous		
image	border	(none)	onabort
	complete		onerror
	height		onload
	hspace		
	lowsrc		
	name		
	src		
	vspace		
	width		
link	hash	(none)	onclick
	host		onmousedown
	hostname		onmouseout
	href		onmouseover
	pathname		onmouseup
	port		
	protocol		

Continued

Object	Properties	Methods	Event handlers
	search target		
location	hash host hostname href pathname port protocol	assign(*"URL"*) reload(*booleanvalue*) replace(*"URL"*)	(none)
Math	E LN2 LN10 LOG2E LOG10E PI SQRT1_2 SQRT2	abs(*value*) acos(*value*) asin(*value*) atan(*value*) atan2(*value1, value2*) ceil(*value*) cos(*value*) exp(*value*) floor(*value*) log(*value*) max(*value1, value2*) min(*value1, value2*) pow(*value, power*) random() round(*value*) sin(*value*) sqrt(*value*) tan(*value*)	(none)
navigator	appCodeName appName appVersion platform userAgent	javaEnabled() taintEnabled()	
Number	MAX_VALUE MIN_VALUE NaN NEGATIVE_INFINITY POSITIVE_INFINITY	toString() valueOf()	
password	defaultValue form name type	blur() focus() select()	onblur onchange onfocus onkeydown

Continued

Object	Properties	Methods	Event handlers
	`value`		`onkeypress`
			`onkeyup`
			`onselect`
`radio`	`checked`	`click()`	`onclick`
	`form`		`onmousedown`
	`length`		`onmouseup`
	`name`		
	`type`		
	`value`		
`reset`	`checked`	`click()`	`onclick`
	`form`		`onmousedown`
	`name`		`onmouseup`
	`type`		
	`value`		
`screen`	`availHeight`	(none)	
	`availWidth`		
	`colorDepth`		
	`height`		
	`pixelDepth`		
	`width`		
`select`	`length`	`blur()`	`onblur`
	`name`	`focus()`	`onchange`
	`options[`*`i`*`]`		`onfocus`
	`options[`*`i`*`].defaultSelected`		
	`options[`*`i`*`].index`		
	`options[`*`i`*`].selected`		
	`options[`*`i`*`].text`		
	`options[`*`i`*`].value`		
	`selectedIndex`		
	`type`		
`String`	`length`	`anchor("`*`anchorname`*`")`	
		`big()`	
		`blink()`	
		`bold()`	
		`charAt(`*`index`*`)`	
		`charCodeAt(`*`i`*`)`	
		`concat(`*`anotherString`*`)`	
		`fixed()`	
		`fontcolor(#`*`colornumber`*`)`	
		`fontsize(`*`sizenumber`*`)` (where *sizenumber* = 1 to 7)	
		`fromCharCode(`*`charNum1, charNum2,...`*`)`	

Continued

Object	Properties	Methods	Event handlers
		indexOf(*searchString, startIndex*)	
		italics()	
		lastIndexOf(*searchString, startIndex*)	
		link()	
		match(*regularExpression*)	
		replace(*regularExpression, replaceString*)	
		search(*regularExpression*)	
		slice(*startIndex [, endIndex]*)	
		small()	
		split("*splitCharacter*")	
		strike()	
		sub()	
		substr(*startIndex [, length]*)	
		substring(*startIndex, endIndex*)	
		sup()	
		toLowerCase()	
		toString()	
		toUpperCase()	
		valueOf()	
submit	checked	click()	onclick
	form		onmousedown
	name		onmouseup
	type		
	value		
text	defaultValue	blur()	onblur
	form	focus()	onchange
	name	select()	onfocus
	type		onkeydown
	value		onkeypress
			onkeyup
			onselect
textarea	form	blur()	onblur
	name	focus()	onchange
	type	select()	onfocus
	value		onkeydown
			onkeypress
			onkeyup
			onselect
window	closed	alert("*message*")	onblur
	defaultStatus	blur()	onerror
	document	clearInterval(*intervalID*)	onfocus

Continued

Object	Properties	Methods	Event handlers
	frames[*i*]	clearTimeout(*timeoutID*)	onload
	history	close()	onresize
	location	confirm(*"message"*)	onunload
	name	focus()	
	navigator	moveBy(*xvalue, yvalue*)	
	opener	moveTo(*xvalue, yvalue*)	
	parent	open(*URL*,*"name"*,*"specifications"*)	
	screen	prompt(*"message"*, *"reply"*)	
	self	resizeBy(*xvalue, yvalue*)	
	status	resizeTo(*width, height*)	
	top	scroll(*xvalue, yvalue*)	
	window	scrollBy(*xvalue, yvalue*)	
		scrollTo(*xvalue, yvalue*)	
		setInterval(*function, milliseconds [,options]*)	
		setTimeout(*function, milliseconds [,options]*)	

Common HTML and JavaScript Errors

Throughout each chapter we indicated errors to watch out for with the Error Alert icon. These alerts were also summarized at the end of each chapter, so remember to review them there. In this appendix, we list a number of the most common errors for HTML, XHTML, and JavaScript, plus error messages for Internet Explorer.

Common HTML and XHTML Errors

(See also Appendix C on the requirements for converting an HTML document into a valid XHTML document.)

1. *Leaving off the* <html> *tag or the .htm (or .html) extension, or saving the source document with a .txt extension.* These errors in an HTML document cause some (but not all) browsers to display the actual HTML code of the source document, instead of the web page the code is supposed to create. In XHTML, the <html> element is required.

2. *Leaving off a* </table> *or* </frameset> *tag.* It's easy to leave off the ending tag of almost any container, but these two examples cause particular problems. If the </table> or </frameset> isn't there, many versions of Navigator will show nothing on the page. (Most versions of Explorer just ignore the missing tags and display the table or frame anyway.) So if you view your page in Navigator and a lot of it is blank, it's likely that you left off one of these tags.

3. *Leaving off a* </p> *tag in paragraph elements.* The ending </p> tag is required in XHTML (as are ending tags for all non-empty elements). It's also required in general when you define a paragraph style, otherwise the style won't work.

4. *Leaving off the slash (/) in empty elements.* To be XHTML-compliant, empty elements (elements that don't have an ending tag) must have a slash at the end. For example, it's <br /> not <br> and

```
<img src="dogpicture.jpg" alt="picture of dog" />
```

not

```
<img src="dogpicture.jpg" alt="picture of dog">
```

5. *Typographical errors in style definitions.* Any error in a style definition, no matter how minor, will usually cause the browser to ignore the definition. So if you specify a style but it doesn't appear as expected in the browser, the first things to check are the spelling (watch the hyphens!) and the semicolons that separate the style definitions.

Common JavaScript Errors

1. *Forgetting to put quotation marks around literal strings (i.e., actual characters).* For example:

```
alert(Hello)
```

vs.

```
alert("Hello")
```

Or:

```
document.myForm.nameBox.value = George
```

vs.

```
document.myForm.nameBox.value = "George"
```

In the first case of each of these examples, JavaScript tries to interpret `Hello` and `George` as variable names, not literal string values.

Another case where it's easy to leave off a string's quotation marks is in a conditional statement:

```
if (userName == Ginger) {
    alert("Would you like to dance?")
}
```

Again, without the quotation marks around "`Ginger`", JavaScript interprets `Ginger` as a variable name, and therefore tries to compare the contents of the variable `userName` with the contents of the supposed variable named `Ginger`.

2. *Quotation marks that aren't nested properly or that don't match.* For example:

```
alert("He said, "Hello"")
```

vs.

```
alert("He said, 'Hello'")
alert('He said, "Hello"')
```

Or:

```
document.myForm.nameBox.value = "George'
```

vs.

```
document.myForm.nameBox.value = 'George'
document.myForm.nameBox.value = "George"
```

The first example in each of the two cases is incorrect. It doesn't matter in JavaScript which type of quotation marks you use, single or double, but if you have more than one pair, the types must alternate. Otherwise, as in the first alert example, JavaScript will match up the second double quotation mark just before the Hello with the first quotation mark and thereby think that it marks the end of a string. In the example of the Georges, it's simply that a pair of quotation marks must be either single or double, but not mixed.

3. *Problems with curly braces.* It is very easy to leave off a curly brace someplace. For example, can you see what's wrong with the code below?

```
if (temperature == "hot") {
    alert("Let's go swimming!")
else {
    alert("Time to hit the books.")
}
```

The conditional statement is missing a right curly brace just before the else. In this case JavaScript will recognize that there should be one before the else statement. But in other cases it won't recognize one is missing until later in the code, because it will try to match up left and right curly braces until it gets to the end and finds itself with a curly brace without a match.

A misplaced curly brace can lead to problems such as our next error, infinite loops.

4. *Loop problems.* We gave several examples of infinite loops in Chapter 14. A misplaced curly brace, for example, can leave the line of code where the counter is incremented outside the loop:

```
counter = 1
while (counter <= 4) {
    alert("The count is: " + counter)
}
counter = counter + 1
```

It's also possible to get an infinite `for` loop if you don't type the conditions correctly. For example:

```
for (counter=0; counter; counter++) {
    //some code here
}
```

Note that the loop has no ending condition (it's just `counter`, not something like `counter <= 10`). Also, while we're on the subject of `for` loops, don't forget to type semicolons, not commas, to separate the three conditions at the beginning of the loop. And make sure to always check the first and last iterations of the loop to avoid off-by-one errors, where the loop iterates one more or one less time than you want it to.

5. *Mixing up single-equal signs and double-equal signs.* Remember that a single-equal sign (=) is used in assignment statements and a double-equal sign (==) in comparison conditions. One way to remember that a double-equal denotes a comparison is to remember that two of the other comparison operators use a double symbol: <= for less than or equal and >= for greater than or equal.

Nevertheless, it's still very easy to type or write a single-equal when you should use a double-equal, especially in conditional statements. For example:

```
if (temperature = "hot") {
    alert("Let's go swimming!")
}
else {
    alert("Time to hit the books.")
}
```

This is a very difficult error to catch, not only because it's easy to miss while you're reading through the code, but because JavaScript will *not* generate an error message for this code. Instead, the (`temperature = "hot"`) expression will *always be true* (because it's an assignment statement) and thus the `"Let's go swimming"` message (or whatever code is there) will *always* appear and the `"Time to hit the books"` message will never appear.

6. *Nested conditional statements.* Consider the following code:

```
if (sky == "blue") {
  if (waves == "high") {
    alert("Cowabunga!")
    //do this if sky is blue and waves are high
  }
}
else {
```

```
            alert("The sky must be cloudy and the waves
               must be low.")
            //do this if the sky isn't blue and the waves
            //aren't high
        }
```

The problem with this code is that if sky is not equal to "blue", then the else statement will execute no matter whether the value of waves is "high" or not (despite what the comment says). In other words, the message "The sky must be cloudy and the waves must be low" will also appear in the case where the value of sky is "cloudy" and the value of waves is "high".

7. *Variable names, function names, or reserved words misspelled or differently spelled.* Remember that JavaScript is case sensitive, so the variable name firstAnswer is different from FirstAnswer. Note also that reserved words, method names, and property names must be spelled correctly, including capitalization. Most reserved words are all lowercase characters. When you're declaring a function, for example, it's function not Function. Some prominent exceptions, however, are the constructor functions for arrays, dates, and images. To create an array, you must write:

```
    var sampleArray = new Array(50)
```

not

```
    var sampleArray = new array(50)
```

Method names and property names often use internal capitalization, such as the bgColor property of the document object (so it's document.bgColor, not document.bgcolor) or the parseFloat() function.

8. *Forgetting the* new *keyword in constructor function calls.* When using a constructor function to create an array, a date object, an image object, or one of your own objects, it's very easy to forget to include the new keyword. It should be:

```
    var sampleArray = new Array(50)
```

not

```
    var sampleArray = Array(50)
```

9. *Errors involving the* var *keyword and mixups between local and global variables.* Only use the var keyword with a variable when you are declaring it for the first time. If you use it more than once with the same variable name, it's possible to end up with two separate variables with the same name, one a local variable and one a global variable.

10. *Trouble with boolean values.* Never enclose the boolean values `true` and `false` in quotation marks, otherwise they will be treated as strings.

11. *Leaving off the square brackets when referring to arrays.* An array always has a pair of square brackets after its name, e.g., `sampleArray[27]`.

12. *Leaving off the parentheses when declaring or calling functions with no parameters.* Functions always have parentheses after their names, whether or not they have any parameters. For example, given the following function declaration:

```
function sampleFunction() {
    //code goes here
}
```

The proper way to call this function is

```
sampleFunction()
```

not

```
sampleFunction
```

13. *Unterminated multiple-line comments.* In a multiple-line comment, it's easy to leave off the ending `*/` .

14. *Improper use of the* `value` *property.* Many beginning JavaScript students are confused about when to use the `value` property. Very simply, never stick a `value` on the end of a string variable. The `value` is the name of a property for certain input elements, but not for strings. We have used it mainly for text boxes, but it also is a valid property of text areas, radio buttons, and check boxes. So to display a message in a text box named `outputBox` (belonging to a form named `myForm`) you write:

```
document.myForm.outputBox.value = "Greetings!"
```

And to put the same message into a string variable named `testString` you write:

```
testString = "Greetings!"
```

But never write:

```
testString.value = "Greetings!"
```

15. *The cryptic "Object Expected" error message in Explorer.* Perhaps the most common JavaScript (JScript) error message you will receive in Explorer is Object expected. (See the section "Browser Error Messages" in Chapter 7 for a review of how error messages are displayed in Explorer and Navigator.) The problem can be any number of things, but most often it's simply a case of something being mis-

spelled. So before you assume that it's something complicated, check your spelling and syntax.

16. *Passing a property value as a parameter and trying to change it in a function.* Remember that when you pass an object's property (e.g., the `value` property of a text box) to a function, only a copy is sent. So any changes made to this value inside the function don't affect the actual object property. For example, if you pass the `value` property of a text box to a function (such as `document.myForm.outputBox.value`) and store it in a formal parameter named `outputValue`, any changes made to `outputValue` in the function's code will have no effect on the actual value of `outputBox`. (See the section "Passing by Copy vs. Passing by Address" in Chapter 10 for details.)

JavaScript (JScript) Error Messages in Internet Explorer

The two lists below catalog the JScript run-time error messages and syntax error messages that may be displayed by Internet Explorer. Navigator's messages are similar (though not identical). Although some of the messages refer to advanced problems, the messages provide a nice reminder of the things that can go wrong. A fuller description of each error message may be found at http://msdn.microsoft.com/library (choose Web Development in the menu on the left, then Scripting, then Documentation, then JScript, then Reference, and finally Errors).

JScript Run-time Errors

JScript run-time errors are errors that occur when Explorer attempts to execute the code but finds it cannot.

Error Number	Description
5029	Array length must be a finite positive integer
5030	Array length must be assigned a finite positive number
5028	Array or arguments object expected
5010	Boolean expected
5003	Cannot assign to a function result
5000	Cannot assign to 'this'
5006	Date object expected

Continued

Error Number	Description
5015	Enumerator object expected
5022	Exception thrown and not caught
5020	Expected ')' in regular expression
5019	Expected ']' in regular expression
5023	Function does not have a valid prototype object
5002	Function expected
5008	Illegal assignment
5021	Invalid range in character set
5014	JScript object expected
5001	Number expected
5007	Object expected
5012	Object member expected
5016	Regular Expression object expected
5005	String expected
5017	Syntax error in regular expression
5026	The number of fractional digits is out of range
5027	The precision is out of range
5025	The URI to be decoded is not a valid encoding
5024	The URI to be encoded contains an invalid character
5009	Undefined identifier
5018	Unexpected quantifier
5013	VBArray expected

JScript Syntax Errors

JScript syntax errors are errors that occur when your JavaScript code does not follow the proper grammatical rules of the language. The browser catches them before attempting to execute any of the code.

Error Number	Description
1019	Can't have 'break' outside of loop
1020	Can't have 'continue' outside of loop
1030	Conditional compilation is turned off

Continued

Error Number	Description
1027	'default' can only appear once in a 'switch' statement
1005	Expected '('
1006	Expected ')'
1012	Expected '/'
1003	Expected ':'
1004	Expected ';'
1032	Expected '@'
1029	Expected '@end'
1007	Expected ']'
1008	Expected '{'
1009	Expected '}'
1011	Expected '='
1033	Expected 'catch'
1031	Expected constant
1023	Expected hexadecimal digit
1010	Expected identifier
1028	Expected identifier, string or number
1024	Expected 'while'
1014	Invalid character
1026	Label not found
1025	Label redefined
1018	'return' statement outside of function
1002	Syntax error
1035	Throw must be followed by an expression on the same source line
1016	Unterminated comment
1015	Unterminated string constant

Publishing a Web Page on the Internet

There are three basic steps to making a web page or multiple-page website available on the Internet so that anyone may view it.

1. *Obtain an Internet account that includes web hosting services.* If you connect to the Internet through an Internet Service Provider (ISP), you probably already have access to web hosting services. Many ISPs offer free storage space for a small website on their web server as part of the regular monthly fee. In this case, the URL for your web page will probably be a combination of the URL of the ISP plus a directory name that corresponds to your username. For example, if your ISP was someISP.com and your username for your ISP account was webguru, then the URL for your website might be something like:

   http://www.someISP.com/webguru

   Most ISPs also offer the option to pay a few dollars more per month and receive a higher level of web hosting services. The usual benefits are more storage space plus the possibility of using your own domain name, so that the URL for your website would be something like:

   http://www.javascriptgenius.com

   This assumes that you have previously registered the domain name "javascriptgenius" with one of the domain name registrars, such as netsol.com or register.com. (See the section "TCP/IP and Domain Names" in Chapter 1 for a few more details about domain names and registrars.)

   If you don't have an account with an ISP, or if your ISP doesn't offer web hosting services, other options exist. Some educational institutions let their students post basic web pages via their student accounts, so if you're a student it's worth it to check out the possibilities. Alternatively, some companies offer free hosting services for small websites. The best known is www.geocities.com (now part of Yahoo). Others (free or not) may be found by consulting sites such as www.freewebspace.net, www.webhostingratings.com, and www.10-best-web-site-and-domain-hosting-services.com.

2. *Prepare your web page/site.* To prepare your web page or site for publication on the Internet, you should first make sure that all the relevant source documents and image files are contained in the same folder. (It's also easiest if you don't have any other sub-folders within that folder, but it's okay if you do.) You should also check your website thoroughly for bugs, broken links, and so on. It's easier to fix them now than later. Finally, the source document for the initial page of the site should be named index.htm or index.html. This name indicates that it's the default page for the site. (Some web hosting services prefer the name default.htm instead of index.htm, so check with your service.) If you have to change the document's name to index.htm or default.htm, don't forget to change the code for any links elsewhere in your site that reference your home page.

3. *Transfer the source documents for your website from your computer to your web hosting account (i.e., to a computer at your web hosting service that is connected to the Internet and acts as a web server).* The normal method to accomplish this transfer is to use FTP (file transfer protocol) software. Your ISP or web hosting service will probably have instructions on exactly how to do this. But if not, you can find basic information on using FTP software at http://help.yahoo.com/help/us/geo/gftp (part of the geocities site). If you're using a school computer, it may already have FTP software installed on it. If you're using your own computer, you can download FTP software from sites like www.download.com and www.tucows.com. Among the most popular Windows programs are WS_FTP and Absolute FTP. For Macintosh users the programs Fetch and Transmit are well regarded. Or your web hosting service may recommend and/or provide FTP software.

If you have designed your website such that the source documents and image files are stored in multiple sub-folders, you may have to recreate those folders (or directories) in your web hosting account. The FTP software will usually allow you to do this.

Once you have transferred your source documents and files and have your website up and running, make sure to test it thoroughly. Remember that it's there for all the world to see, and a website with broken links and/or JavaScript errors is embarassing, to say the least.

Tools and Resources

Web Page Development Tools

There are dozens of software tools available that help you create websites. We list some of the most popular ones below.

Text-based HTML Editors

Text-based HTML editors improve greatly on the simple capabilities of text editors like **Notepad** and **SimpleText**. They allow you, for example, to point and click to insert HTML elements into the document without having to type all the <s and >s, and they will display the HTML elements in color so the code is easier to read. One of the most popular medium-priced HTML Editors for Windows is **Macromedia's HomeSite**, available from www.macromedia.com for about $100. (A demonstration copy is also available.) A less expensive alternative, albeit with many fewer features, is **TextPad** (about $30 from www.textpad.com). Or you can get a free HTML editor by choosing **NoteTab Light** (www.notetab.com) or **1st Page 2000** (www.evrsoft.com). A program named **Arachnophilia** also has many devotees and is available as careware (see www.arachnophilia.com for the interesting requirements of careware). On the Macintosh side, **BBEdit** is very highly rated. It's available from the website www.bbedit.com for about $120 and comes as well in a Lite version that's free.

WYSIWYG HTML Editors

WYSIWYG (what you see is what you get) editors allow you to create web pages without knowing any HTML. The most popular medium-priced choice in this category is **Microsoft FrontPage** ($175–200). If you have Microsoft Office on your PC, you may already have it installed on your computer, because it often comes bundled with Office. Its latest versions also allow more savvy web designers to write HTML code directly. Another good choice is **NetObjects Fusion**, which runs about $100 (www.netobjects.com). Most professional web

581

designers, however, prefer powerful, do-it-all programs like **Macromedia Dreamweaver** (www.macromedia.com) or **Adobe GoLive** (www.adobe.com). Both are available in PC or Mac versions and cost in the range of $300 to $400.

Graphics Tools

Adobe Photoshop is the software of choice for image editing (about $500–600), although less expensive, shareware programs exist. (One good site for more information about these programs and related issues can be found at graphicssoft.about.com.) **Macromedia Flash** (www.macromedia.com, about $400–500) is used by many web designers to create sophisticated web page animations with a minimum of effort. Both come in PC and Mac versions.

Software Download Sites

Many useful and relatively inexpensive utility programs can be found by searching download sites like **www.download.com** and **www.tucows.com**.

Official HTML and JavaScript Documentation

HTML and XHTML

The **World Wide Web Consortium**, at www.w3.org, is the place to visit when you want the official word on HTML and related matters.

JavaScript (Netscape Navigator)

The **DevEdge** site at **developer.netscape.com** has a number of useful links to JavaScript as well as HTML information. JavaScript manuals and articles may be found at developer.netscape.com/docs. Because this documentation refers to older versions of Navigator, there is no direct link from the DevEdge site to it. But it's still very useful information, so it's worth it to type the given URL directly into the browser (i.e., developer.netscape.com/docs). The browser engine underlying Netscape Navigator is now an open-source software project named Mozilla, so another good official site for information on JavaScript can be found at www.mozilla.org/docs/web-developer (scroll down to the section on Scripting).

JScript (Internet Explorer)

Documentation on JScript, Microsoft's version of JavaScript that is implemented in Internet Explorer, may be accessed at **msdn.microsoft.com/library** (in the table of contents on the left side of the screen, click on Web Development and then on Scripting).

ECMAScript

Although it's not in a very friendly format for web developers, the documentation for ECMAScript (the standardized version of JavaScript) may be found at www.ecma.ch/ecma1/stand/ECMA-262.htm.

Document Object Model

The **World Wide Web Consortium** site at www.w3.org has the official word on the Document Object Model. (Click on the link for DOM in the index on the left side of the page.)

HTML and JavaScript Websites

The **HTML Writers Guild** at www.hwg.org is a nonprofit organization that in 2002 merged with the **International Webmasters Association**. Together they have over 147,000 members world-wide. Although some of the HTML information at the www.hwg.org site is accessible by members only (at $49 per year), much of it is open to all.

Other HTML and JavaScript sites may be found by using your favorite web index or search engine, such as www.yahoo.com, www.lycos.com, www.ask.com, or www.google.com. We list some results below. But one group of sites that is worth your while to check out is found through about.com. The premise of about.com is to have a human expert or "guide" constantly search for and catalog the best sites on any given subject. In addition, the guide usually provides other pertinent information on the subject, such as software reviews. For HTML the sites to visit at about.com are **html.about.com** and **webdesign. about.com**, while for JavaScript it's **javascript.about.com**. For general news on Internet trends and technologies, see **internet.about.com**.

Another major site to bookmark for general computing news plus hardware and software reviews is **www.cnet.com**, while the aptly named **www.internet. com** focuses on the Internet itself. A site associated with www.cnet.com that focuses on web design and development is **Builder.com** at **www.builder.com** (or builder.com.com). Click on the link for Web Design Library in the navigation menu on the left, then scroll down and you will find links to Authoring and Site Design, Graphics and Multimedia, Programming and Scripting, and more.

In addition, there are any number of good sites on HTML or JavaScript or both. The hard part is deciding which one to frequent most often. Several nice sites are connected with www.internet.com: **www.webreference.com** provides general information and **www.javascript.com** and **javascript.internet.com** provide JavaScript information, including many sample scripts.

Other good sites include **www.webmonkey.com**, **www.jsworld.com**, **www.javascriptgate.com**, and **www.docjs.com**. On issues of website design and especially what not to do, see **www.useit.com** and **www.webpagesthatsuck.com**.

Finally, don't forget to bookmark the site that goes along with this textbook, at **www.mhhe.com/lagerstrom**.